The Structure of Wages

A National Bureau
of Economic Research
Conference Report

The Structure of Wages: An International Comparison

Edited by   **Edward P. Lazear and
Kathryn L. Shaw**

The University of Chicago Press

Chicago and London

EDWARD P. LAZEAR is currently serving as chairman of the Council of Economic Advisers. He is also the Morris Arnold Cox Senior Fellow at the Hoover Institution; the Jack Steele Parker Professor of Human Resources Management and Economics at the Graduate School of Business, Stanford University; and a research associate of the National Bureau of Economic Research. KATHRYN L. SHAW is the Ernest C. Arbuckle Professor of Economics at the Graduate School of Business, Stanford University and a research associate of the National Bureau of Economic Research.

The University of Chicago Press, Chicago 60637
The University of Chicago Press, Ltd., London
© 2008 by the National Bureau of Economic Research
All rights reserved. Published 2008
Printed in the United States of America

17 16 15 14 13 12 11 10 09 08   1 2 3 4 5
ISBN-13: 978-0-226-47050-4 (cloth)
ISBN-10: 0-226-47050-4 (cloth)

Library of Congress Cataloging-in-Publication Data

The structure of wages : an international comparison / edited by
   Edward P. Lazear and Kathryn L. Shaw.
      p. ; cm. — (National Bureau of Economic Research conference
   report)
   Includes bibliographical references and index.
   ISBN-13: 978-0-226-47050-4 (cloth : alk. paper)
   ISBN-10: 0-226-47050-4 (cloth : alk. paper) 1. Wages. 2. Wages—
Effect of labor mobility on. 3. Wage differentials. I. Lazear, Edward
P. II. Shaw, Kathryn.
   HD4909.S77   2008
   331.2′1—dc33
                                                        2008006593

♾ The paper used in this publication meets the minimum requirements of the American National Standard for Information Sciences— Permanence of Paper for Printed Library Materials, ANSI Z39.48-1992.

Relation of the Directors to the
Work and Publications of the
National Bureau of Economic Research

1. The object of the NBER is to ascertain and present to the economics profession, and to the public more generally, important economic facts and their interpretation in a scientific manner without policy recommendations. The Board of Directors is charged with the responsibility of ensuring that the work of the NBER is carried on in strict conformity with this object.

2. The President shall establish an internal review process to ensure that book manuscripts proposed for publication DO NOT contain policy recommendations. This shall apply both to the proceedings of conferences and to manuscripts by a single author or by one or more coauthors but shall not apply to authors of comments at NBER conferences who are not NBER affiliates.

3. No book manuscript reporting research shall be published by the NBER until the President has sent to each member of the Board a notice that a manuscript is recommended for publication and that in the President's opinion it is suitable for publication in accordance with the above principles of the NBER. Such notification will include a table of contents and an abstract or summary of the manuscript's content, a list of contributors if applicable, and a response form for use by Directors who desire a copy of the manuscript for review. Each manuscript shall contain a summary drawing attention to the nature and treatment of the problem studied and the main conclusions reached.

4. No volume shall be published until forty-five days have elapsed from the above notification of intention to publish it. During this period a copy shall be sent to any Director requesting it, and if any Director objects to publication on the grounds that the manuscript contains policy recommendations, the objection will be presented to the author(s) or editor(s). In case of dispute, all members of the Board shall be notified, and the President shall appoint an ad hoc committee of the Board to decide the matter; thirty days additional shall be granted for this purpose.

5. The President shall present annually to the Board a report describing the internal manuscript review process, any objections made by Directors before publication or by anyone after publication, any disputes about such matters, and how they were handled.

6. Publications of the NBER issued for informational purposes concerning the work of the Bureau, or issued to inform the public of the activities at the Bureau, including but not limited to the NBER Digest and Reporter, shall be consistent with the object stated in paragraph 1. They shall contain a specific disclaimer noting that they have not passed through the review procedures required in this resolution. The Executive Committee of the Board is charged with the review of all such publications from time to time.

7. NBER working papers and manuscripts distributed on the Bureau's web site are not deemed to be publications for the purpose of this resolution, but they shall be consistent with the object stated in paragraph 1. Working papers shall contain a specific disclaimer noting that they have not passed through the review procedures required in this resolution. The NBER's web site shall contain a similar disclaimer. The President shall establish an internal review process to ensure that the working papers and the web site do not contain policy recommendations, and shall report annually to the Board on this process and any concerns raised in connection with it.

8. Unless otherwise determined by the Board or exempted by the terms of paragraphs 6 and 7, a copy of this resolution shall be printed in each NBER publication as described in paragraph 2 above.

Contents

Acknowledgments

We enlisted many authors from a number of countries to achieve two goals: first, we hoped to enrich our understanding of human resources and personnel economics by looking simultaneously within firms, across firms, and across countries. Second, we believed it is important to make greater use of the new employer and employee matched data sets. The international comparisons allow us to understand how wage and employment structures vary across and within countries. The key to this project was the focus on firms and variations in wages, hiring, and promotion practices across firms within a country. Additionally, the large number of country data sets allowed us to document some variations among the countries. We believe that this is the first analysis of its kind and that it will motivate more research into the human resources structure of firms.

We thank the many authors who contributed to these goals with their own chapters, with data analysis for the introduction, and with their dedicated work over several years. We gratefully acknowledge the extensive support of the Alfred P. Sloan Foundation and, in particular, thank Gail Pesyna for her vision and support on this project and many others of this nature. We also thank Diane Lee and Khine Williams for their superb research assistance throughout the project.

Wage Structure, Raises, and Mobility
An Introduction to International Comparisons of the Structure of Wages within and across Firms

Edward P. Lazear and Kathryn L. Shaw

Introduction

The variance of wages across individuals is a summary statistic that means many things. Wage variance is an indicator of income inequality: high variance suggests high income inequality. But the "wage structure" of an economy—or the mean and the variance of wages—is also an indicator of the degree to which some individuals invest in human capital, the degree to which they work hard in response to incentives, the rates of return to human capital investments, and institutional factors that shape wage determination. Thus far, economists have had data on the distribution of wages across individuals in the economy, but not on the distribution of wages across individuals within firms. Now with new matched employer-employee data sets, we can look at the structure of wages within firms as well as across firms. New questions can be raised and addressed empirically.

Every country has wage variation across individuals. Not all workers earn the same amount. Think about the following questions:

Edward P. Lazear is currently serving as chairman of the Council of Economic Advisers. He is also the Morris Arnold Cox Senior Fellow at the Hoover Institution; the Jack Steele Parker Professor of Human Resources Management and Economics at the Graduate School of Business, Stanford University; and a research associate of the National Bureau of Economic Research. Kathryn L. Shaw is the Ernest C. Arbuckle Professor of Economics at the Graduate School of Business, Stanford University; and a research associate of the National Bureau of Economic Research.

We thank the Alfred P. Sloan Foundation for their generous and longstanding support for this work, and we thank the seminar participants at the American Economic Association (AEA), Society of Labor Economics, National Bureau of Economic Research, and university seminars.

1. Is there wage variance because workers find themselves in different firms, some of which are high-wage firms, while other firms are low-wage firms? That is, is there a high variance of mean wages across firms, or are mean wages of firms quite similar across firms?

2. Is there wage variance across individuals because within every firm, some workers are highly paid and others are less well paid?

3. Do all firms have the same wage structure, or are wage structures widely varying across firms? That is, do some firms have a wage structure that is very compressed—paying low- and high-wage workers very similar wages—while other firms have a very dispersed or high-variance structure of wages within the firm? If some wage structures within firms are more compressed than others, what factors account for differences across firms? Do most firms specialize in a narrow range of jobs, so the structure of pay looks very different across firms? Does the boundary of the firm matter? When there is pay compression, does it result in losses of the most able workers or of the retention of the least able?

4. The distribution of income is always skewed across individuals within a country—it has a long upper tail. Is this because salaries within firms are skewed, or does the skewness result from a few firms paying high wage levels? Skewness is relevant in the context of tournament theory, which suggests that there should be skewness within firms because salary jumps at the higher end of the skill hierarchy are greater than salary jumps at the lower end of the hierarchy as a reward for effort.

We can ask similar questions about wage growth rates, or pay raises, for individuals:

1. Are average pay raises very different across firms so that finding employment in a high-growth firm insures a person of high wage growth?

2. Are pay raises uniform within firms, or are some workers treated very differently from others? It is possible that workers' raises within firms are nearly identical—moving lockstep across workers when conditions change for the firm—so that differences in wage growth across workers in the economy is accounted for primarily by firm differences in mean growth rates. It is also possible that mean wage growth rates are very similar across firms, but that significant within-firm variation produces the economy's variation in wage growth rates.

Answers to these questions are revealing. For example, if wage levels are very different across firms, then firms must be sorting workers based on individual workers' levels of human capital or their effort levels, and, moreover, workers can improve their pay only by moving across firms. On the other hand, if mean wages are very similar across firms but wage variance is high within firms, then human capital development within firms and promotions within firms are predominant features of the labor market. Furthermore, if pay increases are very different across workers within the same firm, then effort and skills are being heavily rewarded within firms.

Finally, do the answers to these questions vary across countries? Do wage structures appear to vary significantly across countries as a function of different institutions or human capital? Ultimately, the answers might reflect difference sources of productivity in firms. So do the patterns help explain differences in productivity across countries?

Until very recently, it would be impossible to answer these questions because the answers would require data on all of the workers in a firm for a large number of firms. Now this required data is available from a number of different countries to answer many of these questions and more. The employer-employee matched data sets, from many European countries and from the United States, either contain information on nearly all workers and firms in that country or information on all workers within a large subset of firms. As a result, it is possible to examine the worker's position in the context of his or her entire firm. Additionally, the existence of data for a large number of firms permits new questions, like those listed in the preceding, to be addressed.

This is not the first time such questions have been asked. The first economics paper on this subject is Lazear (1992). That study made use of a complete data set on one large firm and studied both wages and mobility. The work was followed by similar papers by Baker, Gibbs, and Holmstrom (1994a,b). They studied a different company and also examined the structure of promotion, ports of entry, and wages. The advantage of those analyses is that it is possible to examine the entire firm, thereby analyzing promotion paths, determinants and consequences, as well as wage determination and structure. The disadvantage is that because the studies only cover two different firms, it is difficult to generalize the results, and not all results are consistent across papers.

It is important, therefore, to have data not only on entire firms and all workers in them, but also on a large number of firms so that results can be generalized. The authors in this book have used the new style of data to ask and answer questions that cannot be answered with traditional data sets. For example, many of these data sets can be used to calculate returns to experience and tenure and can perhaps do it better because of their richness. In this book, we have steered away from some questions because they are addressed well by traditional individual-level panel data sets that use the individual as the unit of analysis and sample randomly from a large population. Those data sets have very few observations from the same firm and, in most cases, the identity of the firm is unknown. As a consequence, neither a firm's wage structure nor its hiring and promotion patterns can be gleaned from traditional data. Our focus is on exactly the questions that could not be answered historically using individual panel data.

In this introduction, we set out to do two things. First, we use the data from all countries to address the questions, drawing out general patterns about firm wage structure, promotion, hiring, and mobility patterns to answer the questions posed in the preceding and more. Second, because this kind of analysis is new and because we are covering a large number of countries and studies in this introduction, we aim to raise as many questions as we provide answers. But the questions themselves may be useful, if for no other reason than they cast light on the kinds of issues that can be addressed with this type of data.

This study is based on the extensive empirical work done by all of the country-specific authors in this book. The authors provided to us statistics that they each constructed to be as comparable as possible across countries so that we might identify patterns across countries (though differences in the underlying data sets do not make these statistics perfectly comparable, as described in the following). However, in this introduction, we make no attempt to delve deeply into the sources of differences across countries. The individual country chapters describe the primary institutional features of the countries and the macroeconomic conditions. In addition, the country chapter authors provide much greater expertise and analysis of data that is specific to the countries (such as the occupational structures of firms or productivity information). After the following broad description of the data, we then look at the structure of wage levels and at alternative models of interpreting these structures. After that, we turn to wage growth rates and mobility.

The Data

The data come from all of the Scandinavian countries (Denmark, Finland, Norway, Sweden) and from Belgium, France, Germany, Italy, the Netherlands, as well as the United States. The sampling frames are different across countries. In a broad fashion, we can group the data of the countries into five basic sampling schemes, as shown in table I.1. The sequence of data is as follows. At the top of the list are the country data sets that cover most of the populations, and then descending in the table are data sets that cover subsets of the population covered in the data. For example, at the top of the list are Denmark, Norway, and the United States because they have data on all workers in all firms in the economy (though for a subset of states in the United States). Next, Finland, Sweden, and Belgium have data on all workers in large firms; Germany and Norway (using more matched data) have data on all workers in manufacturing. Italy and France cover all firms, but within firms they have only a sample of workers, not data on every worker.[1] Finally, additional analysis is done for Norway

---

1. Italy has a 1/90 sample within firms, so the Italian authors provide information on synthetic firms by taking data from similar industries and locations and blending them into cells, which they treat as firms. France has a 1/25 sample, so we correct statistics for this sampling.

Table I.1   **Country classifications by type of data**

Data type	Country details
All private firms, all employees	United States—all firms, all employees, wages plus bonuses, quarterly data annualized Denmark—all firms, all employees, wages plus bonuses, annual (November) The Netherlands—all firms (including nonprofit, government), all employees, wage plus bonuses, annual (September)
Firms in employer associations, all employees	Finland—employer association (TT; large firms), all employees, wages plus bonuses, annual Belgium—random sample of firms, all employees, 1995, wages plus bonuses, annual Sweden (plants)—all industries, plants only, all employees, annual
Employer associations, some industries, all employees	Germany—manufacturing and services (IAB; large firms), plants only, top-coded wages are input, annual (June) Norway—heavy manufacturing (industry 38), all employees
All private firms, sample of employees	Italy—private sector, large employers, permanent employees, 1/90 sample of workers, annual (May) France—all firms, 1/25 sample of workers in firms, wages plus bonuses
Firms in employer associations, all employees, but only white- or blue-collar	Norway—white-collar, employer association (NHO), manufacturing and services (more manufacturing), all employees, but only employees, wage plus bonuses Sweden (firm)—white-collar, employer association (SAF); blue-collar, employer association (SAF)

Note: TT = Confederation of Finnish Industry;
IAB = Institute for Employment Research;
NHO = Confederation of Norwegian Business and Industry; and
SAF = Swedish Employer's Federation.

and Sweden for white- and blue-collar workers because additional detailed matched data is available for these groups.

Table I.1 also provides a brief summary of the key wage variables and the age or time restrictions on the data, but for more detailed analysis of the country-specific differences, see appendix table I.A.1. Inevitably, variables differ, as in how wages are measured (with or without bonuses, hourly or salary, monthly or annual), and these differences naturally enter the statistical comparisons that we make. In addition to the descriptions in appendix table I.A.1, each chapter describes its own data in detail.

Appendix tables I.A.2 and I.A.3 contain basic descriptive statistics for all the countries for the key variables that are used in the following figure.

The key to constituting an employer-employee matched data set is that there is substantial information on a cross section of workers without firm spanning many firms. This is essential to drawing inference within wage structure, worker mobility, and promotion and hiring patterns and across firms.

Primary Findings

The main finding is that countries are remarkably similar in their structures of wage levels and of wage changes. Given the similarity of the wage structures across countries, we reach some general conclusions based on the data. The discussion section at the end of the chapter introduces more policy conclusions on why these empirical regularities matter.

1. There is a striking amount of wage variation within firms: the within firm wage variation is about 60 to 80 percent of the wage dispersion across all individuals in the economy. There is also variation across firms in the mean wages they pay: the standard deviation of the mean wages of firms is about 60 percent of the standard deviation across all individuals. However, when we scale the mean wages firms pay relative to the average worker's wage in the economy, one standard deviation in firm means is only 15 to 20 percent of the average wage: firms don't differ that much in what they pay. Overall, despite very different labor institutions across countries, the evidence favoring high within-firm wage dispersion appears across countries.

2. The across- (or between-) firm differences in wages appears to be growing over time. That is, for a significant number of countries, the firm-specific fixed effects are explaining a larger percent of the distribution of wages across firms. This may be because firms are increasingly segregated according to the skills that they require. Or it may be that firms that pay high-level efficiency wages (in exchange for skills or low turnover) are increasingly diverging from those that are pushed to low-level market clearing wages in lower-skilled or highly competitive industries. Or it may also reflect the boundaries of the firm associated with outsourcing: the high-skill firms now use more outsourcing for their low-skill jobs.

3. With respect to wage growth, although firms differ in the average raises they give in a particular year, firms do not tie all workers to the same percentage point raise within the firm. The standard deviation of raises within firm is between 10 and 20 percentage points, even when the average wage increase for the firm is close to zero. This is most consistent with the view that firms respond to outside pressure (either market or governmental) to raise workers' wages commensurate with some occupational or skill standard; firms are not raising all workers' wages equally in response to the conditions within the firm.

4. Mobility levels differ across countries, but even here, mobility patterns seem relatively consistent. High-wage firms have low turnover. Large firms are higher wage and lower entry.

Composing Wage Variance

Turn to the question raised at the outset, how much do firms differ? 1 depicts the two extremes views of the variance of wage levels

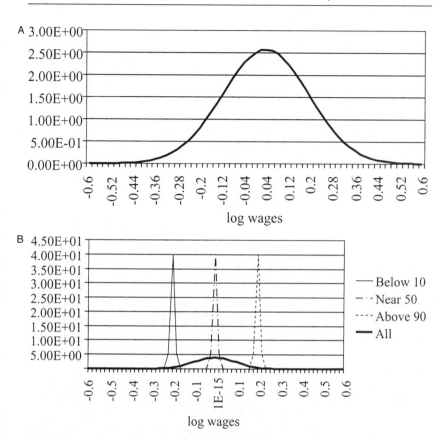

Fig. I.1 **Wage distributions within and between firms: _A_, All firms have identical wage distributions: Firms have the same within-firm wage variation and no between-firm variation. The probability density function for the country is the same as that for the median firm and extreme firms. _B_, All firms have similar within-firm wage distributions and different between-firm wage distributions.**

within and across firms. In panel A of figure I.1, all firms are identical, so the variance of wages for each firm is the same as the variance of wages for the country. At the other extreme, in panel B of figure I.1, all firms differ, so the variance of wages within firms is very narrow, and the variance of wages for the country arises from differences in the variance of mean wages across firms.

The different sources of wage variation in figure I.1 can be decomposed more systematically, which is useful later in interpreting the sources of wage variation. Decompose the variance of wages across individuals into the contribution of firms:

$$(1) \qquad \sigma^2 = \sum_{j=1}^{J} p_j \sigma_j^2 + \sum_{j=1}^{J} p_j (\overline{w}_j - \overline{\overline{w}}_{.})^2,$$

where p_j is the share of workers in the economy who are working in firm j, σ_j^2 is the variance of wages in firm j, $\overline{w}_j$ is the mean wage for firm j (across its workers), $\overline{\overline{w}}$ is the mean wage for the entire economy (across its workers and firms). Thus, the variance of wages for the economy will be high if (1) mean wages differ across firms, so $|\overline{w}_j - \overline{\overline{w}}|$ is large (as in panel B of figure I.1) or if (2) the within-firm variance of wages, σ_j^2, is large (as in panel A of figure I.1), or if both are true (not drawn in a figure).

The wage structure underlying figure I.1 assumes that firms have identical wage variance within each firm. Figure I.2 depicts a more likely structure. In that figure, the variance of wages is not only different across firms, but also rises with the mean wage of the firm. There are numerous reasons for the positive correlation between wage level and variance, such as rising levels of human capital in firms, that are introduced later.

The Structure of Wages: Wage Levels

To get started, let us point out some initial observations. There are two (among many) ways in which data have been displayed by the authors of this book. The first is to use the individual as the unit of analysis. The second, and way most unique to this structure, is to use the firm as the unit of analysis. Table I.A1 does the comparison. Here, the average level of wages, the standard deviations, and 90th and 10th percentile are displayed. The units are own-country currencies, so comparisons cannot be made across countries without conversions to ratios or other unit-free numbers. The mean level of average wages in the firm-based data is always lower than that of the mean for the individual-based data, although there is some variation in ratios across countries (see tables in the country chapters). This reflects

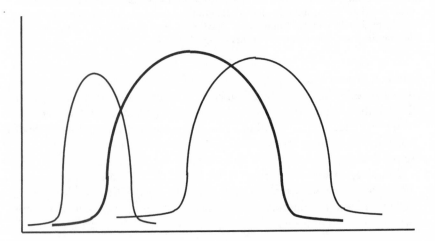

Fig. I.2   Positive correlation in within-firm mean wages and variance

weighting. If all firms were of identical size, then the firm average would equal the individual average. The fact that the firm mean is below the individual mean implies that the largest firms, which account for disproportionately more workers, have higher average wages than the smaller firms. The firm average, which does not weight by firm size, puts relatively more emphasis on the small firms and pulls the average wage down. That firm size and average wage are correlated is not a new result (Brown and Medoff 1989; Fox 2007).

The key question raised in the preceding is, how does the variation in wages within and across firms contribute to the variation in wages for the country? First, if all firms were alike, then their wage distributions would be identical to the distribution for the country as a whole as shown in panel A of figure I.1. At the other extreme, firms might treat their workers very similarly within the firm, and the variation in wages throughout the country could be accounted for by differences in the mean value of wages between firms, as shown in panel B of figure I.1.

We begin by displaying wage distributions for some typical countries. Consider the patterns illustrated by Norway, France, and Denmark (as typical countries) in figure I.3. In figure I.3, there are wage distributions displayed for three typical firms. The Low Wage Below 10th percentile distribution represents the wage distribution for firms in the sample that have mean wages below the 10th percentile of the wage distribution of firms' mean wages.[2] The other two firm types are the firms Around Median Wage (in the 45th to 55th percentile of the firm mean wage distribution) and the High Wage Above 90th percentile. The bold line is the distribution for all individuals in the data.

Norway's situation is typical and is a compromise between panels A and B of figure I.1. Firms have very considerable wage dispersion within them, though not as high as the wage dispersion across all individuals in the economy. The typical firm is not the almost spiked distribution as shown in panel B of figure I.1. However, the wage distribution for the typical firm that is below the 10th percentile is tighter than that for the country as a whole. The same is true for the wage distribution of the typical firm around the median and for the firm with mean wages in the top 10 percent of firms.[3] While wage dispersion within firms is very high, firms have many different jobs within the firm. As a result of differences in the means, the wage distributions of high-wage and low-wage firms are by and large disjoint. At the mean, some of these firms have low pay, low skill; some have

2. In these figures, each distribution is a graph of the normal distribution given the mean wage and standard deviation for that subsample.
3. The typical firm was constructed by averaging the mean log wage and the within-firm standard deviation of log wages for firms in the 0 to 10th percentile, the 45th to 55th percentile, and the 90th and above percentile. The distributions were constructed assuming that wages are distributed log normally.

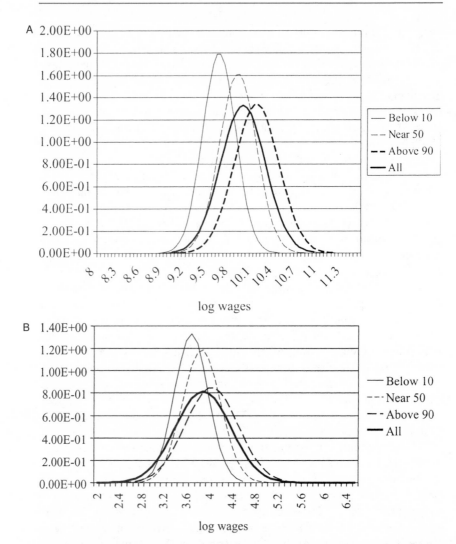

Fig. I.3   **Wage distributions for some typical countries: *A*, Norway 1997; *B*, France 1996; *C*, Denmark 2000**

Notes: Below 10 refers to the subsample of firms for which each firm has its mean wage of the firm below the 10th percentile of the mean wages of all firms. Near 50 refers to the subsample of firms for which each firm has its mean wage of the firm near the 50th percentile of the mean wages of all firms. Above 90 refers to the subsample of firms for which each firm has its mean wage of the firm above the 90th percentile of the mean wages of all firms. All refers to all firms.

high pay, high skill (or high variance). But the high variance of wages within firms causes wage distributions of firms with very different means to overlap.

Figures I.4 through I.6 summarize these primary results across countries on the structure of wages. Figure I.4 graphs the ratio of the average of the

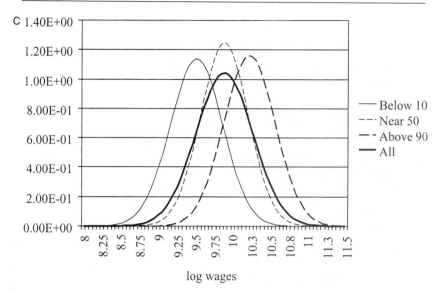

Fig. I.3   (cont.)

within-firm standard deviation of wages divided by the country's standard deviation of wages. Figure I.4 shows that, on average, the dispersion of wages within firms is about 60 percent to 80 percent of the total wage dispersion for the country (across individuals). Figure I.5 graphs the ratio of the standard deviation of the mean wages of the firms divided by the country's mean wage. By this measure, it appears that firms don't differ much in their mean wages—the standard deviation is only 10 percent to 20 percent of the average wage for the country. However, the dispersion of mean wages for firms is high relative to the overall dispersion of means: the standard deviation of mean wages of the firms is about 60 percent of the total wage dispersion for the country (figure I.6).

Thus, these figures show that—across all countries—the structure of wages is a compromise between panels A and B of figure I.1. There is very high wage dispersion within firms. But the mean wages of firms also differ considerably: there are high-wage firms and there are low-wage firms. The figure for Norway, figure I.3, is very representative of the structure of wages across countries.

What is especially striking about these results is that it is true across all countries.[4] Figure I.7 expands upon these two points by providing the average coefficients of variation for within firms across all countries. Countries are remarkably similar: for the average firm, the standard deviation of wages is about 25 percent of the mean wage. For example, Finland has

4. The low number belongs to Italy and the Italian data contain synthetic firms that are closer to a random draw from the overall population. This reduces reported dispersion below the amount that would be present in real firms.

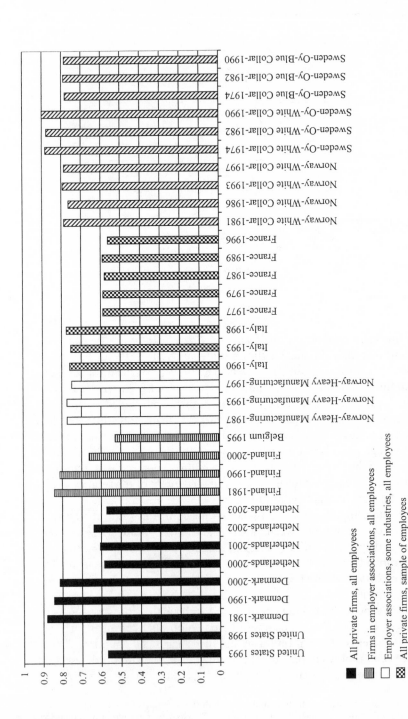

Fig. I.4   Ratio of the average within-firm standard deviation of wages to the standard deviation of wages (across all individuals)

■ All private firms, all employees

▥ Firms in employer associations, all employees

☐ Employer associations, some industries, all employees

▨ All private firms, sample of employees

▨ Firms in employer associations, all employees, but only white or blue collar

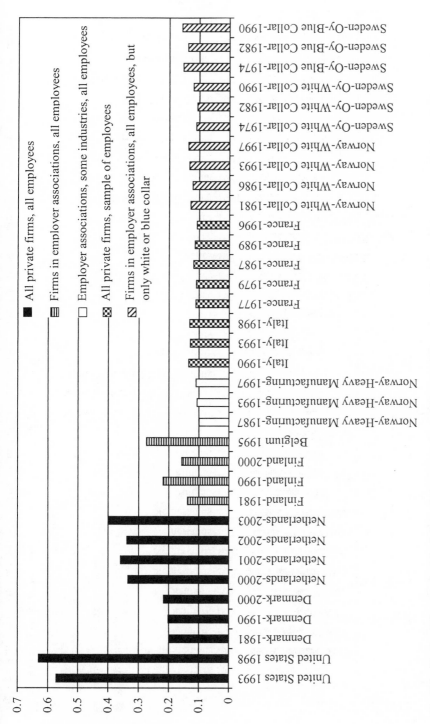

Fig. I.5 Ratio of the standard deviation of the mean wages of firms to the mean wage for the country (across all individuals)

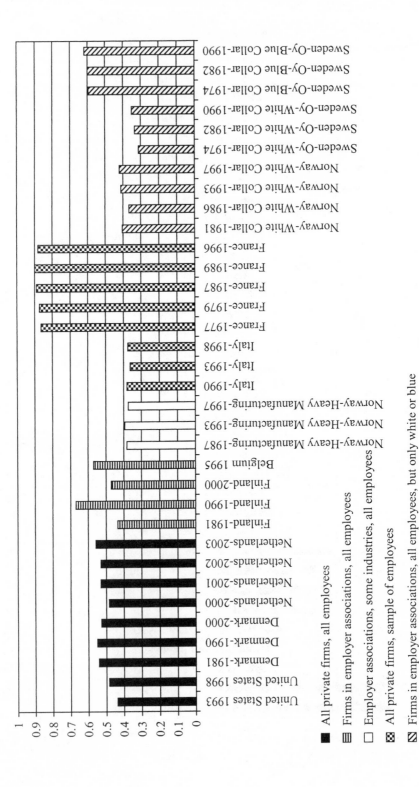

Fig. I.6 Ratio of the standard deviation of the mean wages of firms to the standard deviation of wages for the country (across all individuals)

■ All private firms, all employees

▥ Firms in employer associations, all employees

☐ Employer associations, some industries, all employees

▨ All private firms, sample of employees

▨ Firms in employer associations, all employees, but only white or blue

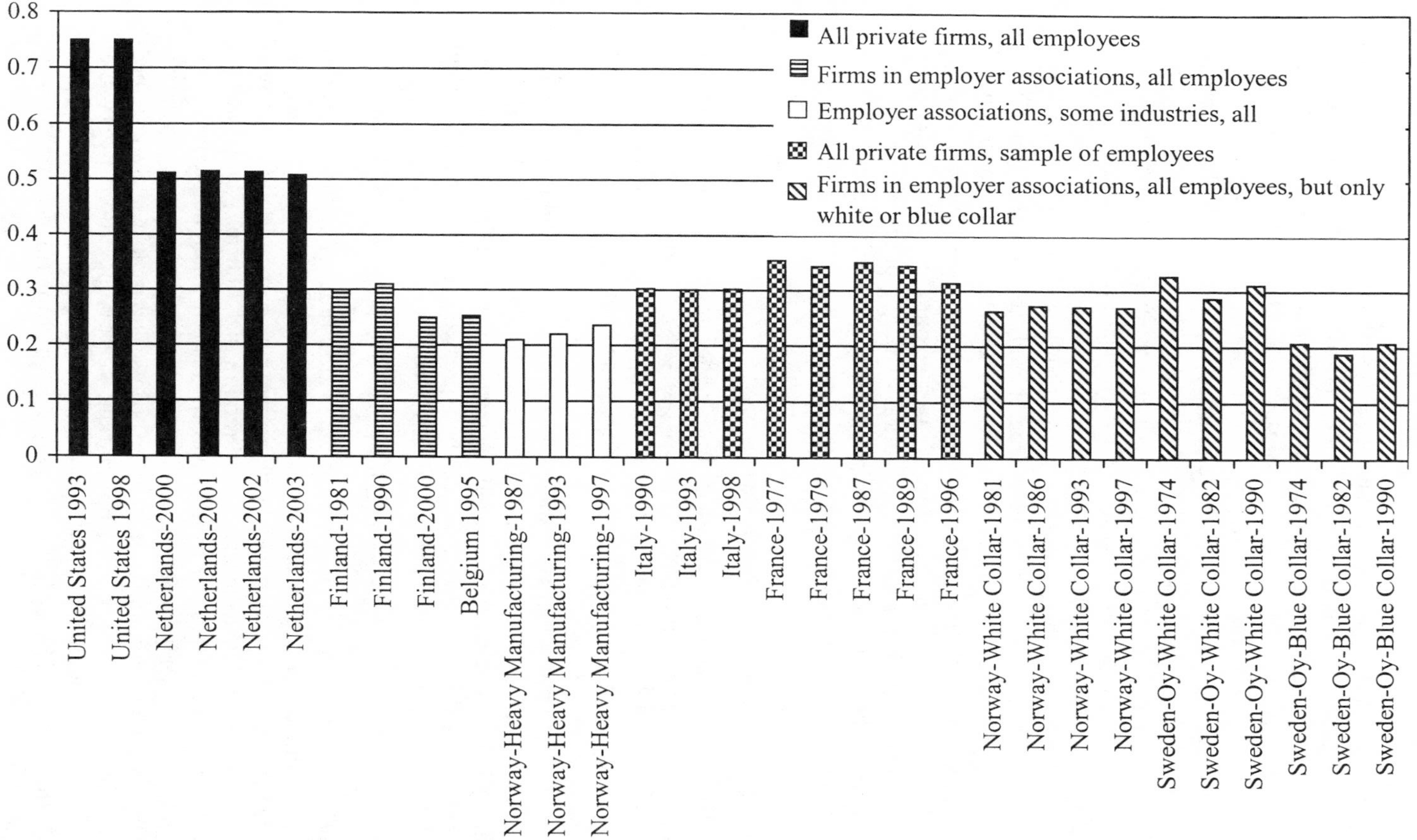
0.8
0.7
0.6
0.5
0.4
0.3
0.2
0.1
0
All private firms, all employees
Firms in employer associations, all employees
Employer associations, some industries, all
All private firms, sample of employees
Firms in employer associations, all employees, but only white or blue collar
United States 1993
United States 1998
Netherlands-2000
Netherlands-2001
Netherlands-2002
Netherlands-2003
Finland-1981
Finland-1990
Finland-2000
Belgium 1995
Norway-Heavy Manufacturing-1987
Norway-Heavy Manufacturing-1993
Norway-Heavy Manufacturing-1997
Italy-1990
Italy-1993
Italy-1998
France-1977
France-1979
France-1987
France-1989
France-1996
Norway-White Collar-1981
Norway-White Collar-1986
Norway-White Collar-1993
Norway-White Collar-1997
Sweden-Oy-White Collar-1974
Sweden-Oy-White Collar-1982
Sweden-Oy-White Collar-1990
Sweden-Oy-Blue Collar-1974
Sweden-Oy-Blue Collar-1982
Sweden-Oy-Blue Collar-1990

Fig. I.7 Within-firm coefficient of variation of wages

considerably different firms in that the firms with larger internal wage dispersion have coefficients of variation equal to about .35, whereas those with little internal wage dispersion have coefficients of around .15. But the average is around .25, which is about the same value as the average value for almost all countries. The average firm across Europe has a standard deviation of wages that is about one-fourth the wage of that firm. This is slightly higher in some countries and slightly lower in others, but the variation is small relative to the within-country differences in coefficients of variation for wages. Whether this reflects some kind of universal constant remains to be determined.

Thus, despite different labor market institutions, countries do not differ dramatically in their wage patterns. Does it imply that there is a typical skill distribution for all countries and these are reflected in the coefficient of variation that is seen for the country as a whole? Or does it imply that wage policies vary across firms, but tend to average out at the country level because firms adopt the same distribution of wage polices irrespective of country? These questions remain open ones, but we turn to themes that describe the wage patterns.

The Structure of Wages: Some Themes

What do these results tell us about our basic models of the determination of wages and productivity across workers? To answer, we begin by identifying three different models of wage setting that permeate the literature. Given these models, we then ask, why do workers differ within firms, and why do firms differ?

The best known theory of wage setting is human capital theory, which states in its most basic form that workers are paid on the basis of their general skills and that these skills can be measured as a scaler, meaning that there is one skill, and everything can be expressed in efficiency units of that skill. The wage equation for individual wages is:

$$(2) \qquad w_{ijt} = \beta_0 + \beta_1 \, \text{Educ}_{ijt} + \beta_2 \, \text{Exper}_{ijt},$$

where wages for person i in firm j at time t are a function of his or her education and experience. Were human capital the only determinant of wages, then it would not matter at all in which firm a worker finds him- or herself. The competitive labor market would require that all firms pay the worker exactly the same thing, irrespective of the firm in which he or she works. Otherwise, other firms could easily steal him or her away by paying a slightly higher wage and capturing the profits. This is most easily described as a spot market view of the labor market, where competition forces workers to be paid on the basis of the productivity, which is in turn reflected perfectly in measurable skills. The β_1 and β_2 in equation (2) measure the rates of return to skills.

Table I.2   **Models of wage setting that would produce figures I.1**

	Wages vary within firms: Broad dispersion of skill or effort within the firm.	Wages vary across firms: Workers sort into firms based on their skill or effort levels.
	Panel A of figure I.1: All firms alike, but high within-firm wage dispersion $\overline{w}_j = \overline{\overline{w}}$; $\sigma_{\overline{w}l} = 0$	Panel B of figure I.1: All workers paid same within firm; Panel firms differ in mean wages. $\overline{w}_j \neq \overline{\overline{w}}$; $\sigma_{\overline{w}l} > 0$; σ_{wl}, low;
Wage setting based on occupation (human capital skills)	All firms have a broad distribution of occupations within the firm (same distribution of human capital).	Wage structures differ across firms because there is one occupation per firm. Workers sort into firms by occupation or by skill level.
Wage setting based on wage policy aimed incentive pay (e.g., piece rates or tournaments) or at wage compression	Workers identical skills; tournament or piece rates create pay dispersion. Or workers differ in ambition, but distribution of types identical in every firm.	Workers sort across firms according to preferences for piece rate pay. Narrow wage dispersion implies no tournaments; there is pay compression within the firm.
Institutional wage setting (such as unions) for sharing rents between worker and firm	All firms have a broad distribution of occupations or job titles on which wages are based, or a steep seniority structure on which wages are based.	Wage structures differ across because workers sort by firms occupation, or because pay is a function of the profitability of the firm.

The human capital model of wage setting does not tell us why wages differ within or across firms because firms are irrelevant. Firms matter if we add a model of worker sorting across firms and thus of differences in the underlying production functions of firms. Table I.2 lays out the alternatives. In column (1), there is large wage dispersion within firms, and all firms are identical (mimicking panel A of figure I.1). There is high wage dispersion within firms if the within-firm production function requires a combination of workers with different skills to optimally produce output. The appropriate model of the firm would be one in which workers within the firm have complementary skills, as in models of teamwork or of hierarchy.[5] In contrast, if firms differ by occupation, then workers are likely to be sorted by occupation or skill: the within-firm wage dispersion is low, but there are large differences in mean wages across firms (as in column [2] of table I.2). Last, it is likely that mean wages and the variance of wages are positively correlated: high-human-capital firms (like law firms or large businesses) are more likely to have teams or hierarchies that produce higher wage variance than low-wage, low-human-capital firms. A law firm will

---

5. See Lazear (1999) for a model of complementary team workers and Hubbard (2000) for a model of complementary workers within a hierarchy.

have high-wage lawyers and lower-wage assistants and janitors, but a janitorial service firm will have few high-paid managers. This theoretical positive correlation between the mean wage and variance is displayed in figure I.2.

An alternative model of wage setting, a purely institutional theory of wage determination, also has the implication that a worker's wage is independent of the firm in which he or she is employed. Suppose that wages were set by a central authority and the authority set the wage based on the worker's occupational title, where his or her occupational title was determined by his or her worker characteristics. For example, a particular level of experience and educational background could be used to determine occupational status using some index, such as

(3) $w_{ijt} = \beta_0 + b \, \text{Educ}_{ijt} + c \, \text{Exper}_{ijt}.$

Although the index might look similar to a human capital wage function, there need be no direct relation of the coefficients b and c to anything having to do with productivity. The central authority, such as a union, might simply determine that the selected weights b and c are appropriate in some sense, based on equity or any other consideration. In the institutional model, the sharing of rents between the worker and firm is determined by institutional rules (such as those set by union negotiations).

As in the human capital model, the institutional model predicts wage dispersion within firms if firms contain many occupations, or, alternatively, predicts very different mean wages across firms if firms are organized by occupation or industry (comparing the predictions of columns [1] and [2] of row [2] in table I.2). The institutional model differs from the human capital model in that the underlying model of wage setting is quite different despite similar predictions. In an institutional model of wage setting, pay dispersion may arise within the firm if pay rises with seniority, even if all workers have the same level of human capital. Alternatively, workers may have very different levels of human capital, but the same wages within the firm, if unions compress all wages to be equal. Firm profitability also enters. If negotiated pay is a function of the profitability of the firm, there will be little wage dispersion within the firm, but very different mean wages across firms as a function of profits. In this case, "a rising tide lifts all boats": rising profits raise the pay for all workers in the firm, and there is no wage dispersion within the firm.

Finally, firms can have "wage policies" that are aimed at incentives for effort or at optimal sorting and that thereby affect wage dispersion. Most wage policies that are aimed at pay for performance will increase wage dispersion within firms. That is true of piece-rate policies or of implicit contract theories that create divergence between wages and productivity. Consider first the piece-rate model, in which a firm pays a piece rate that is given by

(4) $Pay_{ijt} = a + b \, Output_{ijt}.$

The higher is b, the greater is the amount of effort that a worker puts into a job.[6] Thus, if workers differ in skills or in effort, then piece-rate pay accentuates the variance of pay within firms. Similarly, tournament models increase within-firm pay variance as well. Tournament models (Lazear and Rosen 1981), which are most applicable to white-collar workers, suggest that wage structures within firms serve incentive purposes and that it is the hierarchical structure of accelerating wages at each level, rather than the current wage, that determines the strength of the incentives. In tournament theories, workers at higher levels of the firm's hierarchy receive pay that has impacts on those below them. Lower-level workers want to become higher-level workers, and their desire to climb the internal job ladder depends on the raise that workers receive when they are promoted (nonmonetary as well as monetary). Because the optimal size of the raise depends on internal conditions like the riskiness of the activity and the shape of the firm's hierarchy and the firm's production function, tournament theory suggests that workers will be treated differently in different types of firms, even when the workers have the same basic characteristics. Overall, tournaments increase pay dispersion within firms, holding fixed the level of human capital.

Wage policies, such as forms of incentive pay, can also cause striking differences in mean wages across firms due to worker sorting.[7] Firms offering incentive pay are also the high-wage, high-effort firms. Those firms without incentive pay are low wage, low effort, and thus there is variance of mean wages across firms when workers preferring the high effort firm sort to those and others do not (as summarized in column [2] of table I.2). These differences in mean wages and incentives reflect differences in the production environment that determines the value of incentive pay.

In sum, these models suggest at least two possible reasons why firms might have significant within-firm variation in wages. First, and most obvious, is that workers are different. The workers that firms employ within are not identical, and, as a result, wages reflect the skill heterogeneity of the workers within the firm. Those wages might be determined completely externally, either by a competitive labor market process, in the extreme by a spot market, or by a centralized wage setter, like a government or tripartite (labor, management, government) body. If worker skills are different within firms and wages are set externally, then wages within firms will reflect the underlying skill distributions within them.

---

6. The worker maximizes $a + b \, (output) - C(output)$, where $C(output)$ is the effort cost of producing a given output level and where $C' > 0$. The first order condition is $C'(output) = b$. Because $C' > 0$, increasing b increases the amount of effort.

7. For example, see McLeod and Malcolmson (1989) and Stole and Zweibel (1996) for models of bargaining theories, where the outside alternatives as well as the worker's value to the firm affect the actual wage level, and thus create differences in what firms pay.

Alternatively, the wage variance within the firm might reflect wage policy, not skill heterogeneity. Even if all workers were identical ex ante, a wage policy could result in paying different wages to different people. This happens in a tournament, for example, where pay is more dispersed than ex ante talent and where the relation of pay to ex post output is positive, but with a correlation far from 1. In the other direction is that wages may be more compressed than ex ante ability. Pay compression might simply reflect wage policy of the firm. It is well known, for example, that certain institutions, like labor unions, compress wages relative to nonunion firms. It is also possible that wage setting in a centralized or negotiated environment might result in wage compression that brings up the wages of the least skilled and cuts the wages of the most skilled. There is no reason why this pattern would necessarily be uniform across firms, industries, or occupations. Thus, pay policy is another variable that lies behind the within-firm wage distribution.

It is key to try to disentangle these alternative explanations. That takes us beyond this introductory analysis, but in the next sections, we will describe evidence that speaks to these differences and will try to suggest additional questions or lines of research that might assist in obtaining answers.

The Structure of Wages: Disentangling the Themes

The data show that across all countries there is very significant wage dispersion within firms. However, firms are different: mean wages vary considerably.

We cannot identify whether the wage dispersion within firms is due to the heterogeneity of skills within firms or due to wage policies of incentive pay that increase pay variance. However, some forms of wage policies can be rejected. We have two pieces of evidence rejecting the possibility that firms compress pay within the firm (relative to market-level wage rates). The first is the correlation between firms' mean wages and firms' spread in wages within each firm. Second is the correlation between the wage spread in the firm and worker mobility.

Wage Level and Wage Variance

There is a positive correlation between the log wage and the within-firm variance of the log wage (figure I.8). The correlation ranges between .1 and .3 across countries. There are a number of interpretations of this finding. Two are worth mentioning. The first is causal; the second is statistical.

One causal explanation is the human capital story: firms that have high levels of human capital are more likely to have a high within-firm variance of human capital. The second causal explanation is more subtle, regarding wage policy. Apparently, firms are rejecting policies of pay compression in favor of policies of within-firm incentives and human capital growth. A

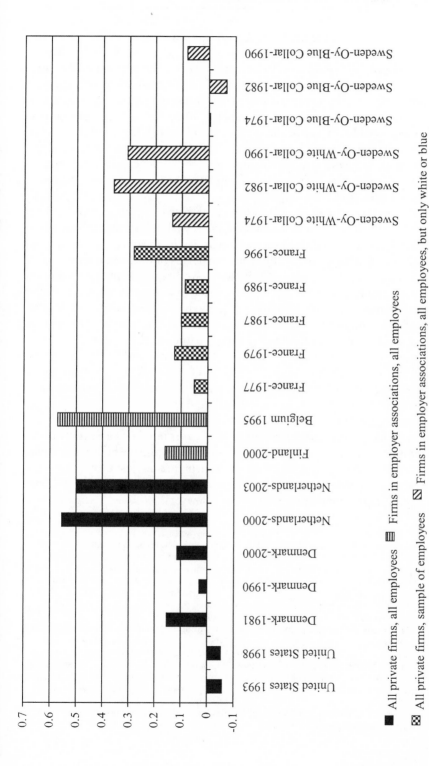

Fig. I.8 Correlation of the within-firm standard deviation of log (wages) and the within-firm mean log (wage)

■ All private firms, all employees   ▦ Firms in employer associations, all employees

▨ All private firms, sample of employees   ▨ Firms in employer associations, all employees, but only white or blue

policy of pay compression—or egalitarian pay and compressed incentives—could arise in large firms with high mean wages. Such a policy of pay compression could increase performance if it enhances teamwork and workers are very complementary (or have high amounts of firm-specific human capital). However, such a policy could be harmful to productivity—it would induce adverse sorting and adverse incentives: the top performers would sort out of the firm and would work less hard if the firm lacks tournaments or piece-rate pay.[8] The data rejects pay compression: high-wage firms are also high-incentive, high human capital firms. In the next subsection, we provide evidence on mobility that also rejects the pay compression model.

A second explanation for the correlation between average wage and its standard deviation is purely statistical. It is well known that the distribution of wages is positively skewed: there is significant positive skew in worker ability. Suppose that firms are partitions of the overall income distribution. A positive correlation between average and standard deviation of wage would result. For example, suppose that wage distribution is partitioned into two firms: the bottom 50 percent of wage earners work for the low-wage firm, and the top 50 percent worked for the high-wage firm. The high-wage firm would have higher variance due to the positive skew of the overall income distribution. Thus, if there are low- and high-wage firms due to people sorting by human capital levels across firms, the skewness of the wage distribution will produce a positive correlation between wages levels and variance.[9]

Finally, the basic results—of positively correlated mean and wage variance—rule out the "extreme sorting" of workers into firms according to either their occupation, skill, or effort level. Even within the high-wage firms, there are lower-wage workers: high-wage firms are not just firms of lawyers or high-tech programmers. Law firms must have janitors, but building cleaning contracting firms need not have lawyers.

---

8. The sorting mechanism is more important at the firm level than at the country level. Between country there is less sorting than between firms within a country. Workers who do not like pay compression in Sweden might choose to move to Denmark, but less readily than those at Volvo move to Saab. As a result, the correlation between average wage and variance in wage might be expected to be stronger within county than between. (It is difficult to compare wages across countries because of exchange rates, purchasing power parity [PPP] issues of nontradeable goods, etc.)

9. The positive skew could be due to luck or effort, or both. Assume the firm has a wage policy of incentive pay. When the firm gets "lucky," the incentive pay rewards all those within the firm, but it rewards the highest paid the most. An extreme example of this would be stock options. For example, Microsoft was a high wage and a high wage variance firm due to options and incentive pay. When Microsoft got lucky, many within Microsoft did well. Because greater amounts of stock options and incentives are given out to those at the highest pay levels, there is a positive correlation between pay level and variance. Researchers could examine the role of luck by looking more closely at the role of individual fixed effects versus firm effects in contributing to high variance income.

Wage Level and Worker Mobility

A key determinant of whether within-firm wage variation reflects wage policy or underlying characteristics is the pattern of mobility. For example, consider a firm that has a small standard deviation of the log of wages. This could reflect a policy of pay compression, or it could reflect a homogeneous workforce. If it is pay compression that hurts the top relative to the bottom, then the top workers should be more likely to leave the firm than the bottom workers. If we find a pattern where firms with tight wage distributions also have disproportionate exit of the highest paid workers, then the inference that we would draw is that the pay compression is policy. Conversely, if low-wage workers have their pay increased relative to the market in such firms, then they should be less likely to leave. There would be no reason for top workers to leave disproportionately nor for bottom workers to stay disproportionately if all were paid their competitive wage.

Figure I.9 provides some evidence. The exit rates of workers who are highly paid but work in compressed pay firms are lower than the exit rates of top workers in noncompressed firms. If these findings hold up, they would suggest that the pattern observed reflects worker heterogeneity more than it does wage policy. That is, firms that have more compressed wages have a more homogeneous workforce, and within that workforce there is less difference between the top workers and the median workers. As a result, top workers are less likely to be underpaid in that environment and less likely to exit. Overall, we do not find evidence that pay compression in firms is pushing out more skilled workers. We leave it to future research to disentangle the relationship between compression and mobility.[10]

In sum, firms that allow high wage spread also have higher wages. This pushes a productivity interpretation: firms that allow disparate wage treatment also reap the benefit through incentive and selection effects of higher productivity. Firms that compress wages drive out their best workers and stifle incentives to produce. However, workers don't exit more in compressed wage firms. Apparently, firms with compressed wages also have higher wage levels or lower skill levels. But across all countries, we find no evidence that policies of pay compression are reducing productivity.

The general conclusion from this section is that there is considerable within-firm variance in wages in all countries. Although firms differ considerably within a country, both in terms of average wage and in terms of wage spread, there is a significant amount of variation within each firm.

---

10. Why is pay compression and exit rate negatively correlated? It could be because large firms have high exit rates and have high but compressed wages. In these data, exit rates are lower in large firms that have compressed wage structures. It could also be because highly skilled workers avoid compressed pay firms. Or it could be that unions compress wages and raise wages.

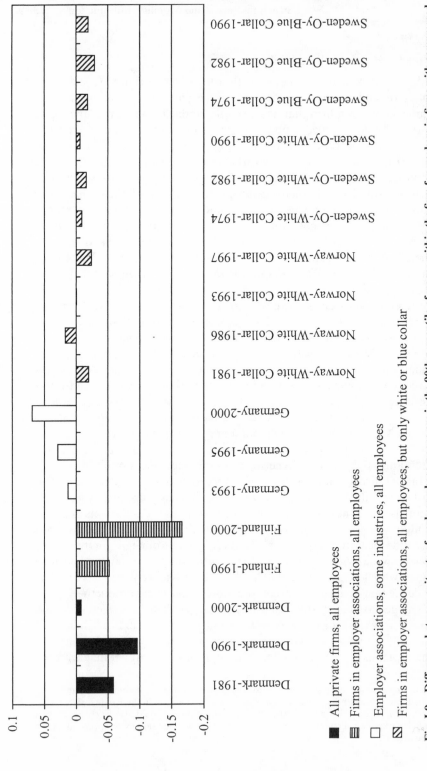

Fig. I.9 Difference between exit rate of workers whose wages are in the 90th percentile of wages within the firm for workers in firms with compressed wages, minus the exit rate for workers in the 90th percentile in firms with noncompressed wages

Notes: "Compressed wages" means the firm's wage variance is below the median. "Noncompressed" means the firm's wage variance is above the median.

Legend:
- All private firms, all employees
- Firms in employer associations, all employees
- Employer associations, some industries, all employees
- Firms in employer associations, all employees, but only white or blue collar

Categories:
Denmark-1981, Denmark-1990, Denmark-2000, Finland-1990, Finland-2000, Germany-1993, Germany-1995, Germany-2000, Norway-White Collar-1981, Norway-White Collar-1986, Norway-White Collar-1993, Norway-White Collar-1997, Sweden-Oy-White Collar-1974, Sweden-Oy-White Collar-1982, Sweden-Oy-White Collar-1990, Sweden-Oy-Blue Collar-1974, Sweden-Oy-Blue Collar-1982, Sweden-Oy-Blue Collar-1990

Some of this reflects differences in workers within each firm, but some may reflect wage policy. At this point, it is difficult to distinguish, but the wage compression evidence points more to heterogeneity than to wage policy.

Wage Growth

Alternative views of the sources of wage growth build directly from the themes developed in the preceding in studying the variation in wage levels across and within firms. Imagine figure I.1 as a picture of the distribution of wage growth rates rather than wage levels. At one extreme is panel B of figure I.1, in which firms have very different mean pay raises. Firm-specific differences in pay raises would arise: when occupational segregation or skill heterogeneity within firms causes some firms to pay high raises in response to hot occupational labor markets; when some firms with a policy of pay compression pay lower raises due to lower performance; or when the profitability of the firm translates into pay differences through institutions or union bargaining. At the other extreme is panel A of figure I.1, in which firms have extreme heterogeneity of wage growth rates within the firm. These within-firm differences in wage growth would arise when workers build human capital at different rates within their careers in the firm; when firms respond to the external labor market pressures for wage growth that vary across the occupations within the firm; when tournaments or incentive structures introduce pay raises for effort; or when institutional seniority-based pay structures vary across occupations.

Raises within and across Firms

The data reveal extensive heterogeneity of wage growth both within each economy and within most firms. Within the economy, workers experience very different outcomes: the standard deviation of the growth of log wages is much larger than the average level of wage growth for most countries (figure I.10). In most economies, the average growth of wages is 2 to 5 percent, but the standard deviation of wages is about 10 to 30 percentage points. Workers in the 90th percentile of wage increases obtained increases in the range of 15 to 20 percent in most countries (figure I.A.1). Even when wages were not growing that rapidly, on average, some workers experienced very high wage increases. This is an interesting fact and one that could have been learned from standard panel data sources. The advantage of the new data is they enable us to look next at how the firm influences these wage changes.

Within the firm, wage dispersion is also very high. The within-firm standard deviation in wage increases is always larger than the mean wage change and, in many countries, very much larger: mean wage dispersion ranges from 5 to 15 percentage points (figure I.11). The within-firm dispersion of wage growth is often about 50 percent of the dispersion of wage

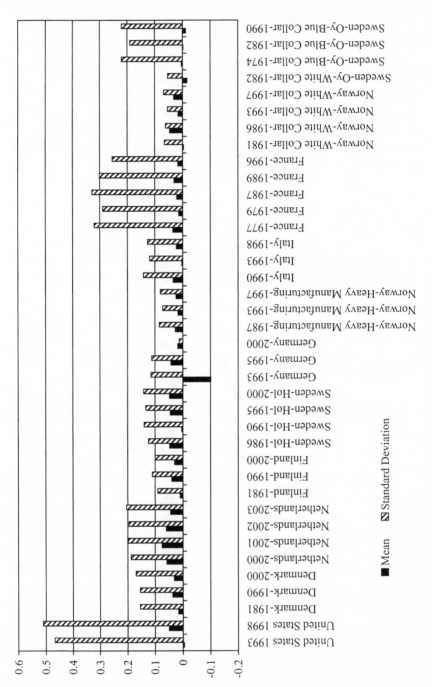

Fig. I.10   Mean and standard deviation of wage growth (across all individuals)

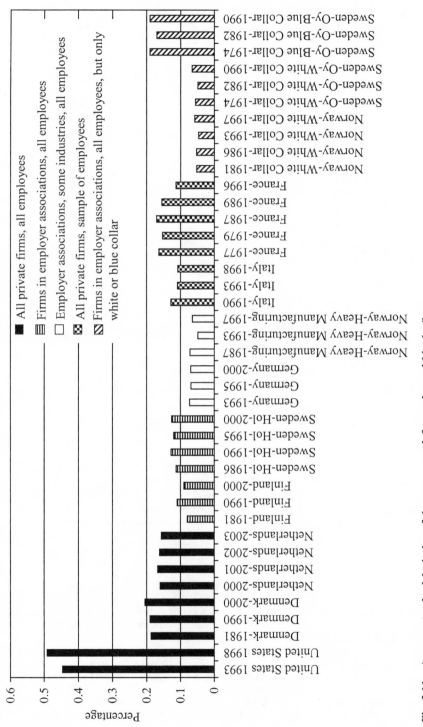

Fig. I.11 Average standard deviation of the wage growth for workers within the firm

Note: Wage growth = log (wage$_t$) – log (wage$_{t-1}$), annual change.

growth for the country. But it is often more than twice the mean wage growth for the firm. For example, in Denmark, in 2000, average wage growth for the firm was 3.4 percent. The within-firm standard deviation of growth rates was 8 percent.

Overall, a very interesting pattern emerges. The picture for wage levels is mirrored and amplified in wage growth. Figure I.12 is the wage growth counterpart to figure I.3 for wage levels. Figure I.12 shows wage growth distributions for low-wage-growth firms and high-wage-growth firms. France has higher wage growth dispersion than does Norway (according to these measures). But for all three countries, the firm is a "microcosm" of

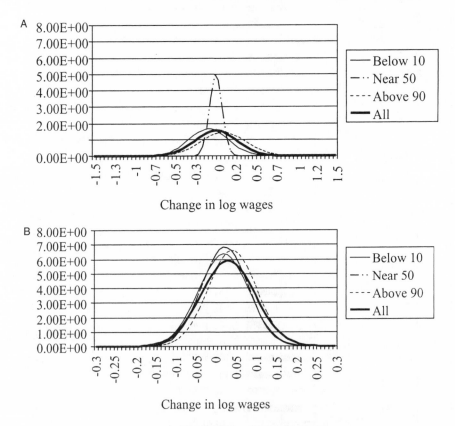

Fig. I.12   Wage growth distributions for low-wage-growth firms, median-wage-growth firms and high-wage-growth firms for some typical countries: *A*, France 1996; *B*, Norway 1997

Notes: Below 10 refers to the subsample of firms for which each firm has its mean wage growth rate of the firm below the 10th percentile of the mean wage growth rate of all firms. Near 50 refers to the subsample of firms for which each firm has its mean wage growth rate of the firm near the 50th percentile of the mean wage growth rate of all firms. Above 90 refers to the subsample of firms for which each firm has its mean wage growth rate of the firm above the 90th percentile of the mean wage growth rate of all firms. All refers to all firms.

the economy—the dispersion of wage growth within the firm is strikingly similar to wage growth across firms and individuals.

Modeling wage growth introduces a role for business cycles. One common view of business cycles and economic growth is that when things are good for some, they are good for all. When the economy is good, wages grow for the economy as a whole, and every firm and every worker experience the same increase in wage growth. In this extreme view, firms change wages in lockstep: wages rise or fall at the same rate and same time for all firms. At the other extreme, the relevant unit of analysis is the worker and the state of the economy has little effect on wage growth. Each worker's annual wage increase is an independent draw from some distribution that is a function of skills or effort. The firm wage increase is then an aggregation of its workers' increases and the economy as a whole an aggregation of the firms' increases. Of course, neither extreme will be true. But what our data shows us is that even though mean wage growth varies over time with the state of the economy, most workers' wage increases do not move in lockstep with the state of the economy, but vary widely in every year regardless of the state of the economy.

The fact that within-firm variation in wage growth is high suggests a number of things. First, a rising tide does not lift all boats, at least to the same extent. Second, the fact that wage growth is quite varied within the firm suggests that raises are tied to some other factor, like the outside labor market. Lazear and Oyer (2004) find that occupation is a much more important determinant of wage growth than is the firm. At least in Sweden, workers' wages are more closely related to their skill set than to their firms' fortunes. The same appears to be true of other countries, because the within-firm variation in wage growth is so high. High variance of wage growth within the firm also suggests high variation in human capital growth or effort across workers within the firm.

Firms are different, however, in that some firms have much more of a lockstep approach to raises than others. Figure I.13 plots the standard deviation of the change in log wage for firms that have very high within-firm variation, specifically are in the 90th percentile of firms' standard deviations of the change in the log wage. It does the same for firms in the 10th percentile. For example, in 2000 in Finland, the firms that treated workers most disparately with respect to raises had a standard deviation of Δ log wage equal to .15, whereas those that treated workers most similarly with respect to raises had a standard deviation of .05. Some firms have a lockstep raise policy. What one worker gets as a raise, the other workers get as well. Other firms do not have much within-firm conformity.

One key area for future investigation is whether the standard deviation of wage changes within the firm is fairly stable over time. Figure I.13 shows that it is remarkably constant over time for the country as a whole. Whether and why the within-firm standard deviation of raises is stable is an area for

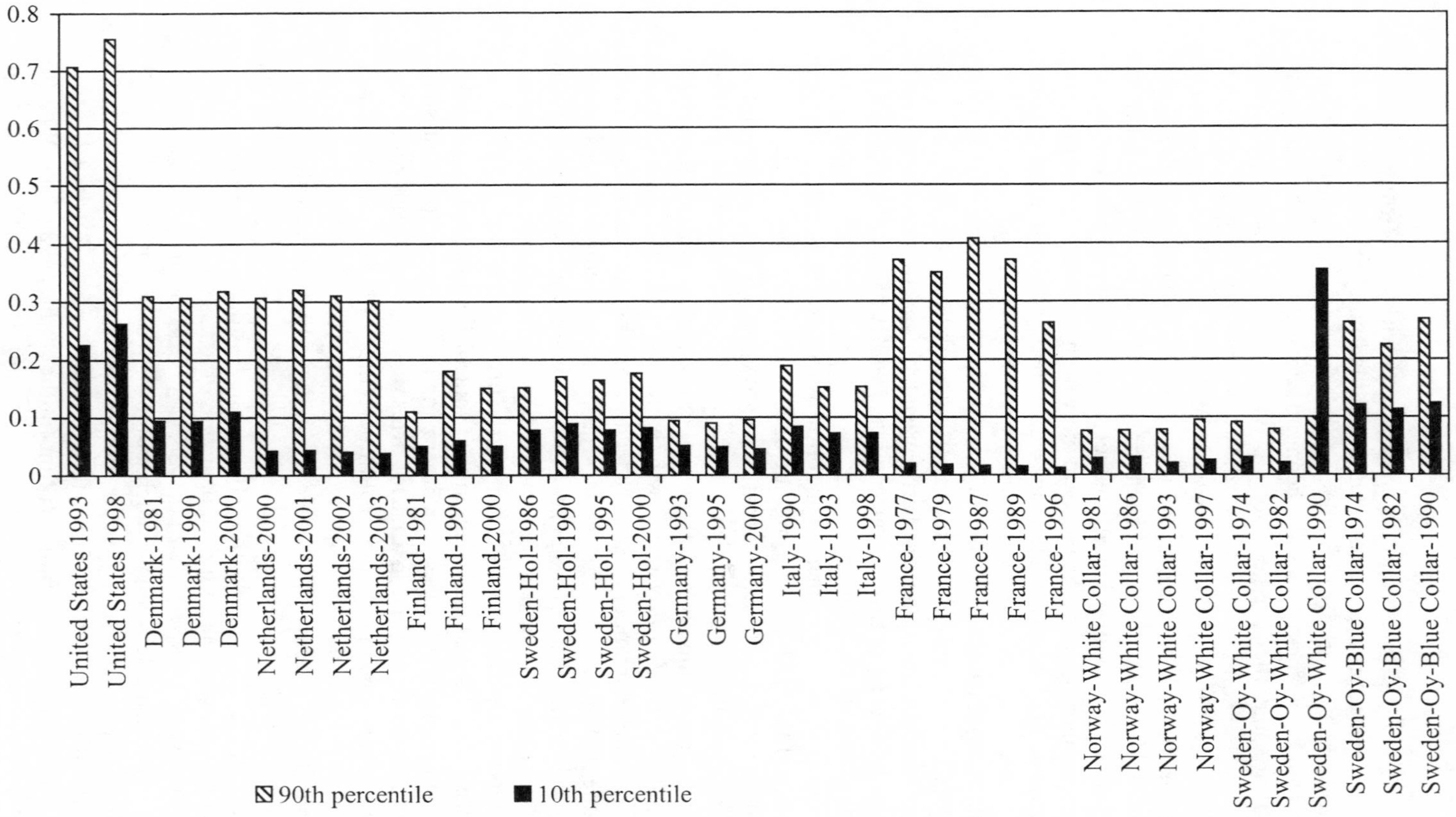

Fig. I.13   The 90th percentile and the 10th percentile of the distribution of the standard deviation of within-firm wage growth rates

future research, but a conjecture is that the structure of the firm remains relatively constant over time.[11] One way of examining this would be to estimate firm fixed effects in the wage growth equation and see if these firm effects are fixed over time and whether they contribute equally to the variance of firm growth over time.[12]

Raises and Tenure

Standard in the literature on human capital is that wage growth is more rapid during the early years of career than during the later years. The average wage increase is larger for young workers than older workers. This can come about through a variety of mechanisms. One is that young workers move across more firms than old workers. The other is that within firms, there is a policy to give larger wage increases to young workers than to older ones. That policy could reflect incentive rewards for early effort or human capital growth. Most academics experience this firsthand: academic deans invariably send out a letter each year bemoaning the small pool available for raises and justifying small senior professor raises by stating that the pool must be reserved to increase the wages of more junior professors. Is this a valid characterization of the typical firm, and how general is this policy across firms and countries?

Figure I.14 shows the difference between the wage growth rate of high-tenure workers and low-tenure workers within the firm, averaged across firms in the economy. The difference is almost always positive, and in some country years, it is large. Of course, this is wage growth for those who stay in the firm. Much of the difference in wage growth at the individual level that occurs over the life cycle may work through mobility across firms.

Young workers who are "stars" also receive considerably higher raises than older workers who are the stars within the firm. Taking the difference in the wage growth rate among the 90th percentile raises among low-tenure workers from that of the 90th percentile of high-tenure workers within the firm, this difference is positive and often 2 to 8 percentage points. This suggests more positive skew in the distribution of raises among the young than among the senior. Some young workers do very well and may be on a fast track. To ascertain that, it would be necessary to examine the pattern of

11. Wage growth dispersion within the firm should reflect the fact that some occupations enjoy relatively large increases in demand during some years, whereas other occupations enjoy large demand increases in other years. Although it is not the same occupation that experiences high wage growth over time, it is true that firms with many occupations are more likely to have more disparate wage growth than firms with few occupations. If so, there will be relative stability in the within-firm variance in wage growth, even if occupations switch places in terms of which are treated well or poorly in a given year.

12. Another question is whether firms that have little wage change also have small variance in wage change. It has long been known that at the national level, inflation and cross-sectional variation in prices are positively correlated; there is a higher variance of wage growth during periods of high inflation. We have not yet investigated this phenomenon, but it is possible to do so with these data.

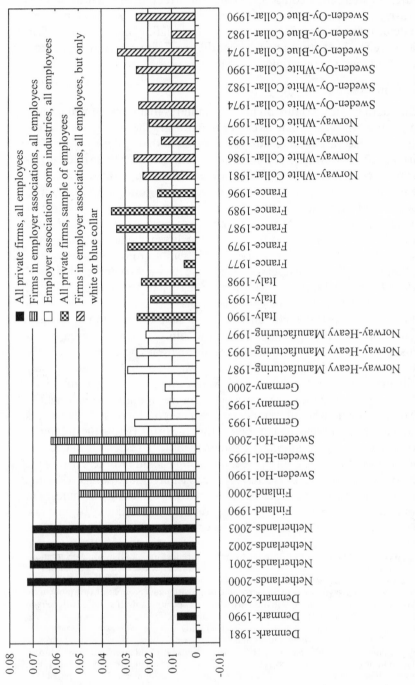

Fig. I.14 Difference in wage growth by tenure group: Low-tenure (< 3 years) wage growth rate minus high-tenure (≥ 3 years) wage growth rate

serial correlation of raises for a given worker over time, which is possible in these data but left for another study.

Mobility

Exit rates vary substantially across firms and countries. The typical firm's exit rate varies from lows of around 15 percent in Norway, Sweden, Finland, and early observations for Germany, to highs of 35 percent in France. However, we caution against comparing exit-rate levels across countries for these data. Because the different data sets measure exit over different time intervals and types of jobs, exit levels are not comparable.[13] Instead, we focus on within-country correlations. For example, in countries where exit rates are high, entry rates are also high (figure I.15). This must be true to provide an equilibrium where approximately the same number of workers are employed over time.[14]

Mobility and Wage Levels

There is a negative correlation between both exit and entry rates and wage levels (figure I.16). Firms that are high-wage firms are also low-turnover firms. This could reflect one of two phenomena. First, high-wage firms may pay above the market. Workers queue for jobs in those firms. When they finally land a job in a high-wage firm, they keep it because their alternatives are rarely better. Low-wage firms scrape for workers, lose them whenever something better comes along, and must have high hiring rates to compensate for the high quit rates.

An alternative explanation is that high-wage firms have more skilled workers, and the turnover rates for the less skilled are higher than those for the more highly skilled. Work experience could account for this alone. A firm with many high-tenure workers would be expected to have lower turnover rates than those with low-tenure workers.

A very interesting new fact comes from figure I.17. Growing firms tend to be low-wage firms. The firms with the high entry rates also have the lowest average wages. The pattern holds across countries and over all years but is stronger in some cases than others. This finding makes sense. New firms are likely to be growing more rapidly than older firms, and new firms are also likely to be smaller than mature firms. It is also interesting that the pattern holds across countries.

---

13. For example, exit rates based on monthly data will be much higher than those based on annual data because one job can have many workers turn over in that job within one year.
14. There are some notable exceptions. Germany, during the early 1990s, had exit rates that far exceeded entry rates. This invariably reflects the reunification and fundamental changes in the labor market that occurred during that period.

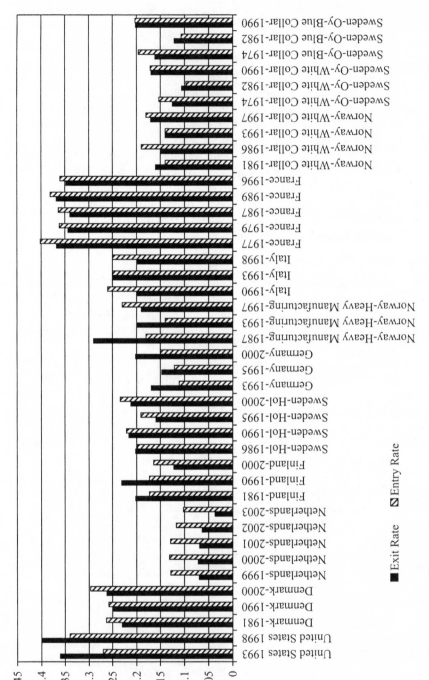

Fig. I.15 Entry and exit rates

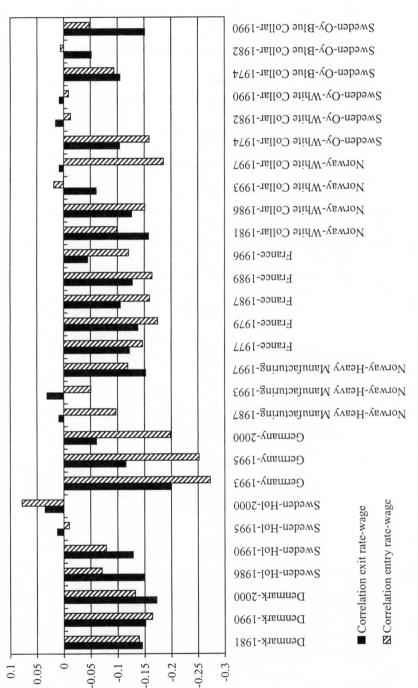

Fig. I.16   Correlation of firms' entry and exit rates with firms' average wage rate

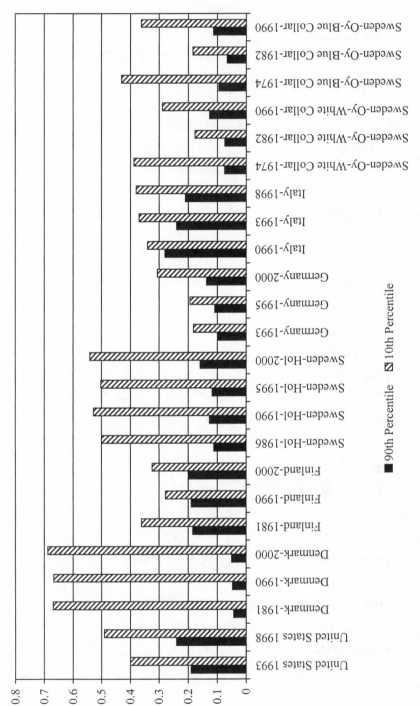

Fig. I.17 Entry rate for workers in the firm for those workers in the top 90th percentile of wages in the firm and entry rate for workers in the bottom 10th percentile of wages within the firm

Mobility and Firm Size

Another related and new fact is that exit rates and entry rates in big firms are lower than the exit and entry rates in the average firms. Figure I.18 shows that the exit rates at big firms are about 80 to 90 percent of the exit rates at average firms. The pattern is strikingly consistent across countries (with a few exceptions). The same is true of entry rates; there is less hiring at big firms and more hiring at small firms relative to the size of the firms. Figure I.19 shows the net entry rate (entry-exit rates) and then taking the difference between all firms and big firms. There is no consistent pattern. This neither supports nor rejects Gibrat's law. In some country years, there is a pattern of growth being lower in large firms. In other country years, the reverse is true. But the difference is rarely zero, which would be the prediction of Gibrat's Law. (Given the number of firms in each subsample, the differences shown in figure I.19 are most likely significant in almost all cases.) Apparently other factors are important in determining the size distribution of growth rates, and the statement that growth is independent of firm size seems to be inaccurate. A more accurate statement is that growth rates vary with firm size across time and location. The causal nature remains unknown at least for this study.

The determinants of firm turnover rates (industry, occupation, wage, skill, average tenure, etc.) could be investigated. Although we present no evidence on those factors here, it is possible to perform an analysis of this sort using the countrywide data sets used in this book.

Firm Mobility and Wage Growth

If the typical labor market allows for some rent sharing between capital and labor, worker wages should rise when firm profits rise. It is also reasonable to expect that profits and employment would be positively related. Firms that are profitable are likely to be doing more net hiring than firms that are unprofitable. When profits are down, firms typically cut the size of their labor force. As a result, good times might be accompanied by supernormal wage growth and also by supernormal employment growth. The cross-country data provide evidence on the correlation between wage and employment policy, and we believe that this is the first evidence of this sort that cuts across many firms.

Figure I.20 reports that the correlation between wage change and entry rates tends to be positive. In a given country year, firms that are raising wages are also likely to have higher than average entry rates. But firms that are raising wages do not consistently (across country years) have lower exit rates. In the most open countries, like Denmark, the finding is strong. High wage growth and low exit rates move together. But in Sweden, the results are weak and in the opposite direction. This might reflect the "dot.com boom" phenomenon. During the dot.com boom, the typical view was that

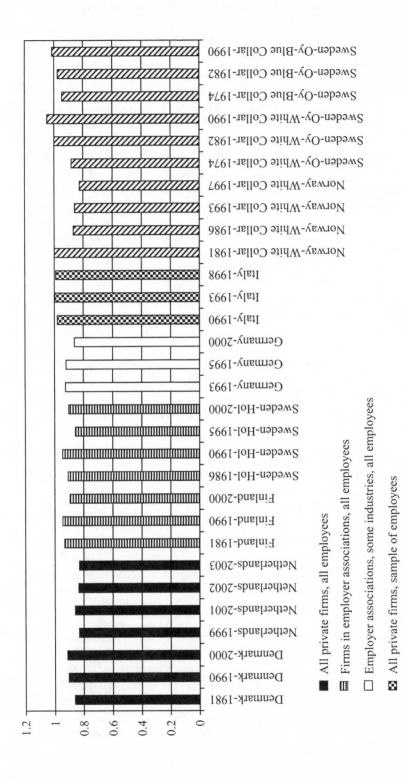

Fig. I.18 Exit rates of workers from big firms (employees ≥ 100) divided by exit rates of all firms

■ All private firms, all employees

▥ Firms in employer associations, all employees

☐ Employer associations, some industries, all employees

▦ All private firms, sample of employees

▨ Firms in employer associations, all employees, but only white or blue collar

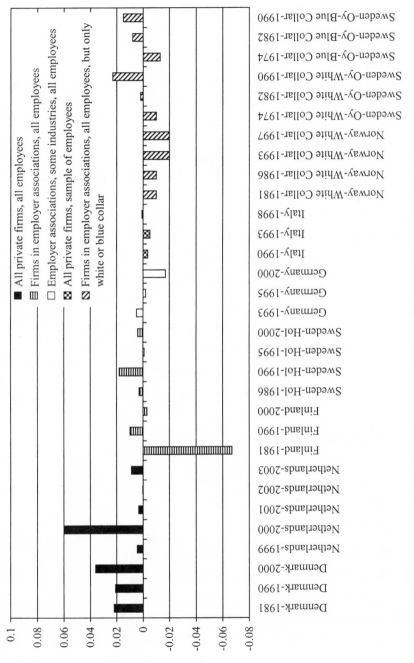

Fig. I.19 Entry rate minus exit rate of workers in all firms minus entry rate minus exit rate of workers in big firms (employees ≥ 100)

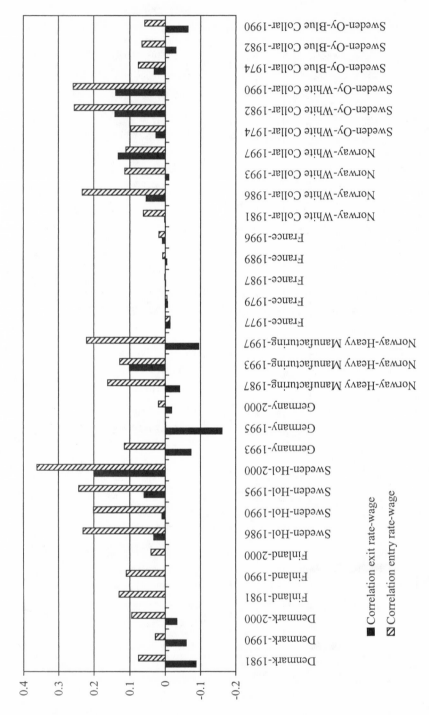

Fig. I.20 Correlation of the firms' exit rate and wage change and correlation of the firm's entry rate and wage change

- Correlation exit rate-wage
- Correlation entry rate-wage

the Silicon Valley labor market was in a talent war. Programmers and other skilled technical workers moved from firm to firm frequently, as demand shifted to reflect the fortunes of one company or another. Firms with rapidly growing wages hired many workers, but also lost them to other firms with rapidly growing wages because of the nature of industrial structure. Turnover rates were lower and wages were increasing less rapidly in more traditional parts of the economy, where the situation was closer to stable. So exit rates and high wage growth might go together if they characterize firms that are in industries that are undergoing rapid change. Again, this is a question that requires additional evidence, obtainable in these data sets, but not presented here.

The Structure of Wages: Why Care? Discussion and Summary

Several results in these data have revealed key features of the employment and wage structure of firms that were not previously known.

- The general structure of wages is remarkably similar across all countries. No previous study has had the data on employees within firms to assess wage structures across countries.
- The wage dispersion within firms is nearly as high as the wage dispersion overall. The standard deviation of wages within the firm is about 80 percent of the standard deviation across all workers in the economy (figure I.4). In addition, the variance in wage growth rates across individuals within the firm is very high. Even when the average raise is 4 percent within the firm, the top 10 percent of workers will typically receive increases of 8 percent. Wage levels and raises vary considerably across workers within the firm.
- Firms are more similar than they are dissimilar. The standard deviation of mean wages across firms is only about 20 percent of the average worker's wage for the economy (figure I.5). But firms are not identical: the standard deviation of mean wages is about 60 percent of the standard deviation of all individual wages (figure I.6).

In sum, most firms have many different jobs within the firm; wage variance is high within firms. But the jobs differ across firms. Janitorial firms have lawyers, but few. Law firms have janitors, but few. Consequently, mean wages differ across firms. Firms are not microcosms of the entire economy, and yet most firms do reflect a subsample of many of the jobs done in the economy. Figure I.2 is the more accurate depiction of the sources of wage variance from within and across firms; the extremes of panels A and B of figure I.1 are not evident in the data. Recalling equation (1), the variance of wages for the economy combines a high within-firm variance and significant gaps in mean wages across firms.

What do we learn about wage-setting policies and worker sorting across firms? First, there is no evidence of extreme sorting of workers across firms. That is, most firms contain a broad mixture of workers' skills or effort levels within the firm: wage levels vary greatly within the firm, and wage growth rates vary greatly within the firm. Moreover, an average worker moving from a low-wage firm to a high-wage firm would increase his or her wages by only about 20 percent. Having said this, one can look at the same data and reach a different conclusion. There are differences in mean wages across firms: law firms do not pay the same as cleaning-service firms, and people do sort by occupation or industry.

Second, there is sorting within the firm. High-effort or high-skilled workers are sorted into jobs that pay more within the firm. High-effort workers are rewarded with pay increases and are thus sorted into the jobs where they are the most productive. Again we know this to be true because there is a high variance of pay levels and pay increases within firms: firms do not have policies of equal pay for all. Instead, what they have is some combination of heterogeneous teamwork within the firm, systems of incentive pay that reward for effort, and sensitivity of wages to outside market conditions for each occupation or individual. Firms are more hierarchical than homogeneous. Of course, a law firm would not be expected to have the same average wage as a cleaning-service firm. The differences in skill between these two firms is obvious. There is also likely to be a difference in wage policy: law firms may by choice introduce tournament models; cleaning-service firms may have compressed wages from unionized bargaining. It may be possible to distinguish skill heterogeneity if we estimate models with individual specific and firm effects; given individual effects, the residual wage variation across firms represents policy. We leave it to future researchers to work on the underlying wage-setting models (extending the work of Abowd, Kramartz, and Margolis 1989). Why does all this matter? We highlight three reasons.

One reason to care about within-firm variation in wages and even more to the point, worker characteristics, is that it may help us learn about the nature of the firm's production function. One possibility (as shown in panel B of figure I.1) is that workers are almost identical within firm, both in wages and in characteristics. The need for different skills to produce a product might be handled by the market, say, where low-skilled workers sell the commodity that they produce to more highly skilled workers who know how to market and distribute the product. Alternatively, team production may make it essential to have many different types of workers within the same firm. It may be difficult to use the discipline of the market to supervise workers within one firm by workers in another firm. The evidence here is that firms comprise workers that are more heterogeneous than homogeneous, but further work should be done.

Some analysis suggests that firms are becoming more dissimilar over time. That is, firms that specialize in high-end skills are increasingly different from firms that specialize in low-end skills (Kremer and Maskin 1995). The evidence for this is from regressions with firm fixed effects. In the chapters that estimated wage regressions with firm fixed effects, the firm fixed effects are contributing more to the R-squared of the wage regression over time. Thus, increasingly the firm matters more: high-wage firms are selecting or rewarding the highest skill. This is an interesting technological change. Kremer and Maskin (1996b) posit that in recent years firms require more skill segregation across firms as a response to skill-biased technological change. In all the countries that study this, we have evidence lending support to this hypothesis. In general, a deeper understanding of the wage distribution within firms might give us a clue as to the labor ingredients required to produce—how those ingredients vary over time and among industries—and might shed some light on the nature of team production.

The ultimate question is whether wage policy specifically and labor policy in general has an effect on productivity. It is conceivable that data of this type might allow investigation of this issue within countries and among countries. Within a country, firms that (randomly) adopt different policies with respect to the types of workers they hire and how they pay them might experience different levels of productivity. For example, some have suggested that firms that limit the levels of top salaries relative to its median levels are less productive. Because the unit of analysis is the pay policy of the firm, only these employer-employee data can address issues such as this. By attaching measures of firm productivity or profitability, or in the absence of profitability, firm survival, we may get some hints as to the effects of various policies. For example, if it were found that firms with either a too compressed or too disparate wage policy were more likely than firms in the middle to go out of business, this would be a starting point. Then an examination of the detailed nature of turnover at those firms might shed additional light.

Finally, these data shed new light on workers' careers. The fact that there is considerable wage variation within firm means that, at least potentially, workers are not locked into a particular wage slot as a function of their first job assignment. If wages were compressed within firms, mobility would be necessary to change one's position, both over the life cycle and relative to other workers. Luck might play an important role. If a worker landed in a low-wage firm like the one pictured at the far left of panel B of figure I.1, he or she would have no hope of changing his or her income without leaving the firm. In an economy where mobility is costly (either as a result of market forces or government mandated severance pay that makes firms reluctant to hire), young workers who begin in low-wage firms suffer significant lifetime losses on their human capital. On the other end, those who start in high-wage firms experience a windfall. Thus, if firm effects dominated the market (as in panel B of figure I.1), then a bad initial "draw" of one's firm has a huge income effect for the rest of the worker's career.

In this context, if all of the variation in wages within firms were accounted for by person effects, then there would be constancy over time in a worker's position in the firm, given his or her initial position. Workers care that their position can improve in the firm as a result of experience and promotion. If there is no within-firm residual variation, then the only way for a worker to improve his or her relative position is to move. Given our evidence on the high levels of variance of individual wage growth rates within firms, the data suggests significant promotions and little evidence of getting stuck in one position, but further work expanding on these points would be highly valuable.[15]

15. One interesting extension is to estimate wage growth models as a function of individual specific fixed effects in wage growth rates.

Appendix

Table IA.1   **Data sources and criteria**

	United States	Denmark	The Netherlands
Source Surveys	All employees in the population for a subsample of states, based on unemployment insurance (UI) records filed quarterly with every state.	IDA—database kept by Statistics Denmark. This is a longitudinal database from 1980–2001. Register data supplemented with data from the 1970 Census and reports from all educational institutions (educational register).	Social Statistical Database of jobs (SSB Banen) kept by Statistics Netherlands. This is an event history database of all employment relationships bringing together information from tax and social security authorities combined with demographic information about Dutch inhabitants and their households from the joint register of Dutch municipalities.
Population	Workers are included in analysis if real monthly earnings exceed $100 and are less than $100,000.	All workers 18–66 years of age and all workplaces and enterprises. The link between workers and employer is established every year on a day in November. Data used are only on primary employment.	All firms (incl. nonprofit and government), all employed workers.
Variables	For each person: gender, age, compensation. For each establishment can calculate wage and entry and exit given all person-level data for the establishment.	Demographics, education, labor market experience, tenure, and earnings.	Demographics, tenure, and earnings.
Years	1993, 1998	1980–2001	1999–2003
Wage definitions and parameters	Earnings are from UI wage records. UI wage records measure "gross wages and salaries, bonuses, stock options, tips, and other gratuities, and the value of meals and lodging, where supplied" (Bureau of Labor Statistics 1997, 44). They do not include Old Age, Survivors, and Disability Insurance (OASDI), health insurance, workers compensation, unemployment insurance, and private pension and welfare funds.	Gross hourly wages, with bonuses and overtime. Register data containing tax-based information on the total earnings paid to each individual worker during the year (considered high quality data). Earnings are for the employer in November. Wage records constitute deductible labor costs for the employers (what makes information more reliable). Working hours: IDA computes annual number of working hours from employer's contributions to the pension scheme (contributions to the pension scheme are proportional to the number of hours worked). Hourly wage rates are calculated by dividing the earnings at a particular employer with the estimated annual hours at the employer.	Gross monthly wages including bonuses. Data contains tax-based information on total earnings per individual and firm combination. Earnings are calculated for the most important employer only, if multiple employers exist. Monthly wages have been calculated on the basis of the annual salary multiplied with fraction of months worked.

(continued)

Table IA.1   (continued)

	United States	Denmark	The Netherlands
Mobility			
Entry rate	Entry (accession) and Exit (separation) rates reflect links across years for unit of observations defined as PIK SEIN year observations (persons linked to a state unemployment insurance account number [SEIN] in a given year). Entry refers to workers who have zero earnings with SEIN in prior year ($t-1$) and have positive earnings in current year (t). Workers are only counted for purposes of computing rates if they satisfy above earnings thresholds. Note, however, that a worker who has positive earnings in year $t-1$ and t but in one year earnings do not satisfy thresholds is not counted as an entrant.	Entry rate calculated as the proportion of new employees in the firm in the end-of-November year t as compared to mean employment in firm over the year.	Entry rate calculated as the proportion of new employees in the firm during the calendar year (t) compared to previous year ($t-1$).
Tenure	No measure.	Tenure is calculated as contiguous time employed at workplace, firm, and industry.	Tenure is calculated based on the first day of employment (as observed by the fiscal authorities) relative to the third Thursday in September of a year (cut date for annual data).
Exit rate	Exit refers to workers who have positive earnings in year t at SEIN and zero earnings in year $t+1$. Workers are counted for purposes of computing rates if they satisfy above earnings thresholds. Note, however, that a worker who has positive earnings in year $t-1$ and t but in one year earnings do not satisfy thresholds is not counted as an exit. Note the timing difference—entry refers to flow into firm from $t-q$ to t; exit refers to flow out of firm from t to $t+1$. Hence, inappropriate to compute net flow from entry and exit given timing differences.	Exit rates are calculated as the proportion of employees who have exited from the firm over the year (since the comparisons are between end-of-Novembers, and this will neglect intermittent short-term jobs, the entry rate and exit rates are downward biased).	Exit rate calculated as the proportion of employees leaving a firm during the calendar year (t) compared to previous year ($t-1$)
	Finland	Belgium	Sweden—Edin, Holmlund, Nordström-Skans's chapter
Source Surveys	Wage survey of the Confederation of Finnish Industry (TT)—about 30% of private-sector employees. Complete wage records on blue- and white-collar workers are available from 1980–2002. Excludes top management.	Two surveys conducted by Statistics Belgium and merged using the form social security number: • 1995 Structure of Earnings Survey (SES) • 1995 Structure of Business Survey (SBS) October 1995.	Registered Manufacturing Data (RAMS), provided by Statistics Sweden, contains data on all individual workers that were employed at each plant sometime during the year.

Population	All employees in all large TT member firms, excludes small firms with less than 25 employees. Most TT firms are in manufacturing and construction. Excludes top management and trainees. Workers whose usual weekly hours exceed 30. All persons aged greater than 15.	All firms with 10+ workers. Economic activity in mining and quarrying; manufacturing; electricity and water supply; construction; wholesale and retail trade; repair of motor vehicles, motorcycles, and personal and household goods; hotels and restaurants; transport, storage, and communication; financial intermediation; and real estate, renting, and business activities. Final sample = 34,969 individuals in 1,498 firms.	16–65 years of age residing in Sweden sometime between 1990 and 2000, ages 16–60 in 1985, and ages 16–64 in 1989. This chapter is focused on the corporate sector, including only establishments with at least 25 employees. Annual data (November). Workers employed full time, in job with person's highest wage.
Variables	Worker demographics and details on all forms of compensation. Annual data (December).	SES: firm characteristics and individual employee demographics. SBS: (firm-level survey) sales, value added, production value, gross operating surplus, and value of purchased goods and services.	Total annual earnings, first and last salaried month for each employee. Year of birth, gender, education, and immigration status for each individual. Sector and industry for each establishment.
Years	1980–2002: data analyzed was mainly from 1981, 1990, and 2000.	1995 only.	1985–2000, more detailed for 1986, 1990, 1995, and 2000.
Wage definitions and parameters	Gross hourly wages, with bonuses and overtime, and real wage 2000. Payroll records. Blue-collar workers (hourly wage) from the last quarter of each year, and white-collar workers (monthly salary) from each December. Wage is calculated with all wage components (bonuses, overtime, etc.) and dividing the total wages by total hours. White-collar worker wages: hourly wages are calculated based on monthly wages and usual weekly hours. All wages are deflated to year 2000 euros using the consumer price index. Wage dynamics obtained by calculating the firm averages in year t and $t-1$, taking the difference, and then the across-firm average of these differences. This calculation does not necessarily have the same employees in both years.	Gross hourly wages (without bonuses) calculated by dividing total gross earnings (including overtime and premiums) in the reference period by the corresponding number of total paid hours (including paid overtime). Gross hourly wage (with bonus) calculated by adding to the gross hourly wages (without bonuses) the annual bonuses dived by: 1) the number of months to which the bonuses correspond, and 2) the number of total paid hours in the reference period, respectively. Thus, *average wage, observation = a person wage*. The individual grossly hourly wages (in EUR) include overtime paid, premiums for shift work, night work, or weekend work.	Monthly wage is calculated by dividing total earnings during the year by the number of remunerated months, including only employment spells that cover November of each year. Employment definition: a person is employed if and only if the wage for November exceeds 75% of the mean wage of a janitor employed by a local municipality according to Statistics Sweden's information on monthly wages. An individual is only allowed to be employed by one plant each year, and priority is given to the observation generating the highest wage. Data set is based on information collected to calculate taxes. Data contains earnings of all employees including CEOs (possible outliers). Wages of the top earners (see table 1.2) have a large impact on the standard deviation of monthly wages, while the mean hardly is affected at all (see text).
Tenure	Wage growth and entry rates calculated from year $t-1$ to t. Wage growth for the workers that enter the firm as well as the wage growth by tenure are calculated using the information on the date when the employee was hired to the current firm.	Not available.	When calculating wage change or plant change, they only counted those who switched between firms that were 25+ employees (if the firm size was less, the subject was dropped).

(continued)

Table IA.1   (continued)

Finland	Belgium	Sweden—Edin, Holmlund, Nordström-Skans's chapter
Current year – entry year.	Not available.	Tenure is calculated within the sample (tenure = the number of consecutive years a person has his or her main employment at the same plant). Thus, the fraction on long-tenured workers may be lower than if calculated from the year of hiring as tenure is broken by absence and only the main employer is used.
Calculated from the year t to the year $t + 1$. Any restrictions on the firm size (25 employees) will refer to the base year. Therefore, it is not required that a firm would have had at least 25 employees or even that a firm would have existed in year $t − 1$ or year $t + 1$.	Not available.	Calculated exit rates will not include plant closings because the authors require that establishments have at least 25 employees in both years.

	Germany	Norway	Italy
Source Surveys	Plants: IAB Establishment Panel conducted by the Institute for Employment Research (since 1993; annual survey based on a register of the Federal Employment Service—entry, exits, and wages are all mandatory reports for the social security system) Employees: all employees in Germany covered by the social insurance and who work at least one day in a plant of the IAB Establishment Panel in the respective year.	Data sets are linked employer-employee from administrative files from Statistics Norway. Plant-level information is from the annual census for manufacturing. White-collar data sets are from the Confederation of Norwegian Business and Industry (NHO). Blue-collar data sets from the Federation of Norwegian Manufacturing Industries (TBL)	WHIP data set (Workers Histories Italian Panel) by LABORatorio R. Revelli. It is built from a randomized sample drawn from INPS (Italian National Social Security Institute). More information available at www.laboratoriorevelli.it/whip. Administrative data set on employees.
Population	The register covers more than 90% of all employees in the manufacturing and 75% in the service sector. Excluded: civil servants, self-employed, and those not eligible for social security; apprentices; switchers from part to full ftime and opposite. All employees in plants with a valid interview in the respective years and at least 25 full-time workers. Number of observations varies from year to year. Workers are age 15–65.	White-collar sample: all workers in all NHO member firms; N = 97,000 white-collar workers per year in different industries during the period 1980–1997. Restrictions on white-collar sample: the number of hours worker per week is 30+ (full-time only); the number of full-time employed white-collar workers (ages 16+) in each firm is at least 25 in year t and in year $t − 1$. Blue collar sample: N = 34,000 blue-collar workers per quarter. Data managed much the same way as white-collar workers.	Employees ages 14–75. INPS archives: employee population: all dependent workers in the nonagricultural private sector. Firms population: all firms in the nonagricultural private sector with at least one dependent. WHIP data set: a sample is drawn selecting all employees born in four fixed dates of the year (sample rate ~1:90) and matching them with all firms where they have been employed. As a result, there are ~130,000 individuals, ~90,000 firms per year. Inclusion criteria here: individuals reported to have a job spell during the month of May of the year of interest, blue- and white-collars working full-time only; thus a cross section of workers for each referred years.

Variables	Primary job in June. Employees: demographics, entries and exits, occupation (3-digit), gross daily precise wages (including all bonus payments), a unique plant identifier and the industry code, since 1999: regional information. Nominal wages are deflated by the consumer price index and are written as euros in 2000. Employers: detailed information about total employment (also for different skills), standard and overtime hours, wage recognition, output, exports, investment, urbanicity, and ownership.	White-collar workers: organized hierarchically with 22 different combinations of groups and levels. Both plant and firm identifiers are available. See the section "Defining Plant and Firm" in the Norwegian chapter for details. The person identification number is used as merging variable when adding in plant and firm information from the employer-employee register.	Annual data (May), full-time jobs. Employee: register—employee ID; date of birth; gender; place of birth. For every year and every job: employee ID; place of work; months paid; number of salaried weeks/days; job start/end date; salary year; wage supplements paid by employer; status full time/part time/temporary; code of contractual agreement and position in contractual ladder; wage supplements on behave of INPS (1989–). Employer (firm): register—employer ID; economic activity (NACE rev. 2, 3 digit), dates of registration and termination; for every month—number of employees, salaries paid, contributions paid, total days for which salary was paid, wage supplements paid for social security, and rebates on contributions.
Years	The survey is conducted annually since 1993 to present. In the text only the years 1993, 1995, and 2000 are observed (meanwhile worker data are applicable until 2002).	1980–1997: specifically 1981, 1986, 1993, and 1997.	1985–1998.
Wage definitions and parameters	All wages are gross wages. The information about wages is censored because payments for the social security system are limited to a certain amount. This threshold varies from year to year. Thus, the observed wage at the threshold are imputed with predicted values using a Mincerian earnings function augmented by ten sector and ten occupation dummies and adding an error term. Varying from year to year 10–15% of all observations are imputed. In the group of employees with a university degree, 50% of all observations are censored.	White-collar: monthly salary (per Sept. 1st) including the value of fringe benefits and exclusive of overtime and bonuses. Indirect costs to the firm such as employers' fee, pensions, etc. are not included. Nominal wages were transformed to real wages using the Consumer Price Index (CPI) with base year 1990.	Defined as the total amount of the earnings paid to the worker: basic wage, cost-of-living allowance, residual fees, overtime plus back pay, bonuses, supplement holiday pay, and sick pay. Wages reported in the tables are defined as average daily retributions, referring to a single job spell/year. This is computed as the total annual wage earned in the firm divided by the number of paid working days. Nominal daily wages are deflated by the CPI index and are expressed in 1990 Italian liras (1 euro = 1936.27 Italian liras).
Mobility **Entry**		For each firm in year t, how many of the workers were not present in year $t − 1$? This number is then divided by firm size in year t.	
Tenure	Job tenure was computed by checking the appearance of the employee identifier in t, $t − n$ ($n \in N$) with the condition of the duration equal 365 (366) days. With larger n they have less plant observations because of panel attrition. Therefore, they calculated the job tenures only up to 3 years. Also, to be in the group job tenure >3 years, there must be full time employment in t and $t − 1$, and the individual identifier in the plant must be observed in all 3 years. In addition, there has to be an annual job duration in these 3 years of 365 (366) days.	Tenure is based on the variable "job start date" (i.e., the date when the worker was first employed with his current employer). Note: there is some censoring with the year 1978 as the censoring point.	Job start and job end are imputed by a procedure that identifies continuing work spells of a worker within the same firm, taking into account possible brief interruptions due to suspensions, illness, and maternity leaves, temporary layoffs. The procedure starts from the first year of the panel so that tenure is left-censored at 1985.

(continued)

Table IA.1 (continued)

	Germany	Norway	Italy	Sweden—Oyer's chapter	France
Exit rate		They look at each firm in year $t-1$ and ask how many workers in the firm leave the firm by year t. This number is then divided by firm size in year $t-1$.			
Source Surveys				Swedish Employer's Federation (SAF) provided employment data.	DADS (Déclaration Annuelles de Données Sociales): longitudinal employee-firm matched data collected by National Institute for Statistics and Economic Studies (NSEE). Tax-based employer mandatory reports.
Population				White- and blue-collar data is on separate databases—there is no way to match the two groups. There are more blue-collar firms than white-collar firms. Firms = every private-sector industry. Firm = white-collar workers at a company or the blue-collar workers at a company.	All statutory employed persons. Final sample = 13,770,082 observations, corresponding to 1,682,080 individuals and 515,557 firms. Sample selection procedure: persons born in October of even-numbered years.
Variables				GDP data presented in dollar terms. Data set variables include occupation, age, and wages. "Levels within firms" white-collar worker occupation codes used to observe hierarchy within firm.	Demographics for each person: number of days worked in the firm, employment status (full time, part time, intermittent), gender, date of birth plus place, occupation, total net earnings year, year, gross nominal earnings. Nominal values were deflated by the CPI.
Years				1970–1990. Mainly 3 points: 1974, 1982, and 1990.	1977, 1979, 1989, 1996. 1987 only used when it was useful to compute 10-year-long differences.
Wage definitions and parameters				Actual wages paid in monthly units.	Minimum wage: since 1951, indexed to the rate of change in consumer prices and to the average blue-collar wage rate. Total annualized net real wage (excluding employer and employee taxes, but including bonuses). French CPI used, base year = 1980.
Mobility					
Entry					
Tenure				Tenure calculations are limited by the entry of individual firms.	Based on observed firm identifier for all jobs starting after 1976 (first year of data). For jobs already started in 1976, imputation is based on the wage structure survey of 1978 (see Abowd, Kramarz, and Margolis 1999, data appendix).
Exit rate					

Table I.A.2   The structure of wage levels within and between firms

	United States (1998)	Denmark (2000)	The Netherlands (2003)	Finland (2000)	Belgium (1995)	Sweden-Hol (2000)	Germany (2000)
Average wage, observation = a person	3,253	21,097	2,767	10	15	17,843	3,314
Standard deviation	4,230	8,674.6	1,986	3.46	7.056	7,040	1,144.24
90th percentile	5,925	31,858.6	4,211	14.82	22.274	26,716	4,844.97
10th percentile	855	12,456.	1,485	5.95	9.055	11,208	2,175.74
No. of workers	40,110,897	1,081,555	4,600,000	380,644	31,788	860,581	
Average of firm average wage, observation = a firm (weights observations differently from previous row)	3,020	20,473	2,206	9.01	13.1851		
Standard deviation	2,051	4,572.9	1,107	1.63	4.018		
90th percentile	5,070	26,584.2	3,066	11.13	18.037		
10th percentile	1,336	15,336.2	1,249	7.01	9.317		
No. of firms	202,528	13,999	71,445	1,863	1,445		
Average of Standard deviation of wage, observation = a firm	2,434	7,065	1,135	2.29	3.7197		
Standard deviation	2,452	2,736.6	1,764	.94	3.382		
90th percentile	4,888	10,764.	1,799	3.6	7.503		
10th percentile	732	3,980.4	535.6	1.15	.802		
No. of firms	202,528	13,995	70,736	1,863	1,445		
Average coefficient of variation of wages, observation = a firm	0.75		0.5081	0.25	0.2531		
Standard deviation	.37		.21	.08	.154		
90th percentile	1.2		.758	.36	.461		
10th percentile	.42		.282	.15	.083		
No. of firms	202,528		70,736	1,863	1,445		
Correlation (average wage, Standard deviation of wage), observation = a firm	0.7856	0.672	0.7299	0.53	0.831		
Average of firm average wage, observation = a plant						17,245	2,861.15
Standard deviation						3,663	677.69
90th percentile						22,497	3,806.67
10th percentile						13,413	2,007.83
No. of plants						9,067	1,569

(continued)

Table I.A.2 (continued)

	United States (1998)	Denmark (2000)	The Netherlands (2003)	Finland (2000)	Belgium (1995)	Sweden-Hol (2000)	Germany (2000)
Average of Standard deviation of wage, observation = a plant						5484	818.24
Standard deviation						2,222	226.69
90th percentile						8,635	1,113.54
10th percentile						2,936	522.29
No. of plants						9,067	1,565
Average coefficient of variation of wages, observation = a plant						0.312	0.293
Standard deviation						.088	.071
90th percentile						.429	.387
10th percentile						.2	.196
No. of plants						9,067	1,565
Correlation (average wage, Standard deviation of wage), observation = a plant						0.768	0.616
Average wage for workers between 25 and 30, observation = a person	2,618	19,556		9.77	12.6091	16,258	2,832
Standard deviation	4,325	6,334.9		3.08	3.768	4,929	740.02
90th percentile	6,822	27,067.9		13.72	17.113	22,121	3,688.77
10th percentile	891	12,935.1		5.82	8.901	11,009	2,062.87
No. of workers	6,589,276	169,120		51,046	7,004	138,219	
Average wage for workers between 45 and 50, observation = a person	3,932	23,044		10.68	16.811	19,169	3,438.98
Standard deviation	9,164	8,796.8		3.56	8.7	7,772	1,204.48
90th percentile	6,989	34,613.3		15.24	26.779	29,579	5,048.48
10th percentile	1,037	14,731.6		6.13	9.98	12,108	2,211.54
No. of workers	5,306,977	132,563		70.212	4.873	116,080	105

	Norway—Heavy Manufacturing (1997)	Italy (1998)	France (1996)	Norway White collar (1997) (1990)	Sweden—Oy White collar (1990)	Sweden—Oy Blue collar
Average wage, observation = a person	18,311	95	56	21,838	15,990	10,571
Standard deviation	5,374	33,359	34.28	7,084	5,435	2,690
90th percentile		140.307	92.1	31,958.9	23,475	14,041
10th percentile		61.751	29.9	14,625	10,400	7,223
No. of workers	25,446	47,173	639,671	79,259	296,782	372,621

Average of firm average wage, observation = a firm (weights observations differently from previous row)	16,877	85.53	50.6	20,395	15,660	10,176
Standard deviation	2,010	12.52	30.2	2,977.008	1,908	1,664
90th percentile		99.774	81.3	24,359.63	17,970	12,400
10th percentile		70.903	28.7	16,685.75	13,329	8,140
No. of firms	139	775	213,493	565	2,493	3,931
Average of Standard deviation of wage, observation = a firm	4,026	25.87	19.3	5,566	4,895	2,112
Standard deviation		7.117	21.868	1,640.82	1,164	656
90th percentile		34.762	44.9	7,421.265	6,335	3,012
10th percentile		16.772	2	3,743.561	3,393	1,366
No. of firms	139	731	68,997	565	2,493	3,930
Average coefficient of variation of wages, observation = a firm)	0.236	0.30	0.314	0.2703342	0.311	0.207
Standard deviation	.054	.001	.235	.057	.058	.054
90th percentile		.397	.647	.334	.382	.276
10th percentile		.221	.051	.204	.235	.145
No. of firms	139	731	68,997	565	2,493	3,930
Correlation (average wage, Standard deviation of wage), observation = a firm	0.59	0.59	0.744	0.72	0.657	0.561
No. of firms	731	731				
Average of firm average wage, observation = a plant						10,192
Standard deviation					2,020	1,706
90th percentile						
10th percentile						
No. of plants					2,956	4,866
Average of Standard deviation of wage, observation = a plant					4,926	2,103
Standard deviation					1,205	663
90th percentile						
10th percentile						
No. of plants					2,956	4,865

(continued)

Table I.A.2   (continued)

	Norway—Heavy Manufacturing (1997)	Italy (1998)	France (1996)	Norway White collar (1997) (1990)	Sweden—Oy White collar (1990)	Sweden—Oy Blue collar
Average coefficient of variation of wages, observation = a plant					0.31	0.21
Standard deviation					.061	.053
90th percentile						
10th percentile						
No. of plants					2,956	4,865
Correlation (average wage, Standard deviation of wage), observation = a plant					0.623	0.582
Average wage for workers between 25 and 30, observation = a person	16,571	83.74	48.0	17,630	13,244	10,642
Standard deviation	2,999	23.969	22.819	3,546.809	2,813	2,671
90th percentile		115.076		22,202.05	16,787	14,143
10th percentile		59.756		13,386.13	10,100	7,373
No. of workers	3,781	9,318	117,395	9,123	37,423	54,590
Average wage for workers between 45 and 50, observation = a person	19,338	105.80	67.3	23,262	17,699	11,020
Standard deviation	5,959	35.541	39.133	7,844.934	5,949	2,707
90th percentile		154.642		34,460.62	26,395	14,511
10th percentile		67.378		15,250	11,500	7,639
No. of workers	3,988	7,489	95,650	13,962	46,722	39,175

Note: See country chapters for detailed discussion of these data and variables.

Table IA.3   Change in log wages [(log wage in year *t*) − (log wage in year *t* − 1)]

	United States (1998)	Denmark (2000)	The Netherlands (2003)	Finland (2000)	Sweden—Hol (2000)	Germany (2000)	Norway—Heavy manufacturing (1997)	Italy (1998)	France (1996)	Norway—white collar (1997)	Sweden—Oy-White collar (1990)	Sweden—Oy-Blue collar (1990)
Average change in wage												
observation = a person	.0496	0.031	0.04464	0.03	0.048	0.018	0.024	0.02	0.017	0.031724	−0.004	−0.011
Standard deviation	.511	.17	.204	.1	.142	.013	.08	.127	.254	.068	.7	.22
90th percentile	.495	.2	.175	.16	.207	.131		.136	.198	.093	.07	.26
10th percentile	−.379	−.125	−.063	−.1	−.085	−.089		−.081	−.142	−.007	−.06	−.27
No. of workers	35,607,319	799,463	3,800,000	312,968	704,360		19,489	43,377	519,770	69,210		
Average of firm average change												
in wage, observation = a firm	0.0558	0.034	0.04726	0.03	0.053	0.021	0.022	0.02	0.022	0.0298882	0.001	−0.011
Standard deviation	.191	.08	.143	.06	.059	.034	.026	.025	.217	.023	.031	.12
90th percentile	.215	.109	.148	.08	.114	.055		.051	.185	.057	.04	.124
10th percentile	−.112	−.036	−.039	−.02	.001	−.012		−.011	−.113	.006	−.031	−.139
No. of firms	202,335	11,383	90,709	1,321	9,063		139	734	148,995	565		
Average of Standard deviation												
of change in wage,												
observation = a person	0.4917	0.205	0.1567	0.09	0.126	0.07	0.065	0.11	0.114	0.0585112	0.066	0.19
Standard deviation	.206	.093	.125	.05	.039	.024	.031	.035	.136	.037	.029	.061
90th percentile	.755	.318	.302	.15	.176	.096		.153	.263	.095	.355	.269
10th percentile	.262	.11	.038	.05	.082	.045		.073	.012	.026	.1	.124
No. of workers	202,335	11,366	85,396	1,307	9,054		139	687	46,573	565		
Average change in wage for												
people who change firms,												
observation = a person	0.1031	0.043		0.05	0.053	n.a.	0.023	0.06	−0.004		0.02	−0.003
Standard deviation	.786	.313		.16	.213	n.a.	.14	.244	.441		.097	.267
90th percentile	.997	.376		.26	.319	n.a.		.327	.477		.14	.319
10th percentile	−.799	−.296		−.16	−.218	n.a.		−.209	−.487		−.055	−.324
No. of firms	10,522,612	240,362		14,473	40,217	n.a.	697	3,496	68,164			

Note: See country chapters for detailed discussion of these data and variables.

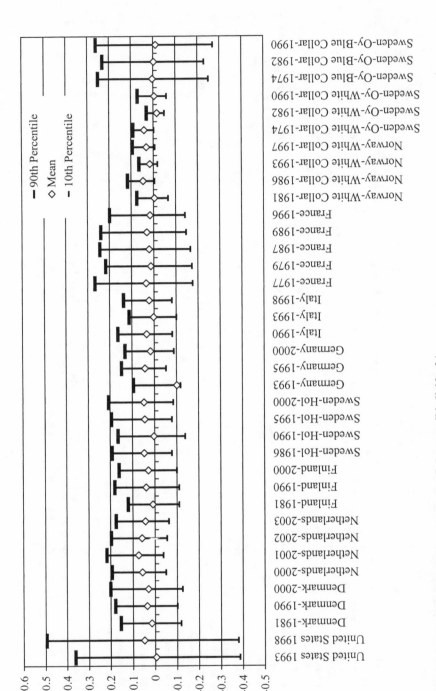

Fig. IA.1   Distribution of mean wage growth (across all individuals)

Note: Wage Growth = log (wage$_t$) − log (wage$_{t-1}$), annual change.

References

Abowd, John M., Francis Kramarz, and David N. Margolis. 1999. High wage workers and high wage firms. *Econometrica* 67 (2): 251–334.

Baker, George P., Michael Gibbs, and Bengt Holmstrom. 1994a. The internal economics of the firm: Evidence from personnel data. *Quarterly Journal of Economics* 109 (November): 881–919.

———. 1994b. The wage policy of a firm. *Quarterly Journal of Economics* 109 (November): 921–55.

Brown, Charles, and James Medoff. 1989. The employer size wage effect. *Journal of Political Economy* 97 (5): 1027–59.

Bureau of Labor Statistics. 1997. *Handbook of methods.* Washington, DC: U.S. Department of Labor, Office of Publications and Special Studies. http://www.bls.gov/opub/hom/home.htm.

Fox, Jeremy T. 2007. Explaining firm size wage gaps with equilibrium hierarchies, The University of Chicago, Working Paper.

Hubbard, Thomas N. 2000. The demand for monitoring technologies: The case of trucking. *Quarterly Journal of Economics* 115:533–60.

Kremer, Michael, and Eric Maskin. 1995. Segregation by skill and the rise in inequality. Hoover Institution Paper no. e-95-7. Stanford, CA: Hoover Institution, Stanford University.

———. 1996a. Wage inequality and segregation. Harvard Institute of Economic Research Working Paper no. 1777. Cambridge, MA: Harvard Institute of Economic Research.

———. 1996b. Wage inequality and segregation by skill. Massachusetts Institute of Technology Working Paper no. 96-23. Cambridge, MA: MIT.

Lazear, Edward P. 1992. The job as a concept. In *Performance measurement, evaluation, and incentives,* ed. William J. Bruns, Jr., 183–215. Boston: Harvard Business School Press.

———. 1999. Personnel economics: Past lessons and future directions: Presidential address to the Society of Labor Economists, San Francisco, May 1, 1998. *Journal of Labor Economics* 17 (2): 199–236.

Lazear, Edward P., and Paul Oyer. 2004. The structure of wages and internal mobility. *American Economic Review* 94 (2): 212–16.

Lazear, Edward P., and Sherwin Rosen. 1981. Rank-order tournaments as optimum labor contracts. *Journal of Political Economy* 89 (5): 841–64.

Macleod, Bentley W., and James Malcomson. 1989. Implicit contracts, incentive compatibility and involuntary unemployment. *Econometrica* 56 (2): 447–80.

Stole, Lars A., and Jeffrey Zwiebel. 1996. Intra-firm bargaining under non-binding contracts. *Review of Economic Studies* 63 (3): 375–410.

Adjusting Imperfect Data
Overview and Case Studies

Lars Vilhuber

1.1 Introduction

This book combines an astonishing variety of data sets in a coherent analytical framework. Data have been extracted from the administrative systems of countries with very different uses for the data contained in these systems: from tax administration in countries such as France and Sweden, to calculation of unemployment benefits in the United States, to administration of centralized bargaining agreements in Norway and Sweden. The size of the countries and, thus, the data sets, ranges from countries with as few as 5 million inhabitants (Finland, Norway, Denmark) to the 293 million inhabitants of the United States. Some statistical agencies conduct coordinated surveys to gather the data; others rely on purely administrative tasks to coincidentally gather the data.

The ease with which the reader can compare the analyses presented in this book was purchased through much hard work by the authors from each country. In particular, each set of authors had to adjust their data for quirks, problems, and issues that are inevitable when working with large administrative data sets and handled them in what their experience told them was the best manner, given the constraints both of their data and the

Lars Vilhuber is a senior research associate at the Cornell University School of Industrial and Labor Relations (ILR), and a senior research associate in the Longitudinal Employer-Household Dynamics program at the U.S. Census Bureau.

I am indebted to all the authors of the country-specific chapters for having provided me with detailed data descriptions, allowing me to write this chapter. Juhana Vartiainen, Lia Pacelli, Roberto Leombruni, Claudio Villosio, and Bruno Contini provided valuable contributions beyond their data descriptions. I am thankful to all of the preceding, John Abowd, and Julia Lane for comments on drafts of this text. All errors, of course, remain mine.

homogenization imposed on all by this project. It goes without saying that not all solutions are identical, and how they differ may affect how the data are to be interpreted. Furthermore, some known issues with the data were left untouched in order to make the data more comparable between countries. Finally, some elements of the data, such as the unit of observation, remain fundamentally different, and it is important to keep that in mind when comparing data across countries. However, although the starting points vary widely, the end result of the authors' efforts is a very high degree of comparability of the analytical data sets across countries, as evidenced by the different chapters in this book.

In this chapter, instead of using the similarity in the cleaned data sets to investigate economic fundamentals, we focus on the steps undertaken by each chapter's authors and their respective data providers to render the data both usable and comparable. We describe two data elements that remain fundamentally different across countries—the sampling or data collection methodology and the basic unit of analysis (establishment or firm)—and the extent to which they differ. We then proceed to document some of the problems that affect longitudinally linked administrative data in general, and we describe some of the solutions analysts and statistical agencies have implemented and some that they did not implement. In each case, we explain the reasons for and against implementing a particular adjustment, and explore, through a select set of case studies, how each adjustment or absence thereof might affect the data. By giving the reader a look behind the scenes, we intend to strengthen the reader's understanding of the data. Thus equipped, the reader can form his or her own opinion as to the degree of comparability of the findings across the different countries.

The structure of this chapter is as follows. A first section provides an overview of select data elements of all data sets and discusses the similarities and differences. The next several sections discuss longitudinal and other linking issues, outline why it is important to properly handle such issues, and provide examples of applications in the data sets underlying the other chapters of this book. Case studies are summarized where appropriate and available. The case studies differ from the applications in that they (typically) do not use the same data sets, but provide a deeper analysis of the same method used on the data sets in this book. They are thus able to provide some empirical insight into the importance of the data adjustment.

1.2   Overview of Data Sets

We start out with a brief overview of all data sets used in this book. The reader is referred to each chapter itself for a detailed description of each data set. Some of the data sets used in this book have also been described previously in Abowd and Kramarz (1999), which also contains an exhaustive list of other matched employer-employee data sets.

1.2.1   Sampling Schemes

The data sets used in this book were derived from administrative sources that essentially have three "sampling schemes": worker-and-firm universe files, worker-based samples, and firm-based samples (see tables I.1 and I.2 in the introduction to this book, by Edward P. Lazear and Kathryn L. Shaw, for more details). In some cases, the sampling scheme is the result of the underlying fundamental structure of the administrative data upon which the data set is based; in other cases, researchers' access mode is restricted to data sets derived using the sampling scheme observed.

Worker-and-firm universe files are not samples, though there may be some smaller coverage issues. Workers and firms appear in the data set because they are covered by a universal entitlement or tax system. The Danish Center for Corporate Performance (CCP) data, the Swedish RAMS data, and the U.S. Longitudinal Employer-Household Dynamics (LEHD) data are examples of such files. However, while the Scandinavian data are national registers and thus cover all firms and workers within each country, the U.S. data are compiled from state-level wage record registers and only covers a select number of states within the United States. Within those states, the LEHD covers almost all firms and workers within those states (Stevens 2002).

The German and the remaining Nordic data sets (Finland, Norway, and the Swedish [SAF; Swedish Employer's Federation] data set) are firm-based samples. For a select number of firms, all workers can be identified, but if those workers work for a firm outside of the sample frame, that employment is not captured. Transitions to firms outside of the sampling frame are also not captured. The remaining Nordic data sets are in fact similar to the worker-and-firm universe files used in the United States, with a critical difference. Whereas the LEHD data set covers all workers within a certain geographic area, but does not cover the full geographic area of the United States, the Nordic data sets cover all firms within each respective country that are members of national employer organizations and have data on all workers working for those firms. From an economy-wide perspective, this more closely resembles a firm-based sample than a universe file. In fact, if not for the sectoral coverage, the sample obtained looks very similar to the German data, which is an explicitly stratified firm sample of all firms in the economy. The firm-based samples have in common that, in principle, data on all workers working for the firms in the sample are available, although some authors have chosen to work with a subsample of workers. Note that a Norwegian national register does exist, and a selection of it is used in conjunction with the selected firm sample in the chapter on Norway, but the full Norwegian register is not used in this book.

The French Déclaration Annuelles de Données Sociales (DADS) and the Italian work histories (WHIP) data are worker-based samples. For some fraction of workers, all jobs with all employers are tracked. Whenever a worker changes firms, his or her move to another employer is included in the database, no matter what the activity or sector of the next employer. The constraint of worker-based sampling is that not all workers within a given firm show up in the sample, imposing some restrictions on analysis of the within-firm structure. For this reason, instead of using firms as the basic unit of analysis for within-unit wage levels and wage changes, the Italy chapter chose to compute these statistics on cells, where cells are defined by unique combinations of four geographic areas by six firm size classes by eight industry sectors. The technical appendix to the Italy chapter addresses the issue of cell-level versus firm-level statistics.

How does the sampling frame affect the analysis? Worker-based samples provide excellent data to provide worker-based statistics. The amount of work experience a worker accumulates is well documented, nonemployment is well captured, and the earnings trajectory, and earnings changes associated with employer changes, can be followed accurately. On the other hand, firm-based statistics are less well defined. The computation of firm size, if not reported by the firm itself, can be noisy for small firms, and small firms themselves may not be well represented in the data. For instance, consider a ten-person firm, and one-in-twenty-five worker sample. Naive estimates for the size of this firm can range from 25 to 250 workers, conditional on at least one worker being sampled, and there is a 66 percent probability that the firm never appears in the data—that is, none of its workers get sampled. Proper adjustments can be made, but for small firms, firm size estimates will remain noisy. Turnover rates, where employment enters the denominator, and estimates of the within-firm variation can be particularly noisy. The chapter on French data contains some further discussions and analysis of the bias introduced by worker-based sampling.

On the other hand, firm-based samples capture most of the firm measures well, while performing less ably for the worker-based statistics. For instance, the earnings of workers who switch firms can only be measured if workers stay within the sample. Differences will arise here between the German and Scandinavian samples, both of which use firm-based samples. The latter will most likely capture only workers who stay within the sector, whereas the former will capture more of the industry-switchers, while missing some of the industry-stayers. How this will affect the estimates of earnings changes will depend on whether industry switchers predominantly have larger or smaller earnings differentials than stayers. Neal (1995), using U.S. data, reports average wage losses for industry switchers of 14 percent, for industry stayers of 6 percent (see also Parent 2000). For France and Germany, the literature seems to indicate that workers tend to have earnings gains rather than losses (Bender et al. 2002), but whether there is a differential gain between stayers and switchers is unknown. For Italy, Leombruni and Quaranta (2002) report average wage changes for industry switchers about 3 percentage points lower than those of job movers within the same industry, although Contini and Villosio (2003) find small wage gains for industry switchers.

1.2.2   Aggregation Levels and the Concept of an Employer

The data sets also differ substantially in another dimension. Whereas the unit of observation on the person side is always well defined, the entity represented in the data on the employer side is not as clearly specified. Although all entities are "employers" in the sense that they have hired the workers, different levels of aggregation are present in the data. Some correspond to physical plants, some are administrative units that may be smaller or larger than any single plant, and some are "firms" or "enterprises" that are better defined by ownership relationships than physical location. Each aggregation level typically has a different identifier, though link files may exist.

The administrative data for each country typically have observations on one specific level of aggregation, although additional variables or links to other data sets may allow for higher-level aggregations. Furthermore, because some of the data are merged from different sources, not all the detail may be available at the lowest aggregation level. Table I.1 in the introduction to this book, by Edward P. Lazear and Kathryn L. Shaw, tabulates what the lowest level of aggregation is for data on employer characteristics for each country. The aggregation level on the files containing job characteristics, if different, is pointed out in the following discussion.

The Nordic data, for the most part, report employer and job characteristics at the level of a physical plant or establishment. This allows allocating an individual to a particular plant at least once a year. However, the data obtained from employer associations may have the feature that only the workers of a particular type (blue- or white-collar) are identifiable. While in Norway, blue- and white-collar data sets can be recombined by firm, this is not feasible in the Swedish SAF data, and is an imperfect process in Finland. On the other hand, the Norwegian, Finnish, and the Swedish RAMS data can typically identify both the firm and the plant a worker is associated with and can thus explore both within-firm and within-plant variation in wages and other measures.

In Italy and the United States, the smallest unit of observation on the employer characteristics file is a reporting unit, respectively, for the social security pension system and for the unemployment insurance system, which typically corresponds to a plant, but may be either larger or smaller. In both countries, the choice is up to the employer, and some employers report all establishments within a large geographic area (a state) on a single record. Furthermore, the records can be aggregated up to a "firm." In the American data, only a state-specific identifier identifies this firm, and the data used in this book cannot identify which firms in different states are actually the same employer. In Italy, as in France, the firm is defined at the national level. However, whereas in Italy a worker's job can be associated with a particular reporting unit, this is not possible for the United States and France.

Finally, in Belgium, as in France, only a "employer" can be identified and associated both with additional details on the firm as well as with the worker.

In summary, the Nordic data, in general, report statistics calculated at both the firm and the plant level in this book, whereas France, Belgium, Italy, the Swedish SAF data, and the United States calculate statistics at the firm level. This aspect of the data needs to be taken into account when comparing "firm" size statistics, turnover, and the variability of earnings within a "firm" or "plant." The difference between plant and firm is a critical distinction and is discussed in more detail in many other locations in this book.

1.3   Longitudinal Linking (Identifier Issues)

1.3.1   Coding Errors in Person Identifiers

The data used in this book are typically used for administrative purposes, and the widespread perception is that administrative data are objective and comprehensive. However, that does not ensure that they are perfect. One particular problem affecting the millions of person records in each of the administrative databases is coding errors. And although coding errors can occur in every item on the "wage record," the variable analysts are most worried about is the person identifier.

When Do Coding Errors Occur?

Coding errors occur for a variety of reasons. A survey of fifty-three state employment security agencies in the United States over the 1996 to 1997 time period found that most errors are due to coding errors by employers, but that when errors were attributable to state agencies, data entry was the culprit (Bureau of Labor Statistics 1997, ii). The report noted that 38 percent of all records were entered by key entry, while another 11 percent were read in by optical character readers (OCRs). The OCR and magnetic media tend to be less prone to errors. Similar errors are known to be present in European data as well, but the extent will vary considerably from one country to the next.

The types of errors differ by the source of the error. When a record is manually transcribed by an employer onto a paper form, scanned, or entered by hand when entering the state agency's data warehouse, the most likely error is a random digit coding error for a single record in a worker's job history. Errors that occur persistently over time will typically be the result of recording a wrong or mistyped person identifier in an employer's data system, which is then repeatedly transmitted to the state agency.

Check digits allow the verification of the validity of a person identifier without reference to any external data and generally prevent, or at least highlight, the presence of coding errors, allowing for easy correction at data entry. However, most person identifiers do not incorporate check digits. In the data used in this book, only the Norwegian and Italian data are known to have checksums on the person identifier.

One last reason why such errors persist and are not corrected is that none of the involved parties has a strong incentive to actively search for and obtain more accurate records on an ongoing basis. The primary focus of the data collection is typically cross-sectional. In the United States, the wage records are collected in the course of the administration of payroll taxes and unemployment insurance systems. Only the sum of wages by firm is used by the collecting agency at the time of collection, ensuring that the firm identifier is generally considered very reliable (but see the next section for exceptions to that statement). In Italy, the primary purpose of collecting the contribution data is for the national pension system. In both cases, for the ultimate beneficiary, the worker, longitudinal consistency only becomes relevant when filing an unemployment or pension benefit claim, possibly years after the coding error was entered into the database. Absences in contributions are corrected using workers' copies of contribution reports and, at least in the United States, are known not to flow back into the actual wage record database. The Italian data typically do not have the coding problem, in part because incentives may be properly aligned, in part because of the presence of a check digit on the person identifier number (Revelli 1996).

What Is the Impact?

Most flow variables (accessions, separations, length of tenure at a firm, etc.) are constructed by associating a person entity—a human being—with a particular person identifier and constructing job histories based on that identifier. Continuity of employment for a given person is inferred from the presence of two records at different points in time bearing the same person identifier. Coding errors in the person identifiers will generate spurious job interruptions that affect all flow variables. Systematic and random errors in the person identifier will generally lead to an upward bias in flow statistics, but result in a downward bias in tenure measures.

The necessity of making a valid longitudinal integration of information for the same individual collected at two different points in time with incomplete linking information is not a new problem in economic measurement. Indeed, probabilistic record linking applications have flourished as a part of research programs that seek to improve such measures. For example, there is a large literature discussing the difficulty of inferring the continuing employment status of an individual between two reference dates using consecutive months of the Current Population Survey (CPS; Fienberg and Stasny 1983; Abowd and Zellner 1985; Poterba and Sommers

1985; and others). Flows into employment, unemployment, and nonparticipation are biased by incorrect longitudinal linkage for exactly the same reason as the accession and separation statistics based on the unemployment insurance (UI) wage records are potentially biased.

Solutions

Methods exist that can avoid or correct for such coding errors. The national person identifiers in some countries have a check digit, which allows the identification at data entry of whether the person identifier was correctly entered. However, for many countries and administrative systems, changing a pervasive identifier without a checksum to a more stable identifier system is not a feasible alternative, or at least a very costly one, and certainly won't work with historical data files.

The practical solution to most coding error problems is automatic and manual editing procedures. Most wage record databases contain names, and inspection and matching of records based on names is a reliable, though not perfect, method of linking records into one consistent job or employment history. Additional information, such as demographic information on the file with the miscoded record and matching information on other files, may facilitate the matching exercise and improve the match rate. The problem is the sheer number of records, which at least for person identifiers makes regular manual editing impossible and has only made automatic editing procedures feasible in the last couple of years, at great computational cost. Often, the simplest solution is to simply drop records that are identifiable as being miscoded. This is the case in Finland, whereas most other countries continue to include such records.

Application: Imputation to Correct for Coding Errors in France

In the French data, a different approach was taken to tackle the same problem (coding errors in the person identifier [NNI] due to keypunch error). As before, as a consequence of coding errors, some job observations, identified by a NNI-SIREN (firm identifier) combination, appear only for a single year in the data. Furthermore, this job is the only one ever registered for this particular NNI. Other job histories will present a single one-period interruption. Consider now the case of a worker with observations in, say, 1978 and 1980 in the same firm (SIREN) but no observation for 1979. If true, this history would mean that the worker was employed until some date in 1978 (depending on the number of days worked, most likely December 31) and also employed after some date in 1980 (depending on the number of days worked, most likely January 1) in this firm but not employed at all during year 1979. This is very improbable. The National Institute for Statistics and Economic Studies (INSEE) thus adopted the following solution: whenever an observation was missing in a given year while the same NNI-SIREN combination exists for the preceding and the following year, an observation is created for the missing year with the same NNI-SIREN combination. Earnings are computed as the geometric mean of the preceding and following wages (in real terms). All other variables are taken at lagged values. For the entire French data set, this procedure added 193,148 observations, or about 1.2 percent of all records.

Case Study: The Sensitivity of Economic Statistics to Coding Errors in Personal Identifiers in the United States (Abowd and Vilhuber 2005)

Abowd and Vilhuber (2005) describe the method used by the LEHD Program at the U.S. Census Bureau to identify coding errors in the person identifier (Social Security Number [SSN] and provide an analysis of the impact that correcting for such errors has on statistics generated from the corrected and the uncorrected data. Their analysis only covered one of the states that are used in the U.S. data chapter of this book, but are generalizable.

First, job histories (the unique combination of an employer identifier [SEIN] and a person identifier [SSN]) are constructed. It is posited that the most likely coding error (random transposition of identifiers) results in (a) a single-period job history for some SSN-SEIN combination and (b) a job history with a single-period interruption. Records are extracted from the wage record database that fit one or the other of the job history profiles. A probabilistic matcher is then used to compare names, the miscoded SSNs themselves, as well as earnings to identify matches.

The process verified over half a billion records. The number of records that are recoded is slightly less than 10 percent of the total number of unique individuals appearing in the original data and only a little more than 0.5 percent of all wage records. Trials in the late 1980s using UI wage records found an average error rate of 7.8 percent, with significant variation across states (Bureau of Labor Statistics 1997). The authors estimate that the true error rate in their data is higher, in part due to the conservative setup of the process. Over 800,000 job history interruptions in the original data are eliminated, representing 0.9 percent of all jobs, but 11 percent of all interrupted jobs.

Despite the small number of records that are found to be miscoded, the impact on flow statistics can be large. Accessions in the uncorrected data are overestimated by 2 percent, and recalls are biased upward by nearly 6 percent. Payroll for accessions and separations are biased upward by up to 7 percent.

1.3.2   Quality of Firm Links, Measures Undertaken and Not Undertaken to Improve Links

The same mechanisms that generate coding errors in person-level data can work on employer data as well. Whether mistyping a person or a firm identifier when transferring information from paper to electronic format, the result is a break in the time series for the affected entity. However, several factors combine to make this a problem both less pervasive and more difficult to correct for in firm-level data.

Administrative versus Economic Identifier Changes:
The Concept of a "Firm" in Administrative Data

People can and do change names, and possibly other theoretically permanent physical attributes, but they always remain a single human entity. The numeric person identifier attributed to a person is only changed in very rare and exceptional instances.

That same intertemporal uniqueness does not necessarily hold for firms. Tracking firms in data and, in particular, administrative data thus poses additional challenges. Firms can be born, split, merge, and disappear. Changes in ownership, of legal and organizational form, and changes in products and services offered can all lead to legitimate and legal changes in administrative identifiers. The very boundaries of what constitutes a single economic entity called a "firm" are often fluid.

For the purposes of the chapters in this book, the fundamental focus is on firms as places of work for workers, that is, the firm as employer. As such, the fundamental economic activity that the authors have attempted to isolate is the employment of a set of individuals that, taken together, constitute the "firm." Under that premise, the tenure of a worker should not be affected by purely administrative changes of the employer identity. But should it be affected by a merger or the transfer of a plant from one firm to another? The identification of an economic, rather than legal, successor to a firm becomes an important distinction.

Impact of Failure to Properly Link Firms

One of the focal statistics used in this book is the "average change in wage from workers who change firms." The failure to properly link firms that change administrative identifiers without an underlying economic event can, under certain circumstances, bias that statistic. Consider an economy with strongly hierarchical firms having few ports of entry and positive returns to tenure. The literature describes various theories and provides examples of firms that have at least some aspects of such a personnel policy (Baker, Gibbs, and Holmstrom 1994; Lazear 1995). By definition, these ports of entry will be at the lower end of the firm-internal pay scale. A worker entering this firm will typically do so at one of the ports of entry and, thus, receive a wage that is below the firm average. As a consequence, the average wage of *all* workers entering this firm will most likely be below the firm-average wage.

Now consider a firm that changes legal form, thus changing its administrative ID in the system, and for some reason, this is not captured in the administrative follow-up. No workers leave the firm, and no workers join the firm. The average change in wage from workers changing firms calculated from this particular subset will be equal to the firm-average wage, substantially higher than if firm changes were measured accurately. If such occurrences are frequent enough, the entire statistic can be biased upward by a significant margin. For instance, Jacobson, LaLonde, and Sullivan (1993a) estimate that in Pennsylvania administrative data for the 1980s, such "bogus job changes" would have been the primary source of all worker movements between employers within industries (Jacobson, LaLonde, and Sullivan 1993a, 39).

Other research would also be affected. An extensive literature shows that a large fraction of workers who are part of a mass layoff have some difficulty reentering the labor market, showing significantly negative effects on the earnings history (Jacobson, Lalonde and Sullivan 1993b) or difficulties in finding a new job (Margolis 1999). An identifier change results necessarily in the observation of a mass layoff, albeit not a real one. However, the workers of such an identifier-induced "mass layoff" do not suffer any earnings problems because, in fact, they are never laid off. Measures of turnover—separation and accession rates—are also driven by the quality of the link, with missing links biasing both measures upward (Spletzer 2000; Benedetto et al. 2007; Vartiainen 2004).

Methods of Linking Firms

To counter the linkage problem identified in the preceding, a variety of methods are used. All corrective methods reduce the linkage failure to varying degrees, but it matters who performs the corrective measure—the researcher or the administrative. Because their motives differ, the goals achieved by corrective measures will also vary.

Following up with firms. Administrations are interested in linking firms for reasons other than longitudinal consistency of research data sets. In particular in the United States, payroll taxes are often experience rated; that is, the tax rate increases as firms lay off large numbers of workers. Firms with a higher payroll tax rate have an incentive to change identity and become an apparently new entity not subject to the predecessor's higher tax rates. To prevent this form of tax evasion, administrations follow up on firms, and the U.S. administrative data contain a field that identifies a possible legal or legally obligated successor. In Italy, the Italian Institute for Social Security (INPS) distinguishes "insurance records" (the basic entity on the firm-level file) from "firms," identified by a single (firm) social security number. The level of disaggregation, that is, the number of insurance records that a firm decides to have, is arbitrary and at the discretion of the firm. But all insurance records can be linked back to the same legal entity, identified by a social security number.

Thus, administrations typically have incentives to properly identify the firm, both at any point in time and across time periods. Most administrative data sets on firms contain some information about a firm's legal predecessors and successors, and this can, if so desired, be used to link firms. This mechanism is known to be used in the United States (Spletzer 2000). In other jurisdictions, administrative follow-up may simply mean that no new identifier gets assigned if the firm or establishment is economically the same (Vartiainen 2004).

The method relies on accurate information on the firms involved being available and (typically) substantial expenses for clerical review. In particular in the United States, where the data are administered by individual states, the success rate of such linkages will vary across states. It is likely to work better in smaller states and for larger firms, where information about individual firms is more easily obtained. It is known to be used by the Finnish and Italian data sources used in this book.

Reverse engineering code changes. In some cases, changes to the coding system have radically altered the identifying codes, resulting in a discontinuity in the time series. One of the reasons this may arise is that the agency collecting the data is not obligated to provide continuity, as in the case of the Finnish employer organization (Vartiainen 2004). Also, the purpose of collecting data may (again) be primarily cross-sectional, with little benefit to the agency of maintaining longitudinal consistency. Finally, extraction and transcription problems when accessing or retrieving historical data series may introduce errors to all records of certain time periods.

When such coding changes occur, researchers do not always have access to the historical documentation detailing the code changes and need to reverse-engineer the coding changes. Many of the methods described subsequently in this section (probabilistic matching, flow analysis) can be used as intermediate tools, rather than actual corrective measures, to identify the way in which coding conventions have changed. Vartiainen (2004) used flow measures to identify pairs of likely "stayers," workers who did not change employers despite a change in their employer's identification code. The resulting pairs of consecutive-year records for the same worker combined with visual inspection allowed the researchers to correct algorithmically for the changes in the establishment codes that had occurred in several years of the Finnish data (Vartiainen 2004).

Using probabilistic matching again. Statistical agencies and researchers also employ probabilistic name matching techniques to link firms. The U.S. Bureau of Labor Statistics attributes about one-third of the quarter-to-quarter matches that are not directly linked through firm identifiers to each of (a) the use of the administrative follow-up described in the preceding paragraph, (b) probabilistic matching, and (c) clerical review of otherwise unmatched records (Pivetz, Searson, and Spletzer 2001; Clayton and Spletzer 2004). Davis, Haltiwanger, and Schuh (1996), and Abowd, Corbel, and

Kramarz (1999), among others, have also used probabilistic name matching in research using U.S. and French data, respectively. In this book, the French data incorporate knowledge gained from the previous probabilistic name-matching exercise.

Correcting by sample selection. The fundamental problem with not correcting for administrative ID changes remains pollution of statistics based on changes in employers. In order not to misclassify the disappearance of administrative numbers as plant closings, most researchers in this book only include plants that existed in two consecutive years when studying changes. Thus, the calculated exit rates will not include plant closings, but will also not include administrative ID changes misclassified as plant closings. To the extent that misclassified plant closings bias the statistics upward, the usual bias described earlier is eliminated. However, to the extent that the earnings changes of workers that are part of true plant closings differ from workers separating for other reasons, a new bias is introduced.

Using worker flows to correct for firm identifier changes. Most of the merged employer-employee data used in all these chapters allow for a further solution to the problem. If workers can be followed from one employer to the next, then worker flows can be used to identify firms that are economically identical despite changing administrative identifiers. At the extreme, if all workers of firm A simultaneously "separate," to then be collectively hired by firm B, where they constitute the totality of employment, then firms A and B are very likely to be the same firm having changed administrative identifiers. More generally, in order for a firm B to be considered the economic successor of firm A, most researchers require that at least one of the following two conditions holds: (1) A large fraction f(A) of workers leaving firm A can be traced to firm B, and (2) a large fraction f(B) of workers at firm B must have come from firm A. How high to set the cutoff levels f(A) and f(B) is the subject of academic discussion, and no clear consensus arises.

Among the data sets used in this book, Denmark, Italy, Finland, and the United States are known to apply such mechanisms. The cases of Finland, Italy, and the United States are described in more detail in the following, but table 1.1 describes how each of these countries handles linking firms in terms of the cutoff levels f(A) and f(B) just described.

Several researchers have also linked firms longitudinally into time-coherent "hiring entities." Because the technique is richer than the simple longitudinal linking that will be described here, it can also be used to identify changes in firm relationships such as mergers, acquisitions, and outsourcing. Using worker flows to identify predecessor-successor links has been used in Italian data (Revelli 1996; Contini 2002), French data, Swedish data, Finnish data (Vartiainen 2004), and U.S. data (Benedetto

Table 1.1   Worker flows between firms, as a percentage of firm employment required to link firms

Country	Predecessor cutoff level: No. of workers leaving predecessor firm and moving to the same successor firm, as fraction of employment level (firm A)	Successor cutoff level: No. of workers coming from predecessor firm and newly hired at successor firm, as fraction of successor's employment level (firm B)
Denmark (CCP)	50%	any
Finland	75%	any
United States (LEHD)	80%	80%
Italy (WHIP)	~100 workers	any
France (DADS)	n.a.	n.a.
Germany (IAB Panel)	n.a.	n.a.
Sweden (SAF)	n.a.	n.a.
Norway (NHO)	n.a.	n.a.
Belgium	n.a.	n.a.
Sweden (RAMS)	n.a.	n.a.

Notes: Firms A and B are linked (firm B is classified as a successor of firm A) if flows of workers between A and B satisfy both the predecessor cutoff level and the successor cutoff level criteria. The predecessor cutoff level is the flow of workers between the two firms, expressed as a fraction of firm A's employment before the flow occurs. The successor cutoff level is the flow of workers between the two firms, expressed as a fraction of B's employment after the flows occurred. Example: 85 workers move from A to B in the United States. Prior to the move, firm A has 100 workers. After the move, firm B has 170 workers. The flow of workers satisfies the predecessor cutoff level, but does not surpass the successor cutoff level. It is not classified as a link between firms A and B. If the same movement were to occur in Finland, it would be classified as a link. n.a. = not available.

et al. 2007). We will discuss some of these approaches and their results in the next sections.

Application: Using Worker Flows to Link Firms

Among the data sets presented in this book, the Danish, Finnish, and Italian data have used worker flows to link firms. In this section, we describe results for these three data sets and summarize the detailed analysis performed by Benedetto et al. (2007). We point out that the U.S. data set used in this book predates the implementation of the worker flow method at the U.S. Census Bureau.

The Italian Case

The Italian WHIP data, which is a one-in-ninety extract of the underlying universe, uses weighting and a cutoff in absolute numbers to define flow-based links. The fundamental hypothesis is that it is unlikely to observe large numbers of workers simultaneously and within a short period of time (one month) moving between two different firms. Because each record in the WHIP worker file represents ninety workers, observing two workers move between firms in the WHIP extract is equivalent to the movement of approximately 180 workers. Such an event is defined a link, and all movements in preceding and succeeding months between the firms linked in this way are classified as spurious movements. About 3.4 percent of all job spells have been corrected according to the spurious movements identifier.

Case Study: Firm Identifier Changes in the United States and the Concept of the Firm (Benedetto, Haltiwanger, Lane, and McKinney 2007)

This section draws on Benedetto, Haltiwanger, Lane, and McKinney 2007 (Benedetto et al. 2007). For eighteen states, some of which are also used in the U.S. chapter of this book, Benedetto et al. (2007) track all movements between firms with more than five employees at the time of the movement between 1992 and 2001. About 2.5 billion such movements are observed. Four conditions are defined. Two characterize the life cycle of predecessor and successor; two characterize the movements between predecessors and successors. The link quality is defined on how many of these conditions are met. A predecessor-based link is of the highest rank if (1) the predecessor exits within two quarters of the movement that defines the link, and (2) 80 percent of the predecessor's prelink employees move to the successor. Not meeting one or the other condition reduces the quality rank attributed to the link. Equivalent conditions characterize the successor link. Benedetto et al. (2007) use these link variables to identify successor-predecessor relationships related to a change in administrative ID, merger-acquisition activity, and the presence of outsourcing. The relation type of relevance to the analyses presented in this book is the "ID change" relation, which depends only on the second condition for both predecessor- and successor-based links. Thus, an ID change occurs when at least 80 percent of a predecessor's employees move to a successor, where they constitute at least 80 percent of the successor's employees (Benedetto et al. 2007, table 2).

Events characterized as "ID changes" account for about 12 percent of all events that meet at least one of the conditions (Benedetto et al. 2007, table 3). More important, movements of this type account for 1 to 2 percent of all accessions in the data. It can be speculated that this symmetrically holds for separations as well. Benedetto et al. (2007) also find significant number of smaller clusters moving between firms. Such movements can be due to small portions, possibly individual establishments, being transferred between firms or for movements of workers across divisions of a firm that appears under multiple identifiers. Additional linkage to the Census Business Register, which allows the identification of more complex firm relationships, indicates that about a fifth of all ID changes occur within the same firm.

Using worker movements to identify predecessor-successor relationships of firms is not the only way to establish such links. Benedetto et al. (2007) compare the worker flow-based links with information present on the ES202 data establishing such links from administrative information. Among "ID changes," more than half of all link events prior to 1998, and approximately half of link events after 1998 are not identified in the administratively defined links. Independent research by other researchers at the U.S. Census Bureau has shown that some of the links defined administratively do not have a corresponding flow.

Overall, the research reported in Benedetto et al. (2007) highlights that using flow-based links as well as administrative information is an important element in accurately defining flows in U.S. data. In the absence of such controls, the bias in separation rates can be as high as 2.5 percent in state-level aggregates.

Application: Firm Identifier Changes in Finland, Flow-Based Identifiers, and Worker Separation Rates (Vartiainen 2004)

Vartiainen (2004) describes the impact of using flow-based identifier correction on the computation of worker separation rates from firms and establishments in Finnish data. In a first step, flow analysis was used to help in reverse engineering identifier code changes (see the section "Application: Using Worker Flow to Link Firms." One particularly problematic problem was the change in the coding systems between 1989 and 1990. Although about two-thirds of all firms as identified by their 1990 identifier have a clear flow of workers from a single firm as identified by the 1989 firm identifier and could thus be readily classified as being the same firm, enough problematic firms, both with multiple predecessors and multiple successors, remain. These problematic firms are likely true mergers or firm splits commingled with the identifier change. As a result, the Finnish authors in this book decided not to report exit rates for 1989 to 1990 as such data would have been too unreliable.

For the remainder of the Finnish employer organization data, Vartiainen analyzes the impact of two different firm and establishment identification strategies on separation rates. The administrative identify of a firm is defined as a unique identifier in the data. In the sample of worker records, a worker is recorded as having separated from a firm in year Y, and thus contributing to the separation rate, if the code of his or her employer in year $Y + 1$ is different than the employer code in year Y, or if the worker no longer appears in the data in the following year. Yearly separation rates based on this criterion are tabulated in column (1) of table 1.2, adapted from Vartiainen (2004).

The flow-based identity of a firm is established by considering the movements of groups of workers. A link between two firms is established if at least 80 percent of ABC's workers in Y reappear at a single firm DEF in year $Y + 1$, and constitute 80 percent of DEF's employment in year $Y + 1$. Note that DEF might or might not be called ABC—the flow criterion ignores the actual administrative identifier code. A worker I at firm ABC is considered a stayer if he or she then also is observed working for DEF in year $Y + 1$. All other workers are considered to have separated. Separation

Table 1.2   Separation rates, based on administrative vs. flow-based firm linkage in Finnish data (%)

Year	Administrative criterion (1)	Pure flow-based (2)	Stayers by flow, exiter by code (3)	Exiter by flow, stayer by code (4)	Administrative criterion + flow criterion (5)
1980	16	17	-0.01	1.46	16
1981	15	17	0.00	1.94	15
1982	16	19	0.00	2.88	16
1983	17	21	0.00	3.82	17
1984	18	20	-0.01	2.37	18
1985	19	25	0.00	6.37	19
1986	23	33	-0.01	9.77	23
1987	22	29	0.00	6.44	22
1988	24	32	-0.56	8.29	24
1989	n.a.	n.a.			
1990	26	29	-0.26	3.07	26
1991	23	26	-0.38	3.64	23
1992	33	37	-0.38	4.20	33
1993	21	25	-0.13	4.52	21
1994	22	26	-1.82	5.51	22
1995	21	23	-0.06	1.81	21
1996	16	17	-0.04	1.55	16
1997	15	15	-0.34	0.82	15
1998	19	20	-0.60	1.83	19
1999	18	19	-1.26	2.31	18
2000	24	27	-0.22	3.74	24
2001	22	24	-0.04	2.08	22

Notes: Adapted from Vartiainen (2004), workers separating from his or her employer in Year + 1, based on different definitions of firm identifiers. n.a. = not available. Blank cells indicate data not available.

rates using only the flow-based criterion are tabulated in column (2) of table 1.2.

The difference between the two columns varies between 1 and 10 percentage points. For the bulk of separating workers, whether administrative or economic entities are tracked is irrelevant. However, for a significant fraction of workers, it does matter. The reason for the difference is broken out in columns (3) and (4). Column (3) tabulates the portion of column (2) that is due to a worker being qualified as a stayer by the flow criterion, but as a separating worker by the administrative criterion. A worker is observed changing identifiers between two years, but moves with over 80 percent of his or her old and new colleagues to the new identifier. This may be a pure administrative code change, or it could be a large spin-off or demerger. It turns out that only a small portion of the separation rate is due to such movements.

Column (4) considers the portion of the separation rate in column (2) that is due to workers being classified as stayers by the administrative criterion but exiters by the flow criterion. Such a situation may arise when a large layoff, affecting over 20 percent of a firm's workforce, occurs. By the flow criterion, no successor firm exists because no group, including the surviving workforce, qualifies for the double-80 percent criterion. Thus, by the flow criterion, such a firm died. The successor or survivor by the administrative criterion is a new firm by the flow criterion, and all workers, whether part of the layoff or part of the surviving workforce, are classified as separators. This situation accounts for almost the entire difference between columns (1) and (2).

Clearly, the situation captured by columns (column 4) is not necessarily the desired outcome as most analysts would consider the administratively surviving firm to be legitimately in continuous existence. Column (5) thus adopts the following strategy. A firm is in continuous existence if a continuous administrative identifier exists (administrative criterion). If a firm death occurs by the administrative criterion but a successor entity exists by the flow criterion, then the firm is still in continuous existence. Only if no administrative and no flow successor can be found does a firm cease to exist. A worker is only counted as an exiter if leaving a firm for an administrative entity that is not a successor either by the administrative or by the flow criterion. In essence, column (5) is obtained by combining columns (1) and (3). Because the Finnish data seem to track administrative successors quite well by maintaining a single identifier throughout time, the difference between a purely administratively based "firm death criterion" and one moderated by worker flows is insignificant. One can conclude that in the Finnish data, the administrative codes seem to track the economic entity quite accurately.

1.3.3   Crossing Borders and Boundaries: The Concept of a Firm Again

In most of the data sets used here, the firm and person identifiers are national identity numbers. This defines a particular concept of a firm. Both finer and broader definitions of a "firm" typically exist but are invisible in this data. For instance, most data sets do not allow the connection of firms in a parent company-subsidiary relationship.

Exceptions, however, appear even here. The Swedish SAF data has person and firm identifiers that are internal to each of the two distinct data sets (blue- and white-collar) it encompasses. Thus, a worker can be followed within the sample of firms reporting data for blue-collar workers even when they switch firms. But a worker switching from a blue-collar occupation to a white-collar occupation within the same firm will appear as an exit from the blue-collar sample and an accession to the white-collar sample. Neither the firm nor the worker can be linked between the blue- and white-collar samples.

In the U.S. data, firms are represented by a state-specific account number within the state unemployment insurance system. Thus, although workers can be traced across state lines, firms cannot be linked across states using the data from the unemployment insurance system (it is feasible to do this using Census-internal data links). A worker transferring from one unit in state A to another unit owned by the same "company" in a different state will be identified as a separation.

Again, as before, the interpretation of certain statistics depends on the granularity of the entity definition, that is, whether a firm or an establishment is the basic unit of accounting on the employer side. Intrafirm transfers between establishments show up in countries that are able to pinpoint employment to an establishment but are hidden in data that can only identify worker movements at the firm level. Thus, turnover statistics—separation and accession rates—will appear higher in establishment data than in firm-level data.

1.4   Missing Data and Related Issues

Data captured by most data sources go back up to three decades. Inevitably, computer systems are no longer the same today as they were at the start of the data collection period. The same applies to the legal environment in which data are collected.

One manifestation of the changing environment is that in many cases, certain portions of the data are no longer available today for reasons outside of the control even of the data collectors. Norway, France, and others all had to face this problem, and there are as many solutions as there are problems.

1.4.1   Application: Tackling Unavailable Data in France

The French DADS was not collected in some years surrounding the 1982 and 1990 Censuses. As a result, data for 1981, 1983, and 1990 were missing. Data were imputed in the same way as in the case of the person identifier miscoding described in the section "Application: Imputation to Correct for Coding Errors in France," thus adding 759,017 observations to the data, equivalent to approximately 4.7 percent of all records.

1.4.2   Application: Tackling Unavailable Data in Norway

In the Norwegian Confederation of Norwegian Business and Industry (NHO) data, the year 1987 is no longer available. However, all years of the NHO data contain lagged values, and so most of the 1987 data can be reconstructed from 1988 data. The only records that cannot be reconstructed are those for workers who left the data in 1987 and for which no lagged values are available

1.4.3   Censoring Issues

For the most part, the data used in this book are collected not to produce data for researchers, but to administer a government program, to collect payroll taxes or unemployment insurance contributions from firms, or to compute income taxes for workers. In particular, the insurance contributions often have a top code, beyond which contributions are no longer computed. The data then only record that top-code value, rather than the true income or wage earned by that worker.

In the German Institute for Employment Research (IAB) data, gross monthly earnings are censored at a time-varying threshold defined by the limitation of payments into the social security system. The following procedure was used to circumvent the censoring problem. A Mincerian earnings equation is estimated, including sector and occupation dummies. From the parameters of this regression, predicted earnings are computed and replace the top-coded values. Across time, between 10 and 15 percent of all observations are imputed, but within some more narrowly defined demographic groups, this percentage increases dramatically. Among workers with a university degree, about 50 percent of all observations are found to be censored.

Although the most frequent censoring issues affect earnings, other variables can be incompletely recorded as well. In particular, the tenure variable suffers from such problems. In most data sets, tenure is computed as the number of years an individual appears in the data, starting at the earliest date. However, if an individual is present in the first year of the data, his or her actual start date is unknown, and thus tenure is censored at a point that varies by individual.

Individuals for whom the first year of observation was in 1976, the start of the data set, and who had worked 360 days in that year, the actual start date is unknown. Abowd, Kramarz, and Margolis (1999) estimated the expected length of the in-progress employment spell by regression analysis using a supplementary survey, the 1978 Enquête sur la Structure des Salaires (ESS; Salary Structure Survey). In this survey, respondent establishments provided information on seniority, occupation, date of birth, industry, and work location for a scientific sample of their employees. Separate regressions were used for men and women. The coefficients were then used to predict (impute) seniority for the in-progress spells in 1976 with 360 days worked. The procedure has been used for most subsequent research papers using the French data, in particular the research reported in this book's chapter on France. The impact of the procedure greatly improves estimates requiring knowledge of the full tenure of workers.

1.5 Conclusion

In this chapter, we have taken a look at the data underlying the other chapters in this book, with an eye for the adjustments that needed to be made in order to make the data both usable and comparable. Each administrative data set, in each state, country, or other organization, has its particularities, including differences in coverage, basic definitions of entities, and data quality. These differences can have a significant impact on the comparability of results obtained from such data. Precisely because the data collection is administrative in nature and beyond the control of most researchers, any attempt to make the actual data collection comparable across countries is bound to fail. An exception to this rule is the collection of administrative surveys coordinated by Eurostat (Structure of Earnings Survey), the Belgian portion of which was used in the chapter by Thierry Lallemand, Robert Plasman, and François Rycx. Such specially administered surveys are costly to produce and coordinate. To wit, the Structure of Earnings Survey, while providing comprehensive cross-sectional coverage, is administered only every four years, and releases can take up to three years to become available to the public.

Researchers accessing the longer time series of conventional administrative data thus need to take extra steps in order to make the data meaningful for analysis and comparable to the data used by others. For the data used in this book, this chapter has outlined their methods and provided, where available, the results of comparing the data used in this book to data produced using alternate scenarios and processing methods. The reader of this chapter should take away a better appreciation of the methods needed to make the data comparable across so many countries and the reassurance that the data can be combined and compared in meaningful ways because of the application and use of these methods.

References

Abowd, John M., Patrick Corbel, and Francis Kramarz. 1999. The entry and exit of workers and the growth of employment: An analysis of French establishments. *Review of Economics and Statistics* 81 (2): 170–87.

Abowd, John M., and Francis Kramarz. 1999. The analysis of labor markets using matched employer-employee data. In *Handbook of labor economics*. Vol. 3, ed. Orley Ashenfelter and David Card, 2629–2710. Amsterdam: North-Holland.

Abowd, John M., Francis Kramarz, and David Margolis. 1999. High-wage workers and high-wage firms. *Econometrica* 67 (2): 251–333.

Abowd, John M., and Lars Vilhuber. 2005. The sensitivity of economic statistics to coding errors in personal identifiers. *Journal of Business and Economics Statistics* 23 (2): 133–52.

Abowd, John M., and Arnold Zellner. 1985. Estimating gross labor force flows. *Journal of Business and Economics Statistics* 3:254–83.

Baker, George, Michael Gibbs, and Bengt Holmstrom. 1994. The internal economics of the firm: Evidence from personnel data. *Quarterly Journal of Economics* 109 (4): 881–919.

Bender, Stefan, Christian Dustmann, David Margolis, and Costas Meghir. 2002. Worker displacement in France and Germany. In *Losing work, moving on: International comparisons of worker displacement*, ed. Peter Kuhn and Randal Eberts, 375–470. Kalamazoo, MI: Upjohn Institute.

Benedetto, Gary, John Haltiwanger, Julia Lane, and Kevin McKinney. 2007. Using worker flows in the analysis of the firm. *Journal of Business and Economics Statistics* 25 (3): 299–313.

Bureau of Labor Statistics. 1997. *Quality improvement project: Unemployment insurance wage records.* Washington, DC: U.S. Department of Labor.

Clayton, Richard, and James Spletzer. 2004. Presentation made at the 2004 NBER Summer Institute. July, Boston.

Contini, Bruno, ed. 2002. *Labour mobility and wage dynamics in Italy.* Turin, Italy: Rosenberg.

Contini, Bruno, and Claudia Villosio. 2003. Worker mobility, job displacement and wage dynamics: Italy 1985–91. LABORatorio Revelli Working Paper no. 24. Turin, Italy: LABORatorio R. Revelli.

Davis, Steven J., John C. Haltiwanger, and Scott Schuh. 1996. *Job creation and destruction.* Cambridge, MA: MIT Press.

Fienberg, Stephen E., and Elizabeth A. Stasny. 1983. Estimating monthly gross flows in labour force participation. *Survey Methodology* 9:77–102.

Jacobson, Louis S., Robert J. LaLonde, and Daniel G. Sullivan. 1993a. *The costs of worker Dislocation.* Kalamazoo, MI: W.E. Upjohn Institute.

———. 1993b. Earnings losses of displaced workers. *American Economic Review* 83 (4): 685–709.

Lazear, Edward P. 1995. *Personnel economics.* Cambridge, MA: MIT Press.

Leombruni, Roberto, and Roberto Quaranta. 2002. The unemployment route to versatility. LABORatorio Revelli Working Paper no. 16. Turin, Italy: LABORatorio R. Revelli.

Margolis, David. 1999. Part-year employment, slow reemployment, and earnings losses: The case of worker displacement in France. In *The creation and analysis of employer-employee matched data,* ed. J. Haltiwanger, J. Lane, J. Spletzer, and J. Theeuwes, 375–416. Amsterdam: North-Holland.

Neal, Derek. 1995. Industry-specific human capital: Evidence from displaced workers. *Journal of Labor Economics* 13 (4): 653–77.

Parent, Daniel. 2000. Industry-specific capital and the wage profile: Evidence from the National Longitudinal Survey of Youth and the Panel Study of Income Dynamics. *Journal of Labor Economics* 18 (2): 306–23.

Pivetz, Timothy R., Michael A. Searson, and James R. Spletzer. 2001. Measuring job and establishment flows with BLS longitudinal microdata. *Monthly Labor Review* 124 (4): 13–20.

Poterba, James M., and Lawrence H. Summers. 1986. Reporting errors and labor market dynamics. *Econometrica* 54 (6): 1319–38.

Revelli, Ricardo. 1996. Statistics on job creation: Issues in the use of administrative data. In *Job creation and loss: Analysis, policy, and data development.* Paris: Organization for Economic Cooperation and Development

Spletzer, James R. 2000. The contribution of establishment births and deaths to employment growth. *Journal of Business and Economic Statistics* 18:113–26.

Stevens, David. 2002. Employment that is not covered by state unemployment. LEHD Technical Paper no. TP-2002-16. Washington, DC: U.S. Census Bureau, Longitudinal Employer-Household Dynamics.

Vartiainen, Juhana. 2004. Measuring interfirm mobility with an administrative data set. National Institute for Economic Research. Mimeograph.

2

Wage Structure and Labor Mobility in the United States

John M. Abowd, John Haltiwanger, and Julia Lane

2.1 Introduction

The new availability of linked employer-employee data in the United States has led to an explosion of interest in research about the outcomes of the labor market interactions of firms and workers. The long history of the examination of worker-based data has revealed the fundamental heterogeneity of worker outcomes, even with rich information on worker characteristics. Similar, but more recent, examination of firm-based data has revealed startling heterogeneity of firm outcomes, despite similarly rich information on industry and firm structure. One of the most interesting, although perhaps not surprising, results from the very recent access to linked

John M. Abowd is the Edmund Ezra Day Professor of Industrial and Labor Relations at Cornell University, and a research associate of the National Bureau of Economic Research. John Haltiwanger is a professor of economics at the University of Maryland, and a research associate of the National Bureau of Economic Research. Julia Lane is program director of the Science of Science and Innovation Policy (SciSIP) at the National Science Foundation.

This document reports the results of research and analysis undertaken by the U.S. Census Bureau staff. This document is released to inform interested parties of ongoing research and to encourage discussion. This research is a part of the U.S. Census Bureau's Longitudinal Employer-Household Dynamics Program (LEHD), which is partially supported by the National Science Foundation Grants SES-9978093 and SES-0427889 to Cornell University (Cornell Institute for Social and Economic Research), the National Institute on Aging Grant R01 AG018854, and the Alfred P. Sloan Foundation. The views expressed on technical issues are those of the authors and not necessarily those of the U.S. Census Bureau, its program sponsors, or data providers. Some or all of the data used in this paper are confidential data from the LEHD Program. The U.S. Census Bureau supports external researchers' use of these data through the Research Data Centers (see http://www.ces.census.gov). For other questions regarding the data, please contact Jeremy S. Wu, Assistant Division Chief, U.S. Census Bureau, LEHD Program, Center for Economic Studies, 4600 Silver Hill Road, Suitland, MD 20233, USA (see Jeremy.S.Wu@census.gov; http://lehd.ces.census.gov).

employer-employee data has been that researchers can explain much more when they have information on both sides of the labor market, rather than one or the other.

In this chapter, we exploit this access to examine the sources of variation in two core outcomes of interest to economists—the earnings distribution and mobility patterns. We particularly focus on the contribution of within and between employer variation in these outcomes. In what follows, we provide a brief literature review and institutional background. We also briefly describe the new database infrastructure, as well as present some basic statistics about the structure of wages within and between firms as well as job mobility patterns.

2.2   Review of the Literature

The increased earnings inequality in the United States that was so evident in the 1980s and early 1990s has not been so apparent in the mid- to late 1990s (Card and DiNardo 2002). Although the consensus in the literature is that skill-biased technical change was the primary driver behind the increased inequality (see, e.g., Acemoglou 2002), Card and DiNardo cast doubt on this because the mid- to late 1990s has been characterized by enormous technological advances without commensurate increases in inequality.

Rising wage inequality in the 1980s in the United States has been attributed in part to increasing returns to education. However, increases in wage dispersion among similar workers suggest that returns to unobservable skill or individual life chances have also increased (Katz and Autor 1999; Levy and Murnane 1992). Despite the overall increase in wage inequality in the United States since the late 1970s, changes in wage structures vary widely across states and across industries. Increases in wage inequality across states are highly correlated with shifts in industrial composition, particularly the decline in manufacturing (Bernard and Jensen 1998).

Changes in the distribution of wages may partly reflect changes on the firm (or demand) side of the labor market. Numerous studies have established the role of firm effects on wages and on wage inequality. Important early work in this area is Groshen (1991), who explored the role of demand side effects from the Bureau of Labor Statistics (BLS) Occupational Wage Surveys. She found that establishment wage differentials account for a substantial fraction of the variation in wages. Related work has examined the establishment and firm characteristics that matter. For example, firm size is an important determinant of wages, and wage inequality has increased both among and within manufacturing plants (Davis and Haltiwanger 1996, 1991). Differences in industry employment shares across states partially explain differences in wage inequality across states (Bernard and Jensen 1998). High-wage firms, or firms that seem to pay a wage premium or markup, and high-wage workers, or those who earn a premium, can be identified (Abowd, Kramarz, and Margolis 1999). Changes in the allocation of workers to jobs could affect the wage distribution; if high-wage workers are more likely to sort toward firms that pay a high wage premium and low-wage workers more likely to sort toward firms that pay workers a discount, then the earnings distribution will become more unequal.

Indeed, earlier work (Andersson, Holzer, and Lane 2005) that focused on the low-wage labor market found that where low-wage workers work can have a major impact on their earnings and, indeed, that the process by which workers are matched to firms in the low-wage labor market has large and important effects on the outcomes we observe for these workers. This very detailed analysis also found that there is considerable mobility into and out of low earnings categories over time, that the characteristics of employers are highly correlated with earnings and with transitions out of low earnings status, and that the characteristics and behaviors of particular firms affect opportunities for low earners.

Work by Davis, Faberman, and Haltiwanger (2006) has directly examined the way in which changes in workforce composition, firm entry and exit, and job reallocation affect industry-specific earnings distributions between 1998 and 2003. They found that worker entry and exit had very little impact on changes in the earnings distributions: despite the ample opportunities for firms to change their workforce composition, industry workforces remained, by and large, very similar, and earnings gains due to experience tended to be higher at the lower end of the distribution. This does not lend credence to the notion that individual firms are changing their production technologies in a way that is biased toward skill. Changes in observable characteristics, which mainly involved the aging of the workforce within each industry, tended to shift the earnings distributions of all industries to the right. The net impact of firm entry and exit is to reduce the dispersion of earnings for all industries. Sorting of workers based on the "human capital" measures over time tended to increase the dispersion of industry earnings distributions between 1992 and 2003. This is consistent with the idea that the driving force of economic change is the entry and exit of firms and can be linked to the selection of new technologies and the associated workforce by new firms. Their results suggest that the underlying dynamics of earnings inequality are complex and are due to factors that cannot be measured in standard cross-sectional data.

2.3 Background

The United States has had lower unemployment than most Organization for Economic Cooperation and Development (OECD) countries in the 1980s and 1990s: below 7 percent for almost all of the past decade. Although there was weak growth and a mild recession in the early 1990s, the

Table 2.1   Macroeconomic conditions

	1990	1991	1992	1993	1994	1995	1996	1997	1998	1999	2000
Unemployment rate	5.6	6.8	7.5	6.9	6.1	5.6	5.4	4.9	4.5	4.2	4.0
Change in GDP											
1 year	0.5	0.9	4.0	2.6	4.1	2.2	4.1	4.3	4.8	4.3	2.3
2 year	1.6	0.7	2.5	3.3	3.3	3.1	3.1	4.2	4.6	4.6	3.3
5 year	2.8	2.4	2.4	2.1	2.4	2.7	3.4	3.4	3.9	3.9	4.0

mid- to late 1990s were characterized by strong growth—between 2 and 5 percent in the two years selected for this chapter. See table 2.1 for a summary of the macroeconomic conditions in the United States during this time period.

A number of labor market changes took place during the period. First, U.S. unionization rates dropped markedly from 20.1 percent for all workers in 1983 to 12.9 percent in 2003. The decline is even more in the private sector, where unionization is now at 8.2 percent; public-sector unionization rates are around 37 percent (Card, Kramarz, and Lemieux 1998). Several researchers (DiNardo, Fortin, and Lemieux 1996; Card, Kramarz, and Lemieux 1998) find that this decline explains at least part of the increase in the variance of log wages.

Second, there has been substantial immigration. More than 15 percent of the workforce is foreign born, and immigrants account for more than half of the growth in the workforce in the 1990s. These workers are disproportionately employed in jobs that require little education—particularly the 40 percent who came from Mexico and Central America (Congressional Budget Office 2005).

Third, the growth in the rate of labor force participation slowed substantially from earlier decades: from a 3.6 percent annual increase in the 1970s to 2.8 percent in the 1980s to a scant .6 percent rate of increase in the 1990s, although this is due to complex offsetting factors. On the one hand, the substantial increase in the prime-age twenty-five to fifty-four-year-old population (from approximately 50 percent of the over-sixteen-year-old population in 1975 to nearly 58 percent in 1996), acted to increase participation rates. In addition, the flat participation rates of never-married mothers increased dramatically in the mid 1990s after the passage of Personal Responsibility and Worker Opportunity Reform Act of 1996 (PRWORA) and the expansion of the Earned Income Tax Credit program (EITC). On the other, male labor force participation rates continued to decline, and the increases in the participation of married mothers, which had had so much impact in the 1970s and 1980s, slowed substantially in the 1990s (Juhn and Potter 2006).

Finally, the real value of the minimum wage declined systemically over the period (see Blackburn, Bloom, and Freeman 1990; DiNardo, Fortin, and Lemieux 1996; Lee 1999).

These changes were accompanied by rising wage inequality in 1980s and 1990s. The general characterization of this increase is its "fractal" nature: that a large component of the level and growth in dispersion is within-group (Levy and Murnane 1992; Moffitt 1990; Burtless 1990). In addition, the college–high school premium increased much less in the 1990s than in the 1980s despite the fact that relative supply kept increasing at the same rate (see Card and DiNardo 2002; Beaudry and Green 2003a; and Lemieux 2004).

The United States example is particularly instructive in that a great deal of research has been devoted to decomposing the earnings distribution into observed and unobserved factors by Abowd and coauthors (see Abowd, Lengermann, and McKinney [2002] for the most recent summary). Briefly, using data and methodology described in detail in the following, Abowd, Lengermann, and McKinney approach permits the decomposition of the wage rate into time varying characteristics, person effect (unobserved and measurable), firm effect, and residual. The results of this decomposition using the data used in the basic statistics discussed later in the chapter are reported in table 2.2. Unlike other versions of this table (e.g., Abowd, Lengermann, and McKinney), this one has been weighted to be representative of the U.S. workforce in 1990 to 2000. Table 2.2 also presents simple correlations of the wage components. By construction, the wage residual is orthogonal to all other wage components.

Intuitively, the person effects, which include some factors that are often observable to the statistician, such as years of education and sex; and some factors that are often not, such as innate ability, people skills, problem solving skills, perseverance, family background, and educational quality, can be thought of as their human capital; the firm effects can be thought of as the pay premium as a result of unionization, rent sharing, or compensating differentials.

There are several striking results to be found from an examination of the table. Most obviously, person and firm heterogeneity are both highly correlated with annualized wages, despite only being mildly positively correlated with each other. In addition, the correlation between time varying individual characteristics and annualized wages, while positive, is smaller than the correlation between either person or firm effects and wages. It is also interesting that both the observed constant person effects and the unobserved person effects are important components of the variation in log wages across individuals.

Abowd, Lengermann, and McKinney (2002) have also examined changes in human capital over time. They find a pronounced right shift in the overall distribution of human capital over the five year period of 1992 to 1997. This is due to increased labor market experience of the existing

Table 2.2   Decomposition of the real wage rate standard deviations and correlations of components (weighted)

	Standard deviation	Log real wage	Time varying characteristics	Person effect	Unobserved person effect	Constant person characteristics	Firm effect	Residual
Log real wage	1.914	1.000	0.732	0.225	0.216	0.483	0.470	0.394
Time varying characteristics	1.656	0.732	1.000	0.347	0.200	0.627	0.141	−0.008
Person effect	1.502	0.225	0.347	1.000	0.914	−0.513	0.074	0.001
Unobserved person effect	1.417	0.216	0.200	0.914	1.000	−0.576	0.059	0.001
Constant person characteristics	1.808	0.483	0.627	−0.513	−0.576	1.000	0.068	−0.009
Firm effect	0.798	0.470	0.141	0.074	0.059	0.068	1.000	0.000
Residual	0.769	0.394	−0.008	0.001	0.001	−0.009	0.000	1.000

workforce, offset slightly by a net reduction in human capital from entry and exit. Their analysis notes that these changes took place despite the fact that the overall wage distribution remained largely unchanged over the same period, largely reflecting the tendency of labor force entrants to sort into firms with below-average internal wages and of continuers to sort into firms with above-average internal wages, thereby exacerbating preexisting wage differences.

Abowd, Lengermann, and McKinney (2002) also examined the human capital distributions for firms in both 1992 and 1997 and found a pronounced tendency for firms to employ workers at the ends of the human capital distribution rather than the middle—even within firms in the same industry. Between 1992 and 1997, between-firm variation in the employment shares of low-skilled workers declined, while the average firm in virtually every industry upskilled considerably. Employment shares in the bottom two skill deciles fell by 7.7 percent and 5.2 percent, respectively, but increased by 6 percent in each of the two highest skill deciles.

2.4   The Structure of the LEHD Program Data

The LEHD database infrastructure is complex. The core integration records are state unemployment insurance (UI) wage records (which are described in detail elsewhere). The integration of the business and demographic data by means of these records, which takes place under strict confidentiality protection protocols,[1] can be visualized by examining figure

---

1. The data are anonymized before use and may only be used for statistical purposes and for approved projects by Census Bureau employees. In addition, the data are protected by Title 13 of the U.S. Code: employees who disclose the identity of an individual or business are subject to a penalty of five years in jail, a $250,000 fine, or both.

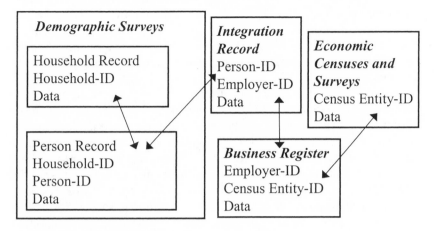

Fig. 2.1   The LEHD program

2.1. These UI records, from now more than forty-eight partner states representing more than 95 percent of U.S. employment, consist of quarterly reports filed by employers every quarter for each individual in covered employment. These records permit the construction of a database that provides longitudinal information on workers, firms, and the match between the two. The coverage is roughly 96 percent of private nonfarm wage and salary employment; the coverage of agricultural and federal government employment is less comprehensive. Self-employed individuals and independent contractors are also not covered.[2] Although the administrative records themselves are subject to some error, staff at the LEHD program has invested substantial resources in cleaning the records and making them internally consistent.[3]

The U.S. Census Bureau information that is integrated into this infrastructure backbone consists of basic demographic information: date of birth, place of birth, sex, and a crude measure of race and ethnicity for almost all workers in the data set—the nonmatch rate is about 4 percent. Other demographic survey data are integrated if the use is permitted under Title 13 of the U.S. Code. While the Census Business Register is the core integration file for business data, other business surveys are also included and integrated (again if the use is permitted under Title 13 of U.S. Code—more information on the microbusiness data integrated can be found at the Center for Economic Studies Web site at http://www.ces.census.gov). To sum up, for the universe of employers and employees, the range of infor-

---

2. See David Stevens (2002). The LEHD program is currently working on using administrative data to track self-employment.
3. The approach is described in John Abowd and Lars Vilhuber (2005).

mation is limited to earnings histories, earnings, employment matches, and basic information such as gender and age of the worker and the location and industry of the business. However, for subsamples of records integrated with Census demographic and business data, additional detailed information is available.

In the current chapter, we present some summary statistics of the structure of wages within and between firms as well as patterns of worker turnover. There are some conceptual issues that need to be made clear. Although we typically refer to the employer as a "firm," the actual reporting unit in the data is an administrative, rather than an economic entity, as the filing unit reflects an employer identification number, rather than a specific firm. The distinction is immaterial for about 70 percent of workers, who work for a single establishment employer—but those who work for a multiple establishment employer, the use of the term "firm" in this book is less well-defined. In addition, no occupation information is available. We observe a "job" as an employer-employee match, and we can only observe internal earnings mobility—not occupational mobility.

An important issue to address is that of earnings. According to the *BLS Handbook of Methods* (1997), UI wage records measure "gross wages and salaries, bonuses, stock options, tips, and other gratuities, and the value of meals and lodging, where supplied." They do not include Old-Age, Survivors, and Disability Insurance (OASDI), health insurance, workers compensation, unemployment insurance, and private pension and welfare funds. In addition, because neither hours nor weeks worked are available on the data, there is no information on hourly or weekly earnings. Consequently, low earnings in a given year (or quarter) can be due to low hourly wages, low hours, or both. Thus, some industries, like retail trade, will show up as low earnings industries at least partly because so much of the work in that industry is part time. Note that hours or weeks worked are typically not reported by employers.

In this chapter, the dependent variable is based on the annualized full-year, full-time wage rate developed in Abowd, Lengermann, and McKinney (2002). It is, essentially, the sum of full-quarter income for four consecutive quarters over the calendar year. When full-quarter income is missing, it is estimated based on the expected full-quarter income for that quarter given the pattern of employment in the six-quarter window that includes the last quarter from the previous year, the four quarters of the current year, and the first quarter of the next year. We derived monthly income by dividing the annualized measure by 12, and deflated it by the CPI-U (base 1990 = 1.00). Only the observation for the dominant employer (the one with whom the individual had the largest earnings [not wage rate] in a given year). Only full-time employees are used (based on the first implicate of the full-time imputation).

A change in the monthly wage rate is computed for individuals with two consecutive years of full-time employment. The change in the wage rate is $w(t) - w(t - 1)$. Only those observations present in $t - 1$ enter the change tables. The weight used is for period t. In computing entry, we define individuals as "entrant" in year t if this year's dominant employer is different from last year's. Similarly, an individual is defined as an "exiter" in year t if this year's dominant employer is different from next year's.

Finally, in the results we reported in table 2.2, we used this data to estimate measures of individual and firm fixed effects, following the methodology described in Abowd, Lengermann, and McKinney (2002).

$$(1) \qquad \ln w_{it} = \theta_i + \psi_{J(i,t)} + x_{it}\beta + \varepsilon_{it},$$

where the dependent variable is the log wage rate of an individual i working for employer j at time t, and the function $J(i,t)$ indicates the employer j of individual i at date t. The first component of equation (1) is the time-invariant person effect, the second component is the time-invariant firm effect, the third component is the contribution of time varying observable individual characteristics, and the fourth component is the statistical residual, orthogonal to all other effects in the model. The econometric methodology and estimates of human capital used in this chapter are discussed and described in detail in Abowd, Lengermann, and McKinney (2002).[4]

More complete details of the database used in this chapter are provided in appendix A. For the current chapter, we use a limited number of states for the years 1993 and 1998. However, as described in appendix B, we have developed weights so that the statistics here can be interpreted as nationally representative.

2.5   Analysis

The key purpose of this chapter is to describe wage structure and individual mobility within and across firms over the period in question. The first panel of table 2.3 provides the individual analysis by describing the distribution of real monthly wage rates and log real monthly wage rates for individuals—the summary statistics include the average, standard deviation, and 90th and 10th percentiles wages in that distribution.[5]

The first thing to note is that the entire distribution of earnings shifted to the right, as already noted by Abowd, Lengermann, and McKinney (2002): average wages increased over the period, as did the wages for workers at the top and bottom end of the distribution (the 90th, 75th, 25th, and 10th percentiles). It is also clear that the dispersion of earnings across workers is enormous. The standard deviation of log earnings is about 80

---

4. Recent research has extended this type of analysis to permit a mixed effects specification—see Abowd, Stephens, and Vilhuber (forthcoming).

5. An individual is included in the analysis if that person had a dominant employer in 1993 or 1998 and worked full time at that employer.

Table 2.3   Structure of wages within and between firms (US$1990)

	Monthly full-time wages		Log monthly wages	
	1993	1998	1993	1998
Average wage[a]	3,074	3,253	7.6848	7.7323
SD	4,015	4,230	0.81	0.82
90th percentile	5,555	5,925	8.6225	8.687
75th percentile	3,671	3,774	8.2083	8.2359
25th percentile	1,319	1,389	7.1847	7.236
10th percentile	798	855	6.6824	6.7513
No. of workers	26,403,031	40,110,897	26,403,031	40,110,897
Average of firm average wage[b]	2,819	3,020	7.6111	7.6639
SD	1,758	2,051	0.4968	0.5157
90th percentile	4,649	5,070	8.228	8.304
75th percentile	3,464	3,645	7.956	7.9988
25th percentile	1,719	1,791	7.2591	7.3018
10th percentile	1,284	1,336	6.9757	7.0129
No. of firms	132,659	202,528	132,659	202,528
Average of SD of wage[b]	2,280	2,434	0.5923	0.5966
SD	2,354	2,452	0.1708	0.1741
90th percentile	4,403	4,888	0.8038	0.8132
75th percentile	2,595	2,848	0.6815	0.6866
25th percentile	1,030	1,062	0.48	0.4813
10th percentile	711	732	0.402	0.4043
No. of firms	132,659	202,528	132,659	202,528
Average coefficient of variation of wages[b]	0.75	0.75	0.0782	0.0783
SD	0.39	0.37	0.024	0.024
90th percentile	1.2	1.2	0.1079	0.1082
75th percentile	0.87	0.88	0.0904	0.0903
25th percentile	0.52	0.52	0.0626	0.0624
10th percentile	0.42	0.42	0.0521	0.0522
No. of firms	132,659	202,528	132,659	202,528
Correlation (average wage, SD of wage)[b]	0.7622	0.7856	−0.0561	−0.0515

Note: SD = Standard deviation.
[a] Employed persons.
[b] Firms, U.S. operations.

log points. Using an alternative measure of dispersion, the worker at the 90th percentile in 1998 has log wages that are about 200 log points larger than those of the worker at the 10th percentile, and this pattern is relatively stable between the two periods.

The second panel, the firm-level analysis,[6] permits the quantification of the between versus within variation in wage patterns, as it shows the aver-

6. A firm is included in the analysis if that firm had positive average month three ES-202 employment during the year of twenty-five or more.

age wage and the variation in wages across firms. Note that the average wage in the average firm is lower than the average individual wage—reflecting the skewed size distribution of firms. In other words, although most workers work in large firms, most firms are small. Because small firms pay less than large, a wage distribution based on firms as the unit of analysis will inevitably have a lower mean than one with individuals as the unit.

As with the individual analysis, it is clear that the entire distribution has shifted to the right during the period in question. In addition, the standard deviation of log wages between firms is large—about 50 log points in 1993 and 1998. The 90-10 differential between firms is also large—around 130 log points. Although this is substantially less than the standard deviations associated with the individual distribution, it is clear that one of the key patterns for understanding the structure of wages is the earnings differences across firms.

The third issue is examining the within-firm wage dispersion, which is presented in the third panel. This shows tremendous variation in the dispersion of log wages within firms. Using as the metric the within-firm standard deviation of wages, the third panel shows that the mean standard deviation within firms is around 60 log points, or about three-fourths of the individual earnings distribution.[7] Those firms with the least compressed distribution, those at the 90th percentile, have a standard deviation of 80 log points, and even in those firms with quite compressed earnings distribution, namely those at the 10th percentile of firms, the within-firm standard deviation is about 40 log points. Interestingly, the distribution of standard deviations also shifted to the right (albeit slightly) during the period.

The fourth panel, which performs the same analysis for a different statistic, the average coefficients of variation across firms, shows similar patterns in terms of the earnings distribution. However, the dispersion of earnings relative to the mean wage is remarkably high: the standard deviation of earnings is about 75 percent of the mean wage. Even for the most compressed firms (the 10th percentile), the standard deviation is about 40 percent of the mean wage; for the least compressed, (the 90th percentile), it is a startling 120 percent.

Both of these panels make it clear that there is substantial within-firm variation at all points of the distribution and that this variation is a sizable fraction of individual variation. As a result, understanding within-firm dispersion in wages is likely to be an important component to understanding the individual earnings distribution. The large spread of earnings within firms is also consistent with the popularly held notion that the spread between top and bottom earnings within a U.S. firm is substantially greater than in their European counterparts.

---

7. Some caution must be used in comparing average standard deviation within firms to overall standard deviation across individuals because the average standard deviation within firms is not employment-weighted across firms.

At the very bottom of table 2.3 is the simple statistic showing the correlation between the within-firm standard deviation of wages and the average wages of the firm. In dollars, the correlation is positive, but this reflects scale effects on the standard deviation measured in dollars. When wages are measured in logs, the correlation is slightly negative and essentially zero. Thus, for the entire United States there is little systematic relationship between within-firm dispersion of wages and average wages. This pattern is likely sensitive to industry and occupation. For example, in a study of the software industry and software engineers and managers, Andersson, Holzer, and Lane (2005) find a positive relationship between within-firm dispersion of earnings and average earnings. However, as argued in the latter paper, this pattern reflects the "winner take all" product mixes in some parts of the software industry such as in computer games.

The fact that the data are linked longitudinally at the individual level permits an analysis of wage dynamics by examining changes in the wage rate and changes in the log wage rate.[8] A set of summary statistics is presented in table 2.4.

An examination of the individual earnings distribution in the first panel reveals that the typical wage change in 1993 was negative and in 1998 positive. This result is consistent with the macroeconomic environment in both periods, as the former is likely to reflect recessionary pressures, while the later expansionary pressures. It is noteworthy that many workers did get sizable raises even in the recessionary periods, as the order of magnitude of the dispersion of wage changes is quite large—about 50 log points—and the order of magnitude did not change much in the expansion. This finding is consistent with the notion that macroeconomic conditions affect the level but not the distribution of wage changes.

The wage growth distribution is quite remarkable. An analysis of this distribution shows that even when economic activity is strong, as in 1998, a substantial portion of the population actually experienced quite substantial earnings declines. Indeed, even at the 25th percentile, log earnings declined by 6 points, and at the 10th percentile, log earnings declined by a startling 38 points. At the top end of the distribution, earnings increased by as much as 50 percent. In keeping with this finding, the standard deviation is quite large—about 50 log points.

The fact that the linked employer-employee data are also linked longitudinally at the firm level enables us to calculate the change in mean firm log wages. An analysis of the results of this calculation, which are presented in the second panel, mirrors the individual distribution in that the mean log wage of firms actually declined in the first period and increased in the

8. An individual is included in the analysis if that person had a dominant employer in 1992 and 1993 or 1997 and 1998 and worked full time in both years. A firm is included in the analysis if that firm had positive average month three ES-202 employment during the year of twenty-five or more.

	Change in monthly full-time wages		Change in log monthly wages	
	1993	1998	1993	1998
Average change in wage[a]	−18	152	−0.0039	0.0496
SD	2,844	3,041	0.467	0.511
90th percentile	837	1,120	0.362	0.495
75th percentile	262	408	0.106	0.17
25th percentile	−231	−144	−0.093	−0.064
10th percentile	−869	−784	−0.386	−0.379
No. of workers	17,614,249	35,607,319	17,614,249	35,607,319
Average of firm average change in wage[b]	−1	166	−0.0017	0.0558
SD	991	1,109	0.183	0.191
90th percentile	426	675	0.1404	0.2153
75th percentile	152	300	0.0661	0.1261
25th percentile	−191	−92	−0.0641	−0.0181
10th percentile	−459	−337	−0.1567	−0.1124
No. of firms	106,732	202,335	106,732	202,335
Average of SD of change in wage[b]	1,621	1,782	0.4462	0.4917
SD	1,858	2,021	0.202	0.206
90th percentile	3,192	3,625	0.707	0.7554
75th percentile	1,836	1,993	0.5504	0.6012
25th percentile	675	738	0.3072	0.3499
10th percentile	442	496	0.2255	0.2623
No. of firms	106,732	202,335	106,732	202,335
Average coefficient of variation of change in wages[b]	2.50	2.49	−1.3944E+12	9.15283E+12
SD	40.69	105.29	1.2939E+15	3.6786E+15
90th percentile	15.55	15.19	16.561	14.4548
75th percentile	5.72	6.3	6.2325	6.18
25th percentile	−6.36	−4.64	−5.6833	−2.8749
10th percentile	−15.91	−13.83	−15.9834	−11.4428
No. of firms	106,732	202,335	106,732	202,335
Average change in wage for people who change firms[a]	−9	195	0.0243	0.1031
SD	3,506	3,664	0.789	0.786
90th percentile	1,660	1,880	0.918	0.997
75th percentile	666	805	0.391	0.46
25th percentile	−548	−394	−0.327	−0.238
10th percentile	−1,716	−1,460	−0.895	−0.799
No. of workers	3,718,398	10,522,612	3,718,398	10,522,612

Notes: SD = Standard deviation. Percentiles for individuals were computed without using person weights due to computer memory limitations. Change in monthly wages is defined as wage in year t − (wage in year t − 1). Change in log monthly wages is defined as log wage in year t − (log wage in year t − 1).

[a] Employed persons.

[b] Firms, U.S. operations.

second.[9] Just as in the individual distribution, there are substantial differences across firms: more than 25 percent of firms actually decreased their mean log wage in both periods, and there were large changes in mean log wages for some firms in both periods. Indeed, the 90th percentile firm actually increased mean log wages by 14 log points in the first and by more than 21 log points in the second period. The summary standard deviation statistics shows that between firm dispersion in log wage changes is around 19 log points.

Because the data are linked longitudinally in both firms and workers, we can also calculate the distribution of the change in log wages for workers within each firm and calculate the standard deviation of this statistic. We provide summary information about the distribution of the standard deviation of this measure of the within-firm wage dispersion in panel three. What is especially striking is the large within-firm dispersion in wage changes. On average, within-firm dispersion in wage changes is 45 log points in 1993 and 49 log points in 1998. In other words, some workers are doing much better within firms than others in terms of wage growth. Even in firms that kept the spread of their wage changes relatively compressed (the 10th percentile), the standard deviation was 20 log points; at the other end of the distribution (the 90th percentile), the standard deviation was a substantial 70 log points. The fourth panel, which reports a similar measure of spread—the coefficient of variation, reflects the same basic facts.

The last panel of table 2.3 sheds light on the structure of wage changes for those who changed firms. In contrast to the distribution of individuals as a whole, on average, the wage change is positive, especially in 1998, suggesting that the average worker gained from job change. However, the dispersion in wage changes is very large across those who changed firms, and clearly some workers lose substantially. At the 90th percentile, the average wage change is almost 100 log points in 1998, while at the 10th percentile it is about –80 log points.

The counterpart of the analysis of wage changes within and across firms is clearly an analysis of mobility, and the results of just such an analysis are presented in table 2.5. We find a very high pace of accessions and separations.[10] We also find that workers are much more mobile at bottom end of distribution than at top—both in 1993 and 1998. Interestingly, despite the differences in macroeconomic activity in both periods, both entry and exit rates increased in 1998.

---

9. Of course, it remains an open question how much of this change is due to changes in wages for continuing workers and how much is due to changes in the workforce at the firm.

10. These rates are averages across firms and have not been employment-weighted, so they are somewhat larger than analogous accession and separation rates that are employment-weighted. In addition, these measures of worker turnover are higher than measures that use point in time changes or only count transitions for workers with some minimum duration of employment. There is an implicit duration requirement in that average real monthly earnings must exceed $100 for a worker to be counted in these statistics, but this might still include a substantial number of short duration jobs.

Table 2.5 Mobility (all jobs)

	All firms with 25+ employees	
	1993	1998
Employees	150	156
	(782)	(817)
Employment growth	0.14	0.17
	(0.48)	(0.49)
Exit (separation) rate	0.36	0.40
	(0.24)	(0.24)
Top quartile of firm wages	0.28	0.31
	(0.27)	(0.28)
Bottom quartile of firm wages	0.49	0.53
	(0.27)	(0.26)
Top decile of firm wages	0.28	0.30
	(0.32)	(0.32)
Bottom decile of firm wages	0.57	0.61
	(0.31)	(0.30)
Entry (accession) rate	0.27	0.34
	(0.24)	(0.24)
Top quartile of firm wages	0.20	0.26
	(0.26)	(0.27)
Bottom quartile of firm wages	0.36	0.45
	(0.27)	(0.26)
Top decile of firm wages	0.19	0.24
	(0.29)	(0.32)
Bottom decile of firm wages	0.40	0.49
	(0.31)	(0.31)
No. of firms (sum of weights)	503,990	547,462

Note: Numbers in parentheses are standard deviations.

2.6   Summary

This chapter has provided an initial examination of the earnings distribution both within and between firms at two different points of the business cycle. There is enormous variation in earnings across workers in the United States. A decomposition into the factors underlying this dispersion suggests that about half of the variation is associated with worker characteristics and about half due to firm effects. Thus, both who you are and where you work are very important in the determination of earnings. While there is substantial between firm variation in earnings, the within-firm variation of earnings is very large in terms of both levels and changes of earnings over time. So while where you work matters substantially, there is enormous variation in earnings within where you work as well. Accompanying the substantial between- and within-firm variation in earnings levels and changes is a high pace of worker turnover. The earnings dynamics and turnover are not surprisingly connected with workers that change jobs having on average a positive increase in earnings. However, underlying this positive average is substantial variation with the 25th percentile of job changers exhibiting over a 20 percent decline in earnings and the 75th percentile exhibiting a 40 percent increase in earnings. Putting all the pieces together suggests a rich and continuous ongoing matching and sorting of heterogeneous firms and workers with a wide variation in outcomes in the U.S. labor market.

Appendix A
Summary of U.S. Statistics Measurement

The nature of administrative data means that a number of technical issues arise in the creation of measures that are sensible for economic analysis. There is extensive documentation on the LEHD Web site (http:// lehd.ces.census.gov) on the characteristics of the data and the methods used to standardize information from different states. What follows is a brief summary of the approach used to prepare the data for this chapter.

Data from seven states are used in this analysis: California, Florida, Illinois, Maryland, Minnesota, North Carolina, and Texas, comprising about 40 percent of U.S. employment. The employer is the dominant employer in a given year (although multistate employment is not eliminated for a given year).

The earnings data are from quarterly UI wage records from each participating state. Unemployment insurance wage records measure "gross wages and salaries, bonuses, stock options, tips, and other gratuities, and the value of meals and lodging, where supplied" (Bureau of Labor Statistics 1997, 44). They do not include OASDI, health insurance, workers compensation, unemployment insurance, and private pension and welfare funds.

The following steps are taken in creating the earnings measures used in this chapter. First, earnings are converted to real earnings using the CPI. They are then annualized using the approach described in Abowd, Lengermann, and McKinney (2002) and converted to monthly earnings by dividing annualized earnings by 12. Workers are included in analysis if real monthly earnings exceed $100 and are less than $100,000.

The unit of observation for the firm is the state unemployment insurance account number (SEIN). For single-unit establishment firms, the SEIN defines both the establishment and the firm. For multiple establishment firms, the SEIN typically includes all establishments within the state that are owned by this firm. For firms that operate in multiple states, the SEIN does not capture all activities of the firm but rather the operations for the state in question. Firms are included in the analysis if employment is larger than twenty-five.

National person and firm weights have been developed for the U.S. statistics in a manner described in appendix B.

Worker flows are calculated as follows. Entry (accession) and exit (separation) rates reflect links across years for jobs, where the unit of observation is defined as an individual-SEIN year observations (persons linked to a SEIN in a given year). Entry refers to workers who have zero earnings with SEIN in prior year ($t - 1$) and have positive earnings in current year (t). Workers are only counted for purposes of computing rates if they satisfy above earnings thresholds.[11] Exit refers to workers who have positive earnings in year t at SEIN and zero earnings in year $t + 1$. Workers are counted for purposes of computing rates if they satisfy above earnings thresholds.[12] There is an important timing difference—entry refers to flow into firm from $t - 1$ to t; exit refers to flow out of firm from t to $t + 1$. It is thus inappropriate to compute net flows from entry and exit.

Employment measures—average employment and employment growth—are based on Quarterly Census of Employment and Wages (QCEW) 202[13] employment from the third month of each quarter. Average employment is computed as the average across the four quarters of the third month QCEW/202 employment measure. Net growth across years is based on the difference between the average value in time t and $t + 1$.

Appendix B
The Construction of the National Weights

Person Level

The control source is the final individual weights from the March Current Population Survey (CPS). The population was defined as those eighteen–seventy-year-olds who were part of the employed, domestic, civilian noninstitutional population (ESR = 1 or 2), age eighteen–seventy-year-olds (inclusive). The major industry classifications were the twenty-two CPS major industry categories. In constructing the weights, we used five age categories (eighteen to twenty-four, twenty-five to thirty-four, thirty-five to forty-four, forty-five to fifty-four, fifty-five to seventy), three education categories

---

11. Note, however, that a worker who has positive earnings in year $t - 1$ and t, but whose earnings fail to meet the threshold for inclusion in our analyses, is not counted as an entrant in t.

12. Similarly, a worker who has positive earnings in both year $t - 1$ and t, but whose earnings fail to meet the threshold for inclusion, is not counted as an exit in t.

13. QCEW/202 employment is the number of workers on the payroll for the payroll period including the 12th of the month.

(zero to eleven years, exactly twelve years (completed), more than twelve years), and two sex categories (male, female).

For each year and major industry, we computed the expected number of employed persons inside each education x age x sex cell based on a log-linear probability model with three-way interactions suppressed estimated from the final weighted March CPS Annual Demographic Supplements (public use files). This is the weight numerator.

For each year and major industry, we computed the number of persons in each education $\times$ age $\times$ sex cell from the LEHD sample.[14] This is the weight denominator.

The P-weight used is the ratio of the weight numerator to the weight denominator. P-weight thus performs a poststratification of the state-specific sample to 600 employment cells each year. The weighted person-level data are representative of the employed civilian noninstitutional population in each year.

The variable P-weight was used to weight all person-level estimates. For changes, the t period and not the $t-1$ period weights were used.

Firm Level

The employment measure used was the average month three employment from the QCEW for every quarter that the SEIN had data in a given year. The control source was the Current Employment Statistics national estimates for two-digit Standard Industrial Classifications (SICs). The population used was all nonfarm establishments, with the following exceptions. The SICs for which the LEHD sample was not representative (SICs 01, 02, 08, 43) were excluded by means of assigning missing weights. Certain SICs were pooled (SICs 20–21, 71–72, 88–89, 90–99). Public administration (90–99) was estimated from federal, state, and local government employment exclusive of government-owned establishments in United States Postal Service (USPS), health, education, and social services, which were either excluded (USPS) or included in the correct SIC.

The numerator of the weight was calculated for each year and two-digit SIC from the total average annual employment from the national Current Employment Statistics (CES) series.

The denominator of the weight was calculated for each year and SEIN in the LEHD sample from total employment in the same two-digit SICs. Note that there are no empty cells and the exclusions noted in the preceding take care of industries in which the sample is probably not representative.

F-weight is the ratio of the weight numerator to the weight denominator. The f-weight is a poststratification of the LEHD sample to two-digit SIC

---

14. There are no empty cells.

average annual employment in the CES. This f-weight is used to weight all firm-level statistics in the tables.

References

Abowd, John M., Francis Kramarz, and David N. Margolis. 1999. High wage workers and high wage firms. *Econometrica* 67:251–333.
Abowd, John M., Paul Lengermann, and Kevin McKinney. 2002. The measurement of human capital in the U.S. Economy. LEHD Technical Paper no. TP-2002-09. Washington, DC: U.S. Census Bureau, Longitudinal Employer-Household Dynamics. http://lehd.dsd.census.gov/led/library/techpapers/tp-2002-09.pdf.
Abowd, John M., Bryce Stephens, and Lars Vilhuber. Forthcoming. The LEHD infrastructure files and the creation of the quarterly workforce indicators. In *Producer dynamics: New evidence from micro data*, ed. T. Dunne, J. B. Jensen, and M. J. Roberts. Chicago: University of Chicago Press.
Abowd, John M., and Lars Vilhuber. 2005. The sensitivity of economic statistics to coding errors in personal identifiers. *Journal of Business and Economics Statistics* 23 (2) 133–52.
Acemoglu, Daron. 2002. Technical change, inequality, and the labor market. *Journal of Economic Literature* 40 (1): 7–72.
Andersson, Fredrik, Harry Holzer, and Julia Lane. 2005. *Moving up or moving on: Who advances in the low-wage labor market?* New York: Russell Sage Foundation.
Beaudry, Paul, and David A. Green. 2003. Wages and employment in the United States and Germany: What explains the differences? *American Economic Review* 93 (3): 573–602.
Bernard, Andrew B. and J. Bradford Jensen. 1998. Understanding Increasing and Decreasing Wage Inequality," Unpublished paper (Yale University).
Blackburn, McKinley L., David E. Bloom, and Richard B. Freeman. 1990. The declining position of less-skilled American males. In *A future of lousy jobs?*, ed. by G. Burtless, 31–67. Washington, DC: Brookings Institution.
Bureau of Labor Statistics. 1997. *Handbook of methods.* Washington, DC: U.S. Department of Labor, Office of Publications and Special Studies. http://www.bls.gov/opub/hom/home.htm.
Burgess, Simon, Julia Lane, and David Stevens. 2000. Job flows and worker flows in the life cycle of the firm. *Oxford Bulletin of Economics and Statistics* 62:885–908.
Burtless, Gary. 1990. Earnings inequality over the business and demographic cycles. In *A future of lousy jobs?*, ed. by G. Burtless, 77–122. Washington, DC: Brookings Institution.
Card, David, and John DiNardo. 2002. Skill-biased technological change and rising wage inequality: Some problems and puzzles. *Journal of Labor Economics* 20 (4): 733–83.
Card, David, Francis Kramarz, and Thomas Lemieux. 1999. Changes in the relative structure of wages and employment: A comparison of the United States, Canada, and France. *Canadian Journal of Economics* 32 (4): 843–77.
Congressional Budget Office. 2005. The role of immigrants in the U.S. labor market. http://www.cbo.gov/ftpdocs/68xx/doc6853/11-10-Immigration.pdf.
Davis, Steven J., R. Jason Faberman, and John Haltiwanger. 2006. The flow approach to labor markets, micro-macro links, and the recent downturn. *Journal of Economic Perspectives* 20 (3): 3–26.

Davis, Steven J., and John Haltiwanger. 1991. Wage dispersion within and between manufacturing plants. *Brookings Papers on Economic Activity, Microeconomics:* 115–80.
————. 1996. Employer size and the wage structure in U.S. manufacturing. *Annales D'Economie et de Statistique* (41–42):323–68.
DiNardo, John, Nicole Fortin, and Thomas Lemieux. 1996. Labor market institutions and the distribution of wages, 1973–1992. *Econometrica* 64:1001–4.
Groshen, Erica. 1991. Sources of intra-industry wage dispersion: How much do employers matter? *Quarterly Journal of Economics* 106 (3): 869–84.
Juhn, Chinhui, and Simon Potter. 2006. Changes in labor force participation in the United States. *Journal of Economic Perspective* 20 (3): 27–46.
Katz, Lawrence, and David Autor. 1999. Changes in the wage structure and earnings inequality. In *Handbook of labor economics.* Vol. 3, ed. O. Ashenfelter and D. Card, 1463–1555. Amsterdam: North-Holland.
Lee, David S. 1999. Wage inequality in the United States during the 1980s: Rising dispersion or falling minimum wage. *Quarterly Journal of Economics* 114:977–1023.
Lemieux, Thomas. 2004. Residual wage inequality: A reexamination. University of British Columbia, Working Paper.
Levy, F., and R. J. Murnane. 1992. U.S. earnings levels and earnings inequality: A review of recent trends and proposed explanations. *Journal of Economic Literature* 30:1333–81.
Moffitt, Robert. 1990. The distribution of earnings and the welfare state. In *A future of lousy jobs?,* ed. by G. Burtless, 201–35. Washington, DC: Brookings Institution.
Stevens, David W. 2002. Employment that is not covered by state unemployment insurance laws. LEHD Technical Paper no. TP-2002-16. Washington, DC: U.S. Census Bureau, Longitudinal Employer-Household Dynamics.

3

Wage and Labor Mobility in Denmark, 1980–2000

Tor Eriksson and Niels Westergaard-Nielsen

3.1 Introduction

The aim of this chapter is threefold. First, we give a brief description of some key features of the labor market in Denmark, some of which we argue contribute to the Danish labor markets behaving quite differently from those in many other European countries. Second, we document in some detail an important aspect of the functioning and flexibility of the labor markets in Denmark: the high level of worker mobility.[1] Third, we describe and examine the wage structure between and within firms and changes therein since 1980, especially with an eye on possible impacts of the trend toward a more decentralized wage determination.

3.2 The Institutional Setting

Although the Danish labor market in many respects resembles other labor markets in Europe, and Scandinavia in particular, it has a number of distinguishing features of its own. In the following, we briefly discuss some

Tor Eriksson is a research director at the Center for Corporate Performance, and a professor of economics at the Aarhus School of Business. Niels Westergaard-Nielsen is director of the Center for Corporate Performance, and a professor of economics at the Aarhus School of Business.

The authors are grateful to the Danish Social Science Research Council for funding, to participants in the National Bureau of Economic Research (NBER) Project for helpful comments, and to Anders Aagaard and Jens Therkelsen for able research assistance. The views expressed herein are those of the authors and do not necessarily reflect the views of the NBER.

1. This is one of the cornerstones of the Danish "flexicurity" model for labor market policy that has attracted a lot of attention in recent years; see, for example, chapter 2 in European Commission (2006).

of them. More precisely, we look at ten features of the labor market in Denmark.[2] These are:

1. The high female labor force participation rate, which is among the highest in the world.

2. The retirement age, which used to be relatively high, but has during relatively few years fallen substantially.

3. The replacement ratio of unemployment benefits for low-wage earners, which to the best of our knowledge is the highest in the world. The replacement ratio is considerably lower for high-wage earners, but due to the compressed wage structure, a nonnegligible portion of the employees has a very high replacement ratio.

4. The relatively widespread eligibility for unemployment benefit.

5. Voluntary membership of unemployment insurance funds.

6. Wage bargaining that used to be highly centralized, but has gradually become more decentralized.

7. Trade union membership and the coverage of unions are both high by international standards.

8. Weak job protection for blue-collar workers and only a modest protection for white-collar workers.

9. Indirect wage costs are internationally very low in Denmark, whereas the rate of direct taxation of wage income is among the highest in the world.

10. Compared to many other countries, agreements between employers and trade unions constitute a more important regulatory mechanism than legislation and government interventions. This is one of the key elements in "the Danish mode."

Each of these aspects has consequences for the behavior of people, firms and their employees, and for the functioning of the Danish labor market.

3.2.1   Female Labor Force Participation

The high female participation is a well-known characteristic feature of the Danish labor market. The growing female share of employment has been facilitated by a massive growth in child care facilities. Child care is to a large extent provided by the public sector; six out of ten children in the age group one to six years are in publicly provided daycare. Daycare used to be highly subsidized but is now less so. Female participation started to grow in the 1970s in close connection to the growth of the public sector and the creation of the welfare state. Many of the jobs held by women, particularly in the public sector, were originally part-time jobs. Today only about 8 to 9 percent of women in the age range twenty-five to fifty-five work part

---

2. Some of these specific features make the labor market in Denmark in some, but absolutely not all, respects look more like that in the United States than labor markets in other European countries.

time. The increase in female labor force participation has occurred in parallel with a shift from part-time to full-time work. In recent years, part-time work is common among young women and older women and sectoral differences with respect to the part-time work are small.

3.2.2   Pension Systems and Retirement

Denmark has for many years had a pension system that provides the entire population (and not only the working population) with old age pension, for men from the age of sixty-seven and for women from the age of sixty-five (recently the old age retirement has gradually been lowered to sixty-five also for men). This is a pay-as-you-go system, where benefits are regulated by the parliament and are paid out of current tax revenue. In 1979 an early retirement program was introduced. All members of the unemployment insurance (UI) system could from the age of sixty receive a benefit corresponding to the UI until the recipient is entitled to normal pension. In addition, a publicly provided disability pension is available for all age groups, where eligibility is determined on health grounds. The proportion of the labor force receiving disability pension was in 2000 about 10 percent. Especially as a consequence of the early retirement program, the average retirement age has been falling over time. Thus, in 2004, only a third of the age group sixty to sixty-six were in the labor force.

The early retirement program has been particularly important for older workers because employers are reluctant to hire unemployed workers in their late or mid-fifties because they expect that they will go on early retirement as they become eligible. Bingley and Lanot (2004) have shown that there is no firm effect with respect to the use of the program, indicating that employers are not systematically pushing elderly employees into early retirement. Rather, it is other factors, such as the work situation of the spouse that are important.

3.2.3   Unemployment Benefits

The unemployment benefit system is still partly organized according to "Bismarckian principles." Thus, workers can voluntarily choose to become members of more than thirty different occupational unemployment insurance funds. Membership and eligibility for unemployment benefits are both conditional on the person having had a job for at least one year. The unemployment benefit is 90 percent of the previous wage but with a maximum of 1,800€ per month. Consequently, the replacement ratio for low-wage workers is 90 percent, but is lower for higher-income earners. Unemployment benefits are taxed, but a special tax rate of 8 percent on all earned income does not apply to unemployment benefits. Together, the high replacement ratio and the asymmetric tax treatment create an incentive problem for low-wage workers, as they earn little by working compared to being unemployed. It has been shown that 23 percent of all employed women and 12 percent of all employed men actually earn 80€ less per week by working relative to what would have received as unemployment benefit claimants; see Smith (1998).

Unemployment benefits are obtained from the first day of unemployment and are paid for one year without any obligations other than seeking work. After one year of unemployment, the UI recipient has to take part in an active labor market policy program. A high replacement ratio, coupled with the fact that there is almost no experience rating for either employers or workers, implies that there are many short spells of unemployment. Even in years of low unemployment, more than 20 percent of all wage earners have experienced at least one spell of unemployment. A high proportion of these spells are concentrated around Christmas, New Year, and other vacations. As a result, for low-pay workers, total working hours are about 80 percent of the total normal hours (to be explained in the following).

The UI system is financed by general tax revenue but operated by the private UI funds. The UI funds are formally unrelated to the trade unions, but membership in the UI system is typically considered as part of a package, which also includes union membership. As a consequence, about 80 percent of the wage earners are members of the UI system, and about 85 percent are members of trade unions (Neumann, Pederson, and Westergaard-Nielsen 1991).

3.2.4 The Danish Model for Cooperation

The overall labor market model in Denmark is often called "The Danish Model." The key ingredient in the Danish model is that the trade unions' and the employers' federation (the social partners) make agreements on most regulatory issues, and the role of the government is to "pick up and pay the bill." The social partners take responsibility for wage bargaining and wage setting. They also make agreements concerning normal working hours and set rules for labor protection with respect to overtime and work environment.[3] As a consequence, there is no minimum wage legislation in Denmark. Nevertheless, the social partners have agreed that no member firm will pay less than 89.50 DKK per hour plus 15 percent vacation pay, that is, altogether 13.8€. Although the employers' organizations do not have full coverage, the unions are very keen on identifying workplaces paying less. According to anecdotal evidence, workers are being paid less in the unorganized parts of the retail sector and in the hotels and restaurant industries.

The role of the government in Denmark is to provide unemployment

---

3. When the current Liberal/Conservative government has made several propositions regarding the work environment, both employers' and workers' organizations have been critical of state intervention into the area.

benefits and to retrain workers who have lost their jobs because their productivity in their current job is too low. The government also provides health care and disability pensions. In other words, the government provides the safety net. This is also the case with respect to those who are not covered by unemployment insurance. These workers are in general eligible for social assistance, which is of the same size as the UI benefit. The main difference is that all payments are means tested.

The Danish labor market model has many features in common with the Swedish model, and because of the similarities, they are sometimes grouped together under the label of "the Nordic Labor Market Model." The main idea is that whenever a firm cannot keep workers productive in their current job, the government should take responsibility and retrain workers. After retraining, the workers should now be more productive and can, therefore, be hired in a new firm and thereby increase overall productivity.

There are, however, distinct differences between the Danish and Swedish models. One of these is that the Danish model does not prohibit layoffs, whereas the Swedish model is considerably more restrictive in this respect. The idea behind the Danish model is that firms should not be forced to maintain a large workforce if it is no longer profitable to do so. In such a situation, it is better for society that firms can rehire workers where these workers' labor is more productive. This increases overall flexibility and productivity. Of course, it also puts a burden on the workers, and that is probably the main reason for the relatively high unemployment benefit in Denmark (at least for low-wage earners). Another difference is that the Swedish model builds heavily on a tripartite cooperation between government, unions, and employers. So in Denmark, the government provides income security, while the labor market organizations deliver flexibility. Hence, the system is called "flexicurity."

3.2.5 Working Hours

In Denmark so-called normal working hours are determined as the outcome of the general wage bargaining between the trade unions' and the employers' federation. As elsewhere, the normal working times have been gradually shortened in Denmark, too. The reduction has on average been about 0.7 percent per year (Andersen et al. 2001). Its sources have changed over time. In the late 1960s and in the beginning of the 1970s, the reduction was in weekly hours, followed by a period when the annual vacation was increased from four to five weeks. In the 1990s, the reduction was again implemented as a reduction in the number of weekly hours; from forty to thirty-seven hours. Recently, a gradual expansion of vacation weeks from five to six weeks has begun.

Annual normal working hours in Denmark are among the lowest in the world. Only the Germans work less than the 1,690 hours per year worked on average by the Danes. However, far from all work that much, especially the low-wage earners. The average for low-wage earners is only about 1,140 hours in Denmark, while it was about 1,700 hours in the United States in the same period. The main reason is, no doubt, that the Danish UI system is not only subsidizing the search between two jobs but also temporary layoffs.

3.2.6   Wage Bargaining

Collective bargaining in Denmark has a long history—in fact, the first general collective wage agreement was settled as early as 1889—and for almost a century, this was the predominant mode of wage determination. In recent years, Danish wage setting has undergone large changes, which are briefly described in this chapter's sequel.

Until the beginning of the 1980s, wages were set in biannual national wage negotiations. A key feature of wage determination was an automatic wage indexation system, which linked hourly wages to the consumer price index (CPI) net of indirect taxes and subsidies. Twice per year, hourly wage increases were triggered by each three-point change in the net CPI. Although the indexation was not complete, it accounted for a large share of wage increases.

General wage negotiations took place between the Danish Federation of Trade Unions (LO) and the Danish Employers' Federation (DA), typically every second year. The LO and DA set the pattern for the entire manual workers' labor market. Although only about 40 percent of the private-sector labor force was employed in firms where both the employees and the employer were organized, the great majority of employers and, hence, also of all workplaces, applied the results of the general agreement. The negotiations and the general agreement were split into general and specific issues such as working hours, vacations, and minimum-wage tariffs.[4] For the vast majority of white-collar workers and public-sector employees, the wage-setting mechanism is quite similar regarding negotiations, timing, and so on to that for blue-collar workers. The difference has been that these groups have never received as much in terms of wage drift between the general contracts as blue-collar workers, but have been compensated for the wage drift in the form of larger wage increases in the central bargainings.

From the beginning of the 1980s, there has been a tendency toward more and more decentralization of wage bargaining and wage setting. A first step was the abolishment of wage indexation in 1982. From 1987 to 1993, negotiations concerning wages were done at the industry level. From 1993 onward, the general wage negotiations have mainly focused on working hours, pensions, sickness pay, and vacation. At the same time, wage bar-

---

4. As mentioned in the preceding, Denmark does not have a legally set minimum wage. However, the lowest tariff wage agreed upon in the wage negotiations sets a floor for wages, and changes in the minimum-wage tariff shift the entire wage rate distribution.

gaining proper has moved down to the industry or firm levels, and an increasing share of wage agreements have been made at the individual employee level. In 1993, 71 percent of all agreements in the market for manual labor were of this type.

While wage setting has been decentralized in the private-labor market, wage bargaining in the public sector is still highly centralized, with biannual national-level negotiations. However, a new wage system, called "Ny-løn" (New-wage), has considerably fewer wage tariffs than before, and in the public sector also the intention is to move toward more individualized pay according to qualifications, job functions, and individual performance. The performance pay element in public-sector wages remains rather small, however.

3.2.7   The Labor Market and the Macroeconomy

Figure 3.1 describes the development of unemployment and annual percentage changes in real gross domestic product (GDP) since 1980. As can be seen from the figure, the time series changes in unemployment are chiefly driven by changes in GDP. From the mid-nineties there has been a long period of continuous decline in open unemployment, and so at the end of the period, Denmark is one of the not-so-numerous European countries that have succeeded in lowering their unemployment rates to levels not experienced since the seventies.

It should be noted, however, that as active labor market policies have played an increasingly important role, and as participants in active labor

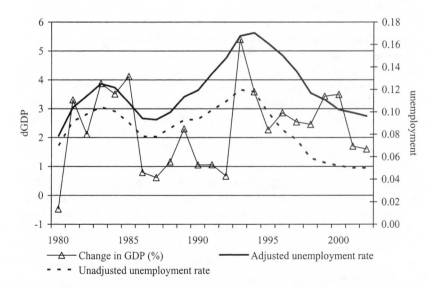

Fig. 3.1   Development in unemployment and annual growth in GDP

market programs are not counted as unemployed, open unemployment has become a more and more dubious measure of the state of the labor market. We have, therefore, in figure 3.1 also included an adjusted unemployment rate that includes individuals in active labor market programs among the unemployed and, consequently, also in the labor force. The main difference is in the levels, while the peaks and troughs are the same. It is worth noting that whereas the rate of unemployment during business cycle upturns is lower at the end of the period than in the mid-eighties, this is not true for the adjusted unemployment rate.

3.2.8 Flexibility

The institutional framework of the Danish labor market implies that there are few barriers to mobility between firms. For employers, the costs of laying off workers are low because of the absence of severance pay legislation and experience rating in the unemployment insurance system, as well as weak job security, particularly of blue-collar workers. For the employees, costs of changing employer or experiencing unemployment spells are reduced by generous unemployment benefits, which are readily available to insured employees, and by the fact that many social benefits, pensions, and vacation are independent of the individual's current employer and are, hence, transferable. As a consequence, the Danish labor market is characterized by both high job mobility and high wage mobility.

3.3 Data Sources

The main data source used in the following empirical analyses is the so-called IDA-database (*Integreret Database for Arbejdsmarkedsforskning*) kept by Statistics Denmark. The IDA is a longitudinal database that contains information about all individuals aged fifteen to seventy-four (demographic characteristics, education, labor market experience, tenure, and earnings) and employees in all plants in Denmark during the period 1980 to 2001. This information has been collected by merging information from several registers in Statistics Denmark with the help of unique identification numbers for individuals and plants. The persons and plants are matched at the end of November in each year. Consequently, only changes between ends-of-Novembers are accounted for (not intermittent changes). Statistics Denmark has aggregated the plant-level information to the level of firms for the first time in the late nineties for the Pay and Performance project at Aarhus School of Business and continues to do so for the Center for Corporate Performance with the help of the unique identification numbers of individuals and plants (firms), additional information from other registers, as well as surveys of firms or individuals that have information about the same identification numbers.

The background data for the IDA consists of various registers, supplemented with data from the latest census in 1970. Thus, data on education come from the Census in 1970 and from reports from all educational institutions on their current population of students and their completion. This means that the educational register contains status and all upgrades after the census.

The wage information is constructed as follows. The point of departure is register data containing tax-based information on the total earnings paid to each individual worker during the year. Earnings may consist of earnings from several employers. The data are considered to be of high quality because the tax authorities use them to assess each employee's earnings. At the same time, the wage records constitute deductible labor costs for the employers.

The number of working hours is estimated as follows. The employers' contributions to a comprehensive pension scheme are determined by the number of hours worked as a fraction of normal annual working hours. Thus, for hourly paid workers—that is, all blue-collar workers—pension contributions up to 1993 were proportional to the number of hours worked. For monthly paid salaried employees, the supplementary pension is computed based on the normal length of the working day according to a three-step scale. The IDA makes use of information about the employers' contributions to the pension schemes to compute the annual number of working hours for each individual. It should be noted that these are estimates. One problem is that the supplementary pay for overtime hours does not yield additional points for the pension schemes. Hence, overtime hours are not properly accounted for.

Hourly wage rates are calculated by dividing the earnings at a particular employer with the estimated annual working hours at that employer. The estimated hourly wage rates are most reliable for the hourly paid workers. However, after 1993, pension contributions have gradually also been paid during sickness and unemployment spells. Consequently, as from the mid-nineties, the hourly wage information is likely to be of poorer quality.

3.4 Worker Mobility

This section looks into worker mobility in somewhat more detail. We start by considering the frequently used measures, entry and exit rates, calculated in the case of entry rates as the proportion of new employees in the firm in end-of-November year t as compared to end-of-November year $t - 1$ and for exit rates the proportion of employees who have exited from the firm since end-of-November in year $t - 1$.[5] Entry and exit rates to and from Danish private-sector firms during 1981 to 2001 are shown in figure

---

5. Because the comparisons are between end-of-Novembers, and thus neglect mobility between intermittent short-term jobs, the entry and exit rates are downward biased.

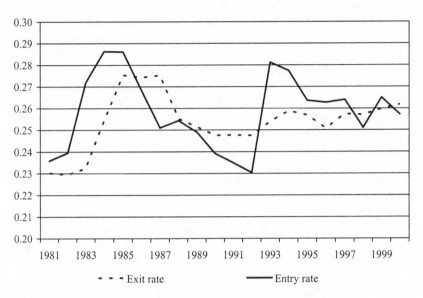

- - - Exit rate   ——— Entry rate

Fig. 3.2   Exit and entry rates

3.2. We can see that the entry and exit rates show no trend and fluctuate around 26 percent. The variations in the entry rate are clearly larger than for exits. The fluctuations appear to be procyclical for both entry and exit rates. Thus, hires and separations both increase in upturns and decrease in downturns. On average, about one third of all annual job exits are to non-employment states; see Frederiksen and Westergaard-Nielsen (2007).

Looking beyond the average entry and exit rates reveals that they differ considerably between different parts of firms' wage distributions. Figure 3.3 shows the entry and exit rates in the top and bottom quartiles of the wage distribution in each firm. Not surprisingly, mobility is substantially higher in the lowest quartile. In the lowest quartile, entry rates exceed exit rates with a wide margin, whereas the relative magnitudes are reversed in the top quartile. Naturally, this reflects the fact that people tend to get hired at the bottom and leave from positions further up in the wage distribution. Mobility out of low-paid work is, in general, high, although it should be noted that a third of transitions out of low-wage jobs is out of the labor force; see Bolvig (2004). The two other thirds are to higher-paid employment within the same firm and to jobs in other firms, respectively. Notably, Bolvig also finds that firms with a higher-than-average share of low-wage workers have a lower workforce turnover than other firms. The entry rates in the bottom quartile vary procyclically and are quite volatile. Entry into the top quartile displays the same pattern, but the variation is less pronounced.

Table 3.1 paints a picture of the composition and development of job

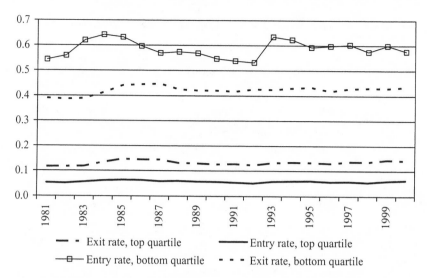

Fig. 3.3   Exit and entry rates for workers from different positions of firms' wage distributions

spells and their duration. The numbers refer to the year 2000. We can see that in that year, out of 1.6 million employees, almost half a million had separated from a job since the previous year. Nearly one third of all employees (a little over half a million) were in another job (actually, at another employer) compared to the previous year. From the third column, it can be seen that in a cross-section, most people employed in Danish private-sector firms—63.2 percent—are in jobs that have lasted less than five years. Less than 10 percent are in jobs that have lasted more than fifteen years. This does not, however, mean that merely about 10 percent of employees end up in jobs lasting fifteen years or more.

The high turnover rates do not necessarily imply that all employees in the firms leave with the same frequency and that, as a consequence, long-tenured jobs are thin on the ground. There are a number of reasons why the cross-sectional picture is misleading (see Hall 1982). First, and obviously, in order to have been in a job lasting for fifteen years or longer the employee has to have been in the labor force for at least fifteen years. Second, an additional reason why the "population at risk" is considerably less than the total workforce is that most of job changes occur in the beginning of workers' labor market careers. Therefore, one should not expect to find many long-term employment relationships before the employees have turned forty. As can be seen from the last three columns in the table, the probability of staying in the same firm for one, five, or ten additional years increases with tenure. Thus, for instance, the probability that a person with ten years of tenure will remain with the same employer for five (ten) addi-

Table 3.1   Distribution of tenure and contemporaneous retention rates in 2000

			Probability of:		
Tenure (in years)	Movers	Stayers	Staying 1 additional year	Staying 5 more years	Staying 10 more years
1	215,638	292,641	0.58	0.35	0.18
2	85,371	169,124	0.66	0.35	0.18
3	50,866	102,096	0.67	0.42	0.21
4	32,284	73,264	0.69	0.47	0.24
5	30,090	60,748	0.67	0.50	0.26
6	13,924	52,413	0.79	0.51	0.27
7	10,274	44,692	0.81	0.51	0.27
8	7,216	35,145	0.83	0.51	0.27
9	5,849	32,988	0.85	0.51	0.27
10	11,934	35,854	0.75	0.51	0.28
11	5,312	26,475	0.83	0.52	0.29
12	3,194	22,083	0.87	0.53	0.31
13	2,816	18,671	0.87	0.53	0.31
14	2,888	19,189	0.87	0.53	0.30
15	2,385	16,880	0.88	0.54	0.29
16	1,962	14,748	0.88	0.56	0.29
17	1,601	11,786	0.88	0.58	0.28
18	1,094	8,599	0.89	0.59	0.29
19	982	7,612	0.89	0.57	0.28
20	836	6,666	0.89	0.54	0.25
20+	10,253	66,655			

tional years is 51 (27) percent. Taking these features into account leads, as has been shown by Hall (1982) for the United States, to a completely different picture of the prevalence of long-term jobs: despite high worker turnover, long job spells can still be common. Does the same apply also to the Danish labor market?

Table 3.2 gives the proportion of five-year age groups with five years of current tenure who go on to reach tenure for twenty years or more. These are calculated using the so-called contemporaneous retention method of Hall (1982). We have computed these shares for two years: 1990 and 2000, respectively. Moreover, for comparison purposes, we include Hall's estimates from the United States in 1978. Three features of the table are worth noting. First, the proportion of individuals whose eventual tenure will exceed twenty years was higher in 1990 than ten years later, and this was true for all age groups. Of course, this difference may simply reflect the fact that 1990 was a business cycle downturn year, whereas 2000 was an upturn year. As we saw earlier, mobility is procyclical. Second, considerably higher proportions of the employees are in lifetime jobs than what is observed in cross sections. Thus, the high annual turnover rates, hovering between 25 and 30 percent, are consistent with the observation that a considerable portion—

Table 3.2   **Proportions reaching 20+ years of tenure**

	Denmark		United States
Age group	1990	2000	1978 (Hall, 1982)
20–24	71.3	58.5	36.6
25–29	34.6	29.6	44.9
30–34	26.9	24.5	39.3
35–39	29.3	25.2	35.9
40–44	28.4	25.9	25.2
45–49	14.1	11.0	8.7
50–54	10.6	7.3	4.3

Note: The numbers show the proportion of those in each age group with five years of tenure who go on to reach tenure of twenty years or more.

between 25 and 35 percent of prime age workers—land jobs in which they stay for substantial parts of their working lives. Third, the percentages for Denmark appear to be somewhat lower than those for the United States. One should be cautious here, as the age structures of the U.S. and Danish labor forces differ somewhat. Still, it is clearly the case that the proportion staying on longer is not larger, but rather smaller, in Denmark than in the United States. This accords with our preceding arguments—that the institutional setup of the Danish labor market strongly facilitates mobility.

3.5   The Changing Wage Structure

Next, we briefly consider some changes in the wage structure and, in particular, changes in the dispersion of wages. The wage concept used is real monthly wages (expressed in 1990 prices), calculated by multiplying each individual's hourly wage rate by the number of a full-time employee's monthly working hours. The population studied is, unless otherwise stated, the private-sector firms with a minimum of twenty employees. In order to reduce measurement errors in the monthly wages, employees who have been in their current jobs for less than one year are omitted.

Figures 3.4 and 3.5 document changes in the distribution of individuals' wages. We may note a clear, albeit not strong, increase in wage dispersion during the twenty-year period. The increase has been about the same magnitude during both the eighties and the nineties. The period when wage differentials widened the most is 1987 to 1994; that is, the first period of a shift toward decentralized wage bargaining. In fact, the changes during the second half of the nineties are relatively small, especially in view of the changes in both wage setting and the increased adoption of new pay practices in firms (Eriksson 2003a). There has been an increase on both sides of the median, but during the nineties, wage dispersion below the median has

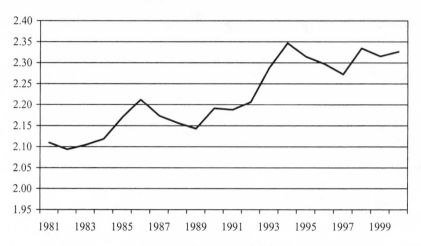

Fig. 3.4   Wage dispersion 1980 to 2000 as measured by the P90/P10-ratio

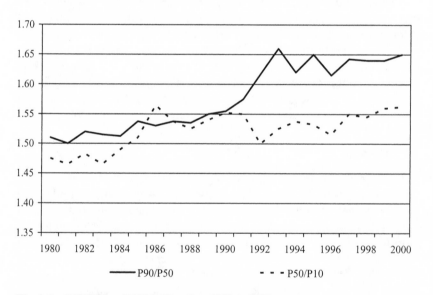

Fig. 3.5   P90/P50 and P50/P10-ratios, 1980 to 2000

been flat, whereas above the median there is a noteworthy jump in the mid-nineties, leading to a stronger increase during that decade; see figure 3.5.

Changes in the dispersion of firm wages have followed a slightly different pattern: from being virtually flat in the eighties, the distribution of firm wages has widened during the second half of the period; see figure 3.6.

Turning next to a decomposition of the wage dispersion into within- and between-firm components, we restrict the sample to firms with fifty or

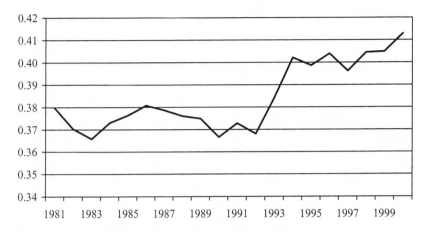

Fig. 3.6   Coefficient of variation of firm average wages

more employees in order to make the within-firm dispersion concept meaningful. Two points emerge from figure 3.7. There has been a trendwise increase in between-firm variance in wages, whereas wage dispersion within firms fell during the eighties up to 1990, from which time on it has been increasing in tandem with that of between-firm wages. By 2000, within-firm wage dispersion has not reached the level of the early eighties. Thus, the observed increase in overall wage dispersion is predominantly due to increasing wage differentials between firms.

3.6   Changes in Wage Setting in Larger Danish Firms, 1980 to 2000

As was discussed in the preceding, Denmark has, during the two most recent decades, experienced a shift in wage bargaining from a highly centralized system to a considerably more decentralized wage setting. The end of the era of centralized wage bargaining came in two steps: first in 1987, when bargaining moved down to the level of industries, and second, and more importantly, involving a larger share of wage setting actually being done at the level of firms, in 1994 to 1995. It seems plausible to assume that as a consequence of the decentralization of the wage-bargaining and wage-setting processes, the relative weights of employer and employee effects for the resulting wage structure may have changed. The aim of this section is to describe and analyze these changes.[6]

A shift to more decentralized wage setting is, however, not the only possible cause of changes in firms' internal wage structure. The much-discussed skill-biased technological change suggests that not only do returns to observable skills increase, but the returns to unobservable skills as picked up

6. This section draws heavily on Eriksson (2003b).

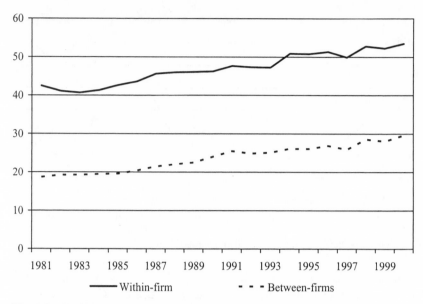

Fig. 3.7   Variation in wages within and between firms, 1980 to 2000

by the firm effects in a standard cross-sectional earnings equation may increase as well (Katz and Autor 1999). Thus, inequality among employers
should rise in tandem with rising returns to observable skills. Another
source of changes in firms' wage structures is changes in firms' local mo-
nopoly power. Deregulation of several markets and increasing international competition, due to the implementation of the European Single
Market Program in 1988 to 1992, and steadily falling transportation and
information transmission costs have eroded firms' product market rents.
When this is the case, we would expect, over time, that inequality among
employers declined.[7]

How could decentralization contribute to changes? One way of thinking
about it is that under centralized wage setting, firm-specific bargaining is
constrained and, hence, local bargaining power is in general low and varies
little across firms. With weakening centralized wage-setting institutions,
local bargaining power rises and, consequently, we would expect to see an
increase in the variability of the firm-specific component of wages.

Next we examine changes in wage setting in Danish firms from the perspective of eventual changes in their internal labor markets. For this reason,
the analysis is restricted to a subsample from the IDA database consisting
of larger private-sector firms. More precisely, the sample we henceforth ex-

---

7. The prediction concerning the impact of increased competition on within-firm inequality is ambiguous; see, for example, Cuñat and Guadalupe (2006).

amine consists of 222 firms that have been above the size of 200 employees in each year during the period 1980 to 2000.[8] The number of observations on individuals varied between 457,821 in 1990 and 417,267 in 1995.

Wage equations, with hourly wage rates as the dependent variable and observable individual characteristics of age, education, gender, and tenure plus employer-specific intercepts as explanatory variables, are estimated. The estimations are carried out for five different cross-sections: 1980, 1985, 1990, 1995, and 2000. In closing, we briefly present and discuss some of the results obtained.

It should be emphasized that not only does the population of firms differ from the one examined in the previous section, but also the wage concept— the hourly wage rate—is different. This explains why we observe from table 3.3 a somewhat different picture of changes in the wage structure: wage dispersion first decreased during the eighties and then increased during the nineties. In 2000, between-persons wage inequality was still smaller than twenty years ago, but had almost returned to its 1985 level. As we will come back to later, during the same period, between-firm wage inequality has grown considerably.

From table 3.4, where the estimates of the returns to the skill variables and gender are collected, we can first of all observe that including the firm fixed effects into the estimating equations does very little to change the estimates to the human capital variables. On the other hand, we see that some of the estimated returns to skill have changed over time. Thus, during the eighties, the age-earnings profiles became successively steeper but have not changed much since. Returns to tenure have also increased, although it should be noted that their magnitude is relatively small: less than 1 percent per year.

The largest changes have occurred with respect to returns to education. The estimated return to one additional year of education has almost doubled during the twenty-year period. The return started to grow from a very low level indeed and has at the end of the period reached about the same magnitude as one additional year of labor market experience. All in all, the estimates indicate that there has been an increase in the returns to observable skills according to several dimensions during the period under study.

For the gender-differential estimates, it makes a difference whether the

---

8. About half of the firms have less than 500 employees, and about the same proportion of the firms are from the manufacturing sector, whereas the remaining 20 and 30 percent are in the trade and services sectors, respectively. The firms differ substantially with respect to employment growth; a little over 40 percent have experienced a decline in employment during the two decades. The workforces in the sample firms consist of 60 percent of males (differing from the whole Danish labor force, where the gender shares are equal—the difference is due to the fact that the firms are from the private sector), and their skill structures have undergone considerable changes during that period, with a notable decline in the share of unskilled blue-collar workers. At the same time, the age structure has remained remarkably stable.

Table 3.3   Between-persons wage inequality

Year	Coefficient of variation (hourly wage)
1980	0.634
1985	0.585
1990	0.504
1995	0.512
2000	0.576

Table 3.4   Returns to skill estimates

Year	Age	Age²/100	Years of school	Tenure	Gender: male
1980	0.041	−0.004	0.028	0.004	0.236
	(0.039)	(−0.004)	(0.030)	(0.003)	(0.181)
1985	0.042	−0.004	0.027	0.004	0.210
	(0.041)	(−0.004)	(0.029)	(0.003)	(0.145)
1990	0.057	−0.006	(0.031	0.006	0.192
	(0.056)	(−0.006)	0.033)	(0.003)	(0.120)
1995	0.055	−0.006	0.044	0.008	0.180
	(0.052)	(−0.005)	(0.045)	(0.006)	(0.113)
2000	0.052	−0.005	0.050	0.008	0.192
	(0.050)	(−0.005)	(0.051)	(0.006)	(0.115)

Notes: Standard errors are omitted because they are all so small. Numbers in parentheses are estimates from equations including firm-fixed effects.

firm effects are included, as entering them leads to a drop in the differential by about one third. During the two decades there was first a decrease in the male-female wage differential, but this decline seems to have leveled off during the nineties. This corroborates what has been found in the gender gap studies. Most of that literature does not, however, account for the demand site.[9] The results in table 3.4 demonstrate that this can be misleading. Moreover, there is an interesting pattern insofar that the gender gap reduction is much larger when firm-fixed effects are controlled for.

Table 3.5 displays the adjusted R^2 statistics from estimations with the firm effects only and with firm-fixed effects and human capital, respectively. We may observe first that on their own the firm-fixed effects explain an increasing portion of differences in individual wage differentials. Second, the "full" model's explanatory power has also increased over time.

The dispersion of "raw" firm-fixed effects has increased; in fact, it has more than doubled; see table 3.6. The increase has been especially pronounced in the nineties. Together with increases in returns to observable

9. Datta Gupta and Rothstein (2005) is an exception, using Danish data.

Table 3.5   **Adjusted R^2**

	1980	1985	1990	1995	2000
Firm fixed effects only	0.190	0.179	0.226	0.267	0.283
Firm fixed effects + human capital	0.308	0.379	0.451	0.498	0.483

Table 3.6   **Dispersion (standard deviation) of firm fixed effects**

Year	Without controls	With controls
1980	0.098	0.081
1985	0.113	0.098
1990	0.152	0.107
1995	0.213	0.192
2000	0.259	0.207

individual characteristics, this is consistent with firm-fixed effects picking up sorting according to unobservable skills.[10]

Although part of the increase goes away when observables are controlled for, a considerable portion remains. Thus, changes in observable skills are not able to explain the whole observed increase in between-firm inequality. The observed pattern is, however, also consistent with an increasing dispersion of bargaining power as a result of weakening of centralized bargaining institutions. In contrast to the changes mentioned in the preceding, the dispersion of the residuals of the wage equations displays no trend, but varies around a stable mean. The fact that the dispersion of fixed effects has not decreased, but rather increased, indicates that increasing competition has not lead to the predicted decline in between-employer inequality.

Let us now consider what has happened to the persistence of firm effects over time. The top panel of table 3.7 answers that question by measuring the "persistence" by means of autocorrelations: corr $[\text{FE}(f,t), \text{FE}(f,t-T)]$ for different time gaps T (five, ten, and fifteen years, respectively).[11] The fixed effects are taken from the wage regressions that include human capital controls.[12] The key message from the table is that there have been no major changes in the persistence in firm-fixed effects over time. There is a slight decline in the five-year correlations, but this provides only limited evidence of a weakening importance of internal labor markets. The persistence is fairly strong and does not decay rapidly as the time gap is widened. The same exercise was also carried out for rank correlations in the bottom

10. Davis and Haltiwanger (1991) have found a similar pattern for U.S. manufacturing during the sixties, seventies, and eighties.
11. The abbreviation FE denotes the firm-fixed effects.
12. Excluding controls leads to somewhat higher correlations, but the pattern observed in the top panel of table 3.7 remains intact.

Table 3.7   Firm fixed effects persistence by autocorrelations and rank correlations

Year	−5 years	−10 years	−15 years
	A. Firm fixed effects persistence		
1985	0.870		
1990	0.837	0.697	
1995	0.836	0.692	0.588
2000	0.824	0.695	0.601
	B. Firm fixed effects persistence—rank correlations		
1985	0.761		
1990	0.794	0.589	
1995	0.727	0.610	0.403
2000	0.795	0.600	0.486

Note: Autocorrelations of fixed effects estimated from wage equations including controls.

panel of table 3.7. The pattern with respect to changes over time is the same, except that the decay associated with lengthening the time differences becomes stronger. At any rate, the results of both tables indicate that firms that pay above (below) the average also are very likely to continue doing that five or ten years later.

Eriksson (2003b) also estimated the wage equations separately for each firm and year and retained the coefficient estimates from each regression and used them as data. The first thing looked at is the changes in their between-firm spread over time. The mean across firms estimates of the return to schooling, say, differs somewhat from those reported in table 3.4, which were based on estimating the equation on all firms. The dispersion of the coefficients for age, schooling, tenure, and gender is set out in table 3.8. From this it can be seen that not only has the mean returns to schooling increased, but its dispersion has, too. The development of the age coefficients is different; they first increase and then decline. The gender wage gap coefficient, which, on average, has first declined and then has stayed flat, displays an increasing dispersion across firms over time. Hence, overall there appears to have been a tendency toward an increase in the spread, not only in firm-fixed effects, but also in how firms reward different observable individual traits of their employees.

A second thing the estimated firmwise coefficients are used for is to look at their persistence, again by means of computed autocorrelations. The five-year autocorrelations for age, schooling, tenure, and gender are collected in table 3.9. Strong internal labor markets would imply highly persistent firm-specific returns. This is also what is found, although the correlations are somewhat lower than for firm-fixed effects. Moreover, for schooling and gender, a decline in the persistence can be observed. Consequently, there is some indication that internal structures have become more flexible. The changes do not appear to be large, however.

Table 3.8   Dispersion (standard deviation) of regression coefficients across firms

Year	βage	βschooling	βtenure	βgender
1980	0.012	0.012	0.017	0.110
1985	0.030	0.017	0.012	0.113
1990	0.020	0.028	0.007	0.139
1995	0.013	0.031	0.013	0.164
2000	0.016	0.028	0.012	0.168

Table 3.9   The persistence of βs over time (5-year autocorrelations)

Year	Age	Schooling	Tenure	Gender
1985	0.579	0.721	0.697	0.836
1990	0.731	0.670	0.655	0.730
1995	0.777	0.692	0.671	0.737
2000	0.724	0.656	0.649	0.685

Summarizing the analysis of the larger firms, it was found that there has been a clear increase in between-firm wage inequality. This is not consistent with the notion that increased competition in the product markets erodes firm-specific rents. Between-employee wage inequality first decreased but increased during the nineties, and at the same time, returns to human capital, in particular schooling, have increased. The dispersion in firm-specific fixed effects has increased over time, which is consistent with both skill-biased technological change and weakened centralized wage bargaining. The employer effects are relatively persistent, and there are no traces of significant changes in this. The same holds for returns to human capital at the level of the firm. Both the observable and the time-invariant unobservable worker and employer characteristics, respectively, have become more important in explaining wage inequality.

3.7   Concluding Remarks

The key messages of this chapter are two. First, the institutional setup of the Danish labor market differs not only from that found in most other European countries but also from that in the neighboring Nordic countries. A main difference is the absence of barriers to mobility. In a sense, this is only natural, as for almost a century Danish wage setting was highly centralized and characterized by a very compressed wage structure that left only limited scope for employers to adjust to changing labor market conditions through wage adjustment. Worker mobility is indeed high. We show that mobility is about as high, or even higher, as in the highly fluid U.S. labor market. But we also document that although labor turnover rates are high, a considerable portion of workers are in long-term employment relationships.

Second, the ongoing process toward increasingly decentralized wage setting, which began in the second half of the eighties, has given rise to an increase, albeit of relatively modest magnitude, in the dispersion of wages. The widening wage distribution seems to be predominantly due to increased wage differentials between firms, and considerably less due to growing within-firm wage dispersion. In parallel, the level and between-firm variance in returns to human capital have increased. The shift toward decentralized wage bargaining has coincided with deregulation and increased product market competition. The evidence appears not to be consistent with stronger competition in product markets eroding firm-specific rents. Hence, the prime suspect is the change in wage-setting institutions.

References

Andersen, T., B. Dalum, H. Linderoth, V. Smith, and N. Westergaard-Nielsen. 2001. *The Danish economy. An international perspective.* Copenhagen: DJØF.
Bingley, P., and G. Lanot. 2004. Employer pay policies, public transfers and the retirement decisions of men and women in Denmark. *European Economic Review* 48:181–200.
Bolvig, I. 2004. Within- and between-firm mobility in the low-wage labour market. In *Job quality and employer behaviour,* ed. S. Bazen and C. Lucifora, 132–56. New York: Palgrave.
Cuñat, V., and M. Guadalupe. 2006. Globalization and the provision of incentives inside the firm. CEPR Discussion Paper no. 5950. London: Centre for Economic Policy Research.
Datta Gupta, N., and D. Rothstein. 2005. The impact of worker and establishment-level characteristics on male-female wage differentials: Evidence from Danish matched employer-employee data. *Labour: Review of Labour Economics and Industrial Relations* 19:1–34.
Davis, S., and J. Haltiwanger. 1991. Wage dispersion between and within U.S. manufacturing plants: 1963–86. *Brookings Papers on Economic Activity, Microeconomics:* 115–200.
Eriksson T. 2003a. *Incitamentsystemer i Dansk personaleledelse* (Incentive systems in Danish personnel policies). In *Total quality management—people—systems—results,* ed. K. Kristensen and H. Sørensen, 1–24. Copenhagen: Børsens Forlag.
———. 2003b. *The potential of firm-level panel data and linked employer-employee microdata for employment analysis.* Report to the European Commission, Directorate General for Employment, Social Affairs, and Equal Opportunities. Brussels: European Commission.
European Commission. 2006. *Employment in Europe 2006.* Brussels: European Commission.
Frederiksen, A., and N. Westergaard-Nielsen. 2007. Where did they go? Modelling transitions out of jobs *Labour Economics* 14:811–28.

Hall, R. 1982. The importance of lifetime jobs in the U.S. economy. *American Economic Review* 72:716–24.

Katz, L., and D. Autor. 1999. Changes in the wage structure and earnings inequality. In *Handbook of labor economics.* Vol. 3A, ed. O. Ashenfelter and D. Card, 1464–1555. Amsterdam: North-Holland.

Neumann, G., P. Pedersen, and N. Westergaard-Nielsen. 1991. Long-run international trends in unionization. *European Journal of Political Economy* 7:249–74.

Smith, N. 1998. Economic incentives to work. In *Work, incentives and unemployment* (in Danish), ed. N. Smith, 179–209. Aarhus, Denmark: Aarhus University Press.

4

Wage Structure and Labor Mobility in the Netherlands, 1999–2003

Lex Borghans and Ben Kriechel

4.1 Introduction

Labor relations in the Netherlands are subject to an intensive system of negotiations between employer associations, trade unions, and the government. Every year, starting at a centralized level, these three parties discuss the economic developments, aiming for agreement on the desirable development of wages. Moderate development of wages to stimulate employment growth has always been an important theme in these negotiations. This agreement serves as advice for negotiations between union and employers' associations at industry level. Collective agreements in industries are generally extended by the Minister of Social Affairs, which means that the agreement applies to all workers and firms within the industry and also to those who are not represented by a trade union or employer association.

This structure suggests that wage development is highly centralized and focused on wage moderation. In contrast, the Dutch labor market also has clearly individualized features. Union membership is low, a high share of employment is in the service sector, while the fraction of workers in the traditionally much more organized industry is small. A large fraction of firms

Lex Borghans is a professor of labor economics and social policy at Maastricht University. Ben Kriechel is a researcher in the Research Centre for Education and the Labour Market (ROA) at Maastricht University.

The authors want to thank Bart Golsteyn, Joan Muysken, Erik de Regt, Bas ter Weel, the editors Edward P. Lazear and Kathryn L. Shaw, and an anonymous referee for their comments on earlier versions of this paper. We thank Statistics Netherlands (CBS) for making available the "SSB Banen" data set, and especially Jan Jonker, Gerhard Meinen, and René van der Poel for their support in accessing and using the data.

explicitly apply some kind of performance pay, and in many more firms, managers have performance interviews with their employees, which may lead to extra wage increases or promotion. Even in the public sector, these modern human resource practices are well developed.

The aim of this chapter is to explain the institutional setting and the main actors of wage determination in the Netherlands, to investigate the influence of the centralized bargaining system on the Dutch wage structure, and to see to what extent individual factors, developments at the firm level, and market developments determine wages. We will also relate wage developments to worker mobility, as this may be a way in which workers respond to rigid wage structures. The analyses are based on administrative data collected by Statistics Netherlands (CBS) from various sources, bringing together wage information about all employment relationships held in the Netherlands. Currently this data set covers the period 1999 to 2003. Our main findings for this period were that the Netherlands clearly experienced an increase in wage inequality, especially among men. This pattern was very similar when comparing firms of different size, while specific industries revealed patterns that substantially deviated from the overall pattern. Young people in all wage categories faced, on average, much higher wage increases than others. Decomposing the wage growth into an industry component, a firm component, and an individual component showed that by far most of the variation in wage growth was individual. On average, only 12 percent of the variance was firm specific. Industry-specific wage growth was almost negligible. In smaller firms, however, the development of wages was much more firm specific. Mobility rates were relatively high among workers in firms with low wage growth as well as firms with high wage growth. This relationship exists when we look at differences both between and within industries in the wage development of a firm.

The period of investigation was characterized by relatively high wage growth (Ter Weel 2003). Although economic performance was already deteriorating after the boom in the late 1990s, the labor market was still heated, especially because of shortages for higher-educated workers in general and low-skilled workers in some specific industries (especially the building industry [ROA 2005]). Our findings, therefore, suggest that wage formation in the Netherlands—at least in this period—was determined mainly by the development of the scarcity of human capital on the one hand, and by individual career developments on the other. Neither collective agreements nor the profitability of firms seemed to have great effects.

We will proceed as follows in this chapter. In section 4.2, we will provide a detailed description of the institutional actors and processes of wage determination in the Netherlands and economic conditions in the period investigated. In section 4.3, we will describe the data. Section 4.4 provides the results of the analyses, and section 4.5 contains our conclusions.

4.2 Institutional Setting

4.2.1 Characteristics of the Dutch Economy

The Dutch economy is a corporative economy in which the government, employers' associations, and trade unions are focused on deliberation and consensus. It can be characterized as a capitalist state of the Rhineland model. The model is based on a regulated market economy and an extensive system of social security. The government, the employers' associations, and the trade unions negotiate about goals and appropriate measures to reach these goals. One of the main aims is sustainable and socially responsible economic growth. Social responsibility and solidarity are some of the main characteristics of this state model.

Until 1982, the Dutch economy was often called the "welfare state without work." In 1982, 13 percent of the Dutch labor force was unemployed, and almost the same number were on social welfare programs, especially early retirement and disability programs. The broad unemployment rate was 28 percent of the labor force (Organization for Economic Cooperation and Development [OECD] 1982). Since 1982, the Dutch economy tackled its labor market problems by applying strict wage moderation, welfare reform, activating labor market policies, and measures to increase labor market flexibility.

From the 1990s onward, the performance of the Dutch economy improved substantially. Some authors refer to wage moderation as the main explanation (Dur 2001; Den Butter and Mosch 2003), others argue that the flexibility of the economy was the main cause (Hartog 1999; Broersma, Koeman, and Teulings 2000), while the third explanation could be that the composition of the Dutch industrial landscape, with many people working in the service industry, explains the favorable situation (OECD 2006).

4.2.2 Wage Negotiations

The legal framework of Dutch industrial relations was put in place in the 1930s. As a consequence of the recession between the wars, the collective agreement received public protection as a measure against unfettered wage competition. After 1945, the role of the state expanded, and for two decades the Netherlands maintained a statutory wage policy. This policy was linked closely to the central union and employers' federations: the *Stichting van de Arbeid*[1] (STAR), the bipartite Foundation of Labor in which unions and employers have been meeting since 1945; and the *Sociaal Economische Raad*[2] (SER), the government's main advisory council on social and economic policies.

---

1. The English translation is "The Labor Foundation."
2. The English translation is "The Social and Economic Council of the Netherlands."

A new wage act in 1970 deprived the government of part of its power. From that time onward, the government was only supposed to intervene during a stalemate of negotiations or to suspend contracts. Nevertheless, between 1973 and 1982, these powers were used seven times, so wage negotiations in that time could hardly be described as bipartite. 1982 was said to be the year of the return to voluntary wage moderation without the threat of government intervention. Dutch unions, although weakened by severe job and membership crises of the early 1980s (Van den Berg 1998) but assured of continued institutional support, have publicly chosen a "jobs before wages" strategy (Visser and Hemerijk 1998).

Actual negotiations on contracts and wages are traditionally done by sector in the Netherlands. This means that for each trade or sector, a separate collective agreement (CAO) is made. However, the trade unions and firms negotiating in a sector or trade are either directly or indirectly guided by their respective central organization. These central organizations are the actors in the national debate on targets, goals, and aims of the bargaining process, set forth in the agreements at the end of every year. This combination of centralized "prebargaining" and goal-setting, combined with decentralized negotiating over the actual form of the new wage contracts, leads to flexibility without overlooking the macroeconomic repercussions of sectoral wage contracts for the rest of the economy. In the context of "globalization," the trend in the Netherlands was to give more leeway to bargaining within a sector to allow for necessary variation across sectors.

The setup of organizations implies that macroeconomic conditions provide major feedback on wage formation. A typical example is the "Wassenaar Agreement" of 1982, which marked the starting point of wage moderation. Instead of a collective agreement, it was an agreement of the centralized trade unions, employers' associations, and the government to implement wage moderation in the collective agreements of the coming year. This was to be the general framework for the collective agreements in different sectors.

Traditionally, the Dutch had tripartite negotiations. Since 1982, negotiations can be called bipartite. But even if the government officially is no longer a direct partner in the bargaining process, the public and political debate plays an important role in the results of the negotiations. The distance between the negotiators is small by any means—physically, socially, and—since the 1980s—also ideologically.

Close cooperation of the parties involved has been institutionalized in the Netherlands through the existence of numerous foundations, councils, committees, and commissions in which parties meet regularly. Because of this system and the small size of the country, trade partners know each other, and meetings may take place in an informal manner. The most important institutions in this context are the aforementioned STAR and the SER.

The STAR was founded 1945 as a private committee by trade union confederations and employers' associations. Its goal was to create a common meeting point to discuss issues relating to social security, pensions, taxes, and wage formation. The STAR publishes proposals and agreements guiding the annual contractual wage negotiations. Part of its advisory function is even laid down in law.[3] The SER is a meeting point for members of STAR with the cabinet and was founded 1950 as an organization under public law and part of a corporatist civil order of the economy. The SER is also the most important council for the government in social and economic issues. The organization of SER is tripartite. Employers and employees each have eleven seats; another eleven seats are for independent members appointed by the government.

The organization of employees in trade unions started between 1905 and 1920, but they were not accepted as negotiation partners for collective bargaining until the 1920s. Today, union membership in the Netherlands is quite low. Nevertheless, a broad majority agrees with the unions' policies. In the Netherlands, there are four trade union federations that cover all sectors. Representing 63 percent of all union members, the Dutch Trade Federation (FNV, *Federatie Nederlandse Vakbeweging*) is the most important one, followed by the Christian National Trade Federation (CNV, *Christelijk Nationaal Vakverbond*), representing 18 percent of all members, the General Trade Federation (AVC, *Algemene Vakcentrale*), and the Trade Federation for Higher Employees and Senior Officials (MHP, *Vakcentrale voor Middelbaar en Hoger Personeel*), both with 9 percent of the total number of members. Trade unions need to cooperate during negotiations to avoid the threat of being excluded. Trade unions are subdivided into units per sector. The largest trade union in this respect is the one for civil servants; the leading trade union within the negotiations is still the industrial federation (IB).

Even though the federations share the same goal, they differ in terms of tradition, religion, and ideology. This differentiation is still a relic from the times of the denominationalism of Dutch society until the seventies. The FNV is a result of a merger of the socialist and the Catholic sections, whereas the CNV's roots are in the Protestant denomination. The important goals of all trade unions include employment growth, wage moderation, reduction of working hours, preventing high wage spread between companies and sectors, and preserving a proper social security system.

The degree of membership among employers is quite high; 60 to 70 percent of all employees in the private sector work in companies that are members of an employers' organization. Of all Dutch employees, 83 percent are covered by a collective contract, 14 percent by company contracts

---

3. The Minister for Social Services and Employment formally has to ask for advice if there is disagreement on the general nature (sanctioning) of a CAO.

(very large companies such as Phillips have their own agreements), while 69 percent are covered by sectoral contracts. In the Netherlands, there are three main employers' associations: *Verbond van Nederlandse Ondernemingen-Nederlands Christelijke Werkgeversverbond* (VNO-NCW) for large companies, *Midden-en Kleinbedrijf* (MKB) for small and medium-sized companies, and *Land-en tuinbouworganisatie* (LTO) Nederland for the agricultural sector.

Despite the decentralization of 1993, many ties can still be found between the approximately 5,000 negotiators involved in bargaining for the 720 collective agreements (Visser and Hemerijk 1998). The bargaining and agreement process typically goes through several stages (de Kam, van Drimmelen, and van Hulst 1994).

The first stage is in the summer of each year. When all collective agreements for the current year have been settled, claims for the coming year start to emerge. This is also to influence the government in its budget planning for the coming year.

The second stage consists of discussions and negotiations within STAR and SER. If these negotiations are successful, they lead to a central agreement within STAR, which provides general guidelines for the sectoral negotiations.

The third stage, usually at the beginning of the new year, is then the actual negotiations for each sector.[4] These negotiations result in the final contractual agreements. The federation usually sets out some guidelines, which are then detailed by the negotiators for the different sectors and levels of negotiation.

The government has the possibility of sanctioning the CAO result, making it binding for all workers involved. This means that even nonunionized employees and firms have to follow the stipulated contract. This is usually done because the CAOs are almost always transferred into law, thus becoming binding for all workers in the sector.

Government influence on wage formation has a long tradition in the Netherlands. Between 1945 and 1970, Dutch wage policies were controlled by the state. All agreements had to be submitted to a body of experts appointed by the government. Agreements became effective after acceptance by this body. Even after 1970, when a new wage law came into force that returned responsibility for wage setting to employers and employees, the state was able to influence wage negotiations in the case of an "economic emergency situation." As mentioned in the preceding, such an "emergency" occurred seven times in the twelve years between 1970 to 1982. Most of the

---

4. Actually, the term "sector" is not entirely correct, because collective agreements are not necessarily negotiated for sectors or industrial branches but can also be on the firm level. The units of collective agreements developed historically and are mutually accepted. They usually follow some sector (e.g., chemical industry), but some firms, such as AKZO, have their own firm-level CAO agreement.

state interventions were necessary because employees and employers were unable to agree. It was not until the Wassenaar Agreement in 1982 that trade partners became autonomous in their wage setting. The power of the government to threaten with state intervention if trade partners could not reach an agreement in their negotiations forced the partners to find a compromise. The possibility of government intervention enabled the trade unions to explain unpopular wage agreements to their members.

At the central level, government is very much involved in Dutch wage negotiations. It is a participant in the discussion on general agreements through the SER, even though it is not directly involved in the drafting of the agreements in the STAR. Through changes in taxes and the social security system, which is set out in the government's budget (*Miljoenennota*), it also influences both the general agreements and the final sectoral collective agreements. These changes must be implemented through the political process and approved by parliament.

At the sectoral level, the government also plays the role of a moderator. For example, the government pointed out that unemployment benefits could not be maintained at the current level if agreed wage increases were too high, as this could lead to a further rise of unemployment. This underlines the solidarity aspect of Dutch culture. Another example is that the government has been lowering the wedge between wage costs and net wages in order to support wage moderation. The government has also restrained wages of civil servants and related employees to a great extent. Direct government involvement follows from the fact that it has to sanction collective agreements at the sectoral level.[5] After government sanctioning, agreements become binding for all those employed in the sector concerned. So even though only about 20 percent of the workers are trade union members, these unions bargain on behalf of all workers and even represent the unemployed. The system of collective agreements that are sanctioned by government, as well as government participation in negotiations and consultations at the central level, is supported explicitly by employers and employees. One of the results is social stability: strikes are very rare in the Netherlands. In addition, the rather implicit role of the government ensures that agreements are based on consensus. Consequently, wage drift is relatively small in the Netherlands.

4.2.3   Wage Flexibility

The institutional setting suggests quite strict and similar wage developments, at least within (sub)sectors. There are, however, reasons why there may be more wage flexibility in practice than these institutional circumstances would suggest.

An important reason is that centrally bargained agreements typically

5. Since 1997, sectoral agreements no longer need to be sanctioned.

have an influence on the wage scales and wage grades that companies use. This shifting of the scales would lead to an equal rise in workers' wages if all workers remained at the same position in these scales. However, the main part of workers' wage development comes from their careers, within or across firms. Throughout their careers, workers move up the wage grades and scales, which leads to higher average wage increases than those that are centrally agreed upon. An example is given in Dohmen (2004): in a large manufacturing firm in the Netherlands, workers move up wage grades and scales, while the underlying matrix of scales are shifted to accommodate centrally agreed wage changes. Many Dutch firms apply modern human resource practices, with performance interviews determining the position of a worker on the wage scale.

Another reason for flexible and divergent development in pay in the Netherlands is the prevalent use of incentive pay. This incentive pay is linked to either quantitative performance measures or qualitative evaluations. At least part of the pay is thus linked to objective or subjective evaluations of performance. Borghans and Kriechel (2006) give an overview of the use of incentive pay and its influence on the moments of wage distribution. They show that the use of incentive pay is quite high across most sectors and that the introduction of incentive pay has had an influence on the distribution within firms. Stegeman (2000) also reports that many Dutch firms use some kind of incentive pay.

4.2.4   Economic Development in 1999 to 2003

In the late 1990s, the Dutch economy was booming, partly as a result of international developments in the information technology (IT) sector. Unemployment decreased rapidly. As the increase in the supply of higher-educated workers diminished while their demand increased, the labor market position of this group improved. Among lower- and intermediately educated workers, the main increase in demand was in the building industry, which experienced a rapid increase in employment of 20 percent between 1996 and 2001 (ROA 2005).

Table 4.1 provides some basic statistics about the development of the labor market in the period 1996 to 2005.[6] The table shows that until 2000, the Dutch economy was doing quite well. Annual gross domestic product (GDP) growth was around 3 percent for some time. Because unemployment was at a high level in the 1980s and, in particular, higher-educated workers had a poor labor market position, it took some time before scarcity was felt in the labor market. In 1998, firms started to have problems recruiting higher-educated workers, vacancy rates increased, and

---

6. The main analysis in section 4.3 is performed for the time period 1999–2003. We have included the other years to show the developments that have led to the examined time period. For the most recent years, the detailed microdata were not yet available.

Table 4.1 Key indicators of the Dutch labor market from 1996–2005

	1996	1997	1998	1999	2000	2001[a]	2002	2003	2004	2005
GDP growth	3.0	3.8	4.3	4.0	3.5	1.4	0.1	–0.1	1.7	0.9
Contract wages (annual growth)	1.9	2.3	3.1	2.9	3.2	4.2	3.5	2.7	1.5	0.8
Incidental wages (annual growth)	0.7	0.7	0.5	0.7	1.6	2.8	0.5	0.8	0.9	0.4
Labor force (x million)[b]	6.686	6.832	6.941	7.069	7.187	7.314	7.337	7.401	7.398	7.401
Labor supply (x million)	5.808	5.992	6.166	6.309	6.423	6.636	6.620	6.563	6.454	6.421
Public sector (x million)	.698	.700	.713	.722	.731	.778	.800	.817	.806	.798
Private sector (x million)	5.110	5.291	5.453	5.587	5.692	5.858	5.819	5.745	5.648	5.623
Employed (x million)	4.338	4.500	4.671	4.825	4.931	5.080	5.050	4.980	4.888	4.859
Self-employed (x million)	.772	.791	.782	.762	.760	.778	.769	.765	.760	.765
Person per full-time year (%)	126	126	126	126	126	125	126	126	126	127
Employed workers (x million)	6.185	6.384	6.587	6.768	6.917	7.020	7.035	7.001	6.919	6.918
Unemployment (%)	7.5	6.6	5.1	4.3	3.8	3.5	4.1	5.4	6.5	6.5
Vacancies (x1,000)	68	85	123	158	188	182	135	99	109	139

Source: Netherlands Bureau for Economic Policy Analysis (CBP; 2006, 178–179, 184–185).

[a]The series were revised in 2001. The figures after revision have been reported here.

[b]The labor force is defined as the sum of the employed and the unemployed labor force

unemployment dropped. The period of 1998 to 2002 was characterized by relatively high wage increases as a response to these developments.

The contractual wage increase indicates the wage increase that workers would receive if the collective agreements were the only cause for a change in wages. In practice, however, workers also experience wage increases due to promotion, change of job, and incidental increases in pay because of good performance. The table shows that contractual wage increases were large from 1998 until 2003. In 2001, 2002, and 2003, these contractual increases were actually larger than the growth of GDP. Usually the incidental component in wage increases equals approximately 0.7, but employers use the possibilities of incidental increases as instruments in the competition for workers. This was obviously the case in 2000 and 2001, which were years characterized by high vacancy rates. The unemployment rate also decreased until 2001 and started to increase from 2002 onward.

4.3   Data and Variables

The analyses in this chapter are based on administrative sources collected by Statistics Netherlands. We have used two administrative data sets.

First, the *Gemeentelijke Basisadministratie* (GBA) contains information about the demographic characteristics and household compositions of all inhabitants of the Netherlands. The data origin from the register is kept within the municipalities. Because all Dutch municipalities use the same unified system for their registers, this joint database is a useful basis for linking various sources. From the GBA, we have used the gender and age of the person.

The second source that we have used is the Social Statistical Database of Jobs (*SSB Banenbestand*). In this data set, Statistics Netherlands has combined information about all Dutch employment relationships from various administrative sources. The two main sources are the social insurance administration (*Verzekeringsadministratie werknemers* [VZA]) and the fiscal database (*Fibase*), which collects information on income taxes. Statistics Netherlands has combined the different sources, verified the information from the different sources, and developed decision rules to combine information in case of inconsistencies. Cases in the database that appear not to reflect a real employment relationship, but are merely financial transactions, have been excluded. An example of this could be a mistake that has been made in the salary of a former employee. Later, when the firm pays the remaining salary, this appears in the administration as a one-day employment relationship with a relatively high salary.

The data is employment-based, so every employment relationship is an observation. Because workers may move from one firm to another within a year and may have multiple employment relationships simultaneously, there are more employment relationships than workers. The data set contains about ten million cases annually. It is organized as a combination of event history and annual data set. For each change in employment relationships, a new observation is generated. Wages, however, are included on an annual basis for each employment relationship separately. Wage changes or a change of job within a firm will not lead to a new observation, but wages earned in different firms are registered separately.

4.3.1   Wages

Within the SSB, the wage information is based on administrative data from the insurance and fiscal authorities. The data set contains all wage earners living in the Netherlands, with their annual incomes.[7] The incomes should be regarded as fiscal, gross salaries. Included in the information from the tax offices are also the number of days a worker has worked.

For some counts (e.g., firm size) a fixed date within a year had to be chosen. We decided to "cut" the data at a specific date. We have used the third Thursday in September, avoiding cut points that have administrative significance or cut points that happen to fall in weekends or major vacations. For the subsequent analysis, in cases where multiple employment relationships for a single worker existed, only the employment relationship within one year that generated the highest income was used for a worker.[8]

We used the gross fiscal annual wages and the number of days a worker was reported to have worked in order to calculate the gross monthly wages in euros. We were unable to control for working hours, but we were able to adjust for the number of days employed within a year.[9] Wage differences were simple deductions of the previous year's wage of the current wage.

It is possible to match various administrative sources using the ID number (*SOFI-nummer*, i.e., the social security number) of people working or living in the Netherlands. For privacy reasons, Statistics Netherlands transforms this ID number into the so-called registrant identification number (RIN) number. In this way, personal information can still be matched, but users of the file cannot search for the social security number of a specific person.

4.3.2   Tenure

Tenure can be measured accurately. It is calculated on the basis of the day of entry into a firm, which is known in the data. We have calculated the tenure in years based on the cutoff point in September.

---

7. The self-employed are not included in this database. Statistics Netherlands is currently developing a similar but separate database for this specific group.
8. An exception is made for the exit and entry rates. These are based on all contracts within a year.
9. Average monthly working hours are reported only for a nonrepresentative subset of the population. Using working hours would halve the population used.

4.3.3   Demographics

The age of a worker is known through the year and month of birth that is available in the data. In addition, there is information on gender, household composition, and changes of a person's address based on the municipal database.

4.3.4   Firm

Firms are identified by a firm ID. The definition of a firm is based on an economic definition developed by Statistics Netherlands. When a holding consists of units that are fairly independent in their daily management, these units are considered to be separate firms.

4.3.5   Mobility

Worker mobility was measured by the number of contracts, with a minimum duration of ninety days, ending within the year. We excluded the prolongation of year-to-year contracts. While most workers have only one contract at a time, it is possible that a worker has several employment contracts simultaneously. Thus, a single worker can, in principal, cause several "exits" within a year.

4.3.6   Selection of the Data

For the analyses, we used only information about employees who were employed for at least three months and had an annual income in excess of one fourth of the annual minimum wage. This excluded short-term contracts and those that contained only very few hours a week. Furthermore, because we are especially interested in differences in wages between workers in the same firm, we excluded from the analyses all workers in firms with less than ten workers.

4.4   Results

The data allow us to investigate the wage structure, wage changes, and mobility patterns of the Dutch economy in the period of 1999 to 2003. Due to the associated firm employee character of the data, the wage structure within the firm can be compared to the overall wage structure.

Table 4.2 presents summary statistics for the distribution of individual wages and the distribution of mean wages of firms. Because smaller firms pay on average substantially lower wages than larger firms, the wage levels of the average firm is lower than the corresponding levels among individuals. Of course, inequality is greater among individuals than among firms. The standard deviation among individuals is about twice the standard deviation of mean wages in firms.

Table 4.3 summarizes the wage distributions within firms. On average,

Table 4.2   The distribution of individual wage and the mean wages within firms

	Individual level					Firm level				
	1999	2000	2001	2002	2003	1999	2000	2001	2002	2003
Median wage	2,176	2,237	2,322	2,384	2,441	1,868	1,919	2,009	2,079	2,142
Mean wage	2,472	2,543	2,646	2,710	2,767	1,923	1,976	2,077	2,142	2,206
SD	1,650	1,759	1,795	1,730	1,986	758	852	951	917	1,107
CV	0.667	0.692	0.678	0.638	0.718	0.394	0.431	0.458	0.428	0.502
P90	3,706	3,821	4,008	4,125	4,211	2,626	2,694	2,857	2,970	3,066
P75	2,785	2,867	2,992	3,083	3,151	2,226	2,284	2,400	2,490	2,571
P25	1,722	1,753	1,799	1,833	1,867	1,502	1,532	1,587	1,631	1,672
P10	1,420	1,431	1,452	1,468	1,485	1,165	1,182	1,201	1,217	1,249

Source: Own calculations based on the job files from the Social Statistical Database (SSB) made available by Statistics Netherlands (CBS).
Note: SD = standard deviation; CV = coefficient of variation.

Table 4.3   Distribution of the coefficient of variation within firms

	1999	2000	2001	2002	2003
Median CV	0.4831	0.4886	0.4910	0.4904	0.4832
Mean CV	0.5055	0.5116	0.5148	0.5133	0.5081
Standard deviation of CV	0.2073	0.2042	0.2064	0.2049	0.2096
P90 CV	0.7487	0.7525	0.7631	0.7613	0.7580
P75 CV	0.6036	0.6104	0.6145	0.6160	0.6107
P25 CV	0.3752	0.3820	0.3835	0.3793	0.3723
P10 CV	0.2845	0.2907	0.2902	0.2874	0.2817

Source: Own calculations based on the job files from the Social Statistical Database (SSB) made available by Statistics Netherlands (CBS).
Note: CV = coefficient of variation.

the coefficient of variation within firms is below the national coefficient of variation. About 25 percent of the firms, however, had a higher wage inequality than the national average, as the 75th percentile equals about this national coefficient of variation of 0.6, as can be found in table 4.2.

Table 4.4 compares the within-firm wage distribution with the overall wage distribution. It confirms that for the average firm, the standard deviation of wages is about half the overall standard deviation of wages. Because firms with a higher average pay also have higher standard deviations, the firms with high wage inequality have about the same inequality as the overall distribution here.

In table 4.5, we take a look at the wage growth measured as the change in log wages. The growth figures approximately reflect the macrofigures presented in section 4.2. As smaller firms especially increased wages between 2001 and 2002, we found large increases at firm level in this period. Both at the individual level and at the firm level, the 10th percentile of the annual change is negative, with the exception of the period 2001 to 2002 at firm level. Because the wages are not deflated, this reveals that a substantial fraction of firms and individuals faced wage decreases every year.

In table 4.6, we present the distribution of exit rates over time. This is done separately for all firms, in the first column of a year, and for large firms with 100 employees or more in the second column of a year. In general, the exit rates diminish from 2000 to 2003, starting at a median of 23.66 percent in 2000 and ending at 17 percent in 2003. This reduction is mainly due to firms at the upper end of the distribution—that is, with the highest exit rates, which is lowered over time. Large firms consistently have 2 to 3 percent lower-than-average exit rates. The exit rate by the position of a firm in the wage distribution shows that the higher exit rates are generated by the lower-paying firms.

The increase in wages was not distributed equally among workers. To investigate the development of wages in greater detail, we split the sample in

Table 4.4   Comparison of overall wage distribution with wage distributions within the firm

	1999	2000	2001	2002	2003
Firm mean SD/country SD	0.5987	0.5839	0.6056	0.6393	0.5715
Firm SD/country mean	0.3067	0.3348	0.3595	0.3383	0.4001
90/10 within firm to 90/10 of country	0.1624	0.1615	0.1530	0.1495	0.1472
90/10 of firm means to 90/10 of country	0.8637	0.8536	0.8618	0.8685	0.8657
Within firm 90% SD relative to the country SD	0.9436	0.9102	0.9566	1.0214	0.9058
Within firm 10% SD relative to the country SD	0.2892	0.2847	0.2880	0.3065	0.2697
Between firm 90% relative to country 90%	0.7086	0.7051	0.7128	0.7200	0.7281
Between firm 10% relative to country 10%	0.8204	0.8260	0.8271	0.8290	0.8411

Source: Own calculations based on the job files from the Social Statistical Database (SSB) made available by Statistics Netherlands (CBS).
Note: SD = standard deviation.

Table 4.5   Distribution of the annual change of individual log wage and the mean log wage within firms

	Individuals				Firms			
	1999–2000	2000–2001	2001–2002	2002–2003	1999–2000	2000–2001	2001–2002	2002–2003
Median	0.046	0.063	0.048	0.038	0.058	0.069	0.135	0.046
Mean	0.058	0.075	0.060	0.045	0.061	0.071	0.162	0.047
Standard deviation	0.188	0.199	0.195	0.204	0.145	0.151	0.127	0.143
P90	0.193	0.217	0.196	0.175	0.171	0.184	0.310	0.148
P75	0.097	0.116	0.098	0.829	0.103	0.114	0.211	0.086
P25	0.013	0.025	0.011	0.002	0.022	0.028	0.077	0.012
P10	−0.050	−0.038	−0.055	−0.063	−0.032	−0.031	0.040	−0.039

Source: Own calculations based on the job files from the Social Statistical Database (SSB) made available by Statistics Netherlands (CBS).

99 percentile groups, based on wages in 2001, with all workers in the 0.5 to 1.5 percentile in the first group, all workers in the 1.5 to 2.5 percentile in the second group, and so on. When comparing different groups, we keep these brackets constant. Figure 4.1 provides the change in wages from 2000 to 2002. Because the percentile groups are based on wages in 2001, we avoided reversal to the mean effects due to measurement error or incidental changes in wages.

The figure compares wage growth of men and women. It shows that there is a general tendency for an increase in wage inequality as wages for workers with high incomes grew more than wages for low-wage workers. This holds especially for men. For women we observed an above-average wage increase for the group in between the 5th and the 40th percentile.

Figure 4.2 makes a similar comparison between age groups. As can be

Table 4.6   Yearly exit rates for all firms and firms with 100 employees or more and at several percentiles of the wage distribution, by year

	2000		2001		2002		2003	
	All firms	>100 firms	All firms	>100 firms	All firms	>100 firms	All firms	>100 firms
Median	0.2000	0.1697	0.1961	0.1635	0.1765	0.1455	0.1343	0.1071
Mean	0.2366	0.2008	0.2318	0.1964	0.2160	0.1817	0.1700	0.1374
Standard deviation	0.1692	0.1225	0.1744	0.1257	0.1771	0.1328	0.1539	0.1088
P90	0.4286	0.3393	0.4286	0.3408	0.4118	0.3200	0.3333	0.2644
P75	0.3015	0.2500	0.3000	0.2479	0.2791	0.2241	0.2286	0.1773
P25	0.1250	0.1204	0.1154	0.1150	0.1000	0.1014	0.0714	0.0692
P10	0.0727	0.0893	0.0667	0.0821	0.0556	0.0717	0.0000	0.0439
Position in wage distribution								
P90	0.189		0.190		0.184		0.140	
P75	0.183		0.175		0.166		0.126	
P50	0.228		0.219		0.204		0.158	
P25	0.275		0.271		0.250		0.202	
P10	0.333		0.331		0.297		0.233	

Source: Own calculations based on the job files from the Social Statistical Database (SSB) made available by Statistics Netherlands (CBS).

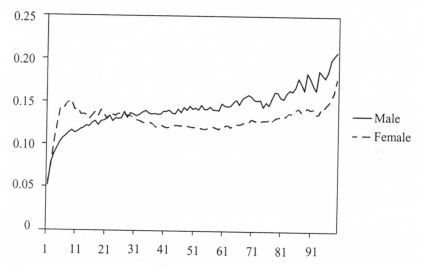

Fig. 4.1 Average wage growth between 2000 and 2002 for male and female employees for 99 percentile groups of the Dutch wage distribution

Source: Own calculations based on the Job files from the Social Statistical Database (SSB) made available by Statistics Netherlands (CBS).

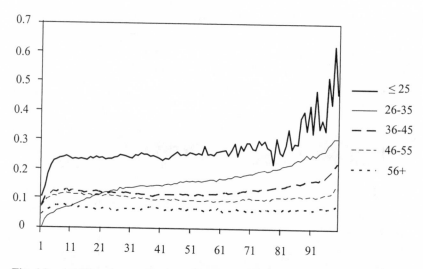

Fig. 4.2 Average wage growth between 2000 and 2002 for employees in different age categories for 99 percentile groups of the Dutch wage distribution

Source: Own calculations based on the Job files from the Social Statistical Database (SSB) made available by Statistics Netherlands (CBS).

expected, young workers faced larger wage increases than older workers. This difference was also very substantial, however, when comparing these figures internationally (Lazear and Shaw 2006). Another interesting feature of the graph is that the wage increase for young workers was high compared to other workers in all percentile groups. This implies that young workers who already earned wages that were very high with respect to the overall wage distribution experienced wage increases far beyond the wage increase of older workers with the same wages.

In figure 4.3, different firm sizes are compared. Although wages are strongly correlated with firm size, the surprising finding here is that the growth of wages—conditional on the wage level—is very similar for all size groups. This result is clearly consistent with a human capital interpretation of wages. When smaller firms pay lower wages because they hire people with lower levels of human capital, but wages only depend on the value of human capital in the market, the change in wages should be the same for all types of firms when conditioning on the wage level.

These findings changed completely when we compared different industries. Figures 4.4 to 4.6 provide the wage growth patterns for ten broad clusters of industries. There are some clear differences between industries. Especially the building industry has a pattern that deviates from the rest. Workers with wages in the lower percentiles of the Dutch wage distribution

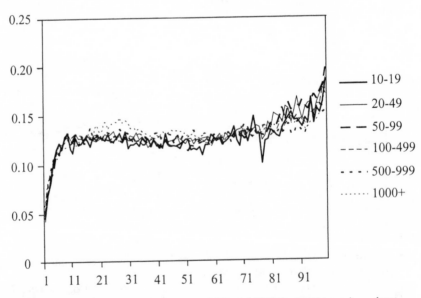

Fig. 4.3   Average wage growth between 2000 and 2002 for employees in various firm-size categories for 99 percentile groups of the Dutch wage distribution
Source: Own calculations based on the Job files from the Social Statistical Database (SSB) made available by Statistics Netherlands (CBS).

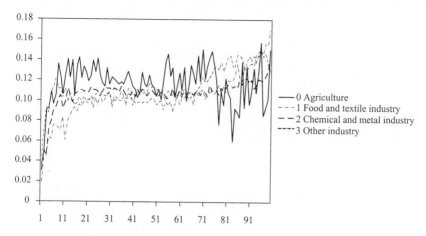

Fig. 4.4   Average wage growth between 2000 and 2002 for employees in agriculture, food and textile industry, chemical and metal industry, and other industries for 99 percentile groups of the Dutch wage distribution
Source: Own calculations based on the Job files from the Social Statistical Database (SSB) made available by Statistics Netherlands (CBS).

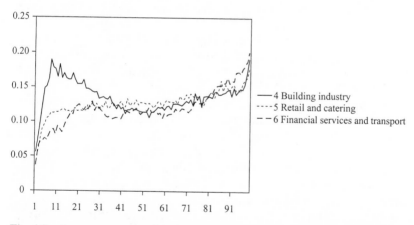

Fig. 4.5   Average wage growth between 2000 and 2002 for employees in the building industry, retail and catering, and financial services and transport for 99 percentile groups of the Dutch wage distribution
Source: Own calculations based on the Job files from the Social Statistical Database (SSB) made available by Statistics Netherlands (CBS).

experienced wage increases that are comparable to the wage increases of the top earners in this industry. Employment in the building industry was expanding rapidly in the period 1996 to 2001, so this wage pattern seems to reflect the increased demand for low-skilled workers in this industry.

The findings, therefore, suggest that the structure of wages in the Nether-

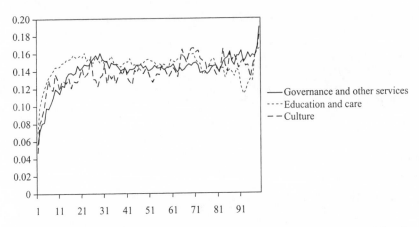

Fig. 4.6   Average wage growth between 2000 and 2002 for employees in public administration and other services, education and care, and culture for 99 percentile groups of the Dutch wage distribution
Source: Own calculations based on the Job files from the Social Statistical Database (SSB) made available by Statistics Netherlands (CBS).

lands is largely related to changes in the scarcity and value of human capital. A remaining question is to what extent these developments are correlated at the firm level and how much they can vary at the individual level. For this reason, we decomposed the wage increase in the period 2001 to 2002 in industry effects, firm effects, and individual effects. The first column of table 4.7 provides the variance of wages if each worker had experienced the same (relative) wage increase within each industry. For these analyses, we used the two-digit industry classification, which consists of fifty-seven different industries. The second column gives the variance of wages, assuming that each worker faced the average wage increase within his firm. The third column provides the individual variance of wages.

Based on this, the contribution to the wage inequality can be split into an industry component, a firm component, and an individual component, as is shown in columns (4) to (6) of the table. These tables provide the corresponding figures for splits of the data in different dimensions.

Overall, an interesting observation is that there was very little variation in wage growth between industries. This implies that either the agreements at the national level dominated the collective agreements at the industrial level or that these collective agreements played only a very small role in wage determination.

Wage growth differences at the firm level contributed on average for 12 percent to the differences in wage growth. The remaining 87 percent of the variation referred to individual differences. Wage growth in the Netherlands was thus mainly determined at the individual level. For men, the individual component was larger than for women. Differences between age

Table 4.7 Decomposition of the variance of wage growth 2001–2002 in between-industry, between-firms, and between-individuals components, by gender, age group, firm size, and industry

	Variance			Percentage		
	Between industries	Between firms	Between individuals	Industry	Firm	Individual
Overall	0.00022	0.00310	0.02456	0.89	11.73	87.38
Gender						
Male	0.00018	0.00258	0.02405	0.74	10.00	89.26
Female	0.00026	0.00366	0.02506	1.05	13.56	85.39
Age						
≤25	0.00022	0.00423	0.03019	0.74	13.25	86.00
26–35	0.00029	0.00433	0.03392	0.86	11.90	87.24
36–45	0.00024	0.00315	0.02368	1.01	12.29	86.70
46–55	0.00019	0.00249	0.01629	1.19	14.09	84.71
55+	0.00019	0.00252	0.01681	1.15	13.87	84.98
Firm size						
10–19	0.00026	0.01147	0.03100	0.82	36.17	63.01
20–49	0.00025	0.00802	0.03034	0.83	25.60	73.57
50–99	0.00025	0.00580	0.02936	0.86	18.90	80.24
100–499	0.00021	0.00281	0.02557	0.81	10.20	88.99
500–999	0.00024	0.00239	0.02501	0.95	8.61	90.45
1,000+	0.00024	0.00103	0.02102	1.16	3.72	95.12
Industry						
0 Agriculture	0.00004	0.00523	0.02376	0.18	21.83	77.99
1 Food and textile industry	0.00010	0.00306	0.02150	0.47	13.76	85.77
2 Chemical and metal industry	0.00007	0.00264	0.01981	0.38	12.95	86.67
3 Other industry	0.00007	0.00246	0.01640	0.43	14.59	84.97
4 Building industry	0.00007	0.00420	0.02309	0.30	17.90	81.80
5 Retail and catering	0.00010	0.00470	0.02774	0.37	16.57	83.06
6 Financial services and transport	0.00049	0.00390	0.02907	1.69	11.71	86.59
7 Governance and other services	0.00029	0.00360	0.02869	1.03	11.52	87.45
8 Education and care	0.00000	0.00142	0.02140	0.01	6.64	93.34
9 Culture	0.00006	0.00524	0.02962	0.20	17.48	82.32

Source: Own calculations based on the job files from the Social Statistical Database (SSB) made available by Statistics Netherlands (CBS).

groups are very small. A substantial difference in this respect was found when we compared firms of different sizes. In the smallest firms, of ten to nineteen employees, 36 percent of the variation in wages was at the firm level, while in the large firms of more than 1,000 employees, this is only 4 percent. This suggests that in small firms, which are in general less involved in negotiations for collective agreements, there was a strong tendency to give all workers approximately the same wage increase. In large firms, which sometimes even have their own collective agreement, not much of a firm effect was observed. Column (2) shows that this difference was to a large part due to the variation in average wage increases at the firm level.

There is much more variation between wage increases of smaller firms than between larger firms.

At the sectoral level (one-digit) the highest firm-specific components were observed in agriculture. In education and care, the between-firm variation was much smaller than in other industries. Here, apparently, firms followed national agreements in wage growth more closely than in other industries.

Apart from negotiating wages with their current employers, employees can of course also influence their wages by changing employer. To investigate whether wage developments at sector and firm levels were related to exit rates, we calculated for each worker the difference between the average wage increase in his or her sector or firm and the average economywide wage increase. We used only wage increases for workers who did not change firm. We determined 99 percentile groups, varying from very low relative wage growth in the sector or firm (0.5 to 1.5th percentile) to very high relative wage growth in the sector or firm (98.5 to 99.5th percentile). The thin line in figure 4.7 provides the exit rates for these 99 groups as a function of the sectoral wage growth. The dashed line provides a similar line for firm-level wage growth. The figure reveals that the exit rate in firms that experienced a relative decrease in wages was higher as the difference in wage development was larger. On the other hand, firms that paid higher wage increases than other firms in the same industry also experienced more

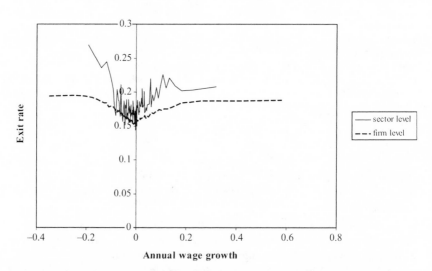

Fig. 4.7   Job mobility in 2001 related to the wage development in a sector or firm relative to the overall wage growth

Source: Own calculations based on the Job files from the Social Statistical Database (SSB) made available by Statistics Netherlands (CBS).

mobility when the difference in wage development was large. At the sector level, we found a similar pattern.

4.5 Conclusions

In this chapter, we documented the wage structure and labor mobility of the Dutch labor market between 1999 and 2003. The analyses are based on the administrative records collected by Statistics Netherlands that became available recently. The data allow for detailed descriptions of the wage structure between and within firms, following workers in time.

In the period 1999 to 2003, wage inequality increased. Especially workers in the lowest wage percentiles experienced lower wage increases than the median workers, while wage increases for top earners were substantially higher. The evidence in this chapter suggests that wage determination in the Netherlands is to a large extent determined by market forces. Workers with similar wages experience similar wage increases, irrespective of firm size. Wages for low-skilled workers in industries with a large increase in demand grow faster than in other industries, and between-industry and between-firm variation in wages is low compared to the individual component.

References

Borghans, Lex, and Ben Kriechel. 2006. Incentive pay and the wage structure of the firm: Evidence from a panel of Dutch firms. Maastricht University. Mimeograph.

Broersma, Lourens, Jan Koeman, and Coen Teulings. 2000. Labour supply, the natural rate, and the welfare state in the Netherlands: The wrong institutions at the wrong point in time. *Oxford Economic Papers* 52 (1): 96–118.

De Kam, C. A., W. van Drimmelen, and W. van Hulst. 1994. *Loonvorming en loonpolitiek in Nederland (Wage formation and wage policy in the Netherlands).* 3rd rev. ed. Groningen, the Netherlands: Wolters-Noordhoff.

Den Butter, Frank, and Robert Mosch. 2003. The Dutch miracle: Institutions, networks, and trust. *Journal of Institutional and Theoretical Economics* 159 (2): 362–91.

Dohmen, Thomas. 2004. Performance, seniority, and wages: Formal salary systems and individual earnings profiles. *Labour Economics* 11 (4): 741–63.

Dur, Robert. 2001. Wage-setting institutions, unemployment, and voters' demand for redistribution policy. *Scottish Journal of Political Economy* 48 (5): 517–31.

Hartog, Joop. 1999. Wither Dutch corporatism? Two decades of employment policies and welfare reforms. *Scottish Journal of Political Economy* 46 (4): 458–87.

Lazear, Edward P., and Kathryn L. Shaw. 2006. Wage structure, raises and mobility.

Netherlands Bureau for Economic Policy Analysis (CPB). 2006. *Central economic plan 2006.* The Hague, the Netherlands: CPB.

Organization for Economic Cooperation and Development (OECD). 1982. *OECD Economic Surveys: Netherlands 1982.* Paris: OECD.

———. *OECD Economic Surveys: Netherlands 2006.* Paris: OECD.

Research Centre for Education and the Labour Market (ROA). 2005. *De arbeids-*

markt naar opleiding en beroep tot 2010 (*The labor market by education and occupation until 2010*). Maastricht, the Netherlands: ROA.

Stegeman, Hans. 2000. Why different pay practices? *CPB Report* 00 (3): 38–43.

Ter Weel, Bas. 2003. The structure of wages in the Netherlands, 1986–1998. *Labour* 17 (3): 361–82.

Van den Berg, Annette. 1998. The ups and downs of trade union membership in the Netherlands. *Journal of European Economic History* 27 (2): 369–94.

Visser, Jelle, and Anton Hemerijk. 1998. *Ein holländisches Wunder* (*A Dutch miracle*). Frankfurt: Campus.

Finland
Firm Factors in Wages
and Wage Changes

Roope Uusitalo and Juhana Vartiainen

5.1 Introduction

5.1.1 General Motivation

The Finnish wage bargaining system has remained roughly unchanged over the last fifty years. Encompassing wage settlements were used as early as 1950 to 1951 to contain the inflationary pressures set off by the Korean war boom. In the 1960s, such cooperation between the labor unions, employer organizations, and the state was established on a more systematic basis. From 1969 onward, the unions and the employer organizations have formally negotiated wage agreements that cover the vast majority of workers. The government has also been actively involved in wage bargaining, and the wage settlements have often included various nonwage issues such as working hours, family policies, unemployment insurance, and pension arrangements.

Thus, and in contrast to the experience of some other countries, the Finnish wage policy has in some sense remained "centralized" up to the present. Yet this "centralization" has always been of a rather limited nature: throughout the post–World War II years, the centralized agreements have had to do with the general pace of wage increases, as well as minimum wage levels associated with specific tasks. Relative wages, however, have largely been determined by market forces. This difference is important,

Roope Uusitalo is research director at the Government Institute for Economic Research, Helsinki. Juhana Vartiainen is an associate professor of economics at Åbo Akademi University, and head of the research division at the National Institute of Economic Research, Stockholm.

We are grateful to Edward P. Lazear, Kathryn L. Shaw, and Lars Vilhuber for comments and suggestions.

because the economic literature on wage coordination has been so incommensurately colored by the Swedish experience of the 1960s and 1970s. In that extremely solidaristic phase of Swedish pay bargaining, centralization came to be synonymous with an attempt to steer the entire structure of relative wages by collective regulations. That phase was transient even in Sweden, but outside commentators do not often realize that such centralistic wage policies were never nearly as strong in the other Nordic countries. In the following, we shall outline the fine print of Finnish pay bargaining in more detail.

The balance between centralized and industry-level agreements has stayed roughly unchanged over time. Perhaps a more significant change is that various firm-specific arrangements have become more common during the 1990s. For example, profit-sharing arrangements and productivity-related pay systems have become popular during the latter part of 1990s.

Indeed, one important conclusion of this chapter is that this largely unchanged pay bargaining system has been able to accommodate large economic restructuring and upheavals. While the wage bargaining system has remained quite stable, the macroeconomic environment within which the firms operate has been extremely unstable. The Finnish economy entered its largest peacetime recession in the beginning of 1990s. The unemployment rate rose from 3.2 percent in 1990 to almost 17 percent in 1994. Real gross domestic product (GDP) declined in four consecutive years. In 1991 alone, real GDP dropped by 6.4 percent. The recovery after the recession was also rapid. The average GDP growth rate between 1994 and 2000 was 4.4 percent.

The bust-boom cycle was also associated with a large reallocation of resources across industries and across firms within industries. These macroeconomic shocks affect all statistics on wage growth and worker mobility reported in this chapter. The post-Depression years have been associated with extremely high productivity growth in some firms and industries and a large reallocation of labor and capital to the growing electronic industry sectors.[1]

Thus, and in contrast to the common "from centralized to individual" narrative of pay bargaining, we argue that such binary simplification is misleading in the Finnish case: collective and individual elements have always been present in a pay bargaining system that has accommodated important structural changes.

Against this institutional background, this chapter presents an econometric analysis of the wage structure in Finnish manufacturing industries. The empirical material presented in this chapter comes entirely from the manufacturing industry. Thus, we cannot lay claim to a complete representativeness of the Finnish labor market. On the other hand, we have at our disposal the complete wage and salary records of all manufacturing

---

1. This has been analyzed in detail by Mika Maliranta (Maliranta 2003).

firms of at least twenty-five employees from 1980 through 2002. This means that we can carry out fairly detailed and reliable analyses on the specific questions that we want to address. Furthermore, as is the case with encompassing register data, sampling problems can be completely ignored, and statistical characterizations of the data apply directly to the universe of wage and salary earners.

Being part of an international comparative project on wage structures, this chapter uses the data material in two ways. The same distinction is reflected in the structure of the chapter.

First, we have computed the comparative tables on wages for Finland, according to the commonly agreed blueprint of the National Bureau of Economic Research (NBER) project on wage structures. To this end, we use the data on the entire Finnish manufacturing workforce for 1981, 1990, and 2000. Our data material, however, come from two separate sources, one for blue-collar hour-wage earners and another for salaried employees remunerated on a monthly basis. These comparative table computations required that these separate records be merged. This merging of blue-collar worker files with salaried employee files yields new insights and makes the tables more comparable to those of other countries, but it is also cumbersome and involves nontrivial decisions that are to some extent arbitrary, as the statistical framework for entering employee information differs between workers and salaried employees. The former group is remunerated by the hour, whereas the salaried employees command a monthly salary. Furthermore, these groups are covered by very different collective agreements and job classification systems.

That is why the other part of the chapter focuses on the group of salaried employees only. To compensate for this loss of generality, we provide a much more detailed analysis of these employees' wage structure in 1980 through 2002. In particular, we describe the changing role of the firm-specific factors as well as the career patterns of individuals.

5.1.2 Structure of the Chapter

The structure of the chapter is as follows. We start by providing a more detailed account of the Finnish collective agreement system and other pay-bargaining institutions. This discussion provides an institutional background against which many of the results reported in the chapter become intelligible.

We then move on to describe the data sets that we have used for this project. As explained in the preceding, these data encompass the entire Finnish manufacturing workforce for 1980 to 2002. For 1981, 1990, and 2000, we have merged the blue-collar and salaried employee files and computed the basic comparative tables motivated in the introductory part of this volume. We also briefly discuss the broad picture that emerges from these tables, in particular as to how the Finnish results compare with other countries.

In the next sections, we move on to report more detailed analyses of the salaried employees' wage structure. In particular, we show how the last ten years have meant a gradual increase in the importance of firm-specific factors in pay determination. We also provide quite detailed estimates of individual mobility across firms and tasks and characterize individual careers as a function of promotions and employer changes. The concluding section discusses the interplay of collective agreements and individual bargaining in the light of the main results and speculates on the future course of pay-bargaining institutions.

5.2   Wage-Setting Institutions

As in the other Scandinavian countries, union density is high in Finland. Union density increased quickly in the 1960s and has been trending upward after that, reaching 82 percent in 1992. Since then, a slow decline has taken place, so that the unionization rate was by 2004 about 70 percent (see Böckerman and Uusitalo 2006).

The Finnish pay bargaining system is often characterized as centralized, but such a one-dimensional depiction is misleading, as wage setting in Finland is a mixture of collective and individual mechanisms. It is actually very hard to find an employee of a privately owned firm whose salary would be directly determined by some collective agreement or other collective intervention. A more accurate description would be to say that pay bargaining is local, but pay increases are coordinated by collectively agreed general wage increases, and, furthermore, there are minimum pay levels for the different occupational categories, as set out in the different collective agreements. There is no minimum wage legislation.

More precisely, the collective constraints put on the local bargaining consist of two elements. First, unions in each industry have established minimum tariff wages for occupational categories and job levels. Thus, when a firm hires an employee and bargains with him or her about the initial salary, both local parties are bound by these minimum tariffs. Most workers and employees of the manufacturing sector are, however, paid more than these minimum levels, so that these minimum tariffs are seldom directly binding.[2]

Second, in each bargaining round, the collective parties—that is, an industrial union and its corresponding employer association—agree on a general wage increase that is as a general rule applied to all workers, regardless of their initial wage. This increase is called the "general increase," and it is most often defined in percentage terms, although the blue-collar unions and their central federation have in most bargaining rounds sought

---

2. Of course, they can indirectly affect the bargaining outcome even if the actual wage exceeds the minimum tariff wage.

to establish a minimum money increase as well, so that the lowest wages would, in fact, be increased relatively more than other wages.[3]

It is important to understand that the general increase is not a binding constraint for the local parties if they both are prepared to deviate from it. Of course, nothing prevents a firm from increasing an individual's wage by more than the general increase. On the other hand, if the firm finds its jobs threatened, it can initiate negotiations on lower pay increases or even pay cuts. If the local parties can agree on such an outcome, they are in general free to do so. The exact legal significance of the general increase is that an industrial peace clause is associated with it: once the union has signed a new collective agreement, the workers have relinquished their right to undertake strikes or other industrial actions. Similarly, the firms whose employer association has agreed on a general increase cannot anymore initiate lockouts or other conflictual actions.

Thus, the local parties can in principle deviate from that general wage increase, but a deviation requires the consent of both parties. Consequently, the general wage increase is in most cases rather mechanically applied to each person's wage. In that sense, the unions can effectively influence the speed of wage increases. The firms, on the other hand, can effectively affect the local wage structure: when recruiting a new worker, the wage can be set according to the firm's own personnel policy, as long as the wage exceeds the minimum tariff listed in the relevant collective agreement.

To sum up, the Finnish wage bargaining system, although centralized as to the determination of wage increases, has not been an instrument that would determine the entire structure of relative wages. Rather, its main and stated objective has been to control the average rate of wage growth while leaving relative wages to decentralized, plant-level, or individual decision making.

The general increases are formally negotiated at the industry level, between the worker and the employer organizations. Collective agreements cover even nonunion members in the sectors where at least half of the employers belong to an employer organization. In practice, this implies that 95 percent of the workers in Finland are covered by the union contracts.

The central labor market organizations have no binding mandate for bargaining on behalf of their members associations. However, most bargaining rounds have started with negotiations between the central employer and employee confederations, creating a high degree of de facto coordination in the individual union contracts. The union bargains have then been negotiated, taking as a starting point the wage increases agreed upon in the central agreement. There has been considerable variation in the degree of centralization between the different bargaining rounds. During the period 1980 to 2002, there have been six bargaining rounds (1980, 1983,

---

3. This is currently a point of contention in the Finnish pay-bargaining debate.

1988, 1994, 1995, and 2000) when no central bargain was reached and bargaining occurred at the industry level.

The outcomes of centralized rounds and industry rounds differ, but the main difference is that decentralized rounds usually generate a higher average rate of wage increases. As we shall see, the variance of pay increases across individuals does not radically differ between those two institutional outcomes. However, as shown in the following, the firm-specific variance component is more important when there is no centralized agreement. Thus, roughly, pay determination becomes slightly more firm- and industry-specific when bargaining is at the industry level, but there is no explosion in the variance of pay increases across individuals, and the main effect is to increase the average level of pay increases (see Uusitalo 2005). This is not surprising, because the industrial unions are able to impose a general level of pay increases on the firms of the industry, even if that general increase is not coordinated by economywide organizations.

The comprehensiveness of centralized bargaining does not necessarily imply a completely rigid structure of relative wages. The starting point for all employee-employer relationships is, of course, a local bargain. As long as a firm complies with the general increases, it can run its own personnel policies. *Wage drift*, defined as the difference between general increases and average actual wage increases, has accounted for approximately 40 percent of the wage growth between 1970 and 2000. This fraction has declined somewhat over time, but wage drift still accounted for 35 percent of wage growth in 1992 to 2000 (see Uusitalo 2005). The unions do not usually attempt to constrain the growth of local or individual wages as long as the minimum tariff levels are met and the general increases (which often hardly exceed the sum of inflation and average productivity growth) are applied. Thus, even when complying with the general increases, firms that can sustain a decent productivity growth rate do have at least some freedom as to their internal wage structures. Some industries operate quite sophisticated collective agreements that condition pay on the complexity of the task and give the firm the right to adjust a person's pay according to his or her individual performance.[4]

Furthermore, various performance-related pay components have become common. In 2000, more than half of the white-collar and about a third of the blue-collar workers in the sample received some performance-related pay components other than traditional piece-rate pay. On average, these components were 4.4 percent of the total pay (see Snellman, Uusitalo, and Vartiainen 2003). For white-collar employees, the inclusion of such performance-related pay elements into a total-compensation mea-

---

4. The collective agreement of the Finnish metalworking industry, nowadays called "technology industry," has such a sophisticated structure. It is described in some detail by Pekkarinen and Vartiainen (2006).

sure imply a far higher likelihood of pay cuts than what an analysis of the monthly salary would imply.

5.3   The Finnish Data Sets and Tables

5.3.1   The Wage and Salary Register of the Finnish Employer Association

The principal data source contains payroll records of all firms that respond to the wage survey of the Confederation of Finnish Industry (TT). In 2000, these companies employed 500,000 employees, which is about a third of all private-sector employees in Finland. Most TT members are large firms in manufacturing and construction industries. The wage statistics cover roughly 70 percent of all employees in these sectors. The data are used to monitor wage growth in the manufacturing sector. The national statistics on earnings growth in manufacturing and construction are based mainly on these data. The data also serve as an information base for collective wage bargaining between the unions and the employer organizations.

The TT gathers information on the blue-collar workers (who receive an hourly wage) from the last quarter of each year and information on the white-collar workers (who receive a monthly salary) from each December. Answering the survey is compulsory for the member companies with more than thirty employees and voluntary for smaller companies. The survey gathers information on all employees of the firm. Only the top management and those working abroad are excluded. In 2000, the data contain information on 255,000 blue-collar and 172,000 white-collar employees. The records are stored at the individual level, and each individual is identified by a personal identity code.

Currently, we have complete wage records for both the blue-collar and the white-collar workers from 1980 to 2002. The last years of data (1996 to 2002) have been used previously by ourselves and by other researchers in Finland. Data up to 1995 have previously been available only for a smaller sample of individuals. Comprehensive data covering all employees and all years have been used only recently, and only in a handful of mainly ongoing studies. Therefore, not much is known about the quality of the data that covers the 1980s and early 1990s. Also, previous analyses have mainly used the white-collar and the blue-collar data separately. Combining white-collar and blue-collar worker data using firm identifiers is possible for the later years of data, but has not been previously done for the earlier period.

The wage records contain basic information on the employees and include details on all forms of compensation. The basic information on employees includes age, sex, job category, education, industry, occupation, and tenure (date of entry). The variable structure of this information differs between the blue-collar and the white-collar employees. The differences are mainly due to the fact that wages are calculated at the hourly level for the blue-collar workers and at the monthly level for the white-collar workers. For both groups of workers, the wages or salaries are reported in great detail. The blue collar data contain wages and hours divided into time-rate, piece-rate, and partial piece-rate (often also called "premium" pay) pay schemes.[5] Overtime pay, Sunday, and shift premiums, as well as performance-related bonuses are reported separately. Most workers receive compensation in several different forms (for example, some time-rate pay, some piece-rate pay, and some overtime pay). For the purposes of this chapter, we have defined the wage as total compensation divided by total hours. To make the white-collar workers data comparable, we have calculated the hourly wages based on the monthly wage and the usual weekly hours also for the white-collar workers.

The register data also contain a firm code and a respondent code that reveals who provided the wage information. Most often this respondent code refers to a plant. It is possible to create firm codes based on the respondent codes, essentially combining the respondent codes that refer to the same firm. For the last years of data, the procedure is reliable; for the early years, we are less certain. The firm code and the plant code have at times been subject to comprehensive registering changes, so that a certain amount of detective work was necessary to create a continuous series of codes that would allow the analysis of interfirm and interplant mobility.

5.3.2   Details on Variable Definitions and the Sample

In the tables based on the merging of blue-collar and white-collar employees files, comparable to the similar tables for the other countries involved in the project, we chose to analyze three years of data, namely 1981, 1990, and 2000. The motivation is to cover as long a time span as possible, skip the years that involve large changes in coding practice, and, at the same time, choose years that are comparable in terms of the business cycle (see figure 5.1 on macroeconomic conditions). To analyze wage growth and entry rates, we calculate all statistics from year $t - 1$ to year t. For exits, we calculate changes from the year t to the year $t + 1$. Any restrictions on the firm size (at least twenty-five employees) will refer to the base year t.

Some employees appear several times in the same year. This may happen, for example, if the employee changes firms during the observation period or if he or she has several employers simultaneously. For these employees, we always select the observation that has the most hours and discard the other observations on the same person. We also require that an employee can be unambiguously identified and, therefore, delete any observations that do not have a valid personal ID number.

---

5. Thus, the idea of premium pay schemes is that there is a fixed base wage upon which a production-related bonus is added.

We calculate wages including all wage components (including bonuses, overtime, etc.) and divide the total wages by total hours. For white-collar workers, we calculate hourly wages dividing monthly wages by the average number of weeks per month and further dividing the result by usual weekly hours. All wages are deflated to year 2000 euros using the consumer price index. To get rid of extreme observations (possibly errors), we delete all observations where the hourly wage is larger than three times the median or less than a third of the median. This rather conservative trimming only affects approximately 0.5 percent of the employees but has a large effect on the estimates for the standard deviations.

We focus on full-time workers and, therefore, delete all observations where the usual weekly hours are less than thirty. We make no restrictions by worker status and retain, for example, trainees and workers with very short contracts.

Only after doing all the data cleaning, we limit the sample to the firms that have at least twenty-five employees. Imposing the size limit has little effect on our data because only the firms with more than thirty employees (this varies slightly by industry) are required to answer the wage survey. Note that in calculating statistics for the high-level and low-level jobs, we make no additional restrictions to the sample. It is, therefore, possible that a firm has only one high-level worker.

When computing the comparative tables on wage dynamics, we perform similar data-cleaning procedures for year $t - 1$, with the exception that we do not require that the firm had twenty-five employees in the previous year. Nor do we impose any limits on the firm's size for year $t + 1$ in calculating the exit rates. The wage growth for the workers that enter the firm as well as the wage growth by tenure are naturally defined using the information on the date when the employer was hired to the current firm. In general, all measures where the observation is a person are easy to define. In contrast, the measures where the observation is a firm can be defined in several ways. For example, we have calculated the "average of firm average change in wage" by calculating the firm averages in year t and $t - 1$, taking the difference, and then the across-firm average of these differences. In this calculation, of course, the firm does not necessarily have the same employees in both years. One could equally well calculate the average growth of wages of individual workers by firm and then take the across-firm average, but it is not clear how one should treat the employees that changed the firm between $t - 1$ and t. See the article by Lars Vilhuber (chapter 1 in this volume) for a more detailed account of the variable definitions.

5.3.3 On Low-Level and High-Level Jobs

The register data also include an occupation code for each employee. The new coding system also identifies a level for each job, but the older codes do not have such a hierarchical structure. There is also a code for the job category that is different for each industry but constant within industries. These job categories are important for wage bargaining, as the union bargains typically set a minimum wage for each job category. In this sense, the job categories are ideal for the analysis of the wage structures because they are defined by the qualifications required for each job, and they are independent of the characteristics of the worker. Of course, these categories are to some extent arbitrary: if the employer wishes to give a worker a raise, he might promote a machinist to a senior machinist position without this change in title implying any changes in the tasks.

Despite the appeal of the job categories, we chose to define high-level and low-level jobs based on the occupation codes. The main reason is that there is a lot less missing data on the occupation codes. We therefore calculated the mean wage for each occupation code, sorted the data according to these occupation mean wages, and defined the employees who have the occupation mean wage in the top 20 percent as being in high-level jobs. In calculating entry and exit rates by quartiles and deciles, we first calculated the relevant percentiles at each firm and selected the high- or low-level jobs after that.

5.4   Macroeconomic Conditions

The Finnish economy has been characterized by rapid but volatile growth, driven by export fluctuations that have often been all but reinforced by domestic fiscal and monetary policy. The volatility of exports is mostly due to the dominant position of a couple of manufacturing sectors like wood and pulp, metal and engineering, and, a latecomer of the 1990s, the electronics sector spearheaded by Nokia. Growth rates and unemployment rates are depicted in figure 5.1.

The 1990s were a particularly turbulent period. The unemployment rate increased from 3.2 percent in 1990 to 16.6 percent in 1994. Real GDP declined by 6.4 percent in 1991, and the recession continued during 1992 and 1993. Recovery from the recession was almost equally rapid. The average growth rate for 1994 to 2000 was 4.4 percent, clearly higher than in other Organization for Economic Cooperation and Development (OECD) economies. With disturbances this large, it is quite difficult to find a "typical" year in terms of business cycle. Our choice of 1981, 1990, and 2000 does not look too bad. In all these years, the unemployment rate remained almost unchanged. In all cases, however, the unemployment rate grew in the following year, which might overstate the exit rates in the "normal" times.

To sum up, it is useful to bear in mind the following rough categorization of the period under study when looking at the tables reported in this chapter:

- The first part of the 1980s: A period of comparatively normal economic growth

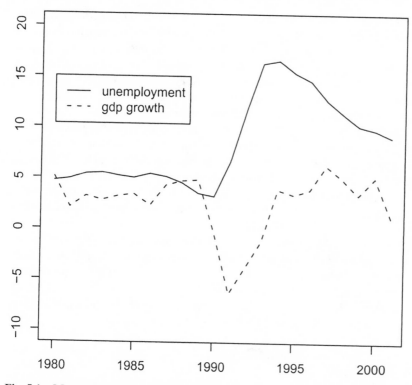

Fig. 5.1   **Macroeconomic environment: GDP growth rates and unemployment rates**
Source: ASTIKA database, Statistics Finland.

- Years 1986 to 1990: An overheated boom with unemployment near 3 percent
- Years 1991 to 1994: An exceptionally severe depression with yearly increases of 4 to 5 percent in the unemployment rate and a wave of bankruptcies
- Years 1995 to 1998: Rapid economic growth as resource use grew again
- Year 1999 and onward: A normalization of economic growth with unemployment stuck at around 9 percent

5.5   Discussion on the Comparison Tables

The comparison tables (see the comparative table section of this volume) yield a picture of wage differentials that is broadly typical of a Nordic country. For example, the wage dispersion entries of table 5.2 are quite similar to the corresponding tables presented in the Sweden chapter. The average wage of the lowest decile is about 57 to 59 percent of the mean wage in Finland, a couple of percentage points lower than in Sweden. This is not unexpected in the light of the Swedish trade unions' more ambitious egalitarian policies. The standard deviation of log wages is almost exactly the same in the two countries.

We explained in the preceding that the bargains on wage increases have been fairly tightly determined by collective agreements that set out a recommendation for general default wage increases. One would consequently expect that the standard deviation of wage changes would be low in Finland. The tables readily confirm this picture. The standard deviation of the year-to-year change in pay is in the order of 0.10, clearly lower than in Sweden, where the corresponding entry varies between 0.14 and 0.16—and manifestly lower than in less neocorporatist countries like France, where the standard deviation estimate is reported to vary between 0.29 and 0.34. In other countries, like Germany and the United States, the corresponding entries are even higher. Thus, whatever the merits or dismerits of this pattern, we see clearly that the Finnish wage-setting institutions lead to fairly uniform wage increases.

The mobility tables reveal fairly high mobility figures, like exit rates that vary between 12 percent and 23 percent. Compared to the United States, for example, these are high figures, and they do not shrink by much even if we only look at high-level jobs. Similar figures emerge in our analyses of salaried employees (see the following).

5.6   Salaried Employees: Decomposing Salaries

In this latter part of the chapter, we take a closer look at the variation of pay in the group of salaried employees. We lose some generality by leaving out hour-remunerated workers, but can instead carry out more detailed analyses on employees. We exploit this by describing our variation measures and other statistics for all years 1980 through 2002.

In an assessment of the workings of a pay-bargaining system as completely steered by collective agreements, as is the case for Finland, an analysis of variance for firm effects is a natural starting point. First, in tables 5.1 and 5.2, we report a variance decomposition for monthly salaries through 1980 to 2002.

We have taken, for each year, the individual log salaries of all full-time salaried employees and projected it to the set of firm dummies. In the tables, the first column, "Raw wage (SD)" reports the standard deviation of log salaries. The "between-R^2" column reports the share of total variance explained by firm dummies.

The third and fourth column repeat the similar analysis, but, this time, for log salary residuals after the original log salaries were projected on three conventional Mincerian covariates: education, age, and gender. The last column reports the number of firms used in the analysis of variance.

The decomposition is carried out separately for the 1980s and 1990s, as

Table 5.1   Variance decomposition for raw log salary and residual log salary for firms (1980–1989)

Year	Raw wage (SD)	Between R^2	Residual wage (SD)	Between R^2	No. of firms
1980	0.36	0.03	0.25	0.04	548
1981	0.34	0.03	0.24	0.04	592
1982	0.34	0.03	0.24	0.04	654
1983	0.34	0.03	0.24	0.04	683
1984	0.34	0.03	0.24	0.04	695
1985	0.34	0.03	0.25	0.04	691
1986	0.34	0.03	0.25	0.05	691
1987	0.34	0.04	0.25	0.05	700
1988	0.34	0.04	0.25	0.05	748
1989	0.34	0.04	0.26	0.06	801

Notes: Monthly salaries, including all bonuses, of white-collar workers working full time in a firm that belongs to the Confederation of Finnish Industry (TT). Residual wage refers to wage dispersion after controlling for gender, age, and education. SD = standard deviation.

Table 5.2   Variance decomposition for raw log salary and residual log salary for firms (1990–2000)

Year	Raw wage (SD)	Between R^2	Residual wage (SD)	Between R^2	No. of firms
1990	0.34	0.10	0.26	0.13	2,690
1991	0.33	0.10	0.25	0.13	2,702
1992	0.33	0.10	0.25	0.13	2,423
1993	0.32	0.10	0.26	0.12	1,404
1994	0.32	0.11	0.22	0.12	1,545
1995	0.32	0.13	0.22	0.15	1,532
1996	0.31	0.12	0.22	0.11	1,568
1997	0.33	0.20	0.22	0.16	1,593
1998	0.33	0.27	0.23	0.18	1,637
1999	0.33	0.27	0.23	0.19	1,601
2000	0.33	0.29	0.24	0.22	1,714
2001	0.33	0.30	0.24	0.22	1,699
2002	0.33	0.27	0.24	0.22	1,679

Note: See table 5.1.

a comprehensive recoding of firms took place between years 1989 and 1990.[6] The recoding implied, inter alia, that the number of firms tripled, so that the firm coding became much less aggregated than what was the case

6. We have analyzed this reorganization of the firm partition of the register and tried to use plant code information to create a continuous time series of firm codes. Unfortunately, this analysis did not reveal sufficiently clear patterns of "linkages" between the old and the new firm codes. Year 1989 was an overheated year in which a lot of splits and mergers took place. These real economic changes are mingled with administrative reforms carried out within the register. Consequently, we have no continuity in firm codes between 1989 and 1990.

in the 1980s. Thus, it is hardly reasonable to draw inferences on the change of the variance components between these two years and, in general, to compare the analysis of variance (ANOVA) results for these two decades. The situation is clearer for plant (establishment) codes, for which we were able to construct a reliable and continuous time series for the entire time span of 1980 through 2002.

We see, first, that the across-firm variance is rather low to start with, in comparison with similar analyses conducted on comparable data sets from other countries (see the other chapters of this volume). The firm effects only explain a paltry 3 to 5 percent of salary variation in the 1980s. Through the 1980s, not very much is going on in these variables: overall salary variation is low and stays put, and mean wage differentials between firms are almost insignificant and do not increase either. Such results rhyme with the stylized facts of organized labor markets, as shown in other papers like that of Holmlund and Zetterberg (see Holmlund and Zetterberg 1991): unexplained wage differentials are low.

In the 1990s, there is more action in these variables. The latter part of the 1990s deserves particular attention. That was a time of large migration between firms, associated with a rapid productivity growth and reallocation of resources to the growing electronic industry (see Maliranta 2003). These trends are probably reflected in the growth of the firm-specific variance component. However, we see that the increase in the between-firms component is clearly larger for raw log wages than for residual log wages. This observation is consistent with the hypothesis that employees are increasingly allocated to firms that employ similar individuals: the highly educated work with highly educated, and the less-educated work with the less educated. Similar empirical results have been reported by Michael Kremer and Eric Maskin (1996), who also present a theoretical argument that explains the increasing sorting of similar skill levels into the same firms.

Another interesting result has to do with the first column of tables 5.1 and 5.2: there is no growth in the aggregate variation of wages. Thus, to sum up, we can say that wage differentials have not increased, but the differences across firms are increasing, and this is only partly accounted for by sorting between firms.

The next figure, figure 5.2, reports the results of the same exercise, computed for establishments. The establishment codes generate a finer partition of the employee material because one firm can consist of many establishments. Furthermore, there are no structural changes in the way the establishments are coded throughout our investigation span of years 1980 through 2002. We can see similar trends: differentials between establishments increased starkly in the buoyant recovery phase of the late 1990s, and this is only partly accounted for by sorting. Figure 5.2 confirms the idea that the massive resource reallocation of the recovery phase of years 1995 to 1998 is a kind of structural break. The share of variance explained by es-

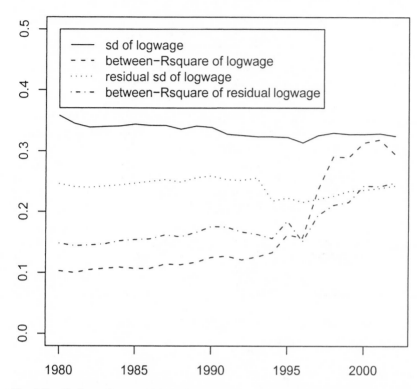

Fig. 5.2   **Variance decomposition of log wages and residual log wages: the share of between- and within-firms components; monthly salaries, including all bonuses, of white-collar workers working full time in a firm that belongs to the Confederation of Finnish Industry (TT)**

tablishment indicators is almost stagnant from 1980 to 1995 but then takes a sharp turn upward. The explained variance share of salary residuals behaves in the same way, but the increase is less dramatic. Thus, again, we can conclude that this period was one of increased sorting of workers to firms according to productive capabilities, but, furthermore, between-establishments salary differentials that cannot be explained by individual characteristics increase as well.

5.7   Mobility between Firms and Establishments

We now turn to the incidence of employer changes and establishment changes. Table 5.3 reports the relative frequencies of an individual changing firm or changing establishment.

Because the exit rates are an interesting variable in intercountry comparisons, it is important to be clear on the procedures used to obtain the

Table 5.3   Probability of firm and establishment exits of white-collar workers in
                   firms that belong to the Confederation of Finnish Industry

Year	Firm exit rate	Estimated exit rate
1980	0.16	0.16
1981	0.15	0.15
1982	0.16	0.16
1983	0.17	0.18
1984	0.18	0.18
1985	0.19	0.19
1986	0.23	0.24
1987	0.22	0.23
1988	0.24	0.24
1989	n.a.	0.31
1990	0.26	0.31
1991	0.23	0.25
1992	0.33	0.41
1993	0.21	0.24
1994	0.22	0.28
1995	0.21	0.25
1996	0.16	0.25
1997	0.15	0.23
1998	0.19	0.22
1999	0.18	0.22
2000	0.24	0.25
2001	0.22	0.28

data of table 5.3. The table is based on a simple criterion: an exit takes place
whenever the firm code or employer code of the individual changes from
the base year to the consecutive year. However, we have also checked that
those events are not based on potential code changes that affect all the individuals of a firm. More precisely, for any "exiter" individual, say individual i in firm j, we checked whether all the individuals in that particular
base year firm j were exiters. If that was the case, we checked whether one
could find at least 80 percent of the base year individuals of that firm j under some same but another consecutive year firm code k, and, furthermore,
whether these "old" individuals coming from j and now in k made up at
least 80 percent of firm k's personnel in the consecutive year (for establishments, we used a 60 percent criterion). Happily, this was never the case. In
other words, whenever there was a complete mass exit from some firm or
establishment code, the exiters were dispersed to a lot of other firm or establishment codes. Therefore, these exits do not simply reflect a change in
the firm code caused by, for example, change in ownership.

For the year pair 1989 to 1990, it was impossible to compute a reliable
estimate of mobility between firms, as a comprehensive overhaul of coding
practices took place between these years, as explained in the preceding. For
the other years, the numbers should be comparable. As seen in table 5.3, the

exit rates increased substantially after the mid-1980s. The exit rates were highest during the recession years in the beginning of 1990s, but seem to remain above the prerecession level even in the end of the century.

We turn next to mobility between tasks. For those who do not change employer or establishment, the probability of a task change (occupation change) is reported in table 5.4. Because task changes are mostly associated with above-average earnings growth, we also call them "promotions," although clearly they may be demotions as well. Even though the promotion rates are exceptionally high in 1992, 1998, and 1997, no clear trend can be seen in table 5.4.

5.8   Job and Promotion Flows and Salary Changes

After documenting the levels of interfirm and intertask mobility, we use these data to describe differentials in wage increases with respect to these events. Throughout the following comparisons, we have defined an indi-

Table 5.4   **Incidence of promotions with unchanged firm and unchanged establishment of white-collar workers in firms that belong to the Confederation of Finnish Industry**

| | Probability of occupation changes | |
Year	Firm unchanged	Estimated unchanged
1980	0.07	0.06
1981	0.06	0.06
1982	0.07	0.07
1983	0.08	0.07
1984	0.07	0.07
1985	0.07	0.07
1986	0.07	0.07
1987	0.08	0.07
1988	0.08	0.08
1989	n.a.	0.08
1990	0.12	0.06
1991	0.09	0.06
1992	0.18	0.07
1993	0.10	0.07
1994	0.12	0.06
1995	0.10	0.06
1996	0.17	0.06
1997	0.17	0.08
1998	n.a.	n.a.
1999	0.06	0.01
2000	0.06	0.04
2001	n.a.	n.a.

Note: n.a. = not available.

vidual's wage growth as the ratio of the money wage increase to the average of base year and subsequent year wage:

(1)
$$\frac{w_{t+1} - w_t}{\dfrac{w_t + w_{t+1}}{2}}$$

Figure 5.3 displays the mean year-to-year real salary increases for two groups of employees: those who remain with their employers and those who change to another firm in the register. When comparing these figures to those of other countries, it is important to bear in mind that we have no information on those who jump to firms outside the manufacturing industry. We have subtracted the increase of the consumer price index from the mean salary increase for each group so that these numbers tell the increase in the real earnings level.

There are quite large swings in the average growth of real earnings, as the numbers vary between –4 and +8 percent. Thus, in the early phases of the

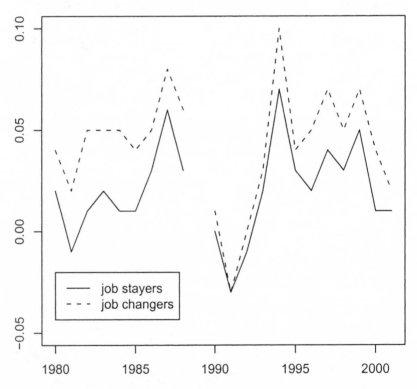

Fig. 5.3   Real wage increases for job stayers and job exiters; monthly salaries, including all bonuses, of white-collar workers working full time in a firm that belongs to the Confederation of Finnish Industry (TT)

1990s recession, average real salaries shrank. The general picture is that salary growth is more rapid for the job changers, but this differential shrinks to zero when the economy is in the deep recession of the early 1990s.

Figure 5.4, in turn, reports salary growth rates for three groups: all job stayers, those job stayers whose occupation code changes, and those who stay under their base year occupation code. Again, the curves are not very surprising: those who change occupation probably get promoted in most cases, and they do better than the rest. In the depression years, the difference is tiny, but it becomes quite large after year 1995. For many years the "non-promoted job stayers" dotted line corresponds exactly to the "all job stayers" continuous line and is therefore not visible in the figure.

It is an obvious hypothesis that job changers or task changers may face higher variability in their earnings growth. Table 5.5 reports the standard deviation of salary changes in all of the five groups discussed here: all individuals, those who stay with their employer, those who change employer, and, finally, two subsets of those who stay with the firm: the ones whose

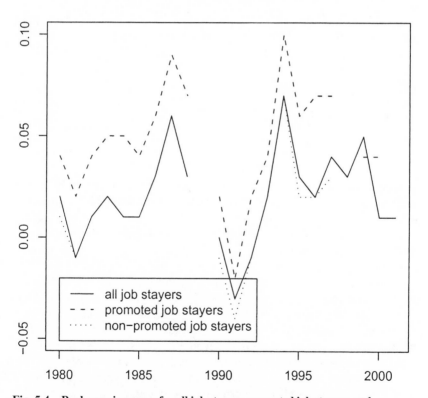

Fig. 5.4   Real wage increases for all job stayers, promoted job stayers, and nonpromoted job stayers; monthly salaries, including all bonuses, of white-collar workers working full time in a firm that belongs to the Confederation of Finnish Industry (TT)

Table 5.5   Standard deviation of variation of monthly changes, including all bonuses, of white-collar workers working full time in a firm that belongs to the Confederation of Finnish Industry

	Workers			Occupation changes	Occupation unchanged
Year	All	Stayers	Changers		
1980–1981	0.07	0.06	0.12	0.09	0.06
1981–1982	0.06	0.06	0.11	0.09	0.06
1982–1983	0.06	0.06	0.11	0.09	0.06
1983–1984	0.06	0.06	0.11	0.09	0.06
1984–1985	0.07	0.06	0.12	0.09	0.06
1985–1986	0.07	0.06	0.11	0.09	0.06
1986–1987	0.07	0.06	0.10	0.09	0.06
1987–1988	0.07	0.07	0.11	0.09	0.06
1988–1989	0.08	0.07	0.11	0.11	0.07
1989–1990	0.08	n.a	n.a.	n.a.	n.a.
1990–1991	0.06	0.06	0.08	0.09	0.06
1991–1992	0.05	0.05	0.06	0.08	0.04
1992–1993	0.06	0.06	0.08	0.09	0.06
1993–1994	0.07	0.06	0.08	0.10	0.06
1994–1995	0.07	0.07	0.08	0.08	0.07
1995–1996	0.07	0.07	0.09	0.10	0.06
1996–1997	0.08	0.08	0.12	0.13	0.07
1997–1998	0.08	0.08	0.13	0.11	0.07
1998–1999	0.09	0.09	0.12	n.a.	n.a.
1999–2000	0.09	0.09	0.12	0.10	0.09
2000–2001	0.09	0.09	0.10	0.11	0.08
2001–2002	0.09	0.09	0.11	n.a.	n.a.

Note: n.a. = not available.

task changes and the ones with an unchanged task. As expected, those who change occupation or employer are, in general, exposed to higher variation of earnings growth.

These differences between groups may seem relatively low, and it is clear that they conceal important differences between the age groups. We know from the economic literature that younger employees typically gain more by changing jobs or occupations. Thus, repeating the same exercise separately for all age groups but aggregating over all years should yield additional information. Such a computation is reported in figure 5.5. For that figure, we have used the entire panel of employees and computed a similar breakdown of salary increases in the groups of firm stayers, firm changers, and firm stayers who change occupation (we leave out the curve for all employees because it is almost identical to that of firm stayers whose occupation is unchanged). A clear pattern emerges: young workers gain a lot by changing employers, but also by being promoted within the firm. After age fifty, promotions and job exits hardly make any difference, and, for the old-

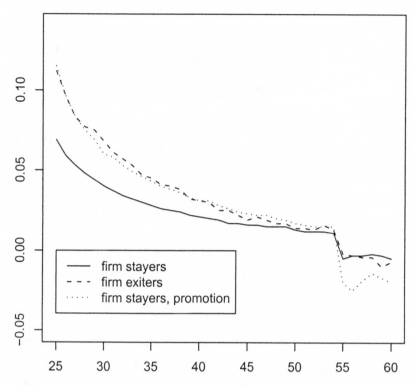

Fig. 5.5 **Real wage increases according to age for all job stayers, job changers, and promoted job stayers; monthly salaries, including all bonuses, of white-collar workers working full time in a firm that belongs to the Confederation of Finnish Industry (TT)**

est workers, being allocated to new tasks within the firm is associated with a drop in real earnings.

5.9 The Variance of Wage Increases

As far as the "tightness" of the collective agreement system is concerned, one of the most interesting questions is the extent to which individual firms can steer their internal pay structures and to what extent they are just compelled to keep the existing pay structure and pay the general increase to everybody.

To shed light on this, figure 5.6 reports an ANOVA decomposition of yearly salary increases, with firm indicators as the conditioning variable, as in the computations reported in tables 5.1 and 5.2. We can see a slow increase in the overall variance of salary increases. As to the share of salary increase variation explained by firm indicators, one might also detect a

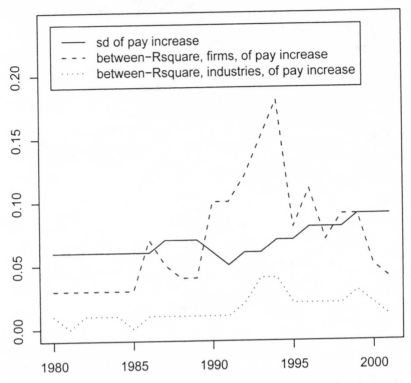

Fig. 5.6   ANOVA for salary increases: The standard deviation of salary increases for job stayers and the share of variance (*R*-squared) explained by firm indicators and industry indicators; monthly salaries, including all bonuses, of white-collar workers working full time in a firm that belongs to the Confederation of Finnish Industry (TT)

weak but increasing trend, but it is overwhelmed by upward and downward movements that seem to be associated with the outcome of centralization efforts. There were no centralized wage agreements in years 1993 and 1994. In the boom years of the late 1990s, economic policymakers again resorted to coordinated wage settlements in order to put a brake on inflation, and we can see a corresponding downward shift in the firm variance component in these years.

These shifts in the firm salary increase differentials are partly based on shifts in interindustry differentials in salary increases: when there is no centralized agreement on a general pay increase, different industries implement different pay increases that might still be fairly uniform between firms. However, as is apparent from figure 5.6, the interindustry differentials do not account for a large part of the pay increase variance, even in those years when the interfirm differentials are large. The shifts in the variance component of industry differentials are far weaker.

Thus, one natural interpretation of the result is that noncentralized rounds do, in general, result in higher pay increases in all the industries. This is also the result obtained by Uusitalo in an earlier study (2005). However, as we see a much stronger upward shift in the firm variance component in those very same years in which there is no centralized agreement, it seems that these industrywide agreements are written in such a way that they leave more room at firm-specific arrangements.

Thus, seen from the point of view of individual firms, noncentralized industry agreements are a mixed bag. They lead to more firm-specific adjustment in wages, but they also result in higher overall pay increases, which is probably particularly disadvantageous for those firms that suffer from below-average labor productivity growth. This is a classic feature of Nordic pay-bargaining models: they reward firms with high productivity growth, as local wage claims are controlled by central organizations, but they penalize entrepreneurs whose productivity growth is below average.

Anyway, we see that quite substantial shifts in variance components can occur within an unchanged institutional framework for wage determination. This does not mean that wage increases would be particularly firm specific in an international comparison. However, it shows that the firms can to some extent at least use wage changes as individual incentives and group incentives within a pay-bargaining system that aims at steering the overall pace of wage change.

5.10   Job and Occupation Transitions and Career Profiles

Finally, we characterize the career dynamics of a couple of cohorts of new entrants into the industry. We select two cohorts, one that enters the industry in 1981 and another that enters in 1987. We select all the entrants that were under thirty-five years of age in the initial year and who were not observable in the panel in the year preceding the initial year. From these cohorts, we further select all those who are observed in the industry for eleven consecutive years after the initial year. For each individual, we compute the sum of job changes within a current employer (promotion) and a change of employer (job exit). We measure the effect of such cumulated changes on the relative position of the employee. To this end, we start the analysis by computing, for each employee, his or her percentile rank in each year in the aggregate salary distribution. Note that we have used the entire salaried employee workforce to compute these ranks, not only the chosen cohort.

Our career variable is then the gain in the relative position of the employee during the eleven years of interest. This procedure abstracts from aggregate productivity and inflation shocks and other business-cycle phenomena and focuses solely on the relative performance of the employees.

We report two tables for both cohorts, one that reports the average relative position improvement as a function of promotions and job changes, and another that reports the headcounts in each group. Table 5.6 reports the average increase in the relative position of the employees in the 1981 cohort. In each cell, the number in parentheses displays the standard deviation of the relative position change for that particular exits-promotion combination. The next table, table 5.7 reports the headcounts of all promotion-job exit combinations, from year 1981 to 1991. As one can see by comparing the two tables, we do not report the mean and standard deviation estimates for cells with less than five individuals.

The next tables, tables 5.8 and 5.9, report a similar exercise for the 1987 cohort.

For the earlier cohort, it seems clear that about four employer changes plus a few promotions lead to a high relative salary gain. The most interesting difference between the two cohorts has to do with the first column of tables 5.6 and 5.8. For the earlier cohort, it was not that advantageous to change employer many times without being promoted in the firm. This tells of a more traditional economy, in which tenure and internal career progress play a main role. The latter cohort has experienced the large interfirm mobility of the 1995 to 1997 recovery years, and for that cohort it is possible to improve one's performance a lot by changing employer but without any promotions.

We also note that the standard deviation figures are quite high, although one has to bear in mind that they are not directly related to uncertainty as to the money salary: we measure progress by the person's position in the distribution, and in the thick parts of the salary distribution, it is, of course, easier to move a lot in the salary distribution of employees without the

Table 5.6   **Cohort relative wage gains as a function of job changes (vertical direction downward) and internal promotions (horizontal direction) of white-collar workers who entered the industry in 1981**

	No. of promotions within firm							
No. of exits	0	1	2	3	4	5	6	7
0–2	9 (15)	13 (25)	18 (21)	21 (28)	17 (29)	27 (29)		
3	10 (18)	15 (23)	14 (27)	25 (29)	26 (36)			
4	14 (24)	21 (25)	20 (26)	30 (23)				
5	12 (25)	20 (30)	23 (29)	24 (11)				
6	14 (30)	22 (31)	28 (20)					
7	18 (19)	4 (30)						
8								
9								

Notes: Each entry in the table reports the average percentile increase (standard deviation in brackets) within the wage distribution. For example, the first entry in the top left corner of the table shows that between 1981 and 1992 the worker who changed employee never, once, or twice and was not promoted while working with the same employer increased his or her relative position, on average, by 9 percentage points of the wage distribution.

Table 5.7   Cohort headcounts according to number of job changes (vertical direction downward) and internal promotions (horizontal direction) of white-collar workers who entered the industry in 1981

No. of exits	No. of promotions within firm							
	0	1	2	3	4	5	6	7
0–2	690	425	199	73	23	8	1	1
3	464	341	104	47	10	5	0	0
4	218	132	47	19	1	0	1	0
5	93	83	27	7	0	1	0	0
6	40	21	7	1	1	0	0	0
7	9	8	3	0	0	0	0	0
8	2	0	0	0	0	0	0	0
9	0	1	0	0	0	0	0	0

Notes: Each entry reports the number of individuals whi experience a particular combination of employer changes and promotions. For example, there are 464 people who changed employer thrice but were never promoted within one employer.

Table 5.8   1987 cohort relative wage gains as a function of job changes (vertical direction downward) and internal promotions (horizontal direction)

No. of exits	No. of promotions within firm							
	0	1	2	3	4	5	6	7
0–2	13 (14)	20 (15)	23 (19)	28 (20)	34 (25)			
3	18 (17)	24 (19)	32 (22)	38 (21)				
4	21 (18)	26 (18)	27 (20)					
5	25 (17)	28 (23)	29 (25)					
6	35 (22)	34 (13)						
7								
8								

Note: See tables 5.6 and 5.7 notes.

Table 5.9   1987 cohort headcounts according to number of job changes (vertical direction downward) and internal promotions (horizontal direction)

No. of exits	No. of promotions within firm							
	0	1	2	3	4	5	6	7
0–2	327	161	92	35	6	0	0	1
3	251	161	59	15	5	0	0	0
4	138	71	47	5	3	0	0	0
5	43	27	11	5	0	0	0	0
6	19	10	4	0	0	0	0	0
7	2	3	0	0	0	0	0	0
8	1	0	0	0	0	0	0	0

Note: See table 5.7 notes.

salary changing a lot. This notwithstanding, the standard deviations are quite high—even the groups of individuals who have mostly stayed with the same employer and have experienced several promotions have, on average, a standard deviation of the career measure variable that is of the same order of magnitude as the value of the measure variable itself.

5.11 New Pay Forms and Pay Flexibility

We have so far confined our analyses to a narrowly defined base monthly salary. In the 1990s, new pay forms related to firm profits or some group or firm performance measures became increasingly popular in Finnish manufacturing. This may be due to at least two factors. Production technologies may evolve in a way that makes the measurement of individual performance more difficult at the same time when productivity becomes increasingly dependent on group performance. Another motivation for an increased use of performance-related pay may be disinflation: when inflation is low, maintaining a given downward real wage flexibility necessitates a higher propensity of nominal pay cuts (see Macleod and Malcomson 1993). Pay cuts are probably easier to carry out for such pay components as performance pay and profit sharing as they are not regulated by collective agreements and are at the discretion of management.

In the context of this chapter, one would expect that such new pay forms would also increase the firm-specific component in wage variation. We illustrate this with a table on the incidence of nominal pay cuts, computed for both narrowly defined monthly salary and the total salary, which is a sum of the narrow salary and eventual performance pay.

Table 5.10 shows that this effect can be quite important for salaried employees. In a similar vein, if we carry out an analysis of variance, similar to that reported for wage increases but this time taking into account new per-

Table 5.10   Probability of a wage cut from base year to next and the coefficient of variation of pay changes, both computed for narrow and wide pay, job stayers of monthly salaries of white-collar workers working in a firm that belongs to the Confederation of Finnish Industry

	Prob(salary cut) and CV(salary change), job stayers			
Year	Salary no PP	Salary with PP	CV(salary no PP)	CV(with PP)
1996–1997	0.04	0.13	2.10	2.06
1997–1998	0.02	0.07	1.21	1.23
1998–1999	0.04	0.14	1.45	1.63
1999–2000	0.02	0.06	1.04	1.11

Notes: Prob = probability; CV = coefficient of variation. Columns "with PP" indicate the performance-related pay components that are typically based on the firm's economic result in the previous year.

Table 5.11   Probability of a wage cut from base year to next and the coefficient of variation of pay changes, both computed for narrow and wide pay, job stayers of hourly wages of blue-collar workers in firms that belong to the Confederation of Finnish Industry

	Prob(wage cut) and CV(wage change), job stayers			
Year	Timewage	Timewage with PP	CV(timewage)	CV(timewage with PP)
1996–1997	0.22	0.21	1.88	1.81
1997–1998	0.19	0.19	1.60	1.52
1998–1999	0.25	0.27	2.06	2.13
1999–2000	0.15	0.15	1.31	1.28

Note: See table 5.10 notes.

formance pay schemes, we see that these new pay schemes greatly reinforce the move to a larger firm specificity of wage changes.

This trend is not general, however: for hourly paid blue-collar workers, there is no such effect, and the incidence of pay cuts is fairly high to start with. This is shown in table 5.11, in which we report the same exercise for blue-collar workers. There is much more downward flexibility in the worker wages to start with, and the introduction of performance pay schemes does not mean a momentous change in this respect.

5.12   Conclusions

We have surveyed the wage structure and wage dynamics of Finnish manufacturing employees in the last twenty-two years. One interesting background factor for this analysis is that the institutions of the wage bargaining system have hardly changed at all in that period. Consequently, we can regard the structural changes that we detect in the empirical material as due to the behavior of firms and individuals instead of institutional reforms.

In our view, the most important stylized facts that emerge out of these analyses are the following:

- The overall cross-section variance of salaries has changed very little. This is true for the distribution of final salaries but almost true even for salary residuals.
- In the 1980s, differences in the mean salaries of firms were very low. This was true both for final salaries as well as residuals after the salaries were projected to conventional Mincer-type regressors like education, age, and gender.
- The differentials between firms started to increase at the end of the 1980s, and this process accelerated after the deep slump of the 1990s. In other words, salaries became more firm specific.

- A large part of this increased importance of the firm-specific variance component is explained by a stronger sorting of employees according to productive characteristics.
- The increased importance of differentials between firm holds true even for Mincer wage residuals. In other words, there are more firm-specific wage differentials between similar individuals who work in different firms.
- A slight but similar development has taken place for the distribution of salary increases. Firm differentials in salary increases are more important now than in the 1980s. However, this trend is not monotone.
- Salary increase differentials between firms increase markedly when there is no centralized wage agreement. Firm differentials in salary increases were particularly large in the mid-1990s when no centralized agreements on salary increases were concluded, but they diminished again when centralized incomes policy again became operative from year 1996 onward.
- Salary increases differ between those who stay and those who leave a firm. In recessions, that difference is not large, but leavers do better in times of boom.
- A similar characterization holds for those who change occupation within a firm. In general, occupation changers increase their pay more than those who stay in their occupation.
- Both of the aforementioned effects depend starkly on age. Firm exits and promotions increase earnings up to the age of fifty years, after which such events do not, on average, improve a person's relative position.
- Finally, an analysis of individual careers over eleven years revealed that both exits and promotions play a role in salary growth. The variance of individual final pay after a career of ten years is large. Macroeconomic conditions can dramatically affect the expected pay and the variance of pay over the career span of an individual. After the deep slump of the early 1990s, employer changes even without internal promotions might have become a more attractive career pattern.

To sum up, wage setting is becoming a bit more firm specific, while centralized agreements on pay increases continue to be the main force that affects the growth in average pay. This kind of modest evolution toward more firm-specific pay firm seems to be well accommodated by the institutional and legal framework of pay bargaining.

There is no necessary contradiction between these trends of more microflexibility and macrocentralization. Indeed, according to some accounts, they would be a rational response to the economic environment. Recent theoretical research on the interplay of central bank policy and wage bargaining suggests that the advent of the euro makes it even more important to coordinate the wage claims of unions. This conclusion has come out of several papers (see Coricelli, Cukierman, and Dalmazzo 2000; Holden 2005). The authors of these papers argue that the introduction of the single currency means that monetary policy becomes more accommodating from the point of view of national wage setters. This means that the incentives to coordinate wage claims increases, as there is no national central bank anymore that would discipline wage setters by threatening with high interest rates if wage claims are excessive. The same point has been made in the empirical industrial relations literature. Anke Hassel (2002) notes that European governments have been keen to use the collective wage bargaining system to get a better macroeconomic grip on average wage growth.

At the same time, it is not surprising that firms want to increase the scope for their specific personnel policies and wage schemes. As the importance of sheer physical labor recedes and production processes become more complicated, it becomes more important for the firm to introduce increasingly sophisticated incentive schemes. This means that pay is increasingly conditioned on team performance, which warrants the introduction of performance pay or even profit sharing. In our blue-collar register data, for example, we can observe a steady decrease in the share of pure individual piece-rate work and a corresponding increase in partial piece-rate or premium pay that is often based on team performance. Such trends in production techniques make it increasingly important for firms to design sophisticated incentive structures.

Against these two general trends, the gradual increase in microflexibility within the confines of an otherwise centralized macroeconomic control of wage increases might be at least a reasonable second-best reaction to economic circumstances. In this respect, Finland is hardly alone among the small European countries, of course. Recent institutional developments in Sweden tell a similar story: collective agreements are increasingly written so that relative wage differentials at the firm level are left to local negotiations, while the macroeconomic control of the speed of wage increases is tightened with the help of new neocorporatist institutions like the new National Mediation Office.[7] In the Netherlands, typical wage bargains also keep a centralized control of general wage increases but otherwise leave wage determination to the local level.[8]

---

7. This new organization was established in year 2000, and its aim is to enhance bargaining coordination and set guidelines for reasonable wage settlements.

8. See Teulings and Hartog (1998) for a sophisticated theoretical rationale of the Dutch wage bargaining model, not unlike the arguments that we have advanced in this paper.

References

Böckerman, P., and Uusitalo, R. 2006. Union membership and the erosion of the Ghent system: Lessons from Finland. *British Journal of Industrial Relations* 44 (2): 283–303.

Coricelli, F., A. Cukierman, and A. Dalmazzo. 2000. Monetary institutions, monopolistic competition, unionized labour markets and economic performance. CEPR Technical Report no. 2407. London: Centre for Economic Policy Research.

Hassel, A. 2002. A new going rate? Co-ordinated wage bargaining in Europe. In *Wage policy in the euro zone*, ed. P. Pochet, 149–76. Brussels: Peter Lang.

Holden, S. 2005. Monetary regimes and the coordination of wage setting. *European Economic Review* 49:833–43.

Holmlund, B., and J. Zetterberg. 1991. Insider effects in wage determination: Evidence from five countries. *European Economic Review* 35 (5): 1009–34.

Kremer, M., and E. Maskin. 1996. Wage inequality and segregation by skill. NBER Working Paper no. 5718. Cambridge, MA: National Bureau of Economic Research.

Macleod, W. B., and J. M. Malcomson. 1993. Investments, holdup, and the form of market contracts. *American Economic Review* 83:811–37.

Maliranta, M. 2003. Micro level dynamics of productivity growth. ETLA Working Paper no. A38, Helsinki, Finland: Research Institute of the Finnish Economy.

Pekkarinen, T., and J. Vartiainen. 2006. Gender differences in promotion on a job ladder: Evidence from Finnish metalworkers. *Industrial and Labor Relations Review* 59 (2): 285–301.

Snellman, K., R. Uusitalo, and J. Vartiainen. 2003. *Tulospalkkaus ja teollisuuden muuttuva palkanmuodostus* (*The role of profit sharing schemes in the evolution of wage institutions in manufacturing*). Helsinki, Finland: Sitra/Edita.

Teulings, C., and J. Hartog. 1998. *Corporatism or competition? Labour contracts, institutions and wage structures in international comparison.* Cambridge, UK: Cambridge University Press.

Uusitalo, R. 2005. Do centralized bargains lead to wage moderation? In *Collective bargaining and wage formation*, ed. H. Piekkola and K. Snellman, 121–32. Heidelberg, Germany: Labour Institute for Economic Research.

6

Wage Structure and Firm Productivity in Belgium

Thierry Lallemand, Robert Plasman, and François Rycx

6.1 Introduction

Relative wages are often considered as a key determinant of the workers' effort. Indeed, because workers often compare their wages with those of their coworkers, it is argued that the intrafirm wage dispersion has an impact on the individual worker's productivity and thus on the average firm performance. However, there is no consensus regarding the precise impact of intrafirm wage dispersion on firm productivity. On the one hand, the single-period rank-order version of the tournament models (e.g., Lazear and Rosen 1981) stresses the positive influence of wage inequality within a firm on the worker's effort. This model suggests that firms should implement a differentiated prize structure and award the largest prize to the most

Thierry Lallemand is a lecturer, teaching assistant, and research fellow in the Department of Applied Economics (DULBEA) and the Center for Accounting and Management (Centre de Comptabilité et Contrôle de Gestion) at the Free University of Brussels. Robert Plasman is a professor and head of the Department of Applied Economics (DULBEA) at the Free University of Brussels. François Rycx is an associate professor of economics in the Department of Applied Economics (DULBEA) at the Free University of Brussels.

This paper is produced as part of a Targeted Socio-Economic Research (TSER) program on Pay Inequalities and Economic Performance (PIEP) financed by the European Commission (Contract no. HPSE-CT-1999-00040). It has evolved from earlier versions presented at the PIEP meetings (July 2003, London School of Economics; and January 2004, Université Libre de Bruxelles), the 9th Annual Meeting of the Society of Labor Economists (April 2004, San Antonio, Texas), the National Bureau of Economic Research (NBER) "Empirical Personnel Economics" workshop (August 2004, Cambridge, Massachusetts), and the European Commission "Employment, Productivity and Wage Structures in Europe: New Evidence from Linked Employer-Employee Data" workshop (April 2005, Brussels). We are most grateful to D. Cecchi, C. Dell'Aringa, C. Lucifora, and D. Marsden for helpful suggestions. We also thank Statistics Belgium for giving access to the Structure of Earnings Survey and the Structure of Business Survey. This paper is an extension of Lallemand, Plasman, and Rycx (2004).

productive worker. On the other hand, other theories argue for some wage compression within a firm by emphasizing the importance of fairness and cooperation among the workforce (e.g., Akerlof and Yellen 1990; Levine 1991).

Empirical studies, focusing on the relationship between wage disparities and firm performance, are not very numerous, and their results vary significantly. Due to a lack of appropriate data, these studies often rely on economy-wide inequality indicators or use self-constructed indicators of firm performance. Moreover, they are generally restricted to a specific segment of the labor force (e.g., the top management level) or a particular sector of the economy (e.g., the manufacturing sector, academic departments, professional team sports). In sum, the available evidence does not appear to be very compelling yet (Frick, Prinz, and Winkelmann 2003).

The aim of this chapter is twofold. First, we analyze the structure of wages within and between Belgian firms. Next, we examine how the productivity of these firms is influenced by their internal wage dispersion. Our study is based on a unique matched employer-employee data set. This data set derives from the combination of the 1995 Structure of Earnings Survey and the 1995 Structure of Business Survey. The former contains detailed information on firm characteristics (e.g., sector of activity, size of the firm, and level of wage bargaining) and on individual workers (e.g., gross hourly wages, bonuses, age, education, sex, and occupation). The latter provides firm-level information on financial variables (e.g., gross operating surplus, value added, and value of production).

To analyze the impact of wage dispersion on firm productivity, we followed the methodology developed by Winter-Ebmer and Zweimüller (1999). It rests on a two-step estimation procedure. First, we compute conditional intrafirm wage differentials by taking the standard errors of wage regressions run for each firm. Next, we use these conditional wage differentials as an explanatory variable in a firm-level productivity regression. However, as a sensitivity test, we also analyze the impact of unconditional indicators of intrafirm wage dispersion on firm productivity. These indicators include the standard deviation, the coefficient of variation, and the max-min ratio of the gross hourly wages within the firm. The productivity of a firm is measured by the value added per employee. We address the potential simultaneity problem between wage dispersion and firm productivity using information from the Belgian income tax system. More precisely, we apply two-stage least squares (2SLS) and instrument the dispersion of wages, *including* bonuses, by the intrafirm standard deviation of income taxes on gross earnings *excluding* bonuses.

To our knowledge, this chapter is one of the first to examine the effect of intrafirm wage dispersion on firm performance in the private sector using both a conditional wage inequality indicator and direct information on firm productivity. It is also one of the few, with Bingley and Eriksson (2001) and Heyman (2002), to consider potential simultaneity problems. Empirical findings, reported in this chapter, support the existence of a positive and significant relationship between wage inequality and firm productivity. Moreover, we find that the intensity of this relationship is larger for blue-collar workers and within firms with a high degree of monitoring. These results are more in line with the tournament models than with the fairness, morale, and cohesiveness models.

The remainder of this chapter is organized as follows. Section 6.2 reviews the literature (both theoretical and empirical) dealing with the impact of intrafirm wage dispersion on firm productivity. Section 6.3 summarizes the main features of the wage-bargaining process in the Belgian private sector. Sections 6.4 and 6.5 describe the data and variables as well as structure of wages within and between Belgian firms. The impact of intrafirm wage dispersion on firm productivity is analyzed in section 6.6. The last section concludes.

6.2   Review of the Literature

6.2.1   Theoretical Findings

A first interpretation of the relationship between within-firm wage dispersion and firm performance has been provided by Akerlof and Yellen (1988). On the basis of the effort version of the efficiency wage theory (Solow 1979), the authors argue that, in a firm where the workers' characteristics are not totally observable and where the monitoring of their actions is not perfect, employers have to find well-suited incentives to maximize the workers' effort. According to Akerlof and Yellen (1988), the effort function of a worker can be written as follows: $e = e[\sigma^2(w)]$, where e denotes the level of effort and $\sigma^2(w)$ the variance of wages within the firm. This expression shows that the worker's effort does not only depend on the wage level but also on the degree of salary dispersion within the firm. Using this expression, the authors argue that a compressed wage distribution improves labor relations and stimulates the average worker's effort. To put it differently, firms should achieve a greater output per worker if their wage dispersion is low.

Later, Akerlof and Yellen (1990) developed the fair wage-effort hypothesis. This hypothesis clarifies their previous reasoning by developing in greater detail the notion of fairness and introducing the concept of relative wages.[1] The basic idea is that workers often compare their wages either internally (i.e., with workers within the same firm) or externally (i.e., with

---

1. The fair wage-effort hypothesis is based on the social exchange theory in sociology (e.g., Blau 1955; Homans 1961) and on the equity theory in psychology (e.g., Adams 1963). Both theories show the existence of a relationship between effort and fairness.

workers in other firms or industries). Therefore, Akerlof and Yellen (1990) consider the following worker's effort function: $e = \min [(w / \hat{w}), 1]$, with w the actual wage, $\hat{w}$ the fair wage, and e equal to 1 if the level of effort is normal. This expression shows that workers reduce their effort if their actual wage falls short of the wage they regard as fair. According to the authors, a wage is generally considered as fair if the pay spread is lower than the performance differential. This means that a worker would act so as to preserve a certain equilibrium between the subjective value of input and the subjective value of return. Levine (1991) put forward this argument by stressing that pay compression within a firm where teamwork among employees is essential (i.e., participatory firms) sustains and stimulates cohesiveness, which increases the firm's total productivity.

The preceding notions of fairness, morale, and cohesiveness led Hibbs and Locking (2000) to define the following firm-level production function: $Q = \mathrm{Ef}[\sigma^2(w)]F(L, \ldots)$, with Q the real value added, $\mathrm{Ef}(.)$ the labor effectiveness depending on the within-firm wage dispersion, F a standard production function, and L the labor inputs to production. This expression shows that the performance of a firm depends positively upon the efficiency of labor, which is negatively correlated with the intrafirm wage dispersion (i.e., $\mathrm{Ef}' < 0$, $\mathrm{Ef}'' > 0$). As a result, this model of fairness, morale, and cohesiveness suggests that firms have a strong incentive to implement a wage distribution that is more compressed than the variation in workers' productivities.

A complementary theory promoting wage compression to increase firm performance has been developed by Milgrom (1988) and Milgrom and Roberts (1990). The authors emphasize that (white-collar) workers have incentives to (1) withhold information from managers in order to increase their influence and (2) engage in costly rent-seeking activities instead of productive work. They also argue that the implementation of some wage equity can reduce the potential tendency of workers to take personal interest decisions, which may not be profitable for the organization as a whole. Moreover, they stress that it is more costly to monitor the actions of white-collar workers. Therefore, lower levels of wage dispersion would be even more important for the latter.

In contrast to the previous literature, the relative compensation or *tournament* model, developed by Lazear and Rosen (1981), points to the benefits of a more dispersed wage structure, deriving from a performance-based pay system. This model suggests that managers should introduce a large spread in the rewards of workers in order to stimulate their effort. In other words, firms should establish a differentiated prize structure and award the largest prize to the most productive worker.[2] Formally, Lazear and Rosen

---

2. There is some ambiguity in the literature about the definition of a prize. It can be seen either as a promotion (i.e., to get a task with higher responsibilities and to rise in the firm hierarchy) or as a bonus.

(1981) consider two identical risk-neutral workers and a risk-neutral firm, with a compensation scheme such that the most productive worker receives a high wage (W_H) and the least productive a low wage (W_L). On the basis of these assumptions, the authors show that, ceteris paribus, workers' optimal level of effort (1) increases with prize dispersion ($W_H - W_L$) and (2) decreases with the random component of output (e.g., luck).[3] This model has been generalized by McLaughlin (1988) for n players. The author shows that the number of players matters and that the probability to win a game decreases with the number of contestants. Consequently, to stimulate workers' effort, there should be a positive correlation between the prize spread and the number of contestants.

Lazear (1989, 1995) argues, however, that high within-firm wage dispersion generates more competition between the workers, which may negatively affect firm performance. Indeed, considering an organization in which several workers are noncooperative or have a sabotage behavior (hawks), and others who are less aggressive (doves), the author shows that wage compression is crucial for firm performance.[4] The point is that the noncooperative activities adopted by hawks reduce the total effort level of the workers. In other words, the positive impact of an output-based pay system on firm performance may be offset by a lower level of work cohesion due to the sabotage behavior of hawks. As a result, it appears profitable for a firm to (1) adequately sort out workers before hiring them and (2) adjust the compensation scheme to the hierarchical level.

A further strand of the literature, developed by Frey (1997) and Frey and Osterloh (1997), focuses on the interplay between wage dispersion and intrinsic motivation.[5] This literature shows that the implementation of explicit incentive contracts (e.g., performance-based pay systems) can crowd out the intrinsic motivation of the workers by generating excessive external monitoring (in particular, for workers who need autonomy in their job and who have high responsibilities). However, it can also enhance intrinsic motivation by supporting the workers' own motivation, self-esteem, and feeling of competence. In sum, this literature emphasizes the importance of a correct match between the compensation scheme and the monitoring environment within a firm (Belfield and Marsden 2003).

6.2.2   Empirical Findings

Empirical studies examining the relationship between wage disparities and firm performance are not very numerous, and their results vary

---

3. For a discussion of Lazear and Rosen's (1981) model, see Gibbons and Waldman (1999).

4. According to Lazear (1989, 1995), hawks are often found at the top level of the organization; that is, mainly among white-collar workers. His arguments are thus in line with those of Milgrom (1988) and Milgrom and Roberts (1990). The counterproductive effect should be greatest within the higher echelons of the hierarchy.

5. It derives from the psychological literature that suggests that intrinsic motivation is the main driving force of workers' effort.

markedly. Due to a lack of appropriate data, these studies often rely on economy-wide inequality indicators or use self-constructed indicators of firm performance. Moreover, they are generally restricted to a specific segment of the labor force (e.g., the top-management level) or a particular sector of the economy (e.g., the manufacturing sector, academic departments, professional team sports). In what follows, we review the main features of these studies.[6]

A first strand of the empirical literature provides evidence in favor of the fairness, morale, and cohesiveness theory, developed by Akerlof and Yellen (1990) and Levine (1991). Cowherd and Levine (1992), for instance, examine the relationship between interclass pay equity and the performance of business units by integrating the body of equity, relative deprivation, and quality management theories.[7] Their study is based on data collected from 102 business units with more than 59 employees, in North America (72 percent) and Europe (28 percent). The performance of a business unit is measured by the quality of its production.[8] According to the authors, product quality is a good indicator of firm performance because it is (1) difficult for managers to control and (2) a function of the willingness of lower-level employees to contribute more than can formally be asked from them. Their empirical findings show the existence of a substantial positive relationship between interclass pay equity and product quality. The authors attribute this result to the impact of pay equity on three aspects of lower-level employee motivation: commitment to managerial goals, effort, and cooperation.

Pfeffer and Langton (1993) analyze how within-academic departments wage dispersion and pay schemes affect the individual's satisfaction, research performance, and cooperation, using a large sample of college and university faculty in the United Kingdom.[9] Their data set contains information on circa 17,000 college and university professors from 600 academic departments located in some 300 institutions.[10] Salary dispersion is measured by an unconditional indicator—that is, the coefficient of variation (the standard deviation divided by the mean) in salaries within a given academic department. Controlling for numerous predictors, the authors observe statistically and substantively significant negative effects of pay

---

6. For a summary, see appendix A.
7. Interclass pay equity is measured by the pay relation of hourly paid employees to top-three levels of management, controlling for the business size effect. A business unit is defined as any autonomous organizational unit that has top management with decision-making authority in areas like manufacturing and sales.
8. The latter is measured by customers in relative terms; that is, in comparison with the product quality of the main competitors of each business unit.
9. The data come from the Carnegie Commission's 1969 survey of college and university faculty.
10. The authors confined their attention to respondents in departments with a size of twenty or larger that had a response rate to the questionnaire greater than 50 percent.

dispersion. To put it differently, they find that, on average, people are less satisfied, do less collaboration on research, and have a lower productivity when the pay distribution is more dispersed. Moreover, results show that the extent to which wage dispersion produces adverse effects depends on one's position in the salary structure and factors such as information, commitment, consensus, and the level of certainty in the evaluation process.

A number of studies, essentially concentrated on the United States, have been devoted to the interaction between salary dispersion and performance in the team sports industry. Using mainly unconditional measures of wage inequality (e.g., the Gini index), these studies generally conclude that pay compression is beneficial for team performance (e.g., the win-loss percentage).[11] The study of Frick, Prinz, and Winkelmann (2003) is the first to attempt to measure the impact of pay inequalities on the performance of professional team sports across different leagues. Their approach enables them to implicitly control for the influence of different institutional regimes and production technologies. Using panel data from the four major North American sports leagues (i.e., baseball, basketball, football, and hockey), their study supports neither the fairness, morale, and cohesiveness hypotheses nor the tournament theories. Indeed, findings vary substantially between the four leagues. According to their estimates, a higher degree of intrateam wage dispersion is beneficial to the performance of professional basketball and hockey teams.[12] However, the reverse relationship is found for football and baseball teams; that is, a team is more successful if its pay distribution is more compressed. The authors attribute the diversity in their results to the different degrees of cooperation requirements in the four leagues.

Another strand of the empirical literature offers evidence in favor of the tournament theory developed by Lazear and Rosen (1981). Winter-Ebmer and Zweimüller (1999), for instance, investigate the impact of intrafirm wage dispersion on firm performance using panel data covering the whole Austrian workforce for the period 1975 to 1991.[13] They measure within-firm wage inequality by the standard errors of firm-level wage equations. This conditional indicator controls for the composition of the workforce within each firm.[14] Unfortunately, the authors did not observe the financial performance of the firms. As a result, they have constructed their own per-

11. For professional baseball teams, see Bloom (1999), DeBrock, Hendricks, and Koenker (2001), Depken (2000), Harder (1992), or Richards and Guell (1998). For soccer and hockey teams, see, respectively, Lehmann and Wacker (2000) and Gomez (2002).

12. For hockey teams, the coefficient is positive but not significantly different from zero.

13. Their sample is restricted to firms with more than twenty employees and with at least four data points.

14. The data report monthly earnings that are top coded. The explanatory variables in the tobit wage regressions, run separately for each firm, include age, age squared, and dummies for sex, blue-collar, foreigner, and two tenure dummies. Information on education levels is not available.

formance indicator—that is, standardized wages. Of course, this instrument is not perfectly adequate. Be it as it may, controlling for several predictors, their findings suggest the existence of a positive and hump-shaped relationship between intrafirm wage dispersion and firm performance, for both blue- and white-collar workers. Yet the overall pattern appears more monotonic for blue-collar workers. These findings are in line with the hypothesis that too little wage inequality negatively affects firm performance due to a lack of incentives. However, they also suggest that excessive wage dispersion can be harmful for productivity because of fairness effects. According to the authors, the contrasting results for blue- and white-collar workers appear to be consistent both with theories of intrinsic motivation and rent-seeking and with the prevalence of piece rates in blue-collar jobs.

Hibbs and Locking (2000) examine the effects of changes in the overall wage dispersion during the periods 1964 to 1993 and 1972 to 1993 on the productive efficiency of Swedish industries and plants. To do so, they first decompose the total variance in individual wages *within* and *between* plants (and industries). Next, they integrate the squared coefficients of variation of these components at the plant (or industry) level in an Akerlof and Yellen's (1990) type of production function. The dependent variable in this equation—that is, their performance indicator—is the log of real value added at the plant (or industry) level.[15] Their empirical findings do not confirm that wage leveling within plants and industries enhance productivity. Therefore, they do not support the fairness, morale, and cohesiveness theories.

Bingley and Eriksson (2001) analyze the impact of pay spread and skewness on two performance indicators—that is, firm productivity and employee effort. Their study uses longitudinal matched employer-employee data comprising information on Danish medium and large private-sector firms during the period 1992 to 1995. It is the first to address potential simultaneity problems using information from the income tax system. Firm productivity and employee effort are estimated by the total factor productivity and the sickness absence, respectively. Differences in firm productivity effects between the occupational groups and types of firms give support to the theories of fairness, tournaments, and tastes for skewness. In contrast, individual effort effects only back up the tournament theory.

Finally, a number of papers present evidence on the interaction between the pay structure of top executives and firm performance. Focusing on managers in large U.S. firms, Leonard (1990) finds no significant relationship between the standard deviation of pay and firm performance—that is,

---

15. Their production function is as follows: $\ln (Q) = \ln [Ef[\sigma^2(w)] F(.)]$, where $Ef[\sigma^2(w)] = Ef[CV^2(W), CV^2(B)]$. In this expression, Q represent the real value-added, $Ef(.)$ the labor effectiveness depending on $\sigma^2(w)$ (i.e., the total variation in individual wages), and $F(.)$ a standard production function (e.g., Cobb-Douglas, CES, or Translog). $CV^2(W)$ and $CV^2(B)$ stand, respectively, for the within and between components of the total variance of individual wages (squared coefficient of variation) among workers' assortment by plants (or industries).

the return on investment. In contrast, using respectively U.S. and Swedish data, Main, O'Reilly, and Wade (1993) and Eriksson (1999) report a positive impact of top executive pay dispersion on firm performance. The latter is measured by returns on assets and the profits-sales ratio, respectively. The paper of Heyman (2002) is the first to explicitly control for firm differences in human capital when testing several predictions from the tournament theory for white-collar workers and, in particular, managers.[16] Potential endogeneity problems are addressed using lagged predetermined values of wage dispersion. On the basis of a large matched employer-employee data set for the Swedish economy in 1991 and 1995, the author finds a positive effect of wage dispersion on profits.

6.3   Wage Bargaining in Belgium

Before describing our data set and turning to the empirical analysis, we briefly summarize the main features of the wage bargaining process in the Belgian private sector.

In the countries of North America, the legal provisions offer workers the possibility of voting for or against their companies' joining a union in elections supervised by the public authorities. This means that the union can earn the exclusive right to represent all the workers, whether union members or not, in bargaining with the employers. Yet as the majority of the collective agreements are negotiated at the level of the individual companies, the institutional system leads to a clear distinction between the unionized establishments—in other words, those that are subject to a collective agreement—and the nonunionized establishments. Hence, the rate of unionization provides a good approximation of the coverage rate or the bargaining regime.

In Belgium, as in the majority of European countries, the situation is very different. The point is that wage bargaining in the Belgian private sector occurs at three levels: the national (interprofessional) level, the sectoral level, and the company level. They generally occur every two years on a pyramidal basis. In principle, they are inaugurated by a national collective agreement defining a minimum level in wage terms. This national agreement can be improved within every sector of activity. Then we have the company negotiations, where the sectoral collective agreements may be renegotiated, except where there is a so-called imperative clause. However, these cannot give rise to a collective agreement that would run counter to the sectoral or national agreements. In other words, the wage bargained at the firm level can only be greater or equal to the wage set at the national or industry level.

---

16. His conditional indicator of wage dispersion is the same as in Winter-Ebmer and Zweimüller (1999).

Belgium is characterized, in addition, by a coverage rate of about 90 percent (Organization for Economic Cooperation and Development [OECD] 1997, 2002). This stems from the fact that nonunionized workers, like employers not members of an employers' organization, are generally covered by a collective labor agreement. The point is that Article 19 of the law dated 5 December 1968 specifies that a collective agreement is automatically binding on the signatory organizations, employers who are members of those organizations or who have personally concluded the agreement, employers joining those organizations after the date of the conclusion of the agreement, and finally, all workers, *whether unionized or not*, who are employed by an employer so bound. Moreover, most of the sectoral collective agreements have been rendered obligatory by Royal Decree. This means that they apply compulsorily to all companies in the sector and to their workers, *whether or not they are members* of the signatory organizations (employers' organizations or unions).[17]

To sum up, unlike in the United States or Canada, the bargaining regime in companies in the Belgian private sector does not derive directly from the latter's union membership. It is reflected more through the level of wage bargaining. The heart of the wage bargaining lies at the sectoral level in Belgium. However, in certain cases, sectoral agreements are renegotiated (improved) within individual companies.[18]

6.4   Data and Variables

Our analysis is based on a unique combination of two large-scale data sets. The first, conducted by Statistics Belgium,[19] is the 1995 Structure of Earnings Survey (SES). It covers all Belgian firms employing at least ten workers and with economic activities within sections C to K of the Nace Rev. 1 nomenclature. It thus encompasses the following sectors: mining and quarrying (C); manufacturing (D); electricity and water supply (E); construction (F); wholesale and retail trade; repair of motor vehicles, motorcycles, and personal and household goods (G); hotels and restaurants (H); transport, storage, and communication (I); financial intermediation

17. The trade union density in Belgium stands at around 54 percent (OECD 1997, 2002).
18. These institutional features are crucial to understand why Belgium has a relatively compressed wage distribution and how the wage setting system could be changed to generate more wage inequalities. Although the literature on wage dispersion and collective bargaining in corporatist countries is still limited and to some extent mixed (Dell'Aringa and Lucifora 1994; Dell'Aringa and Pagani 2007; Dominguez and Rodriguez-Gutiérrez 2004; Plasman, Rusinek, and Rycx 2007; Rycx 2003), results for Belgium suggest that company collective agreements increase (slightly) wage dispersion compared to multi-employer agreements. Hence, one way to raise intra-firm wage inequalities might be to decentralise the wage bargaining process from the sectoral to the firm level. Yet, great caution is required as results on the relationship between wage inequality and the level of collective wage bargaining are still fragile.
19. This is according to the instructions given by Eurostat (E-U regulation Nr. 2744/95).

(J); and real estate, renting, and business activities (K). The survey contains a wealth of information, provided by the management of the firms, both on the characteristics of the firms (e.g., sector of activity, number of workers, level of collective wage bargaining, type of economic and financial control, region) and on the individual employees (e.g., age, educational level, tenure, gross earnings, paid hours, sex, occupation, type of contract, annual bonuses).[20] Gross hourly wages, *without* bonuses,[21] are calculated by dividing total gross earnings (including earnings for overtime hours and premiums for shift work, night work, or weekend work) in the reference period (October 1995) by the corresponding number of total paid hours (including paid overtime hours). In contrast, gross hourly wages, *with* bonuses, are obtained by adding to the gross hourly wages (without bonuses) the annual bonuses divided by (1) the number of month to which the bonuses correspond and (2) the number of total paid hours in the reference period, respectively.

Unfortunately, the SES provides no financial information. This is why the SES has been combined with the 1995 Structure of Business Survey (SBS). It is a firm-level survey, conducted by Statistics Belgium, with a different coverage than the SES in that it includes neither the financial sector (Nace J) nor the firms with less then 20 employees. Both data sets have been merged by Statistics Belgium using the firm social security number. The SBS provides firm-level information on financial variables such as sales, value added, production value, gross operating surplus and value of purchased goods and services.

The final sample, combining both data sets, covers 34,969 individuals working for 1,498 firms.[22] It is representative of all firms employing at least twenty workers within sections C to K of the Nace Revision 1 nomenclature, with the exception of the financial sector.

20. The SES is a stratified sample. The stratification criteria refer respectively to the region (NUTS1), the principal economic activity (NACE-groups) and the size of the firm (determined by the data obtained from the Social Security Organisation). The sample size in each stratum depends on the size of the firm. Sampling percentages of firms equal respectively 10, 50, and 100 percent when the number of workers is lower than 50, between 50 and 99, and above 100. Within a firm, sampling percentages of employees also depend on size. Sampling percentages of employees reach respectively 100, 20, and 10 percent when the number of workers is lower than 50, between 50 and 99, and above 100. The consequence of these stratification criteria is that the number of data points depends upon firm size. For this reason, wage inequality indicators computed in sections 6.5 and 6.6 may be slightly biased. Finally, let us also notice that no threshold at the upper limit of wages is to be found in the SES. To put it differently, wages are not censored. For an extended description of the SES, see Demunter (2000).

21. Annual bonuses include irregular payments that do not occur during each pay period, such as pay for holiday, thirteenth month, or profit-sharing.

22. If we only consider full-time employees (i.e., individuals working a minimum thirty hours per week) and firms with at least twenty-five workers, our sample still covers 31,788 individuals working for 1,445 firms.

6.5   Structure of Wages within and between Firms

In this section, we analyze the structure of gross hourly wages, with and without bonuses, in the Belgian private sector. In particular, we focus on the dispersion of wages within and between firms. Between firms, wage dispersion is measured by the standard deviation of each firm's mean wage. Within firms, wage inequality is estimated by the mean over all firms of each firm's standard deviation, coefficient of variation, and max-min ratio of wages, respectively. As agreed, we only consider full-time employees (i.e., individuals working a minimum thirty hours per week) and firms with at least twenty-five workers. Statistics on the structure of wages have been computed for the overall sample as well as by firm size (i.e., number of employees below *or* above 100), level of collective wage agreement (i.e., only national or sectoral collective agreement *versus* firm-level collective agreement) and composition of the workforce (i.e., majority of blue- *versus* white-collar workers). Qualitative results are similar for gross hourly wages with and without bonuses. Therefore, in what follows, we solely comment on the latter.[23]

6.5.1   Overall Sample

Table 6.1 shows that, for the overall sample, the mean individual gross hourly wage stands at 12.25 EUR, with a standard deviation equal to 5.38. We also find that the dispersion of wages between firms is slightly higher than within firms (3.01 versus 2.90). Moreover, there appears to be a positive and significant correlation between the average and standard deviation of wages within firms. Thus, results suggest that high-paying firms are characterized by a more dispersed wage structure.

6.5.2   Firm Size

Besides, we see that the mean and dispersion of wages increase with firm size. We also notice that for both small and large firms (1) the correlation between the average and standard deviation of wages within firms remains positive and significant, and (2) the wage inequality between firms is slightly larger than the wage inequality within firms. However, wage dispersion within and between firms rises with firm size.

The positive relationship between wages and firm size is in line with neoclassical and institutional arguments supporting the existence of a positive size-wage premium. These arguments suggest inter alia that large employers (1) hire more qualified workers (e.g., Hamermesh 1980; Kremer and Maskin 1996; Troske 1999), (2) compensate for bad working conditions, (3) have more market power and share their excess profits with their workers (e.g., Mellow 1982; Slichter 1950; Weiss 1966), (4) avoid or mimic

---

23. Statistics on the structure of gross hourly wages with bonuses are reported in appendix B.

Table 6.1 Structure of wages (without bonuses) within and between firms, 1995

	Overall sample[a]	Firm size		Level of wage bargaining			Workforce composition	
		Small firms (25–99 workers)	Large firms (≥100 workers)	CA only at national and/or sectoral level	Firm level CA	Other or no CA	Majority blue-collar workers	Majority white-collar workers
Average wages[c]	12.25	11.03	12.77	11.67	12.88	11.75	n.a.	n.a.
SD[b]	5.38	4.80	5.53	5.65	5.00	5.56	n.a.	n.a.
25th percentile	9.10	8.45	9.50	8.62	9.88	8.58	n.a.	n.a.
75th percentile	13.52	11.82	14.12	12.59	14.24	12.63	n.a.	n.a.
No. of workers	31,788	9,450	22,338	14,123	15,713	1,952	n.a.	n.a.
Average of firm average wage[d]	11.10	10.80	11.91	10.93	11.60	10.68	9.92	12.22
SD	3.01	2.83	3.33	3.06	2.76	3.21	1.73	3.51
25th percentile	9.16	9.08	9.68	9.10	9.88	8.90	8.70	9.69
75th percentile	12.47	12.07	13.38	12.11	12.91	12.08	10.87	13.80
No. of firms	1,445	590	855	795	530	120	760	685
Average of SD[b] of wage[d]	2.90	2.79	3.21	2.87	2.96	2.94	1.80	3.95
SD	2.53	2.38	2.88	2.61	2.36	2.46	1.33	2.92
25th percentile	1.19	1.15	1.27	1.12	1.44	1.02	0.82	1.82
75th percentile	4.03	3.76	4.45	4.04	3.93	4.28	2.30	5.20
No. of firms	1,445	590	855	795	530	120	760	685
Average CV of wage[d]	0.24	0.24	0.24	0.24	0.24	0.25	0.17	0.30
SD	0.14	0.14	0.15	0.15	0.14	0.15	0.11	0.15
25th percentile	0.13	0.13	0.13	0.12	0.14	0.11	0.09	0.19
75th percentile	0.33	0.32	0.34	0.33	0.32	0.33	0.23	0.38
No. of firms	1,445	590	855	795	530	120	760	685

(continued)

Table 6.1 (continued)

	Overall sample[a]	Firm size		Level of wage bargaining			Workforce composition	
		Small firms (25–99 workers)	Large firms (≥100 workers)	CA only at national and/or sectoral level	Firm level CA	Other or no CA	Majority blue-collar workers	Majority white-collar workers
Average max.-min. ratio of wage[d]	2.61	2.63	2.58	2.56	2.62	2.99	2.04	3.16
SD	1.58	1.62	1.45	1.44	1.64	2.13	1.06	1.78
25th percentile	1.54	1.56	1.50	1.54	1.54	1.46	1.39	1.91
75th percentile	3.16	3.14	3.22	3.15	3.12	3.37	2.36	3.76
No. of firms	1,445	590	855	795	530	120	760	685
Correlation (average wage, SD of wage)[d]	0.820***	0.812***	0.840***	0.832***	0.800***	0.832***	0.630***	0.821***

Notes: CA = collective agreement on wages; SD = standard deviation; CV = coefficient of variation of wage (SD of wage/average of wage); n.a. = not applicable.

[a]These statistics refer to the weighted sample only covering full-time workers in firms employing at least twenty-five employees.

[b]Individual gross hourly wages (in EUR) include overtime paid, premiums for shift work, night work, and/or weekend work.

[c]Observation = a person.

[d]Observation = a firm.

***Indicates that the Pearson correlation coefficient is significant at the 1% level.

unionization (e.g., Brown, Hamilton, and Medoff 1990; Voos 1983), and (5) substitute high monitoring costs with wage premiums (e.g., Eaton and White 1983; Garen 1985; Lucas 1978; Oi 1983; Stigler 1962).[24] How are we to explain that both within- and between-firms wage dispersion increases with firm size? Davis and Haltiwanger (1996) argue that because large firms are more technologically diversified (horizontally and vertically), their workforce is more heterogeneous. Hence, within-firms wage dispersion is likely to rise with employer size. However, in contrast to our findings, the authors expect between-firms wage dispersion to fall with firm size (due to the life-cycle dynamics of firms). Another factor that can explain higher wage dispersion within large firms is linked to the tournament theory (Lazear and Rosen 1981). The tournament theory points to the benefits of a more dispersed wage structure, deriving from a performance-based pay system. In other words, this theory suggests that firms should establish a prize structure and award the largest prize to the most productive worker. Moreover, according to McLaughlin (1988), to stimulate the workers' effort, there should be positive correlation between the prize spread and the number of contestants. Because the number of contestants is likely to rise with firm size, one may expect a more dispersed wage structure within large firms.[25]

6.5.3   Level of Wage Bargaining

As expected, table 6.1 indicates that, on average, workers, whose wages are renegotiated collectively at the firm level, earn higher wages. This result is in line with earlier findings for Belgium. Using the Oaxaca-Blinder decomposition, Rycx (2003) reports indeed that, ceteris paribus, workers covered by a company collective agreement (CA) earn 5.1 percent more than their opposite numbers who are (solely) covered by the national or sectoral CAs. A similar finding is found by Plasman, Rusinek, and Rycx (2007). Table 6.1 also shows that while within-firms wage dispersion is higher when wages are renegotiated collectively in house, between-firms wage dispersion is larger when wages are solely covered by a national or sectoral CA. Although caution is required, these findings suggest that the bargaining regime has a significant impact on the structure of wages even in a corporatist country like Belgium.[26]

---

24. Empirical evidence on the firm-size wage premium in Belgium and across European countries is provided by Lallemand, Plasman, and Rycx (2005a, b).
25. Davis and Haltiwanger (1996) for the United States and Lallemand and Rycx (2006) for European countries provided empirical evidence on how and why the wage distribution differs among firms of different sizes.
26. For more evidence on this issue, see, for example, Card and de la Rica (2006), Dell'Aringa and Pagani (2007), Dominguez and Rodriguez-Gutiérrez (2004), Rodriguez-Gutiérrez (2001).

6.5.4   Composition of the Workforce

Finally, let us also note that (1) the mean wage is around 2.3 EUR higher within firms employing a majority of white-collar workers, and (2) the structure of wages is more compressed when blue-collar workers compose the majority of the workforce.

6.6   Wage Inequality and Firm Productivity

In this section, we analyze the impact of intrafirm wage dispersion on firm productivity in the Belgian private sector.

6.6.1   Methodology and Indicators

There are several ways to compute intrafirm wage inequality. On the one hand, wage dispersion can be measured between unequal workers by unconditional indicators (e.g., the Gini index, the white-collar–blue-collar wage ratio, or the pay gap between managers and the rest of the workforce). On the other hand, it can be defined for workers with similar observable characteristics. In this case, wage dispersion is measured by the residual inequality, after controlling for human capital variables.

Although unconditional indexes may have appeal if the analysis focuses on the effect of the chief executive officer's (CEO) pay on firm performance, many theories like tournaments or hawks and doves refer to wage differentials between similar workers (Winter-Ebmer and Zweimüller 1999). As a result, a conditional indicator appears more appropriate for our study. Hence, we follow the methodology developed by Winter-Ebmer and Zweimüller (1999). However, as a sensitivity test, we also analyze the impact of three unconditional indicators of intrafirm wage dispersion on firm productivity. These indicators include the standard deviation, the coefficient of variation, and the max-min ratio of the gross hourly wages within the firm.

The methodology of Winter-Ebmer and Zweimüller (1999) rests upon a two-step estimation procedure. In the first step, we estimate by ordinary least squares (OLS) the following wage equation for each firm:

$$(1) \qquad \ln W_{ij} = \alpha_0 + \alpha_1' \, \mathbf{Y}_{ij} + \varepsilon_{ij},$$

where W_{ij} is the gross hourly wage (with bonuses) of worker i in firm j; $\mathbf{Y}_{ij}$ is a vector of individual characteristics including age, age squared, sex, education (two dummies), and occupation (one dummy); and ε_{ij} is the usual error term. The standard errors of these regressions (σ_j) are used as a measure of conditional intrafirm wage dispersion.

In the second step, we estimate by OLS the following firm-level performance regression:

$$(2) \qquad \ln P_j = \beta_0 + \beta_1' \sigma_j + \beta_2' X_j + \beta_3' Z_j + \upsilon_j,$$

where P_j is the productivity of firm j, σ_j is the conditional indicator of the intrafirm wage dispersion, X_j contains aggregated characteristics of workers, Z_j includes employer characteristics, and υ_j is the usual error term. The productivity of a firm (P_j) is measured by the value added (at factor costs) per employee. It is obtained by dividing the firm annual gross operating income (plus subsidies, minus indirect taxes) by the number of workers in the firm. The main explanatory variable in equation (2) is the conditional intrafirm wage dispersion (σ_j) estimated in step 1. Equation (2) contains numerous control variables for the composition of the workforce (X_j) as well as for firm characteristics (Z_j). These control variables include the share of the workforce that (1) at most has attended lower secondary school, (2) has more than ten years of tenure, and (3) is younger than twenty-five and older than fifty years, respectively. The share of women, the share of blue-collar workers, the share of workers supervising coworkers, sectoral affiliation (five dummies), the size of the firm (the number of workers), and the level of wage bargaining (two dummies) are also included.

An important problem to consider is the potential simultaneity between productivity and wage dispersion. Indeed, it may be argued that highly productive firms pay larger bonuses, which in turn leads to more wage inequality. We address this issue using information from the income tax system. More precisely, we use two-stage least squares (2SLS) and instrument the dispersion of wages *including* bonuses by the intrafirm standard deviation of income taxes on gross earnings *excluding* bonuses. Of course, it is very difficult to find an appropriate instrument for intrafirm wage inequality. However, we believe that our instrument is of potential interest for breaking the simultaneity problem between productivity and wage dispersion because it is less affected by rent sharing. In other words, we expect the intrafirm standard deviation of income taxes on gross earnings *excluding* bonuses to be uncorrelated (or at least less correlated) with the error term and highly correlated with the endogenous variable (i.e., wage dispersion). Statistics on workers' income taxes, available in our data set, have been estimated by Statistics Belgium. To do so, Statistics Belgium relied on individual gross annual earnings, excluding bonuses and social security contributions (13.07 percent). After deduction of professional costs, they obtained the assessable income. From this, they derived the base income tax (seven different scales), the municipality taxes (7 percent),[27] the supplementary crisis contribution (3 percent), and the special social security contribution (six different scales). The sum of these four elements provides an estimation of the individual income taxes.[28]

---

27. Statistics Belgium had no information on the workers municipality of residence. Therefore, they applied the average municipality tax (7 percent) to all employees.
28. The most important restriction of these estimates is that they do not consider the specific situation of the employee, for example, composition of the family. For more information, see Demunter (2000).

6.6.2   Descriptive Statistics

The first step of our estimation procedure requires a large number of data points per firm. Therefore, our sample has been restricted to firms with at least 200 workers. This restriction guarantees a minimum of ten observations per firm. Our definitive sample is representative of all firms employing at least 200 workers within sections D to K of the Nace Rev. 1 nomenclature, with the exception of hotels and restaurants (H) and the financial sector (J).[29] It covers 17,490 individuals working for 397 firms. The mean number of data points per firm is forty-four, and for 75 percent of the firms, there are between ten and forty-one observations.

Table 6.2 depicts the means and standard deviations of selected variables.[30] We note that, on average, the value added per employee amounts to 61,344 EUR and that the residual pay inequality is equal to 0.17. Moreover, we find that the estimated intrafirm wage dispersion is highest when measured by the max-min ratio, that the mean age is around thirty-seven years, and that, on average, approximately 26 percent of the workers are women, 48 percent are blue collar, and 42 percent have a low level of education (i.e., lower secondary school at most). Finally, table 6.2 shows that, on average, firms employ 480 workers and are essentially concentrated in the manufacturing sector (64 percent); wholesale and retail trade, repair of motor vehicles (19 percent); and real estate, renting, and business activities (11 percent).

6.6.3   Empirical Analysis

Basic Specification

Table 6.3 reports our estimates of the effect of wage dispersion on firm productivity. These estimates are obtained by applying respectively OLS and 2SLS, with White (1980) heteroscedasticity consistent standard errors, to equation (2).

Findings, obtained from OLS regressions, emphasize the existence of a positive and significant relationship between intrafirm wage dispersion and firm productivity. Overall, the point estimates range between 1.25 and 0.08, which yields an elasticity of between 0.25 and 0.14 at sample means. These results suggest that, on average, a rise of 10 percent in wage inequal-

---

29. Our sample is representative of all firms employing at least 200 workers within the following sectors: (1) manufacturing (D), (2) electricity, gas, and water supply (E), (3) construction (F), (4) wholesale and retail trade; repair of motor vehicles, motorcycles, and personal and household goods (G), (5) transport, storage, and communication (I), and (6) real estate, renting, and business activities (K). The mining and quarrying sector (C) and the hotels and restaurants (H) are not part of our final sample because almost all firms in these sectors employ less than 200 workers.

30. For a detailed description, see appendixes C and D.

Table 6.2   **Means and standard deviations of selected variables**

	Mean	SD
Value-added per employee at factor costs[a] (in thousands of EUR)	61.34	1,618.9
Residual pay inequality[b]	0.17	0.07
Standard deviation of wages[c]	0.24	0.10
Coefficient of variation of wages[c]	0.29	0.14
Max.-min. ratio of wages[c]	3.17	1.60
Age (years)	37.2	9.6
Female	25.9	
Education		
No degree, primary/lower secondary	41.5	
General upper secondary, technical/artistic/prof. upper secondary	38.8	
Higher nonuniversity, university, and post graduate	19.7	
Blue-collar workers	48.4	
Size of the firm (no. of workers)	480.4	621.1
Sector		
Manufacturing (D)	63.5	
Electricity, gas, and water supply (E)	0.2	
Construction (F)	3.6	
Wholesale and retail trade; repair of motor vehicles (G)	18.6	
Transport, storage, and communication (I)	3.7	
Real estate, renting, and business activities (K)	10.6	
No. of employees		17,490
No. of firms		397

Notes: The descriptive statistics refer to the weighted sample.

[a]Estimated by the firm annual gross operating income per worker (plus subsidies, minus indirect taxes).

[b]Conditional measure of the intrafirm wage dispersion (i.e., standard errors of wage regressions run for each firm separately).

[c]Individual gross hourly wages include overtime paid, premiums for shift work, night work, and/or weekend work and bonuses (i.e., irregular payments that do not occur during each pay period, such as pay for holiday, 13th month, and profit sharing).

ity increases firm productivity by between 2.5 and 1.4 percent.[31] Yet it could be argued that because of the potential simultaneity between productivity and wage dispersion, OLS estimates are not only biased but also inconsistent.[32] To account for this problem, we run 2SLS regressions instrumenting the dispersion of wages *including* bonuses by the intrafirm standard deviation of income taxes on gross earnings *excluding* bonuses. Results from these regressions, presented in table 6.3, confirm the positive

31. Similar positive and significant results have been found for the unconditional indicators when we extended our sample to all firms with twenty workers or more. These results are available on request. Yet due to a limited number of data points within small firms, we were not able to determine whether this is also the case using a conditional indicator.

32. Hausman's (1976) specification error tests, reported in table 6.3, support the existence of a simultaneity problem.

Table 6.3 Effect of wage inequality on firm productivity, OLS versus 2SLS

| | Value added per employee[a] (ln) | | | | | | | |
	OLS				2SLS			
Intercept	7.22***	7.20***	7.27***	7.49***	6.92***	7.05***	7.12***	7.60***
	(0.27)	(0.27)	(0.27)	(0.26)	(0.26)	(0.27)	(0.28)	(0.27)
RPI[b]	1.25***				4.38***			
	(0.45)				(0.72)			
SD of wages[c]		1.03***				2.09***		
		(0.27)				(0.36)		
CV of wages[c]			0.48***				1.47***	
			(0.20)				(0.27)	
Max.-min. ratio of wages[c]				0.08***				0.13***
				(0.02)				(0.02)
Worker characteristics[d]	Yes	Yes	Yes	Yes	Yes	Yes	Yes	Yes
Firm characteristics[e]	Yes	Yes	Yes	Yes	Yes	Yes	Yes	Yes
Adjusted R^2	0.53	0.54	0.53	0.55	0.44	0.52	0.48	0.53
F-stat	130.43***	136.62***	126.69***	134.75***	138.59***	145.04***	132.77***	143.03***
Hausman test: p-value					0.00	0.00	0.00	0.00
No. of employees	17,490	17,490	17,490	17,490	17,490	17,490	17,490	17,490
No. of firms	397	397	397	397	397	397	397	397

Notes: Dependent variable = value added per employee (ln). RPI = residual pay inequality; SD = standard deviation; CV = coefficient of variation. White (1980) heteroscedasticity consistent standard errors are reported in parentheses.

[a]Estimated by the firm annual gross operating income per worker (plus subsidies, minus indirect taxes).

[b]Conditional measure of the intrafirm wage dispersion (i.e., standard errors of wage regressions run for each firm separately).

[c]Individual gross hourly wages include overtime paid, premiums for shift work, night work, and/or weekend work and bonuses (i.e., irregular payments that do not occur during each pay period, such as pay for holiday, 13th month, and profit sharing).

[d]Share of the workforce that (1) at most has attended lower secondary school, (2) has more than ten years of tenure, and (3) is younger than twenty-five and older than fifty years, respectively. The share of women, the share of blue-collar workers, and the share of the workers supervising coworkers are also included.

[e]Sectoral affiliation (five dummies), size of the firm (number of workers), and level of wage bargaining (two dummies).

***Significant at the 1 percent level.

and significant impact of wage dispersion on productivity. Moreover, we find that the elasticity between wage dispersion and productivity is significantly larger when using 2SLS. At sample means, the elasticity now stands at between 0.75 and 0.43. This means that, on average, when wage dispersion increases by 10 percent, firm productivity rises by between 7.5 and 4.3 percent.[33]

How are we to interpret these results? The positive impact of wage dispersion on firm productivity tends to support the tournament models (Lazear and Rosen, 1981). Indeed, these models demonstrate that if the workforce is relatively homogeneous, wage differentials stimulate workers' effort and their productivity. To put it differently, these models suggest that firms should establish a differentiated prize structure and award the largest prize to the most productive workers. Lazear's model (1989, 1995) of hawks and doves suggests that it is profitable for a firm to (1) adequately sort out workers at the hiring stage and (2) adjust the compensation scheme to the characteristics of the workforce (i.e., the hierarchical level). This model shows that if the majority of the workforce adopts a sabotage or noncooperative behavior, a more compressed wage structure should be preferred. According to this theory, our sample is essentially composed of doves. To put it in another way, it is because the majority of the workforce adopts a cooperative behavior that firms can achieve a higher productivity by implementing a more dispersed wage structure. However, our findings offer no support to the fairness, morale, and cohesiveness theories (Akerlof and Yellen 1990; Levine 1991). Indeed, these theories suggest a negative relationship between intra-firm wage dispersion and firm productivity.

Composition of the Workforce

According to the "new economics of personnel" (Lazear 1995), we should expect the elasticity of firm productivity with respect to pay inequality to be influenced by the composition of the workforce. In particular, various theories suggest that the relationship between pay dispersion

33. To test for a hump-shaped relationship, three methods have been used. Firstly, we added within-firm wage inequality indicators in quadratic form to our regression model. Results obtained with OLS were inconclusive because of a strong multicollinearity between indicators in level and squared. However, 2SLS estimates showed a significant positive and hump-shaped pattern for three instrumented wage inequality indicators, that is, the standard deviation, the coefficient of variation, the max-min ratio of wages. Next, we divided our sample into two homogeneous parts containing low and high inequality firms, respectively. The idea was to test whether the impact of wage inequality on firm productivity is larger in low inequality firms. Using OLS, we found no significant differences in the elasticities for both subsamples (with the exception of the max-min ratio of wages). In contrast, 2SLS estimates supported, for all instrumented wage inequality indicators, the existence of a positive and hump-shaped relationship between wage dispersion and firm productivity. Finally, we tested for a nonlinear relationship using dummy variables (two or more) indicating the magnitude of the intrafirm wage inequality. This methodology led to insignificant results using both OLS and 2SLS regressions. In sum, we found some evidence in favor of a hump-shaped relationship. However, results (available on request) were not very robust.

and firm productivity depends upon the proportion of white- and blue-collar workers within the firm. In this section, we test this hypothesis by letting our intrafirm wage dispersion indicators interact with a dummy variable that is equal to 1 if the share of white-collar workers within the firm is larger than 50 percent and zero otherwise. The results of this new specification are presented in table 6.4.

Whatever the indicator used for intrafirm wage dispersion, OLS estimates show that the intensity of the relationship between pay dispersion and productivity is significantly lower in firms that are essentially composed of white-collar workers. Indeed, the point estimates vary between 1.70 and 0.09 for blue-collar workers and between 0.79 and 0.05 for white-collar workers. At sample means, this yields an elasticity of between 0.39 and 0.26 for blue-collar workers and of between 0.14 and 0.06 for white-collar workers. In sum, results suggest that following a 10 percent rise in wage inequality, productivity increases by approximately 2.1 percentage points more within firms that are essentially composed of blue-collar workers. The 2SLS estimates, reported in table 6.4, confirm that the elasticity between wage dispersion and productivity is positive and substantially larger within firms with a majority of blue-collar workers. Yet caution is required because regression coefficients associated to the interaction variables are only significant at the 15 percent level. As in the basic specification, 2SLS point estimates are larger than those obtained by OLS. Using 2SLS, the elasticity, at sample means, ranges between 0.57 and 0.30 for white-collar workers and between 0.91 and 0.55 for blue-collar workers, respectively. These findings suggest that if wage dispersion rises by 10 percent, productivity increases by approximately 2.9 percentage points more in firms essentially composed of blue-collar workers.

Why is the effect of pay dispersion on firm performance different for blue- and white-collar workers? As suggested by Winter-Ebmer and Zweimüller (1999), a first possible explanation is that piece rates are more frequently used in firms with a majority of blue-collar workers. The point is that the implementation of piece rates increases wage dispersion but also productivity because, in general, workers will put in more effort, and top performers will stay in these firms. Another argument may be that, on average, white-collar workers have a higher degree of autonomy in their jobs, more responsibilities, and superior career prospects (Winter-Ebmer and Zweimüller 1999). Therefore, their level of effort is thought to be more determined by their intrinsic motivation. To put it differently, strong incentive schedules such as pay-for-performance, which in general need more monitoring, could be seen as a threat to their autonomy by white-collar workers and, as such, crowd out their intrinsic motivation and reduce the intensity of their effort (Frey 1997). Our findings can also be interpreted on the basis of the theory of Milgrom (1988) and Milgrom and Roberts (1990). Indeed, monitoring costs are likely to be higher for white-collar workers.

Table 6.4   Effect of wage inequality on firm productivity—interaction with the composition of the workforce, OLS versus 2SLS

	Value added per employee[a] (ln)							
	OLS				2SLS			
Intercept	7.32***	7.30***	7.35***	7.61***	7.00***	7.13***	7.20***	6.71***
	(0.26)	(0.26)	(0.26)	(0.26)	(0.26)	(0.26)	(0.26)	(0.67)
RPI[b]	1.70***				4.53***			
	(0.50)				(0.72)			
RPI · white-collar[c]	−0.91**				−0.61†			
	(0.40)				(0.41)			
SD of wages[d]		1.36***				2.20***		
		(0.30)				(0.35)		
SD · white-collar[c]		−0.69***				−0.41†		
		(0.24)				(0.26)		
CV of wages[d]			0.79***				1.56***	
			(0.24)				(0.25)	
CV · white-collar[c]			−0.55***				−0.34†	
			(0.20)				(0.21)	
Max.-min. ratio of wages[d]				0.09***				0.14***
				(0.02)				(0.02)
Max.-min. · white-collar[c]				−0.04**				−0.03*
				(0.02)				(0.02)
Worker characteristics[e]	Yes	Yes	Yes	Yes	Yes	Yes	Yes	Yes
Firm characteristics[f]	Yes	Yes	Yes	Yes	Yes	Yes	Yes	Yes

(continued)

Table 6.4 (continued)

	Value added per employee[a] (ln)							
	OLS				2SLS			
Adjusted R^2	0.53	0.54	0.53	0.55	0.57	0.57	0.57	0.57
F-stat	126.89***	131.88***	123.69***	132.05***	136.48***	137.15***	137.11***	137.49***
Hausman test: p-value					0.00	0.00	0.00	0.00
No. of employees	17,490	17,490	17,490	17,490	17,490	17,490	17,490	17,490
No. of firms	397	397	397	397	397	397	397	397

Notes: See table 6.3 notes.

[a] Estimated by the firm annual gross operating income per worker (plus subsidies, minus indirect taxes).

[b] Conditional indicator for within-firm wage dispersion (i.e., standard errors of wage regressions run for each firm separately).

[c] "White-collar" is a dummy variable that is equal to 1 if the share of white-collar workers within the firm is larger than 50 percent and 0 otherwise.

[d] Individual gross hourly wages include overtime paid, premiums for shift work, night work, and/or weekend work and bonuses (i.e., irregular payments that do not occur during each pay period, such as pay for holiday, 13th month, and profit sharing).

[e] Share of the workforce that (1) at most has attended lower secondary school, (2) has more than ten years of tenure, and (3) is younger than twenty-five and older than fifty years, respectively. The share of women, the share of blue-collar workers and the share of the workers supervising coworkers are also included.

[f] Sectoral affiliation (five dummies), size of the firm (number of workers), and level of wage bargaining (two dummies).

***Significant at the 1 percent level.

**Significant at the 5 percent level.

*Significant at the 10 percent level.

†Significant at the 15 percent level.

Therefore, white-collar workers may have more incentives to (1) withhold information from managers in order to increase their influence and (2) engage in costly rent-seeking activities instead of productive work. This could be an additional reason explaining why the elasticity between wage dispersion and productivity might be lower for white-collar workers.

Monitoring Environment

Another important question is whether the relationship between wage dispersion and firm productivity is affected by the degree of monitoring within the firm. To address this question, we have let our intrafirm wage dispersion indicators interact with a dummy variable that is equal to 1 if the share of the workforce with supervising authority over coworkers is lower than or equal to 20 percent and zero otherwise.

The OLS estimates relative to this new specification, presented in table 6.5, show that the elasticity of productivity to pay dispersion is positive and significantly higher among firms with a high degree of monitoring (supervising firms). At sample means, the elasticity of productivity to intrafirm pay dispersion ranges between 0.37 and 0.23 in firms with a high degree of monitoring and between 0.20 and 0.10 in firms with a low degree of monitoring. The 2SLS estimates also show a positive and significant effect of wage dispersion on firm productivity. However, while coefficients associated to the interaction variables remain negative, none of them are significantly different from zero. This result suggests that findings from OLS regressions have to be interpreted with care. Yet it should be noted that our instrumenting procedure may have led to some loss of information.

Overall, findings reported in table 6.5 emphasize the importance of a correct match between the compensation scheme and the monitoring environment within a firm. To put it differently, results appear to be consistent with the hypothesis that "it is not so much the choice of pay system that drives the organisational outcomes, but the combination of pay system and monitoring environment" (Belfield and Marsden 2003, 469). It is also noteworthy that our descriptive statistics indicate that supervising firms have a greater proportion of blue-collar workers (66 percent versus 43 percent) and that their mean conditional pay inequality is larger (0.20 versus 0.15). Hence, our findings seem to be consistent with Milgrom (1988) and Milgrom and Roberts (1990), who suggest a lower pay spread within firms that are mainly composed of white-collar workers.

6.7   Conclusion

The objective of this chapter is twofold. First, we analyze the structure of wages within and between Belgian firms. Next, we examine how the productivity of these firms is influenced by their internal wage dispersion. To do so, we rely on a unique combination of two large-scale data sets (i.e., the

Table 6.5   Effect of wage inequality on firm productivity—interaction with the monitoring environment, OLS versus 2SLS

	Value added per employee[a] (ln)							
	OLS				2SLS			
Intercept	7.27***	7.23***	7.50***		6.95***	7.07***	7.13***	7.60***
	(0.26)	(0.27)	(0.26)		(0.26)	(0.26)	(0.26)	(0.26)
RPI[b]	1.66***				4.42***			
	(0.47)				(0.71)			
RPI * low monitoring[c]	−0.71**				−0.26			
	(0.32)				(0.33)			
SD of wages[d]		1.21***				2.12***		
		(0.30)				(0.93)		
SD * low monitoring[c]		−0.29†				−0.09		
		(0.17)				(0.21)		
CV of wages[d]			0.64***				1.48***	
			(0.22)				(0.24)	
CV * low monitoring[c]			−0.25†				−0.04	
			(0.16)				(0.18)	
Max.-min. ratio of wages[d]				0.09***				0.14***
				(0.02)				(0.02)

Max.-min. * low monitoring^c				-0.03* (0.01)				-0.01 (0.02)
Worker characteristics^e	Yes	Yes	Yes	Yes	Yes	Yes	Yes	Yes
Firm characteristics^f	Yes	Yes	Yes	Yes	Yes	Yes	Yes	Yes
Adjusted R^2	0.54	0.54	0.53	0.55	0.57	0.57	0.57	0.57
F-stat	128.41***	129.52***	120.02***	130.51***	136.29***	135.21***	134.89***	135.31***
Hausman test: p-value					0.00	0.00	0.00	0.00
No. of employees	17,490	17,490	17,490	17,490	17,490	17,490	17,490	17,490
No. of firms	397	397	397	397	397	397	397	397

Notes: See table 6.3 notes.

[a] Estimated by the firm annual gross operating income per worker (plus subsidies, minus indirect taxes).

[b] Conditional indicator for within-firm wage dispersion (i.e., standard errors of wage regressions run for each firm separately).

[c] "Low monitoring" is a dummy variable that is equal to 1 if the share of the workforce with supervising authority over coworkers is lower than or equal to 20 percent and 0 otherwise.

[d] Individual gross hourly wages include overtime paid, premiums for shift work, night work, and/or weekend work and bonuses (i.e., irregular payments that do not occur during each pay period, such as pay for holiday, 13th month, and profit sharing).

[e] Share of the workforce that (1) at most has attended lower secondary school, (2) has more than ten years of tenure, and (3) is younger than twenty-five and older than fifty years, respectively. The share of women, the share of blue-collar workers and the share of the workers supervising coworkers are also included.

[f] Sectoral affiliation (five dummies), size of the firm (number of workers), and level of wage bargaining (two dummies).

***Significant at the 1 percent level.

**Significant at the 5 percent level.

*Significant at the 10 percent level.

†Significant at the 15 percent level.

1995 Structure of Earnings Survey and Structure of Business Survey). The former contains detailed information on firm-level characteristics (e.g., sector of activity, size of the firm, and level of wage bargaining) and on individual workers (e.g., gross hourly wages, bonuses, age, education, sex, and occupation). The latter provides firm-level information on financial variables (e.g., gross operating surplus, value added, and value of production).

Our methodology is consistent with that of Winter-Ebmer and Zweimüller (1999). It rests on a two-step estimation procedure. First, we compute conditional intrafirm wage differentials by taking the standard errors of wage regressions run for each firm separately. Next, we use these conditional wage differentials as an explanatory variable in a firm-level productivity regression. As a sensitivity test, we also analyze the impact of unconditional indicators of intrafirm wage dispersion on firm productivity. These indicators include the standard deviation, the coefficient of variation, and the max-min ratio of gross hourly wages within the firm. The productivity of a firm is measured by the value added per employee. The potential simultaneity problem between wage dispersion and firm productivity is addressed using information from the Belgian income tax system. More precisely, we apply two-stage least squares (2SLS) and instrument the dispersion of wages *including* bonuses by the intrafirm standard deviation of income taxes on gross earnings *excluding* bonuses.

To our knowledge, this chapter is one of the first to examine the effect of intrafirm wage dispersion on firm performance in the private sector using both a conditional wage inequality indicator and direct information on firm productivity. It is also one of the few, with Bingley and Eriksson (2001) and Heyman (2002), to consider potential simultaneity problems. Empirical findings, reported in this chapter, support the existence of a positive and significant relationship between wage inequality and firm productivity. Moreover, we find that the intensity of this relationship is stronger for blue-collar workers and within firms with a high degree of monitoring. These findings are more in line with the tournament models (Lazear and Rosen 1981) than with the fairness, morale, and cohesiveness models (Akerlof and Yellen 1990; Levine 1991).

Future research in this area should rely on matched employer-employee panel data so as to control for the nonobserved characteristics of the workers or firms. Unfortunately, at the moment, such data do not exist for Belgium. It would also be interesting to extend the analysis to small firms using a conditional measure of intrafirm wage dispersion. However, this option requires a rich data set with a larger number of observations per firm.

Appendix A

Table 6A.1 Intrafirm wage dispersion and firm performance—some empirical results

Study	Countrie(s)	Data/Coverage	Wage dispersion	Firm performance	Methodology	Results
Cowherd and Levine (1992)	North America, Europe	OASIS program: 102 business units ≥ 59 workers	Semiunconditional: pay of employees relative to top 3 management level	Product quality	Cross-section (OLS)	Negative relationship between wage spread and firm performance → fairness and cooperation theory + relative deprivation theories
DeBrock, Hendricks, and Koenker (2001)	United States	Professional baseball teams, 1985–1998	Several unconditional measures and standard error of earnings regression	Win-loss percentage by team	Cross-section (OLS) and fixed effects	Negative impact of wage dispersion on team performance → fairness theory
Eriksson (1999)	Denmark	2,600 managers from 210 Danish firms, 1992–1995	Unconditional: coefficient of variation	Profits/sales ratio	Cross-section (OLS) and fixed effects	Weak positive relationship between these variables among executives → tournament theory
Frick, Prinz, and Winkelman (2003)	United States	Professional baseball, basketball, football, and hockey teams, data for min. 7 years in each league	Unconditional: GINI index of wage inequality	Win-loss percentage by team	Cross-section (OLS), fixed effects or random effects	Ambiguous result. For basketball and hockey teams, a higher degree of wage dispersion is beneficial for team performance but the reverse is found for football and baseball teams.
Gomez (2002)	United States	Professional hockey teams, 1993–1998	Unconditional: GINI coefficient	Win-loss percentage by team and season-ending point totals	Cross-section (OLS) and fixed effects	Negative relationship between these variables → fairness theory
Harder (1992)	United States	Professional baseball teams, data for 4 seasons (1976, 1977, 1987, 1988). Professional basketball (1987)	Two separate continuous measures of inequity (% overrewarded and % under-rewarded players)	Technical measures for baseball (e.g., runs created, total average) and for basketball (e.g., points scored)	Cross-section (OLS) and lagged dependent values as explanatory variables	Negative relationship between these variables for basketball, results less clear for baseball → partial support of pay equity theory (underreward leads to selfish behavior, overreward to cooperative behavior)

(continued)

Table 6A.1 (continued)

Study	Countrie(s)	Data/Coverage	Wage dispersion	Firm performance	Methodology	Results
Heyman (2002)	Sweden	Panel data for white-collar workers and approximately 10,000 managers in 1991 and 1995	Conditional: standard error of wage regression	Profits	Cross-section (OLS) and fixed effects (lagged value of wage spread as instrumental variable)	Positive relationship between these variables among white-collar workers and managers → tournament theory
Hibbs and Locking (1995)	Sweden	Aggregated individual wage data, 1974–1993	Unconditional: squared coefficient of variation	Real value added	Cross-section (OLS) and instrumental variable (lagged value of output)	Positive relationship between these indicators → tournament theory
Leonard (1990)	United States	439 large corporations, 1981–1985	Unconditional: standard deviation of pay	Return on investment	Cross-section (OLS) and fixed effects	No significant relationship between these indicators for top executives
Main, O'Reilly, and Wade (1993)	United States	Executives in 210 firms, 1980–1984	Unconditional: coefficient of variation	Return on assets	Cross-section (OLS)	Positive relationship between these indicators for executives → tournament theory
Pfeffer and Langton (1993)	United Kingdom	17,000 college and university professors from 600 academic departments	Unconditional: coefficient of variation	Workers' satisfaction, productivity, and cooperation	Cross-section (OLS)	Negative relationship between wage spread and (1) satisfaction, (2) productivity, (3) cooperation → fairness and cooperation theory
Richards and Guell (1998)	United States	Professional baseball teams, 3 seasons (1992, 1993, 1995)	Unconditional: variance of team salaries	Win-loss percentage by team	Cross-section (OLS) and fixed effects	Negative effect of wage spread on the win percentage but not on the probability to win a title → partial support of fairness theory
Winter-Ebmer and Zweimüller (1999)	Austria	Panel of Austrian firms (≥ 20 workers with at least 4 data points), 1975–1991	Conditional: standard error of wage regression	Standardized wage for white- and blue-collar workers	Cross-section (OLS) and fixed effects	Positive relationship between these variables. Stronger for blue-collar workers → results more in line with tournament theory

Note: OLS = ordinary least squares.

Appendix B

Table 6B.1   Structure of wages (with bonuses) within and between firms, 1995

	Overall sample[a]	Firm size		Level of wage bargaining			Workforce composition	
		Small firms (25–99 workers)	Large firms (≥100 workers)	CA only at national and/or sectoral level	Firm level CA	Other or no CA	Majority blue-collar workers	Majority white-collar workers
Average wage[b,c]	13.85	12.36	14.49	13.14	14.63	13.21	n.a.	n.a.
SD[b]	6.67	6.01	6.83	7.10	6.08	6.90	n.a.	n.a.
25th percentile	9.94	9.17	10.43	9.27	10.92	9.22	n.a.	n.a.
75th percentile	15.39	13.43	16.11	14.31	16.21	14.45	n.a.	n.a.
No. of workers	31,788	9,450	22,338	14,123	15,713	1,952	n.a.	n.a.
Average of firm average wage[d]	12.46	12.11	13.44	12.25	13.11	11.94	10.81	14.04
SD	3.80	3.59	4.16	3.89	3.35	4.15	2.08	4.35
25th percentile	9.98	9.82	10.58	9.80	10.83	9.40	9.45	10.91
75th percentile	14.02	13.74	15.41	13.80	14.75	13.47	11.89	16.03
No. of firms	1,445	590	855	795	530	120	760	685
Average SD[b] of wage[d]	3.52	3.38	3.89	3.51	3.53	3.50	2.14	4.83
SD	3.20	3.08	3.48	3.35	2.83	3.12	1.63	3.73
25th percentile	1.40	1.39	1.48	1.29	1.64	1.17	0.99	2.16
75th percentile	4.80	4.60	5.36	4.81	4.75	5.00	2.80	6.38
No. of firms	1,445	590	855	795	530	120	760	685
Average CV of wage[d]	0.25	0.25	0.26	0.25	0.25	0.26	0.19	0.32
SD	0.15	0.15	0.16	0.16	0.14	0.15	0.12	0.16
25th percentile	0.13	0.13	0.13	0.13	0.14	0.11	0.10	0.19
75th percentile	0.34	0.34	0.35	0.34	0.33	0.35	0.25	0.40
No. of firms	1,445	590	855	795	530	120	760	685

(continued)

Table 6B.1   (continued)

	Overall sample[a]	Firm size		Level of wage bargaining			Workforce composition	
		Small firms (25–99 workers)	Large firms (≥ 100 workers)	CA only at national and/or sectoral level	Firm level CA	Other or no CA	Majority blue-collar workers	Majority white-collar workers
Average max.-min. ratio of wage[d]	2.79	2.81	2.74	2.76	2.76	3.11	2.14	3.42
SD	1.80	1.88	1.59	1.74	1.79	2.22	1.09	2.11
25th percentile	1.63	1.64	1.56	1.64	1.58	1.46	1.43	2.03
75th percentile	3.27	3.26	3.45	3.31	3.18	3.53	2.49	4.04
No. of firms	1,445	590	855	795	530	120	760	685
Correlation (average wage, SD of wage)[d]	0.831***	0.829***	0.839***	0.844***	0.800***	0.866***	0.642***	0.825***

Notes: CA = collective agreement on wages; SD = standard deviation; CV = coefficient of variation of wage (SD of wage/average of wage); n.a. = not applicable.

[a] These statistics refer to the weighted sample only covering full-time workers in firms employing at least twenty-five employees.

[b] Individual gross hourly wages (in EUR) include overtime paid, premiums for shift work, night work, and/or weekend work.

[c] observation = a person.

[d] observation = a firm.

***Indicates that the Pearson correlation coefficient is significant at the 1 percent level.

Appendix C

Table 6C.1   Means and standard deviations of variables—workers' level (first step)

	Mean	SD
Gross hourly wage (in EUR)	13.5	262.6
Age (years)	37.2	9.6
Female	25.9	
Education		
No degree, primary/lower secondary	41.5	
General upper secondary, technical/artistic/prof. upper secondary	38.8	
Higher nonuniversity, university, and postgraduate	19.7	
Blue-collar workers	48.4	
No. of employees	17,490	
No. of firms	397	

Notes: The descriptive statistics refer to the weighted sample. Gross hourly wage includes overtime paid, premiums for shift work, night work, and/or weekend work, and bonuses (i.e., irregular payments that do not occur during each pay period, such as pay for holiday, 13th month, profit sharing, etc.).

Appendix D

Table 6D.1   Means and standard deviations of variables—firm level (second step)

	Mean	SD
I. Firm productivity[a]	61.34	1,618.89
II. Intrafirm wage dispersion		
Residual pay inequality[b]	0.17	0.07
SD of wages[c]	0.24	0.10
CV of wages[c]	0.29	0.14
Max.-min. ratio of wages[c]	3.17	1.60
III. Control variables		
A) Share of the workforce		
Age < 25 years	10.2	11.5
Age > 50 years	9.3	8.5
Female	30.1	27.0
Low educated (no degree, primary, or lower secondary)	40.6	31.0
Blue-collar workers	52.4	34.2
Tenure > 10 years	42.2	23.4
Supervising their coworkers (monitoring)	15.1	13.4
B) Firm characteristics		
Size (no. of workers)	480.4	621.1
Level of wage bargaining		
CA only at national and/or sectoral level	41.7	
CA at the company level	53.5	
Other	4.8	

(*continued*)

Table 6D.1   (continued)

	Mean	SD
Sector		
Manufacturing (D)	63.5	
Electricity, gas, and water supply (E)	0.2	
Construction (F)	3.6	
Wholesale and retail trade; repair of motor vehicles (G)	18.6	
Transport, storage, and communication (I)	3.7	
Real estate, renting, and business activities (K)	10.6	
No. of employees		17,490
No. of firms		397

Notes: The descriptive statistics refer to the weighted sample. CA = collective labor agreement; SD = standard deviation; CV = coefficient of variation.

[a]Firm productivity is estimated by the value added per worker (in thousands of EUR). The value added is approximated by the firm annual gross operating income per worker (plus subsidies, minus indirect taxes).

[b]Intrafirm wage dispersion is the conditional measure of the intrafirm wage dispersion (i.e., standard errors of wage regressions run for each firm separately)

[c]Individual gross hourly wages include overtime paid, premiums for shift work, night work and/or weekend work and bonuses (i.e., irregular payments that do not occur during each pay period, such as pay for holiday, 13th month, and profit sharing)

References

Adams, J. 1963. Toward an understanding of inequity. *Journal of Abnormal and Social Psychology* 517:422–36.
Akerlof, G. A., and J. L. Yellen. 1988. Fairness and unemployment. *American Economic Review* 78 (Papers and Proceedings): 44–49.
———. 1990. The fair wage-effort hypothesis and unemployment. *Quarterly Journal of Economics* 105:255–83.
Belfield, R., and D. Marsden. 2003. Performance pay, monitoring environments, and establishment performance. *International Journal of Manpower* 24:452–71.
Bingley, P., and T. Eriksson. 2001. Pay spread and skewness, employee effort and firm productivity. Department of Economics, Faculty of Business Administration. Working Paper no. 01-2. Aarhus, Denmark: University of Aarhus.
Blau, P. M. 1955. *The dynamics of bureaucracy: A study of interpersonal relations in two government agencies.* Chicago: Cambridge University Press.
Bloom, M. 1999. The performance effects of pay dispersion on individuals and organizations. *Academy of Management Journal* 42:25–40.
Brown, C., J. Hamilton, and J. Medoff. 1990. *Employers large and small.* Cambridge, MA: Harvard University Press.
Card, D., and S. de la Rica. 2006. Firm-level contracting and the structure of wages in Spain. *Industrial and Labor Relations Review* 59:573–92.
Cowherd, D. M., and D. I. Levine. 1992. Product quality and pay equity between lower-level employees and top management: An investigation of distributive justice theory. *Administrative Science Quarterly* 37:302–20.

Davis, S. J., and J. Haltiwanger. 1996. Employer size and the wage structure in U.S. manufacturing. *Annales d'Economie et de Statistique* 41/42:323–67.

DeBrock, L., W. Hendricks, and R. Koenker. 2001. Pay and performance: The impact of salary distribution on firm-level outcomes in baseball. University of Illinois, Urbana-Champaign, Department of Economics. Unpublished Manuscript.

Dell'Aringa, C., and C. Lucifora. 1994. Wage dispersion and unionism: Do unions protect low pay? *International Journal of Manpower* 15:150–70.

Dell'Aringa, C., and L. Pagani. 2007. Collective bargaining and wage dispersion. *British Journal of Industrial Relations* 45:29–54.

Demunter, C. 2000. Structure and distribution of earnings survey: Analysis 1995. *Statistics Belgium Working Paper.* Brussels, Belgium: Statistics Belgium.

Depken, C. A. 2000. Wage disparity and team productivity. Evidence from major league baseball. *Economics Letters* 67:87–92.

Dominguez, J., and C. Rodriguez-Gutiérrez. 2004. Collective bargaining and within firm wage dispersion in Spain. *British Journal of Industrial Relations* 42:481–506.

Eaton, B. C., and W. D. White. 1983. The economy of high wages: An agency problem. *Economica* 50:175–81.

Eriksson, T. 1999. Executive compensation and tournament theory: Empirical tests on Danish data. *Journal of Labor Economics* 17:262–80.

Frey, B. S. 1997. *Not just for the money: An economic theory of personal motivation.* Cheltenham, UK: Edward Elgar.

Frey, B. S., and M. Osterloh. 1997. *Sanktionen oder seelenmassage? Motivationale grundlagen der unternehmesführung* (Sanctions or gentle persuasion? Foundations of incentives for firm management). *Die Betriebswirtschaft* 57:307–21.

Frick, B., J. Prinz, and K. Winkelmann. 2003. Pay inequalities and team performance: Empirical evidence from the North American major leagues. *International Journal of Manpower* 24:472–88.

Garen, J. 1985. Worker heterogeneity, job screening, and firm size. *Journal of Political Economy* 93:715–39.

Gibbons, R., and M. Waldman. 1999. Careers in organizations: Theory and evidence. In *Handbook of labor economics.* Vol. 3, ed. O. Ashenfelter and D. Card, 2373–2437. Amsterdam: North-Holland.

Gomez, R. 2002. Salary compression and team performance: Evidence from the National Hockey League. *Zeitschrift für Betriebswirtschaf: Ergänzungsheft 'Sportökonomie'* 72:203–20.

Hamermesh, D. S. 1980. Commentary. In *The economics of firm size, market structure, and social performance,* ed. J. Siegfried, 383–88. Washington, DC: Federal Trade Commission.

Harder, J. W. 1992. Play for play: Effects of inequity in a pay-for-performance context. *Administrative Science Quarterly* 37:321–35.

Hausman, J. A. 1976. Specification tests in econometrics. *Econometrica* 46:1251–71.

Heyman, F. 2002. Pay inequality and firm performance: Evidence from matched employer-employee data. FIEF Working Paper no. 186. Stockholm, Sweden: Trade Union Institute for Economic Research.

Hibbs, D. A., and H. Locking. 2000. Wage dispersion and productive efficiency: Evidence for Sweden. *Journal of Labor Economics* 18:755–82.

Homans, G. C. 1961. *Social behavior: Its elementary forms.* New York: Harcourt Brace Jovanovich.

Kremer, M., and E. Maskin. 1996. Segregation by skill and the rise in inequality. NBER Working Paper no. 5718. Cambridge, MA: National Bureau of Economic Research.

Lallemand, T., R. Plasman, and F. Rycx. 2004. Intra-Firm wage dispersion and firm performance: Evidence from linked employer-employee data. *Kyklos* 57:541–66.

———. 2005a. The establishment-size wage premium: Evidence from European countries. IZA Discussion Paper no. 1569. Bonn, Germany: Institute for the Study of Labor.

———. 2005b. Why do large firms pay higher wages? Evidence from matched worker-firm data. *International Journal of Manpower* 26:705–23.

Lallemand, T., and F. Rycx. 2006. Establishment size and the dispersion of wages: Evidence from European countries. *Applied Economics Quarterly* 52:309–36.

Lazear, E. P. 1989. Pay equality and industrial politics. *Journal of Political Economy* 97:561–80.

———. 1995. *Personnel economics.* Cambridge, MA: MIT Press.

Lazear, E. P., and S. Rosen. 1981. Rank-order tournaments as optimum labor contracts. *Journal of Political Economy* 89:841–64.

Lehmann, E., and U. Wacker. 2000. *Messung und steuerung von einkommensungleichheiten in organisationen* (Measurement and management of income inequalities in organization). In *Flexibilisierungstendenzen in der betrieblichen personalpolitik,* ed. U. Backes-Gellner, 109–28. Munich: Hampp.

Leonard, J. 1990. Executive pay and firm performance. *Industrial and Labor Relations Review* 43:13–29.

Levine, D. I. 1991. Cohesiveness, productivity and wage dispersion. *Journal of Economic Behavior and Organization* 15:237–55.

Lucas, R. E. 1978. On the size distribution of business firms. *Bell Journal of Economics* 9:508–23.

Main, B. G., C. A. O'Reilly, and J. Wade. 1993. Top executive pay: Tournament or teamwork? *Journal of Labor Economics* 11:606–28.

McLaughlin, K. 1988. Aspects of tournaments models: A survey. *Journal of Labor Economics* 15:403–30.

Mellow, W. 1982. Employer size and wages. *Review of Economics and Statistics* 54:495–501.

Milgrom, P. 1988. Employment contracts, influence activities and efficient organisation design. *Journal of Political Economy* 96:42–60.

Milgrom, P., and J. Roberts. 1990. The efficiency of equity in organisational decision processes. *American Economic Review* 80 (Papers and Proceedings): 154–59.

Oi, W. Y. 1983. The fixed employment costs of specialized labor. In *The measurement of labor cost*, ed. J. Triplett, 63–116. Chicago: University of Chicago Press.

Organization for Economic Cooperation and Development (OECD). 1997. *Employment Outlook.* Paris: OECD.

———. 2002. *Employment Outlook.* Paris: OECD.

Pfeffer, J., and N. Langton. 1993. The effect of wage dispersion on satisfaction, productivity, and working collaboratively: Evidence from college and university faculty. *Administrative Science Quarterly* 38:382–407.

Plasman, R., M. Rusinek, and F. Rycx. 2007. Wages and the bargaining regime under multilevel bargaining: Belgium, Denmark and Spain. *European Journal of Industrial Relations* 13:161–80.

Richards, D. G., and R. C. Guell. 1998. Baseball success and the structure of salaries. *Applied Economics Letters* 5:291–96.

Rodriguez-Gutiérrez, C. 2001. Wage dispersion within firms and collective bargaining in Spain. *Economics Letters* 72:381–86.

Rycx, F. 2003. Industry wage differentials and the bargaining regime in a corporatist country. *International Journal of Manpower* 24:347–66.

Slichter, S. H. 1950. Notes on the structure of wages. *Review of Economics and Statistics* 32:80–91.
Solow, R. 1979. Another possible source of wage stickiness. *Journal of Macroeconomics* 1:79–82.
Stigler, G. J. 1962. Information in the labour market. *Journal of Political Economy* 70:94–105.
Troske, K. R. 1999. Evidence on the employer-size wage premium from worker-establishment matched data. *Review of Economics and Statistics* 81:1–12.
Voos, P. 1983. Union organizing: Costs and benefits. *Industrial and Labor Relations Review* 36:576–91.
Weiss, L. 1966. Concentration and labour earnings. *American Economic Review* 56:96–117.
White, H. 1980. A heteroscedasticity-consistent covariance matrix estimator and a direct test for heteroscedasticity. *Econometrica* 48:817–30.
Winter-Ebmer, R., and J. Zweimüller. 1999. Intra-firm wage dispersion and firm performance. *Kyklos* 52:555–72.

7

Wage Dispersion between and within Plants
Sweden 1985–2000

Oskar Nordström Skans, Per-Anders Edin, and Bertil Holmlund

7.1 Introduction

Over the period lasting from the late 1960s to the mid-1980s, Sweden experienced a sharp decline in wage inequality. Overall wage inequality fell along with educational wage differentials and wage differentials between younger and older workers. This development came to a halt in the mid-1980s, and the subsequent years have seen a reversal of previous trends. The rise in wage inequality since the mid-1980s has been particularly marked for private-sector workers (le Grand et al. 2001).

The causes of the fall of Swedish wage inequality have been discussed in Edin and Holmlund (1995), Hibbs (1990), and other contributions. Institutional factors almost certainly played a role. The so-called solidarity wage policy pursued by the major trade union confederation was clearly attempting to reduce wage differentials and appeared to have been successful in these ambitions. However, there is also evidence that the usual supply and demand factors played some role, in particular concerning the evolution of educational wage differentials. Changes in the university wage premium (college versus high school) are strongly negatively correlated with changes in the relative supply of university educated people in the labor force up to the mid-1990s. From the mid-1990s, however, this pattern no

Oskar Nordström Skans is an associate professor of economics at the Institute for Labour Market Policy Evaluation (IFAU), Uppsala. Per-Anders Edin is a professor of economics at Uppsala University, and a researcher at the Institute for Labour Market Policy Evaluation (IFAU), Uppsala. Bertil Holmlund is a professor of economics at Uppsala University.

The research reported in this paper has been part of the National Bureau of Economic Research (NBER) personnel economics program. Helpful comments from Edward P. Lazear, Kathryn L. Shaw, Nils Elvander, Anders Forslund, Eva Mörk, participants at NBER workshops, and seminar participants at IFAU are gratefully acknowledged.

longer holds. The university wage premium has continued to increase despite a continuous increase in the relative supply of university-educated people in the labor force (Gustavsson 2006).

Earlier studies of changes in Swedish wage inequality have been silent on the question as to what extent the changes are attributable to changes in dispersion between and within firms or plants. The main contribution of the present chapter is to document how wage dispersion between and within plants has evolved since the mid-1980s. We use hitherto largely unexploited data and find a continuous rise in between-plant wage inequality. This development may reflect increased sorting of workers by skill levels, so that high-skilled and low-skilled workers to a greater extent are found in different plants. Another possibility is that the importance of rent sharing at the plant level has increased, perhaps reflecting stronger local unions or more scope for differential wage outcomes due to a greater between-plant variation in the ability to pay. Our data do not allow clean tests of alternative hypotheses, but they suggest that both sorting and genuine plant effects may have become more important.

Our chapter also includes a fairly detailed descriptive analysis of the associations between worker mobility at the plant level and various measures of wage inequality within and between plants. This analysis confirms some well-known stylized facts: most mobility takes place in the lower part of the plant's wage distribution, both in terms of exit and entry; mobility rates are strongly procyclical; and smaller plants experience higher mobility.

The plan of this chapter is as follows. We begin in section 7.2 by giving a brief overview of the Swedish labor market institutions, the turbulent macroeconomic events of the 1990s, and evolution of labor mobility and fixed-term contracts as a background to the later analysis of wages and mobility.[1] Section 7.3 describes the data, section 7.4 provides snapshots of plant wages and mobility, and section 7.5 portrays in some detail the evolution of the wage structure. Section 7.6 provides a discussion, and section 7.7 concludes.

7.2 Background

7.2.1 Employment Protection Legislation

Swedish legislation on employment protection dates back to the 1974 Employment Protection Act, which has remained largely intact over the past three decades. The law presumes that an employment contract is valid until further notice, unless stated otherwise. An employer must provide a valid reason for terminating a contract. "Lack of work" is a valid reason,

---

1. This section draws on various sources, in particular Holmlund (2003) and Holmlund and Storrie (2002).

and the employer's assessment of whether there is lack of work cannot be disputed in court. Workers have to be notified of layoffs several months ahead of their implementation and layoffs must, in general, proceed according to seniority. No redundancy pay is stipulated in the law, although such pay may be part of employer-union deals at the plant level.

The legislation allows for temporary (fixed-term) contracts. For example, the law has always permitted the use of temporary contracts to replace an absent worker. Another common form of temporary contract involves project work in construction or research. Contracts for probationary periods are also allowed.

During the 1990s, there have been no significant reforms of the Employment Protection Act concerning the termination of open-ended contracts. There have, however, been several changes to the statutory regulation of fixed-term contracts. In January 1994, the maximum permitted duration for probationary contracts and those motivated by a temporary increase in labor demand were prolonged from six to twelve months. However, this was immediately repealed in January 1995. The reforms of 1997 were arguably more important. The employer was now given the opportunity to hire for a fixed duration without having to specify a particular reason. However, an employer could only use a maximum of five such contracts, and a particular individual could not be employed under such a contract for more than twelve months during a three-year period. If the plant is newly established, the period may be extended to eighteen months.

Another important element of the 1997 law was the opportunity to strike collective agreements on derogations from statutory law regarding fixed-term contracts at the local level, provided that the parties had a central agreement in other matters. Prior to 1997, these agreements could only be made at the central level.

Comparisons with employment protection in other countries suggest that the Swedish legislation is relatively stringent, although not as stringent as in several Southern European countries (see Organization for Economic Cooperation and Development [OECD] 2004).

7.2.2   Collective Bargaining

Union density in Sweden has hovered above or around 80 percent of the number of employees over the past couple of decades. The coverage of collective agreements is even higher, as the collective agreements typically are extended to nonunion workers. A high degree of union membership is an integral part of what has been referred to as the Swedish Model. Indeed, labor legislation concerning employment protection and worker codetermination is based on the presumption that the overwhelming majority of the workers are union members.

The fact that the provision of unemployment insurance is closely linked to union membership is almost certainly an important explanation of the high unionization rate. Three other Nordic countries with very high union density—Denmark, Finland, and Iceland—also organize their unemployment insurance through union-affiliated insurance funds. There is by now a reasonable amount of evidence suggesting that such institutional details explain some of the country differences in unionization (see, e.g., Boeri, Brugiavini, and Calmfors 2001).[2]

Postwar wage determination in Sweden has frequently been associated with centralized wage bargaining as well as so-called solidarity wage policy. Nationwide coordination of wage negotiations was implemented from the mid-1950s and continued for almost three decades. The key players in these negotiations were the Swedish trade union confederation (LO) and the Swedish employers' federation (SAF). The guiding principle for LO's wage policy, as laid out in several influential documents by their economists Gösta Rehn and Rudolf Meidner, was "equal pay for equal work." One implication of this principle was that wages should not be made dependent on the ability to pay among particular plants or industries. In theory, the policy recognized the need for wage differentials among workers so as to reflect differences in qualifications. In practice, there was always a clear egalitarian ambition in LO's wage demands.

The centralized wage negotiations came under increasing stress during the late 1970s, when some employer organizations argued that the central frame agreements left too little room for flexibility at the local and industry level. A significant step toward more decentralized wage bargaining came in 1983, when the metalworkers' union and their employer counterpart sidestepped the national negotiations and opted for an industry agreement. Wage negotiations after 1983 have mainly taken place at the industry level, albeit with exceptions in the early 1990s when double-digit inflation and an emerging macroeconomic crisis led the government to initiate a coordinated "stabilization drive" so as to achieve a deceleration of wage inflation. The drive took the form of a government-appointed commission that delivered a proposal for economy-wide wage restraint for the period 1991 to 1993. This involved negotiations with over 100 organizations, and the proposal was finally accepted across the whole labor market. The following years involved a return to largely uncoordinated industry-wide bargaining.

In the summer of 1996, several blue-collar unions in the manufacturing sector launched an important initiative that eventually materialized as the

2. Union density has fallen sharply over the period 2006 to 2007. By October 2007, union density stood at 72 percent according to data from the labor force surveys (Kjellberg 2007). This development can almost certainly be largely explained by new policies concerning the financing of unemployment insurance that came into effect in 2007. The policies raised the cost of being insured and has resulted in a sharp fall in membership in unemployment insurance funds. A substantial number of workers leaving the unemployment insurance funds have also chosen to leave the unions.

so-called Industrial Agreement (IA) of 1997. The agreement was struck by the blue- and white-collar unions as well as employer organizations in the industrial sector and was mainly concerned with procedural "rules of the game." It represented an attempt to establish consensus around timetables for negotiations, the role of mediators, and rules for conflict resolution. A group of "impartial chairs" have been appointed, and the agreement states rules for when and how these chairs could intervene in the negotiation process.

The IA has served as a model for similar agreements in the public sector (and also in parts of the service sector). As of 2002, over 50 percent of the labor force is covered by IA-type agreements. The IA also came to serve as a model for government policies concerning industrial relations. A new national mediation institute (*Medlingsinstitutet*) has been created (in operation from June 2000) with the power to appoint mediators even without the consent of the parties concerned.

The IA innovations that emerged in the late 1990s represent a move toward more informal coordination in wage bargaining. Perhaps paradoxically, the move toward informal macro-coordination in wage bargaining has taken place simultaneously with a clear shift toward stronger local influence over the distribution of wage increases. Pay setting in the public sector is a case in point. Previous rigid wage scales have been abandoned, and there is, at least in theory, substantial room for wage adjustments tailored to the needs of recruiting and retaining employees.

7.2.3   The Macroeconomy in Turmoil

During the 1980s, Swedish labor market performance was widely appreciated as a remarkable success story. Whereas unemployment in Western Europe climbed to double-digit figures, the Swedish unemployment rate remained exceptionally low by international standards. The average unemployment rate during the 1980s was around 2 percent, and by the end of the decade, it had fallen to 1.5 percent. Employment-to-population rates were also exceptionally high by international standards. In 1990, total employment had risen to 83 percent of the working age population, whereas the average European figure was 61 percent, and the OECD average was 65 percent.

In the early 1990s, the picture of outstanding Swedish labor market performance changed dramatically. Between 1990 and 1993, unemployment increased from 1.6 percent to 8.2 percent, and total employment declined to 73 percent of the working age population (see table 7.1). The level of gross domestic product (GDP) fell from peak to trough by 6 percent over a three-year period. For five successive years in the mid-1990s, official unemployment was stuck at around 8 percent, whereas extended measures of unemployment reached double-digit figures.

Why did Swedish unemployment rise so sharply in the early 1990s? It can

Table 7.1   **Macroeconomic conditions**

Year	Unemployment[a]	Employment[b]	Economic growth[c]		
			1 year	2 year	5 year
1980	2.0	79.9	1.67	5.57	6.83
1981	2.5	79.4	−0.19	1.47	5.51
1982	3.2	79.1	1.24	1.05	8.55
1983	3.5	79.0	1.88	3.14	8.68
1984	3.1	79.4	4.31	6.27	9.18
1985	2.8	80.3	2.22	6.62	9.77
1986	**2.7**	**80.9**	**2.79**	**5.07**	**13.04**
1987	2.1	81.4	3.40	6.28	15.45
1988	1.7	82.2	2.60	6.09	16.27
1989	1.5	82.9	2.75	5.42	14.53
1990	**1.6**	**83.1**	**1.03**	**3.80**	**13.20**
1991	3.0	81.0	−1.08	−0.06	8.94
1992	5.2	77.3	−1.18	−2.25	4.11
1993	8.2	72.6	−2.00	−3.15	−0.56
1994	8.0	71.5	4.16	2.09	0.82
1995	**7.7**	**72.2**	**4.05**	**8.39**	**3.84**
1996	8.1	71.6	1.29	5.40	6.32
1997	8.0	70.7	2.44	3.76	10.22
1998	6.5	71.5	3.65	6.17	16.56
1999	5.6	72.9	4.58	8.39	17.03
2000	**4.7**	**74.2**	**4.33**	**9.10**	**17.33**
2001	4.0	75.3	0.92	5.29	16.91

Note: Numbers in bold refer to the years studied in section 7.4.
[a]Share of labor force.
[b]Share of working aged (sixteen to sixty-four) population.
[c]Change in real GDP.

be argued that the main causes were a series of adverse macroeconomic shocks, partly self-inflicted by bad policies and partly caused by unfavorable international developments. The policy failures date back to the 1970s and include an inability to pursue a sufficiently restrictive aggregate demand policy so as to bring inflation under control. This inflationary bias in policy was especially pronounced in the late 1980s, when it was fueled by financial liberalization. The timing of financial liberalization and a major tax reform in 1990 to 1991, which contributed to a slump in the housing market, was not well designed. When macroeconomic policy finally took a firm anti-inflationary stand in 1991, the economy was already edging toward recession. The depth of the recession was reinforced by the international recession of the early 1990s and by increasing real interest rates.

Although the prospects for a sustained labor market improvement appeared remote in the mid-1990s, a strong recovery was, in fact, around the corner. From 1997 and onward, employment exhibited a marked increase and unemployment fell precipitously. By the end of 2000, unemployment had reached 4 percent of the labor force, and it remained fairly constant at this level during 2001 and 2002. To some degree, this recovery reflects the unwinding of earlier shocks and a return to what may be close to the equilibrium unemployment rate. There is little doubt that the extremely low unemployment rate around the 1990s was not sustainable. Over the 1990s, several reforms may have facilitated a return to lower equilibrium unemployment. For example, unemployment insurance became less generous, a number of deregulations in product markets took place, and labor market reforms opened up for temporary work agencies.

7.2.4 Labor Mobility and Temporary Contracts

Available measures of labor mobility in Sweden reveal strong cyclical patterns. However, any statements about cycles versus trends are problematic considering the exceptionally deep and prolonged slump of the early 1990s. A noticeable change is the rapid growth of fixed-term employment contracts.

One source of information on labor mobility is the retrospective labor force surveys. Data on external job mobility—change of employer at least once during the past year—reveal annual mobility rates hovering between 6 and 12 percent since the mid-1960s. There is some evidence that internal mobility—change of position without changing employer—has shown a slight trend increase, at least up to the late 1980s.

Overall labor turnover has been markedly procyclical, with quits accounting for the overwhelming share of the total number of worker separations. For blue-collar workers in mining and manufacturing, the annual quit rate amounted to 22 percent over the period 1968 to 1988, to be compared with an average annual layoff rate of only 2 percent.[3] The importance of layoffs increased substantially during the slump of the 1990s, but separate data on quits and layoffs are not available after 1988. Other evidence, such as information on unemployment inflow and advance notification of layoffs, indicates sharply rising layoff rates in the early 1990s.

The distinction between quits and layoffs is often fuzzy, and especially fuzzy for fixed-term contracts that have grown relentlessly during the 1990s. As shown in figure 7.1, the sharp fall in total employment in the early 1990s was due to sharply falling employment in open-ended contracts. The number of fixed-term contracts stood at approximately the same level in the first quarter of 1994 as it did four years earlier. When the economy approached the cyclical peak in the late 1980s, we observe rising permanent employment along with a decline in the number of fixed-term contracts.

---

3. Quits are worker separations "initiated by the employee," whereas layoffs are separations "initiated by the employer." The data are based on surveys to firms and were collected by Statistics Sweden. Empirical studies of worker mobility in Sweden up to the early 1980s are reported in Holmlund (1984).

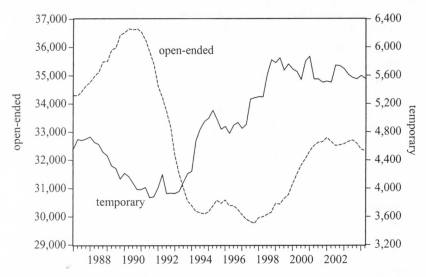

Fig. 7.1   Wage and salary employment (100s) by type of contract, seasonally adjusted quarterly data 1987Q1 to 2004Q2
Source: Labor force surveys, Statistics Sweden.

From the early 1990s and during most of the rest of the decade, there is a remarkable increase in fixed-term contracts that amounts to roughly 50 percent. Measured relative to total wage and salary employment, the number of temporary workers rose from 10 percent to 16 percent; see figure 7.2. Note, however, the declining share of fixed-term contracts in the late 1980s and the late 1990s, periods with falling unemployment.[4]

The prevalence of fixed-term contracts is particularly visible among women, the young, and foreign-born residents. By the turn of the century, 18 percent of the female employees were on fixed-term contracts, a figure to be compared with 13 percent for the male employees. The trend rise in temporary work is striking for both men and women. Among young female workers aged sixteen to twenty-four, close to 60 percent were in temporary work by the end of the century; the corresponding share for young men was around 40 percent.

Temporary work has increased in every broad sector of the economy. Two sectors stand out. Financial and business services exhibit both the greatest increase in fixed-term contract rate and share of all fixed-term contracts, while health and care show the lowest growth rates in both these figures.

The most frequent form of fixed-term contracts involves replacement of

4. Fixed-term contracts account for a much higher share of the total flow of new hires than of the total stock of employment. Available data for the private sector reveal that fixed-term contracts accounted for roughly 50 percent of all new hires in the late 1980s. By the late 1990s, they accounted for some 70 percent.

Fig. 7.2   Temporary work (percent of total wage and salary employment) and un-employment (percent of the labor force), seasonally adjusted quarterly data 1987Q1 to 2004Q2

Source: Labor force surveys, Statistics Sweden.

absent workers. Sweden has a generous allowance for many forms of leave, particularly parental leave and long statutory holidays. The incidence of leave replacements has, however, remained roughly constant at around 4 to 5 percent of total wage and salary employment. The entire rise in temporary work is accounted for by other categories, namely on-call contracts, project work, and probationary employment.

Why did fixed-term contracts exhibit such rapid growth during the 1990s? Holmlund and Storrie (2002) discuss this issue and conclude that legislative changes are unlikely to be crucial. Changes in the industrial structure of employment, or in the demographic composition of the labor force, have likewise negligible explanatory power. A more promising explanation focuses on the consequences of adverse macroeconomic conditions. A recession is associated with relatively more hirings on temporary contracts, reflecting weaker incentives on the part of firms to offer long-term contracts when workers are easier to find as well as an increased willingness on the part of workers to accept temporary work when job offers are in short supply. The Swedish experience as well as the developments of temporary work in the other Nordic countries lends support to this hypothesis. The share of temporary work has been relatively stable in Norway (with stable or falling unemployment) but increased sharply in Finland over the 1990s—that is, a period when Finnish unemployment skyrocketed.

The trend rise in temporary work over the 1990s may thus to a significant degree reflect changes in the macroeconomic environment and, in particular, the rise in unemployment from the exceptionally low (and unsustainable) levels in the late 1980s to the much higher (and presumably sustainable) levels prevailing in recent years. In addition, other, more "structural" forces may have tilted employers' preferences toward more flexible staffing arrangements, but it is difficult to pinpoint the exact causes. Hiring labor on a fixed-term contract can accommodate fluctuations in the workload associated with a volatile market environment, but evidence on *increased* volatility is hard to come by.[5]

7.3   Data

In order to study wage dispersion, wage changes, and mobility, we use a linked employer-employee database containing information on all workers and plants in both the private and public sectors. From the database, we derive measures of wage levels, wage changes, mobility, and tenure. Through the employer-employee link, we are able to derive plant aggregates of these measures as well as measures of wage dispersion at the plant level. In addition to these core measures, we also use information on observable characteristics (age, gender, immigrant status, and education) of the workers.

The basic data source is a version of a register database (RAMS) provided by Statistics Sweden. The RAMS database contains yearly plant-level data on all workers that were employed at a plant some time during each year, irrespectively of whether they were employed on a fixed-term or a permanent contract. The data include information on total annual earnings as well as the first and the last remunerated month for each employee. We construct monthly wage data by dividing total earnings during the year by the number of remunerated months, including only employment spells that cover November each year. Thus, we use the average monthly wage-bill paid to an employee by a single employer as our measure of the employee's wage.

The data are yearly and cover the period 1985 to 2000. The underlying population consists of all individuals aged sixteen to sixty-five who resided in Sweden anytime between 1990 and 2000. This implies that the oldest workers as well as workers who emigrated or died before 1990 are missing during the first five years. Thus, in effect, we have an age restriction of sixteen to sixty in 1985 and sixteen to sixty-four in 1989.

The data do not contain information on hours worked, so in order to focus on workers that are reasonably close to full-time employment, we consider a person to be full-time employed if and only if the wage for No-

---

5. Houseman (2001) reports from a survey of U.S. employers that flexible staffing arrangements are mainly used to accommodate fluctuations in workload or absences.

vember exceeds a minimum wage.[6] Furthermore, an individual is only counted as employed by at most one plant each year, with priority given to the observation generating the highest wage.

The data set is based on information on total labor earnings collected for the purpose of calculating taxes. Thus, the data include the earnings of *all* employees, including top chief executive officers (CEOs), which implies that some of the observations are extreme outliers. It should be noted that there is great persistence over time in the recorded wages of these individuals, suggesting that the extreme values are not due to errors. As is evident from table 7.2, the wages of the top earners have a large impact on the standard deviation of monthly wages, while the mean hardly is affected at all (this pattern is, of course, even more noticeable when looking at wages in levels). It might be misleading if a very small number of workers influence the statistics in such a dramatic way, especially when comparing to other data sets where this group may be excluded by construction. On the other hand, wages of top earners within each plant are the focus of parts of this chapter. Considering this, we retain all but the top 0.5 percent in the wage distribution in the relevant years. In an effort to reduce the impact of measurement errors in changes, we also rank individuals according to their log wage change and drop the highest and lowest half-percentile each year.

Table 7.3 compares the constructed wage distribution to the "actual" wage distribution, calculated from the 3 percent random sample in the Longitudinal Individual Data Base (LINDA; see Edin and Fredriksson 2000). The constructed data correspond reasonably close to the actual data when looking at log wages but appear to contain some noise in the estimated dispersion of both wages and wage changes.

The individual identifiers are based on official personal identification numbers, which should be very accurate and consistent over time. However, plant identifiers may change over time for administrative reasons. In order not to misclassify the disappearance of administrative plant numbers as plant closings, we only include plants that existed in two consecutive years when studying changes (and, for comparability, throughout section 7.4). Thus, the calculated exit rates (i.e., the fraction of employees in a plant that leave within a year) does not include plant closings. Because our tenure variable is calculated within the sample, changes in administrative plant numbers will probably mean that we underestimate the fraction of long-tenured workers. When calculating wage changes for people who change plants, we only include people who changed between plants with at least twenty-five employees in both years in order to get consistency with the definition used elsewhere in this analysis.

6. The minimum wage is defined as 75 percent of the mean wage of janitors employed by local municipalities, according to Statistics Sweden's information on monthly wages; the cutoffs are available upon request.

Table 7.2   The importance of extreme values (2000)

	Log of nominal monthly wage in 2000		
Highest included percentile	Mean	Standard deviation	Max.
95	9.820	0.283	10.54
99	9.855	0.328	10.98
99.5	9.862	0.338	11.19
99.9	9.868	0.351	11.75
All	9.870	0.359	15.07

Note: Total sample size is 3,040,555 individuals.

Table 7.3   Actual and constructed nominal monthly wages (2000)

	Log (wages)		Changes in log wage (from 1999)	
	Constructed	Actual	Constructed	Actual
Mean	9.860	9.876	0.051	0.054
Standard deviation	0.336	0.283	0.149	0.116
10th percentile	9.453	9.585	−0.093	−0.022
Median	9.821	9.818	0.042	0.037
90th percentile	10.309	10.258	0.216	0.165
N	2,999,065	105,633	2,602,351	88,864

Note: The observations with the largest (and smallest for the actual data) 0.5 percent of wages as well as the largest and smallest 0.5 percent of log wage changes are excluded from the data.

Our analysis is focused on the corporate sector,[7] and in order to get a meaningful description of the wage dispersion within establishments, we include only plants with at least twenty-five employees. Table 7.4 displays the relative size of the corporate sector for the years 1985 and 2000.[8] We include both a measure where we use the entire corporate sector and one where we restrict the analysis to the private corporations. It is shown that the size of the corporate sector, as measured in number of employees, increased slightly between 1985 and 2000 (from 63 to 66 percent).

Table 7.4 also shows the share of workers in each sector who worked in plants with at least twenty-five employees. It is shown that 59 percent of individuals employed in the corporate sector in 2000 worked in 25+ sized plants; the corresponding number for 1985 was 57 percent. Figure 7.3

7. The main reason is to get comparability with other studies in the volume.
8. The sector definitions are based on Statistics Sweden (SCB; 2001) and SCB (2002) and comply with European Union (EU)-standard classifications.

Table 7.4   **Sector and size**

	Relative size of sector (no. of employees)		Share of all employees in sector working in size 25+ plants
	All plants and employees	Employees in size 25+ plants only	
1985			
All corporate	0.63	0.62	0.59
Private	0.52	0.48	0.55
Public and nonprofit	0.37	0.38	0.63
2000			
All corporate	0.66	0.62	0.57
Private	0.60	0.54	0.55
Public and nonprofit	0.34	0.38	0.68

Note: Size is the total number of employees each year.

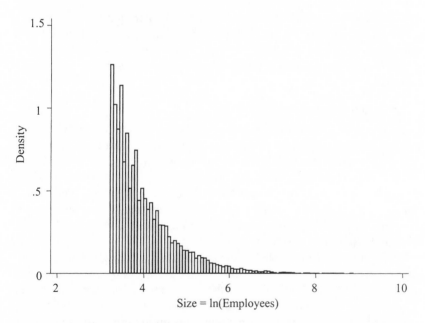

Fig. 7.3   Plant size distribution for 2000: Corporate sector

shows the log plant-size distribution for 2000. It is obvious that most 25+ sized plants have close to twenty-five employees, and, as a consequence, a significant fraction of plants move around the twenty-five limit between years. However, as noted in the preceding, we will condition on plants having at least twenty-five employees in both years whenever we calculate changes.

7.4   Snapshots of Plant Wages and Mobility

This section provides detailed descriptive evidence of wages, wage changes, and mobility at the plant level in the Swedish private corporate sector for the years 1986, 1990, 1995, and 2000. The purpose of the analysis is to provide an overview of the role of plants in shaping wages, wage changes, and labor mobility in Sweden since the 1980s, in order to facilitate comparisons with other countries and depict the most important changes that have occurred during the period under study.

The analysis is based only on plants in *privately owned* firms in the corporate sector. It is worth noting that the period under study was characterized by a steady increase in the share of workers in private plants within the corporate sector: in 1986, only 77 percent of workers worked in plants owned by private firms, whereas the corresponding share was 87 percent in 2000 (see table 7.4).

Because the focus of this section is on describing the pattern and changes in wages and turnover at the plant level, most statistics are calculated with one plant as one observation, implying that all included plants have an equal weight. Thus, small plants are up-weighted compared to an analysis based on individuals.

7.4.1   Wage Levels

Figure 7.4 shows the log real wage distribution for the four years studied (wages are deflated by the consumer price index). The figure reveals a steady increase in real wages, but also an increase in dispersion. This is also shown by the first panel of table 7.5, where the standard deviation of log wages increases from 0.307 to 0.340 between 1986 and 2000. This reproduces what is a well-known fact from several previous studies, namely that the wage dispersion in Sweden started to increase in the mid-1980s after several decades of wage compression.[9]

The second panel of table 7.5 shows that the *between*-plant dispersion, measured as the standard deviation of plant average wages, increased over time. As a contrast, the third panel shows that the *within*-plant dispersion, measured as the mean of the within-plant standard deviation of wages, remained relatively constant over time. This impression also holds in the fourth panel showing statistics for the coefficient of variation within plants. Thus, it appears as though the prime source of increased dispersion is between, rather than within, plants. We will return to this issue at length in section 7.5 of the paper.

The fifth panel of table 7.5 reveals a positive correlation between the wage *level* in a plant and the wage *dispersion* within the plant. This result is

---

9. See, for example, Le Grand, Szulkin, and Thålin (2000), Edin and Holmlund (1995), and Gustavsson (2004).

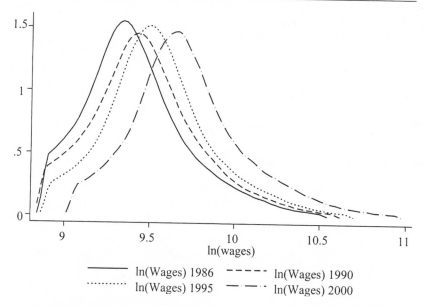

Fig. 7.4   **The distribution of log real wages**
Note: Deflated by CPI to 1990:SEK.

probably, at least partly, driven by the skewness of the wage distribution (see figure 7.4). The wage dispersion among high-paid people is larger even in relative terms.[10]

The last two panels of table 7.5 show the evolution of wage dispersion for young (twenty-five to thirty) and old (forty-five to fifty) workers. The results show that the increase in wage dispersion was larger for young workers than for prime-aged workers. However, if we compare the log wages for youths to the average log wages displayed in the top panel, we see that youth wages appear to have remained relatively stable at approximately 90 percent of the average wage over the period.

7.4.2   Wage Changes

In this subsection, we study wage changes within and between plants. In doing so, we only look at changes for workers that are employed by plants in the sample (i.e., by plants with at least twenty-five employees in the private corporate sector) in two consecutive years. Figure 7.5 shows the distribution of wage changes for the four years studied. It can be noted that many workers experienced a real wage decline between 1989 and 1990.

10. Some caution is warranted when comparing these numbers to other data sources because the used data are rather unique in including the earnings of all people receiving remuneration from each plant, including top CEOs. Note, however, that we, as explained in section 7.3, excluded the top 0.5 percent of wages each year.

Table 7.5   Structure of wages within and between plants

	Wages (1990-SEK)[a]				Log wages (1990-SEK)[a]			
	1986[b]	1990	1995	2000	1986	1990	1995	2000
1. Average wage	12,976	13,797	14,865	17,843	9.420	9.477	9.553	9.727
SD	4,572	4,996	5,346	7,040	0.307	0.322	0.318	0.340
90 percentile	18,832	20,069	21,606	26,716	9.843	9.907	9.981	10.193
75 percentile	14,544	15,649	16,711	20,055	9.585	9.658	9.724	9.906
Median	11,848	12,696	13,668	16,070	9.380	9.449	9.523	9.685
25 percentile	9,992	10,525	11,462	13,437	9.210	9.262	9.347	9.506
10 percentile	8,519	8,728	9,570	11,208	9.050	9.074	9.166	9.324
No. of workers	692,870	800,332	739,378	860,581	692,870	800,332	739,378	860,581
2. Plant average wage	12,678	13,490	14,432	17,245	9.396	9.455	9.521	9.692
SD	2,088	2,266	2,679	3,663	0.145	0.152	0.169	0.188
90 percentile	15,699	16,680	18,143	22,497	9.603	9.664	9.751	9.959
75 percentile	13,664	14,586	15,855	19,008	9.478	9.541	9.624	9.801
Median	12,228	13,076	13,935	16,397	9.376	9.440	9.505	9.665
25 percentile	11,239	11,953	12,554	14,698	9.297	9.353	9.407	9.561
10 percentile	10,448	11,003	11,501	13,413	9.227	9.272	9.318	9.472
No. of plants	7,047	8,306	7,526	9,067	7,047	8,306	7,526	9,067
3. Plant SD of wages	3,820	4,168	4,404	5,484	0.266	0.279	0.273	0.279
SD	1,387	1,416	1,626	2,222	0.064	0.060	0.066	0.069
90 percentile	5,830	6,219	6,678	8,635	0.355	0.361	0.361	0.371
75 percentile	4,702	5,029	5,459	6,917	0.308	0.317	0.317	0.326
Median	3,595	3,924	4,151	5,047	0.260	0.274	0.267	0.272
25 percentile	2,775	3,119	3,159	3,794	0.220	0.238	0.226	0.228
10 percentile	2,206	2,546	2,474	2,936	0.186	0.207	0.192	0.195
No. of plants	7,047	8,306	7,526	9,067	7,047	8,306	7,526	9,067
Plant CV of wages	0.296	0.305	0.300	0.312	0.028	0.030	0.029	0.029
SD	0.076	0.072	0.080	0.088	0.007	0.006	0.007	0.007
90 percentile	0.392	0.399	0.406	0.429	0.037	0.038	0.037	0.038
75 percentile	0.349	0.356	0.356	0.371	0.033	0.033	0.033	0.033
Median	0.294	0.302	0.298	0.306	0.028	0.029	0.028	0.028
25 percentile	0.240	0.253	0.242	0.247	0.024	0.025	0.024	0.024
10 percentile	0.197	0.212	0.196	0.200	0.020	0.022	0.020	0.020
No. of plants	7,047	8,306	7,526	9,067	7,047	8,306	7,526	9,067
4. Correlation (average wage, SD of wage)	0.782	0.758	0.742	0.768	0.591	0.499	0.480	0.499
5. Wages for workers aged 25–30	11,910	12,716	13,318	16,258	9.358	9.419	9.467	9.657
SD	2,950	3,321	3,456	4,929	0.230	0.249	0.243	0.276
90 percentile	15,521	16,772	17,305	22,121	9.650	9.727	9.759	10.004
75 percentile	13,293	14,381	14,994	18,364	9.495	9.574	9.615	9.818
Median	11,466	12,335	12,922	15,469	9.347	9.420	9.467	9.647
25 percentile	9,961	10,508	11,086	13,073	9.206	9.260	9.313	9.478
10 percentile	8,649	8,861	9,449	11,009	9.065	9.089	9.154	9.306
No. of workers	103,277	125,836	127,035	138,219	103,277	125,836	127,035	138,219
6. Wages for workers aged 45–50	14,251	15,453	16,255	19,169	9.508	9.585	9.638	9.795
SD	5,236	5,770	6,002	7,772	0.327	0.339	0.332	0.351
90 percentile	21,462	23,417	24,497	29,579	9.974	10.061	10.106	10.295

Table 7.5   (continued)

	Wages (1990-SEK)[a]				Log wages (1990-SEK)[a]			
	1986[b]	1990	1995	2000	1986	1990	1995	2000
75 percentile	16,254	17,854	18,562	21,767	9.696	9.790	9.829	9.988
Median	12,820	13,974	14,680	16,948	9.459	9.545	9.594	9.738
25 percentile	10,773	11,600	12,304	14,193	9.285	9.359	9.418	9.561
10 percentile	9,162	9,690	10,455	12,108	9.123	9.179	9.255	9.402
No. of workers	91,500	120,626	121,496	116,080	91,500	120,626	121,496	116,080

Notes: SD = standard deviation; CV = coefficient of variation.
Data only include employees of plants with 25+ employees in year t and $t-1$.
[a]Deflation by CPI to 1990-SEK.
[b]Data for 1986 do not include workers older than sixty-two or workers that emigrated or died before 1990.

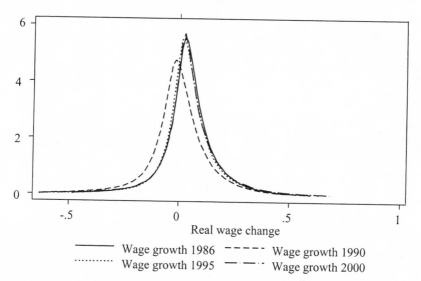

Fig. 7.5   Distribution of log real wage changes
Note: Deflated by CPI to 1990:SEK.

Table 7.6 looks at wage changes. The top panel shows the mean and distribution of individual wage changes: the average real wage change was between 4 and 5 percent, except in 1990 when it was close to zero. As for the dispersion, there appears to be some variation over time, but not much to indicate a trend.

Figure 7.6 and the second panel of table 7.6 show the distribution of plant average wage changes using information on the workers that remained in the plant for two consecutive years (from $t-1$ to t). We see that

Table 7.6   **Wage changes**

	Δ Wages (1990 SEK:s)[a]				Δ ln(Wages) (1990 SEK:s)[a]			
	1986[b]	1990	1995	2000	1986[b]	1990	1995	2000
1. Change in wages	610	46	638	898	0.048	0.004	0.045	0.048
SD	1,559	1,890	2,018	2,633	0.124	0.140	0.134	0.142
90 percentile	2,356	2,174	2,803	3,668	0.191	0.164	0.193	0.207
75 percentile	1,283	922	1,428	1,826	0.103	0.068	0.098	0.105
Median	503	−27	476	626	0.040	−0.002	0.034	0.038
25 percentile	−108	−830	−195	−177	−0.009	−0.059	−0.014	−0.011
10 percentile	−956	−1,920	−1,160	−1,434	−0.078	−0.139	−0.079	−0.085
No. of workers	586,057	665,982	623,679	704,360	586,057	665,982	623,679	704,360
2. Plant wage change[c]	666	122	565	948	0.054	0.010	0.041	0.053
SD	541	680	799	1,141	0.042	0.049	0.053	0.059
90 percentile	1,255	860	1,366	2,088	0.099	0.063	0.094	0.114
75 percentile	914	440	878	1,292	0.073	0.033	0.063	0.076
Median	617	90	484	763	0.052	0.008	0.037	0.047
25 percentile	368	−232	162	384	0.032	−0.016	0.014	0.024
10 percentile	138	−549	−148	30	0.013	−0.039	−0.008	0.001
No. of plants	7,037	8,296	7,521	9,063	7,037	8,296	7,521	9,063
3. Within plant SD	1,402	1,713	1,738	2,197	0.113	0.128	0.120	0.126
SD	483	553	690	980	0.029	0.033	0.035	0.039
90 percentile	2,008	2,393	2,614	3,417	0.151	0.170	0.164	0.176
75 percentile	1,627	1,986	2,059	2,605	0.130	0.147	0.140	0.147
Median	1,322	1,632	1,615	1,975	0.111	0.127	0.117	0.122
25 percentile	1,078	1,346	1,275	1,553	0.093	0.107	0.096	0.100
10 percentile	890	1,112	1,000	1,231	0.078	0.089	0.078	0.082
No. of plants	7,035	8,294	7,519	9,054	7,035	8,294	7,519	9,054
4. Wage change if changed plant	524	−129	742	1,069	0.037	−0.015	0.047	0.053
SD	2,302	2,671	3,179	4,026	0.174	0.194	0.197	0.213
90 percentile	3,243	2,979	4,382	5,727	0.254	0.221	0.292	0.319
75 percentile	1,703	1,358	2,347	3,133	0.135	0.099	0.155	0.175
Median	452	−110	664	913	0.035	−0.008	−0.044	0.051
25 percentile	−700	−1,595	−789	−1,049	−0.055	−0.122	−0.053	−0.063
10 percentile	−2,168	−3,348	−2,771	−3,525	−0.184	−0.269	−0.195	−0.218
No. of workers	23,659	28,824	21,477	40,217	23,659	28,824	21,477	40,217
5. Wage change if tenure 1–3 years		444	1,073	1,542		0.037	0.083	0.089
SD		1,984	2,316	2,965		0.155	0.163	0.164
90 percentile		2,769	3,765	4,837		0.228	0.292	0.292
75 percentile		1,460	2,186	2,793		0.118	0.165	0.170
Median		336	845	1,178		0.027	0.063	0.073
25 percentile		−569	−30	108		−0.044	−0.002	0.007
10 percentile		−1,659	−1,046	−1,151		−0.128	−0.075	−0.071
No. of workers		230,789	172,967	224,083		230,789	172,967	224,083
6. Wage change if tenure ≥3 years		−168	458	555		−0.013	0.029	0.027
SD		1,726	1,773	2,192		0.121	0.113	0.115
90 percentile		1,635	2,213	2,637		0.113	0.142	0.141
75 percentile		603	1,150	1,312		0.043	0.078	0.075

Table 7.6   **Wage changes**

	Δ Wages (1990 SEK:s)[a]				Δ ln(Wages) (1990 SEK:s)[a]			
	1986[b]	1990	1995	2000	1986[b]	1990	1995	2000
Median	–175		378	446	–0.013	0.027	0.027	
25 percentile		–915	–233	–252	–0.064	–0.016	–0.015	
10 percentile		–1,950	–1,131	–1,387	–0.136	–0.077	–0.081	
No. of workers		403,369	429,235	440,060	406,369	429,235	440,060	

Notes: See table 7.5 notes.
[a]Deflation by CPI to 1990-SEK.
[b]Data for 1986 do not include workers older than sixty-two or workers that emigrated or died before 1990.
[c]Average change in wage (or log wage) for workers that worked in the plant in both t and $t-1$.

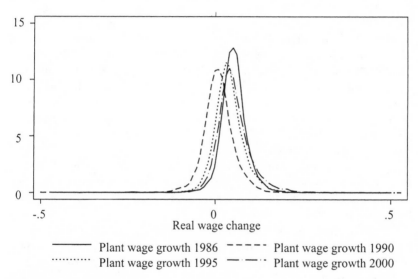

——— Plant wage growth 1986   ⁻ ⁻ ⁻ ⁻ ⁻ Plant wage growth 1990
·········· Plant wage growth 1995   — · — · · Plant wage growth 2000

Fig. 7.6   Distribution of plant average log wages for workers who remain in the same plant
Note: Deflated by CPI to 1990:SEK.

the dispersion of wage changes *between* plants, as measured by the standard deviation of plant wage changes, increased over time. As a contrast, it is shown in the third panel that the dispersion of wage changes *within* plants (the mean of the standard deviation of wage changes within a plant) was relatively stable. Thus, the results suggest that the rate of real wage changes increasingly varies between plants, but that the variation of wage changes has remained stable within plants.

The bottom three panels of table 7.6 show the distribution of wage changes separately for different tenure groups: (1) for those that changed plants (from one plant in the sample to another), (2) for those with short (one to three years) tenure, and (3) for long-tenured (> three years) workers. The tables show, as expected, that wage increases are smaller for workers with long tenure than for workers with shorter tenure. The wage increases for workers that change plants are smaller than average at the start of the period, but larger at the end of the period. This observation seems consistent with the observed increase in the importance of plant effects. However, it should also be noted that the dispersion of wage changes is much larger for those that change plants, suggesting important differences between voluntary and involuntary worker separations. It is important to keep in mind that the analysis is based on raw differences and that the probability of changing plants may be correlated with other characteristics that may affect the rate of wage growth, such as age or education.

7.4.3 Mobility

We now take a look at worker mobility at the plant level. The *entry rate* is defined as the share of workers in a plant in year t that did not work in the plant in $t - 1$. Correspondingly, the *exit rate* is defined as the share of workers in a plant in year $t - 1$ that did not remain in the same plant in year t.

The top panels of table 7.7 shows some background statistics. We see an increase in the number of plants over time (top panel) and some decrease in the average number of employees per plant (the second panel) consistent with the declining average plant size we described in section 7.3. The third panel shows the employment growth rates of the plants and by comparing the left part of the table (all 25+ sized plants) with the right side (only 100+ sized plants) it is clear the smaller plants had higher growth rates than larger plants during this period.

Comparing the exit rates depending on the size of the plant in the fourth and fifth panels, we see that there are fewer exits in the largest plants; presumably this is because they can provide more career opportunities than smaller organizations.

In the following panels (6 and following), we show exit and entry rates for different parts of the plant wage distribution. It is clear that most of the mobility takes place in the lower part of a plant's wage distribution, both in terms of exit and entry. Exit rates in the top quartile are in the order of 13 to 18 percent, whereas exit rates in the bottom quartiles are between 26 and 36 percent. The corresponding numbers for entry rates are 10 to 14 percent in the top quartile and 40 to 44 percent in the bottom quartile. Thus, there is relatively more entry than exits at the lower part of the plant wage distribution and relatively more exits than entry at the higher part of the wage distribution, suggesting that workers to some extent enter at lower wage levels and get promoted to higher wage levels before leaving the plant.

Table 7.7   Mobility, all jobs

	All Plants				Plants with 100+ employees			
	1986	1990	1995	2000	1986	1990	1995	2000
1. No. of plants	7,047	8,306	7,526	9,067	1,341	1,566	1,420	1,650
2. Employees/plant	98.3	96.4	98.4	95.2	311.5	303.1	315.3	301.6
	(232.1)	(222.6)	(219.1)	(206.7)	(474.3)	(456.0)	(441.2)	(424.4)
3. Employment growth/plant	0.015	0.028	0.056	0.059	0.001	−0.006	0.051	0.040
	(0.241)	(0.245)	(0.228)	(0.319)	(0.172)	(0.160)	(0.193)	(0.249)
By individual—a person is one observation								
4. Exit rate	0.199	0.217	0.151	0.204	0.182	0.208	0.132	0.186
If wage >90 percentile	0.165	0.176	0.174	0.231	0.153	0.167	0.155	0.222
If wage in 45–55 percentile	0.135	0.159	0.099	0.142	0.120	0.151	0.081	0.123
If wage <10 percentile	0.475	0.457	0.336	0.422	0.462	0.454	0.314	0.403
By plant—a plant is one observation								
5. Exit rate	0.202	0.216	0.159	0.212	0.183	0.204	0.136	0.191
	(0.124)	(0.124)	(0.120)	(0.141)	(0.107)	(0.107)	(0.100)	(0.124)
6. Exit rate, top quartile of plant wages	0.131	0.148	0.127	0.174	0.116	0.139	0.110	0.164
	(0.147)	(0.154)	(0.148)	(0.174)	(0.116)	(0.121)	(0.111)	(0.141)
7. Exit rate, bottom quartile of plant wages	0.355	0.353	0.259	0.316	0.338	0.349	0.230	0.288
	(0.190)	(0.184)	(0.180)	(0.194)	(0.138)	(0.135)	(0.131)	(0.147)
8. Exit rate, top decile of plant wages	0.143	0.160	0.148	0.191	0.133	0.154	0.137	0.188
	(0.192)	(0.201)	(0.197)	(0.224)	(0.144)	(0.144)	(0.142)	(0.169)
9. Exit rate 45–55 percentile, of plant wages	0.156	0.179	0.127	0.178	0.130	0.159	0.100	0.153
	(0.201)	(0.212)	(0.190)	(0.218)	(0.134)	(0.137)	(0.121)	(0.153)
10. Exit rate, bottom decile of plant wages	0.454	0.432	0.340	0.396	0.444	0.437	0.314	0.376
	(0.272)	(0.270)	(0.268)	(0.278)	(0.161)	(0.159)	(0.164)	(0.173)

(continued)

Table 7.7   Mobility, all jobs

	All Plants				Plants with 100+ employees			
	1986	1990	1995	2000	1986	1990	1995	2000
	By plant—a plant is one observation							
11. Entry rate	0.198	0.221	0.191	0.234	0.176	0.191	0.169	0.209
	(0.126)	(0.129)	(0.127)	(0.153)	(0.105)	(0.102)	(0.110)	(0.135)
12. Entry rate, top quartile of plant wages	0.103	0.116	0.105	0.144	0.090	0.100	0.096	0.134
	(0.134)	(0.140)	(0.136)	(0.164)	(0.102)	(0.108)	(0.111)	(0.137)
13. Entry rate, bottom quartile of plant wages	0.398	0.432	0.392	0.438	0.366	0.388	0.353	0.399
	(0.212)	(0.212)	(0.227)	(0.235)	(0.169)	(0.165)	(0.177)	(0.199)
14. Entry rate, top decile of plant wages	0.112	0.127	0.118	0.159	0.103	0.115	0.115	0.155
	(0.170)	(0.182)	(0.176)	(0.206)	(0.121)	(0.135)	(0.133)	(0.161)
15. Entry rate 45–55 percentile of plant wages	0.135	0.156	0.127	0.168	0.112	0.125	0.106	0.142
	(0.193)	(0.207)	(0.189)	(0.224)	(0.124)	(0.125)	(0.129)	(0.160)
16. Entry rate, bottom decile of plant wages	0.500	0.528	0.502	0.541	0.461	0.478	0.463	0.504
	(0.288)	(0.282)	(0.294)	(0.295)	(0.195)	(0.189)	(0.198)	(0.215)
17. percent of workers with 5+ years of tenure		0.316	0.414	0.364		0.351	0.459	0.423
		(0.218)	(0.262)	(0.249)		(0.225)	(0.257)	(0.258)
18. Correlation (size, average tenure)[a]	-0.004	0.072	0.052	0.045		0.092	0.032	0.022
19. Correlation (size, average age)	-0.184	0.014	-0.004	-0.011	-0.063	-0.038	-0.064	-0.035
20. Correlation (exit rate, average wage)	0.050	-0.166	-0.034	-0.019	-0.136	-0.128	0.037	0.084
21. Correlation (exit rate, average wage change)	0.054	-0.002	0.040	0.181	0.098	-0.028	0.079	0.272
22. Correlation (exit rate, SD of wage)	-0.100	0.097	0.177	0.215	0.110	0.114	0.299	0.340
23. Correlation (entry rate, average wage),	0.249	-0.118	-0.051	0.026	-0.107	-0.051	0.021	0.054
24. Correlation (entry rate, average wage change)	0.110	0.206	0.249	0.362	0.383	0.199	0.330	0.414
25. Correlation (entry rate, SD of wage),		0.135	0.181	0.239	0.192	0.251	0.248	0.310

Notes: Numbers in parentheses are standard deviations (SD). All statistics are at the plant level with one plant as one observation except as otherwise noted. Separate tables for high and low level jobs can be found in appendix A. Correlations are with average log wages in plants, average log wage changes for workers remaining in the plant, and standard deviation of log wages within plants.

[a]Note that tenure is calculated from 1985 onward, and thus truncated at different values for different years.

The most important development over time seems to be some procyclicality, in terms of entry rates and exit rates. In both the (relative) slump years of 1986 and 1995, we see that exits as well as entries were relatively uncommon (panels 5 to 16) and the fraction of high-tenured workers was relatively large in 1995 (panel 17).

The six bottom panels (18 to 25) of table 7.7 show correlations between entry and exit rates and different aspects of the plants wage distributions. In calculating these correlations we use the log wages, the standard deviation of log wages, and the log wage changes (for those remaining in the plant between year t and $t - 1$). The purpose is to describe the relationship between wage levels and wage structures on one side and mobility on the other side.

The correlations between average wage and exit rates are negative in the first years, but they grew over time, and for the large plant sample, they are positive for the last two years. The correlation between average wage change and exit rates fluctuates substantially between the years and even change signs. Exit rates are in all cases positively correlated with the standard deviation of wages, and this correlation appears to be growing over time.

As for the entry rates, the correlation with the average wage is similar to that for exit rates; it starts out negative but is positive at the end of the period. High entry rates also appear to be positively correlated with wage growth as well as with within-plant wage dispersion, and at least in the case of dispersion, increasingly so over time.

Appendix A shows tables that depict high- and low-level jobs separately. *High-level jobs* are defined as jobs paying more than the 80th percentile of the wage distribution in the data and *low-level jobs* are defined as the jobs paying less than the 20th percentile of the distribution. The story told by these numbers is essentially the same as in table 7.7: both entry and exits are more common for low-level jobs and less common for high-level jobs, with a more pronounced pattern for entries. The main difference seems to be that the correlation between mobility and the plant wages, wage changes, and wage dispersion all are more positive for high-level jobs.

This concludes the snapshots of wages and mobility. The most noteworthy observation is the rise in between-plant wage dispersion, whereas the within dispersion has remained largely constant. The next section takes a closer look at this development.

7.5   The Evolution of the Wage Structure

Figure 7.7 shows the overall log wage variance throughout the time period for the entire economy, for the corporate sector, for the private corporate sector, and for manufacturing. The figure clearly shows that the wage dispersion has increased quite consistently for all of these except for manufacturing, where the dispersion has been relatively stable.

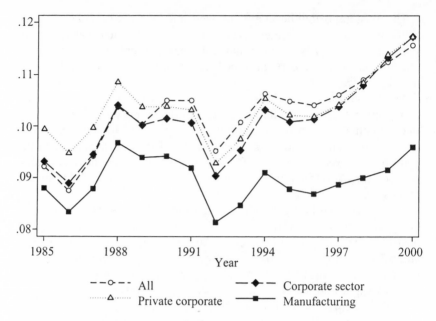

Fig. 7.7   Overall log (wage) variance

The description in the previous section suggested that differences be-tween plants may play an important role in explaining the growing wage dispersion in Sweden since the mid-1980s. The purpose of this section is to study in some detail the changing role that plants have played in explaining the growing wage dispersion between workers in the Swedish economy.

7.5.1   Within- and between-Plant Components

We start by looking at how the share of log wage variance that can be at-tributed to plant-specific factors has changed over time. Figure 7.8 shows that the between-plant variance as a share of overall variance has increased steadily throughout the period. The development is equally visible when studying the entire economy as when studying only the corporate sector. There is also a steady increase in the importance of plant effects when fo-cusing only on the manufacturing sector, even though the increase is less pronounced in that sector. Throughout the rest of this section, we will fo-cus on plants in the corporate sector. However, we will include the entire corporate sector regardless of ownership (see the discussion in the begin-ning of the previous section).

Interestingly, it is the increase in between-plant variance that makes up the entire increase in wage dispersion over the period. Figure 7.9 shows the evolution of within-plant variance, which contains a slightly cyclical pat-tern, but has no trend.

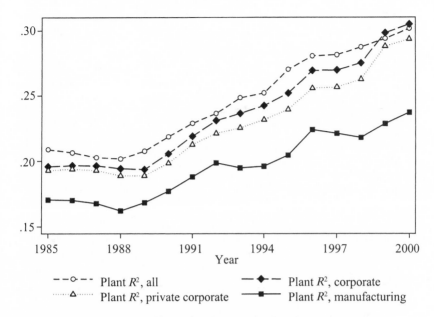

Fig. 7.8   Fraction of total variance explained by plant effects

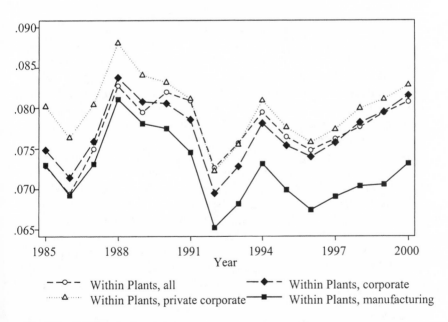

Fig. 7.9   Within-plant variance

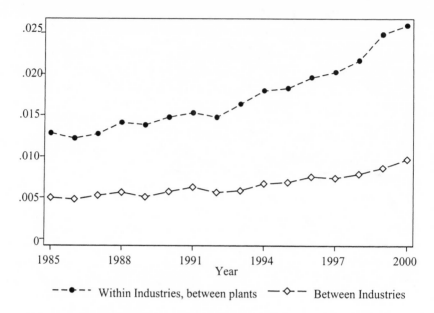

Fig. 7.10   **Between-plant components: Corporate sector**

It is possible that the increase in between-plant variance is due to changes in the industry composition. Thus, in figure 7.10 we decompose the between-plant variance in two parts, between plants within the same two-digit industry and between two-digit industries.[11] The figure clearly shows an increase in both the wage variances between plants in the same industry and between industries. We have also looked at the variance between plants within the same firm; this variance is small (because many firms just have one plant) but increasing.

As a (very) rough formal analysis of time trends for different industries, we estimated time trend estimates for the entire economy as well as separately for all one-digit industries. The results (not displayed) showed that all industries had positive trends in between-plant variances, while only three industries had trends in within-plant variances. To further assess the role of structural change, we have looked separately at all plants that existed in 1985 or 2000, as well as divided these plants by employment growth rates. All the results from these experiments suggested that the growing difference between plants is driven by increased differences between plants in the wages they pay, rather than by changes in the composition of plants in the economy.

11. We use "reduced" two-digit industry codes that are the lowest level at which it is possible to get consistent industry classifications throughout the period (new codes were issued in 1992). Thus, the corporate sector is divided into thirty-nine industries.

7.5.2   The Role of Sorting and Observed Human Capital Attributes

The increased between-plant wage inequality may have occurred for two very different reasons. First, it may be due to increased sorting of workers by observed and unobserved skills so that high-skilled and low-skilled workers to an increasing degree are found in different plants. Another possibility is increased importance of "true" plant effects, such as effects operating via rent sharing at the plant level. For example, between-plant wage dispersion is likely to rise if wages at the plant level become more responsive to plant-specific price and productivity conditions.

To get a first look at the importance of sorting according to skill, we will include traditional observable human capital variables (age, age squared, education, gender, and immigration status) in a Mincer-type regression. The results from the regressions can be found in appendix B. As has already been shown in, for example, Gustavsson (2006), the explanatory power of observable characteristics has declined over time.

We proceed by including plant-fixed effects in the Mincer equation and calculate the fixed effects R^2 (explanatory power), defined as the fraction of total residual variance attributed to the plant effects. This fraction captures the additional explanatory power of plant effects after controlling for observable characteristics.[12] The results displayed in figure 7.11 show that the plants play an increasingly important role after controlling for observable skills: there is a trend increase in the fraction of residual variance attributed to plant effects. We also calculate the correlation between the fixed effects and the prediction from observables and take this as a measure of the degree of sorting on observables in order to answer the question: to what extent do individuals with high earnings potential work in plants with large plant effects? Figure 7.11 reveals an increase in the degree of sorting: workers with favorable observed human capital attributes show an increasing tendency to work in high paying plants.

How should these patterns be interpreted? There is clearly evidence of increased sorting on observed skills, and there is a presumption that this also is associated with more sorting on unobserved skills. Conclusions about the development of true plant effects are more problematic, however, because such conclusions would require that the observed human capital characteristics capture all skill differences between individuals, which seems like a rather strong assumption.[13]

---

12. The fraction is formally equivalent to what Kremer and Maskin (1996) refer to as an index of segregation (or correlation) by worker skill.

13. Figure 7.11 also shows that observed human capital variables can explain less of the within-plant variance over time. However, using the within-estimated coefficients to calculate the between R^2, we see no evidence of a trend, suggesting that the between-plant variance of observables has increased relative to the within-plant variance. We interpret this as further support to the notion of increased sorting.

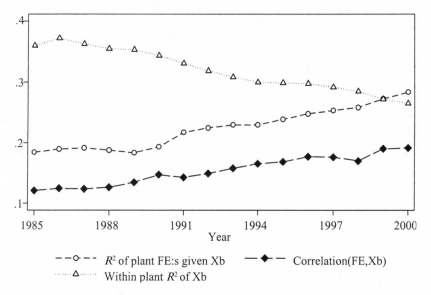

— — o — — R^2 of plant FE:s given Xb   — ◆ — Correlation(FE,Xb)
······ △ ······ Within plant R^2 of Xb

Fig. 7.11   Plant effects when controlling for observables
Notes: The estimated (year-specific) model is $\ln W(i,j,t) = X(i,t) b(t) + \text{FE}(j,t) + e(i,j,t)$, where X is education (six dummies), age, age squared, gender, and immigration status. FE is a plant fixed effect and e the error term. For estimates, see appendix C.

7.5.3   Plant Effects and Skill Levels

We noted already in section 7.4 that the variance of log wages within a plant is correlated with the average log wage of that plant and that this may reflect the skewness of the log wage distribution. Thus, we may be interested in the changing role of plants in different parts of the skill distribution. We study this by dividing the sample of individuals into quartiles of predicted wages from the estimated ordinary least squares (OLS) Mincer equations. Figure 7.12 shows an interesting pattern; the plant effects become increasingly important for all quartiles except the top predicted quartile.[14] Thus, it appears that the increasing importance of plant effects is a feature of all parts of the skill distribution *except* at the most highly skilled quartile. Plant effects were clearly most important for the highest-skilled workers at the beginning of the time period; but at the end of the period, there were little or no differences between different parts of the skill distribution. This suggests that changes in bargaining institutions may have been a factor of importance. For white-collar workers in the top of the earnings distribution, there has typically been considerable scope for indi-

---

14. It should be noted that the pattern of increased plant effect R^2s can be replicated using only males. Thus, it is not likely that the differences between predicted wage quartiles are driven by different time patterns for men and women.

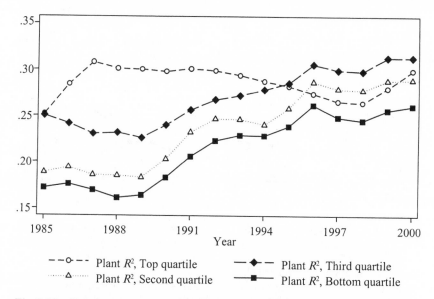

Fig. 7.12   Fraction of variance explained by plant effects by predicted wage quartile in the corporate sector
Note: Quartiles of predicted wages from regressions on education (six dummies), age, age squared, immigration status, and gender.

vidual bargaining with the employer, and the national wage agreements have been less relevant for those workers than for other groups. A speculative interpretation of figure 7.12 would be that a gradual erosion of the bite of national wage agreements has made wage-setting processes more similar across skill groups, with a tendency to emulate practices among the workers with the highest pay.

7.5.4   Wage Changes and Mobility

So far this section has focused entirely on wage levels. However, changes in the variance between plants in wages may have implications for both wage changes and mobility. In figure 7.13 we study the fraction of wage growth variance that can be attributed to plant effects for the different years (using only workers who remain in the same plant). The pattern is less obvious than when studying wage levels, but there is a marked shift in plant-specific wage growth in the beginning of the 1990s. This pattern also remains after controlling for observables. The strongest pattern emerging from the figure is, however, an increased sorting on observables (measured as the correlation between observed human capital and plant-fixed effects) starting in the mid-1990s, where workers with high predicted wage growth rates (e.g., young workers) increasingly sort themselves to plants with high residual wage growth rates. However, it should be noted that, as is evident

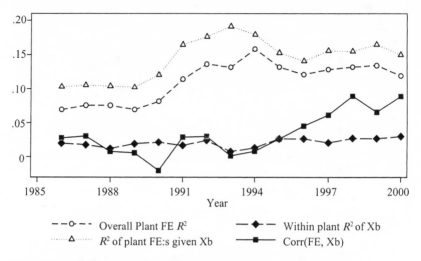

Fig. 7.13   Real wage growth and plant effects

Notes: The overall plant R^2 is the between-plant variance of changes divided by total variance of changes in log wages. The other statistics are based on the estimated (year-specific) model $d \ln W(i,j,t) = X(i,t) b(t) + \text{FE}(j,t) + e(i,j,t)$, where i is for individual, j for plant, and t for time (year). X includes education (six dummies), age, age squared, gender, and immigration status. FE is a plant-fixed effect and e the error term.

from figure 7.13, the within-plant predictive power of the observables is quite small (in the order of 1 to 3 percent).

In section 7.4, we noted what appeared to be increased wage changes for those who changed plants relative to the average wage change. However, when studying the time pattern throughout the period, it is apparent that the difference is highly volatile, with little evidence of a trend (in most cases, the differences are insignificant), a picture that also remains after controlling for observable characteristics. What appears to be a robust pattern, however, is a procyclicality of the fraction of workers observed in the data in two consecutive years who have changed plants between the years (see figure 7.14). The fraction of workers changing jobs in 1993 is roughly half that in 1988 and 2000.

7.5.5   The Dynamics of Plant Wages

It appears clear that wages have become more dispersed between plants in the cross-section. In this subsection, we study whether the same is true for the time dimension—that is, does the apparent increase in cross-sectional flexibility also mean that average plant wages are more volatile over time? We have computed the year-by-year correlations of plant log wages. The correlations are displayed in figure 7.15 and vary between 0.92 and 0.96 with a marked procyclical pattern—the four years with the lowest correlations are 1991 to 1994—but with no trend. Thus, plant-specific wages do

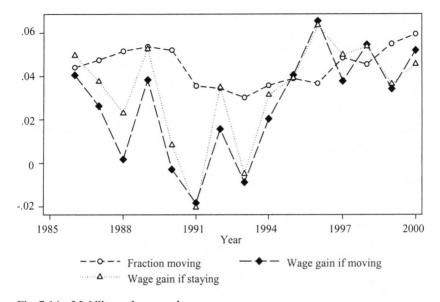

Fig. 7.14   Mobility and wage gains

Notes: Data include only workers in plants with 25+ employees in year t and $t-1$. "Fraction moving" is fraction of included workers that changed plant between t and $t-1$.

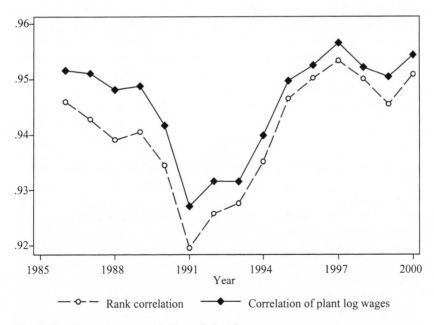

Fig. 7.15   Year-to-year correlations of plant log wages

not *fluctuate* more in 2000 than they did in 1985, even though wages are more dispersed in the cross section.

A main drawback of our data is the lack of information on productivity at the plant level. It is not possible, therefore, to examine how plant wages respond to changes in value productivity. However, because our results show that wages do not fluctuate more, but are more dispersed in the cross-section, it is suggested that either wages do not follow productivity more closely now (on a year-by-year basis at least), *or* wages follow productivity more, but the time variability in productivity has been reduced.

7.6 Discussion

We have documented a continuous increase in between-plant wage inequality since the mid-1980s. This increase holds in the raw data but also after controls for observable human capital attributes. It holds within industries as well as between plants in different industries. It is also interesting to note that the development is visible in all parts of the (observed) skill distribution except for the most highly skilled workers.

How can this development be explained? One possibility is increased sorting of workers by skill. Other possibilities revolve around rent sharing and what we have referred to as true plant effects. Suppose that wage negotiations have gradually become more decentralized, with increased bargaining power for local unions. This could cause an increase in wage dispersion as wages adjust to plant-level productivity, recognizing that plant productivity levels typically are much more dispersed than wages. Another twist on the rent-sharing theme is that the dispersion of plant productivity has increased, something that would translate into more wage dispersion to the extent that there is some scope for rent sharing at the plant level. We discuss these possibilities in turn.

7.6.1 Sorting by Skill

The segregation by skill theory of Kremer and Maskin (1996) is concerned with the idea that a rise in the overall (mean) skill levels may be accompanied by a rise in wage inequality as well as a rise in segregation across plants of workers of different skills. Key assumptions are that workers of different skills are imperfect substitutes, different tasks within a plant are complementary, and different tasks differ in their sensitivity to skill. The distribution of worker skills is exogenous, and the competitive economy operates under constant returns. The equilibrium wage distribution depends on skill distribution, but also on how workers of different skills are matched with one another. The model predicts that a rise in the dispersion of the skill distribution will cause increased segregation of workers. Moreover, a rise in the mean of the skill distribution increases wage inequality across plants when the skill distribution is sufficiently dispersed.

Kremer and Maskin (1996) provide empirical evidence that suggests that segregation by skill has become increasingly prevalent in the United States, the United Kingdom, and France over the 1980s and the 1990s. There is, furthermore, some evidence from data on U.S. states that segregation by skill is amplified by increased variance of skills, consistent with the theory.

The level of education has increased substantially in Sweden in recent decades. Between 1970 and 2000, the fraction of the population with upper-secondary education increased from 30 to 50 percent, and the fraction with tertiary education from 7 to 30 percent (Björklund et al. 2005). Has there also been an increase in the dispersion of education? If so, the Kremer and Maskin (1996) theory would predict increased segregation by skill, consistent with what we observe in the Swedish data.

We have transformed our data on education levels into years of schooling and computed the variance of schooling using all individuals in the data. The results are displayed in figure 7.16 and reveal a marked increase in the variance of schooling from the early 1990s and onward (but a slight decline in the late 1980s). Although this pattern is broadly consistent with the Kremer and Maskin (1996) theory, the exercise certainly does not demonstrate a causal relationship between the dispersion of education and segregation of workers by observed and unobserved skill, or between the

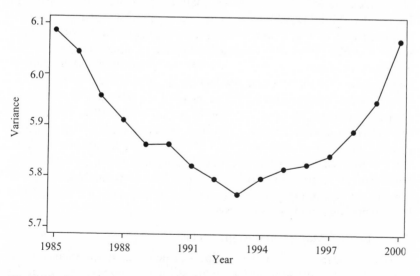

Fig. 7.16   Variance in years of schooling
Notes: Years of schooling calculated as less than compulsory, eight years; compulsory, nine years; two-year high school, eleven years; three-year high school, twelve years; some university, thirteen years; university, fifteen years; graduate studies, nineteen years. Data is for the entire Swedish population aged sixteen to sixty-five each year.

dispersion of skills and between-plant wage inequality. At the very least, the results suggest that future work on the sources of increased wage inequality in Sweden should explore how changes in the level and dispersion of schooling have affected employers' incentives to match workers of different skills in the same plants.

7.6.2   Decentralization of Wage Bargaining

In a standard bargaining framework, the bargained wage is determined by "inside" and "outside" factors. The former include measures of the plant's ability to pay, the latter overall labor market conditions. Imagine a plant-level wage negotiation between an employer and a local union. The stronger the local union is, the more responsive would the bargained wage be with respect to the plant's ability to pay. The power of the local union will be constrained not only by a strong bargaining position of the employer but also by a central union that is able to strike wage agreements at the national or industry level. The more centralized the wage bargaining system, the weaker the links between plant-specific productivity factors and wage agreements at the local level. And, conversely, the less centralized the bargaining system, the more scope for local rent sharing.

A number of studies have examined this hypothesis using data on plants or industries.[15] By and large, most studies find that rent sharing has been of limited importance in Sweden. There is so far little hard evidence that increasingly decentralized wage negotiations have changed this pattern. Forslund and Lindh (2004) used plant data for Swedish mining and manufacturing and looked at the cross-sectional relationship between plant wages and plant productivity, measured as the nominal value added per employee. In regressions for each year for the period 1970 to 1996, they related log wages to log productivity. The estimated coefficient on productivity was closely centered on 0.05. The mean of the estimates was 0.055 for the period 1970 to 1982 and 0.051 for the period 1983 to 1996. The authors report that panel data regressions produce similar estimates. There is no indication in this study that wages have become more responsive to plant-level productivity despite the fact that wage negotiations arguably have become more decentralized since the mid-1980s. Unfortunately, because our data do not include any plant-level productivity measures, it is not possible to shed new light on this hypothesis.

7.6.3   Product Markets and Ability to Pay

An increase in the productivity dispersion across plants may cause an increase in between-plant wage inequality as long as there is some scope for local rent sharing. The recent paper by Dunne et al. (2004) brings new ev-

---

15. Holmlund and Zetterberg (1991) exploit industry data, whereas firm data are used by Arai (2003), Forslund (1994), and Forslund and Lindh (2004).

idence on this issue in a study of wage and productivity dispersion in U.S. manufacturing. The study exploits establishment data over the 1975 to 1992 period and finds that almost all of the increase in hourly wage dispersion is accounted for by an increase in the between-plant component. Interestingly, the study also documents an increase in the between-plant distribution of productivity over the same period. Moreover, wages and productivity at the plant level are strongly positively correlated, both in levels and changes. The paper also finds that an important source of the rise in wage and productivity dispersion between plants is accounted for by changes in the distribution of computer investment across plants.

Data on the evolution of the productivity dispersion across Swedish plants are rare. Some information is offered by Forslund and Lindh (2004), who computed a productivity measure (the standard deviation of log value productivity) for mining and manufacturing. Interestingly, there is a trend rise in productivity dispersion, especially from the early 1980s and onward. To the extent that this development holds for the private sector as a whole, it may help explain the rise in between-plant wage inequality.

7.7   Concluding Remarks

This chapter has provided new evidence on the evolution of wage dispersion in Sweden, with particular focus on dispersion within and between plants. We use linked employer-employee data and find a striking trend increase in between-plant wage inequality since the mid-1980s. Interestingly, this trend in between-plant variance makes up the entire increase in wage dispersion over the period.

The increase in wage dispersion between plants is not only present in the raw data, but also when we control for workers' human capital characteristics. Thus, sorting by observed characteristics can only explain part of the increase. We find that the basic pattern holds within industries as well as between plants in different industries. Also, increasing between-plant wage dispersion has been substantial throughout the individual wage distribution, except for individuals at the top of the distribution. Overall, our results suggest that the growing difference between plants is driven by increased differences between plants in the wages they pay, rather than by changes in the composition of plants in the economy.

It lies close at hand to suspect that a gradual evolution toward more decentralized wage-bargaining practices is a factor of importance. Our data are, however, not rich enough to test alternative hypotheses concerning the mechanisms behind the rise in wage inequality between plants. It is premature, therefore, to identify the causes of the rise in between-plant wage inequality. To make progress on this front, we need more information on plant characteristics and, in particular, measures of (value) productivity at the plant level.

Appendix A
Mobility of High- and Low-Level Jobs

Table 7A.1   Mobility: High-level jobs

	All plants				Plants with 100+ employees			
	1986	1990	1995	2000	1986	1990	1995	2000
No. of plants	6783	8025	7137	8475	1338	1560	1418	1640
Employees	100.6	98.4	101.7	99.1	311.6	303.8	315.4	302.6
	(236.1)	(226.1)	(224.5)	(213.2)	(474.7)	(456.8)	(441.5)	(425.5)
Employment growth	0.016	0.029	0.057	0.062	0.002	−0.005	0.051	0.040
	(0.243)	(0.247)	(0.230)	(0.327)	(0.171)	(0.160)	(0.193)	(0.249)
Exit rate, observ = person	0.136	0.149	0.136	0.182	0.133	0.153	0.131	0.197
Exit rate	0.141	0.158	0.144	0.190	0.125	0.152	0.130	0.191
	(0.202)	(0.210)	(0.206)	(0.237)	(0.140)	(0.150)	(0.139)	(0.179)
Top quartile of firm wages	0.167	0.183	0.179	0.220	0.161	0.190	0.182	0.239
	(0.285)	(0.293)	(0.293)	(0.320)	(0.201)	(0.213)	(0.213)	(0.259)
Bottom quartile of firm wages	0.128	0.147	0.128	0.177	0.113	0.128	0.105	0.159
	(0.249)	(0.266)	(0.252)	(0.282)	(0.185)	(0.188)	(0.184)	(0.217)
Top decile of firm wages	0.186	0.204	0.208	0.239	0.188	0.229	0.236	0.279
	(0.339)	(0.352)	(0.353)	(0.375)	(0.263)	(0.288)	(0.291)	(0.333)
Bottom decile of firm wages	0.141	0.156	0.122	0.192	0.115	0.130	0.095	0.170
	(0.289)	(0.301)	(0.267)	(0.323)	(0.233)	(0.233)	(0.196)	(0.269)

	(1)	(2)	(3)	(4)	(5)	(6)	(7)	(8)
Entry rate	0.116	0.129	0.128	0.169	0.107	0.114	0.118	0.167
	(0.183)	(0.191)	(0.197)	(0.227)	(0.133)	(0.136)	(0.138)	(0.181)
Top quartile of firm wages	0.130	0.147	0.146	0.181	0.126	0.148	0.151	0.191
	(0.253)	(0.268)	(0.271)	(0.300)	(0.182)	(0.202)	(0.208)	(0.243)
Bottom quartile of firm wages	0.117	0.125	0.122	0.179	0.102	0.096	0.105	0.149
	(0.241)	(0.244)	(0.242)	(0.289)	(0.182)	(0.163)	(0.182)	(0.221)
Top decile of firm wages	0.144	0.160	0.159	0.194	0.152	0.171	0.180	0.222
	(0.304)	(0.320)	(0.321)	(0.347)	(0.243)	(0.260)	(0.273)	(0.311)
Bottom decile of firm wages	0.128	0.141	0.139	0.200	0.094	0.095	0.111	0.154
	(0.279)	(0.289)	(0.285)	(0.330)	(0.201)	(0.201)	(0.209)	(0.254)
% of workers with 5+ years of tenure	0.452	0.485	0.447	0.447		0.472	0.529	0.468
	(0.344)	(0.355)	(0.347)	(0.347)		(0.310)	(0.308)	(0.299)
Correlation (exit rate, average wage),	0.105	0.106	0.134	0.158	0.174	0.117	0.196	0.193
Correlation (exit rate, average wage change)	0.045	0.047	0.072	0.131	0.074	0.084	0.121	0.141
Correlation (exit rate, SD of wage)	0.072	0.109	0.120	0.161	0.096	0.074	0.146	0.117
Correlation (entry rate, average wage)	0.103	0.129	0.150	0.165	0.088	0.165	0.229	0.182
Correlation (entry rate, average wage change)	0.027	0.044	0.056	0.090	0.084	0.085	0.069	0.083
Correlation (entry rate, SD of wage)	0.087	0.128	0.117	0.129	0.037	0.141	0.118	0.122

Notes: High-level jobs are jobs with wages above the 80th percentile of the sample wage distribution. All statistics are at the plant level with one plant as one observation except as otherwise noted. Tables for all jobs can be found in the text. Correlations are with average log wages in plants, average log wage changes for workers remaining in the plant, and standard deviation (SD) of log wages within plants. Numbers in parentheses are standard deviations.

Table 7A.2   Mobility: Low-level jobs

	All plants				Plants with 100+ employees			
	1986	1990	1995	2000	1986	1990	1995	2000
No. of plants	6964	8195	7415	8868	1340	1565	1420	1650
Employees	99.1	97.2	99.4	96.4	311.6	303.2	315.3	301.6
	(233.3)	(223.9)	(220.6)	(208.8)	(474.4)	(456.1)	(441.2)	(424.4)
Employment growth	0.016	0.028	0.057	0.060	0.001	−0.006	0.051	0.040
	(0.242)	(0.246)	(0.228)	(0.320)	(0.172)	(0.160)	(0.193)	(0.249)
Exit rate, observ = person	0.394	0.395	0.270	0.346	0.376	0.387	0.246	0.319
Exit rate	0.387	0.382	0.286	0.345	0.369	0.377	0.258	0.321
	(0.212)	(0.216)	(0.219)	(0.233)	(0.135)	(0.138)	(0.146)	(0.160)
Top quartile of firm wages	0.303	0.318	0.217	0.276	0.257	0.290	0.168	0.230
	(0.314)	(0.316)	(0.296)	(0.318)	(0.189)	(0.191)	(0.181)	(0.207)
Bottom quartile of firm wages	0.521	0.485	0.393	0.456	0.525	0.496	0.385	0.460
	(0.353)	(0.352)	(0.349)	(0.352)	(0.209)	(0.214)	(0.231)	(0.245)
Top decile of firm wages	0.291	0.306	0.208	0.272	0.249	0.274	0.159	0.226
	(0.385)	(0.387)	(0.352)	(0.380)	(0.247)	(0.255)	(0.224)	(0.267)
Bottom decile of firm wages	0.579	0.537	0.443	0.517	0.584	0.545	0.451	0.518
	(0.409)	(0.413)	(0.411)	(0.415)	(0.312)	(0.313)	(0.320)	(0.321)

Entry rate	0.428	0.463	0.417	0.463	0.393	0.414	0.378	0.424
	(0.239)	(0.239)	(0.256)	(0.264)	(0.167)	(0.162)	(0.181)	(0.201)
Top quartile of firm wages	0.333	0.375	0.320	0.361	0.280	0.319	0.273	0.309
	(0.336)	(0.345)	(0.347)	(0.359)	(0.210)	(0.216)	(0.237)	(0.262)
Bottom quartile of firm wages	0.544	0.568	0.541	0.583	0.510	0.515	0.500	0.538
	(0.357)	(0.355)	(0.358)	(0.356)	(0.234)	(0.230)	(0.238)	(0.263)
Top decile of firm wages	0.318	0.364	0.305	0.347	0.262	0.300	0.259	0.285
	(0.400)	(0.414)	(0.402)	(0.417)	(0.264)	(0.276)	(0.282)	(0.306)
Bottom decile of firm wages	0.570	0.604	0.585	0.618	0.523	0.538	0.546	0.567
	(0.413)	(0.407)	(0.409)	(0.405)	(0.328)	(0.323)	(0.322)	(0.332)
% of workers with 5+ years of tenure	0.137	0.235	0.203			0.170	0.278	0.262
	(0.169)	(0.232)	(0.222)			(0.147)	(0.196)	(0.210)
Correlation (exit rate, average wage)	−0.175	−0.139	−0.186	−0.217	−0.123	−0.069	−0.229	−0.249
Correlation (exit rate, average wage change)	−0.015	−0.048	−0.024	−0.020	−0.044	−0.084	−0.014	−0.073
Correlation (exit rate, SD of wage)	0.044	0.053	0.076	0.099	0.061	−0.014	0.064	0.162
Correlation (entry rate, average wage)	−0.153	−0.116	−0.122	−0.148	−0.177	−0.058	−0.069	−0.168
Correlation (entry rate, average wage change)	0.110	0.083	0.132	0.130	0.225	0.215	0.252	0.139
Correlation (entry rate, SD of wage)	0.045	0.033	0.055	0.079	−0.015	−0.002	−0.053	0.021

Notes: Low-level jobs are jobs with wages below the 20th percentile of the sample wage distribution. All statistics are at the plant level with one plant as one observation except as otherwise noted. Tables for all jobs can be found in the text. Correlations are with average log wages in plants, average log wage changes in plants, and standard deviation (SD) of log ages within plants. Numbers in parentheses are standard deviations for workers remaining in the plant, and standard deviation (SD) of log ages within plants.

Appendix B

Mincer Equation Estimates

Table 7B.1   OLS Mincer equation results for corporate sector workers in 25+ sized plants

	1985	1986	1987	1988	1989	1990	1991	1992	1993	1994	1995	1996	1997	1998	1999	2000
2-year high school	0.052	0.056	0.057	0.057	0.059	0.064	0.072	0.062	0.064	0.062	0.059	0.060	0.058	0.053	0.052	0.048
3-year high school	0.159	0.163	0.164	0.158	0.160	0.166	0.173	0.161	0.165	0.163	0.154	0.159	0.157	0.156	0.161	0.161
Some univ.	0.210	0.216	0.222	0.223	0.225	0.233	0.241	0.230	0.235	0.235	0.232	0.246	0.252	0.257	0.271	0.277
3-year univ.	0.403	0.421	0.425	0.430	0.421	0.429	0.441	0.431	0.429	0.435	0.427	0.437	0.438	0.441	0.452	0.458
Post grad.	0.561	0.578	0.578	0.598	0.582	0.588	0.592	0.584	0.576	0.556	0.565	0.552	0.549	0.552	0.565	0.617
Age	0.041	0.040	0.041	0.042	0.041	0.041	0.039	0.033	0.035	0.040	0.040	0.041	0.043	0.044	0.044	0.044
Age$^2 \cdot$ 100	-0.041	-0.040	-0.041	-0.042	-0.041	-0.041	-0.038	-0.032	-0.034	-0.039	-0.040	-0.040	-0.042	-0.044	-0.044	-0.044
Female	-0.206	-0.192	-0.201	-0.216	-0.211	-0.213	-0.215	-0.206	-0.214	-0.219	-0.219	-0.215	-0.211	-0.207	-0.199	-0.197
Immigrant	-0.051	-0.056	-0.062	-0.070	-0.076	-0.082	-0.073	-0.058	-0.057	-0.058	-0.061	-0.064	-0.069	-0.074	-0.090	-0.097
Constant	8.158	8.238	8.287	8.323	8.439	8.526	8.640	8.810	8.801	8.735	8.769	8.809	8.804	8.815	8.825	8.865
R^2	0.4	0.41	0.4	0.39	0.39	0.38	0.37	0.36	0.35	0.35	0.35	0.35	0.35	0.34	0.33	0.33

Notes: All estimates are significant at the 1 percent significance level (all standard errors are 0.003 or less). Reference for education is "less than high school."

Table 7B.2   Plant-fixed effects Mincer equation results for corporate sector workers in 25+ sized plants

	1985	1986	1987	1988	1989	1990	1991	1992	1993	1994	1995	1996	1997	1998	1999	2000
2-year high school	0.042	0.045	0.045	0.045	0.047	0.050	0.053	0.049	0.049	0.048	0.046	0.048	0.046	0.042	0.039	0.036
3-year high school	0.122	0.125	0.124	0.119	0.121	0.123	0.126	0.119	0.119	0.117	0.110	0.115	0.113	0.112	0.112	0.111
Some univ.	0.154	0.160	0.163	0.165	0.167	0.172	0.176	0.168	0.169	0.169	0.164	0.172	0.176	0.177	0.182	0.184
3-year univ.	0.326	0.343	0.342	0.347	0.338	0.339	0.347	0.339	0.335	0.340	0.329	0.334	0.331	0.328	0.325	0.321
Post grad.	0.490	0.507	0.503	0.523	0.505	0.507	0.513	0.508	0.500	0.505	0.489	0.493	0.485	0.482	0.483	0.490
Age	0.038	0.037	0.038	0.039	0.038	0.038	0.035	0.031	0.032	0.036	0.037	0.037	0.040	0.041	0.040	0.040
Age² · 100	-0.038	-0.037	-0.037	-0.038	-0.037	-0.037	-0.034	-0.029	-0.030	-0.034	-0.036	-0.036	-0.039	-0.040	-0.039	-0.039
Female	-0.216	-0.205	-0.214	-0.224	-0.218	-0.220	-0.221	-0.211	-0.219	-0.219	-0.215	-0.210	-0.207	-0.203	-0.197	-0.194
Immigrant	-0.056	-0.059	-0.064	-0.070	-0.077	-0.078	-0.068	-0.056	-0.052	-0.052	-0.055	-0.057	-0.059	-0.064	-0.068	-0.073
Constant	8.222	8.311	8.366	8.400	8.517	8.623	8.732	8.888	8.903	8.845	8.866	8.911	8.897	8.907	8.946	8.986
No. of Plants	8381	8680	9226	10109	10243	10552	10296	9431	9191	9816	10501	10720	10997	11575	12138	12820
Within R^2	0.36	0.37	0.36	0.35	0.35	0.34	0.33	0.32	0.31	0.3	0.3	0.3	0.29	0.28	0.27	0.26
Between R^2	0.505	0.523	0.508	0.518	0.513	0.536	0.500	0.502	0.514	0.523	0.524	0.522	0.511	0.490	0.491	0.469
Variance-share of plant effect (u)	0.184	0.189	0.191	0.188	0.183	0.193	0.217	0.225	0.229	0.229	0.239	0.248	0.253	0.258	0.272	0.283
Corr ($X b, u$)	0.121	0.124	0.124	0.126	0.135	0.147	0.143	0.149	0.156	0.165	0.174	0.177	0.176	0.170	0.190	0.196

Notes: All estimates are significant at the 1 percent significance level (all standard errors are 0.005 or less). Reference for education is "less than high school." Estimated model is ln $W = Xb + \theta + e$, where θ is the fixed-plant effect and e is an error term. Between R^2 are based on squared correlations of actual and predicted plant averages (predictions are based on plant average X and within-estimated parameters).

Appendix C
Additional Tables

Table 7C.1   Means and standard deviations of wages and wage changes

	Log wages				Log wage change			
	1986	1990	1995	2000	1986	1990	1995	2000
	Plants by wage decile				*Plants by wage change decile*			
>90 percentile plants								
Mean wage (or change)	9.690	9.753	9.845	10.068	0.128	0.092	0.137	0.156
Average within plants SD	0.343	0.345	0.338	0.348	0.133	0.150	0.146	0.168
45th to 55th percentile plants								
Mean wage (or change)	9.376	9.440	9.505	9.666	0.051	0.006	0.036	0.046
Average within plant SD	0.255	0.270	0.263	0.264	0.111	0.128	0.116	0.121
<10 percentile plants								
Mean wage (or change)	9.178	9.213	9.249	9.411	−0.012	−0.073	−0.037	−0.034
Average within plant SD	0.217	0.240	0.238	0.236	0.122	0.138	0.131	0.134
	Plants by distance to the plant with median wage				*Plants by distance to the plant with median wage change*			
Decile around 1 SD above median								
Mean wage (or change)	9.542	9.606	9.690	9.880	0.094	0.055	0.094	0.108
Average within plant SD	0.317	0.317	0.313	0.324	0.124	0.138	0.139	0.152
Decile around 1 SD below median								
Mean wage (or change)	9.250	9.302	9.351	9.504	0.013	−0.040	−0.012	−0.007
Average within plant SD	0.228	0.253	0.239	0.247	0.116	0.131	0.121	0.128
No. of plants by decile	704	831	753	906	704	831	753	906

Notes: All statistics are at the plant level with one plant as one observation and calculated for one decile in the distribution of plant wages (left-hand side) or in the distribution of wage changes (right-hand side). SD = standard deviation.

Table 7C.2   Exit rates in plants with compressed and dispersed wages

	1986	1990	1995	2000
Plants with compressed wages (90th/50th wage percentile ratio below average)				
Exit rate	0.197	0.207	0.149	0.193
	(0.123)	(0.121)	(0.114)	(0.132)
Exit rate in top within-plant decile	0.127	0.142	0.123	0.158
	(0.182)	(0.187)	(0.175)	(0.200)
Exit rate in bottom within-plant decile	0.456	0.432	0.340	0.389
	(0.272)	(0.269)	(0.267)	(0.273)
Plants with dispersed wages (90th/50th wage percentile ratio above average)				
Exit rate	0.209	0.228	0.174	0.238
	(0.125)	(0.128)	(0.127)	(0.149)
Exit rate in top within-plant decile	0.165	0.185	0.184	0.236
	(0.204)	(0.215)	(0.220)	(0.245)
Exit rate in bottom within-plant decile	0.452	0.431	0.341	0.406
	(0.270)	(0.270)	(0.268)	(0.284)

Notes: All statistics are at the plant level with one plant as one observation and calculated for one decile in the distribution of plant wages (first half) or in the distribution of wage changes (second half). Numbers in parentheses are standard deviations.

References

Arai, M. 2003. Wages, profits, and capital intensity: Evidence from matched worker-firm data. *Journal of Labor Economics* 21:593–618.

Björklund, A., M. A. Clark, P.-A. Edin, P. Fredriksson, and A. Krueger. 2005. *The market comes to education in Sweden: An evaluation of Sweden's surprising school reforms.* New York: Russel Sage Foundation.

Boeri, T., A. Brugiavini, and L. Calmfors. 2001. *The role of unions in the twenty-first century.* Oxford, UK: Oxford University Press.

Dunne, T., L. Foster, J. Haltiwanger, and K. Troske. 2004. Wage and productivity dispersion in United States manufacturing: The role of computer investment. *Journal of Labor Economics* 22:397–429.

Edin, P.-A., and P. Fredriksson. 2000. LINDA—Longitudinal INdividual DAta for Sweden. Department of Economics. Working Paper no. 2000:19. Uppsala, Sweden: Uppsala University.

Edin, P.-A., and B. Holmlund. 1995. The Swedish wage structure: The rise and fall of solidarity wage policy? In *Differences and changes in wage structures*, ed. R. Freeman and L. Katz, 307–44. Chicago: University of Chicago Press.

Forslund, A. 1994. Wage setting at the firm level—Insider versus outsider forces. *Oxford Economic Papers* 46:245–61.

Forslund, A., and T. Lindh. 2004. Decentralization of bargaining and manufacturing employment: Sweden 1970–96. Uppsala University, Department of Economics. Unpublished Manuscript.

Gustavsson, M. 2006. The evolution of the Swedish wage structure: New evidence for 1992–2001. *Applied Economics Letters* 13 (5): 279–86.

Hibbs, D. 1990. Wage dispersion and trade union action in Sweden. In *Generating equality in the welfare state: The Swedish experience*, ed. I. Persson, 181–200. Oslo: Norwegian University Press.

Holmlund, B. 1984. *Labor mobility.* Stockholm: Industriens Utredningsinstitut.

———. 2003. The rise and fall of Swedish unemployment. CESifo Working Paper no. 918. Munich: Center for Economic Studies-Ifo Institute for Economic Research.

Holmlund, B., and D. Storrie. 2002. Temporary work in turbulent times: The Swedish experience. *Economic Journal* 112:F245–F269.

Holmlund, B., and J. Zetterberg. 1991. Insider effects in wage determination: Evidence from five countries. *European Economic Review* 35:1009–34.

Houseman, S. 2001. Why employers use flexible staffing arrangements: Evidence from an establishment survey. *Industrial and Labor Relations Review* 55:149–70.

Kjellberg, A. 2007. *Det fackliga medlemsraset i Sverige Oktober 2006–Oktober 2007: En första översikt* (The fall in union density in Sweden from October 2006–2007). University of Lund, Department of Economics. Unpublished Manuscript.

Kremer, M., and E. Maskin. 1996. Wage inequality and segregation by skill. NBER Working Paper no. 5718. Cambridge, MA: National Bureau of Economic Research.

Le Grand, C., R. Szulkin, and M. Thålin. 2001. *Lönestrukturens förändring i Sverige* (Changes in Swedish wage structure). In *Välfärd och arbete i arbetslöshetens årtionde (Welfare and work in the decade of unemployment)*, 121–74. SOU Report no. 2001:53. Stockholm: Fritzes.

Organization for Economic Cooperation and Development (OECD) 2004. *OECD Employment Outlook.* Paris: OECD.

Statistics Sweden (SCB). 2001. *Standard Classification by Institutional Sector, 2000, INSEKT 2000, Standard Classification by Ownership Control, 2000, ÄGAR 2000, Classification by Type of Legal Entity, JURFORM.* MIS Report no. 2001:2. Örebro, Sweden: SCB.

———. 2002. *En longitudinell databas kring utbildning, inkomst och sysselsättning (LOUISE) 1990–1999. Bakgrundsfakta till arbetsmarknads—och utbildningsstatistiken.* MIS Report no. 2002:2. Örebro, Sweden: SCB.

Wage Structure and Labor Mobility in the West German Private Sector, 1993–2000

Holger Alda, Lutz Bellmann, and Hermann Gartner

8.1 Introduction

Since the early 1990s, West German firms have had to deal with sharp changes of the economic environment. The German Unification and the emerging competitors in Eastern European countries seem to be the most important ones. At the same time, some labor market institutions in Germany became less rigid—for example, regulation on temporary work. But other institutions are unchanged, so that by and large Germany remains a country with highly regulated labor markets. Thus, international literature characterizes the German economy as a coordinated one (for example, Hall and Soskice 2003). Our study gives an overview of the West German wage structure (their dynamics) and of the mobility in firms of the West German private sector during the 1990s and sheds light on the role of labor market institutions in Germany.

The following are the main questions of our analyses: How much of the German wage dispersion can be attributed to firm and worker characteristics? Are there differences if firms are confronted with different institutions? We address especially the system of collective agreements and the apprenticeship training system. The role of collective agreement in setting wages is seen in Germany as very strong, especially in combination with works councils, because it links the aims of unions—normally formulated on the branch level and negotiated in collective contracts—directly to single

Holger Alda is head of the Data Research Center of the Federal Institute for Vocational Education and Training. He is a research affiliate of the Sociological Research Institute (SOFI) at University Goettingen, Germany. Lutz Bellmann is the head of the Establishments and Employment department and a researcher at the Institute for Employment Research (IAB), Germany. Hermann Gartner is a senior researcher in the Business Cycle and Working Time department at the Institute for Employment Research (IAB), Germany.

firms. The Organization for Economic Cooperation and Development (OECD) states that the German wage-bargaining system is centralized on a medium level (the single Federal States of Germany, *Bundesländer*) and coordinated on a high level (OECD 1997). According to Calmfors and Driffill (1988), this system leads to suboptimal labor market performance because wages do not react sufficiently to macroeconomic shocks.

To examine this point, we will compare separately for different years wages and turnover of firms covered by collective contracts with firms not covered by collective contracts, using propensity score matching. We found that the difference of wages and turnover between firms with and without collective contracts alternates sharply during the business cycle. For example, the workers' wage changes during a boom in firms without collective contracts are higher than in firms with collective contracts, whereas during a recession, they are lower, suggesting that firms without collective contracts can react more flexibly to macroeconomic shocks.

The second property of German labor market institutions we address is the system of vocational training. This system certifies a large range of occupations. For firms covered by collective agreements, the wages are negotiated specifically for occupational groups. Furthermore, if the occupational structure of a national workforce reflects the scale of worker productivity, then there might be reasons for firms to set wages according to occupations. It may be, therefore, expected that wages and wage changes are tied to occupations.

To dig deeper into the role of occupations for wage differences, we ask the following: Can occupational wage differences be explained by differences in observed or unobserved characteristics of firms that employ workers within certain occupations? Or can they be explained by differences in unobserved characteristics of the workers? To answer these questions, we use the method of Abowd, Kramarz, and Margolis (1999). We find that a large part of the occupational wage differences can be explained by unobserved personal characteristics. This means workers with good unobserved characteristics are sorted into high-wage occupations.

With rapidly growing technological and organizational change, we assume that the instrument of setting wages by rather rigid defined occupations loses its power in predicting or signaling single worker productivity. Therefore, we examine the development of the role of occupations in wage setting by analysis of variance technique. The results support our assumption.

The chapter proceeds as follows. In the next section, we describe the macroeconomic environment for German firms in the 1990s and refer more deeply to labor market institutions that are affecting the wage and mobility patterns. The data are described in section 8.3. In section 8.4, we discuss the empirical results. Section 8.5 summarizes and concludes the chapter.

8.2   Macroeconomic Environment and
Labor Market Institutions in Germany

8.2.1   Macroeconomic Environment in the 1990s

For a first glance, the macroeconomic situation is described in table 8.1 by the development of the West German gross domestic product (GDP) and the respective unemployment rates during the 1990s.

In the first years after the German Unification, the West German economy benefited from the growing demand for goods and services in the former German Democratic Republic. The West German GDP grew substantially from 1990 to 1992, but not enough to lower or at least stabilize the unemployment rate. Then, in 1993 there was a slump in economic activities. In 1994 and 1995, the GDP grew again slightly. Since 1998, the growth of the GDP is joined with a decrease of the unemployment rate. The peak of the GDP growth rate was reached in 2000 with about 3 percent. In order to map a business cycle, we choose for our empirical study the years 1993, 1995, and 2000; 1993 is a slump year, 2000 a boom year. In 1995, the growth rate is average, and the unemployment rate remains almost stable.

8.2.2   Labor Market Institutions in Germany

On the OECD scale of rigidities and employment protection, Germany ranks in the midfield (OECD 1999). Despite the trend of deregulating the German labor market in the 1990s, there are still several institutions that enforce the position of insiders. Outsiders have, especially during recessionary periods, only small chances to enter or reenter the (internal) labor

Table 8.1   GDP and unemployment rate in West Germany (1991–2000)

Year	GDP	Growth GDP 1 year (%)	Unemployment rate
1991	1,567,693		.063
1992	1,594,951	1.74	.066
1993	1,557,562	−2.34	.082
1994	1,578,491	1.34	.092
1995	1,600,479	1.39	.093
1996	1,607,803	0.46	.101
1997	1,629,703	1.36	.110
1998	1,664,769	2.15	.094
1999	1,697,689	1.98	.088
2000	1,749,554	3.06	.078

Sources: For GDP, German Central Statistical Office. For unemployment rate, Federal Employment Service.

Note: Gross domestic product (GDP) is at 1995 prices in millions of euros (West Germany only).

market. Four of the most important institutions in Germany affecting wage setting and worker mobility are the system of vocational training, works councils, collective wage contracts, and the protection of workers against dismissal.

The System of Vocational Training

The German system of vocational education is called a dual system because the apprentice is trained partly in the firm and partly in a vocational school. The system has developed from preindustrial apprenticeship roots and prevails not only in Germany, but similarly in Austria, Denmark, and Switzerland (compare with Winkelmann 1997). The training continues between two and three and a half years, so firms invest remarkable time and money in the training of apprentices. The German vocational system reduces the mobility of employees, especially in the group of young, skilled blue-collar workers in the first years after finishing their training, because establishments try to amortize their investment in human capital by longer job tenure of their trainees (Schwerdt and Bender 2003). In several branches, collective agreements guarantee that apprentices can stay for at least one year in the firm after the training.

The German apprenticeship system has deep impacts on the skill composition of the workforce, on tenure tracks, and, consequently, on the wage setting and wage changes of employees. The apprenticeship system and the resulting occupational composition of the workforce is responsible for a clear distinction between skilled and unskilled workers. The occupational characteristics are institutionalized by certificates and occupation regulations—especially in manufacturing and trades, but also in the private and public sector.[1]

In general, the German workforce can be roughly divided into low-, medium-, and high-skilled workers (unskilled, skilled, and workers with a university degree). The apprenticeship system and the resulting occupational structure are mainly a matter of medium skills. In section 8.4, we estimate for all three skill levels of manufacturing, private and public service occupations, the average wage return rate using different sets of covariates, and worker and firm characteristics, respectively. Furthermore, we decompose the variance of workers' average wage change according to firm and occupation.

Works Councils

Another notable institution is the setup of works councils. They have a strong legal base in Germany. A works council is guaranteed by law in all firms with more than five employees, if the majority of the firms' employ-

---

1. An occupational scheme with fewer distinctions also exists for unskilled workers, but this is often only regulated in collective contracts.

ees want to elect one. Furthermore, in firms with more than twenty employees, the works council must agree to dismissals. In case of mass dismissals, the regional labor office and the firms have to draft a social plan to avoid cases of social hardships, if possible. Lots of studies have been made about the effect of works councils on wages and mobility of employees (e.g., Addison et al. [2004]). Nearly all studies conclude that the mobility of workers is hampered by this institution.

Collective Wage Contracts

Especially in larger firms, works councils often coincide with collective agreements. Table 8.2 shows the proportions of full-time workers covered by collective agreements on the firm or branch level[2] and shows for the years 1998 and 2002 how many of these covered full-time workers are working in a firm with a works council.[3]

The coverage of works councils and collective agreement on full-time workers in larger firms is above 90 percent. Firms that are members in an employers' association can deviate from paying collectively agreed wages only by negotiating with the workers on the firm level, but nevertheless, the branch union must agree to the result of the bargaining. Firms that are not members in an employers' association have no restrictions in setting wages. Statutory minimum wages exist only in the construction sector. Negotiated wages must be paid only for union members, but, in fact, negotiated wages are paid to all employees in a firm. The coverage of collective agreement is higher in manufacturing than in the private service sector. Also, the increase of bargained wage is often higher in manufacturing. A high-level coordinated bargaining needs some kind of standards to deal with firm and regional heterogeneities in the branches. This could be occupations, for instance.

Some firms pay more than negotiated wages, especially for high-wage jobs. This additional payment is a component of flexibility in wage setting in rigid labor markets (Kohaut and Schnabel 2003).[4] In this perspective, paying higher wages than fixed by collective agreements will cause larger wage dispersions *within* firms. On the other hand, for example, Büttner and Fitzenberger (1998) show that wages are equal to collective arrangements, especially at the bottom of the wage distribution. If both are present in a

2. Approximately 10 percent of all private firms have wage arrangements on the firm level. The share is rising. For table 8.2, we group both outward forms of collective agreement into one category.

3. In 1993 and 1995, the information is not available. We choose the years 1998 and 2002 in order to show that the coverage of collective agreement over full-time workers is still decreasing.

4. Another form of additional flexibility in paying workers could be employee participation in asset formation or share ownership. In the year 1998, 5 percent of all West German firms use this form of payment (Möller 2001) covering about 15 percent of the total West German workforce.

specific firm, we may find no difference in the within-wage dispersion because in unionized firms, the whole within-wage dispersion might be shifted to the right.

As table 8.3 shows, the proportion of firms paying more than fixed by collective agreement decreases between 1993 and 2000 by 14 percentage points. These firms pay in 1993, on average, 13.4 percent more than bargained; in 2000, they pay 11.5 percent more.

In section 8.4 we will test by nonparametric propensity score matching, whether unionized and nonunionized firms differ in their average wage level, their wage change, the within-firm wage dispersion, and in their mobility patterns (entry and exit rates, percentage of core workers).

Table 8.2   Works councils and collective agreement: Coverage on full-time employees in the West German private sector

	Coverage of collective agreement		Coverage of collective agreement and works councils[a]	
Class size of employees	1998	2002	1998	2002
1–4	.46	.45	Not possible	Not possible
5–19	.65	.55	.05	.05
20–99	.73	.62	.24	.29
100–199	.79	.72	.60	.61
200–499	.85	.81	.79	.76
500+	.96	.94	.95	.92
Total	.78	.71	.51	.48

Source: IAB-Establishment-Panel 1998 and 2002, weighted values.
[a]100 percent are the proportions of the rows on the left.

Table 8.3   Proportion of firms paying more than collectively agreed wages, average, and distribution of this payment (in percent above tariff wage) on firm level (proportion: firms covered by collective agreement in the West German private sector)

Year	Proportion	Mean	Standard deviation	10th percentile	90th percentile
1993	.41	.134	.076	.05	.25
1995	.32	.112	.073	.05	.20
1998	.23	.111	.066	.05	.20
2000	.27	.115	.071	.05	.20

Source: IAB Establishment Panel 1993–2000, weighted values.
Notes: Reading example: In the year 2000, 27 percent of all German unionized firms pay at least to some of their workers higher wages than collectively bargained. On average, this additional payment is 11.5 percent higher than fixed by the respective collective contract. The standard deviation is about 7 percent. The 10th percentile of *these* firms are paying 5 percent higher wages than fixed by collective agreement, the 90th percentile is 20 percent.

The Protection of Workers against Dismissal

A prominent example for the protection of insiders is the German Protection Against Dismissal Acts (PADA), which applies for all firms with more than five (between 1996 and 1998 and since 2004 for firms with more than ten) employees. In the field of application of the PADA, firms are obliged to take into account for their dismissals fairness considerations to avoid cases of social hardship. As a result, if an employer wants to dismiss employees, it has to select young employees (workers with short job tenure) instead of others, especially older, married workers and employees with children. In all of the firms included in the analysis, this law is valid. Thus, we can expect that the mobility of individuals is mainly determined by younger persons with shorter job durations (for an investigation of worker flows and dismissal protection, see Bauer, Bender, and Bonin [2004] and Verick [2004]).[5]

Other Institutions

In Germany, there is a large wedge between labor costs and net wages. Because of the cost of German Unification, the wedge increased during the 1990s: According to the OECD (2005), the income tax plus employee and employer contributions for social security for a single person without children increased in Germany from 46.4 in 1993 to 51.8 in 2000 (as percentage of labor costs). This may be the main reason that, despite a moderate development of wages, unemployment did not fall during the 1990s.

A further institution affecting unemployment and wages is unemployment benefits. Compared to OECD countries, the replacement ratio ranges in the midfield in the 1990s, but the duration of benefits was very high. With a sufficient work history, older unemployed workers are entitled to unemployment benefits for up to thirty-two months. The strictness of work availability conditions are criticized as lax. The duration of benefit entitlement and the criteria for benefit receipt was thoroughly reformed only after 2000.

Some other institutions of the German labor market are deregulated already in the middle of the 1990s: the Federal Employment Service loses the exclusive right of placing workers in jobs. Restrictions for temporary work agencies are relaxed, and it becomes easier for firms to employ workers by fixed-term contracts—resulting in a increasing proportion of fixed-term workers (compare with table 8.4 in section 8.3). We expect, therefore, that a rising part of wage dynamics during the 1990s could be explained by the mobility of workers instead of the adjustment of wages for stayers.

---

5. Both studies found no significant differences in the level of employment between firms in which the PADA is valid and in which it is not. But there are differences in the structure of employment.

8.3   Data Section

We use the German linked employer-employee data of the Institute for Employment Research (LIAB), the LIAB data link firm-level data from the IAB Establishment Panel (a survey), to administrative individual data from the employment statistics register.[6]

The employment statistics register is based on the integrated notification procedure for the health, pension, and unemployment insurances, which was introduced in 1975. Employers are obliged to report information about all employees covered by social security to the social security agencies. They submit the notifications at the beginning and the end of any employment period as well as each year on December 31st. The notifications include the date of employees' entry and exit, wages, gender, qualification, and the current occupation (defined by a three-digit code). There are legal sanctions for misreporting. The employment statistics register covers more than 90 percent of all employees in manufacturing and 75 percent in the service sector. Freelancers, civil servants, self-employed persons, and workers with earnings below a minimum level are not eligible for the social security system and, therefore, are not included in the worker-level data.

The IAB Establishment Panel is a survey conducted since 1993. The unit "Establishment" refers not to an enterprise or company as a commercial aggregate, meaning that we are not able to identify multiplant firms in our data.[7] Our observation unit firm is smaller than in linked employer-employee data from many other countries. The IAB Establishment Panel is a sample drawn from the so-defined establishments included in the employment statistics register according to stratification cells of the establishment size class (ten categories) and the industry (sixteen categories).[8] These stratification cells are also used for weighting the data set. The population for the survey are all firms with at least one employee covered by the social security system.

To correct for panel attrition, exit of firms, and newly founded units, the samples are augmented regularly, leading to an unbalanced panel. The attrition of the largest firms can only be corrected by an increasing number of medium-sized firms. The reason for this is not only the absence of appropriate larger firms. Especially due to outsourcing activities during the 1990s, the average firm size in Germany was decreasing.

The IAB establishment oversamples larger firms, meaning that there is al-

6. Appendix A gives a short description of the two data sets that are linked to the LIAB.
7. In this sense, we make hereafter no difference between the terms *firm, establishment,* and *employer.*
8. From 2000 onward, the stratification is done according to twenty industries.

Table 8.4   Weighted and unweighted proportions of selected forms of employment on firm level (population: firms with at least 25 full-time employees)

| | Proportion of: | | | |
| | Part-time workers | | Fixed-term contracts | |
Year	Unweighted	Weighted	Unweighted	Weighted
1993	.09	.13	.02	.03
1995	.17	.22	n.a.	n.a.
2000	.20	.28	.08	0.9

Source: IAB Establishment Panel 1993, 1995, 2000.
Note: n.a. = not applicable.

ways a difference between weighted and unweighted results.[9] To illustrate the effect of the weighting procedure for the firm-level data, table 8.4 shows the weighted and unweighted values of the proportion of part-time workers and fixed-term contracts. Smaller establishments are sampled with a lower probability so that weighting increases their proportion. The weighted values for the proportions of both employment forms are higher because small firms employ a higher share of part-time and fixed-term contract workers.

A short note to the result: the increase in the share of part-time workers is mostly driven by the rising participation rate of females in the labor market, whereas fixed-term contracts are distributed more equally between males and females. However, both forms of employment are characterized in the literature as one instrument of firms in order to gain more employment flexibility. Due to the increasing proportions of both forms of employment, we expect higher mobility on firm level at the end of our observation period.

The LIAB data are constructed by merging the IAB Establishment Panel with the data of the employment statistics register using an administrative firm identifier. The IAB has developed two types of the LIAB: the cross-section model and the longitudinal model. An overview about the LIAB, the two data models, and the several versions is given by Alda, Bender, and Gartner (2005); further details are described in Data Reports (Alda 2005a,b,c,d). We compute the descriptive statistics with the LIAB cross-sectional model, version 1. This data set includes in each year the employment spells of the persons employed at June 30th in a firm surveyed by the IAB Establishment Panel.[10]

9. As a rule of thumb, a small establishment with, say, less than five workers, represents approximately 3,000 firms of the national economy, while the largest ones, say, with more than 1,000 employees, represents, on average, only 1.2 firms.
10. June 30th is the reference date of the questions in the IAB Establishment Panel.

The construction of the cross-sectional LIAB allows us to identify movers and stayers as well as compute job duration and the change in wages only by identifying the workers in the same firm on June 30th in two sequenced years.[11] We constructed the tenure variable by checking whether an employee in year t appears also in the same firm in $t - n$ ($n \in$ 1,2, . . .). With larger n, we observe fewer firms due to panel fluctuation. Therefore, we differentiate only between workers with tenure of more or less than three years. Furthermore, in the cross-sectional LIAB, we cannot observe employees after leaving a surveyed firm. It follows that we are not able to compute the change in wages for workers who change their employer with this data model.[12]

The firm size is constructed by aggregating the number of workers covered by the social security system in the employment statistics register. We include in the analysis only firms with at least twenty-five employees in t, where part-time workers, apprentices, and workers not covered by the social insurance system do not count.

Results from tables 8.6, 8.7, 8.8, and 8.10 are computed with the LIAB longitudinal model, version 1. The longitudinal model, version 1, is based on all surveyed firms interviewed between 1999 and 2001 in each year. The corresponding employee data contain all persons who work at least one day between 1996 and 2001 in these firms. The complete working histories of these persons are applicable for the time period 1990 to 2001.

Although both samples—the LIAB cross-sectional and longitudinal model—are representative of the German economy, they differ in some technical aspects and the time period covered. While we restrict the cross-sectional data to firms in the private sector with at least twenty-five full-time employees, the analyses based on the LIAB longitudinal model covers all firms, including the public sector, with at least three full-time employees.[13] Consequently, the results for the average wage and other statistics differ slightly between the two data models. All key variables and definitions (appendix B) are—if applicable—the same in both data models.

However, independent of the LIAB model, two problems occur in the administrative employee data:

First, all wages in the employment register are left-truncated and right-censored. The observable gross wages are left-truncated because workers

---

11. This means first, identify firms, which are in the t and $t - 1$ part of the panel. Second, identify the employees, who are observed in t and $t - 1$. They are defined as stayers. Third, identify workers with only one observation. Workers only observed in t are entries; workers only observed in $t - 1$ are exits. For the first year of the panel, 1993, we use another procedure. For this year, we calculate entries, exits, and wage changes by drawing additional information from the employment register that are not included in the cross-sectional LIAB. This is also the reason why we have the highest number of observations in 1993.

12. With the exception of employees moving to another surveyed firm, the number of these movers is too small for calculating the change in wages for persons changing their employer.

13. The private sector is identified via the legal form of the surveyed firms.

with wages below a certain limit are not obliged to pay contributions for social security. More important is that the wages are also right-censored because the contribution to the social security system must only be paid up to a contribution limit, meaning that this threshold is the highest observable wage in the respective year. The contribution limit rises from year to year. For example, in the year 2000, it corresponds to a gross monthly wage of 3,427 euros. Between 8 and 15 percent of all observations of a year are censored. In the group of employees with a university degree, 50 percent of their wages are censored.

The right-censoring of the wage has implications on the distribution of wages and, therefore, for our wage statistics. To correct this, we impute the censored wages using a tobit estimation of a Mincerian earnings function augmented by ten sector and ten occupation dummies. The imputed wage is calculated as the expected wage ($x'\beta$) plus an error term drawn from a truncated normal distribution.[14]

The second problem is the employment statistics differ only between full- and part-time workers, without further information about working hours. Therefore, part-time workers and switchers from part-time to full-time (and opposite) are excluded from our analyses.

We also exclude apprentices from our data set.[15] All descriptive wage statistics for the cross-country comparison are based on continuing workers in continuing firms. Appendix B gives an overview for all the key variables (and their definitions) we apply in this chapter.

8.4   Empirical Findings

We present each descriptive table of wage levels, wage changes, and the mobility patterns for the cross-country comparison twice, with weighted and unweighted values. They are printed in appendix C. We focus least on the wage statistics of the unweighted results because they are more precise. The weighted values give an impression of how the oversampling of larger firms in the IAB Establishment affects the results. All figures and tables show monthly gross wages in euros. We deflated the wages with the official consumer price index with the base year 2000.

Additionally, to describe statistics on wage structure, we use an analysis of variance (ANOVA) technique. We ask especially how much of the variance of wages can be explained by firm-fixed effects and by human capital and how much of the variance of wage changes can be explained by firm effects and by occupational group.

We analyze the role of occupational group in wage setting more deeply

---

14. The method is described in Gartner (2005).
15. Apprentices work full time and receive wages fixed by collective agreements. Their wages are much lower even than those of unskilled blue-collar workers.

by applying a similar method as developed by Abowd, Kramarz, and Margolis (1999) and applied by Andrews, Schank, and Upward (2004). The method allows us to differ between occupational effects, observed and unobserved firm effects, and observed and unobserved person effects.

A further topic we address more deeply is the effect of collective agreements on wages and worker mobility. To identify this effect, we apply a nonparametric kernel matching algorithm and bootstrap standard errors of the treatment effect with 200 repetitions. Our sample contains 120 firms without collective agreements in 1993 (91 in 1995 and 193 in 2000). The probit estimation of the propensity scores uses as covariates the average age of workers in a firm; a dummy for workers council; one regional dummy; and proportions of females, of fixed-term workers (not included in 1995), of blue-collar workers, and of six different qualification groups. The results are listed in appendix table 8F.1 and discussed in the following subsections.

Before discussing wage and mobility patterns at the firm level, we should take a glance at demographic firm patterns: table 8.5 shows the number of West German firms, their average size, and the employment growth on firm level. During the 1990s, the number of firms is increasing. At the same time, the firm size decreases. The negative growth of employment on firm level refers only partly to a negative macroeconomic growth of employment, because the negative employment growth on firm level is partly compensated by the increasing number of firms. Comparing the growth rates, it seems that firms substitute a part of employees covered by social security

Table 8.5   Number of firms, average firm size, and employment growth on firm level in Germany (1993–2000)

		Firm size				Employment growth	
		All employees		Employees covered by social security			
Year	No. of firms	Mean	CV	Mean	CV	All employees	Employees covered by social security
1993	1,596,596	18.50	0.13	14.78	0.10		
1994	1,608,418	18.24	0.12	14.72	0.10	–1.9	1.1
1995	1,624,600	18.21	0.14	14.63	0.12	1.9	–1.1
1996	1,633,744	17.85	0.14	13.93	0.12	1.6	0.0
1997	1,639,029	17.46	0.14	13.62	0.12	1.4	–5.2
1998	1,643,586	17.41	0.14	13.48	0.12	2.0	–4.3
1999	1,652,821	17.19	0.15	13.58	0.13	–3.2	–2.4
2000	1,712,406	16.65	0.15	13.28	0.12	0.5	–3.8

Source: IAB Establishment Panel 1993–2000, weighted values.
Note: Firms with at least one employee covered by social security are included. CV = coefficient of variation.

by workers with no connection to the social security system—for example, freelancers or low wage earners. But due to the increasing coefficient of variation, one cannot be sure about this. Concerning their average number of employees, German firms became more heterogeneous during our observation period.[16]

Organizational change is responsible for the increasing number of newly founded firms and the downsizing of the existing firms. There were many outsourcing activities in Germany, especially at the end of the 1990s. The newly founded firms have a more homogenous workforce than the "old" firms had before the outsourcing. Therefore, we expect that the wage dispersion between firms is increasing during the 1990s, while the within-firm wage variance in decreasing. In other words, we expect larger firm effects at the end of our observation period due to more (and smaller) high- and low-wage firms.

8.4.1 Structure of Wages within and between Firms

In this section, we discuss the development of wages on firm level and worker level during the 1990s. The descriptive statistics are presented in the appendix tables 8C.1 (unweighted values) and 8C.2 (weighted values). In figure 8.1, we plot the kernel densities of the workers' log wage distribution in the years 1993, 1995, and 2000 and in figure 8.2 the distribution of the firm average wage for the same years.[17]

The distribution of workers' wages shifted to the right, and the dispersion of wages is increased. This means that higher wages increased more than lower wages. The distribution of firm average wage shifted also to the right and exhibits a higher dispersion. Germany has, in the year 2000, more high- and low-wage firms than in 1993. Appendix table 8C.1 supports this result: the standard deviation of the employees' and firms' average wage increases in our observation period. Workers' and firms' wages became more unequal in Germany during the 1990s.

How is the observed within-firm wage dispersion affected by our example of a labor market institution, namely collective contracts?

The results of matching firms with and without collective contracts (second row in appendix table 8G.1) shows no significant wage compression in firms covered by collective contracts compared to nonunionized firms. The average wage in firms with a collective contract is higher, but significantly only in the boom year 2000. Collective contracts shift the within-wage distribution to the right, on the upper bound of wages as well as on the lower bound. The mean comparison shows that for discussing the descriptive

---

16. Details of the firm size distribution shows especially large firms downsize during the 1990s. The increase of the coefficient of variation is, therefore, determined by medium-sized firms.

17. We cut off all censored wages for figure 8.1.

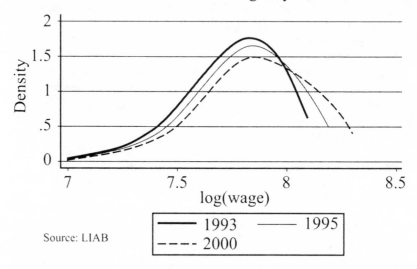

Fig. 8.1 German workers' and firms' wage distribution in 1993, 1995, and 2000: Individual wage by year

Source: LIAB cross-sectional model, version 1.

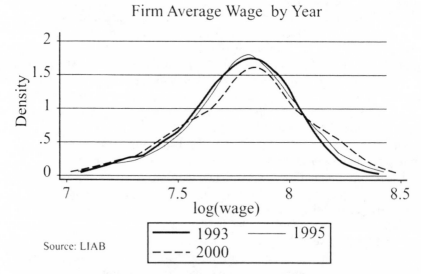

Fig. 8.2 German workers' and firms' wage distribution in 1993, 1995, and 2000: Firm average wage by year

Source: LIAB cross-sectional model, version 1.

results, we do not have to take especially into account a clear difference between unionized and nonunionized firms.

Table 8C.1 shows the following:

- The higher standard deviation is mostly driven by the development at the upper bound of wages on individual *and* firm level. The logs of individuals' and firms' wages were rising by about 0.1 log points in the 90th percentile, but in the 10th percentile, the individual wage rises by 0.05 log points, and the firm wage even decreased slightly.
- While at the upper bound of the firms' wage distribution the within-wage dispersion became more unequal (column: average standard deviation of firms' average wage), at the lower bound of the firms' wage distribution, the within-wage dispersion became more equal.
- The average standard deviation of firms' average wage was about 30 percent of the overall average wage. This means that still a bulk of wage variation in the German economy was within firms, not between firms, but the latter became more important during the end of the observation period.
- The distribution of the individual wage shifted to the right. That is, the weight of higher wages has increased, which is also true for the distribution of firms' average wage, because the proportion of high-wage firms increased from 1993 onward. The contrast between the distributions for the years 1993 and 2000 is very clear, whereas the 1995 distribution is in-between.
- Workers aged twenty-five to thirty and workers aged forty-five to fifty exhibited a similar development of wages (appendix table 8C.1). Again, wages at the upper bound of the wage distribution increased much more than at the lower bound.
- The wages for persons aged forty-five to fifty were higher than for younger people. This can only partly be explained by the fact that larger firms pay higher wages and employ older workers. The correlation between the log size and the average age of workers in firms is 0.111 in 1993, 0.026 in 1995, and only 0.02 in 2000 (but all coefficients are significant on the 5 percent level). Wage regressions show the usual U-shaped wage return rate for age. One year older corresponds, ceteris paribus, to a higher wage for workers aged thirty of 2.8 percent (aged forty: 1.6 percent; aged fifty: 0.4 percent).[18]
- The correlation between the average tenure and the firm size decreases. The (log) size correlates with the average tenure on firm level in the year 1996 with 0.375 and in 2000 with 0.284 (1993, 1995 not applicable). One interpretation of this result is that in stable or slump years, larger firms keep their workers with longer job duration more

---

18. These results refer to the observation period 1996 to 2001.

than in boom years. Another interpretation is simply that large firms grow in boom years.[19] We have to leave open here whether the weaker correlation in 2000 also corresponds with worker mobility mostly driven by employers or the respective employees (we come back to this point by discussing the mobility results). However, wage regressions show that the average wage return for one additional year of job duration is, ceteris paribus, 2.1 percent in the time period 1996 to 2001.

Beside these descriptive results, linked employer-employee data allow computing the proportion of the variance of wages that can be explained by the variance of human capital and by the variance of firm-specific effects (Groshen 1989, 1991; Stephan 2001). Table 8.6 shows the coefficient of determination, R^2, which can be attributed to human capital, firm-specific effects, and their interaction by estimating a Mincerian earnings function.

For the years 1993 to 2000, a clear trend emerges: the importance of the firm-specific effect increases, whereas that of the human capital effect decreases. This means that unobserved firm effects or sorting to firms according to unobserved personal characteristics affect more and more the distribution of wages, whereas sorting according to observed personal characteristics plays a smaller role. This may be driven by the decreasing firm size, which is accompanied by more within-homogeneity of firms. The R^2 related to the interaction of firm-specific and human capital effects remains almost stable over that time period. These results fit very well into the results of our descriptive analyses of the wage structure.

Wage levels and within-firm wage variance are correlated positively (appendix table 8C.1). Of course, larger firms pay higher wages and use a wider range of different occupations, but the increasing within variance of wages in the observation period can only be partly explained by a wider range of occupations.[20]

8.4.2   Occupational Wage Differentials and Heterogeneity of Workers and Firms

We analyze more deeply the relation between occupations and wages: What is the reason for wage differentials between occupations? Can occupational wage differentials be explained by the following?

- Differences in the productivity of occupations
- Observed differences in characteristics of firms that have a demand for these occupations

---

19. This seems unlikely. A comparison of the weighted and unweighted values in appendix table 8C.5 shows that the employment growth in 2000 is "larger" (in the sense of a less negative growth) in smaller establishments.

20. This can be seen in table 8C.5: firms use less occupations at the end of our observation period than at the beginning. The nearly unchanged weighted values for the observed time period show that only larger firms reduced their number of occupations.

Table 8.6   Analysis of variance of workers' wages

	Adjusted R^2 of ANOVA		
	1993	1995	2000
Firm effects	0.273	0.284	0.347
Human capital	0.448	0.445	0.386
Human capital + firm effects	0.587	0.586	0.595

Source: LIAB cross-sectional model, version 1.
Note: Firms with at least twenty-five full-time employees are included.

- Unobserved differences in characteristics of firms that have a demand for these occupations
- Unobserved differences in employees that work in this occupation

To answer this question, we estimate wage regressions using the LIAB longitudinal data.[21] The first regression model (1) includes ten covariates of personal characteristics x_{it} (like job tenure, education level, job experience, and others) and dummies B_{it} for ten occupational groups. The second model (2) uses in addition twenty-one different observable firm characteristics w_{jt} (like their reorganization activities, the existence of a workers council or collective agreement, worker flow characteristics [i.e., the churning rate], and many others).[22] Model (3) includes additionally unobserved firm heterogeneity ψ_j and unobserved person heterogeneity θ_i. The three models are, therefore, formulated as[23]

(1) $$y_{it} = \mu + x_{it}\beta + B_{it}\zeta \qquad\qquad + \varepsilon_{it}$$

(2) $$y_{it} = \mu + x_{it}\beta + B_{it}\zeta + w_{jt}\gamma \qquad + \varepsilon_{it}$$

(3) $$y_{it} = \mu + x_{it}\beta + B_{it}\zeta + w_{jt}\gamma + \theta_i + \psi_j + \varepsilon_{it}.$$

The time index t refers to June 30th of each year between 1996 and 2001. To estimate model (3), we sweep out the unobserved heterogeneities on firm and worker level by subtracting averages on spell level (a spell is defined by an unique worker-firm combination). A short description of this "spell-fixed-effect" regression gives us appendix F. The models (1) and (2) are pooled ordinary least squares (OLS) regressions. The wage regressions are based on 2,282,926 observations (worker years) of 673,606 full-time workers. We are interested in the zeta coefficients of the occupation groups (table 8.7).

21. In order to downsize the wide range of occupations, we recode the three-digit occupational code into ten occupational groups. The original three-digit-code does not fit well into up-to-date international classifications (ISCO-88 would be possible with the applicable three-digit code).
22. All covariates for the models (1) to (3) are listed in appendix D.
23. Symbols and indexes are explained in appendix E.

Table 8.7   ζ coefficients for occupational groups in West Germany (1996–2001)

	Coefficients from model:		
	(1)	(2)	(3)
Unskilled manual occupations		Reference	
Skilled manual occupations	0.196	0.146	0.019
Technicians, engineers	0.293	0.284	0.058
Unskilled service occupations	n.s.	−0.004	n.s.
Skilled service occupations	0.148	0.045	0.031
Semiprofessionals	0.303	0.146	0.059
Professionals	0.467	0.342	0.100
Unskilled civil servant occupations	0.058	0.047	0.003
Skilled civil servant occupations	0.262	0.223	0.048
Managers	0.458	0.426	0.127

Source: LIAB longitudinal model, version 1 for 1996 to 2001.
Notes: Uses 2.28 million y_{it}-observations; all coefficients are significant on a level of $\alpha < 0.01$; n.s. = not significant; models are explained in the text.

The occupational returns in column (1) control only for observed worker characteristics. The results in column (2) control additionally for observed firm characteristics. The more the specific occupational group is—relative to the unskilled manual occupations—sorted into high-wage firms (expressed by $w_{ji}\gamma$), the lower is the zeta coefficient of model (2) compared to model (1). But they differ only slightly. Accordingly, only a small part of occupational wage differentials can be explained by differences in observed characteristics of firms that have a demand for these occupations. Exceptions of the small, observable firm effects are the skilled service occupations and semiprofessionals or professionals, meaning that especially high-wage firms employ workers with such occupations.

Model (3) controls additionally for unobserved heterogeneity of workers and firms. The interpretation of the differences between the zeta coefficients from model (2) and (3) is quite similar. The more the occupational wage differentials could be explained by unobserved characteristics of workers and firms, the lower is the zeta coefficient in model (3) compared to model (2). In most cases, the zeta coefficient is even substantially lower. Only for skilled service occupations do the unobserved worker and firm characteristics have just a small effect on the wage return rates in this occupational group.

To summarize, if we control for unobserved firm and worker characteristics, there are often only small wage differences between different occupational groups. Thus, we can conclude that firms set wages not only by occupations but also for other observed and unobserved person and firm characteristics.

Table 8.8   Correlation between observed and unobserved worker and firm characteristics

	$\hat{\theta}_i$	$\hat{\psi}_j$	$x_{it}\hat{\beta}$	$w_{jt}\hat{\gamma}$
Unobserved worker characteristics ($\hat{\theta}_i$)	1.0000			
Unobserved firm characteristics ($\hat{\psi}_j$)	−0.0960	1.0000		
Observed worker characteristics ($x_{it}\hat{\beta}$)	0.3787	0.0002	1.0000	
Observed firm characteristics ($w_{jt}\hat{\gamma}$)	−0.0276	−0.2376	−0.0417	1.0000

Source: LIAB longitudinal model, version 1 for 1996 to 2001.
Note: The table uses 673,606 averages on the level of persons, based on 2,282,926 y_{it}-observations.

To investigate this further, table 8.8 shows the correlations of the observed and unobserved workers' and firms' characteristics.

Like in many countries,[24] the correlation between unobserved firm and worker characteristics, corr($\hat{\theta},\psi$) = −0.0960, has the wrong sign if one expects that "good" employers have "good" workers.[25] Also, the correlation between unobserved firm characteristics, ψ, and observed worker characteristics, $w_{jt}\hat{\gamma}$, looks somewhat skewed.[26] Whereas a plausible result is that observed and unobserved worker characteristics correlate positively, corr($\hat{\theta}, x_{it}\hat{\beta}$) = 0,3787. This means that high-skilled workers also accumulate unobserved abilities for which employers pay higher wages.

The correlation of the observed firm characteristics with the observed and unobserved worker characteristics is weak. This suggests that the estimated coefficients of one side of the labor market are not affected if we ignore the other side. But, on the other hand, as shown for the occupational groups in table 8.7, the returns for observable workers' characteristics sometimes differ remarkably if we control for observed and unobserved firm characteristics.

Referring to the unobserved worker heterogeneities, further investigations (Alda 2006) show that unobservable good workers are more likely to

24. Abowd, Creecy, and Kramarz (2002) reports a strong negative correlation of −0.283 for the French and −0.025 for Washington State data. Goux and Maurin (1999) estimate (depending on the time period) +0.01 to −0.32. Gruetter and Lalive (2003) report −0.543 for Austria, and Barth and Dale-Olsen (2003) −0.47 to −0.53 for Denmark.
25. Andrews, Schank, and Upward (2004) report for Germany a correlation of nearly zero (−0.0172) in the time period 1993 to 1997 with comparable LIAB data, but fewer and different covariates. One reason for their weak correlation is that they did not use characteristics of individuals that describe their labor market behavior (e.g., times of unemployment and leave of absence for family phases). These covariates are positive correlated with the unobserved person effects (meaning that the higher the integration in the labor market and the less there are events and times of unemployment, the higher is the unobserved person effect on wages). The correlation with the vector of covariates referring to labor market integration and the unobserved person effect θ_i is + 0.1526.
26. The reason might be too little turnover between the firms in the sample.

be sorted into larger firms, in firms that reduce hierarchies and increase workers' responsibilities, in firms that have less turnover, and those who are tied by collective agreement on the firm level.[27]

8.4.3   Wage Dynamics

The statistics for the wage dynamics are printed in appendix tables 8C.3 and 8C.4. Figure 8.3 shows the kernel densities for the change in wages on individual, figure 8.4 on the firm level.

The change in wage for workers (figure 8.3) and the change of the firms' average wage (figure 8.4) give no clear picture. Both distributions shift to the right from 1993 to 1995. Between 1995 and 2000, there is a slight shift to the left. The peak of the density function changes only for individuals. On the firm level, the peaks are in all years nearly on the same level.

The change of wages varies not only between firms. There is also a wide range of within variation in the change of wages, increasing during the observation period. The 90/10 ratio of the standard deviation of the change in firms' average wage is 2.383 in the year 1993, 2.545 in 1995, and 2.814 in the year 2000. Two interpretations are possible:

First, rising wage growth rate differences might reflect wage-level differences. Maybe the wages in human capital-intensive firms grew very fast, while wages remain nearly unchanged in nonintensive firms. A tied argument is that heterogeneous firms have a large mixture of skills. Then there would be a high variance of wage growth rates within firms and little variation in the means across firms.

Second, the growth rate differences might reflect institutional or sectoral differences. These could be unions or industries. Collective contracts, for instance, might compress wages as well as their growth rates. To test this hypothesis, we estimate the effect of collective contracts on change in wages by a matching approach (appendix G). But the results only partly support the second hypotheses, because firms with and without collective contracts do not differ significantly in their average change in wages in any observed year. Only the coefficient of variation of the change in wages is in all years lower in unionized firms, significantly in the year 1993 and in 2000. Firms covered by collective contracts treat their workers regarding the wage change more equally than nonunionized firms.

However, depending on the year, the standard deviation of the change in firms' average wage is higher than the average change in workers' wage. Further analyses are needed to interpret this. From the rough tenure variable in the LIAB cross-sectional model (appendix table 8C.3), we can deduce no clear interpretation for the results. If wages within a firm grow

27. If firms pay wages by collective agreement on branch level, the averages of the unobserved person effects on firm level are smaller, but, nevertheless, higher than in firms not covered by unions. Hence, the wage regressions control for the observable average effect of collective agreement on the firm and branch levels.

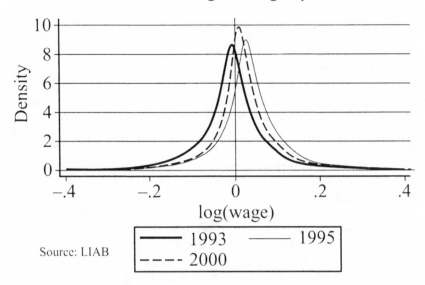

Fig. 8.3 Change in log wages on worker and firm level: Individual wage change by year
Source: LIAB cross-sectional model, version 1.

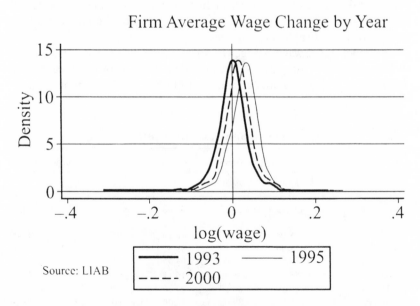

Fig. 8.4 Change in log wages on worker and firm level: Firm average wage change by year
Source: LIAB cross-sectional model, version 1.

differently, the *average* change in wages for workers is not able to tell us what drives this development. The high standard deviation of wage changes supports this argument. It seems that within firms, winners and losers (in terms of their wage change) coexist at the same time. Different working conditions might be a reason, for example, fixed in the design of the working contract at the date of entrance assuming it is a firm's reaction of a yearly changing economic environment.

In table 8.9, we investigate this further by looking at the change in wages using the LIAB longitudinal model due to a more precise record of the tenure variable. The table summarizes the change in wages by years of job duration.

We distinguish between males and females. The reason for this is that—despite that males have, on average, higher wage growth rates than fe-males—we can observe a fairly clear trend for male workers. An entrance cohort at a certain time can be identified by diagonals. Each year an en-trance cohort is going one group downward until they finally reach the group with job duration of over five years. The male entrance cohort 1997 to 1998 (this is the category tenure one to two years in the year 1999) has in all years the highest growth rates relative to all other groups. It follows that wage growth rates are joined with the date of entrance in a firm. Rising wage differentials between otherwise equal workers (e.g., regarding their skills or occupation) *within* firms are, therefore, to some extent a conse-quence of their date of entrance into the firm, meaning that rising wage dif-ferentials between firms for workers with comparable human capital are partly a result of firm heterogeneities.

How much of the wage change variance is attributed to firms' fixed effect and how much to occupations? We again use analysis of variance, but in-stead of a vector of human capital, we apply the information of workers'

Table 8.9   Change in wages by job tenure (1999–2001)

	Males			Females		
	1999	2000	2001	1999	2000	2001
All employees	126.75	54.51	46.03	86.64	35.93	24.62
Tenure						
Less than 1 year	88.08	−5.82	−9.19	47.25	37.75	40.09
1–2 years	178.93	99.14	99.51	97.52	91.63	64.62
2–3 years	150.89	130.96	95.27	49.41	65.12	56.26
3–4 years	158.46	95.35	116.11	87.93	41.84	58.05
4–5 years	97.17	86.50	67.76	62.83	50.19	28.90
5+ years	125.64	89.08	72.00	67.60	28.60	17.54

Source: LIAB longitudinal model, version 1.

Note: Monthly gross average wage change in euros.

Table 8.10   Analysis of variance of changes in workers' log wages referring to occupation and firm fixed effects

| | Adjusted R^2 of ANOVA | | |
	1993	1995	2000
Occupation	0.1801	0.1383	0.1689
Firm	0.0856	0.1275	0.1341
Occupation + firm	0.2171	0.2214	0.2474

Source: LIAB cross-sectional model, version 1.
Note: About 330 occupations according to the three-digit classification in the administrative data are included.

occupation. We estimate three regression models: the first regresses the change in wages only on fixed effects for about 330 occupations. The second includes only fixed-firm effects. The third includes occupational as well as firm-fixed effects. Table 8.10 shows the adjusted R^2 for the regression models.

In 1993, the occupation has a much larger effect on the change in wages than the firm. This suggests that firms set wages more by occupations than due to their own heterogeneities. In 1995, there is nearly no difference between firm and occupational effects on the change in wages. In 2000, the influence of both, firms and occupation, on the average wage change is rising. The firm effect on wage changes became higher during the observation period, which is a similar development for wage levels (table 8.6). Also, the interpretation is quite the same. Firm heterogeneities became more important for the development of workers' wages. The occupation effect on the change in wages exhibits no clear time trend. However, in each year, the occupation better explains the variance in the change of wages for workers than the firm.

The analysis of table 8.10 allows us to come back to the interpretation that firm heterogeneities are more important for the change of worker wages within specific entrance cohorts. Table 8.11 repeats the analyses of variance of table 8.10, but now we run separate regressions for each entrance cohort.[28]

For most of the entrance cohorts—especially for the later ones—the picture changed, compared to table 8.10. As suggested by discussing table 8.9, the firm better explains the variance of wage changes of employees with shorter durations. Only for workers with job durations of more than eight years in 1997 does the occupation better predict the change in wages than the firm. Comparing 1997 and 2000 exhibits the same picture as the

28. The results of tables 8.10 and 8.11 are not directly comparable because we have to switch between the LIAB data models.

Table 8.11   Analysis of variance of changes in workers' log wages referring to occupation and firm effects by tenure

Adjusted R^2 of ANOVA

Entrance cohort	Occupation 1997	Occupation 2000	Firm 1997	Firm 2000	Firm + occupation 1997	Firm + occupation 2000
1999/2000		0.209		0.266		0.381
1998/1999		0.110		0.183		0.228
1997/1998		0.121		0.174		0.240
1996/1997	0.216	0.141	0.232	0.143	0.328	0.227
1995/1996	0.129	0.135	0.186	0.157	0.235	0.222
1994/1995	0.151	0.125	0.178	0.158	0.254	0.230
1993/1994	0.159	0.107	0.157	0.145	0.234	0.207
1992/1993	0.144	0.146	0.185	0.172	0.233	0.247
1991/1992	0.123	0.145	0.134	0.147	0.202	0.241
1990/1991	0.127	0.141	0.149	0.169	0.210	0.231
1990 and earlier	0.115	0.114	0.093	0.137	0.175	0.203

Source: LIAB longitudinal model, version 1.

other statistics: in 2000, the firm effects are more important than in 1997, and the human capital (here approximated by occupation) can explain less of the change of workers wages. The combination of the occupation and the firm explains the variance of the wage change of earlier entrance cohorts in 2000 better than in 1997.

To conclude, wage growth rates are joined with the date of entrance by the employer. In addition, firms employ a large mixture of skills. This means there is a lot of within-variance of the change in wages and less variation in the means across firms, as shown in figures 8.3 and 8.4.

8.4.4   Mobility

This section discusses exit and entry rates on the establishment level. The differences between weighted and unweighted values are here more important, because in a smaller firm, one exiting worker increases the proportion of exits more than in a larger one. Due to the oversampling of larger firms in our sample, weighted values reflect the mobility for the typical German firm; unweighted values express the mobility in larger firms.

The growth rate of the firm size is computed as $2(N_t - N_{t-1})/(N_t + N_{t-1})$ with N as the total number of full-time workers. Entry and exit rates were constructed as $2E_t/(N_t + N_{t-1})$. E is the total number of exits or entries in the firm. The correlations are computed with the log wages on the firm level. We calculated the mobility patterns separately for high-wage jobs, low-wage jobs, and for all jobs.

Mobility: All Jobs

Appendix table 8C.5 presents the results for all jobs. As mentioned in section 8.3, the average firm size decreases during the 1990s (table 8.5), but the decreasing firm size in our sample is also partly a result of sample attrition. The weighted values correct for this selectivity. The large firm size and the large standard deviation of the firm size in the unweighted values compared with the weighted values is a typical result of the oversampling. However, according to other studies, larger German firms especially became smaller in the second half of the 1990s because of in- and outsourcing. Therefore, we observe a negative growth of full-time jobs on the establishment level. As noted in section 8.2, this decline in the number of full-time jobs is partly compensated by an increasing number of part-time jobs.

The number of occupations declines during the period in larger firms by approximately 30 percent. This may be a result of the declining firm size, but could also reflect the old-fashioned occupational classification system of the 1970s. Occupations in the declining industrial sector are more microscopically classified than occupations in the expanding service sector. Last but not least, firms sometimes really drive down their number of occupations to concentrate on their core business.

The exit rate for all jobs rises from 0.19 to 0.23 in our observation period. These values are slightly higher than in Norway and Sweden, but still lower than in Denmark, France, or Italy. The entry rate rises from 0.16 to 0.18. This is comparable to the Nordic countries. The rising entry and exit rates may be attributable to the flexibilization of the labor market institutions. Furthermore, the exit rates are higher than the entry rates, reflecting the decline of full-time employment in the 1990s.

Could the rising firm turnover be connected to the declining coverage of collective contracts?

As the matching of firms with and without collective contracts (appendix table 8G.1) shows: exit rates in firms with collective contracts are by 7.7 percent significantly lower in the slump year 1993. At other points of the business cycle, there are no differences between unionized and nonunionized firms. Also, the entry rates differ in both types of firms. In 1993 and 2000, firms with a collective contract hire significantly fewer employees (on average, about 3 percent). These mean comparisons show that especially in more turbulent economic times, collective contracts influence mobility patterns. They are protecting insiders, at least in the years 1993 and 1995 (last column of appendix table 8G.1).

However, despite the institutional treatment, as expected, high- and low-wage firms differ in their mobility patterns. Firms in the top decile of firm wages exhibit lower exit and entry rates than firms in the bottom decile. This is shown by the unweighted as well as the weighted results.

The growing mobility of workers has consequences for the percentage of core workers (defined as persons with job tenure over three years). There are fewer core workers in the year 2000 than in former years. Collective contracts could not prevent this development, as the mean comparison of the propensity score matching shows (appendix table 8G.1, last column): Firms with collective contracts protect—compared to firms without collective contracts—insiders in the years 1993 and 1995 better than in 2000, and, consequently, the difference between the two groups diminishes.

Finally, the correlation patterns in Mobility: All Jobs show:

- The correlation of the exit and entry rates with the average firm wage is negative. This means that high-wage firms have a lower turnover. The reason for this may be that firms try to keep their human capital. But the correlation is getting weaker at the end of the observation period.
- As expected, exit rates are lower and entry rates are higher if firms raise the wages for their workers. This suggests that growing firms raise wages to attract new workers.
- Firms with a higher variance of wages exhibit higher worker mobility, shown by the positive correlation between the entry/exit rate and the standard deviation of the average wage.

Mobility: High-Level Jobs and Mobility: Low-Level Jobs

The mobility patterns of all jobs, high-level jobs, and low-level jobs differ in some points. The definition of high- and low-level jobs is based on the occupational classification (on a three-digit level). We rank occupations by their median wage. High-level jobs are above the 80th percentile of the wage distribution. Low-level jobs are below the 20th percentile.

The following are the main results:

- High- and low-level jobs are a matter of larger establishment. Therefore, the number of high- and low-level jobs differs strongly between weighted and unweighted values.
- As expected, high-wage earners are less mobile in high-wage firms and more mobile in low-wage firms (low-level jobs and vice versa). In all kind of firms, the exit and entry rates of low-level jobs are higher than the rates of high-level jobs. This is consistent with predictions of human capital theory. High-wage workers have accumulated more firm-specific human capital and receive, therefore, higher returns if they stay in the firm.
- In 2000, the entry rate of low-level jobs is higher than the exit rate. This suggests an expanding sector of low-wage jobs in Germany.
- High-wage firms have a lower turnover of high-level jobs and a higher turnover of low-level jobs. If high-wage firms can be regarded as high human capital firms, they have little reason for a high turnover.
- The correlation between the average wage change and the entry rates is for both kinds of jobs negative in 1995 and positive in 2000. If firms

Table 8.12   Exit rates of top, middle, and bottom earners

	1993	1995	2000
90th percentile wage (top earners)	0.133	0.131	0.178
Median-wage (middle earners)	0.129	0.118	0.158
10th percentile wage (bottom earners)	0.232	0.219	0.283
Exit-90th percentile wage (compressed)	0.139	0.145	0.211
Exit-90th percentile wage (spread out)	0.126	0.116	0.142

Source: LIAB cross-sectional model, version 1.

grow in boom years, then these firms may raise their wages to attract workers. A supporting argument is—as already discussed in section 8.4.2 (table 8.8)—that the change in wages for the new hires (with job duration of one to three years) is higher than for employees with longer job tenure.

The relation between the wage dispersion in a firm and the turnover of the high-level jobs is more complicated. The turnover of high- and low-level jobs is lower if the wages within firm are more compressed—with only one exception (entry rate of high-level jobs in 1993). We can expect this only for the low-level jobs. As stated in section 8.2, in firms with workers councils or collective contracts, the wages are more compressed, and low-wage workers are better protected against dismissals. It seems that high-wage earners more often leave firms with compressed wage structures (table 8.12).

There are two differences between the appendix tables 8C.6 and 8C.7 and table 8.12. First, the top, middle, and bottom earners are not calculated by the median wage of occupations but by the wage of people.[29] Second, we calculate the 90th percentile instead of the 80th percentile. However, table 8.12 shows that middle earners are the group with the most stable employment. This may be an effect of the strong insider position of skilled blue-collar workers resulting from the German apprenticeship system. The wages for skilled blue-collar workers are fixed by collective agreements, and unemployment for this skill group is low. Many firms that are not covered by unions also pay tariff wages if they require these skills, so that blue-collar workers—who are the majority of middle earners—have no incentives to change their employer.

The mobility of bottom earners is often induced by the employer, while top earners more often exit from firms with a compressed wage structure.[30] This suggests that they quit more often to seek their chances elsewhere.

29. Middle-wage earners are in the 45th to 55th percentile of the wage distribution.
30. A firm has a compressed wage structure if the value of the 90/50 ratio of the within-firm wage distribution is below the average of the 90/50 ratio of all firms in the German economy. A spread out wage structure is defined for firms who have a 90/50 ratio above this average.

8.5   Summary and Outlook

The West German private sector is characterized by a rising inequality of wages during the 1990s. At the same time, firm heterogeneities became more important for the wage setting and the within- and between-firm variation of wages. To understand the development of wages, we must, therefore, ask, what do the firms do?

There were a lot of reorganization activities in German firms in the 1990s. Outsourcing, new customer-producer relationships, and changes in the work organization were necessary for making firms more competitive. Such activities change the wage structure between and within firms. Wage structures in Germany are rather rigid, and payment adjustments can be more expected via the mobility of workers. Skill-biased technological change affects both the risks of job loss and the wage development of different skill groups (e.g., Bauer and Bender 2002; Kölling and Schank 2003). The institutional frame of the German labor market can be described more or less as protecting insiders. But during the 1990s, employers gain more flexibility in designing fixed-term contracts and employing temporary workers. All this is resulting in a large mixture of heterogeneous workers in heterogeneous firms, in the sense that some of them are more affected by new developments than others. This explains a part of the rising wage inequality and the larger wage dispersion.

The following are further results of analyzing the within and between-variance of wage levels:

- The rising within-variance of wages can only be partly explained by a change in firms' mixture of occupations.[31] The occupational wage differentials are affected by sorting and unobserved characteristics of workers. If we controlled for unobserved firm and worker characteristics, there are only small occupational wage differentials. This means that firms set wages not only by occupations but also for other observed and, especially, unobserved human capital. For example, unobservable good workers work more often in firms that reduce hierarchies, improve worker responsibilities, and have fewer worker flows.
- The wage structure of firms is only partly affected by unions. Unionized firms pay in 2000, on average, significantly higher wages and have in 1995 a more compressed wage structure, whereas in other years, we find no significant differences between unionized and nonunionized firms.
- A decomposition of the variance of wages shows that the importance of the firm-specific effect increases, whereas that of the human capital effect decreases. The R^2 attributed to the interaction of both human

31. We estimate an average wage return rate for workers of, ceteris paribus, 1 percent, if their employer drives down the proportion of different occupations in his or her firm by 5 percent (relative to all of his or her employees).

capital and firm-specific effects remains almost stable during the years 1993 to 2000.

Analyses of the wage changes show that firms exhibit a wide range of change in wages:

- In general, workers with shorter job durations receive higher wage changes than workers with longer job durations.
- The range of the change in wage, especially on the individual level, is getting wider during the 1990s. The 90/10 ratio of the standard deviation of the change in firms average wage is 2.383 in 1993 and 2.814 in the year 2000, whereas the mean remains nearly unchanged.
- Referring to all employees, it looks like wage changes are affected more by occupation than by firm. But wage growth rates are connected with the date of entry in a firm—and the wage growth rates of the same entrance cohort differ between heterogeneous firms. If we control for the date of entry, the firm explains the change in wages better than the occupation.
- We find nearly no significant differences between unionized firms and nonunionized ones. Only in 1995 is the change in wages for workers more compressed if wages are collectively bargained.

The worker mobility increased in the second half of the 1990s and suggests that this is not only driven by the business cycle but also by a trend of deregulation of the German labor market. On the other hand, several institutions tend to protect insiders. It can be concluded that a notable part of the higher mobility in the second half of the 1990s was undertaken by a minority of employees, while the majority of employees still remained in stable employment.

Such mobility patterns also become obvious in our tables for the cross-country comparison (appendix tables 8C.5 to 8C.7):

- While the entry rates in most cases grew moderately (but, nevertheless, there was more mobility), the exit rates become higher during the 1990s.
- Nevertheless, stable employment is still normal in Germany. The protection of insiders became most obvious in the percentage of workers with a duration of job tenure of more than three years. Especially in stable years, the proportion of core (full-time) workers rises in German establishments.

What can be topics for future research? There are two general aspects: the development of the data, and questions about wages and mobility patterns.

The linked employer-employee data from Germany (LIAB) take major steps forward. New technologies allow the building up of better data sets, making a wider range of investigations possible. In the foreground of the further development of the LIAB is the association of the two LIAB data models. This means the integration of workers' histories with the cross-sectional model for all firms of the IAB establishment panel. Meanwhile, over 10,000 firms join in the West and nearly 5,000 in the East Germany panel. Integrating key variables to the associated administrative individual data—like daily precise job durations, the wage of workers by the former employer, durations of unemployment, participation on programs of active labor market policy, and many more—will make research with LIAB data not only easier, but also more fruitful.

To better understand the structure and dynamics of wages and the mobility of employees in Germany, we would like to take a deeper look into the firms in order to understand what is happening *between* them. Maybe this includes firm closing and how newly founded units develop over time, with special attention given to the in- and outsourcing activities of other firms.[32] What is the impact on the skill-wage premium? What follows for the mobility of workers in an economy? Such questions might also give a partial answer to how internal labor markets change over time. Do workers become more equal within firms and more different between firms?

At the end, we would like to note that—and this seems to be consistent in a cross-country comparison—unobservable worker and firm characteristics become more important. They are correlated with the observables and possibly can be regarded as a key for the understanding of wage dispersion as well as the sorting on (national) labor markets, especially whether countries become more equal in labor market mechanisms.

Appendix A
Description of the Data

Description of the data comes from Andrews, Schank, and Upward (2004, 13–14).

The IAB Establishment Panel (*Betriebspanel*)

The IAB Establishment Panel covers the period 1993 to the present of firms located in West and 1996 to the present in East Germany. Establishments are selected by using a fairly complicated weighting procedure. The IAB Establishment Panel covers, unweighted, 1 percent of all firms (but nearly every larger one) and about 8 percent of all employees. Information on each establishment includes, among others:

---

32. An investigation of wage structures in newly founded units with LIAB data is given by Brixy, Kohaut, and Schnabel (2007).

- Total employment
- Standard and overtime hours
- Output
- Exports
- Investment
- Urbanity
- Ownership
- Technology (subjective measure)
- Organizational change
- Profitability
- Age of firms and whether parent is a single firm

The Employment Statistic Register (*Beschäftigtenstatistik*)

For the other side of the labor market, the IAB has access to the federal employment statistics register. It starts in 1975 in West Germany and 1992 in East Germany. It contains about 400 million records, covering about 46 million employees. Information on each worker includes the following:

- Gender, age, and nationality
- Start and end of every employment spell
- Occupation (three-digit)
- Daily gross wages (left-truncated and right-censored)
- Qualifications (education/apprenticeship)
- Industry, region
- Establishment identification number
- Information about multiple jobs and times of unemployment

By using the establishment identification number, the IAB is able to associate each worker in the employment statistics register with an establishment in the IAB Establishment Panel.

Appendix B
Variables and definitions

Remark

The structure of the linked employer-employee data sets of the IAB is described in the data sections in this chapter and in IAB Discussion Paper no. 6/2005. Hereafter, we describe how the applied key variables are defined.

Wages

Wages are gross wages and include all bonus payments. The wages are applicable on a precise daily base. They are multiplied by 30.5 to get monthly wages. Wages are truncated at a lower bound and censored at an upper bound. Censored wages are imputed as described by Gartner (2005). We deflate all wages by the consumer price index (2,000 = 100). All wages and statistics refer to full-time employees. The monthly wages are restricted to the interval [500; 22,026] euros (in log wages [5.5;10]).

Full-Time Employees

The employee data contain no information about the working hours, only whether they are full-time or part-time workers. Therefore, we include only full-time workers. Apprenticeships are excluded from all analyses.

Movers

We use the LIAB cross-sectional data. In this model, movers can only be identified if they move to another firm, which is also part of the IAB Establishment Panel in the following year. We did not use this information for the cross-country comparison. In the longitudinal model, it is possible to follow the working history of people. The correlations of observed and unobserved employer and employee characteristics are based on this LIAB longitudinal data.

Tenure

In the cross-sectional model, it is only possible to check whether the individual identifier occurs in three consecutive years. In the longitudinal model, it is possible to compute job durations on a precise daily base (left-censored at January 1st, 1990). We use this information to report the correlation of the firm size with tenure.

Sector Classification

We use the sector classification from the IAB Establishment Panel. We excluded all firms in the public sector and all firms in public ownership. In the manufacturing sector—which is a subpopulation of the whole sample—we exclude the agrarian sector as well as mining and construction firms. The number of remaining firms in manufacturing are as follows: 1993: 1,161; 1995: 915; 2000: 730).

Mobility and Growth Rates

All mobility rates are based on the formula $2 \times E_t/(N_{t-1} + N_t)$, where E is the event (entries, exits), and N is the total number of employees. This means, for example, that the exit rate of high-level jobs is based on all exits of high-level jobs times two, divided by the sum of all existing high-level jobs at time t and at time t_{-1}. Growth rates are quite similarly constructed: $2 \times (N_t - N_{t-1})/(N_t + N_{t-1})$.

High- and Low-Level Jobs and Top, Middle, and Bottom Earners

To define high- and low-level jobs, we compute for each occupation (on a three-digit level) the median wage. High-level jobs are those jobs in the top 80 percent decile of the wage distribution, low-level jobs are in the bottom 20 percent decile.

Top earners are people in the 90th percentile of the yearly wage distribution, bottom earners are in the 10th percentile, and middle earners are in the 45th to 55th percentile.

Coefficient of Variation

This is constructed as $r = \sigma/|\bar{y}|$, where r is the coefficient, σ the standard deviation, and y the (change in) wage on firm level. For the tables about wage dynamics, the coefficient of variation is much higher than for the structure of wages. In the tables about wage dynamics, the coefficient is, therefore, divided by 100.

Size

All size information used is based only on full-time employees excluding apprenticeships. For the cross-country comparison, there have to be at least twenty-five full-time employees in a firm, for analyses with the longitudinal LIAB data, three.

Switch Rate

The switch rate measures a change in the occupational code of a full-time employee between t and $t - 1$ of all nonmovers in a firm.

Appendix C
Tables on Wage and Mobility Patterns

Table 8C.1   Structure of wages within and between firms (unweighted values; in euros)

	Monthly wages			Log monthly wages		
	1993	1995	2000	1993	1995	2000
Average wage[a]	3,089.97	3,187.36	3,314.24	7.989	8.018	8.052
Median	2,855.75	2,934.31	3,054.59	7.957	7.984	8.024
SD	995.96	1,048.59	1,144.24	0.303	0.308	0.328
90th percentile	4,438.33	4,606.65	4,844.97	8.398	8.435	8.486
75th percentile	3,569.87	3,697.24	3,850.25	8.180	8.213	8.256
25th percentile	2,408.41	2,469.87	2,543.85	7.787	7.811	7.841
10th percentile	2,076.52	2,126.95	2,175.74	7.638	7.662	7.685
No. of workers	1,613,662	1,059,419	622,307	1,613,662	1,059,419	622,307
Average of firm average wage[b]	2,774.89	2,875.68	2,861.15	7.869	7.884	7.878
Median	2,758.07	2,845.02	2,820.62	7.890	7.895	7.897
SD	557.49	601.23	677.69	0.213	0.220	0.251
90th percentile	3,493.73	3,664.33	3,806.67	8.115	8.145	8.192
75th percentile	3,144.38	3,263.71	3,251.82	8.021	8.037	8.038
25th percentile	2,408.39	2,478.56	2,430.48	7.747	7.758	7.747
10th percentile	2,078.78	2,145.13	2,007.83	7.589	7.611	7.547
No. of firms	2,163	1,709	1,578	2,163	1,709	1,578
Average of SD of wages[b]	790.99	818.24	829.83	0.267	0.266	0.274
Median	790.18	821.16	833.26	0.264	0.264	0.271
SD	210.66	226.69	265.19	0.062	0.064	0.076
90th percentile	1,061.06	1,113.54	1148.94	0.346	0.345	0.366
75th percentile	929.03	973.55	1014.69	0.306	0.304	0.315
25th percentile	648.77	663.67	657.91	0.226	0.225	0.225
10th percentile	524.44	522.29	473.57	0.191	0.190	0.189
No. of firms	2,163	1,709	1,578	2,163	1,709	1,578

Average CV of wages[b]	0.288	0.284	0.293	0.034	0.034	0.035
Median	0.286	0.286	0.291	0.033	0.033	0.034
SD	0.067	0.071	0.081	0.008	0.009	0.010
90th percentile	0.370	0.372	0.387	0.044	0.044	0.047
75th percentile	0.329	0.327	0.339	0.039	0.039	0.040
25th percentile	0.245	0.245	0.243	0.029	0.029	0.028
10th percentile	0.206	0.202	0.196	0.024	0.024	0.024
No. of firms	2,163	1,709	1,578	2,163	1,709	1,578
Correlation (average wage, SD of wage)[b]	0.571**	0.589**	0.616**	n.a.	n.a.	n.a.
Average wage for workers between 25 and 30[a]	2,708.43	2,731.13	2,832.01	7.878	7.887	7.916
Median	2,628.39	2,647.54	2,738.93	7.874	7.881	7.915
SD	639.17	634.27	740.02	0.227	0.224	0.257
90th percentile	3,483.24	3,504.48	3,688.77	8.156	8.161	8.213
75th percentile	3,003.81	3,038.16	3,190.57	8.007	8.019	8.067
25th percentile	2,293.15	2,319.55	2,360.98	7.737	7.749	7.767
10th percentile	2,023.95	2,053.61	2,062.87	7.612	7.627	7.631
No. of workers	292,220	172,243	69,017	292,220	172,243	69,017
Average wage for workers between 45 and 50[a]	3,280.06	3346.05	3,438.98	8.046	8.064	8.086
Median	3,040.57	3,095.89	3,161.72	8.019	8.038	8.059
SD	1,072.67	1,115.22	1,204.48	0.313	0.318	0.336
90th percentile	4,706.99	4,833.69	5,048.48	8.457	8.483	8.527
75th percentile	3,920.19	3,981.54	4,082.18	8.274	8.289	8.314
25th percentile	2,514.67	2,560.34	2,612.21	7.829	7.847	7.867
10th percentile	2,136.32	2,166.89	2,211.54	7.667	7.681	7.701
No. of workers	227,483	158,982	105,460	227,483	158,982	105,460

Source: Linked employer-employee data of the Institute for Employment Research/Germany, cross-sectional model, version 1.

Notes: SD = standard deviation; CV = coefficient of variation.

[a]Observation = a person.

[b]Observation = a firm.

**Significant at the $\alpha < 0.005$ level.

Table 8C.2 Structure of wages within and between firms (weighted values; in euros)

	Monthly wages			Log monthly wages		
	1993	1995	2000	1993	1995	2000
Average wage[a]	2808.99	2874.33	3,021.66	7.882	7.904	7.947
Median	2614.68	2662.79	2,778.85	7.869	7.887	7.929
SD	984.09	1025.72	1,130.84	0.343	0.347	0.368
90th percentile	4150.29	4284.84	4,552.66	8.331	8.363	8.423
75th percentile	3291.25	3361.08	3,576.89	8.099	8.120	8.182
25th percentile	2151.25	2194.55	2,267.37	7.674	7.693	7.726
10th percentile	1776.12	1813.39	1,858.69	7.482	7.503	7.527
No. of workers	9,083,054	8,187,154	4,652,141	9,083,054	8,187,154	4,652,141
Average of firm average wage[b]	2,535.99	2,595.01	2,645.80	7.773	7.780	7.795
Median	2,507.45	2,546.38	2,623.53	7.779	7.801	7.809
SD	555.01	597.57	690.68	0.233	0.242	0.269
90th percentile	3,251.58	3,347.32	3,616.41	8.045	8.073	8.148
75th percentile	2,895.55	2,925.65	3,044.09	7.931	7.935	7.972
25th percentile	2,171.04	2,220.07	2,151.13	7.644	7.648	7.618
10th percentile	1,847.67	1,875.74	1,799.47	7.465	7.482	7.455
No. of firms	292,220	172,243	69,017	292,220	172,243	69,017
Average of SD of wage[b]	703.75	708.16	760.17	0.269	0.265	0.286
Median	695.81	693.25	762.97	0.265	0.261	0.277
SD	224.42	248.17	289.53	0.076	0.084	0.105
90th percentile	992.09	1,038.20	1,110.95	0.367	0.363	0.416
75th percentile	850.89	862.11	972.49	0.320	0.316	0.335
25th percentile	547.89	533.42	556.28	0.218	0.209	0.218
10th percentile	414.79	388.57	362.78	0.173	0.160	0.160
No. of firms	292,220	172,243	69,017	292,220	172,243	69,017

Average CV of wages[b]	0.281	0.278	0.289	0.035	0.034	0.037
Median	0.277	0.276	0.288	0.034	0.033	0.035
SD	0.082	0.091	0.095	0.010	0.011	0.014
90th percentile	0.384	0.386	0.416	0.047	0.047	0.054
75th percentile	0.334	0.327	0.346	0.041	0.041	0.043
25th percentile	0.226	0.218	0.226	0.028	0.027	0.028
10th percentile	0.177	0.167	0.164	0.023	0.020	0.020
No. of firms	292,220	172,243	69,017	292,220	172,243	69,017
Correlation (average wage, SD of wage)[b]	0.498**	0.480**	0.604**	n.a.	n.a.	n.a.
Average wage for workers between 25 and 30[a]	2,472.50	2,490.99	2,571.29	7.779	7.786	7.809
Median	2,395.12	2,425.38	2,451.72	7.781	7.794	7.804
SD	650.78	657.61	765.63	0.261	0.263	0.299
90th percentile	3,286.77	3,299.86	3,515.17	8.097	8.101	8.164
75th percentile	2,795.77	2,822.11	2,956.56	7.935	7.945	7.991
25th percentile	2,049.23	2,066.89	2,084.02	7.625	7.633	7.642
10th percentile	1,763.34	1,767.69	1,766.04	7.475	7.478	7.476
No. of workers	2,075,194	1,402,819	548,181	2,075,194	1,402,819	548,181
Average wage for workers between 45 and 50[a]	3,033.17	3,069.02	3,142.69	7.956	7.964	7.982
Median	2,828.37	2,842.27	2,890.66	7.947	7.952	7.969
SD	1,071.39	1,121.66	1,197.33	0.357	0.364	0.381
90th percentile	4,459.18	4,583.83	4,743.76	8.402	8.431	8.464
75th percentile	3,683.26	3,689.56	3,776.64	8.211	8.213	8.236
25th percentile	2,289.23	2,306.39	2,339.59	7.736	7.743	7.757
10th percentile	1,853.41	1,857.98	1,879.18	7.525	7.527	7.538
No. of workers	1,327,249	1,159,054	770,242	1,327,249	1,159,054	770,242

Source: Linked employer-employee data of the Institute for Employment Research/Germany, cross-sectional model, version 1, weighted values.

Notes: SD = standard deviation; CV = coefficient of variation.

[a]Observation = a person.

[b]Observation = a firm.

**Significant at the $\alpha < 0.005$ level.

Table 8C.3 Wage dynamics (unweighted values; in euros)

	Change in monthly wages			Change in log monthly wages		
	1993	1995	2000	1993	1995	2000
Average change in wage[a]	−29.82	136.08	63.13	−0.101	0.043	0.018
Median	−26.67	105.48	43.21	−0.100	0.039	0.016
SD	486.69	482.26	601.42	0.115	0.112	0.013
90th percentile	294.74	476.43	444.63	0.094	0.147	0.131
75th percentile	80.89	238.19	171.86	0.296	0.083	0.059
25th percentile	−144.83	11.08	−48.33	−0.051	0.004	−0.017
10th percentile	−372.37	−163.01	−299.75	−0.118	−0.053	−0.089
No. of workers	1,612,065	1,058,246	621,576	1,612,065	1,058,246	621,576
Average of firm average change in wage[b]	−9.44	103.43	53.67	−0.004	0.038	0.021
Median	−1.01	100.52	48.46	−0.001	0.038	0.019
SD	80.57	95.16	90.83	0.027	0.034	0.034
90th percentile	75.83	214.74	148.51	0.025	0.072	0.055
75th percentile	39.28	154.22	94.99	0.013	0.055	0.035
25th percentile	−49.55	51.81	10.87	−0.017	0.023	0.006
10th percentile	−109.31	5.97	−34.62	−0.039	0.004	−0.012
No. of firms	2,163	1,709	1,578	2,163	1,709	1,578
Average of SD of change in wage[b]	217.41	210.17	207.16	0.073	0.069	0.070
Median	209.51	203.61	199.28	0.071	0.066	0.067
SD	71.37	73.77	81.81	0.019	0.020	0.024
90th percentile	311.77	307.57	317.35	0.094	0.090	0.096
75th percentile	264.51	255.27	254.62	0.083	0.079	0.081
25th percentile	168.29	157.57	151.62	0.060	0.057	0.055
10th percentile	130.83	120.84	112.77	0.051	0.049	0.045
No. of firms	2,163	1,709	1,578	2,163	1,709	1,578

Average CV[c] of change in wages[b]	4.814	3.849	6.086	0.228	0.231	0.294
Median	3.423	2.755	3.822	0.223	0.219	0.284
SD	107.33	26.309	385.056	0.058	0.069	0.097
90th percentile	9.127	7.639	15.978	0.307	0.313	0.392
75th percentile	5.487	4.219	8.046	0.249	0.259	0.336
25th percentile	2.189	1.742	1.553	0.186	0.188	0.238
10th percentile	0.989	0.816	-4.934	0.159	0.161	0.191
No. of firms	2,163	1,709	1,578	2,163	1,706	1,578
Average change in wage for people with tenure <3 years[a]	34.75	156.25	94.51	0.012	0.053	0.030
Median	18.09	117.59	54.61	0.007	0.046	0.021
SD	443.73	467.19	558.82	0.118	0.118	0.138
90th percentile	336.82	500.61	461.33	0.119	0.163	0.149
75th percentile	137.28	258.54	197.19	0.054	0.095	0.073
25th percentile	-84.71	23.55	-26.61	-0.036	0.009	-0.010
10th percentile	-254.06	-134.86	-203.64	-0.093	-0.048	-0.071
No. of workers	236,672	165,071	105,938	236,672	165,071	105,938
Average change in wage for people with tenure ≥3 years[a]	-40.93	132.36	56.68	-0.014	0.042	0.017
Median	-33.54	103.45	41.10	-0.012	0.038	0.015
SD	492.86	484.90	609.62	0.105	0.111	0.120
90th percentile	284.58	471.55	440.42	0.083	0.144	0.121
75th percentile	68.94	234.15	166.52	0.026	0.081	0.156
25th percentile	-154.89	8.64	-53.66	-0.046	0.003	-0.018
10th percentile	-392.05	-168.39	-321.58	-0.107	-0.054	-0.092
No. of workers	1,375,393	893,175	515,638	1,375,393	893,175	515,638

Source: Linked employer-employee data of the Institute for Employment Research/Germany, cross-sectional model, version 1.

Notes: SD = standard deviation; CV = coefficient of variation.

[a]Observation = a person.

[b]Observation = a firm.

[c]Divided by one hundred.

Table 8C.4   Wage dynamics (weighted values; in euros)

	Change in monthly wages			Change in log monthly wages		
	1993	1995	2000	1993	1995	2000
Average change in wage[a]	−13.82	103.49	57.08	−0.005	0.036	0.016
Median	−13.71	78.86	37.22	−0.006	0.032	0.014
SD	405.27	398.19	485.91	0.108	0.104	0.129
90th percentile	255.01	378.33	364.73	0.092	0.131	0.127
75th percentile	81.05	188.90	148.10	0.033	0.073	0.056
25th percentile	−110.37	−1.84	−38.67	−0.043	−0.001	−0.015
10th percentile	−294.32	−144.37	−215.48	−0.104	−0.053	−0.075
No. of workers	9,069,945	8,187,154	4,646,177	9,069,945	8,187,154	4,646,177
Average of firm average change in wage[b]	6.51	73.33	36.94	0.003	0.031	0.018
Median	6.35	71.29	36.26	0.003	0.032	0.018
SD	94.71	98.65	105.52	0.038	0.039	0.041
90th percentile	115.87	177.89	143.22	0.047	0.071	0.060
75th percentile	54.48	124.58	87.27	0.022	0.051	0.036
25th percentile	−43.16	18.91	−10.21	−0.017	0.012	−0.001
10th percentile	−95.49	−35.57	−69.94	−0.041	−0.009	−0.021
No. of firms	292,220	172,243	69,017	292,220	172,243	69,017
Average of SD of change in wage[b]	189.82	180.21	185.73	0.072	0.068	0.071
Median	181.54	166.99	168.60	0.069	0.062	0.065
SD	76.26	78.41	93.09	0.027	0.027	0.038
90th percentile	296.17	285.94	310.75	0.108	0.097	0.105
75th percentile	236.89	222.80	243.11	0.085	0.082	0.084
25th percentile	135.12	121.86	126.14	0.053	0.051	0.048
10th percentile	96.84	90.27	80.85	0.043	0.040	0.037
No. of firms	292,220	172,243	69,017	292,220	172,243	69,017

Average CV[c] of change in wages[b]	1.213	0.061	0.163	0.214	0.074	0.510
Median	0.048	0.027	0.039	0.045	0.024	0.034
SD	31.55	0.156	2.322	0.262	0.040	4.712
90th percentile	0.217	0.119	0.182	0.093	0.092	0.207
75th percentile	0.095	0.052	0.088	0.092	0.047	0.078
25th percentile	0.025	0.017	0.021	0.022	0.014	0.019
10th percentile	0.152	0.011	0.014	0.014	0.010	0.014
No. of firms	292,220	172,243	69,017	292,220	172,243	69,017
Average change in wage for people with tenure <3 years[a]	27.61	115.40	73.78	0.011	0.044	0.026
Median	13.48	85.01	46.08	0.067	0.037	0.019
SD	356.03	374.94	481.62	0.113	0.111	0.133
90th percentile	283.85	388.67	389.21	0.114	0.144	0.137
75th percentile	119.53	199.81	167.38	0.052	0.082	0.067
25th percentile	-74.59	6.64	-29.35	-0.033	0.003	-0.013
10th percentile	-223.79	-128.74	-183.85	-0.091	-0.051	-0.073
No. of workers	2,089,873	2,002,997	1,160,379	2,089,873	2,002,997	1,160,379
Average change in wage for people with tenure ≥3 years[a]	-26.22	99.64	51.65	-0.009	0.033	0.016
Median	-21.28	77.17	36.60	-0.008	0.303	0.014
SD	418.09	405.36	517.64	0.106	0.102	0.119
90th percentile	242.58	374.98	360.59	0.829	0.126	0.114
75th percentile	67.77	185.52	143.07	0.026	0.069	0.052
25th percentile	-121.17	-4.019	-36.78	-0.046	-0.002	-0.014
10th percentile	-317.24	-150.51	-223.47	-0.107	-0.054	-0.073
No. of workers	6,980,071	6,184,157	3,486,152	6,980,071	6,184,157	3,486,152

Source: Linked employer-employee data of the Institute for Employment Research/Germany, cross-sectional model, version 1, weighted values.

Notes: SD = standard deviation; CV = coefficient of variation.

[a]Observation = a person.

[b]Observation = a firm.

[c]Divided by one hundred.

Table 8C.5   Mobility: All jobs

	Unweighted values			Weighted values		
	1993	1995	2000	1993	1995	2000
Employees	812.415	696.544	453.927	100.315	94.229	86.165
SD	2119.559	1552.058	1286.649	395.994	310.298	374.508
No. of occupations	35.012	33.351	26.455	13.776	13.152	13.013
SD	27.262	25.798	21.565	11.056	10.612	10.356
Employment growth	-0.049	-0.020	-0.047	-0.017	-0.002	-0.042
SD	0.153	0.163	0.237	0.151	0.158	0.231
Exit rate	0.169	0.147	0.202	0.187	0.163	0.227
SD	0.135	0.132	0.204	0.132	0.128	0.195
Exit rate, top decile of firm wages	0.154	0.156	0.226	0.183	0.137	0.223
SD	0.183	0.182	0.246	0.177	0.142	0.199
Exit rate, top quartile of firm wages	0.147	0.139	0.193	0.161	0.127	0.213
SD	0.158	0.152	0.210	0.144	0.133	0.182
Exit rate, bottom decile of firm wages	0.246	0.209	0.338	0.247	0.228	0.292
SD	0.153	0.140	0.213	0.153	0.147	0.184
Exit rate, bottom quartile of firm wages	0.209	0.179	0.306	0.219	0.191	0.291
SD	0.127	0.150	0.229	0.134	0.139	0.181
Entry rate	0.111	0.121	0.150	0.159	0.157	0.179
SD	0.102	0.113	0.156	0.125	0.141	0.177

Entry rate, top decile of firm wages	0.097	0.109	0.137	0.200	0.227	0.161
SD	0.101	0.139	0.155	0.152	0.194	0.151
Entry rate, top quartile of firm wages	0.090	0.096	0.125	0.137	0.117	0.150
SD	0.085	0.105	0.135	0.125	0.118	0.148
Entry rate, bottom decile of firm wages	0.182	0.194	0.306	0.200	0.227	0.248
SD	0.143	0.169	0.271	0.152	0.194	0.234
Entry rate, bottom quartile of firm wages	0.147	0.162	0.261	0.181	0.187	0.250
SD	0.123	0.143	0.231	0.132	0.166	0.218
Percentage of employees who switch jobs[a] internally	0.027	0.021	0.020	0.024	0.014	0.015
SD	0.048	0.035	0.045	0.052	0.030	0.034
Percentage of workers who have been at firm 3+ years	0.664	0.665	0.590	0.585	0.584	0.545
SD	0.194	0.275	0.337	0.217	0.282	0.324
Correlation (exit rate, log average wage)[b]	-0.225**	-0.143**	-0.109**	-0.248**	-0.267**	-0.165**
Correlation (exit rate, log average wage change)[b]	-0.017***	-0.118***	0.015	0.006	-0.026***	-0.025***
Correlation (exit rate, SD of log wage)[b]	0.079***	0.079***	0.062***	0.114**	0.125***	-0.080***
Correlation (entry rate, log average wage)[b]	-0.321***	-0.291***	-0.244***	-0.218***	-0.292***	-0.183***
Correlation (entry rate, log average wage change)[b]	0.205***	0.069***	0.073***	0.142**	0.089***	0.014
Correlation (entry rate, SD of log wage)[b]	0.139***	0.128***	0.093***	0.057**	0.073***	-0.118**

Source: Linked employer-employee data of the Institute for Employment Research/Germany, cross-sectional model, version 1.

Notes: SD = standard deviation. All statistics are on the establishment level.

[a]Change in the 3-digit occupational code.

[b]Observation = a firm.

**Significant at the α <0.005 level.

Table 8C.6   Mobility: High-level jobs

	Unweighted values			Weighted values		
	1993	1995	2000	1993	1995	2000
Employees	157.661	131.322	68.213	29.900	28.225	21.523
SD	313.019	257.689	123.875	72.246	60.801	42.907
No. of occupations	15.290	14.098	9.595	6.786	6.596	5.495
SD	12.728	11.612	7.740	5.302	4.984	4.103
Employment growth	−0.081	−0.105	−0.080	−0.089	−0.030	−0.099
SD	0.308	0.317	0.385	0.339	0.329	0.387
Exit rate	0.114	0.116	0.159	0.119	0.119	0.156
SD	0.186	0.190	0.242	0.254	0.260	0.292
Exit rate, top decile of firm wages	0.121	0.131	0.182	0.148	0.113	0.175
SD	0.173	0.178	0.223	0.175	0.127	0.185
Exit rate, top quartile of firm wages	0.109	0.109	0.156	0.106	0.088	0.167
SD	0.149	0.141	0.192	0.138	0.120	0.180
Exit rate, bottom decile of firm wages	0.134	0.149	0.269	0.159	0.184	0.358
SD	0.307	0.317	0.524	0.410	0.389	0.719
Exit rate, bottom quartile of firm wages	0.116	0.141	0.226	0.127	0.155	0.286
SD	0.232	0.291	0.452	0.323	0.366	0.604
Entry rate	0.060	0.074	0.091	0.079	0.086	0.093
SD	0.111	0.175	0.183	0.171	0.239	0.220

Entry rate, top decile of firm wages	0.062	0.065	0.093	0.092	0.087	0.101
SD	0.080	0.081	0.131	0.121	0.122	0.117
Entry rate, top quartile of firm wages	0.053	0.054	0.081	0.075	0.061	0.089
SD	0.068	0.066	0.118	0.099	0.091	0.139
Entry rate, bottom decile of firm wages	0.104	0.110	0.219	0.127	0.118	0.125
SD	0.229	0.276	0.421	0.304	0.331	0.367
Entry rate, bottom quartile of firm wages	0.079	0.100	0.138	0.096	0.093	0.997
SD	0.169	0.256	0.338	0.234	0.278	0.351
Percentage of employees who switch jobs[a] internally	0.026	0.019	0.019	0.024	0.013	0.014
SD	0.060	0.049	0.068	0.077	0.047	0.055
Percentage of workers who have been at firm 3+ years	0.636	0.669	0.628	0.561	0.627	0.605
SD	0.259	0.310	0.391	0.277	0.330	0.389
Correlation (exit rate, log average wage)[b]	−0.046**	−0.047**	−0.031**	−0.090**	−0.117**	−0.055**
Correlation (exit rate, log average wage change)[b]	−0.004	−0.129**	0.025**	0.007	−0.067**	0.138**
Correlation (exit rate, SD of log wage)[b]	−0.063**	−0.089**	−0.075**	−0.072**	−0.103**	−0.146**
Correlation (entry rate, log average wage)[b]	−0.128**	−0.137**	0.016	−0.096**	−0.143**	−0.013
Correlation (entry rate, log average wage change)[b]	0.118**	−0.004	−0.055**	0.135**	−0.013	0.060**
Correlation (entry rate, SD of log wage)[b]	0.053**	−0.035**	−0.051**	−0.001	0.016	−0.092**

Source: Linked employer-employee data of the Institute for Employment Research/Germany, cross-sectional model, version 1.

Notes: SD = standard deviation. All statistics are on the establishment level.

[a]Change in the 3-digit occupational code.

[b]Observation = a firm.

**Significant at the $\alpha < 0.005$ level.

Table 8C.7   Mobility: Low-level jobs

	Unweighted values			Weighted values		
	1993	1995	2000	1993	1995	2000
Employees	223.284	181.506	111.529	66.920	59.406	54.314
SD	839.317	562.563	494.572	300.380	217.421	301.362
No. of occupations	17.890	16.660	11.807	11.795	10.997	9.409
SD	17.825	16.750	13.458	10.090	9.539	9.223
Employment growth	−0.039	−0.081	−0.060	−0.027	−0.084	−0.044
SD	0.305	0.303	0.360	0.231	0.237	0.348
Exit rate	0.252	0.222	0.317	0.240	0.214	0.313
SD	0.189	0.206	0.319	0.182	0.178	0.264
Exit rate, top decile of firm wages	0.333	0.349	0.450	0.309	0.298	0.451
SD	0.295	0.342	0.429	0.352	0.287	0.367
Exit rate, top quartile of firm wages	0.309	0.298	0.383	0.312	0.288	0.377
SD	0.261	0.291	0.374	0.299	0.273	0.317
Exit rate, bottom decile of firm wages	0.251	0.211	0.316	0.218	0.203	0.327
SD	0.159	0.143	0.211	0.129	0.118	0.168
Exit rate, bottom quartile of firm wages	0.225	0.186	0.289	0.211	0.176	0.262
SD	0.137	0.105	0.237	0.116	0.123	0.197
Entry rate	0.181	0.203	0.352	0.203	0.241	0.373
SD	0.182	0.192	0.363	0.184	0.229	0.329

Entry rate, top decile of firm wages	0.248	0.277	0.476	0.261	0.359	0.420
SD	0.269	0.297	0.495	0.249	0.386	0.465
Entry rate, top quartile of firm wages	0.216	0.245	0.418	0.232	0.313	0.409
SD	0.229	0.258	0.430	0.219	0.321	0.410
Entry rate, bottom decile of firm wages	0.190	0.201	0.306	0.189	0.212	0.369
SD	0.163	0.179	0.287	0.143	0.181	0.335
Entry rate, bottom quartile of firm wages	0.163	0.176	0.267	0.176	0.183	0.322
SD	0.142	0.153	0.244	0.144	0.167	0.305
Percentage of employees who switch jobs[a] internally	0.022	0.015	0.021	0.020	0.012	0.023
SD	0.074	0.054	0.083	0.062	0.051	0.090
Percentage of workers who have been at firm 3+ years	0.831	0.767	0.708	0.835	0.728	0.733
SD	0.234	0.327	0.403	0.202	0.349	0.395
Correlation (exit rate, log average wage)[b]	0.134**	0.193**	0.187**	0.078**	0.099**	0.112**
Correlation (exit rate, log average wage change)[b]	0.024**	-0.025**	0.045**	0.088**	0.016**	-0.022**
Correlation (exit rate, SD of log wage)[b]	-0.057**	-0.087**	-0.083**	-0.051**	-0.035**	-0.104**
Correlation (entry rate, log average wage)[b]	0.046**	0.099**	0.194**	0.135**	0.008	0.156**
Correlation (entry rate, log average wage change)[b]	0.181**	0.083**	0.039**	0.070**	0.055**	-0.015
Correlation (entry rate, SD of log wage)[b]	-0.057**	-0.067**	-0.158**	-0.131**	-0.100**	-0.257**

Source: Linked employer-employee data of the Institute for Employment Research/Germany, cross-sectional model, version 1.

Notes: SD = standard deviation. All statistics are on the establishment level.

[a]Change in the 3-digit occupational code.

[b]Observation = a firm.

**Significant at the α <0.005 level.

Appendix D
Covariates in the Wage Regressions for Table 8.6 and 8.7 (Full Regression Results, Including Coefficients, are Published in Alda [2006, chapter 5])

Worker Characteristics

Time/Spell Variant ($= x_{it}$)

age (age^2/100; age^3/10,000)	tenure (in years)	education level
current occupation group	multiple jobs (yes/no)	days of employment / days of unemployment × 100
days of employment / days unobserved × 100	number of employers	number of unemployment phases

Time/Spell Invariant

gender	nationality	of leave of absence (e.g., sabbaticals)

Firm Characteristics

Time/Spell Variant ($= w_{it}$)

size (ten dummies)	collective agreement (branch/firm level; yes/no)	works council (yes/no)
economic situation (subjective measure)	paying more than tariff wages (yes/no)	sum of investment (log) per capita
weekly worked hours	outsourcing activities	vacancies
organizational change	number of occupations	churning

proportions of fixed-term contracts, females, and university degrees

Time/Spell Invariant

ownership sector (ten dummies) parent is single (yes/no) urbanity

Appendix E
Symbols and Indexes for Wage Regressions

Indexes

i: individuals	j: firms	t: time (years)

Symbols

μ : constant
x : observable time-variant person characteristics
w : observable time-variant firm characteristics
θ_i : unobserved person fixed-effect
ψ_j : unobserved firm fixed-effect
B : occupation groups
Note: θ_i and ψ_j include the time invariant covariates of people or firms.

Appendix F

Estimation of Fixed-Firm and Person Effect

A more detailed description of the regression techniques is given by Andrews, Schank, and Upward (2004):

For the spell-level fixed effect regression (Spell-FE), we define:

(E1) $$\lambda_s = \theta_i + \psi_j$$

for each unique worker-firm combination ($=$ spell). Neither θ_i nor ψ_j vary within a spell. The wage regression is then

(E2) $$y_{it} = x_{it}\beta + w_{jt}\gamma + \lambda_{ijt} + \varepsilon_{it},$$

with

(E3) $$\overline{\lambda}_s = \sum \frac{\lambda_{ijt}}{n} = \lambda_{ijt}.$$

n is the number of observations (worker years) within a specific spell. Computing the mean deviations for each observation within a spell is:

(E4) $$y_{it} - \overline{y}_s = (x_{it} - \overline{x}_s)\beta + (w_{jt} - \overline{w}_s)\gamma + (\lambda_{ijt} - \overline{\lambda}_s) + (\varepsilon_{it} - \overline{\varepsilon}_s).$$

Because of (E3), $\overline{\lambda}_s - \lambda_{ijt} = 0$. The estimator is consistent because he sweeps out both unobserved heterogeneities. He is not the most efficient one (because a least square dummy variable regression, LSDV, is).

The time-invariant covariates are constant within a spell and, therefore, swept out. The following example for a standard one-way-fixed model with worker data only shows how the wage effect of the time-invariant covariates are identified. The one-way wage regression is:

(E5) $$y_{it} = \mu + x_{it}\beta + \theta_i + \varepsilon_{it}.$$

The standard fixed effect (FE) estimator of β can be interpreted as an instrumented variable (IV) estimator (Andrews, Schank, and Upward 2004, 10; Verbeek 2004, section 10.2.5). Then we can formulate

(E6) $\hat{\beta}_{FE} = [\Sigma_i \Sigma_t (X_{it} - \overline{x}_i)'(X_{it} - \overline{x}_i)]^{-1} \Sigma_i \Sigma_t (X_{it} - \overline{x}_i)'(Y_{it} - \overline{y}_i)$

$= [\Sigma_i \Sigma_t (X_{it} - \overline{x}_i)' x_{it}]^{-1} \Sigma_i \Sigma_t (X_{it} - \overline{x}_i)' V_{it}.$

Further details for the Spell-FE regression can be found in Andrews, Schank, and Upward (2004, 10–11). All variables correlated with the unobservables are instrumented by their mean deviations. Time-invariant variables are "instrumented with themselves," making the usual random effect assumption. The estimator is a special case of Hausman and Taylors' 1981 estimator.

For explicitly calculating (and not sweeping out) the unobserved fixed effects, we set all firm effects with less than sixteen movers into a single common effect. This allows us to connect all groups (forty-five) into one by constructing an artificial firm that contains all firms (and workers) who experience little turnover. After this procedure, we time-demean the remaining firm dummies (this is what Andrews, Schank, and Upward (2004) call FE_iLSDV_j) and compute θ_i with the estimated values of ψ_j.

Appendix G

Table 8G.1   Firm is covered by collective contract compared to firms without collective contract—average treatment effects on the treated

	1993	1995	2000
Average wage			
Collective contract	2,704.07	2,744.75	2,838.53
Without col. contract	2,656.02	2,736.61	2,711.09
Average treatment effects	48.05	8.13	127.44
t-value	0.64	0.08	2.33
Within firm standard deviation			
Collective contract	772.90	804.97	831.06
Without col. contract	807.61	825.87	815.63
Average treatment effects	−34.71	−20.89	15.42
t-value	−1.16	−0.6	0.7
Change in wage			
Collective contract	19.56	93.71	54.18
Without col. contract	12.73	88.85	60.42
Average treatment effects	6.82	4.86	−6.24
t-value	0.56	0.24	0.72
Coefficient of variation of change in wage			
Collective contract	0.289	0.297	0.294
Without col. contract	0.312	0.307	0.308
Average treatment effects	−0.2288	−0.0099	−0.0139
t-value	−2.47	−0.71	−1.73

Table 8G.1   (continued)

	1993	1995	2000
Exit rate			
Collective contract	0.181	0.170	0.210
Without col. contract	0.257	0.194	0.220
Average treatment effects	−0.077	−0.024	−0.01
t-value	−3.58	−1.03	0.58
Entry rate			
Collective contract	0.160	0.166	0.165
Without col. contract	0.192	0.178	0.190
Average treatment effects	−0.032	−0.012	−0.026
t-value	−2.04	−0.52	−1.95
Percentage of workers who have been at firm 3+ years			
Collective contract	0.587	0.595	0.546
Without col. contract	0.500	0.509	0.519
Average treatment effects	0.087	0.086	0.027
t-value	3.49	2.08	0.95

Source: LIAB, cross-sectional model, version 1.

Notes: Firms with at least twenty-five full-time employees. In 1993, there are 120 (1995: 91; 2000: 193) firms without collective agreement in the sample, whereas firms with collective contract are ten times more. We reverse, therefore, the treatment in the matching procedure. For a better reading, we multiplied the average treatment on the treated times minus one. Between four (in 1993) and seventeen firms (in 2000) are not covered by the region of common support. These firms are excluded.

Bootstrapped t-values according to H_0: identical mean values. Monthly gross wages; mobility variables defined as proportions.

We apply a kernel matching and calculated bootstrapped standard errors with 200 repetitions. The probit estimation of propensity scores uses as covariates the average age of workers in a firm, existence of a workers council, one regional dummy, three dummies for firm size and eight for branches and proportions of females, of fixed-term workers, of blue-collar workers and of six different qualification groups. Pseudo-R^2 is varying between 0.29 and 0.15.

References

Abowd, J. M., R. Creecy, and F. Kramarz. 2002. Computing person and firm effects using linked longitudinal employer-employee-data. U.S. Census Bureau Technical-Paper no. 2002-6. Washington, DC: U.S. Census Bureau.

Abowd, J. M., F. Kramarz, and D. Margolis. 1999. High wage workers—High wage firms? *Econometrica* 67:251–333.

Addison, J. T., L. Bellmann, C. Schnabel, and J. Wagner. 2004. The reform of the German Works Constitution Act: A critical assessment. *Industrial Relations* 43:392–420.

Alda, H. 2005a. *Betriebe und beschäftigte in den linked employer-employee daten* (Firms and employees in the linked employer-employee data [LIAB] of the Institute of Employment Research). FDZ Data Report no. 1. Nuremberg: Institute for Employment Research.

————. 2005b. *Die Verknüpfungsqualität der LIAB daten* (The quality of linking LIAB data). FDZ Methodology Report no. 2. Nuremberg: Institute for Employment Research.

————. 2005c. *Datenbeschreibung der version 1 des LIAB querschnittmodells* (Data description for the first version of the LIAB cross-sectional model). FDZ Data Report no. 2. Nuremberg: Institute for Employment Research.

————. 2005d. *Datenbeschreibung der version 1 des LIAB längsschnittmodells* (Data description for the first version of the LIAB longitudinal model). FDZ Data Report no. 3. Nuremberg: Institute for Employment Research.

————. 2006. *Beobachtbare und unbeobachtbare betriebs- und Personeneffekte auf die Entlohnung: Beiträge aus der Arbeitsmarkt- und Berufsforschung 298* (Observed and unobserved effects of firm and worker characteristics on wages: Features of employment and occupational research 298). Nuremberg: Institute for Employment Research.

Alda, H., S. Bender, and H. Gartner. 2005. The linked employer-employee dataset of the IAB (LIAB). IAB Discussion Paper no. 06/2005. Nuremberg: Institute for Employment Research.

Andrews, M., T. Schank, and R. Upward. 2004. Practical estimation methods for linked employer-employee-data. IAB Discussion Paper no. 3/2004. Nuremberg: Institute for Employment Research.

Barth, E., and H. Dale-Olsen. 2003. Assortative matching in the labour market? Stylised facts workers and plants. Paper presented at the EALE 2003 Conference. 9–11 September, Lisbon, Portugal.

Bauer, T., and S. Bender. 2002. Technological change, organizational change, and job turnover. IZA Discussion Paper no. 570. Bonn: Institute for the Study of Labor.

Bauer, T., S. Bender, and H. Bonin. 2004. Dismissal protection and worker flows in small establishments. IZA Discussion Paper no. 1105. Bonn: Institute for the Study of Labor.

Büttner, T., and B. Fitzenberger. 1998. Central wage bargaining and local wage flexibility: Evidence from the entire wage distribution. ZEW Discussion Paper no. 98-39. Mannheim, Germany: Center for European Economic Research.

Brixy, U., S. Kohaut, and C. Schnabel. 2007. Do newly founded firms pay lower wages? First evidence from Germany. *Small Business Economics* 29:161–71.

Calmfors, L., and J. Driffill. 1988. Bargaining structure, corporatism, and macroeconomic performance. *Economic Policy* 6:14–61.

Gartner, H. 2005. The imputation of wages above the contribution limit with the German IAB employment sample. FDZ Methodenreport no. 2/2005. Nuremberg: Institute for Employment Research.

Goux, D., and E. Maurin. 1999. Persistence of inter industry wage differentials: A reexamination using matched worker-firm panel data. *Journal of Labor Economics* 17:492–533.

Groshen, E. L. 1989. Do wage differences among employers last? Federal Reserve Bank of Cleveland Working Paper no. 8802. Cleveland, OH Federal Reserve Bank of Cleveland.

————. 1991. Five reasons why wages vary among employers. *Industrial Relations* 30:350–83.

Gruetter, M., and R. Lalive. 2003. Job mobility and industry wage differentials: Evidence from employer-employee matched data. University of Zurich. Mimeograph.

Hall, P., and D. Soskice, eds. 2003. *Varieties of capitalism.* New York: Oxford University Press.

Kohaut, S., and C. Schnabel. 2003. *Verbreitung, ausmaß und determinanten der übertariflichen entlohnung* (Coverage, intensity, and determinants of wages above tariff arrangements). *Mitteilungen aus der Arbeitsmarkt- und Berufsforschung* 36:661–71.

Kölling, A., and T. Schank. 2003. Skill-biased technological change, international trade and the wage structure. Chair for Labor Market and Regional Policy Discussion Paper no. 14. Nuremberg: University of Erlangen-Nuremberg.

Möller, I. 2001. *Mitarbeiterbeteiligung: Ein weg zu höherer produktivität* (Employee profit sharing: A way to higher productivity). IAB *Kurzbericht* 9/2001. Nuremberg: Institute for Employment Research.

Organization for Economic Cooperation and Development (OECD). 1997. *Employment Outlook 1997*. Paris: OECD.

———. 1999. *Employment Outlook 1999*. Paris: OECD.

———. 2005. *Taxing wages 2004/2005*. Paris: OECD.

Schwerdt, W., and S. Bender. 2003. *Was tun lehrlinge nach ihrer ausbildung? Eine analyse mit dem linked employee-datensatz des IAB* (What do apprentices do after their training? An investigation with the linked employer-employee data of the IAB). *Mitteilungen aus der Arbeitsmarkt- und Berufsforschung* 36:46–59.

Stephan, G. 2001. *Firmenlohndifferentiale—Eine empirische Untersuchung für die Bundesrepublik Deutschland* (*Firm wage differentials: An empirical investigation for the Federal Republic of Germany*). Frankfurt a. M: Campus.

Verbeek, M. 2004. *A guide to modern econometrics.* 2nd ed. New York: Wiley.

Verick, S. 2004. Threshold effects of dismissal protection legislation in Germany. IZA Discussion Paper no. 991. Bonn: Institute for the Study of Labor.

Winkelmann, R. 1997. How young workers get their training: A survey of Germany versus the United States. *Journal of Population Economics* 10:159–70.

Wage Structure and Labor Mobility in Norway, 1980–97

Arngrim Hunnes, Jarle Møen, and Kjell G. Salvanes

9.1 Introduction

In the 1980s and 1990s, most Western European countries broke the trend of increasing the size of the welfare state and the use of solidaristic wage policies that were developed in the 1950s and continued through the 1970s. Increased and persistent unemployment and budget deficits led many countries to question the size of the welfare state and egalitarian wage policies. Also, Scandinavian countries—most notably Sweden—were forced to reassess their welfare policies, and centralized wage negotiations were abandoned. Norway went in a different direction and resisted the trend observed in other developed countries in this period. In the early 1980s, wages were negotiated at the industry level, but in 1986 to 1987, bargaining was further centralized to the national level. In the early 1990s, the so-called solidarity alternative wage policy was introduced. This strengthened the guarantied negotiated minimum wage for the lowest paid (Wallerstein, Golden, and Lange 1997; Kahn 1998; Freeman 1997). It is notable that the earnings distribution did not increase as in most other countries but stayed compressed until the mid-1990s (Aaberge et al. 2000).[1] The return to education in Norway is fairly low and stable. Ordinary least squares (OLS) estimates from Mincer regressions suggest that the marginal return to one extra year of education is about 5 percent; see, for example, Barth and Røed (2001).

Arngrim Hunnes is a postdoctoral researcher in economics at the Norwegian School of Economics and Business Administration. Jarle Møen is an associate professor of economics at the Norwegian School of Economics and Business Administration. Kjell G. Salvanes is a professor of economics at the Norwegian School of Economics and Business Administration.

1. See Kahn (1998) and Hægeland, Klette, and Salvanes (1999) for explanations for the increased wage compression.

Because of high wage compression and strong labor market institutions, the Norwegian economy differs from most other Western economies. However, we do not know much about the precise workings of the labor market in Norway. To what extent do different firms follow different wage policies? Do such differences relate to how workers move between firms? What are the effects of different wage bargaining regimes? The empirical branch of personnel economics has long been hampered by a lack of representative data sets. Norway is one of a handful of countries that has produced rich linked employer–employee data suitable for such analysis.[2] A special feature of our data is detailed information on occupational hierarchies and very detailed information on wage compensation for normal hours and overtime as well as bonuses. There is also very good information on hours worked. We match these data to the main register-based employer-employee data set, containing detailed information on firm and worker characteristics.[3]

Our chapter is very descriptive in nature, and it should be read as a detailed country study together with the other country studies in this volume. The chapter has three parts. First, we describe the wage setting and employment protection institutions in Norway. Next, we describe the Norwegian data sets. Finally, we document a large number of stylized facts regarding wage structure and labor mobility within and between Norwegian firms. We cover the period from 1980 to 1997. One topic analyzed is within- and between-firm wage dispersion and whether wage dispersion has been stable over time. Although overall wage dispersion has been stable, there might still have been changes in the individual components of the variance both across firms and across worker groups. There might also have been increased sorting of workers across firms. We document these types of patterns and also those of worker mobility for different groups of firms and workers. A unique feature of our data is that we can compare mobility across occupations within firms for white-collar workers as opposed to the more standard mobility patterns across firms. Another feature is the ability to compare wage and worker mobility for white- and blue-collar workers separately. The wage setting institutions are very different for white- and blue-collar workers. There is no centrally bargained wage for white-collar workers, whereas blue-collar workers have a two-tier system with both national (or industry) and firm-level negotiations. In this way, we have an extra institutional "experiment" within the country. Furthermore, the period we analyze was volatile in terms of business-cycle movements. Hence, our

2. Some work on both the job and worker turnover and wage structure has been undertaken before, but very little has been conducted on wage mobility within and between firms. See Salvanes (1997), Salvanes and Førre (2003), and Margolis and Salvanes (2001).
3. See Møen, Salvanes, and Sørensen (2004) for a description of the main employer-employee data set used in several previous studies.

data are well suited for studying the cyclical pattern of wage and worker mobility.

The remainder of the chapter is organized as follows. In section 9.2, we describe the macroeconomic conditions in the period we are analyzing. Section 9.3 presents the institutional setting in Norway, and section 9.4 presents the data we are using. In section 9.5, we look at the wage structure and labor mobility in detail. Section 9.6 summarizes our empirical findings.

9.2 Macroeconomic Conditions

Table 9.1 and figure 9.1 show unemployment and growth rates for Norway for each of the years from 1972 to 2002. We see that the macroeconomic conditions have not been stable in the period covered by our analysis, 1980 to 1997. There was a mild downturn in the early 1980s, with a peak in the business cycle around 1985 to 1987. The unemployment rate was then about 2 percent of the labor force. From 1988 onward, Norway experienced its worst economic recession in the postwar period, when the unemployment rate was about 6 percent. After 1993, growth picked up, and 1997 was a peak year in the relatively stable period after the mid-1990s. Given these business-cycle fluctuations, we have picked 1981 and 1993 as two low-growth years and 1986 to 1987 and 1997 as two high-growth years in our empirical analysis.

The Norwegian government plays an important part in coordinating wage settlements, and this had important implications for wage determination in the period analyzed. For instance, wage negotiations in 1988 were undertaken with considerable concern about the future of the Norwegian economy. Partly because of the oil price fall in 1986, the Norwegian krone had been devalued by 10 percent in May 1986. The largest employer association, the Norwegian Employers Confederation (NAF), the predecessor of the Confederation of Norwegian Business and Industry (NHO), called a lockout that failed, largely because of disagreement among the employers. This led to reductions in work time and high increases in wages in 1986. After the subsequent downturn in the economy, the main labor union, the Norwegian Confederation of Trade Unions (LO), and NAF/NHO agreed to a moderate wage increase in 1988. To ensure that all groups followed suit, the Storting (the Norwegian national assembly) passed a law that wages could not increase by more than 5 percent, in line with the outcome of the wage settlements between the LO and NHO. A similar law was passed in 1989. Therefore, a wage-freeze policy at 5 percent nominal increase was in place in these two years.

In 1990, the income regulation laws expired, yet the LO and NHO agreed that wage increases should still be moderate because of high unemployment and the weak competitive position of the trading sector. In 1992, the agreement among the labor market organizations on wage restraint was

Table 9.1 **Macroeconomic conditions: Unemployment and economic growth**

Year	Unemployment rate	Economic growth (% change in GDP)		
		1 year	2 year	5 year
1971		5.00		
1972	1.7	4.97	4.99	
1973	1.5	4.32	4.64	
1974	1.5	4.11	4.21	
1975	2.3	5.10	4.60	4.70
1976	2.0	5.70	5.40	4.84
1977	1.0	4.18	4.94	4.68
1978	1.8	3.43	3.80	4.50
1979	2.0	4.38	3.91	4.56
1980	1.7	4.83	4.61	4.50
1981	2.0	0.96	2.90	3.56
1982	2.6	0.21	0.58	2.76
1983	3.4	3.52	1.86	2.78
1984	3.2	5.74	4.63	3.05
1985	2.6	5.07	5.40	3.10
1986	2.0	3.54	4.30	3.61
1987	2.1	2.03	2.79	3.98
1988	3.2	−0.04	1.00	3.27
1989	4.9	0.95	0.45	2.31
1990	5.2	2.06	1.51	1.71
1991	5.5	3.55	2.81	1.71
1992	5.9	3.25	3.40	1.95
1993	6.0	2.69	2.97	2.50
1994	5.4	5.12	3.91	3.33
1995	4.9	4.27	4.69	3.78
1996	4.8	5.12	4.69	4.09
1997	4.0	5.06	5.09	4.45
1998	3.2	2.60	3.83	4.43
1999	3.2	2.11	2.35	3.83
2000	3.4	2.80	2.45	3.54
2001	3.6	1.91	2.35	2.89
2002	3.9	0.95	1.43	2.07

Sources: The unemployment rate is taken from the Norwegian Labour Force Survey (AKU) published by Statistics Norway (1974, 1978, 1984, 1997, 2003a). The economic growth numbers are computed based on numbers from Statistics Norway (2003b).

Notes: In the computation of economic growth, the GDP numbers are fixed at 2000 prices. The formula used is growth$_{GDP}$ = 100(lnGDP$_t$ − lnGDP$_{t-yr}$)/yr, where t = 1971, . . . , 2002, and yr ∈ (1,2,5). The years 1981 and 1993 indicate low-growth years. The years 1986 and 1997 indicate high-growth years.

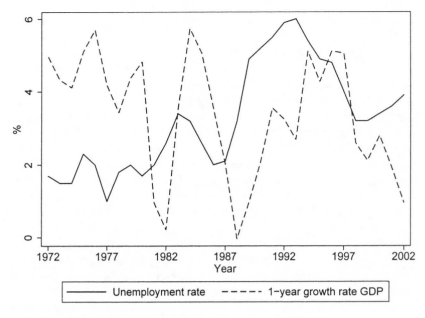

Fig. 9.1   Unemployment rate and one-year growth rate GDP

formalized in the Solidarity Alternative. In 1994, a major revision was undertaken by industry, yet wage growth was moderate, following the lead from the metal industry. In 1996 and 1998, however, proposed agreements in line with the Solidarity Alternative were rejected in ballots. This led to strikes and subsequent agreements on higher wage growth.

9.3   Institutional Setting

This section describes wage setting institutions in Norway for different worker groups and institutions for employment protection.

9.3.1   Wage Setting

In the private sector in Norway, about half of the labor force is covered by collective agreements (Stokke, Evju, and Frøland 2003).[4] Union density, that is, the share of employees who are members of a union, is somewhat lower: 43 percent in the private sector (Stokke, Evju, and Frøland 2003). These figures were very stable in the period we analyze (Wallerstein, Golden, and Lange 1997). Bargaining coverage is higher than union density because firms covered by a collective agreement follow the agreement

4. See Holden and Salvanes (2005) for more details on the wage setting process.

for all employees. However, in contrast to many other European countries, extension mechanisms imposing regulations from collective agreements onto the nonunionized sectors are not used in Norway.

The largest employees' association is the LO, to which about half of all union members belong. The traditional stronghold of the LO is among blue-collar workers in the manufacturing industry, but the LO is also prominent in some private service sectors, and for nonprofessionals and unskilled employees in the public sector. The LO is organized as union branches, to a large degree covering different industry sectors. Other employees' associations are the Confederation of Vocational Unions (YS), covering many of the same workers as the LO; the Confederation of Higher Education Unions (UHO), covering teachers, nurses, the police, and so on; and *Akademikerne* (The Federation of Norwegian Professional Associations), covering employees with higher education. On the employers' side, the NHO is the dominant association in the private sector, being the main counterpart of the LO. The NHO has about 16,000 member companies, employing about 490,000 employees in Norway (Stokke, Evju, and Frøland 2003); that is, about one-quarter of the total workforce of 2.3 million.

For employees covered by collective agreements, wage setting takes place at two levels: national (or industry) and the firm level (wage drift). Central negotiations concern collective agreements, wage regulations, working hours, working conditions, pensions, medical benefits, and so on. Firm-level negotiations determine possible local adjustments and additions to the collective agreements. These negotiations are generally conducted under a peace clause, preventing strikes and lockouts within the contract period of the collective (i.e., central) agreements (Holden 1998). Collective agreements usually last for two years. Since 1964, the main revisions to the collective agreements have been undertaken every second year, in even years (most recently in 2006). The draft agreement in a main revision is subject to a ballot among union members. Occasionally, draft agreements are rejected by the members, leading to a strike and subsequent negotiations during or after the strike. There are also central negotiations in intermediate years, but the scope for these negotiations is usually limited to wages only. Furthermore, negotiations in intermediate years are undertaken at the national level, without any ballot requirements, which usually ensures a more moderate wage outcome. Broadly, we can distinguish three types of collective agreements:

- Minimum wage agreements
- Normal wage agreements
- Agreements without wage rates

Most workers are covered by minimum wage agreements, which specify minimum wage rates, as well as other working conditions. For these workers, there are local negotiations about additions to the central agreements.

Importantly, as the local agreements specify additions to the central agreements, an increase in the centrally specified minimum wage rates raises the wage of all workers, even if they are paid more than the minimum rates. Workers covered by normal wage agreements are not supposed to have local wage negotiations, so their wages and working conditions are fully specified by the central agreements. At the opposite end, there are also agreements without wage rates, specifying only procedures for the local wage setting. These agreements are only used for white-collar workers. Hence, an important feature of the Norwegian wage setting is that white-collar wages are mainly set at the firm level and thus reflect conditions at the firm level. It should also be noted that there is no national, statutory minimum wage for all workers in Norway. Minimum wages only apply to workers covered by collective agreements.

Although blue-collar wages are negotiated centrally, there is considerable variation between sectors with regard to the number of firms with local bargaining and the importance of the wage drift—the change in wages due to local negotiations. Figure 9.2 shows the total wage change in the period 1970 to 1996 for blue-collar workers. As can be seen from the figure, quite a large proportion of total wage gains are realized at the local level; see also Holden and Rødseth (1990). This means that the sector minimum

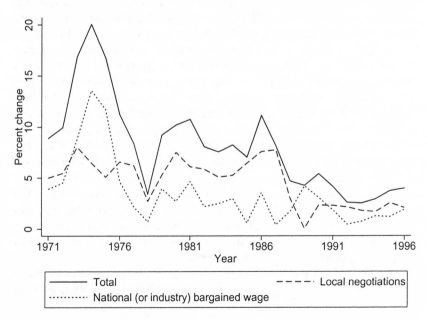

Legend:
——— Total   ---- Local negotiations
·········· National (or industry) bargained wage

Fig. 9.2   Total wage change in Norway decomposed by national (or industry) and locally bargained wage in the private sector in Norway

Source: The Norwegian Technical Calculation Committee for Wage Settlements (TBU).

wage will not be binding for several firms as they have locally contracted higher wages. In our data, a relatively small proportion of the workforce is paid at or near the minimum wage, and local bargaining could be one reason why this is so.

9.3.2   Employment Protection

Rules regarding individual and collective dismissals, as well as those about the flexibility of industrial plants with respect to temporary hiring and the use of subcontractors, are important aspects of employment protection and thus the costs of adjustment for firms.[5] The different types of constraints regulating the hiring and firing of workers are not completely transparent because, in addition to national laws, collective agreements between employers and workers' organizations are also very important in regulating the adjustment of the labor factor. These agreements may differ across industries and workers, depending upon workers' age, tenure, and so on.

Two main laws govern the labor relations in Norway: the law on employment (*Sysselsettingsloven*) and the law on labor relations (*Arbeidsmiljøloven*). The law on employment mainly regulates changes in labor during a period of restructuring and mass layoffs by the firm. The latter was enacted in 1982, and it includes standards for general working conditions, overtime regulations, and legal regulation for employment protection. According to the law on labor relations, dismissals for individual reasons are limited to cases of disloyalty, persistent absenteeism, and so on. In general, it is possible, but very difficult, to replace an individual worker in a given job with another worker. Hence, there is strong employment protection in Norway. The law on employment states that the general rule for laying off a worker for *economic reasons* is that it can occur only when the job is "redundant" and the worker cannot be retained in another capacity. This regulation covers all workers regardless of how long they have been employed. Requirements for collective dismissals in Norway basically follow the common minimum standards for European Union (EU) countries. It is important to note that a firm can dismiss workers not only when it is making a loss but also when it is performing poorly. There is no actual rule on the selection of workers to be dismissed. However, the legal practice narrows down which workers can be dismissed. Conversations with lawyers in the employees' organizations indicate that many, if not most, dismissal cases are taken to court. This is costly for firms.

When it comes to other costs of dismissal, the employment law states that employment is terminable with one month's notice for workers with

---

5. A new law of employment protection and the use of time-limited labor contracts has been proposed by the government and is to be decided upon in 2005. The main proposals are to allow more flexible use of fixed-term contracts and more flexible use of overtime work.

tenure of less than or equal to five years. This one-month notice period is at the lower end of the spectrum compared to many countries. However, most workers have a three-months'-notice requirement for both parties to the contract. Although there is no generalized legal requirement for severance pay in Norway, agreements in the private sector require lump-sum payments to workers aged between fifty and fifty-five. As an example, in the contract between the LO and NHO, a worker who is fifty and has been working for ten consecutive years in the firm, or twenty years in total, is eligible for one to two months' pay. Similar agreements exist for the other unions. Some EU-countries have even stronger job protection rules, including, for instance, general compensation, a social plan for retraining, or transfer to another plant within a firm. Although not mandatory, some of these other requirements are also commonplace in Norway. Note finally that while some costs of reducing the workforce (such as redundancy payments) are related to the size of the reduction, others (such as advance notice requirements, legal, and other administrative costs) may have significant fixed components.

The workforce flexibility of an economy can be enhanced by allowing fixed-term contracts in addition to standard contracts, and by the use of temporary work agencies. In many Organization for Economic Cooperation and Development (OECD) countries, there has been a strong trend toward liberalizing the use of these two schemes. In Norway, the use of fixed-term contracts is allowed only for limited situations, such as specific projects, seasonal work, or the replacement of workers who are absent temporarily. However, it is not as restrictive as it appears, as defining a specific project for a firm is partly open to discretion. Repeated temporary contracts are possible with some limitations, and there is no rule limiting the accumulated duration of successive contracts. In general, the use of temporary work agencies is prohibited, but substantial latitude exists for service-sector occupations. Restrictions for the number of renewals exist, and two years is the maximum for accumulated contracts. Compared to other OECD countries, Norway is ranked a little bit above average for the strictness of the use of temporary employment (OECD 1999). Very few comparative studies of the overall degree of employment protection exist. A much-cited study by Emerson (1987) ranks Italy as having the strongest employment protection rules, while the United Kingdom and, on some criteria, Denmark, are at the other end of the spectrum. Norway is ranked together with Sweden, France, and, to a lesser extent, Germany (when all regulations are taken together) as an intermediate country with a fairly high degree of protection. Obviously, intercountry comparisons are difficult. The most recent comparison was made by the OECD in 1999, where Norway was ranked at number twelve out of nineteen OECD countries in the late 1980s, and as number nineteen out of twenty-six OECD countries in the late 1990s in the degree of restrictiveness (OECD 1999). Evidence on the flexibility of the Norwegian economy from job and worker flows data suggests that it is about average for OECD countries, although worker flows are a bit below average (Salvanes 1997; Salvanes and Førre 2003). The overall impression is that legislation, contracts, and common practice impose important additional costs in Norway when adjusting the labor force downward, and possibly upward as well. See Nilsen, Salvanes, and Schiantarelli (2003) for an analysis of the effect of labor adjustment costs in Norway.

9.4 Data

Like other Scandinavian countries, Norway has rich and high quality linked employer-employee data sets. The sources and structure are basically the same as the data sets used in Denmark, Sweden, and France. The basis of the Norwegian data is administrative files from Statistics Norway and plant-level information from the annual census for manufacturing plus a similar data set for private and public service sectors. Information on research and development (R&D) and trade statistics has been added as well. See Møen, Salvanes, and Sørensen (2004) and Salvanes and Førre (2003) for a general description of the Norwegian linked employer-employee data sets.

In this chapter, we take advantage of two new data sets, one for white-collar workers and one for blue-collar workers. We can match these to the linked employer-employee data as they both use the same series of person identifiers. Both these data sets are from the NHO, the main employers' association in Norway. The white-collar data set is the main data set used in this chapter. Its main advantage over data that has been available so far is that it contains information on hourly wages, overtime hours, pay, and bonus pay as well as detailed information on occupations. The main employer-employee data set contains only information on annual earnings and education, but none about occupations.

9.4.1 White-Collar Data

The white-collar data contain employment and wage data information from the NHO, which has about 16,000 member companies. Seventy-three percent of these companies have fewer than twenty person-years (both blue- and white-collar workers). The member companies employ about 450,000 workers, mainly in construction, services, and manufacturing in Norway (NHO 2004).[6] There is a bias toward manufacturing. Many of the member companies in the NHO operate in export and import competing industries. The total labor force in Norway is about 2.3 million workers, of whom about half were employed in the public sector in the year 2000;

---

6. Note that this data set is very similar to the Swedish data set used in Oyer (chapter 12 in this volume) and the Finnish one used in Uusitalo and Vartiainen (chapter 5 in this volume).

hence, the NHO covers roughly 40 percent of private-sector employment. In terms of private-sector gross domestic product (GDP), the members of the NHO produce about 40 percent.

The data is based on establishment records for all white-collar workers employed by firms that are members of the NHO confederation. Norwegian law requires all employers to report data on wages and employment annually to Statistics Norway. Until 1997, the NHO collected data for their member plants under this law, and Statistics Norway collected data for the rest of the economy. From 1997, Statistics Norway collected data from all sectors. The data set is considered to be very precise, as the wage data were a major source of information for the collective bargaining process in Norway between the NHO and the unions. See Holden and Salvanes (2005) for an assessment of the wage data from this source as compared to other sources of earnings data from Norwegian registers.

Our data cover an average of 97,000 white-collar workers per year in different industries during the period 1980 to 1997.[7] The chief executive officers (CEOs) (and in large firms, vice CEOs) are, in principle, not included. The average number of plants is 5,000, and the average number of firms is 2,700 per year.

As mentioned, we have merged the NHO data set with the main administrative matched employer-employee database. This database contains a rich set of information on workers and plants for the period 1986 to 2002. In principle, this merging allows us to identify CEOs and vice CEOs indirectly. One of the reasons for merging the NHO data set with the administrative register, besides obtaining more information, is that it is unclear whether the information reported in the NHO statistics pertains to plants, firms, or a combination of the two.[8] Compare this with section 9.4.3 for how this problem is solved. On average, we could match 97 percent of workers with plants and 93 percent with firms.

Main Variables

In this section, we briefly describe some of the most important variables in the white-collar worker data set.

Occupation. Each worker is assigned an occupational group and a level *within* the occupational group. The groups are labeled A through F: Group A is technical white-collar workers, Group B is foremen, Group C is ad-

7. The year 1987 is missing. However, the data set for each year contains lagged values; hence, we were able to reconstruct 1987 by using lagged values in the 1988 file. This is, of course, not a perfect reconstruction, as we do not have information on workers who left the data set in 1987 and were not in the 1988 file.

8. The register data covers the year 1986 and onward, and the merging between the NHO data set and the register data is almost perfect. However, we do not have register data for the years 1980 to 1985. In order to construct the link between workers and plants in this period, we used various methods. Important sources of information were the job start date in the 1986 register data and the links provided in the 1980 census data.

ministration, Group D is shops, and Group E is storage. Group F is a miscellaneous group consisting of workers that do not fit in any of the other categories. Hierarchical level is given by a number where zero represents the top level. The number of levels defined varies by group and ranges from 1 (F) to 7 (A). Table 9.2 shows the distribution of workers on the occupational groups. These codes are made by NHO for wage bargaining purposes, and as such they are similar across firms and industries. That information is one of the unique features of this data set, and it gives us a picture of how the hierarchical structure looks within each firm. For example, we are able to study mobility within a firm and questions related to promotion.

We define an occupation as a combination of group and level. That gives us twenty-two occupations.[9] To create a single hierarchy within a firm, we aggregate the twenty-two different occupations into seven different levels. This gives a maximum of seven levels in a single firm.[10] To help in the aggregation, we have carefully utilized the NHO's descriptions of the different occupational groups. Still, such a harmonization across occupational groups is difficult. One problem lies in the fact that some levels are overlapping with respect to responsibility in the organization. For example, even though we aggregate occupational Groups A31 and A32 into the same level (see table 9.3), we know that they differ in responsibility, as A31 involves management of other workers while A32 does not (however, they are both ranked above the A4 level). Furthermore, the levels defined within each group do not necessarily align; for example, level 1 within Group B seems closest to level 1 within Group A, but also overlaps with level 2. Level 2 within Group B is closest to level 3 within Group A, but also overlaps with level 2. Table 9.4 shows the distribution of workers on the seven levels. Note that in terms of white-collar workers, the typical firm is not "pyramid shaped." Most workers are at the middle levels.

Wage. We use monthly salary (on September 1st) for white-collar workers including the value of fringe benefits and excluding overtime and bonuses. Indirect costs to the firm such as payroll tax, pensions, and so on are not included. We transform nominal wages to real wages using the Consumer Price Index with base year 1990 (Statistics Norway 2004).

Hours. The hours reported in the data are average normal hours per week exclusive of lunches and overtime.

Bonuses. This variable gives the monthly average value of bonuses, commissions, and production bonuses during the twelve months prior to September 1st.

9. In the data set, we also have a much richer set of four-digit job codes. These are less consistently used across firms and, perhaps, also within firms across time. We have, therefore, not yet utilized this information.
10. Note that not all firms will have workers on each of the seven levels.

Table 9.2   **Distribution of workers in occupational groups**

	Year			
Occupational group	1981	1986	1993	1997
A0	0.40	0.50	0.51	0.55
A1	2.18	2.58	3.69	4.13
A2	4.80	6.50	6.91	6.89
A31	4.44	5.22	4.34	4.64
A32	5.66	6.64	8.76	8.34
A41	1.45	1.63	1.36	1.19
A42	7.30	7.34	7.34	8.43
A5	4.83	4.80	4.08	4.61
A6	1.79	1.68	1.61	1.33
B1	0.59	0.54	0.68	0.76
B2	2.24	1.93	1.95	1.92
B3	11.96	9.16	7.27	6.35
C0	0.91	1.02	1.07	1.11
C1	5.54	5.51	6.59	6.41
C2	8.82	9.80	10.33	10.61
C3	13.34	14.09	14.60	13.89
C4	9.88	7.92	6.28	5.80
D1	0.33	0.24	0.36	0.29
D2	0.96	0.68	0.92	0.86
E1	1.44	1.20	0.93	0.79
E2	3.04	2.91	1.81	1.91
F	8.09	8.10	8.63	9.20
Total	100.00	100.00	100.00	100.00

Tenure. To create the tenure variable, we used the job start variable that is present in the administrative register data.

Restrictions on the Sample

We put the following restrictions on the sample:

1. To remove outliers in the data, we imposed the restriction that the monthly wage should be at least 2,000 NOK measured in 1980 kroner.

2. The number of hours worked per week is thirty or above; that is, we look at full-time workers.

3. The number of full-time workers in each firm is at least twenty-five in year t.

4. The number of full-time workers in each firm is at least twenty-five in year $t - 1$.[11]

---

11. This restriction, agreed on by all project members present at an National Bureau of Economic Research (NBER) meeting in Boston in April 2004, introduces a selection bias in the entry and exit rates related to firms crossing the twenty-five worker threshold.

Table 9.3   Harmonization of levels

Level	Occupational groups
7 (top)	A0, C0
6	A1, B1, C1
5	A2
4	A31, A32, B2, C2
3	A41, A42, B3, C3, D1, E1
2	A5, F, D2, E2
1 (bottom)	A6, C4

Table 9.4   Distribution of workers in harmonized levels

	Year			
Level	1981	1986	1993	1997
7 (top)	1.32	1.52	1.58	1.66
6	8.31	8.62	10.95	11.30
5	4.80	6.50	6.91	6.89
4	21.16	23.59	25.38	25.50
3	35.82	33.67	31.85	30.94
2	16.92	16.49	15.44	16.58
1 (bottom)	11.67	9.61	7.89	7.13
Total	100.00	100.00	100.00	100.00

Because our data set only contains white-collar workers, this means that we are looking at large firms by Norwegian standards. In 1993, a firm with twenty-five full-time white-collar workers had, on average, sixty blue-collar workers. Table 9.5 shows the effect of our restrictions on the number of workers and firms.

9.4.2   Blue-Collar Data

Our blue-collar data set was obtained from *Teknologibedriftenes Lands-forening* (TBL), (the Federation of Norwegian Manufacturing Indus-tries).[12] The TBL is by far the largest federation within the NHO. As of De-cember 2003, the TBL has about 1,150 member companies employing about 66,000 workers. The member companies operate in industrial sectors ranging from mechanical and electrical engineering to information tech-nology, furnishing, and textile industries (TBL 2004). The data set covers blue-collar workers only, and consists of quarterly observations for the pe-riod 1986 to 1998; that is, a span of thirteen years.[13] Each quarter covers on

12. Because these data are used only in a small part of our analysis, this description will be somewhat briefer than our description of the white-collar data.
13. The 4th quarter of 1987 is missing.

Table 9.5   The effect (i.e., the difference between each row in the table) of restrictions on the number of white-collar workers and firms in the sample

	1981	1986	1993	1997
No. of white-collar workers				
No restrictions	74,075	91,911	100,087	111,336
Outliers	74,074	91,896	99,648	110,516
Hours per week ≥30	73,776	91,695	94,404	104,899
Firmsize ≥25 in year *t*	60,657	78,587	80,831	87,533
Firmsize ≥25 in year *t* − 1	56,838	73,600	76,449	79,259
No. of firms				
No restrictions	2,348	2,622	2,682	3,838
Outliers	2,348	2,622	2,638	3,715
Hours per week ≥30	2,327	2,614	2,509	3,518
Firmsize ≥25 in year *t*	532	591	586	679
Firmsize ≥25 in year *t* − 1	467	506	521	565

average 34,000 workers. Examples of principal variables are pay (fixed, piece, and overtime) and hours worked (regular hours, piece hours, and overtime). Each worker is classified on the basis of a three-digit code describing which working group the worker belongs to; therefore, we have information on what kind of job the worker is doing.

We have linked these data to information from administrative registers in the same way as we have linked the white-collar data; compare with section 9.4.1.

Merging Blue- and White-Collar Data

A logical next step is to merge the blue- and white-collar data sets to get one sample with information about whole firms. This is possible because the TBL is a member of the NHO. Hence, the firms in our blue-collar data set are a subsample of the firms in our white-collar data set. Most member firms in the TBL belong to Sector 38 (Manufacture of fabricated metal products, machinery, and equipment). We, therefore, have constrained the merging of blue- and white-collar data to this sector.[14] When combining the data, we have adjusted for the fact that some of the information is not directly comparable. For example, the TBL data report quarterly wage while the NHO data report monthly wage. Also, because the TBL data span 1986 to 1998 and the NHO data span 1980 to 1997, we are restricted to the period 1986 to 1997.

After cleaning up the merged sample by removing firms with only blue-collar or white-collar workers and putting the same restrictions on the sample as given in section 9.4.1, we are left with a sample of 24,268 work-

14. When talking about blue-collar workers in this chapter, we mean blue-collar workers in Sector 38.

ers in 1987; 26,805 in 1993; and 25,446 in 1997. Numbers of firms are 119, 149, and 139, respectively. This implies that we are able to link approximately 25 percent of the NHO firms with the TBL firms.[15]

9.4.3 Defining Plant and Firm

In this subsection, we explain briefly how we were able to link employees to plants and firms—a link that is crucial. Both the white- and blue-collar data set contain an employer identification number, which is the employer's member number in the TBL (blue-collar data) or NHO (white-collar data).[16] It has not been possible to establish whether this employer identification represents a plant, a firm, or a combination of the two. It is also unclear how plant and firm restructuring is handled. To overcome these obstacles, we take advantage of the National Employer-Employee register, which links employers and employees for administrative purposes related to tax and social benefits.[17] The Employer-Employee register uses the same person identification number as our white- and blue-collar data sets. Hence, we use the person identification number as the merging variable when adding plant and firm information from the Employer-Employee register.[18] In fact, the person identification number is the key variable that allows us to merge the new data sets with other firm and worker information to which we have access.

9.5 Results

In this section, we provide detailed descriptive measures of the wage structure and wage mobility in Norway for both blue- and white-collar workers for the years 1981, 1986 to 1987, 1993, and 1997. These years comprise two peak years and two trough years in the business cycle as explained in section 9.2. The white-collar results consist of all white-collar workers covered by the NHO and include both manufacturing and private services. When we assess both white- and blue-collar workers working in the same firms, we are restricted to one sector within manufacturing only: manufacture of fabricated metal products, machinery, and equipment (Sector 38). This sector comprises about half of the labor force in the man-

---

15. This number is approximate as we look at the number of firms after imposing the restrictions in section 9.4.1.

16. The member numbers in the TBL and NHO are not compatible.

17. To be precise, we do not use the actual numbers from the Employer-Employee register but plant and firm numbers used by Statistics Norway and added to the Employer-Employee register by them.

18. The original person identification number both in the white- and blue-collar data sets and in all national administrative registers is the individuals' social security number. When preparing the various data sets for research use, Statistics Norway recodes the social security numbers in order to preserve anonymity. The link file between the original series and the recoded personal identification numbers used in our data sets is maintained by Statistics Norway only.

ufacturing sector and both high-tech and low-tech firms as explained in section 9.4.2. It is important to distinguish between the wage structures for white-collar and blue-collar workers in Norway, as the institutional setting for wage determination is quite different in the private sector. As explained in section 9.3.1, white-collar workers have their wages mainly set at the firm or plant level, whereas blue-collar workers' wages are mainly set by central bargaining. Robustness tests will be presented where we use plant-level results instead of firm-level results. Recall also that firms included in our analysis have more than twenty-five workers in each year. This means that we are assessing relatively large firms by Norwegian standards.

9.5.1 Wage Structure in Norway

Wage Dispersion for Workers, 1980–1997

Figures 9.3 and 9.4 depict the development of average wage by presenting the average wage and the 90th, 75th, 25th, and 10th percentiles from 1981 to 1997. When we consider white-collar workers alone, we notice that the overall real wage increase has been about 20 percent in the period. Blue-collar workers' wages have had a similar increase. Noticeable in both cases is a slight increase in real wages around 1985 and then a drop in the late 1980s due to the wage freeze at 5 percent nominal rises in 1988 and 1989. Real wages started to rise again in the 1990s. The different portions

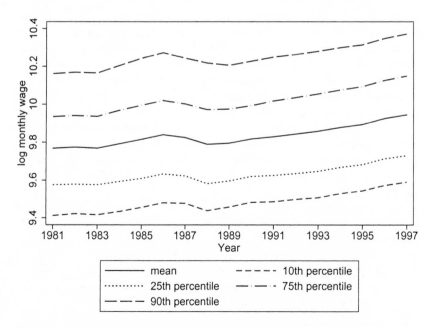

Fig. 9.3   Log monthly wage for white-collar workers in the private sector

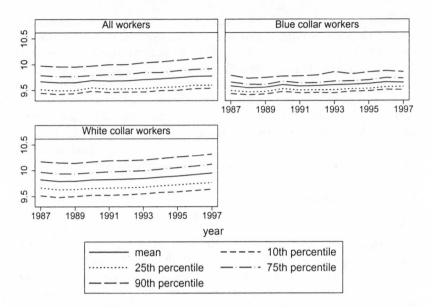

Fig. 9.4   Log monthly wage for workers in the machinery and equipment industry (Sector 38)
Note: Graphs by all workers/blue-collar workers/white-collar workers.

of the wage distribution basically follow the same pattern, and wage dispersion did not increase in this period either within the group of white-collar workers or for all workers taken together. A rather stable wage distribution is also confirmed by the estimated kernel densities presented in figure 9.5 and for both white- and blue-collar workers in figures 9.6, 9.7, and 9.8. The results confirm previous findings (Salvanes, Burgess, and Lane 1999; Aaberge et al. 2000) of no increase in wage dispersion in Norway in this period,[19] and differ substantially from the development in other OECD countries and notably for other Scandinavian countries (see Skans, Edin, and Holmlund [chapter 7 in this volume] and Oyer [chapter 12 in this volume] for Sweden and Uusitalo and Vartianen [chapter 5 in this volume] for Finland).

From figures 9.7 and 9.8, we see that there is more wage variance among white-collar workers than among blue-collar workers. This is to be expected because white-collar workers include high-wage management as well as low-end staff positions. In addition, the wage of white-collar workers is mainly determined locally (so-called wage drift), while the wage of blue-collar workers is mainly determined though centralized collective

19. There is some evidence that wage dispersion increased in the late 1980s. See Faggio, Salvanes, and Reenen (2007), using earnings data going beyond 1997.

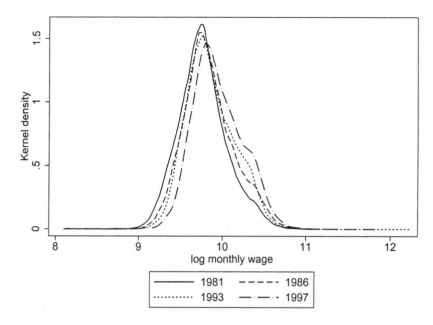

Fig. 9.5   Kernel densities for white-collar workers in the private sector

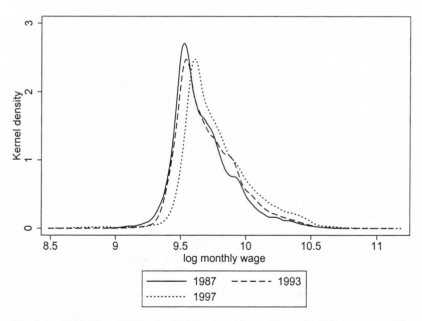

Fig. 9.6   Kernel densities for both blue- and white-collar workers in the machinery and equipment industry (Sector 38)

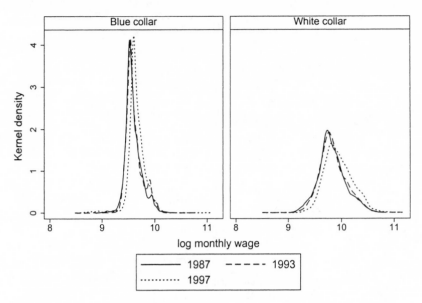

Fig. 9.7 Kernel densities for workers in the machinery and equipment industry (Sector 38)

Note: Graphs by group.

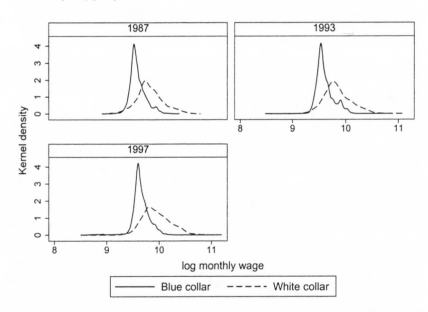

Fig. 9.8 Kernel densities for workers in the machinery and equipment industry (Sector 38) by year

Note: Graphs by year.

agreements. See section 9.3.1 for more about this. Hence, white-collar wages are more strongly influenced by firm heterogeneity.

In table 9A.1 in the appendix, we present more detailed measures for the structure of wage levels for white-collar workers.[20] In table 9A.2 in the appendix, the same type of results are presented for white- and blue-collar workers in the machinery and equipment industry (Sector 38). In these tables, we also report the wage distribution by age. From the lower panel of table 9A.1, we see that older white-collar workers (age forty-five to fifty) have a higher wage level than younger workers (age twenty-five to thirty) as expected but also higher wage dispersion than younger workers. This implies that pay for unobserved characteristics is correlated with the age of the workers. Both groups seem to follow a similar pattern of wage increases over time, but wage dispersion appears to be increasing for older workers.

Within- and Between-Firm Wage Dispersion

In this section, we assess the variation of wages at the firm level. Is the modest and stable overall wage dispersion in Norway representative for all firms, or are there large differences in wage structure across firms? From the institutional setting, we would expect that centralized wage setting induces very similar wage structures across firms, but we also know that wage drift is important (see figure 9.2), particularly for white-collar workers. In addition, we know that technological change, increased international trade, and outsourcing are distributed unequally across firms. These forces have been as important in Norway as in most other countries and may lead to differences in wage dispersion across firms (Salvanes and Førre 2003). Such possible differences may, of course, reflect different factors such as productivity differences, differences in wage policy, or differences in the composition of the workforce.

Recall that the average wage increase is about 20 percent for white-collar workers in the period we are analyzing. In figure 9.9, we present the real wage increase at the firm level for both the mean wage level and different parts of the distribution. We see that the wage increase has been very similar for different parts of the wage distribution of firms. This implies that there has not been any increased wage dispersion across firms over time in Norway. More detailed results, and results for blue- and white-collar workers together in the machinery and equipment industry can be found in tables 9A.3 and 9A.4 in the appendix.

In order to further assess the wage structures within and between firms, we decompose the wage structure. These results are presented in figure 9.10 for white-collar workers only and in figure 9.11 for blue- and white-collar workers in the machinery and equipment industry (Sector 38).

---

20. Table 9A.12 presents the same numbers at plant level instead of firm level.

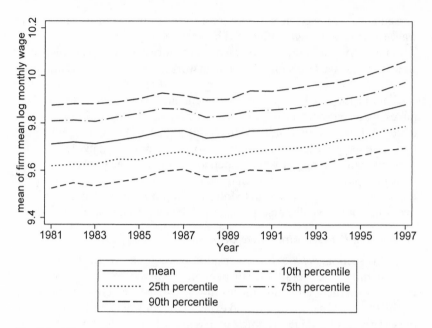

Fig. 9.9   Mean of firm mean log monthly white-collar wage in the private sector

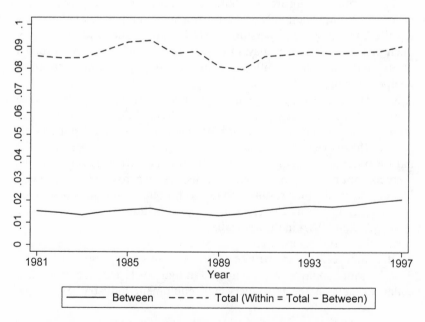

Fig. 9.10   Decomposition of log monthly wages for white-collar workers in the private sector

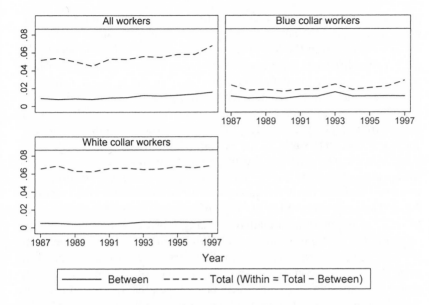

Fig. 9.11   Decomposition of log monthly wage for workers in the machinery and equipment industry (Sector 38)
Note: Graphs by all workers/blue-collar workers/white-collar workers.

Corresponding numbers are given in tables 9A.9 and 9A.10 in the appendix.[21] As expected, only 15 to 20 percent of the wage variation for white-collar workers are between firms. Thus, most of the wage dispersion in Norway is within firms. It is important to note, however, that there was a slight increase in the magnitude of firm wage differences at the end of the period (see also figure 9.13). Somehow, the firms became more different over time. Turning to the results for both white- and blue-collar workers in the same firms, we notice in figure 9.11 that there is a big difference between white- and blue-collar workers and between sectors. First, the total variance is, as expected, much larger for white-collar workers within the same sector. Second, the total variance for white-collar workers is also, as expected, lower within the machinery and equipment industry (Sector 38) than when private services are included as in figure 9.10. Hence, because there is less variance within the machinery and equipment industry and because blue-collar workers are in the majority here, the total variance for both groups taken together is lower than the results shown for white-collar workers only in figure 9.11. However, again the within-firm part dominates the between-firm part, and there is a slight increase in the between-firm

21. Table 9A.13 gives the numbers for white-collar workers, where we use plants instead of firms.

part at the end of the period. One slightly puzzling result, however, is that when we compare the between-firm part for blue- and white-collar workers separately within the machinery and equipment industry (Sector 38), the between-firm part is far bigger for blue-collar workers than for white-collar workers (see the details in table 9A.10 in the appendix). Because firm-level negotiations are much more important for white-collar workers than for blue-collar workers, we would have expected the opposite. As can be seen from figure 9.2, the wage drift part is also very important for blue-collar workers, so this may partly explain the puzzle.

In order to test whether the increased between-firm component for white-collar workers is due to changes in the worker composition on observables, we show the decomposition of the residual wage distribution in figure 9.12 after controlling for type of education, gender, and age in a Mincer wage equation estimated annually (corresponding numbers are given in table 9A.9 in the appendix). Two important findings are evident. We basically get the same result in the first part of the period. Between-firm wage dispersion accounts for about 17 percent of the total dispersion. However, controlling for compositional changes, the increase in the wage dispersion across firms at the end of the period completely disappears. This is made even clearer in figure 9.13, where we report the ratio of the between-firm and total variation. The large increase in differences in wages

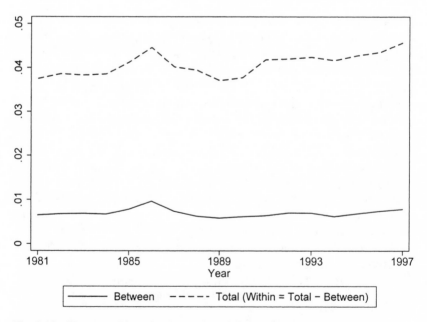

Fig. 9.12   Decomposition of residuals from Mincer equations for white-collar workers in the private sector

Fig. 9.13   Fraction of total variance for white-collar workers in the private sector explained by between-firm effects

due to changes in the workforce composition started in the beginning of the large downturn of the Norwegian economy in the late 1980s. The finding of relatively strong compositional changes in Norwegian firms in this period is also supported by other studies that assess reallocation of jobs and workers (Salvanes and Førre 2003). Salvanes and Førre find that the bulk of reallocation of jobs is between firms *within* five-digit sectors, indicating that structural change at this level has been important in explaining the change in the composition of workers in the firms. The change has been connected to increased technological change and increased international trade.

It is interesting to compare our results with other Scandinavian countries that have different wage setting institutions. Sweden started out with centralized wage bargaining like Norway's, but in the early 1980s it basically decentralized wage bargaining to the industry level and, unlike Norway, did not recentralize. Finland has had partly decentralized wage bargaining at the industry level since the early 1980s, and, as in Norway, plant-level bargaining has been important over the whole period. When we compare total wage dispersion and the importance of the firm level in determining wages, Norway is very similar to Sweden in the 1980s, when the wage bargaining institutions were similar. According to Skans, Edin, and Holmlund (chapter 7 in this volume), the firm-level part constituted about

20 percent until about 1990, and then it increased to about 30 percent of wage dispersion in Sweden around the year 2000. For Norway, it increased less, at least until 1997. A similar pattern is found when controlling for sorting to explain the increased importance of firms in determining wages. Sorting is important both in Sweden and in Norway, but in Sweden, real firm effects also exist. Finland is very different from Norway and Sweden in that the total wage dispersion is much smaller and constant throughout the period. Furthermore, Finland is vastly different when it comes to the importance of firm effects: the firm effect was negligible in the beginning and explains the entire wage dispersion from the late 1990s (Uusitalo and Vartiainen, chapter 5 in this volume).

9.5.2   Firm Size

Davis and Haltiwanger (1996) have shown firm size to be important in explaining wage differences. Figure 9.14 shows the average of log monthly wage for white-collar workers distributed by firm size. Here we use a sample where the firm size restriction is at least two white-collar workers instead of twenty-five white-collar workers. In line with the previous literature, we find that wages increase with firm size. Note that the wage differences between different firm size classes are roughly unchanged over time.

To picture the wage dispersion, we use the coefficient of variation between and within firms.[22] Figure 9.15 shows that wage dispersion within firms tends to increase with firm size, while wage dispersion between firms tends to decrease with firm size.[23]

9.5.3   Wage Dynamics

Figure 9.16 presents the average log wage changes for private-sector, white-collar workers. We notice that wage growth differs strongly over the business cycle for this group of workers. Wage growth is much higher for the two peak periods of 1985 to 1986 and 1996 to 1997 than at the two low-point years. From 1980 to 1981, there is even a decline in real average wages. This procyclical pattern is strong and characterizes all segments of the wage change distribution.

When comparing the group of workers moving between firms to all workers (presented in figure 9.16), the results indicate that most moves are voluntary, as movers have a much higher wage increase than the overall average for almost the whole period. Table 9A.3 in the appendix reports the wage changes for different parts of the distribution, and we see that the

---

22. We have no controls, that is, we look at the raw wage data.

23. Davis and Haltiwanger (1996, 364) write: "The negative relationship of establishment size to wage dispersion [. . .] entirely reflects the behavior of the between-plant component of wage dispersion. [. . .] In contrast, the within-plant coefficient of wage variation tends to rise with establishment size."

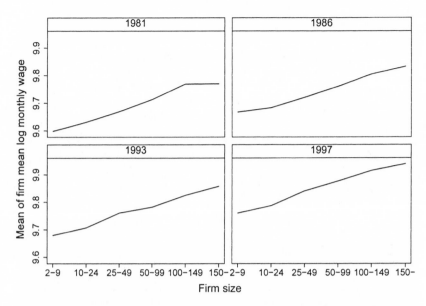

Fig. 9.14   Mean of firm mean log monthly wage by firm size: White-collar workers in the private sector

Note: Graphs by year.

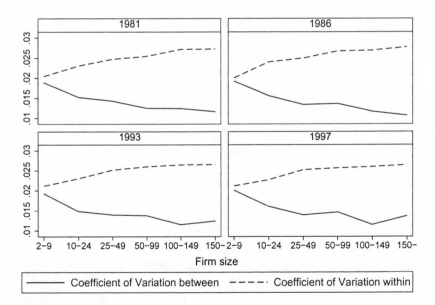

Fig. 9.15   Coefficient of variation within and between firms: White-collar workers in the private sector

Note: Graphs by year.

Fig. 9.16   **Average change in log monthly wage for all white-collar workers and for white-collar workers who switch firms in the private sector**

same pattern is especially strong for the 75th percentile. Again the cyclical patterns are strong, pointing to voluntary moves.

Figure 9.17 presents the wage increases for short- and long-tenured workers. As we would expect, workers with short tenure have much higher wage increases than workers who have stayed with the firm for a while. Again the cyclical pattern is strong.

Turning to the sample of both blue- and white-collar workers presented in table 9A.4 in the appendix, a procyclical pattern is present but much less pronounced. This indicates that white-collar workers are under a more flexible regime in terms of wage setting, whether it has to do with firm-level negotiations or other factors. Results for movers and differences between short- and long-tenured workers hold also for this group of workers.

9.5.4   Worker Mobility within and across Firms

In this section, we present patterns of worker mobility across firms, that is, firings and separations, as well the worker mobility rates within firms, for example, promotions. We want to assess the distribution of worker exit and entry rates both across groups of workers and firms and over the business cycle. A novel feature is that we can calculate internal turnover rates and entry rates for different occupations within the firms. We will focus on the results for white-collar workers in the manufacturing sector and private services.

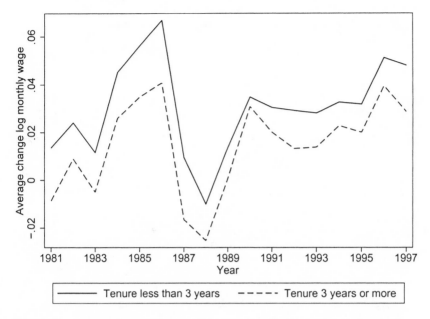

Fig. 9.17   Average change in log monthly wage for all white-collar workers in the private sector, by tenure

Worker Exit and Entry Rates

We start by presenting in figure 9.18 the development and size distribution for all firms defined as 25 or more workers both in t and $t - 1$ in the white-collar data set as well as for large firms defined as 100 or more workers, to make the results comparable across countries. Note that none of these groups will be representative for the Norwegian economy, as firms with 25 or more white-collar workers are relatively large in Norway. However, from figure 9.19, we see that the size distribution for all firms is very stable. For "all firms," that is, 25 or more white collar workers, average firm size increased from 121 employees in 1981 to 139 in 1997. For firms with 100 or more white collar workers, size increased from 287 to 345 employees.

In order to illustrate the patterns of worker mobility, we present in figures 9.20, 9.21, and 9.22 exit and entry rates by year, firm size, and for lower and upper segments of the wage distribution. Tables 9A.5, 9A.6, and 9A.7 in the appendix provide more detailed information.[24] The exit rate or worker separation rate for all white-collar workers taken together is about 15 percent annually for all firms in our sample, and about 10 percent for large firms. Salvanes and Førre (2003), using a data set without a lower

---

24. Table 9A.8 in the appendix provides numbers for both white- and blue-collar workers in the machinery and equipment industry (Sector 38). Table 9A.14 provides numbers for white-collar workers by plant instead of firm.

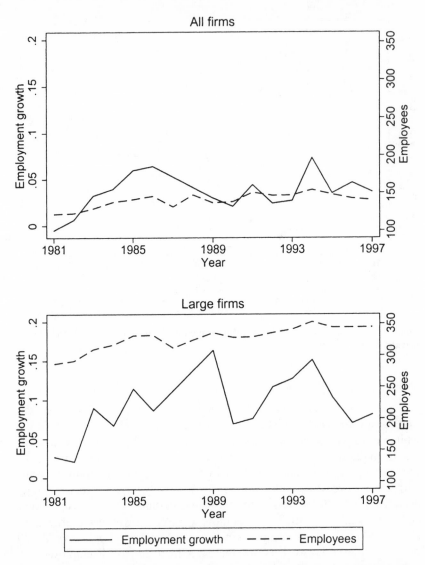

Fig. 9.18   Number of white-collar workers and employment growth for firms in the private sector, by firm size

Note: Large firms defined as at least 100 white collar workers.

limit on firm size, find an exit rate around 25 percent. This is only slightly below results for the U.S. economy. The entry or hiring rate is between 14 percent and 19 percent for all firms and between 9 percent and 12 percent for large firms. One observation, therefore, is that the turnover rates are high for white-collar workers and that they decrease with firm size as

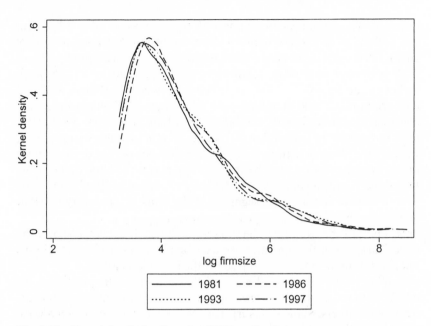

Fig. 9.19   Kernel density log firm size: White-collar data

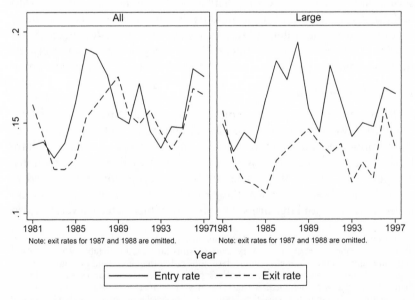

Fig. 9.20   Firm-level exit and entry rates: White-collar workers in the private sector
Notes: Large firms defined as at least 100 white-collar workers. Graphs by all/large firms.

expected. These findings are in line with previous work using other data sets and different parts of the firm size distribution (Salvanes and Førre 2003). Looking at different segments of the workforce, see figures 9.21 and 9.22, we notice that white-collar workers in low-paid jobs have much higher exit and entry rates than workers in high-paid jobs.[25] Thus, low-paid jobs are more volatile than high-paid jobs. Figure 9.23 shows the kernel densities for exit and entry rates at the firm level. The cyclical pattern is quite interesting for worker flows. The exit rate is quite stable over the cycle, whereas the job destruction rate that comprises one part of the exit rate is for many countries found to be countercyclical (for the United States, see Davis and Haltiwanger [1992]; for Norway, see Salvanes [1997]). This pattern appears to be true for all segments of the firms. It is the entry rate that varies over the cycle in a procyclical fashion. Looking at job creation rate only, a part of the entry rate, the standard result is that it is stable over the cycle. This pattern also appears to be true for all segments of the workforce, but it seems to be more pronounced for the lower-level jobs.

In table 9A.5 in the appendix, we see that entry rates are positively correlated with wage growth, suggesting that growing firms raise wages to attract new workers. Somewhat surprisingly, the relationship between wage growth and the worker exit rates is much weaker. One would expect wage growth to be negatively correlated with the exit rate, and to some extent this is so for low-level jobs. For workers in high-level jobs, however, table 9A.6 shows that there is significant, positive correlation between wage growth and exit rates. One explanation could be that managers in successful firms get attractive outside offers. Within-firm wage dispersion does not seem related to exit rates, nor to entry rates with one exception. For high-level jobs, there is significant positive correlation between wage dispersion and entry.

Internal Worker Dynamics

Because we have information on the internal structure of the firms' labor market, we can assess the internal worker turnover rates. Two measures will be presented: internal turnover rates across occupations and the share hired from within the firm.[26] We look at twenty-two different occupations; compare with section 9.4.1. The number of occupations represented in each firm has been stable over the period. The average is thirteen for all firms and sixteen for large firms. The number of hierarchical levels has also

25. Low and high pay is here defined as being in the bottom or top quartile of the within-firm wage distribution, respectively. Very similar results can be found in tables 9A.6 and 9A.7 in the appendix, looking at high- and low-level jobs rather than high- and low-paid workers. High- and low-level jobs are defined as follows: first, we calculate median wages for all jobs; then we rank all jobs by their median wage. High-level jobs are those jobs whose median wage is in the top 20 percent of the wage distribution, and low-level jobs are those in the bottom 20 percent.

26. See Hunnes, Møen, and Salvanes (2003) for more details on this.

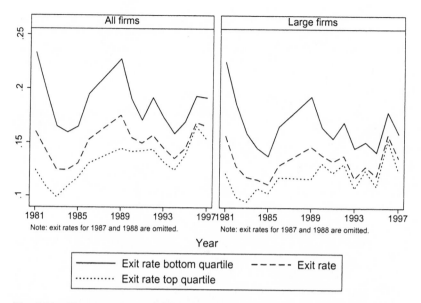

Fig. 9.21 Firm-level exit rates: White-collar workers in the private sector, split by top/bottom quartile of the within-firm wage distribution

Notes: Large firms defined as at least 100 white-collar workers. Graphs by all/large firms.

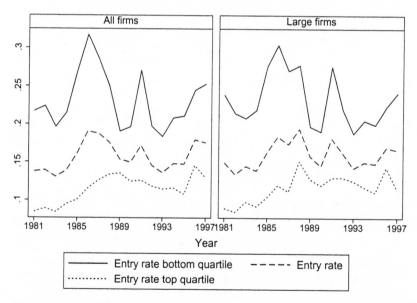

Fig. 9.22 Firm-level entry rates: White-collar workers in the private sector, split by top/bottom quartile of the within-firm wage distribution

Notes: Large firms defined as at least 100 white-collar workers. Graphs by all/large firms.

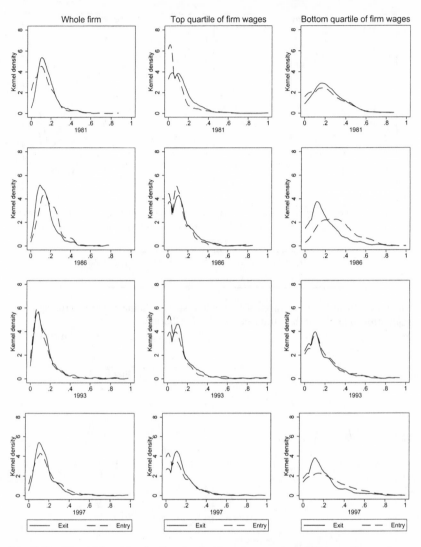

Fig. 9.23   Kernel densities for firm-level exit and entry rates: White-collar workers in the private sector

been stable over time. The average is six for all firms and 6.8 for the 100 or more firms. The number of levels appears to be larger for Norwegian firms than the figure Oyer (chapter 12 in this volume) reports for Swedish firms.

Figure 9.24 shows that about 10 percent of the workers switch jobs internally. The number of new jobs filled internally is about 40 percent for all white-collar workers. The numbers are similar across different firm sizes. Tables 9A.5, 9A.6, and 9A.7 in the appendix present further details. The

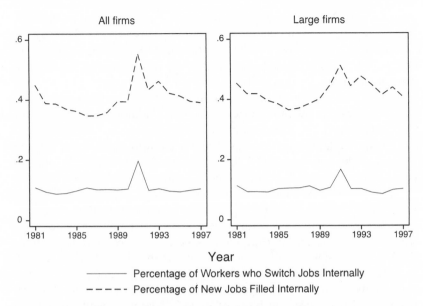

Fig. 9.24   **Percentage of employees who switch jobs internally and percentage of jobs filled internally: White-collar workers in the private sector**
Notes: Large firms defined as at least 100 white-collar workers. Graphs by all/large firms.

number of internally filled jobs is much lower at the lower end of the job-level distribution. We would expect that those jobs are filled externally, as the ports of entry jobs are at the bottom. In table 9A.8 in the appendix, we report results for blue- and white-collar workers together in the machinery and equipment industry. Blue-collar workers comprise the bulk of the jobs because the data are from the manufacturing sector. The external turnover rates are much the same as for white-collar workers. The internal rates are quite different, being also half the rate of white-collar workers. The percentages of jobs filled internally are also much lower. Blue-collar jobs are primarily filled externally.

9.6   Concluding Remarks

To what extent do different firms follow different wage policies? Do such differences relate to how workers move between firms? What are the effects of different wage bargaining regimes? The aim of this chapter has been threefold: first, to describe the Norwegian wage setting and employment protection institutions; next, to describe data sets available for empirical analysis; and, finally, to document stylized facts about the wage structure and the worker mobility patterns in Norway. We analyze within- and between-firm wage differences and worker entry and exit rates in the period

1980 to 1997. Norway is an interesting case to study for several reasons. The Norwegian economy is very open, but wage dispersion in Norway has remained low, while most OECD countries have experienced a strong increase. Also, certain labor market institutions are different from other European countries. Most notably, centralized wage bargaining is quite important. Differences in wage bargaining institutions between white- and blue-collar workers within Norway provide an additional dimension for comparison.

Norway is a high-wage country. Average monthly white-collar wage in the early 1990s was about NOK 20,000, the equivalent of 2,500 EURO. Average monthly wage across both blue- and white-collar workers in the machinery and equipment industry was about NOK 17,000. Real white-collar wages grew 18 percent over the sixteen-year period 1981 to 1997. Wage dispersion was low and stable with a coefficient of variation for white-collar workers of 31.8 percent in 1981 and 32.4 percent in 1997; that is, the standard deviation of white-collar wages was less than a third of the wage level. Country studies from Finland, Germany, Italy, Sweden, and Denmark find coefficients of variation in wages in the interval 33 to 41 percent. We find that wage dispersion among blue-collar workers is much smaller than wage dispersion among white-collar workers. This is to be expected, as blue-collar workers are a much more homogeneous group.

An important question we have analyzed is to what extent firms differ in their wage setting. Numerous economic models portray all firms as similar, using the "representative firm" metaphor. How far from the truth is this simplification? We find that most of the wage variation in Norway is within firms. The average standard deviation of wages within firms is 79 percent of the overall standard deviation. Still, firms vary considerably in their average wage level. The standard deviation of average firm wages is about 13 percent of the overall average wage, and between-firm wage variation represents 17 to 23 percent of the overall wage variation. The between share has increased over time, suggesting that firms are becoming somewhat more dissimilar. This development is related to changes in the workforce composition and disappears when observable worker characteristics are controlled for.

The correlation between the firm's average wage and the standard deviation of wages within the firm is positive and significant, both when we look at the wage level and the log of wages. Hence, high-wage firms have larger within-firm wage dispersion than low-wage firms. Whether this is because high-wage firms are more heterogeneous with respect to the composition of the workforce or because high-wage firms follow a different wage policy is an interesting and important question that we will pursue in future work.

Firms may differ not only with respect to average wage and wage dispersion, but also with respect to average wage growth. Looking into this, we find some heterogeneity. The interquartile range in average wage growth across firms is 3 to 4 percentage points in the 1980s, and about 2 percentage points in the 1990s. These numbers are for white-collar workers. Wage growth is strongly procyclical. When looking at the sample of both blue- and white-collar workers in the machinery and equipment industry, however, the procyclical pattern is less pronounced. This might be related to centralized wage bargaining being more important for blue-collar workers. Workers who change firms have above average wages growth in all years. This finding suggests that there are more voluntary moves than layoffs, even during economic downturns.

In our sample, dominated by relatively large firms, about 15 percent of the workers leave their employer each year. This is a fairly low number compared to other countries. A previous study for Norway, using the entire universe of firms, have found the exit rate to be about 25 percent. We find that the exit rate is very stable over the business cycle. This may seem surprising, but it is in line with previous studies suggesting that higher job destruction rates in bad years are counteracted by less voluntary job changes. The entry rate, on the other hand, is highly procyclical, and varies between 14 to 19 percent. Previous studies suggest that this is driven by more voluntary job changes is good years, while the job creation rates are fairly stable over the cycle. Entry and exit rates are much higher for workers in low-level jobs than for workers in high-level jobs. Hence, low-level jobs have, on average, a shorter duration.

There is substantial heterogeneity in entry and exit rates across firms. Some of this heterogeneity is explained by firm characteristics. First, we find that entry and exit rates are smaller in large firms than in small firms. Obviously, large internal labor markets offer better career opportunities within firms. Second, entry rates are positively correlated with wage growth, suggesting that growing firms raise wages to attract new workers. Somewhat surprisingly, the relationship between wage growth and the worker exit rates is much weaker. One would expect wage growth to be negatively correlated with the exit rate, and to some extent this is so for low-level jobs. For workers in high-level jobs, however, there is significant, positive correlation between wage growth and the exit rate. One explanation could be that managers in successful firms get attractive outside offers.

Having information about the internal structure of firms' labor markets, we are not restricted to analyzing worker mobility across firms. Looking at within-firm job mobility, we find that about 10 percent of white-collar workers change occupation each year. Occupations are broadly defined in our data; hence, these workers should experience a significant shift in their job content. The share of workers changing occupation internally is similar for small and large firms, and the number is also stable over the business cycle. The share of new white-collar jobs filled internally varies between 35 and 46 percent. There is more external hiring in good years. Consistent with the hypothesis that low-level jobs are "ports of entry" into the firms, we find that the share of jobs filled internally is much lower for low-level jobs than for high-level jobs. The difference is particularly large in large firms. Among blue-collar workers, the share of workers who change occupation within firms is much lower than for white-collar workers. The share of new jobs filled internally is also much lower.

Future work on the Norwegian data should go deeper into the importance of sorting and clarify further to what extent different wage structures reflect differences in the workforce composition and to what extent they reflect managerial choices. How has sorting of workers developed over time and what are possible driving forces? How do different managerial choices with respect to wage policy affect firm productivity? A related issue is the effect of technological change and innovativeness on the wage structure. Finally, there is more work to be done on the effect of different wage bargaining regimes, exploiting differences between blue- and white-collar workers, different sectors, and different time periods.

Appendix
Additional Tables

Table 9A.1   Structure of wages within and between firms (white-collar workers in the private sector)

	Monthly wage				Log monthly wage			
	1981	1986	1993	1997	1981	1986	1993	1997
Average wage	18,259	19,694	20,001	21,855	9.768	9.840	9.858	9.945
SD	5,810	6,560	6,455	7,072	0.293	0.305	0.296	0.300
90th percentile	25,872	28,934	29,175	31,959	10.161	10.273	10.281	10.372
10th percentile	12,231	13,090	13,447	14,625	9.412	9.480	9.507	9.590
No. of workers	56,838	73,600	76,449	79,259	56,838	73,600	76,449	79,259
Average of firm average wage	17,226	18,201	18,677	20,395	9.713	9.766	9.791	9.879
SD	2,350	2,404	2,656	2,977	0.135	0.130	0.135	0.141
90th percentile	20,114	21,231	22,023	24,360	9.875	9.926	9.962	10.061
10th percentile	14,042	15,114	15,601	16,686	9.525	9.596	9.622	9.697
No. of firms	467	506	521	565	467	506	521	565
Average of SD of wage	4,568	5,006	5,121	5,566	0.249	0.255	0.253	0.252
SD	1,206	1,381	1,653	1,641	0.048	0.053	0.051	0.048
90th percentile	6,125	6,713	6,852	7,421	0.302	0.312	0.310	0.308
10th percentile	2,999	3,356	3,537	3,744	0.194	0.200	0.197	0.198
No. of firms	467	506	521	565	467	506	521	565
Average CV of wage	0.263	0.273	0.271	0.270	0.026	0.026	0.026	0.026
SD	0.050	0.055	0.061	0.057	0.005	0.005	0.005	0.005
90th percentile	0.323	0.341	0.339	0.334	0.031	0.031	0.032	0.031
10th percentile	0.197	0.208	0.204	0.204	0.020	0.021	0.020	0.020
No. of firms	467	506	521	565	467	506	521	565

(continued)

Table 9A.1   (continued)

	Monthly wage				Log monthly wage			
	1981	1986	1993	1997	1981	1986	1993	1997
Correlation (average wage, SD wage)	0.738	0.732	0.727	0.726	0.203	0.155	0.364	0.333
Significance level	0.000	0.000	0.000	0.000	0.000	0.001	0.000	0.000
Average wage for workers between 25 and 30	15,486	16,984	16,304	17,630	9.627	9.716	9.679	9.757
SD	3,179	3,795	3,282	3,547	0.201	0.216	0.200	0.201
90th percentile	19,725	22,120	20,564	22,202	9.890	10.004	9.931	10.008
10th percentile	11,774	12,626	12,483	13,386	9.374	9.444	9.432	9.502
No. of workers	7,378	11,628	10,833	9,123	7,378	11,628	10,833	9,123
Average wage for workers between 45 and 50	19,970	21,352	21,368	23,262	9.858	9.920	9.919	10.003
SD	6,291	7,182	7,327	7,845	0.290	0.305	0.312	0.316
90th percentile	28,747	32,092	31,592	34,461	10.266	10.376	10.361	10.448
10th percentile	13,576	14,309	14,094	15,250	9.516	9.569	9.554	9.632
No. of workers	7,231	9,031	14,641	13,962	7,231	9,031	14,641	13,962

Notes: The numbers are real wages, transformed from nominal wages using the Consumer Price Index from Statistics Norway with base year 1990. SD = standard deviation; CV = coefficient of variation.

Table 9A.2   Structure of wages within and between firms (all workers in the machinery and equipment industry; sector 38)

	Monthly wage			Log monthly wage		
	1987	1993	1997	1987	1993	1997
Average wage	16,328	16,989	18,311	9.673	9.710	9.779
SD	4,241	4,586	5,374	0.227	0.236	0.261
90th percentile	21,487	22,805	25,364	9.975	10.035	10.141
10th percentile	12,664	12,938	13,873	9.447	9.468	9.538
No. of workers	24,268	26,805	25,446	24,268	26,805	25,446
Average of firm average wage	15,436	15,930	16,877	9.620	9.649	9.703
SD	1,621	1,807	2,010	0.097	0.104	0.109
90th percentile	17,625	18,629	19,383	9.755	9.814	9.847
10th percentile	13,583	14,123	14,787	9.508	9.544	9.585
No. of firms	119	149	139	119	149	139
Average of SD of wage	3,278	3,549	4,026	0.185	0.191	0.212
SD	1,027	1,142	1,219	0.044	0.047	0.044
90th percentile	4,734	4,910	5,464	0.251	0.259	0.274
10th percentile	2,057	2,201	2,487	0.131	0.136	0.153
No. of firms	119	149	139	119	149	139
Average CV of wages	0.210	0.220	0.236	0.019	0.020	0.022
SD	0.052	0.056	0.054	0.005	0.005	0.004
90th percentile	0.278	0.297	0.309	0.026	0.026	0.028
10th percentile	0.141	0.149	0.169	0.014	0.014	0.016
No. of firms	119	149	139	119	149	139
Correlation (average wage, SD wage)	0.718	0.690	0.762	0.501	0.489	0.447
Significance level	0.000	0.000	0.000	0.000	0.000	0.000
Average wage for workers between 25 and 30	15,642	15,650	16,571	9.642	9.643	9.701
SD	2,935	2,836	2,999	0.175	0.171	0.165
90th percentile	19,744	19,658	20,284	9.891	9.886	9.918
10th percentile	12,689	12,671	13,606	9.448	9.447	9.518
No. of workers	3,299	4,654	3,781	3,299	4,654	3,781
Average wage for workers between 45 and 50	17,211	17,888	19,338	9.723	9.755	9.831
SD	4,678	5,341	5,959	0.236	0.259	0.268
90th percentile	23,035	24,954	27,825	10.045	10.125	10.234
10th percentile	13,151	13,200	14,155	9.484	9.488	9.558
No. of workers	3,102	4,474	3,988	3,102	4,474	3,988

Notes: See table 9A.1 notes.

Table 9A.3   Wage dynamics for white-collar workers in the private sector

	Δ monthly wage				Δ log monthly wage			
	1981	1986	1993	1997	1981	1986	1993	1997
Average change in wage	-93	903	329	709	-0.004	0.047	0.016	0.032
SD	1,228	1,263	1,430	1,488	0.065	0.061	0.054	0.068
90th percentile	1,276	2,274	1,241	2,057	0.074	0.116	0.064	0.093
10th percentile	-1,226	-79	-308	-131	-0.066	-0.005	-0.018	-0.007
No. of workers	49,975	60,499	68,162	69,210	49,975	60,499	68,162	69,210
Average of firm average change in wage	-171	820	246	623	-0.008	0.046	0.013	0.030
SD	627	471	369	494	0.036	0.027	0.019	0.023
90th percentile	514	1,396	666	1,186	0.031	0.075	0.034	0.057
10th percentile	-849	267	-176	120	-0.050	0.016	-0.010	0.006
No. of firms	467	506	521	565	467	506	521	565
Average of SD of change in wage	955	1,001	892	1,198	0.052	0.053	0.047	0.059
SD	399	464	823	777	0.024	0.028	0.028	0.037
90th percentile	1,381	1,499	1,434	2,019	0.076	0.077	0.078	0.095
10th percentile	552	562	373	503	0.029	0.031	0.021	0.026
No. of firms	467	506	521	565	467	506	521	565
Average change in wage for workers who change firms	242	1,644	533	1,091	0.015	0.081	0.025	0.050
SD	1,838	2,403	1,708	2,141	0.098	0.117	0.075	0.099
90th percentile	2,405	4,414	2,128	3,424	0.132	0.220	0.100	0.0157
10th percentile	-1,512	-465	-443	-215	-0.068	-0.026	-0.021	-0.011
No. of workers	1,265	814	2,688	2,842	1,265	814	2,688	2,842
Average change in wage for workers with tenure <3	205	1,215	549	1,000	0.014	0.067	0.028	0.048
SD	1,342	1,434	1,260	1,712	0.075	0.075	0.064	0.085
90th percentile	1,750	2,788	1,726	2,808	0.105	0.151	0.091	0.135
10th percentile	-1,109	-32	-300	-137	-0.062	-0.002	-0.016	-0.007
No. of workers	4,766	13,314	10,626	10,829	4,766	13,314	10,626	10,829
Average change in wage for workers with tenure ≥3	-170	815	289	655	-0.009	0.041	0.014	0.029
SD	1,156	1,196	1,454	1,436	0.059	0.055	0.051	0.063
90th percentile	1,116	2,085	1,128	1,873	0.060	0.103	0.058	0.084
10th percentile	-1,236	-84	-310	-131	-0.068	-0.005	-0.019	-0.007
No. of workers	25,065	46,834	57,469	58,295	25,065	46,834	57,469	58,295

Notes: Change in wage is wage in year t minus wage in year $t-1$. The numbers are real wages, transformed from nominal wages using the Consumer Price Index from Statistics Norway with base year 1990. SD = standard deviation.

Table 9A.4   **Wage dynamics for all workers in the machinery and equipment industry (sector 38)**

	Δ monthly wage			Δ log monthly wage		
	1987	1993	1997	1987	1993	1997
Average change in wage	341	308	473	0.027	0.017	0.024
SD	1,423	1,269	1,513	0.084	0.072	0.080
90th percentile	1,686	1,402	1,822	0.112	0.083	0.097
10th percentile	−1,180	−489	−506	−0.060	−0.027	−0.027
No. of workers	20,401	22,957	19,489	20,401	22,957	19,489
Average of firm average						
change in wage	444	175	396	0.034	0.011	0.022
SD	488	364	473	0.031	0.023	0.026
90th percentile	1,054	579	884	0.077	0.035	0.049
10th percentile	−121	−178	−98	−0.004	−0.013	−0.010
No. of firms	119	149	139	119	149	139
Average of SD of change						
in wage	1,127	820	1,146	0.072	0.049	0.065
SD	696	656	610	0.034	0.033	0.031
90th percentile	1,678	1,417	1,956	0.102	0.078	0.097
10th percentile	598	260	473	0.040	0.016	0.031
No. of firms	119	149	139	119	149	139
Average change in wage for						
workers who change firms	297	346	597	0.025	0.016	0.023
SD	1,684	2,222	2,406	0.103	0.114	0.140
90th percentile	2,205	2,679	3,362	0.142	0.157	0.159
10th percentile	−1,355	−1,169	−1,998	−0.084	−0.070	−0.119
No. of workers	609	319	697	609	319	697
Average change in wage for						
workers with tenure <3	617	612	736	0.050	0.039	0.041
SD	1,558	1,573	1,955	0.106	0.095	0.106
90th percentile	2,398	2,234	2,403	0.181	0.141	0.141
10th percentile	−1,073	−505	−545	−0.059	−0.025	−0.031
No. of workers	4,488	3,272	3,289	4,488	3,272	3,289
Average change in wage for						
workers with tenure ≥3	264	257	420	0.021	0.014	0.020
SD	1,373	1,203	1,401	0.075	0.067	0.073
90th percentile	1,492	1,221	1,665	0.099	0.072	0.085
10th percentile	−1,220	−487	−492	−0.060	−0.027	−0.025
No. of workers	15,913	19,685	16,200	15,913	19,685	16,200

Notes: See table 9A.3 notes.

Table 9A.5 Mobility: white-collar workers in the private sector (all jobs)

	All firms				Firms with 100+ employees			
	1981	1986	1993	1997	1981	1986	1993	1997
No. of firms	467	506	521	565	144	170	174	173
Employees	122	145	147	140	287	332	341	345
SD	199	294	293	304	297	453	448	491
No. of occupations	13	13	13	12	16	16	16	15
SD	4	4	4	4	3	3	3	3
No. of levels	6	6	6	6	7	7	7	7
SD	1	1	1	1	0	0	1	1
Employment growth	0.00	0.06	0.03	0.04	0.03	0.09	0.13	0.08
SD	0.23	0.20	0.46	0.27	0.32	0.21	0.74	0.38
Exit rate (all)	0.16	0.14	0.14	0.16	0.11	0.09	0.08	0.10
Exit rate	0.16	0.15	0.14	0.17	0.16	0.13	0.12	0.14
SD	0.10	0.10	0.13	0.12	0.11	0.08	0.08	0.07
Exit rate, top quartile	0.12	0.13	0.13	0.15	0.12	0.12	0.11	0.12
SD	0.12	0.12	0.14	0.14	0.11	0.10	0.10	0.08
Exit rate, bottom quartile	0.23	0.19	0.17	0.19	0.22	0.17	0.15	0.16
SD	0.15	0.15	0.16	0.16	0.13	0.11	0.11	0.10
Entry rate	0.14	0.19	0.14	0.18	0.15	0.18	0.14	0.17
SD	0.11	0.10	0.13	0.13	0.12	0.10	0.14	0.13

Entry rate, top quartile	0.08	0.12	0.11	0.13	0.09	0.12	0.13	0.11
SD	0.12	0.12	0.15	0.13	0.12	0.11	0.17	0.12
Entry rate, bottom quartile	0.22	0.32	0.18	0.25	0.24	0.30	0.19	0.24
SD	0.17	0.17	0.17	0.20	0.16	0.15	0.16	0.18
Percentage of employees who switch jobs internally	0.11	0.11	0.10	0.10	0.11	0.11	0.10	0.10
SD	0.10	0.09	0.08	0.09	0.10	0.07	0.07	0.09
Percentage of new jobs filled internally	0.45	0.35	0.46	0.39	0.45	0.36	0.48	0.41
SD	0.29	0.21	0.26	0.25	0.26	0.18	0.20	0.22
Percentage of workers who have been at firm 5+ years	0.07	0.56	0.67	0.62	0.08	0.56	0.69	0.67
SD	0.15	0.24	0.23	0.24	0.15	0.24	0.20	0.23
Correlation (exit rate, average wage)	-0.158	-0.126	-0.061	0.008	-0.118	-0.143	0.017	0.134
Significance level	0.001	0.005	0.166	0.841	0.159	0.063	0.820	0.079
Correlation (exit rate, average wage change)	0.002	0.054	-0.010	0.132	0.006	-0.065	-0.050	0.223
Significance level	0.963	0.224	0.825	0.002	0.942	0.400	0.512	0.003
Correlation (exit rate, SD wage)	-0.080	-0.033	0.029	0.127	-0.061	-0.098	0.122	0.261
Significance level	0.085	0.453	0.511	0.003	0.467	0.205	0.107	0.001
Correlation (entry rate, average wage)	-0.099	-0.151	0.018	-0.186	0.007	-0.028	0.052	-0.136
Significance level	0.032	0.001	0.674	0.000	0.930	0.716	0.494	0.074
Correlation (entry rate, average wage change)	0.062	0.233	0.114	0.111	0.132	0.254	0.029	0.091
Significance level	0.182	0.000	0.009	0.008	0.115	0.001	0.704	0.233
Correlation (entry rate, SD wage)	0.033	0.058	0.063	-0.056	0.098	0.204	0.000	-0.010
Significance level	0.476	0.192	0.152	0.181	0.243	0.008	0.998	0.891

Note: Top and bottom quartiles are quartiles in the within-firm wage distribution.

Table 9A.6 Mobility: white-collar workers in the private sector (high-level jobs)

	All firms				Firms with 100+ employees			
	1981	1986	1993	1997	1981	1986	1993	1997
No. of firms	465	503	515	546	144	170	174	173
Employees	18	24	29	29	40	56	69	75
SD	29	81	107	141	43	133	177	245
No. of occupations	3	3	3	3	4	4	4	4
SD	1	1	1	1	1	1	1	1
No. of levels	2	2	2	2	3	3	3	3
SD	1	1	1	1	0	0	1	1
Employment growth	0.05	0.13	0.06	0.06	0.10	0.11	0.19	0.05
SD	0.47	0.55	0.65	0.50	0.55	0.33	0.99	0.29
Exit rate (all)	0.14	0.12	0.13	0.15	0.10	0.08	0.09	0.10
Exit rate	0.13	0.14	0.14	0.15	0.12	0.12	0.11	0.13
SD	0.16	0.16	0.17	0.17	0.12	0.11	0.11	0.10
Exit rate, top quartile	0.13	0.15	0.16	0.19	0.13	0.15	0.12	0.15
SD	0.23	0.24	0.26	0.27	0.17	0.17	0.16	0.15
Exit rate, bottom quartile	0.14	0.14	0.14	0.13	0.14	0.10	0.11	0.13
SD	0.24	0.24	0.25	0.23	0.18	0.14	0.16	0.15
Entry rate	0.07	0.11	0.11	0.12	0.08	0.11	0.13	0.11
SD	0.12	0.13	0.17	0.17	0.12	0.12	0.17	0.13
Entry rate, top quartile	0.07	0.12	0.14	0.15	0.07	0.12	0.15	0.14
SD	0.17	0.22	0.25	0.25	0.15	0.17	0.22	0.19

Entry rate, bottom quartile	0.07	0.10	0.11	0.09	0.13	0.11	0.10
SD	0.16	0.21	0.23	0.15	0.16	0.19	0.16
Percentage of employees who switch jobs internally	0.15	0.11	0.11	0.16	0.15	0.11	0.12
SD	0.19	0.15	0.15	0.15	0.13	0.12	0.13
Percentage of new jobs filled internally	0.48	0.39	0.37	0.64	0.56	0.51	0.52
SD	0.44	0.40	0.40	0.37	0.32	0.35	0.35
Percentage of workers who have been at firm 5+ years	0.07	0.67	0.67	0.08	0.62	0.71	0.72
SD	0.19	0.27	0.29	0.18	0.27	0.21	0.24
Correlation (exit rate, average wage)	-0.132	0.015	0.159	-0.062	-0.140	0.044	0.175
Significance level	0.004	0.728	0.000	0.462	0.068	0.565	0.021
Correlation (exit rate, average wage change)	0.108	0.139	0.079	-0.012	-0.089	0.094	0.149
Significance level	0.020	0.002	0.065	0.890	0.247	0.217	0.051
Correlation (exit rate, SD wage)	-0.012	0.109	0.072	-0.036	-0.030	0.063	0.170
Significance level	0.801	0.014	0.101	0.669	0.699	0.405	0.026
Correlation (entry rate, average wage)	-0.018	0.151	0.120	0.045	0.050	0.018	0.032
Significance level	0.707	0.001	0.005	0.595	0.520	0.809	0.677
Correlation (entry rate, average wage change)	0.067	0.034	0.033	0.100	0.144	-0.048	-0.022
Significance level	0.149	0.438	0.437	0.235	0.061	0.529	0.776
Correlation (entry rate, SD wage)	0.115	0.171	0.096	0.086	0.175	0.010	0.164
Significance level	0.014	0.000	0.027	0.306	0.022	0.892	0.031

Notes: See footnote 25 for definition of high-level jobs. Top and bottom quartiles are quartiles in the within-firm wage distribution.

Table 9A.7　Mobility: white-collar workers in the private sector (low-level jobs)

	All firms				Firms with 100+ employees			
	1981	1986	1993	1997	1981	1986	1993	1997
No. of firms	455	493	496	528	144	170	172	167
Employees	20	20	16	15	43	39	33	32
SD	29	29	32	31	42	42	50	50
No. of occupations	2	2	2	2	3	2	2	2
SD	1	1	1	1	1	1	1	1
No. of levels	2	2	1	1	2	2	2	2
SD	0	0	0	0	0	0	0	0
Employment growth	-0.04	0.20	0.09	0.12	0.03	0.13	0.11	0.13
SD	0.56	0.85	0.65	0.63	0.71	0.48	0.69	0.65
Exit rate (all)	0.22	0.17	0.17	0.20	0.14	0.11	0.11	0.12
Exit rate	0.24	0.20	0.16	0.18	0.22	0.17	0.15	0.17
SD	0.19	0.19	0.20	0.21	0.13	0.13	0.15	0.17
Exit rate, top quartile	0.16	0.16	0.13	0.16	0.12	0.14	0.11	0.12
SD	0.25	0.25	0.24	0.27	0.16	0.18	0.19	0.19
Exit rate, bottom quartile	0.31	0.24	0.21	0.22	0.30	0.21	0.20	0.23
SD	0.29	0.29	0.31	0.31	0.21	0.19	0.25	0.26
Entry rate	0.20	0.29	0.17	0.23	0.22	0.29	0.19	0.21
SD	0.21	0.21	0.20	0.24	0.19	0.17	0.18	0.20
Entry rate, top quartile	0.12	0.18	0.13	0.17	0.13	0.19	0.13	0.16
SD	0.23	0.27	0.26	0.28	0.20	0.22	0.22	0.24

Entry rate, bottom quartile	0.32	0.47	0.22	0.31	0.34	0.46	0.26	0.29
SD	0.33	0.35	0.30	0.36	0.28	0.27	0.28	0.29
Percentage of employees who switch jobs internally	0.05	0.06	0.07	0.06	0.05	0.05	0.07	0.06
SD	0.11	0.12	0.13	0.13	0.09	0.08	0.11	0.09
Percentage of new jobs filled internally	0.15	0.13	0.23	0.16	0.19	0.13	0.26	0.20
SD	0.28	0.23	0.34	0.28	0.26	0.20	0.30	0.27
Percentage of workers who have been at firm 5+ years	0.05	0.44	0.64	0.60	0.06	0.45	0.67	0.67
SD	0.13	0.29	0.31	0.33	0.13	0.26	0.27	0.28
Correlation (exit rate, average wage)	-0.199	-0.131	0.011	-0.081	-0.245	-0.287	0.080	-0.155
Significance level	0.000	0.004	0.815	0.062	0.003	0.000	0.296	0.045
Correlation (exit rate, average wage change)	0.036	0.019	-0.100	-0.087	0.019	-0.047	-0.141	-0.059
Significance level	0.445	0.675	0.026	0.050	0.825	0.542	0.065	0.451
Correlation (exit rate, SD wage)	-0.047	0.004	-0.045	-0.043	-0.123	-0.059	-0.182	-0.020
Significance level	0.327	0.927	0.330	0.350	0.145	0.442	0.017	0.800
Correlation (entry rate, average wage)	-0.179	-0.286	-0.122	-0.241	-0.155	-0.317	-0.221	-0.248
Significance level	0.000	0.000	0.007	0.000	0.064	0.000	0.004	0.001
Correlation (entry rate, average wage change)	0.126	0.170	0.048	0.098	0.097	0.196	0.016	0.111
Significance level	0.008	0.000	0.287	0.026	0.248	0.011	0.834	0.154
Correlation (entry rate, SD wage)	0.075	0.154	0.047	-0.054	0.016	0.173	0.046	0.048
Significance level	0.117	0.001	0.311	0.238	0.845	0.024	0.554	0.540

Notes: See footnote 25 for definition of low-level jobs. Top and bottom quartiles are quartiles in the within-firm wage distribution.

Table 9A.8   Mobility: all workers in the machinery and equipment industry (all jobs; sector 38)

	All firms			Firms with 100+ employees		
	1987	1993	1997	1987	1993	1997
No. of firms	119	149	139	55	60	65
Employees	204	180	183	379	370	330
SD	290	265	242	353	338	290
No. of occupations	11	12	12	15	16	15
SD	4	4	4	2	3	3
No. of levels	6	6	6	7	7	7
SD	1	1	1	1	1	1
Employment growth	−0.08	−0.04	0.11	−0.09	0.05	0.21
SD	0.24	0.33	0.35	0.21	0.42	0.45
Exit rate (workers)	0.32	0.21	0.18	0.28	0.16	0.14
Exit rate	0.29	0.20	0.19	0.29	0.19	0.19
SD	0.14	0.15	0.10	0.13	0.13	0.09
Exit rate, top quartile	0.27	0.12	0.13	0.27	0.13	0.13
SD	0.20	0.12	0.10	0.20	0.14	0.08
Exit rate, bottom quartile	0.35	0.27	0.26	0.35	0.25	0.27
SD	0.17	0.20	0.16	0.12	0.17	0.15
Entry rate	0.18	0.14	0.23	0.19	0.17	0.28
SD	0.12	0.11	0.14	0.10	0.14	0.16
Entry rate, top quartile	0.11	0.09	0.13	0.12	0.11	0.16
SD	0.11	0.12	0.11	0.10	0.12	0.12
Entry rate, bottom quartile	0.30	0.21	0.39	0.29	0.25	0.43
SD	0.20	0.18	0.22	0.15	0.19	0.21
Percentage of employees who switch jobs internally	0.05	0.05	0.04	0.05	0.05	0.05
SD	0.05	0.04	0.04	0.05	0.04	0.04
Percentage of new jobs filled internally	0.23	0.29	0.18	0.23	0.30	0.19
SD	0.22	0.22	0.18	0.19	0.20	0.16
Percentage of workers who have been at firm 5+ years	0.54	0.74	0.63	0.56	0.69	0.61
SD	0.27	0.19	0.18	0.27	0.19	0.20
Correlation (exit rate, average wage)	0.009	0.031	−0.152	−0.190	−0.123	−0.320
Significance level	0.923	0.706	0.073	0.166	0.350	0.009
Correlation (exit rate, average wage change)	−0.041	0.101	−0.095	−0.068	−0.213	−0.168
Significance level	0.655	0.223	0.264	0.621	0.102	0.182
Correlation (exit rate, SD wage)	0.021	0.054	−0.134	−0.155	−0.216	−0.255
Significance level	0.825	0.514	0.117	0.257	0.098	0.040
Correlation (entry rate, average wage)	−0.097	−0.051	−0.119	−0.155	−0.326	−0.270
Significance level	0.294	0.537	0.164	0.259	0.011	0.030
Correlation (entry rate, average wage change)	0.161	0.128	0.221	0.133	0.115	0.103
Significance level	0.081	0.119	0.009	0.333	0.381	0.414
Correlation (entry rate, SD wage)	−0.163	0.019	−0.038	−0.227	−0.282	−0.112
Significance level	0.076	0.815	0.655	0.096	0.029	0.374

Note: Top and bottom quartiles are quartiles in the within-firm wage distribution.

Table 9A.9   **Decomposition of log monthly wage (white-collar workers in the private sector)**

Year	Total	Between
1981	0.0857	0.0152
1982	0.0849	0.0145
1983	0.0850	0.0135
1984	0.0884	0.0150
1985	0.0921	0.0158
1986	0.0929	0.0165
1987	0.0869	0.0147
1988	0.0879	0.0140
1989	0.0809	0.0133
1990	0.0797	0.0141
1991	0.0857	0.0157
1992	0.0865	0.0169
1993	0.0877	0.0177
1994	0.0869	0.0173
1995	0.0874	0.0182
1996	0.0879	0.0196
1997	0.0903	0.0207

Table 9A.10   **Decomposition of log monthly wage (all workers in the machinery and equipment industry; sector 38).**

	All workers		White collar		Blue collar	
Year	Total	Between	Total	Between	Total	Between
1987	0.0517	0.0089	0.0657	0.0049	0.0238	0.0115
1988	0.0541	0.0078	0.0689	0.0049	0.0179	0.0092
1989	0.0500	0.0084	0.0630	0.0040	0.0190	0.0099
1990	0.0451	0.0078	0.0625	0.0043	0.0166	0.0087
1991	0.0528	0.0094	0.0660	0.0043	0.0191	0.0111
1992	0.0525	0.0097	0.0664	0.0048	0.0195	0.0113
1993	0.0558	0.0120	0.0648	0.0062	0.0247	0.0160
1994	0.0549	0.0114	0.0654	0.0060	0.0187	0.0113
1995	0.0582	0.0124	0.0679	0.0063	0.0207	0.0115
1996	0.0582	0.0137	0.0668	0.0059	0.0225	0.0115
1997	0.0680	0.0158	0.0693	0.0065	0.0291	0.0114

Table 9A.11   The ratio between the between variation and the total variation (white-collar workers in the private sector)

Year	Log wage decomposition	Residual decomposition
1981	0.1777	0.1738
1982	0.1707	0.1762
1983	0.1587	0.1803
1984	0.1694	0.1752
1985	0.1716	0.1899
1986	0.1773	0.2164
1987	0.1688	0.1842
1988	0.1596	0.1590
1989	0.1641	0.1579
1990	0.1774	0.1638
1991	0.1832	0.1531
1992	0.1956	0.1674
1993	0.2012	0.1653
1994	0.1993	0.1493
1995	0.2083	0.1603
1996	0.2230	0.1712
1997	0.2289	0.1723

Table 9A.12   Structure of wages within and between plants (white-collar workers in the private sector)

	Monthly wage				Log monthly wage			
	1981	1986	1993	1997	1981	1986	1993	1997
Average wage	18,606	19,972	20,378	22,242	9.787	9.854	9.876	9.964
SD	5,901	6,580	6,576	7,130	0.293	0.303	0.297	0.299
90th percentile	26,376	29,280	29,652	32,344	10.180	10.285	10.297	10.384
10th percentile	12,415	13,258	13,632	14,874	9.427	9.492	9.520	9.607
No. of workers	48,226	65,825	65,839	68,900	48,226	65,825	65,839	68,900
Average of firm average wage	17,770	18,658	19,068	20,776	9.743	9.790	9.812	9.898
SD	2,404	2,553	2,723	3,027	0.132	0.134	0.135	0.140
90th percentile	20,618	21,813	22,496	24,696	9.893	9.947	9.985	10.077
10th percentile	14,654	15,344	15,881	17,264	9.566	9.608	9.649	9.731
No. of firms	535	613	614	688	535	613	614	688
Average of SD of wage	4,807	5,182	5,222	5,629	0.252	0.256	0.252	0.250
SD	1,303	1,452	1,774	1,727	0.047	0.053	0.055	0.051
90th percentile	6,420	6,944	7,036	7,468	0.309	0.315	0.313	0.306
10th percentile	3,150	3,410	3,406	3,657	0.193	0.196	0.192	0.189
No. of firms	535	613	614	688	535	613	614	688
Average CV of wages	0.268	0.276	0.271	0.268	0.026	0.026	0.026	0.025
SD	0.053	0.059	0.067	0.061	0.005	0.005	0.005	0.005
90th percentile	0.334	0.346	0.343	0.333	0.032	0.032	0.032	0.031
10th percentile	0.200	0.206	0.201	0.200	0.020	0.020	0.020	0.019
No. of firms	535	613	614	688	535	613	614	688
Correlation (average wage, SD wage)	0.718	0.701	0.693	0.692	0.261	0.198	0.369	0.337
Significance level	0.000	0.000	0.000	0.000	0.000	0.000	0.000	0.000
Average wage for workers between 25 and 30	15,720	17,185	16,457	17,821	9.643	9.729	9.689	9.770
SD	3,180	3,784	3,269	3,460	0.199	0.214	0.197	0.194
90th percentile	19,890	22,298	20,703	22,260	9.898	10.012	9.938	10.011
10th percentile	11,927	12,784	12,647	13,606	9.387	9.456	9.445	9.518
No. of workers	6,232	10,752	9,660	8,050	6,232	10,752	9,660	8,050
Average wage for workers between 45 and 50	20,385	21,725	21,902	23,818	9.879	9.938	9.943	10.027
SD	6,409	7,235	7,496	7,947	0.288	0.304	0.313	0.315
90th percentile	29,510	32,617	32,255	34,960	10.292	10.393	10.381	10.462
10th percentile	13,945	14,614	14,372	15,539	9.543	9.590	9.573	9.651
No. of workers	6,161	7,939	12,419	12,009	6,161	7,939	12,419	12,009

Notes: See table 9A.1 notes.

Table 9A.13 Wage dynamics for white-collar workers in the private sector (plants)

	Δ monthly wage				Δ log monthly wage			
	1981	1986	1993	1997	1981	1986	1993	1997
Average change in wage	−80	917	349	725	−0.003	0.046	0.017	0.032
SD	1,243	1,271	1,489	1,495	0.064	0.060	0.054	0.066
90th percentile	1,316	2,307	1,271	2,085	0.075	0.115	0.066	0.094
10th percentile	−1,237	−80	−306	−112	−0.065	−0.005	−0.017	−0.006
No. of workers	42,734	54,712	59,319	60,755	42,734	54,712	59,319	60,755
Average of firm average change in wage	−150	819	257	620	−0.007	0.045	0.013	0.029
SD	645	483	378	486	0.037	0.026	0.019	0.023
90th percentile	539	1,428	686	1,163	0.032	0.076	0.034	0.055
10th percentile	−849	268	−173	118	−0.047	0.016	−0.009	0.006
No. of firms	535	613	614	688	535	613	614	688
Average of SD of change in wage	950	989	868	1,132	0.050	0.051	0.045	0.054
SD	405	479	994	729	0.022	0.024	0.029	0.033
90th percentile	1,380	1,498	1,456	1,870	0.073	0.074	0.076	0.085
10th percentile	516	532	353	482	0.027	0.029	0.019	0.024
No. of firms	535	613	614	687	535	613	614	687
Average change in wage for people who change firms	168	1,633	645	1,107	0.012	0.081	0.031	0.049
SD	1,713	2,314	1,810	2,072	0.090	0.110	0.081	0.093
90th percentile	2,149	4,317	2,345	3,303	0.123	0.211	0.112	0.145
10th percentile	−1,440	−343	−390	−106	−0.066	−0.016	−0.021	−0.006
No. of workers	1,690	811	2,312	3,261	1,690	811	2,312	3,261
Average change in wage for workers with tenure <3	257	1,251	577	1,023	0.017	0.068	0.030	0.049
SD	1,364	1,417	1,269	1,691	0.075	0.072	0.062	0.082
90th percentile	1,862	2,812	1,742	2,802	0.111	0.152	0.092	0.134
10th percentile	−1,091	−5	−277	−89	−0.060	0.000	−0.014	−0.005
No. of workers	3,769	12,133	9,363	9,494	3,769	12,133	9,363	9,494
Average change in wage for workers with tenure ≥3	−163	822	306	670	−0.008	0.040	0.015	0.029
SD	1,156	1,210	1,522	1,449	0.058	0.055	0.052	0.062
90th percentile	1,135	2,116	1,162	1,907	0.060	0.102	0.059	0.084
10th percentile	−1,242	−93	−310	−114	−0.067	−0.005	−0.018	−0.006
No. of workers	21,769	42,255	49,898	51,202	21,769	42,255	49,898	51,202

Notes: See table 9A.3 notes.

Table 9A.14   Mobility for white-collar workers (all jobs; plants)

	All firms				Firms with 100+ employees			
	1981	1986	1993	1997	1981	1986	1993	1997
No. of plants	535	613	614	688	134	162	169	181
Employees	90	107	107	100	215	267	262	248
SD	106	163	164	161	152	256	252	262
No. of occupations	12	12	12	12	16	15	15	15
SD	3	4	4	4	2	3	3	3
No. of levels	6	6	6	6	7	7	7	7
SD	1	1	1	1	1	1	1	1
Employment growth	0.03	0.08	0.02	0.04	0.10	0.11	0.15	0.10
SD	0.34	0.19	0.64	0.36	0.55	0.18	1.19	0.63
Exit rate (all)	0.12	0.12	0.13	0.17	0.06	0.06	0.07	0.10
SD	0.14	0.13	0.14	0.16	0.12	0.10	0.11	0.15
Exit rate	0.08	0.09	0.12	0.11	0.06	0.06	0.07	0.09
SD	0.11	0.11	0.13	0.15	0.09	0.09	0.11	0.15
Exit rate, top quartile	0.11	0.11	0.13	0.14	0.08	0.09	0.10	0.12
SD	0.21	0.17	0.17	0.18	0.17	0.13	0.13	0.16
Exit rate, bottom quartile	0.15	0.14	0.17	0.15	0.10	0.09	0.11	0.11
SD	0.14	0.18	0.13	0.16	0.15	0.17	0.14	0.17
Entry rate	0.12	0.11	0.12	0.13	0.13	0.10	0.13	0.14
SD	0.09	0.11	0.10	0.12	0.09	0.11	0.12	0.12
Entry rate, top quartile	0.13	0.11	0.13	0.13	0.13	0.10	0.14	0.13
SD	0.21	0.31	0.17	0.24	0.24	0.29	0.18	0.24
Entry rate, bottom quartile	0.18	0.18	0.16	0.20	0.18	0.15	0.14	0.19
SD	0.11	0.11	0.10	0.10	0.12	0.11	0.11	0.09
Percentage of employees who switch jobs internally	0.11	0.11	0.11	0.10	0.11	0.11	0.11	0.09
SD	0.11	0.10	0.07	0.09	0.12	0.09	0.07	0.09

(continued)

Table 9A.14 (continued)

	All firms				Firms with 100+ employees			
	1981	1986	1993	1997	1981	1986	1993	1997
Percentage of new jobs filled internally	0.48	0.37	0.47	0.40	0.48	0.39	0.48	0.40
SD	0.30	0.23	0.27	0.27	0.28	0.21	0.22	0.25
Percentage of workers who have been at firm 5+ years	0.07	0.56	0.70	0.65	0.07	0.56	0.70	0.69
SD	0.16	0.26	0.23	0.25	0.15	0.26	0.21	0.24
Correlation (exit rate, average wage)	-0.155	-0.159	0.006	0.094	-0.116	-0.165	-0.005	0.076
Significance level	0.000	0.000	0.889	0.014	0.182	0.035	0.951	0.310
Correlation (exit rate, average wage change)	0.072	0.108	0.059	0.199	0.062	-0.067	-0.034	0.087
Significance level	0.098	0.008	0.145	0.000	0.476	0.396	0.661	0.245
Correlation (exit rate, SD wage)	-0.036	-0.038	0.028	0.136	0.053	-0.133	0.058	0.072
Significance level	0.400	0.346	0.483	0.000	0.540	0.091	0.452	0.338
Correlation (entry rate, average wage)	-0.079	-0.059	0.047	-0.065	0.018	-0.015	-0.011	-0.025
Significance level	0.067	0.145	0.241	0.087	0.832	0.851	0.891	0.739
Correlation (entry rate, average wage change)	0.072	0.283	0.206	0.220	0.085	0.306	0.179	0.086
Significance level	0.095	0.000	0.000	0.000	0.329	0.000	0.020	0.251
Correlation (entry rate, SD wage)	0.042	0.080	0.080	0.011	0.138	0.169	-0.009	0.049
Significance level	0.337	0.049	0.046	0.779	0.112	0.032	0.903	0.513

Note: Top and bottom quartiles are quartiles in the within-firm wage distribution.

References

Aaberge, R., A. Bjørklund, M. Jannti, P. Pedersen, N. Smith, and T. Wennemo. 2000. Unemployment shocks and income distribution: How did the Nordic countries fare during their crisis? *Scandinavian Journal of Economics* 102:77–100.

Barth, E., and M. Røed. 2001. Education and earnings in Norway. In *Education and earnings in Europe—A cross-country analysis of returns to education,* ed. C. Harmon, I. Walker, and N. Westergaard-Nielsen, 198–212. Cheltenham, UK: Edward Elgar.

Confederation of Norwegian Business and Industry (NHO). 2004. http://www .nho.no/.

Davis, S., and J. Haltiwanger. 1992. Gross job creation, gross job destruction, and employment reallocation. *Quarterly Journal of Economics* 107 (3): 819–63.

———. 1996. Employer size and the wage structure in U.S. manufacturing. *Annales d'Economie Et De Statistique* (41–42):323–67.

Emerson, M. 1987. Labour market flexibility and jobs: A survey of evidence from OECD countries with special reference to Europe: Comments. In *The fight against unemployment: Macroeconomic papers from the Centre for European Policy Studies,* ed. R. Lyard and L. Calmfors, 77–84. Cambridge, MA: MIT Press.

Faggio, G., K. G. Salvanes, and J. V. Reenen. 2007. The evolution of inequality in productivity and wages: Panel data evidence. NBER Working Paper no. 13351. Cambridge, MA: National Bureau of Economic Research.

Federation of Norwegian Manufacturing Industries (TBL). 2004. http://www.tbl.no/.

Freeman, R. B. 1997. Are Norway's solidaristic and welfare state policies viable in the modern global economy? In *Making solidarity work? The Norwegian labour market in transition,* ed. J. E. Dølvik and A. H. Steen, 17–49. Oslo: Scandinavian University Press.

Hægeland, T., T. J. Klette, and K. G. Salvanes. 1999. Declining returns to education in Norway? Comparing estimates across cohorts, sectors and time. *Scandinavian Journal of Economics* 101 (4): 555–76.

Holden, S. 1998. Wage drift and the relevance of centralised wage setting. *Scandinavian Journal of Economics* 100 (4): 711–31.

Holden, S., and A. Rødseth. 1990. Wage formation in Norway. In *Wage formation and macroeconomic policy in the Nordic countries,* ed. L. Calmfors, 237–80. Oxford, UK: Oxford University Press.

Holden, S., and K. G. Salvanes. 2005. Downward nominal wage rigidity in Norway. Norwegian School of Economics and Business Administration. Unpublished Manuscript.

Hunnes, A., J. Møen, and K. G. Salvanes. 2003. Ports of entry: The Norwegian case. Norwegian School of Economics and Business Administration. Unpublished Manuscript.

Kahn, L. 1998. Against the wind: Bargaining recentralisation and wage inequality in Norway, 1987–91. *Economic Journal* 108 (448): 603–45.

Margolis, D. N., and K. G. Salvanes. 2001. Do firms really share rents with their workers? IZA Discussion Paper no. 330. Bonn: Institute for the Study of Labor.

Møen, J., K. G. Salvanes, and E. Ø. Sørensen. 2004. Documentation of the linked employer-employee data base at the Norwegian School of Economics and Business Administration. Norwegian School of Economics and Business Administration. Unpublished Manuscript.

Nilsen, Ø. A., K. G. Salvanes, and F. Schiantarelli. 2003. Employment changes, the structure of adjustment costs, and plant size. IZA Discussion Paper no. 920. Bonn: Institute for the Study of Labor.

Organization for Economic Cooperation and Development (OECD). 1999. *Employment Outlook*. Paris: OECD.

Salvanes, K. G. 1997. Market rigidities and labour market flexibility: An international comparison. *Scandinavian Journal of Economics* 99:315–33.

Salvanes, K. G., S. Burgess, and J. Lane. 1999. Sources of earnings dispersion in a linked employer-employee data set: Evidence from Norway. In *The creation and analysis of employer-employee matched data,* ed. J. C. Haltiwanger, J. I. Lane, J. R. Spletzer, J. J. M. Theeuwes, and K. R. Troske, 261–84. Amsterdam: North-Holland.

Salvanes, K. G., and S. E. Førre. 2003. Effects on employment of trade and technical change: Evidence from Norway. *Economica* 70:293–329.

Statistics Norway. 1974. *Arbeidsmarkedsstatistikk 1974 (Labor market statistics 1974)*. Oslo: Statistics Norway.

———. 1978. *Arbeidsmarkedsstatistikk 1978 (Labor market statistics 1978)*. Oslo: Statistics Norway.

———. 1984. *Arbeidsmarkedsstatistikk 1984 (Labor market statistics 1984)*. Oslo: Statistics Norway.

———. 1997. *Arbeidsmarkedsstatistikk 1997 (Labor market statistics 1997)*. Oslo: Statistics Norway.

———. 2003a. *Arbeidsmarkedsstatistikk 2003 (Labor market statistics 2003)*. Oslo: Statistics Norway.

———. 2003b. *Statistisk Årbok 2003 (Statistical yearbook of Norway 2003)*. Oslo: Statistics Norway.

———. 2004. *Konsumprisindeksen fra 1865 (1998=100)* (The Consumer Price Index from 1865 [1998=100]). Oslo: Statistics Norway. http://www.ssb.no/kpi/1-7t.html.

Stokke, T. A., S. Evju, and H. O. Frøland. 2003. *Det kollektive arbeidslivet: Organisasjoner, tariffavtaler, lønnsoppgjør og inntektspolitikk (Collective labour relations: Organisations, collective bargaining, wage negotiations, and incomes policy)*. Oslo: Scandinavian University Press.

Wallerstein, M., M. Golden, and P. Lange. 1997. Unions, employers' associations, and wage-setting institutions in Northern and Central Europe, 1950–1992. *Industrial and Labor Relations Review* 50 (3): 379–401.

10

Wage Mobility and Dynamics in Italy in the 1990s

Bruno Contini, Roberto Leombruni,
Lia Pacelli, and Claudia Villosio

10.1 Macroeconomic Conditions and Long-Term Trends in Employment, Wages, and Mobility

10.1.1 Employment

From the end of the 1970s to the early 2000s, the employment cycle in Italy had two long periods of growth, from 1983 to 1990 and from 1994 to today, interrupted by a strong recession from 1991 to 1993. The first phase was marked by steady gross domestic product (GDP) growth accompanied by a very modest increase in employment, with 3 to 4 percentage points difference in 1984 to 1989 (it was described as "jobless growth"; see figure 10.1). In the early 1990s, Italy was hit by the most severe recession since the Second World War in terms of job losses. During the crisis of the early 1960s, which put an end to the so-called economic miracle, total employment declined by 640,000 full-time equivalent units; in the early 1990s, the cumulative fall reached 1,080,000 units (Brandolini et al. 2006). The high drop in employment was not mitigated by job creation in the public administration, nor in state-owned companies. Moreover, layoffs were easier—

Bruno Contini is professor at the University of Turin and director of the LABORatorio R. Revelli, Centre for Employment Studies at Collegio Carlo Alberto. Roberto Leombruni is assistant professor at the University of Turin and a research fellow at LABORatorio R. Revelli, Centre for Employment Studies at Collegio Carlo Alberto. Lia Pacelli is an assistant professor of economics and finance at the University of Turin and a research fellow at LABORatorio R. Revelli, Centre for Employment Studies at Collegio Carlo Alberto. Claudia Villosio is partner at Research and Projects (R&P; *Ricerche e Progetti*) and senior researcher at LABORatorio R. Revelli, Centre for Employment Studies at Collegio Carlo Alberto.

Very valuable research assistance has been provided by Matteo Morini and Roberto Quaranta. Thanks to Jennifer Chubinski for her careful reading of the text.

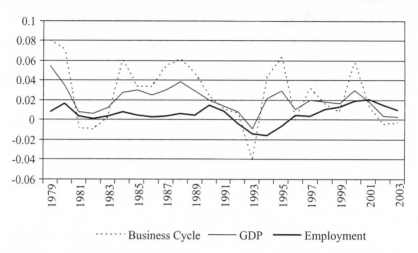

····· Business Cycle ——— GDP ——— Employment

Fig. 10.1   Growth rates of GDP, employment, and Bank of Italy's coincident indicator of the business cycle
Source: Contini and Trivellato (2005).

thanks to the 1991 reform of collective dismissals (see section 10.2)—and a drastic restructuring process continued until 1995.

The subsequent recovery, in contrast with what was observed in the first growth phase, was marked by strong trends in employment—which took advantage of a period of salary moderation and labor market reforms—and a modest increase in GDP. Figure 10.1 shows that from 1996 on, employment started increasing again, with growth rates similar to the GDP. Beginning in 2000, this trend inverted, and the employment growth rate exceeded GDP growth—which, while positive, was clearly in decline. The elasticity of employment to GDP in the years post-1994 was about 0.7 percent, almost double with respect to the 0.38 percent that characterized the phase of jobless growth.

Employment growth since the 1980s is almost completely attributed to women (see figure 10.2). Female employment increased between 1979 and 2003 by 43 percent, while male employment was nearly stagnant.

The unemployment rate constantly increased until the end of the 1980s. After three years of modest decrease between 1989 and 1991, it increased again until 1996—when it reached, according to the old definition,[1] a peak

1. In table 10.1, two unemployment series are reported, before and after the revision of the Labour Force Survey methodology and definitions occurred in 1992. In the old definition, the criteria by which an individual was classified as a job seeker were looser. Job seekers included individuals who completed inactive search actions and whose last search action took place more than four weeks prior to the interview. In line with International Labor Organization (ILO) definitions, these individuals are currently classified as inactive, belonging to the so-

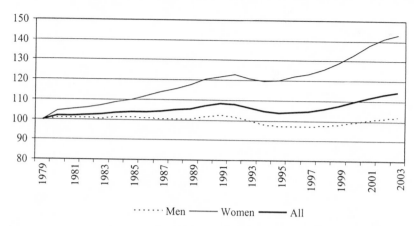

Fig. 10.2   Index numbers of employment by gender, 1979 to 2003 (1979 = 100)
Source: Contini and Trivellato (2005).

of nearly 16 percent. It then began to decrease during the years of intense employment growth, which brought it slightly above 10 percent in 2004 (see table 10.1).

Expansion of the service sector occurred mostly in the 1980s and 1990s, following, with some delay, the physiological pattern of industrialized countries. The service sector, 43 percent of total employment in 1970, swells to 66 percent in 2003, still below the EU average.

A profound transformation in the employment structure has been driven by population aging, which is currently proceeding at a pace more pronounced than in most other OECD countries (OECD 2006). After the "baby boom" of the 1960s and early 1970s, the fertility rate declined steeply: it fell below the replacement rate of 2.1 at the beginning of the 1980s, reaching 1.24 in 2000. At the same time, life expectancy is rising rapidly. Even though a slight recovery in fertility rates is expected in the coming years, the transition process to the new demographic regime is having, and will have, a profound impact on the economy. In the next two decades, the baby boom generations will reach retirement age and will be replaced by new cohorts roughly half in size. By 2050, more than one in three Italians will be over the age of sixty-five.[2]

Aging affects companies in different ways because the mature workforce

---

called potential labor force. There is evidence, however, that their characteristics and behaviors are more similar to the unemployed than to the inactive (see Brandolini, Cipollone, and Viviano 2006; Battistin, Rettore, and Trivellato 2007).

2. See the population projections produced by the Italian Statistical Office (ISTAT), "central" scenario (http://demo.istat.it/index.html).

Table 10.1   Macroeconomic conditions

Year	Unemployment rate Before LFS revision 1992	After LFS revision 1992	GDP (billion euros, 1995 prices)	Change in GDP 1 year	2 year	5 year
1970	5.3		486			
1971	5.3		495	1.9		
1972	6.3		511	3.2	5.1	
1973	6.2		544	6.5	9.9	
1974	5.3		573	5.3	12.2	
1975	5.8		561	-2	3.1	15.5
1976	6.6		598	6.5	4.3	20.7
1977	7.0		612	2.4	9	19.8
1978	7.1		634	3.7	6.1	16.5
1979	7.5		669	5.5	9.4	16.8
1980	7.5		693	3.5	9.2	23.4
1981	8.3		698	0.8	4.3	16.8
1982	9.0		703	0.6	1.4	14.8
1983	10.0		711	1.2	1.9	12.1
1984	10.7		731	2.8	4	9.2
1985	11.0		753	3	5.8	8.6
1986	11.5		772	2.5	5.6	10.5
1987	12.3		795	3	5.6	13.1
1988	12.4		826	3.9	7.1	16.1
1989	12.4		850	2.9	6.9	16.3
1990	11.3		867	2	4.9	15.1
1991	10.9		879	1.4	3.4	13.9
1992	11.5		885	0.8	2.2	11.4
1993	13.7	10.3	877	-0.9	-0.1	6.2
1994	15.0	11.2	897	2.2	1.3	5.5
1995	15.7	11.8	923	2.9	5.2	6.5
1996	15.9	12.0	933	1.1	4	6.2
1997	15.9	12.1	952	2	3.1	7.5
1998	15.7	12.3	969	1.8	3.9	10.4
1999	15.2	11.8	985	1.7	3.5	9.9
2000	14.4	11.0	1015	3	4.7	10
2001	12.4	9.7	1033	1.8	4.8	10.7
2002	11.8	9.3	1037	0.4	2.2	8.9
2003	11.1	9.0	1040	0.3	0.6	7.3
2004	10.2	7.4	1052	1.2	1.5	6.8

concentrates in larger firms. The shift in the age distribution of employment, though, has been remarkable in all firm sizes: between 1988 and 1998, the mode of the distribution among smaller firms shifted markedly from the twenty to twenty-four age group to the twenty-five to twenty-nine group; among larger firms, the shift is toward a bimodal distribution, with one hump at age thirty to thirty-four and the other at age forty-five to forty-nine (see figure 10.3).

1988

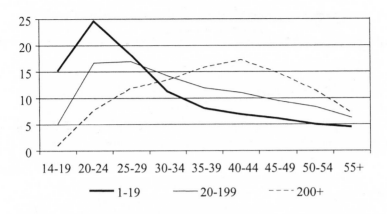

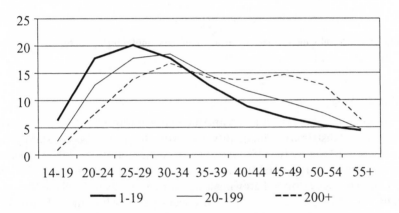

Fig. 10.3   Workforce age distribution by firm size, 1988 and 1998
Source: Our calculations based on WHIP data, 1988 and 1998.

The distribution of dependent employment by firm size did not change much over the last fifteen years: the share of firms with less than twenty employees held steady at around 40 percent of total employment, the share of large firms (> 1,000 workers) dropped by almost 4 percentage points, and that of small-medium firms (20 to 100 workers) increased in proportion. In manufacturing, the shift was huge (see figure 10.4), with the share of firms > 1000 declining from 23 percent in the early 1980s to 16 percent in 1998. Large manufacturers went through a profound restructuring process that caused the loss of about 380,000 jobs, only partially reabsorbed by small and medium firms: the overall employment loss in manufacturing was about 250,000 workers.

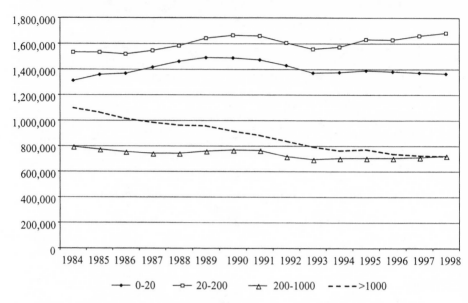

Fig. 10.4   Employment trends by firm size in the manufacturing sector
Source: Our calculations based on WHIP data.

10.1.2   Wages

In table 10.2, we report mean and median real wages 1985 to 1999 and a selection of distribution/inequality indicators. Real earnings constantly increased until the early 1990s. After the recession, and the 1993 collective agreements that reshaped the system of collective bargaining (see section 10.2), real wages stopped growing altogether, and only in 1999 did they attain the prerecession levels. In subsequent years, while most European countries experienced a long phase of real wage growth, in Italy they remained roughly stagnant.

Wages changed with remarkable differences between the tails and the center of the distribution. Over the 1985 to 1999 period, the median individual faced a modest 3.4 percent real increase, while at both ends of the distribution, growth was much faster. In 1985, the ratio between the ninth and the fifth decile (P90-P50) was 1.54; by 1999, it increased to 1.83. At the same time, the ratio between the fifth and the first decile (P50-P10) dropped from 1.52 to 1.44. Likewise, the ratio between the ninth and the first decile (P90-P10) ratio increased from 2.34 to 2.60. This points to a reduction of inequality in the low tail of the distribution and an increase in the high tail. Overall inequality measured by Gini, Theil, and Var-Logs indexes increased significantly in the period.

The relationship between wages and firm dimension is clear in figure 10.5: larger firms, on average, pay higher wages. The wage-firm size relation

Table 10.2   **Real wage distribution**

Year	Median	Mean	Percentiles ratios P90/P50	Percentiles ratios P50/P10	Percentiles ratios P90/P10	Inequality measures Gini	Inequality measures Theil	Inequality measures var-logs
1985	1424	1532	1.54	1.52	2.34	199 (0.6)	71 (0.5)	133 (0.8)
1986	1407	1529	1.55	1.52	2.36	203 (0.7)	74 (0.6)	136 (0.8)
1987	1427	1569	1.61	1.53	2.45	214 (0.7)	82 (0.6)	147 (0.9)
1988	1424	1572	1.63	1.52	2.47	216 (0.7)	83 (0.6)	149 (0.8)
1989	1435	1620	1.68	1.42	2.38	219 (0.7)	87 (0.6)	146 (0.8)
1990	1449	1671	1.73	1.42	2.46	233 (0.8)	102 (0.8)	160 (0.9)
1991	1503	1712	1.70	1.45	2.46	227 (0.7)	96 (0.6)	156 (0.8)
1992	1498	1719	1.72	1.43	2.47	229 (0.7)	97 (0.7)	156 (0.9)
1993	1499	1724	1.72	1.42	2.44	227 (0.7)	96 (0.7)	152 (0.9)
1994	1484	1711	1.73	1.42	2.46	228 (0.8)	98 (0.8)	153 (1.0)
1995	1444	1672	1.77	1.42	2.52	229 (0.7)	97 (0.7)	155 (0.9)
1996	1433	1673	1.79	1.41	2.52	233 (0.7)	101 (0.7)	159 (0.8)
1997	1461	1710	1.79	1.42	2.54	237 (0.7)	105 (0.7)	164 (0.9)
1998	1470	1723	1.80	1.45	2.60	244 (0.8)	112 (0.8)	170 (1.0)
1999	1473	1768	1.83	1.44	2.63	257 (0.9)	134 (1.2)	187 (1.1)
Percent change 1985–1999	3.4	15.4	19.4	−5.7	12.6	28.9	89.7	41.1

Source: Devicienti (2006).

Notes: Wages are monthly wages at 1999 prices, private sector only. Part-time monthly wages have been converted into full-time equivalents. Numbers in parentheses are standard errors.

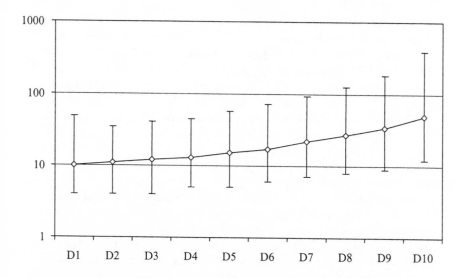

Fig. 10.5   Firm size distribution (P10, median, and P90) by wage deciles—1999
Note: Size in log scale.
Source: Our calculations on WHIP data.

Table 10.3   Monthly wages in 1986 and 1991 and wage growth rate 1986–1991 for movers and stayers

	Movers			Stayers		
	N	Mean	SD	N	Mean	SD
Wage 1986	9,641	1,731.2	548.2	20,526	1,906.7	604.2
Wage 1991	9,641	2,805.2	1,138.3	20,526	3,042.3	1,184.5
Wage growth rate	9,641	1.6	0.4	20,526	1.6	

Source: Contini and Villosio (2003).

also explains the wage dynamics of job changes: workers switching from small to large firms earn wage premiums, while job switches in the opposite direction often lead to wage losses (see Contini and Villosio [2003] and table 10.3).

Table 10.4 displays the results of a decomposition exercise: for all partitions, inequality is predominantely explained by its within-group component. The between-group component is negligible except for age and occupation partitions. In the former, the between component accounts for about 12 to 14 percent of aggregate inequality, while in the latter, it explains about one-fourth. This is consistent with a collective wage-setting process that relies on seniority (here proxied by age) and occupation.

10.1.3   Mobility

Gross worker turnover (GWT) in Italy—the ratio of yearly flows of engagements and separations on average employment—hovered about 60 percent (see table 10.5), indicating that labor force mobility is higher than that of most European countries (Leombruni and Quaranta 2002, 2005). This may appear at odds with the view that Italian labor market legislation is among the most rigid: we will address this point in section 10.2.

As theory suggests (Blanchard and Diamond 1990), GWT appears to move procyclically, with peaks in the expansionary phases and a trough during the recession culminated in 1993.

The GWT, like most mobility indicators, reflects worker age and firm size (Davis and Haltiwanger 1999). Young workers are the most mobile: the search for a "good job" translates into many flows in and out of jobs. Worker flows are much higher in small firms, for a variety of reasons: higher entry and exit rates, limited internal mobility, and few firing constraints due to looser institutional constraints and to the limited presence of unions. Figure 10.6 displays GWT as a function of both variables. Mobility as a function of age is U-shaped in all size classes. In small firms, it is notably shifted upward compared to the large companies and has a flatter shape. Most notably, the "small firm" effect dominates the age factor in determining mobility: individuals aged fifty and over working in small firms

Table 10.4   Inequality decompositions by population subgroups, 1985 and 1996

	Theil index		Shares (%)		Average monthly wage (1999 prices)		Δ wage (%)	Relative average wages (all = 1)	
	1985	1999	1985	1999	1985	1999		1985	1999
A. All	71	134	100	100	1,532	1,768	15.4	1	1
B. Males	67	138	71	66	1,628	1,864	14.5	1.06	1.05
Females	61	115	29	34	1,298	1,579	21.6	0.85	0.89
Within-group inequality	66	131							
Between-group inequality	5	3							
C. Apprentice	49	90	5	6	899	1,003	11.6	0.59	0.57
Blue collar	43	86	65	60	1,431	1,540	7.6	0.93	0.87
White collar	71	115	29	33	1,828	2,212	21.0	1.19	1.25
Managers	36	34	0.6	0.8	4,044	6,393	58.1	2.64	3.62
Within-group inequality	53	97							
Between-group inequality	18	37							
D. North	68	133	60	61	1,535	1,797	17.0	1.00	1.02
Center	74	140	19	19	1,550	1,773	14.4	1.01	1.00
South	74	128	21	20	1,508	1,669	10.7	0.98	0.95
Within-group inequality	71	133							
Between-group inequality	0.0	0.4							
E. Age 15–24	51	79	23	16	1,179	1,244	5.5	0.77	0.70
Age 25–34	47	87	28	35	1,501	1,613	7.5	0.98	0.91
Age 35–49	68	133	35	36	1,716	1,984	15.6	1.11	1.12
Age 50–64	75	168	14	13	1,721	2,244	30.4	1.12	1.27
Within-group inequality	60	118							
Between-group inequality	10	16							

(continued)

Table 10.4   (continued)

	Theil index		Shares (%)		Average monthly wage (1999 prices)		Δ wage (%)	Relative average wages (all = 1)	
	1985	1999	1985	1999	1985	1999		1985	1999
F. Manufacturing	64	149	56	48	1,511	1,795	18.8	0.99	1.02
Building	48	66	12	10	1,512	1,546	2.4	0.99	0.87
Services	89	129	32	42	1,578	1,790	13.4	1.03	1.01
Within-group inequality	70	133							
Between-group inequality	0.2	1							
H. Full time	70	133	99	90	1,531	1,781	16.3	1.00	1.01
Part time	104	137	1	10	1,639	1,651	0.8	1.07	0.93
Within-group inequality	71	134							
Between-group inequality	0.0	0.3							

Source: Devicienti (2006).

Note: For the definition of wage, see table 10.2 notes.

Table 10.5			Yearly worker flows, four subperiods, Italy	
	Separation rate	Association rate	Gross worker turnover	Business cycle
1986–1990	29.86	32.53	62.39	Expansion
1991–1993	28.77	28.01	56.78	Recession
1994–1996	29.68	29.01	58.69	Recovery
1997–1999	33.00	35.00	68.00	Expansion

Note: Percentage values, authors' calculations based on WHIP data.

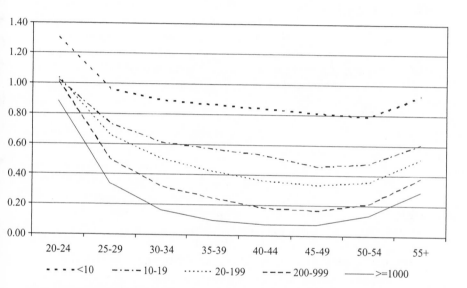

Fig. 10.6   Gross worker turnover by worker age and firm size, 1987 to 1999
Source: Leombruni and Quaranta (2005).

(ten to nineteen employees) have a 50 percent overall turnover, while individuals aged twenty-five to twenty-nine employed in large firms (1000+) slightly exceed 30 percent.

Blue-collar workers are much more mobile than white-collar workers, who in turn are more mobile than managers (but the probability of a direct job-to-job change conditional to a move is much higher for managers than for any of the other categories). Moreover, the difference in mobility of blue-collar workers with respect to white-collars has widened noticeably over the years (Leombruni and Quaranta 2005). While GWT for white-collars has been stable at about 41 percent in the period, that for blue-collars increased from 69 percent in 1987–1989 to 78 percent in 1997–1999.

10.2 Institutional Aspects of the Italian Labor Market

For many years, and at least through the late 1990s, Italy has been renowned as the European country with the most rigid labor market legislation. The OECD has widely contributed to this view. It may, therefore, appear strange, to say the least, that the magnitude of job and worker turnover in Italy (as reported in the previous paragraph and, in more detail, in section 10.3.3) has been among the highest in Europe, second only to the United Kingdom.

There can be no question that Italy's labor legislation has been (and still is today) swamped by a huge number of laws and bylaws, sometimes patently contradictory. Labor jurists sometimes refer to a peculiar dichotomy between the "law in the books" and the "law in action." This dichotomy undoubtedly applies to Italy. Be it because of its internal contradictions, dubious interpretation, fragility of the system of controls, unapplied or inapplicable sanctions, illegal practices, and so on, the degree of labor turnover in Italy by far exceeds what might be reasonably expected under its current legislative apparatus. The magnitude of Italy's labor market flows is, to some extent, counterbalanced by the relative rigidity of the wage structure throughout the 1980s. One might say that the former is a consequence of the latter, because quantities adjust when prices cannot. Also on the wage front, however, there have been interesting innovations in the last decade, as witnessed by the trends toward rapidly increasing differentials of the 1990s (reported in section 10.3 of this report).

What follows is a summary of the most salient features of the institutional aspects of Italy's labor market and its major changes in the last twenty-five years. The data we are presenting in this chapter end with 1998: they are, nevertheless, representative of the abnormal features of the Italian labor market from the preceding perspective. In more recent years—since 2002—Italy's labor legislation has undergone a vast deregulatory process, as in many other European countries.

The early 1980s witnessed the most rigid "snapshot" of Italian labor market legislation that can be taken. It was characterized by centralized bargaining, by an egalitarian mechanism of wage increases, and by severe restrictions both on hirings and firings. Nominal wages were indexed to prices through an automatic mechanism known as *scala mobile* (escalator clause), whose rules were uniform across sectors. Indexation took place quarterly. Hirings involved almost exclusively open-end contracts. Manual workers were selected almost exclusively from the unemployment workers' lists held by the public employment service, and not via direct selection mechanisms. Individual firings in firms with fifteen or more employees were admissible only under a "just cause" rule: workers dismissed without justifiable reason had the right to reinstatement. This rule, given the diffusion of small firms in Italy, actually was not enforceable for about 35 percent of dependent employment; when applicable, it was commonly bypassed either legally by extrajudiciary settlements with severance pay, or by unlawful practices such as forced quits that would go unreported to the judiciary for fear of losing job options offered within the same industrial district.

Collective and temporary layoffs were instead widely utilized by way of ad hoc institutes—the earnings integration scheme (CIG; *cassa integrazione guadagni*) since the 1970s—easily available to large firms during times of industry crises or restructuring.

Starting from the mid-1980s, several reforms have radically reshaped the working of the labor market.

In 1984, restrictions on hirings were markedly reduced with a partial liberalization of direct selection mechanisms; part-time work and work-training contracts (CFL; *contratti di formazione-lavoro*) were introduced. The latter was a mixed contract, aimed at young people aged fifteen to twenty-nine, under which employers had to provide workers with appropriate occupational training. Hires via CFL enabled firms to benefit from a hefty 50 percent rebate on social security contributions. In addition, it was a fixed-term contract, with a predetermined duration of no less than eighteen months and no longer than twenty-four. At termination, the firm had the right, but no obligation, to upgrade the CFL contract into an open-ended one, taking advantage of favorable tax treatment for one additional year.[3]

In 1986, the automatic indexation of wages via *scala mobile* was reduced from quarterly to twice a year, and definitely abolished in 1992.

In 1991, a new institute ("mobility lists") aimed at dealing with collective layoffs was introduced. Dismissed workers were granted long-term unemployment benefits, while fiscal incentives were made available to firms willing to hire from the "lists." In addition, CIG was extended also to small and medium firms of the manufacturing sector (CIGS; *cassa integrazione guadagni straordinaria*). The latter, in principle, was still designed for temporary layoffs, but in practice it allowed mass layoffs at very low costs, as it could be extended several times.

In 1993, at the peak of recession, the unions, Confindustria (the Italian Manufacturers' Association), and the government pledged to act in concert to improve the conditions of the labor market. A new two-level bargaining system was agreed upon, still in rule today. At the national level, wages are set according to the inflation rate targeted by the government for the following twenty-four months. The difference between actual and targeted inflation is not automatically recovered and is to be taken into account at the start of a new bargaining round. At the regional or firm level, additional wage components are introduced to be geared by profit-sharing

---

3. The CFL underwent several reforms during the years that progressively reduced their advantages in terms of social security rebates and flexibility. They were finally abolished in 2003.

considerations. In a few years, firm-level bargaining spread in the majority of large firms, while it was still negligible in the small-firm sector.

The new catchphrase of subsequent policies was "increasing flexibility on all fronts." As a matter of fact, most of the action took place in the labor market, while little was achieved in terms of product market flexibility.

In 1996, the so-called *pacchetto Treu* extended the range of possible work contracts by introducing temporary work, by extending the applicability of part-time and fixed-term contracts, and by regulating the so-called *parasubordinato* contract, a form of disguised self-employment. The portfolio of available contracts was further extended into twenty-one different typologies in 2003, including job sharing, project work, and staff leasing.

As a consequence, from 1996 on, the standard open-end contracts lost importance in favor of atypical ones, which began to represent the most widespread channel for entry into the labor market. In 2002, the share of workers with a fixed-term contract already accounted for 10 percent of total employment—against an EU15 average of 13 percent (European Commission 2003).

10.3   Results

The tables presented in this section have been computed using the Work Histories Italian Panel (WHIP), based on administrative data from the Italian Social Security (INPS) archives.

Wages are average daily earnings paid to the worker, at 1990 prices, expressed in Italian lire (,000), gross of income taxes and payroll taxes paid by workers, and net of payroll taxes paid by employers.[4] Social security payroll records a relatively accurate measure of total earnings, at least when compared to survey-based information. The same does not apply to the measurement of labor input: there is some evidence of underreporting in the number of paid working days, as some firms adjust the reported daily wage to minimum wage requirements. Such underreporting seems to be important mostly in the South of Italy, leading to a potential bias in within-country comparisons (Contini, Filippi, and Malpede 2000). There are no obvious ways of recovering the correct value of the variable. An option could be to approximate the number of days using another available variable in WHIP—the number of paid weeks—which are not affected by such bias. Unfortunately, this would introduce another bias, as they do not accurately measure temporary leaves and the duration of short spells. Because we do not need to drill the data down to the regional level, we used the original value of the variable.

---

4. This is the so-called base wage, on which social security and pension contributions are calculated. It includes basic wage, cost-of-living allowance, residual fees, overtime plus back pay, bonuses, supplements, holiday pay, and sick pay.

For worker-based statistics, we select all blue- and white-collar workers with a job spell active during the month of May of the year of interest, working full-time, in firms employing at least twenty employees. For firm-based statistics, WHIP is a 1:90 random sample of workers. Hence, we do not have a representative sample of the workforce in small- and medium-sized firms. This is not an issue for tables in section 10.3.3 on mobility indicators: the monthly employment stock and the average wage of each firm are reported in WHIP, yielding good approximations of entry and exit rates. For the tables in sections 10.3.1 and 10.3.2, in contrast, we pooled together firms into cells—called "synthetic firms"—in order to have enough individual observations to compute firm wage and wage change distributions. The 800-cells grid is based on the following partition:

* Geography: twenty Italian regions
* Firm size: five classes (20 to 49, 50 to 99, 100 to 199, 200 to 499, 500+ workers)
* Sector of activity: forty-four classes (Nace-70 two-digit sectors)

More details on the data and a discussion on the synthetic firm approach can be found in the methodological appendix.

10.3.1   Structure of Wages between and within Firms

Table 10.6 includes two sets of statistics: worker-based (referred to as "observation = one person") and firm-based (referred to as "observation = one firm").

Worker-based statistics confirm several stylized facts well known in the literature. Average individual wage and standard deviation increase with worker age, reflecting the wider range of career paths experienced as workers grow older. The dispersion of individual wages in Italy is in line with the other countries included in this book. It is not far from that of Norway and Sweden, but it is high with respect to Denmark and Finland: in Italy, the P90-P50 ratio is 1.7, and P10-P50 is 0.7 (in Denmark and Finland, these statistics are much closer to 1).

Firm-based statistics introduce new hints. Average firm wage is lower than average individual wage, reflecting the fact that small firms pay (on average) lower wages than large ones. The ratio of between-firms wage variability relative to the country's average wage is 13 percent, similar to other countries included in this book, except the Netherlands and the United States (see figure I.5 in the introduction of this volume). Within-firm wage variability represents about two-thirds of total variability (25.87 against 33.36 in 1998), and is larger than between-firm variability (12.52 in 1998).[5]

---

5. The true difference between the two, however, may be upward biased, as statistics based on synthetic firms tend to underestimate between-firm variability and overestimate within-firm variability, as a consequence of attributing to "within cell" the variability "between firms belonging to the same cell" (see the methodological appendix).

Table 10.6   Structure of wages between and within firms

	1990	1993	1998
Average wage[a]	94.67	97.76	95.15
SD	33.42	34.77	33.36
CV			0.35
90th percentile	139.99	144.50	140.31
75th percentile	109.57	112.70	111.26
Median	86.75	89.36	87.44
25th percentile	71.63	74.01	72.23
10th percentile	61.48	63.68	61.75
No. of workers	54,794	51,777	47,173
Average of firm average wage[b]	83.61	86.44	85.53
SD	12.74	12.61	12.52
CV	0.15	0.15	0.15
90th percentile	96.97	99.71	99.77
75th percentile	90.07	92.32	90.97
Median	84.12	86.01	85.26
25th percentile	76.85	80.25	78.10
10th percentile	66.65	69.28	70.90
No. of firms (cells)	822	781	775
Average no. of workers per cell (unweighted)	60.88	60.77	57.32
Average SD of no. of workers per cell	69.24	65.71	56.85
Average of SD of wage[b]	25.36	26.21	25.87
SD	6.92	7.56	7.12
90th percentile	33.86	35.50	34.76
75th percentile	29.43	30.73	31.10
Median	25.32	25.88	25.76
25th percentile	20.38	21.53	21.53
10th percentile	16.48	17.30	16.77
No. of firms	763	732	731
Average CV of wages[b]	0.30	0.30	0.30
SD	0.0007	0.0007	0.0007
90th percentile	0.38	0.38	0.40
75th percentile	0.34	0.34	0.33
Median	0.30	0.30	0.30
25th percentile	0.34	0.34	0.25
10th percentile	0.22	0.21	0.22
No. of firms	763	732	731
Correlation (average wage, SD of wage)[b]	0.63	0.69	0.59
p-value	0.0001	0.0001	0.0001
Average wage for workers between 25 and 30[a]	85.03	86.66	83.74
SD	25.02	24.73	23.97
90th percentile	117.17	116.70	115.08
75th percentile	97.34	98.46	95.03
Median	80.14	81.81	79.32
25th percentile	68.21	70.53	68.58
10th percentile	59.77	62.33	59.76
No. of workers	10,365	10,487	9,318
Average wage for workers between 45 and 50[a]	102.57	106.76	105.80
SD	35.70	37.60	35.54
90th percentile	153.15	160.74	154.64

Table 10.6   (continued)

	1990	1993	1998
75th percentile	119.68	124.88	124.51
Median	94.53	97.86	99.00
25th percentile	77.76	80.79	81.16
10th percentile	66.25	68.40	67.38
No. of workers	7,844	8,343	7,489

Notes: CV = coefficient of variation; SD = standard deviation.
[a]Observation = a person.
[b]Observation = a firm.

The ratio of the between-firm wage variability relative to total wage variability is sizeable in all countries, and Italy is no exception (see figure I.4 in the introduction of this volume). In Italy, it is sizeable also with respect to other decompositions (see section 10.1.2). Characteristics like gender, geographical area, and industry account for a negligible part of the total variance of wages. The results presented in section 10.1.2 are not directly comparable with table 10.6, as the one displayed in the latter is not an exact decomposition.[6] However, this is an indication of the importance of firm wage policies in shaping the wage distribution, a point that seems to overrule the importance of individual observable characteristics.

Figure 10.7 adds to the point. Panel A shows P10, P50, and P90 of the within-firm wage distribution at the end of the period (based on firms—here not synthetic firms—of which we observe at least ten workers), ranked by firm-average wage. Indeed "the tide lifts all boats," as all percentiles increase with average firm wage. In addition, the spread becomes larger with increasing average wage, especially in the P90 band. Workers receiving "low" wages (P10) from a high-wage firm are paid more than many workers receiving "high" wages (P90) from a low-wage firm. This is true not only in large firms, like those included in panel A, but also among small firms, as shown in panel B, which refers to firms employing ten or more workers of two Veneto provinces for which we have population data (see appendix for details). This finding strongly suggests that firms do not follow a pay compression model in their wage policy.

Also, the widening of within-firm wage differentials as average wages increase is at odds with the hypothesis that firms are homogeneous with respect to human capital (all workers alike in terms of skills, productivity, effort). It rather points to a substantial amount of worker heterogeneity rewarded according to human capital, at least among the medium-large

---

6. Total variability do not decompose into the within and between components reported in table 10.6, although it is positively correlated with both. An exact decomposition, for instance, is that reported in equation (1) in the introduction to the volume.

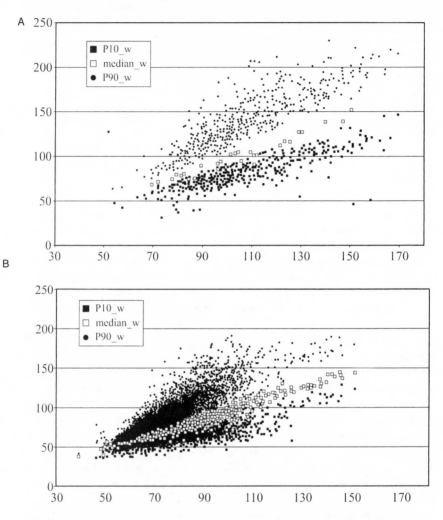

Fig. 10.7   Tide raises all boats: *A*, Mean versus P10-P50-P90; Italy, firms employing more than 1,000 workers, 1998; *B*, Mean versus P10-P50-90; Treviso and Vicenza, firms employing more than ten workers, 1998

firms. It is also consistent with the impact of a bargaining system that has been decentralized during the period under examination (see section 10.2). Today, almost all large firms in Italy bargain over wages with unions at the firm level, holding the nationwide industry contract as a benchmark. This is less frequent among small firms, which at times refer to local agreements at the district level. In addition, both the correlation between firm-average wages and within-firm SD (0.59 in 1998), and the average coefficient of variation increasing from P10 to P90 (table 10.6) confirm that job heterogeneity increases with firm size. In general, the task of ascertaining the source of the firm-specific wage policy (the firm itself or the bargaining process with unions) is hard, but the conclusion still holds: firm wage policy shows its relevance in all of these statistics.

10.3.2 Wage Dynamics

Table 10.7 displays year-to-year absolute and relative wage changes computed for individuals working both in May t and in May t - 1.[7]

Average changes in individual wages roughly follow the business cycle: 3 percent in 1990, 0.3 percent in 1993, and 2 percent in 1998. The whole distribution of individual wage changes follows the same pattern, although different parts of the distribution react differently, the upper tail showing a higher responsiveness to the business cycle. In the low tail, the large negative wage changes observed among movers and short tenure workers stay within 20 to 22 percent and 12 to 14 percent, respectively, all over the period.

Average relative changes are higher for movers than stayers and for low-tenure workers than high-tenure workers. This is consistent with an increasing and convex wage profile over seniority and can be observed in all countries included in this book.[8] Also, the standard deviation of wage changes is larger among movers, decreases among low-tenure workers, and is smaller among long-tenure workers. Different past career paths generate heterogeneity of wage changes at the beginning of one's career; once on the payroll, workers follow a much more predetermined wage path, described mostly by seniority and task.

Firm-based statistics in table 10.7 show that average change in firm wages is very close to the average change in individual wages. This means that individuals employed in small firms and in large firms enjoy the same average wage growth (recall that this does not hold for wage levels, discussed in section 10.3.2). The distribution of firm wage changes is more compressed than that of individual wage changes, as expected, and it is also somewhat more compressed in Italy than in other countries: P90 of the 1998 wage change distribution is 5 percent; P10 is -1 percent. In Denmark, the percentiles are 10 percent and -3 percent, in Finland 8 percent and -2 percent, in Germany 5 percent and 3 percent.

The between-firm variability of wage changes (0.03 in 1998) is lower than the variability of individual wage changes (0.13 in 1998). The within-firm standard deviation of wage change (0.11 in 1998) is almost as high as that of individual wage change. The two statistics are of the same order of magnitude in most countries (compare figures I.10 and I.11 in the introduction in this volume). Most of the discussion on wage levels applies here as well.

---

7. Relative changes are $\ln W_t - \ln W_{t-1}$.
8. It must be recalled that movers are also included in the short-tenure group.

Table 10.7 **Wage dynamics**

	Logs			Levels		
	1989–1990	1992–1993	1997–1998	1989–1990	1992–1993	1997–1998
Average change in wage[a]	0.03	0.003	0.02	3.58	0.21	2.20
SD	0.14	0.12	0.13	11.88	10.26	10.25
90th percentile	0.16	0.11	0.14	16.36	10.78	13.09
75th percentile	0.08	0.04	0.06	8.01	4.06	5.84
Median	0.03	−0.00	0.02	2.29	−0.01	1.47
25th percentile	−0.02	−0.04	−0.02	−1.58	−3.93	−1.93
10th percentile	−0.08	−0.10	−0.08	−7.34	−10.26	−7.65
No. of workers	50,244	48,871	43,377	50,244	48,871	43,377
Average of firm average change in wage[b]	0.03	0.005	0.02	2.86	0.47	2.07
SD	0.03	0.02	0.03	2.32	1.84	2.20
90th percentile	0.06	0.03	0.05	5.48	2.43	4.78
75th percentile	0.04	0.02	0.04	3.89	1.56	3.28
Median	0.03	0.01	0.02	2.64	0.57	2.14
25th percentile	0.02	−0.01	0.01	1.51	−0.38	0.54
10th percentile	0.00	−0.03	−0.01	0.48	−2.08	−0.62
No. of firms (cells)	791	761	734	791	761	734
Average no. of workers per cell (unweighted)	52.81	55.45	49.91	52.81	55.45	49.91
Average SD of no. of workers per cell	63.23	63.35	51.66	63.23	63.35	51.66
Average of SD of change in wage[b]	0.13	0.11	0.11	9.75	8.76	8.50
SD	0.05	0.03	0.04	2.54	2.10	2.09
90th percentile	0.19	0.15	0.16	13.17	11.40	10.99
75th percentile	0.14	0.12	0.12	10.93	10.06	9.57
Median	0.12	0.10	0.10	9.58	8.57	8.32
25th percentile	0.10	0.09	0.09	8.17	7.41	7.30
10th percentile	0.08	0.07	0.07	6.81	6.41	5.99
No. of firms (cells)	739	713	687	739	713	687
Average CV of change in wages[b]	9.03	6.33	0.004	5.50	3.13	4.64
SD	0.76	0.58	0.53	0.18	0.64	0.43
90th percentile	14.42	23.07	14.82	11.91	21.17	14.82
75th percentile	5.76	8.63	5.16	4.88	8.80	4.83
25th percentile	2.38	−6.37	1.61	2.37	−4.90	1.72
10th percentile	1.28	−17.35	−9.42	1.57	−22.82	−6.00
No. of firms (cells)	739	713	687	739	713	687
Average change in wage for peopls who change firm[a,c]	0.06	0.02	0.06	4.91	1.53	3.75
SD	0.25	0.22	0.24	18.17	16.23	16.52
90th percentile	0.35	0.27	0.33	28.40	22.39	25.43
75th percentile	0.17	0.13	0.17	14.25	10.43	13.54
Median	0.05	0.01	0.04	3.69	1.08	3.11
25th percentile	−0.06	−0.09	−0.07	−4.90	−7.60	−6.02
10th percentile	−0.20	−0.22	−0.21	−16.50	−19.23	−17.40
No. of workers	4,775	3,344	3,496	4,775	3,344	3,496

Table 10.7   (continued)

	Logs			Levels		
	1989– 1990	1992– 1993	1997– 1998	1989– 1990	1992– 1993	1997– 1998
Average change in wage for						
people with tenure <3 years[a]	0.05	0.02	0.04	4.50	1.48	3.22
SD	0.19	0.16	0.17	14.06	12.30	12.33
90th percentile	0.23	0.17	0.21	20.57	15.48	17.68
75th percentile	0.12	0.08	0.10	10.02	6.60	8.48
Median	0.04	0.01	0.03	3.22	0.90	2.39
25th percentile	−0.02	−0.04	−0.03	−1.64	−3.63	−2.01
10th percentile	−0.12	−0.14	−0.12	−9.70	−12.05	−9.98
No. of workers	13,305	11,133	10,782	13,305	11,133	10,782
Average change in wage for						
people with tenure ≥3 years[a]	0.03	0.00	0.02	3.25	−0.16	1.87
SD	0.12	0.10	0.11	10.97	9.54	9.44
90th percentile	0.14	0.09	0.11	14.87	9.37	11.50
75th percentile	0.07	0.04	0.05	7.29	3.40	5.08
Median	0.02	0.00	0.01	2.03	−0.24	1.27
25th percentile	−0.02	−0.04	−0.02	−1.56	−3.99	−1.91
10th percentile	−0.07	−0.09	−0.07	−6.66	−9.77	−7.09
No. of workers	36,939	37,738	32,595	36,939	37,738	32,595

Notes: SD = standard deviation; CV = coefficient of variation.
[a]Observation = a person.
[b]Observation = a firm.
[c]These are true firm changes as we don't need to pool together observations into synthetic firms.

Firm wage policy matters in shaping not only the wage level distribution but also the wage change distribution.

10.3.3   Mobility

Focus: Firm Data, Turnover, and Legal Transformations

- The WHIP reports the monthly employment stock and average wage of each firm. The employment stock counts all workers, including part time, apprentices, and managers, excluded from the previous tables.
- We use the monthly employment series to approximate worker flows: positive monthly changes in employment are association, and negative changes are separations. The sum of monthly associations (separations) relative to the average yearly employment is the firm association (separations) rate.
- There are two sources of measurement error. The first is that we miss across-month churning: if a worker exits during a given month and his

or her position is filled in the following month, we do not observe any monthly change in the employment stock, as the latter is measured as the number of heads present in the payroll in a given month. The second one is that it is—not surprisingly—difficult to control for legal transformations. We handle this problem by computing monthly changes from January to November only and reweighting to twelve months, as most legal transformations take place between December and January (end of the Italian fiscal year). Furthermore, we exclude entry and exit rates above 200 percent. The exclusion of spurious movements remains, however, far from perfect.

• The firm-average wage refers to white- and blue-collar workers only. Firms are selected if they employ at least twenty employees.

The sum of entry (associations) and exit (separations) rates measured on worker data yields a gross turnover of about 47 percent in 1998. This is the turnover rate relative to people working in firms with more than twenty employees.[9] When computing the same statistics with firm data, we tend to overestimate all rates. The overestimate in entry and exit rates is larger during the 1993 downturn, while they are more precisely estimated in 1998 and 1990. The imperfect control of legal transformations may explain the upward bias when large reorganizations take place (see preceding bulleted list).

Low-wage firms almost always show the highest positive net flows, which is consistent with what is observed in other countries. This is explained by the correlation between average firm size and firm wages, as in Italy most job creation occurs in the small-firm sector. Top-decile firms have higher net flows than top-quartile ones, due to the better growth performance of firms with highly skilled workforce. The positive correlation between average firm size and firm wages also explains the ranking in turnover levels, with low-wage firms showing the highest turnover.

Finally, the correlation between firm size and within-firm individual seniority is positive, and exit rates decline as wages increase. All this is consistent with the working of internal labor markets that provide opportunities for advancement without leaving the firm and with declining external wage offers that dominate current wages as the latter increase (see table 10.8).

10.4 Conclusions

In spite of the centralized nature of wage bargaining in Italy, we find some evidence suggesting the existence of firm-wage policies. First, the ratio of the between-firm wage variability relative to total wage variability is sizeable and not very dissimilar from that reported for other countries. In

---

9. The same figure is about 60 percent considering all firms; see section 10.1.3.

Table 10.8   **Mobility**

	Entry			Exit			Net		
	1990	1993	1998	1990	1993	1998	1990	1993	1998
Rate (person)	0.22	0.16	0.24	0.21	0.19	0.23	0.01	−0.03	0.01
Rate	0.26	0.25	0.25	0.20	0.25	0.20	0.05	0.01	0.04
SD	0.29	0.30	0.27	0.23	0.30	0.23	0.27	0.28	0.25
Rate, top decile of firm wages	0.28	0.24	0.21	0.16	0.23	0.15	0.12	0.01	0.06
SD	0.36	0.33	0.28	0.24	0.32	0.22			
Rate, top quartile of firm wages	0.25	0.22	0.20	0.17	0.23	0.16	0.08	−0.01	0.04
SD	0.32	0.29	0.25	0.23	0.31	0.22			
Rate, bottom quartile of firm wages	0.30	0.31	0.33	0.23	0.29	0.25	0.07	0.02	0.08
SD	0.31	0.34	0.32	0.23	0.31	0.25			
Rate, bottom decile of firm wages	0.34	0.37	0.38	0.25	0.33	0.29	0.09	0.04	0.09
SD	0.34	0.39	0.37	0.24	0.35	0.28			

	1990	1993	1998
Employees	90.62	87.85	88.25
SD	745.67	670.58	603.96
Correlation (exit rate, average wage)	−0.06	−0.03	0.00
p-value	0.00	0.00	0.56
Corr-size-tenure,[a] obs: person	n.a	n.a.	0.199
p-value			0.00
Exit-90% wage, obs: person	0.170	0.174	0.192
Exit-median-wage, obs: person	0.172	0.189	0.183
Exit 10%-wage, obs: person	0.430	0.378	0.511

Notes: SD = standard deviation; n.a. = not applicable.
[a]Elapsed tenure May 1998, truncated at 161 months.

Italy, it is sizeable also with respect to other decompositions: characteristics like gender, geographical area, and industry account for a negligible part of the total variance of wages. Second, the tide raising all boats is also quite suggestive: not only do individual wages throughout the whole distribution increase as average firm wages increase, but the spread increases too as we move from P10 to P90, indicating that the rewards of high-pay individuals are highly differentiated even within the same employer. This is coherent with the detected positive correlation between firm size and firm wages. In Italy, almost all large firms directly bargain over wages with unions, holding the nationwide industry contract as a benchmark. This is less frequent among small firms, which at times refer to local agreements at the district level.

Firm wage policy matters in shaping not only the wage level distribution but also the wage change distribution. The within-firm standard deviation of wage change is almost as high as that of individual wage change, and much higher than between-firm variability of average change in wages. Worker-based statistics, on the other side, show that relative changes in individual wages follow the business cycle, although different parts of the distribution react differently, the upper tail showing a higher responsiveness. Both facts are at odds with the often-reported rigidity of Italian wages. Indeed, the detected flexibility is mainly driven by movers and short-tenure workers, who show higher and more dispersed relative wage changes. Different past career paths generate heterogeneity of wage changes at the beginning of one's career within each firm. Once workers become insiders, they follow a predetermined wage path according to seniority and task.

The preceding results, and the simple comparisons between stayers' and movers' wages (see table 10.3), are in line with well-established facts: wage growth (on impact) is often higher among movers, while wage levels are lower compared to stayers, before and, often, also after the job switch. Along similar lines suggested by Lazear and Shaw, we find that negative wage growth is more common among movers and short-tenure workers. In addition, worker entry and exit rates are higher at low-pay firms and lower at high-pay firms. This stylized fact is, however, of more difficult interpretation, as composition effects due to the high correlation between firm size and wages may hide the conclusion. Nor do we have any direct evidence that voluntary mobility is higher where wage compression is high. The cross-country comparison suggests that the relatively high degree of wage compression in Italy could be associated with higher entry and exit rates, but, as Lazear and Shaw emphasize in the introduction to this volume, one must be cautious with this comparison, as the different data sets used in this book measure exit over different time intervals and types of jobs.

Methodological Appendix

Data Used

In order to produce the tables presented, we used the Work Histories Italian Panel (WHIP), a database developed at the LABORatorio R. Revelli based on administrative data from the Italian Social Security (INPS).

For the purpose of this chapter, we used the WHIP section on dependent employment, which is a Linked Employer-Employee Database made up of a 1:90 sample of employees over the period from 1985 up to 2001. Details on the database and a public use file can be found at http://www.laboratoriorevelli.it/whip.

Treatment of Legal Transformations, Mergers, and Acquisitions

The use of administrative data on firms poses the problem of the treatment of legal transformations. Administrative archives treat events such as ownership transfers, bequests, donations, and legal transformations as if they were firms' start-ups and closures, even if these events do not produce a real interruption in the life of a firm. These events generate spurious flows of firms, jobs, and workers.

The WHIP database detects and corrects legal transformations first through a longitudinal firm identification algorithm that builds directly on the firm data provided by INPS. This algorithm is particularly suited to correct for mergers and acquisitions involving establishment or plants.

Moreover, the linkage between employees and the firms for which they are working enables to detect other legal transformations tracking simultaneous flows of workers between two or more firms. The key is to discriminate between normal movements, deriving from workers' decisions to change jobs, and spurious movements. It is intuitively unlikely that many workers of a company independently and simultaneously decide to move together to another firm, whereas this event will take place if all, or part of, the activities of the first firm are transferred to the second firm, or if the second firm is just a legal transformation of the first. In order to identify spurious components, a threshold for the intensity of such movements has been established. Given the WHIP sampling ratio, the observation of two workers moving within one month from the same firm (call it A) to a same firm (call it B) would statistically mean that, on average, firm A has handed over about 180 workers to firm B. Thus, if we observe in the same month at least two workers moving from firm A to firm B, we treat it as a spurious movement. Once spurious movements are detected, we reconnect the job spells of every worker involved in the simultaneous job change.

The Synthetic Firm Approach

Because WHIP is a 1:90 random sample of workers, we do not have a representative sample of employees working in small- and medium-sized firms. In addition, we observe the average wage paid to blue and white collars, but not the standard deviation. Only if the firm is sufficiently large is the number of observed workers sufficient to estimate the standard deviation of wages. For 99 percent of firms recorded in WHIP, we have less than ten workers belonging to the same firm; for 83 percent of them, we have just one worker.

In order to compute firm-based statistics in section 10.3, then, we pooled together firms into cells, called "synthetic firms." The synthetic firm approach leads to an underestimation of between-firm variability and to a parallel overestimation of within-firm variability as we attribute to "within cell" the variability between firms belonging to the same cell. To limit this bias, we chose the finest grid granting a sufficient number of observations per cell. After several explorations, we ended up with an 800-cell grid along the following partitions:

- Geography: twenty Italian regions
- Firm size: five classes (20 to 49, 50 to 99, 100 to 199, 200 to 499, 500+ workers)[10]
- Sector of activity: forty-four classes (Nace-70 two-digit sectors)

Each cell has been weighted with the actual number of firms with the same characteristics in the population, as published by "*Osservatorio INPS*," the official aggregate statistics on the population produced by INPS.

The validity of the synthetic firm approach is tested using a data set that covers the whole population of workers and firms located in two provinces of Veneto, in the Italian Northeast (Treviso and Vicenza). On this data set, we mimicked the sampling procedure that generates WHIP and then pooled the resulting firm sample using three different synthetic firm definitions. We are, therefore, in a position to evaluate how within- and between-variance estimates vary at increasing levels of cell disaggregation and how far we are from statistics measured in the firm population.

Results are as follows:

1. Worker-based statistics computed in the sample are quite close to true values (and, obviously, do not change at different synthetic firm definitions).

2. As expected, between-firm variability is always underestimated in synthetic firms with respect to population values, while within-firm variability is overestimated. Comparing the three definitions we have that as cells become smaller, the bias decreases. This is particularly true for the between-firm variability, which increases from 7.32 to 10.11 (the true value being 13.89).

3. The correlation between average wage and standard deviation of wage, at the highest level of disaggregation, is almost equal to the correlation computed at the firm level.

10. Firms under twenty employees have been excluded for cross-country comparability.

Table 10A.1   **Structure of wages between and within firms, year 1990, Vicenza and Treviso**

	Synthetic firms on sample data			Firm population
	Definition (I)	Definition (II)	Definition (III)	
Average wage[a]	78.87	78.87	78.87	79.11
SD	23.64	23.64	23.64	24.11
90th percentile	109.37	109.37	109.37	108.66
10th percentile	57.34	57.34	57.34	57.43
No. of workers	2075	2075	2075	194095
Average of firm average wage[b]	76.21	76.10	76.11	73.45
SD	7.32	8.46	10.11	13.89
90th percentile	84.47	88.48	88.48	90.74
10th percentile	68.34	67.28	62.40	58.44
No. of firms (cells)	28	52	95	4502
Average no. of workers per cell (unweighted)	74	40	22	43
Average SD of no. of workers per cell	91	49	26	106
Average of SD of wage[b]	21.62	21.03	19.81	14.70
SD	6.68	8.69	10.03	8.72
90th percentile	30.61	28.74	29.49	26.80
10th percentile	16.82	15.27	9.40	4.72
No. of firms	28	50	91	4481
Correlation (average wage, SD of wage)[b]	0.38	0.61	0.66	0.68

Notes: Definition (I) = cells are by eight one-digit Nace-70 sectors and five firm size classes. Definition II) = cells are by eight one-digit Nace-70 sectors, five firm size classes and two provinces. Definition III) = cells are by forty-four two-digit Nace-70 sectors, five firm size classes and two provinces.
Observation = a person.
Observation = a firm.

References

Battistin, E., E. Rettore, and U. Trivellato. 2007. Choosing among alternative classification criteria to measure the labour force state. *Journal of the Royal Statistical Society* A (1): 5-27.

Blanchard, O. J., and P. Diamond. 1990. The cyclical behavior of gross flows of workers in the United States. *Brookings Papers on Economic Activity*, Issue no. 2: 85-155. Washington, DC: Brookings Institution.

Brandolini, A., P. Casadio, P. Cipollone, M. Magnani, A. Rosolia, and R. Torrini. 2006. Employment growth in Italy in the 1990s: Institutional arrangements and market forces. In *Social pacts, employment and growth: A reappraisal of Ezio Tarantelli's thought,* ed. N. Acocella and R. Leoni, 31-68. Berlin: Physica-Verlag.

Brandolini, A., P. Cipollone, and E. Viviano. 2006. Does the ILO definition capture all unemployment? *Journal of the European Economic Association* 4 (1): 153-79.

Contini B., M. Filippi, and C. Malpede. 2000. Safari tra la giungla dei salari. Nel mezzogiorno si lavora meno? (Safari in the wage jungle: Do people work less in the South?). *Lavoro e Relazioni Industriali* (2).

Contini, B., and U. Trivellato, eds. 2005. *Eppur si muove. Dinamiche e persistenze nel mercato del lavoro Italiano* (Still, it moves: Dynamics and persistence in the Italian labor market). Bologna: Il Mulino.

Contini, C., and C. Villosio. 2003. Worker mobility, job displacement and wage dynamics in Italy. LABORatorio R. Revelli Working Paper no. 24.

Davis, S. J., and J. Haltiwanger. 1999. Gross job flows. In *Handbook of labor economics*. Vol. 3B, ed. O. Ashenfelter, and D. Card, 2711-2805. Amsterdam: North-Holland.

Devicienti, F. 2006. Earnings mobility in Italy, 1985-1999. *Mimeograph.*

European Commission. 2003. *Employment in Europe 2003.* Luxembourg: Office for Official Publications of the European Communities.

Leombruni, R., and R. Quaranta. 2002. Worker mobility: Structural changes and cyclical behaviour. In *Labor mobility and wage dynamics in Italy,* ed. B. Contini, 91-176. Turin, Italy: Rosemberg & Sellier.

———. 2005. Eppure si muoveva già: Una breve storia della mobilità dei lavoratori in Italia (Still, it already moved: A brief history on workers mobility in Italy). In *Eppur si muove: Dinamiche e persistenze nel mercato del lavoro Italiano,* ed. B. Contini and U. Trivellato, 205-36. Bologna: Il Mulino.

Organization for Economic Cooperation and Development (OECD). 2004. *Ageing and employment policies—Italy.* Paris: OECD.

11

Wage Structure in France, 1977–96

Francis Kramarz and Sébastien Perez-Duarte

11.1 Introduction

The story of wages and mobility, both at the firm and at the worker level, is one that until recently could not have been told. In France, matched employer-employee data was collected since the middle of the 1970s, but only in the past few years has computer power, storage, and ease of use been enough to allow systematic study of the links between employee and firm characteristics. In the spirit of the other contributions to this book, we will sift the wage structure in France during the twenty years between 1976 and 1996 through the sieve of intra- and interfirm heterogeneity. Section 11.2 describes the data used, section 11.3 paints the picture of wage movements, while section 11.4 analyzes wage dispersion and variation through some sample statistics.

11.2 Description of the Data Used: The DADS

The *Déclaration Annuelles de Données Sociales* (DADS) is a longitudinal matched employer-employee data source collected by the *Institut National de la Statistique et des Etudes Economiques* (INSEE) and maintained in the *Division des Revenus/Exploitation des Fichiers Administratifs* at INSEE.

Francis Kramarz is the director of the Center for Research in Economics and Statistics (CREST) at the National Institute for Statistics and Economic Studies (INSEE). Sébastien Perez-Duarte was a researcher at INSEE/CREST when this chapter was prepared. He is currently an economist-statistician at the European Central Bank.

We gratefully acknowledge the irreplaceable help of the Cornell Restricted Access Data Center, without which we would have suffered through our journey across the data; and of John Abowd, whose contribution to the data used in this chapter, and to all the derivative work engendered by it, can never be overstated.

The data are based on a mandatory employer report of the gross earnings of each employee subject to French payroll taxes. The universe includes all statutory employed persons. Our analysis sample covers all individuals employed in French enterprises who were born in October of even-numbered years, with civil servants excluded. Our analysis sample runs from 1976 through 1996, with 1981, 1983, and 1990 excluded because the extracts from the master payroll records were not built for those years. The initial data set contained sixteen million observations. Each observation corresponds to a unique enterprise-individual-year combination. The observation includes an identifier that corresponds to the employee (called NNI in the following) and an identifier that corresponds to the enterprise (SIREN). For each observation, we have information on the number of days during the calendar year the individual worked in the establishment, as well as the full-time/part-time/intermittent/at-home work status of the employee. Each observation also includes, in addition to the variables listed in the preceding, the sex, month, year, and place of birth; occupation; total net nominal earnings during the year and annualized gross nominal earnings during the year for the individual; as well as the location and industry of the employing establishment. Nominal values were deflated by the consumer price index, and are written as thousands of 1980 French francs (FF).

11.2.1 Observation Selection, Variable Creation, and Imputation

An observation is identified by a combination of two identifiers, the firm ID and the person ID. The SIREN number has an internal structure that allows a check for coding errors. But the NNI number has no such internal control. Although 90 percent of current DADS information is filed by the responding firm using an electronic medium (tape or diskette), the situation in the 1980s was quite different. In that era, INSEE had to perform data entry by keypunch from paper forms. Entry errors in the NNI occurred (exchange of two digits of the NNI, error in one of the digits, etc.). This phenomenon is well known at INSEE but, despite many attempts, no general way of solving this problem was found. As a consequence, some observations have a NNI-year-SIREN combination such that no other observation has the same NNI. As a joint product, some NNI-SIREN combinations have a unique missing year. Consider now the case of a worker with observations in, say, 1978 and 1980 in the same enterprise (SIREN) but no observation for 1979. If true, this history would mean that the worker was employed until some date in 1978 (depending on the number of days worked, December 31 most likely) and also employed after some date in 1980 (depending on the number of days worked, January 1 most likely) in this firm but not employed at all during year 1979. This is very improbable, in particular because there is a layoff procedure in France in which workers may be recalled by their firms after some period of unemployment. Suggestions of D. Verger (head of the Division Revenus, in charge of the DADS at the beginning of the 1990s) led us to adopt the following solution.

Whenever an observation was missing in a given year while the same NNI-SIREN combination exists for the preceding and the following year, we created an observation for the missing year with the same NNI-SIREN combination. (This added 193,148 observations.) Earnings are computed as the geometric mean of the preceding and following wages (in real terms). All other variables are taken at their preceding year value.

Because of the 1982 and 1990 Census, the 1981, 1983, and 1990 DADS data were not available. We used the same principle as the one described in the preceding to impute missing observations. Hence, imputation was performed only for those individuals that were present in the same firm in 1980 and 1982 or 1982 and 1984 or 1989 and 1991. (This added 759,017 observations to the sample.) All variables were imputed as in the preceding.

11.2.2 Multiple Jobs

Until now, nothing in our procedure rules out multiple job holding. Multiple jobs are difficult to handle in our data because we only have information on the number of days worked in each NNI-year-SIREN combination. Hence, we do not know the starting and the ending date of the spell in that year (for all spells that last less than 360 days, the maximum). To be able to build spells of employment for each worker, we only kept those individuals who never had strictly more than three employers in any year. We computed the number of employers any worker had in a year. We kept in our analysis file those workers who had at most three different employers in each year. At this stage, our sample only contains workers who hold at most three simultaneous jobs in a given year. Then we computed the sum of all days worked in each year. If this number was strictly larger than 720 days for some year, that is, the worker necessarily had three simultaneous jobs at some point of this year, we deleted the individual from our sample.

We define a job spell as an uninterrupted period of employment for a given NNI in a given SIREN over, possibly, many years.

11.2.3 Beginning and End of Job Spells

Because workers can have at most three types of job spells in a year, the possible sequence of job spells are limited. This allows us to compute exactly the beginning and the ending dates of a job spell. First, we identified for each individual the starting and the end years of a job spell. Then we ordered these sequences. The different cases are the following:

When a job spell starts in year t but ends after December 31 of the same year, we compute the starting date within year t as $(360 - DP_t)/360$, where DP_t denotes the number of days worked in year t.

The end date within year t of a spell is computed symmetrically if the spell started before year t as $(DP_t - 360)/360$.

When a spell starts and ends the same year, and if there is no simultaneous job this year, the spell starts at the beginning of the year (January 1).

When a worker has multiple spells that all start and end the same year, we assume that the sequence of job spells is organized as follows. As long as the sum of days worked in this year is less than or equal to 360, the job spells are put in sequence one after the other, the first one starting January 1. Any spell with a number of days worked, $DP_{1,t}$ such that $DP_{1,t} + DP_{k,t} > 360$ where $k = 2,3$ (the other two potential spells), is also placed January 1. This finishes when the three spells (maximum possible) have been coded.

If a job spell ends in year t but started at some previous date, any other job spell that took place the same year t will start at the end of this spell if the total number of days worked for these two spells is smaller or equal to 360 but starts January 1 otherwise. The third spell, if it exists, is placed after the first of the two spells for which the sum is smaller or equal to 360.

The symmetric principles apply whenever a spell starts in year t and ends after December 31 for all spells that took place in year t.

At the end of this procedure, whenever a worker held three jobs simultaneously (think of a worker with three spells in a given year that all last 200 days), all of his or her observations were deleted. Altogether, both procedures for finding workers holding three simultaneous jobs or more eliminated from the sample 2,223,859 observations that correspond to 115,637 workers.

11.2.4   Job Duration

Individuals fell into two categories with respect to the calculation of job duration: those for whom the first year of observation was in 1976 with 360 worked days in that year and those that appear in the sample after this date or had less than 360 days of work in 1976. For the first category, we estimated the expected length of the in-progress employment spell by regression analysis using a supplementary survey, the 1978 *Enquête sur la Structure des Salaires* (ESS; Salary Structure Survey). In this survey, respondent establishments provided information on seniority, occupation, date of birth, industry, and work location for a scientific sample of their employees. Using this information, Abowd, Kramarz, and Margolis (1999 estimated separate regressions for men and women that we use to predict seniority for the in-progress spells in 1976 with 360 days worked (all coefficients are reported in Abowd, Kramarz, and Margolis; see, in particular, the data appendix).

Finally, as in Abowd, Kramarz, and Margolis (1999), we eliminated observations for which the logarithm of the real annualized total compensation cost was more than five standard deviations away from its predicted value based on a linear regression model of this variable on sex, region, experience, and education (see once more the data appendix in Abowd, Kramarz, and Margolis).

Having done all these selections and imputations, the final data set that we use contains 13,770,082 observations, corresponding to 1,682,080 individuals and 515,557 firms. For international comparison purposes, only observations for full-time jobs were selected. This limits a potential bias because the number of part-time jobs doubled between 1979 and 1996. The share of women in the labor force also increased, by more than 5 percentage points, so we could potentially find different results if we produced separate tables by gender.

The years initially selected were 1977, 1979, 1987, 1989, 1993, and 1996, since the sample period goes from 1976 to 1996. As described in the preceding, the years 1981, 1983 and 1990 are not available, and, unfortunately, there was a complete overhaul of the computerized programs of the DADS in 1993. This last change made 1993 and 1994 too special to be useable. Hence, we selected 1977, 1979, 1989, 1996, and only used 1987 when it was useful to compute ten-year-long differences.

11.2.5   The Effect of the Sampling Scheme on Our Statistics

Our data only includes workers born on October of even-numbered years. Combined with missing information on the year and month of birth for some observations, the data is constructed so that it represents exactly 1/25 of the total number of observations, and hence 1/25 of the number of workers.

This sample selection procedure leads to unbiased worker-dependent statistics and is perfectly appropriate for workercentric models (job changes, wages, work experience, seniority, etc.).

However, some *within-firm*, second-order statistics will be inconsistent, as firm size is fixed in the data. To see this, consider an economy where there are J firms of the same size N, the sampling is uniform, and the size of the firm is large enough that every firm has n sampled workers (the sampling ratio is thus n/N). All (log-) wages are drawn from the same $N(\mu,\sigma^2)$ distribution. This entails that within-firm mean wage follows a $N(\mu, \sigma^2/n)$ distribution. Average within-firm wage is thus $N(\mu, \sigma^2/nJ)$, so this statistic is consistent. The standard deviation of the within-firm mean wage is not consistent, however.

The within-firm mean wage is $X_j = (1/n)\Sigma_i X_{ij}$, and the variance of this within-firm mean wage is:

$$Y = \frac{1}{J}\sum_j X_j^2 - \left(\frac{1}{J}\sum_j X_j\right)^2.$$

Thus,

$$EY = E(X_j^2) - E\left[\left(\frac{1}{J}\sum_j X_j\right)^2\right] = \mu^2 + \frac{\sigma^2}{n} - \left(\mu^2 + \frac{\sigma^2}{nJ}\right) = \frac{J-1}{J}\frac{\sigma^2}{n}.$$

Hence, as the number of firms goes to infinity, the standard deviation of within-firm mean wage will converge to $\sigma/\sqrt{n}$ (recall, n is the firm size). In our case, the sampling ratio is 1/25, thus in this simplistic economy, the standard deviation of the within-firm average wage will be off by a factor of five (compare with figure I.3 in Lazear and Shaw's introduction in this volume, where France is 0.54 versus the average of the other countries at

0.15). Now consider the case where firms have different sizes (n_j), and wages are drawn from the same distribution as before. Then the standard deviation of the within-firm mean wage will be a pure reflection of the distribution of firm sizes. Finally, if firms have varying mean wages and different within-firm dispersions, the statistic will reflect a complex mixture of size, average pay structure, and firm dispersion. This happens in every case, with or without sampling.

By contrast, figure I.5 in Lazear and Shaw's introduction in this volume shows that the average of the standard deviation by firm is not very different in France, as the standard deviation is only affected in its variance by the sampling scheme. In this case, the within-firm variance is:

$$S_j = \frac{1}{n-1}\sum_i X_{ij}^2 - \frac{n}{n-1}\left(\frac{1}{n}\sum_i X_{ij}\right)^2,$$

thus $ES_j = \sigma^2$, and by the law of large numbers the mean of the standard deviation will converge to its true value of σ^2. Note, however, that the variance can only be computed when there are at least two observations for the given year; hence, our statistic will tend to overrepresent larger firms.

11.3   Wage Institutions in France: A Bird's-Eye View

11.3.1   The Minimum Wage

Since 1951, French industry has been subject to a national minimum wage (called the SMIC since the revisions to the relevant law in 1971) that is indexed to the rate of change in consumer prices and to the average blue-collar wage rate.[1]

Figures 11.1 and 11.2 depict the changes in the (real) minima over the sample period (with the minimum wage in the United States as a useful comparison). The French SMIC started its very sharp increase in the beginning of the 1970s. In the rest of the sample period, the French SMIC continued its increase, partly mandated by one-shot increases and partly by formulaic increases. Note, however, that minimum wage rates delivered to the worker do not present the firm's minimum labor costs. Indeed, the structure of payroll taxes that augment wages as a part of labor cost has changed in France. After a constant increase in payroll tax rates from the early 1970s, they dropped sharply in 1994 and even more so in the ensuing years (see Kramarz and Philippon 2001) as a part of an explicit program to lower total labor costs for workers at the minimum wage.

11.3.2   Wage Bargaining: The French Way

During the sample period, the French labor market institutions were also characterized by important changes in the bargaining institutions and

---

1. This section and the following borrow heavily from work by Abowd et al. (2005).

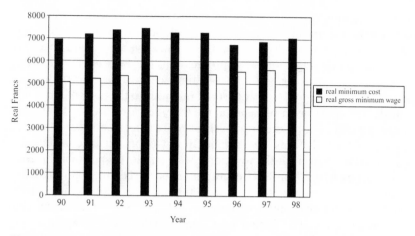

Fig. 11.1   Changes in the real minimum cost
Source: Kramarz and Philippon (2001).

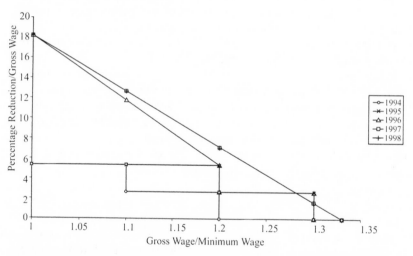

Fig. 11.2   Changes in the real minimum cost and the real minimum wage. Reduction of employer-paid payroll taxes
Source: Kramarz and Philippon (2001).

environment. In the 1970s, centralized collective bargaining agreements (*conventions collectives de branches*) were the basic elements of the negotiation process in France. The different industrial sectors had collective agreements that were negotiated by groups of unions and employer associations. These agreements were binding on the negotiating parties. The complete agreement was then typically extended to cover the entire industry (or region) by the Ministry of Labor and was then made binding on workers and firms that were not party to the original negotiation (see Margolis 1994). More than 95 percent of the workforce was covered by these collective bargaining agreements at the end of the 1980s, while union membership was approximately 10 percent. The collective agreements specified a set of minimum wages and wage progressions for the occupational categories covered by the negotiations (sometimes called a wage grid). But, beginning in 1982, the *lois Auroux* (a set of revisions to the body of labor law named after the Minister of Labor at the time) required firms with at least fifty employees to negotiate firm-level collective agreements (*accords d'entreprise*). Although firms were explicitly not obligated to conclude an agreement, 65 percent of the workforce were employed at establishments or businesses where firm-level negotiations occurred either through the union delegates or some other worker representative. Among this 65 percent of the workforce, only three-quarters of the workers ended up with an agreement as a result of these negotiations. Finally, the percentage of the workforce covered by some establishment or firm-level agreement on wages is approximately 40 percent in 1992. The law required that the firm-level agreements could only improve the conditions stated in the industrial agreement so that, over time, the firm-level agreements have become more important for wage determination than the industry agreements. Although more than 90 percent of French workers are covered by industrial agreements throughout our analysis period (1976 to 1996), firm-level negotiations outpaced renegotiations of industrywide agreements in most industries. The regular increases in the national minimum wage (in particular those driven by the indexation to the average blue-collar wage rate) resulted in the lowest categories on the collective pay scales in most industry contracts for most occupations being below the national minimum by the beginning of the 1990s. When this occurs, it is the national minimum wage, and not the collectively bargained wage, that binds.

11.3.3 Product Markets

Our sample period for France is not one of intense product market competition. Even though France, pushed by European institutions, started in the 1990s to deregulate some industries, the process is far from complete. During our sample period, near-monopolies operated in many industries. Air France (airlines), Seita (cigarettes), Électricité de France (energy), and Gaz de France (energy) are all examples of firms in which the State has a majority equity stake and there are no local competitors (even though France imports cigarettes and allows foreign airlines to land in France). Entry into these industries was, and still is, heavily regulated. Surprisingly, it is also the case in many other apparently competitive industries, such as the retail trade, that entry regulations loomed and are still very important (see Bertrand and Kramarz [2002] for the detrimental effect of the *loi Royer* on employment in the retail trade). Djankov et al. (2000) have also shown that entry regulations, as measured by requirements to starting a new business in France, are common, time-consuming, and costly. This startup process takes sixty-six days and sixteen different legal and administrative steps in France and only seven days and four steps in the United States.

11.3.4 Macroeconomic Conditions

During our sample period, the economy has lived through several cycles, though the labor market has not. The first years in our sample follow the end of *Trente Glorieuses*, the thirty years of golden prosperity after World War II. Unemployment increased steadily from around 3 percent in the beginning of the 1970s to 10 percent in 1985. The years between 1987 and 1989 are two years where the economy returned to growth years (incidentally, 1989 and 1990 are exceptionally good wine years), and the only ones in which unemployment declined significantly. Growth then drastically slowed and unemployment soon increased, reaching 12 percent in 1996, the last year of our sample.

11.4 The Heterogeneity of Wages

We will start first by describing some sample wage statistics before delving into the depths of the distributions.

11.4.1 Levels

The central feature of the wages is that in real terms wages increase by around 0.8 percent per year. The increase is higher for the firm average wage than for the worker average wage. Only when the unemployment rate decreased by a bit more than 1 percent between 1987 and 1989 did real wages fall. (See figure 11.3.)

Wage increases were not shared equally between different categories of workers. Only from 1989 to 1996 did wages for young workers (twenty-five to thirty) increase, whereas for workers aged between forty-five and fifty, the increase was high at around 1 percent per year (except for the 1987 to 1989 period). Youth unemployment was an increasing problem during the whole period and may have held entry wages down during that period. (See figure 11.4)

This increase in the real wage is also not constant across the wages. The wages on the middle half of the distribution of wages increased by 0.7 percent by year, on average, though the average wage increased by 0.8 percent. The difference is explained by the higher increase in the lower wages, 1.0 percent per year. In figure 11.5 we plot the increase in the log wage between 1977 and several years, at each percentile of the distribution. Three results are striking between 1977 and 1996: for wages between percentiles 20 percent and 95 percent: the increase in wages is constant, wage increases were very high for the bottom part of the distribution, while top wages only received a below average increase. Wages were compressed from below, while

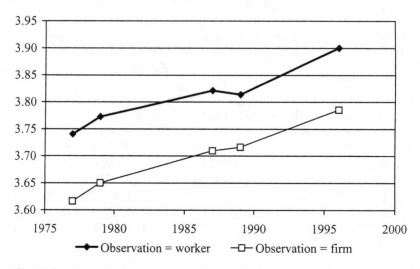

Fig. 11.3   Average log wage across workers or firms

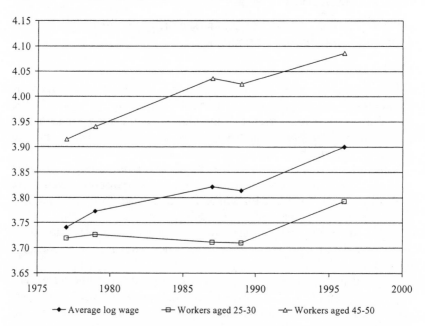

Fig. 11.4   Average log wage and age

most of the rest of the distribution is unaffected: the minimum wage was increased in 1991 and 1992, while payroll taxes were reduced starting in 1994. The firms had clear incentives to compress the wages around the minimum wage so as to benefit from the threshold-based exemptions. Because of this reduction in labor cost, turnover was also lower for low-wage workers.

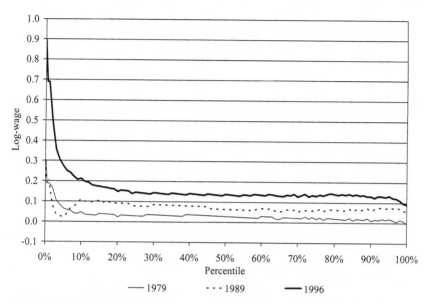

Fig. 11.5   Percentile-based increase in wages. Shift in the distribution of log wages, since 1977 up to year 1996

11.4.2   Variance

Another striking feature in the data is the stability of the wage distribution within firms for most of our sample period. Proof of this is found in the distribution of the coefficient of variation (CV) of wages (figure 11.6). Between 1979 and 1989, the CV of log wages was constant at around 9.5 percent, after a small decline at the beginning of the period. The real change occurs between 1989 and 1996, where the CV decreased to 8.1 percent. The CV of wages (as opposed to log wages) also experiences this stability followed by a strong decrease.

At the end of our sample period, between 1993 and 1996, the large decrease in payroll taxes, concentrated on the lower end of the distribution of wages (up to 1.33 of the minimum wage), had a very sizeable impact on the labor market. Kramarz and Philippon (2001) estimate that the decrease in payroll taxes had a positive impact on the rate of firing of low-wage workers. This cannot be confirmed, however, through the turnover statistics: the exit rate is constant between 1987 and 1996. The concentration of wages, however, was altered, as we saw in the preceding.

11.4.3   Earnings Mobility

Buchinsky et al. (2003), while studying earnings mobility with a variety of different statistics, find that between 1971 and 1977 mobility strongly declined in France, and while the mobility stayed very low, no clear pattern could be seen afterward. In our data, the distribution of wage changes is re-

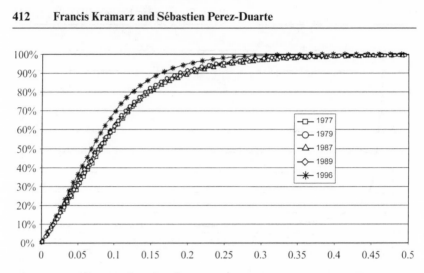

Fig. 11.6   Within-firm wage variance. Cumulative distribution of coefficient of variation, log wage within firm

markably stable throughout our entire sample period, as can be surmised from figure 11.7.

Furthermore, the distribution of wage changes for movers and stayers (figure 11.8) is also very stable during all our sample period: wage change for movers is much more dispersed, both in the upper part of the distribution and in the bottom part.

11.4.4   Turnover

The relationship between job change and wage is studied by Abowd, Kramarz, and Roux (2006) in a model of joint mobility and wages by firm; 30 percent of the variance is explained by the axis high-turnover–low wage–high returns to seniority versus low-turnover–high wage–low returns to seniority.

Correlation between the average wage in the firm and exit and entry rates is consistently negative throughout the years (see table 11.1).

Turnover is mainly procyclical in France (Dares 2003). However, the interaction of different effects renders interpretation difficult. Abowd, Corbel, and Kramarz (1999, 182), with a different data set, conclude that:

> Adjusted establishment growth rates are procyclical (negatively related to changes in the unemployment ratio) with an elasticity of –0.14 (0.02 robust standard error). The employment entry rate is weakly countercyclical with an elasticity of 0.09 (0.04). The employment exit rate is strongly countercyclical with an elasticity of 0.23 (0.06) and the involuntary exit rate displays essentially identical countercyclicality. The employment quit rate is weakly countercyclical with an elasticity of 0.02 (0.004). Finally, the retirement rate is procyclical with an elasticity of –0.22 (0.06).

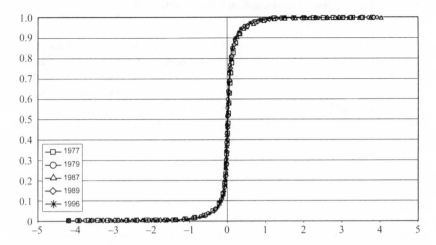

Fig. 11.7   Log wage change. Cumulative distribution of wage change
(observation = worker)

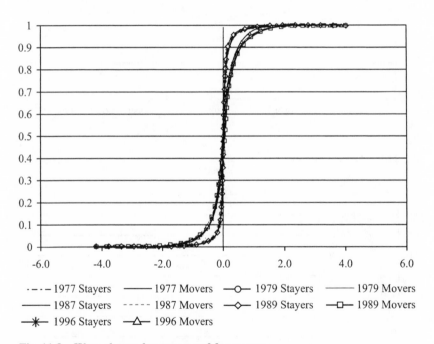

· - · - 1977 Stayers   —— 1977 Movers   —○— 1979 Stayers   —— 1979 Movers
—— 1987 Stayers   - - - - 1987 Movers   —◇— 1989 Stayers   —□— 1989 Movers
—*— 1996 Stayers   —△— 1996 Movers

Fig. 11.8   Wage change for movers and for stayers

Table 11.1   Correlation at the firm level between average wage and exit and
                    entry rates

	1977	1979	1987	1989	1993	1996
Exit rate	–0.12	–0.14	–0.11	–0.13	–0.10	–0.05
Entry rate	–0.15	–0.17	–0.16	–0.16	–0.11	–0.12

In our data, turnover is remarkably higher in 1977 than for all other years in our sample period. For example, for our sample of large firms, the entry rate (the proportion of new workers in each firm) was above 30 percent in 1977 but was at or below 26 percent for all the other years in our sample.

The entry and exit rates in 1977 are high throughout the entire distribution, as can be seen in figures 11.9 to 11.12. This year excepted, the

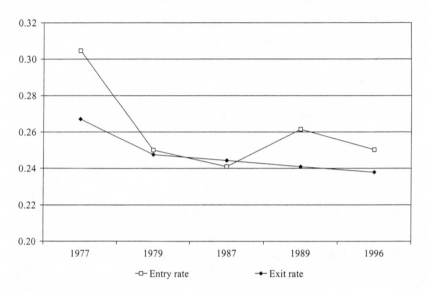

Fig. 11.9   **Average turnover**

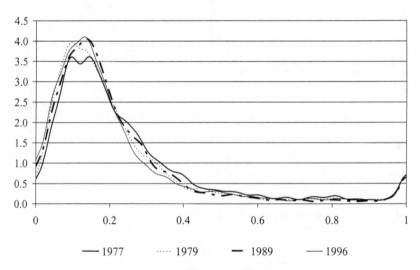

Fig. 11.10   **Distribution of average firm exit rates**

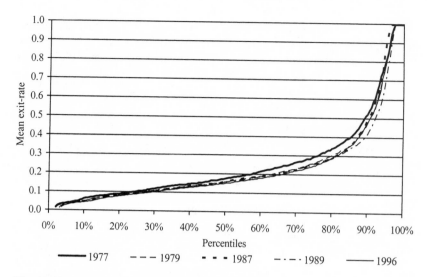

Fig. 11.11 Distribution of average firm exit rates

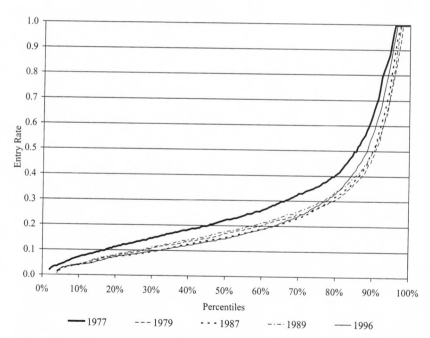

Fig. 11.12 Distribution of average firm entry rates

distribution of exit and entry rates is very similar from one year to the other. We can observe that a positive number of firms exhibit exit rates of one (the firm is destroyed). On average, 3 percent of the firms close every year.

Appendix

Table 11A.1   Macroeconomic conditions

Year	Unemployment rate	GDP (%)	GDP 5 years (%)	Percentage of part-time workers	Percentage of women in labor force
1970	2.5	5.5			35.7
1971	2.7	4.8		5.8	36.1
1972	2.8	4.4		5.8	36.5
1973	2.7	5.4		5.9	36.8
1974	2.8	3.1	4.6	5.9	37.0
1975	4.1	−0.3	3.5	8.1	37.4
1976	4.5	4.2	3.4	8.1	38.0
1977	5.0	3.2	3.1	8.7	38.6
1978	5.3	3.4	2.7	7.9	39.0
1979	5.9	3.3	2.8	8.2	39.5
1980	6.3	1.6	3.1	8.3	39.9
1981	7.4	1.2	2.5	8.4	40.3
1982	8.1	2.6	2.4	9.2	40.8
1983	8.4	1.5	2.1	9.7	41.3
1984	9.8	1.6	1.7	10.3	41.8
1985	10.2	1.5	1.7	11.0	42.2
1986	10.4	2.4	1.9	11.8	42.5
1987	10.5	2.5	1.9	11.8	43.0
1988	10.0	4.6	2.5	12.1	43.1
1989	9.4	4.2	3.0	12.1	43.3
1990	8.9	2.6	3.3	12.0	43.4
1991	9.3	1.0	3.0	12.0	43.7
1992	10.2	1.5	2.8	12.7	44.2
1993	11.5	−0.9	1.7	13.9	44.5
1994	12.1	2.1	1.2	14.8	44.9
1995	11.4	1.7	1.1	15.6	45.0
1996	12.0	1.1	1.1	16.0	45.2
1997	12.1	1.9	1.2	16.8	45.4
1998	11.5	3.4	2.0	17.2	45.6
1999	10.8	3.2	2.3	17.3	45.7
2000	9.5	3.8	2.7	16.9	45.8
2001	8.7	2.1	2.9	16.4	45.9
2002	9.0	1.2	2.7	16.2	46.1

Source: Unemployment rate is taken from the International Labor Organization.

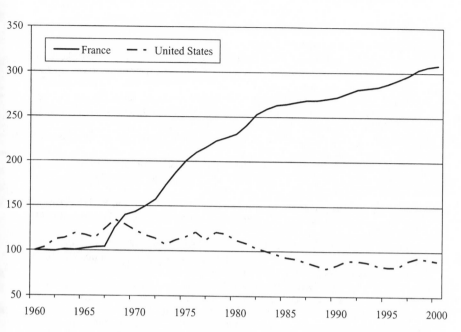

Fig. 11A.1   Real minimum wage in France and in the United States (=100 in 1960)

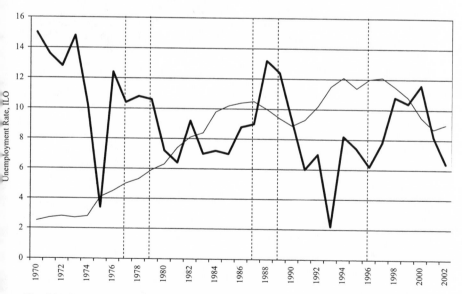

Fig. 11A.2   Macroeconomic conditions in France

Note: Dashed lines represent our sample years.

References

Abowd, J. M., P. Corbel, and F. Kramarz. 1999. The entry and exit of workers and the growth of employment: An analysis of French establishments. *Review of Economics and Statistics* 81 (2): 170–87.

Abowd, J. M., F. Kramarz, P. Lengermann, and S. Roux. 2005. Persistent inter-industry wage differences: Rent sharing and opportunity costs. Center for Research in Economics and Statistics (CREST), Working Paper.

Abowd, J. M., F. Kramarz, and D. N. Margolis. 1999. High wage workers and high wage firms. *Econometrica* 67:251–334.

Abowd, J. M., F. Kramarz, and S. Roux. 2006. Wages, mobility, and firm performance: Advantages and insights from using matched worker-firm data. *Economic Journal* 116:245–85.

Bertrand, M., and F. Kramarz. 2002. Does entry regulation hinder job creation? Evidence from the French retail industry. *Quarterly Journal of Economics* 117 (4): 1369–1414.

Buchinsky, M., G. Fields, D. Fougère, and F. Kramarz. 2003. Francs or ranks? Earnings mobility in France, 1967–1999. CEPR Discussion Paper no. 3937. London: Centre for Economic Policy Research.

Dares. 2003. *Depuis 10 ans, le turnover est en phase avec l'activité économique* (For the last 10 years, turnover has been synchronized with economic activity). Premières Synthèses no. 38.1. Paris: French Ministry of Labor.

Djankov, S., R. La Porta, F. Lopez-de-Silanes, and A. Schleifer. 2000. The regulation of entry. NBER Working Paper no. 7892. Cambridge, MA: National Bureau of Economic Research.

Kramarz, F., and T. Philippon. 2001. The impact of differential payroll tax subsidies on minimum wage employment. *Journal of Public Economics* 82:115–46.

Margolis, D. N. 1994. Government extension of collective bargaining agreements. Center for Research in Economics and Statistics (CREST), Unpublished Manuscript.

12

Wage Structure and Labor Mobility in Sweden, 1970–90

Paul Oyer

12.1 Introduction

Sweden is often thought of as the quintessential social welfare economy. Due to public policies and labor market institutions, Sweden has historically had highly compressed wages and even more compressed after-tax income. Despite the common assumption that there is an equality/efficiency trade-off, Sweden has also had one of the highest average incomes in the world and, until recently, very low unemployment. The period 1970 to 1990 was an interesting time for the Swedish labor market, as it generally prospered but faced several challenges. This chapter uses a large matched employee-employer data set to look at trends in the Swedish labor market during this period.

Several important factors affected the Swedish labor market system during the 1970s and 1980s. One important change was the breakdown in the traditionally centralized wage-bargaining system. From the 1950s through the early 1980s, Swedish unions and employers negotiated wages at a highly centralized level. Individual firms and unions had little leeway to arrange specific wage agreements. However, in 1983, driven by a few firms' inability to find enough skilled labor at the negotiated rate, individual firms and unions began to break away from the collective agreement. Other important changes included a weakening of the Swedish economy in the early

Paul Oyer is an associate professor of economics in the Graduate School of Business, Stanford University, and a research associate of the National Bureau of Economic Research.

The paper is part of the project "Pay and Promotion in Swedish Private Industries, 1970–1990," which is under the leadership of Eva M. Meyersson Milgrom and is financially supported by the Swedish Council for Research in the Humanities and Social Sciences. I thank the Swedish Employers' Federation for access to their data and Eva M. Meyersson Milgrom for help accessing and understanding the data.

1980s, a sharp increase in the use of temporary workers starting in the late 1980s, and an increase in merger and acquisition activity in the late 1980s. As I show in the following, these factors (and possibly others) led to several important trends in the Swedish labor market. There was a distinct decrease in wage inequality from 1974 through 1982, but this decrease was almost exactly reversed by 1990. These changes in wage compression occurred both within firms and across firms. As wages became more compressed from 1974 through 1982, employee turnover became less common. But turnover rates rose sharply after that and, by 1990, were significantly above the 1974 level. The decrease in turnover followed by an increase holds in virtually every group I analyze—blue-collar, white-collar, high-pay, low-pay, and so on. There is little evidence that some firms were more affected by any of these trends than other firms.

Skans, Edin, and Holmlund (chapter 7 in this volume) perform an analysis of the Swedish labor market that is similar in spirit to this chapter. However, there are several important differences. I focus on the 1970s and 1980s, while their study covers 1985 to 2000. This enables them to look at the 1990s which was another turbulent decade for the Swedish labor market, as unemployment increased dramatically. Skans, Edin, and Holmlund (chapter 7 in this volume) use administrative data that is more comprehensive than the union/employers' federation data set I use. However, I have more detailed information on the jobs and occupations of individual workers. So, while both chapters use employee-employer data sets to look at the Swedish labor market, differences in time frame and data details make it possible to gain different and complementary insights from the two studies.

The rest of this chapter provides a few more details on the Swedish labor market and then conducts formal descriptive analyses to document these changes throughout the 1970s and 1980s. The next section provides some institutional background. Section 12.3 describes the matched employee-employer data set that I use. Section 12.4 contains the analysis of wage levels and wage changes. Trends in worker mobility are described in section 12.5. Section 12.6 concludes and discusses how my findings might help motivate future research.

12.2 Institutional Background

During the period I study, Sweden experienced an unusually successful mix of very high standards of living, minimal income inequality, and low unemployment. Also during this period, the central bargaining system underwent important changes with wide-ranging ramifications.[1]

---

1. This section draws heavily from Edin and Topel (1997). See that paper, Ekberg (2004), and Nilsson (1993) for further background.

As of 1950, wage negotiations in Sweden were similar to those in the United States. Many union groups were associated with the Swedish Trade Union Confederation, which represented blue-collar workers, and many employers were affiliated with the Swedish Employers Federation (SAF— the group that provided the data for this study.) However, most bargaining was done on a one employer/one union basis. Apparently at the urging of the SAF, which wanted to avoid pattern bargaining driving wages up as one group after another negotiated, negotiations in the 1950s became broader.

Though at first somewhat reluctant, the union groups agreed to more centralized bargaining by the mid-1950s as they began to more actively seek equality and solidarity among their members. The unions were inspired by the work of economists Gosta Rehn and Rudolf Meidner, who argued that idiosyncrasies in wage negotiations led to pay differences between similar workers and, therefore, impeded the reallocation of jobs. According to Edin and Topel (1997, 158–59), Rehn and Meidner's view promotes the belief that "there is no trade-off between equity and efficiency; instead, they are complements in producing greater social welfare."

This form of bargaining is particularly important in Sweden, relative to other countries such as the United States, because union membership rates are very high throughout the economy. In 1960, about three-quarters of Swedish workers belonged to unions, but that figure reached 90 percent in 1990. During the same time, labor force participation rose. While male participation dropped slightly from 1965 to 1990 (though it was always approximately 90 percent), female participation increased from just over half in the mid-1960s to over 80 percent by 1990. As a result of these two trends and some population growth, union membership in Sweden nearly doubled from 1960 to 1990. The trend toward bargaining at a higher level of aggregation, therefore, led to negotiations over much bigger groups of people.

Collective bargaining in Sweden entered a new era in 1983, however, when one large union (metalworkers) and the engineering firms' employers' federation bargained outside the broader collective negotiations. The firms argued that the prior system underpaid skilled workers, making it difficult to recruit them. According to Edin and Topel (1997, 160), "a tendency toward more bargaining at industry and company levels seems clear."

12.3 Years and Data

I study the Swedish labor market between 1970 and 1990. Most of the analysis looks at three points in time—1974, 1982, and 1990. Table 12.1 provides basic information about the macroeconomic situation in Sweden in the period surrounding each of those years, while figures 12.1 to 12.3 plot similar data for the entire 1970 to 1990 period. Figure 12.1 shows unemployment. As the graph makes clear, unemployment was quite low in Sweden during this period, peaking at approximately 4 percent. During

Table 12.1   Macroeconomic conditions

	1970	1973	1974	1981	1982	1989	1990
Unemployment	1.5	2.5	2.0	2.8	3.5	1.6	1.8
GDP per person (1995 US$)	19,269	20,446	21,038	22,570	22,820	27,166	27,252
Change in GDP (%)							
1 year (total)	6.47	3.97	3.20	−0.17	1.17	2.69	1.10
2 year (total)	11.81	6.35	7.29	1.50	1.00	5.34	3.81
5 year (total)	22.28	20.03	17.96	5.53	8.50	14.29	13.08
1 year (per capita)	5.48	3.78	2.89	−0.29	1.11	2.00	0.32
2 year (per capita)	10.01	5.84	6.78	1.18	0.82	4.18	2.32
5 year (per capita)	17.58	16.74	15.17	4.29	7.55	12.19	10.32

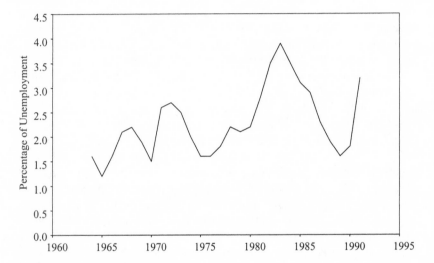

Fig. 12.1   Swedish unemployment

the late 1980s, unemployment dipped under 2 percent, suggesting this was a favorable period for employees. Figure 12.2 plots annual gross domestic product (GDP) growth and figure 12.3 shows per capita GDP in constant dollar terms. These plots show that, though the annual growth rate varied considerably from year to year, there were no long boom or bust periods during the 1970s or 1980s in Sweden, and income grew fairly consistently. The low unemployment, steady growth, and increasing labor force participation in Sweden is quite remarkable, especially given that tax rates (especially payroll taxes) increased significantly during the 1970s and 1980s (Edin and Topel 1997.)

The employment data were provided by the Swedish Employers' Federation (SAF). The SAF assembles detailed and uniform data from

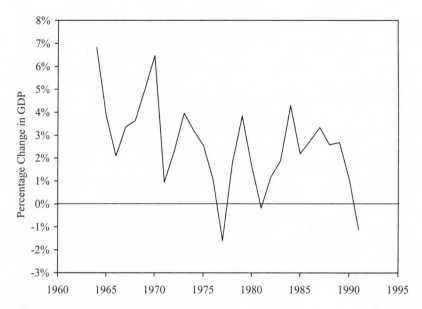

Fig. 12.2 Swedish GDP growth

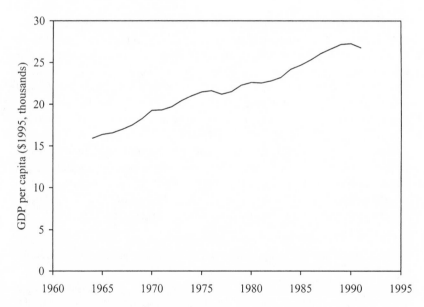

Fig. 12.3 Swedish per capita GDP

establishment-level personnel records.[2] The firms span virtually every private-sector industry (with the exception of financial services). The data are used for wage negotiations and are monitored by employers and labor unions, which ensures a high level of accuracy. Ekberg (2004) discusses some potential measurement issues with the data that are driven by timing of negotiations and other issues. I chose 1974, 1982, and 1990 for the analysis partially because these problems are minimized in these years. For example, negotiations stalled in 1980, so data from that year did not reflect all raises agreed to during the year. If I used 1980 or 1981 as one of the key years, wages or wage changes would not properly reflect labor market conditions.

Some complication is created by the fact that white-collar and blue-collar workers are in separate data sets, and there is no way to match firms across the two groups. As a result, if a firm has a group of white-collar workers and a group of blue-collar workers, I cannot join them together to analyze characteristics of the firm as a whole. It is clearly not perfectly accurate to treat groups of white-collar workers at a single firm or groups of blue-collar workers at a single firm as whole firms. However, due to the fact that firms are not matched across the data and that there are differences in the two data sets in how some variables are defined, I must redefine a "firm" as the white-collar workers within a company *or* the blue-collar workers within a company.[3]

There are far more blue-collar firms than white-collar firms in most industry/year combinations. One reason for this is that the white-collar data do not include the chief executive officer (CEO) and other members of the executive team who negotiate their own wages rather than letting a union negotiate on their behalf. At some firms, there is just a small set of such workers, and the rest of the employees are blue collar. The definition of a firm as the blue-collar workers at a company is, therefore, approximately accurate for many of the blue-collar "firms."

The two data sets contain a wealth of other information. The other variables that I use here include occupation, age, and wages. I use actual wages paid as the primary wage measure and then put this into monthly units. Though the data are generally highly accurate, I minimize the effect of data entry errors or other problems by dropping the highest and lowest 0.5 per-

---

2. See Meyersson Milgrom, Petersen, and Snartland (2001) and Ekberg (2004) for further details about the SAF data.

3. In an earlier version of this chapter, I attempted to form groups approximating actual whole firms by merging firms from each of the two data sets. In each year, I ranked firms within an industry from largest to smallest in both the blue-collar and white-collar data sets. Then I assumed that the firm with the largest set of blue-collar workers in a given year and in a given industry is the same as the firm with the largest set of white-collar workers in that industry and year. I matched the second largest, the third largest, and so on. I subsequently learned that, in order to insure data integrity, the SAF prohibits the merging of the two data sets. Note, however, that conclusions based on the "merged" data set were similar to those I draw in this version of the chapter.

cent of wage observations each year for both the blue-collar and white-collar samples.

Firms enter and exit the data set throughout the whole period studied. Tenure calculations are limited by the entry of individual firms. For example, some of the analyses look at workers who have been at their firm at least three years. These analyses in, for example, 1982 are limited to firms that had entered the data by 1979 because, for firms that entered the data after 1979, it is impossible to determine which workers had been at the firm for at least three years as of 1982.

Occupations in both data sets are determined by a detailed set of codes that are part of the Swedish occupational coding system. When I look at "levels" within firms, I look only at the white-collar employees and use the last digit of their occupation code (also known as the BNT code). This digit can take one of seven values, each of which indicates a different level of responsibility and skill. Within occupations, this precisely identifies the relative level of a job (see Lazear and Oyer [2004] for examples of job classifications). While these levels are not meant to be comparable across occupations, I use the number of relative levels as a rough gauge for the range of the hierarchy of individual firms.

As the kernel density estimates in the top of figure 12.4 suggest, most firms and plants are quite small (though most employees work in fairly large plants and firms). For the rest of this chapter, I restrict the sample to firm-year observations with at least twenty-five employees. As the bottom of figure 12.4 shows, most of these firms are near the twenty-five employee cutoff. However, the average firm in the sample has roughly 100 employees. Much of the analysis further restricts the sample to firms with 100 or more workers. Keep in mind that, in this restriction and throughout the whole chapter, the term "firm" actually means the white-collar workers at a company or the blue-collar workers at a company.

12.4   Wage Structure

Table 12.2 provides numerous details about wages at Swedish firms in 1974, 1982, and 1990. The top panel of table 12.2 provides these details for blue-collar firms, and the bottom panel of table 12.2 provides analogous information for white-collar firms. Before getting to the wage changes, note the changes in composition of the labor force. The number of blue-collar workers at firms with at least twenty-five workers who meet the hours restriction fell throughout the period, with a particularly large drop from 1974 to 1982. The number of workers in the blue-collar sample shrank by about one-sixth from 1974 to 1982. Some of this reduction is because workers move to the white-collar sector, but that only explains a small fraction of the blue-collar reduction. Given that the total number of workers rose steadily in Sweden, this reduction suggests some combination of firms

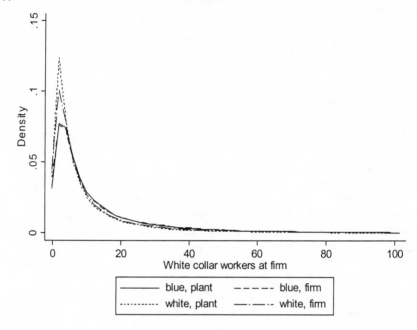

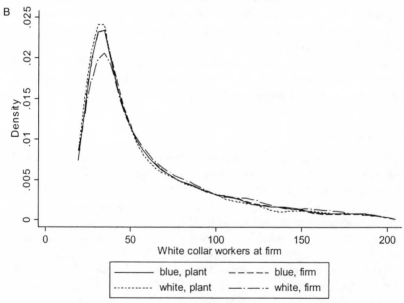

Fig. 12.4 Kernel density of firm and plant size: *A*, **All firms;** *B*, **firms/plants with 25 or more employees**

Table 12.2   **Structure of wages within and between firms**

	Wages in 1990 kroners			Log monthly wages in 1990 kroners		
	1974	1982	1990	1974	1982	1990
	Blue-collar workers					
Average wage[a]	9,860	9,526	10,571	9.16	9.13	9.23
SD	2,546	2,184	2,690	0.27	0.24	0.26
90th percentile	13,088	12,281	14,041	9.48	9.42	9.55
10th percentile	6,589	6,628	7,223	8.79	8.80	8.88
No. of workers	474,857	396,701	372,623			
Average of firm average wage[b] (weight observations different from previous row)	9,636	9,221	10,176	9.14	9.10	9.19
SD	1,514	1,310	1,664	0.16	0.14	0.16
90th percentile	11,619	10,908	12,400	9.33	9.28	9.40
10th percentile	7,686	7,552	8,140	8.92	8.91	8.98
No. of firms	3,708	3,546	3,931			
Average of SD of wage[b]	1,988	1,723	2,112	0.22	0.20	0.21
SD	587	465	656	0.053	0.044	0.051
90th percentile	2,785	2,339	3,012	0.28	0.25	0.28
10th percentile	1,306	1,171	1,366	0.15	0.14	0.15
No. of firms	3,705	3,546	3,930			
Average CV of wages[b]	0.207	0.188	0.207	0.024	0.021	0.023
SD	0.052	0.046	0.054	0.006	0.005	0.006
90th percentile	0.273	0.247	0.276	0.031	0.028	0.030
10th percentile	0.144	0.133	0.145	0.017	0.015	0.017
No. of firms	3,705	3,546	3,930			
Correlation (average wage, SD of wage)[b]	0.523	0.443	0.561	−0.004	−0.066	0.082
Average of firm average wage[c]	9,636	9,227	10,192	9.14	9.10	9.19
SD	1,632	1,381	1,706	0.17	0.15	0.16
90th percentile	11,881	11,105	12,558	9.35	9.29	9.41
10th percentile	7,432	7,371	8,059	8.89	8.88	8.97
No. of plants	4,832	4,526	4,866			
Average of SD of wage[c]	1,969	1,717	2,103	0.22	0.19	0.21
SD	597	471	663	0.052	0.044	0.051
90th percentile	3,044	2,538	3,163	0.31	0.27	0.30
10th percentile	1,308	1,173	1,373	0.16	0.14	0.15
No. of plants	4,826	4,526	4,865			
Average CV of wages[c]	0.20	0.19	0.21	0.024	0.021	0.023
SD	0.05	0.05	0.053	0.006	0.005	0.006
90th percentile	0.29	0.26	0.29	0.034	0.029	0.032
10th percentile	0.15	0.14	0.15	0.017	0.016	0.017
No. of plants	4,826	4,526	4,865			
Correlation (average wage, SD of wage)[b]	0.562	0.485	0.582	0.035	−0.022	0.110
Average wage for workers between 25 and 30[a]	10,129	9,587	10,642	9.19	9.14	9.24

Table 12.2   (continued)

	Wages in 1990 kroners			Log monthly wages in 1990 kroners		
	1974	1982	1990	1974	1982	1990
SD	2,474	2,086	2,671	0.25	0.22	0.25
90th percentile	13,261	12,235	14,143	9.49	9.41	9.56
10th percentile	7,010	6,901	7,373	8.86	8.84	8.91
No. of workers	67,765	55,204	54,590			
Average wage for workers between 45 and 50[a]	10,065	9,797	11,020	9.18	9.16	9.28
SD	2,583	2,207	2,707	0.26	0.23	0.25
90th percentile	13,334	12,545	14,511	9.50	9.44	9.58
10th percentile	6,721	6,817	7,639	8.81	8.83	8.94
No. of workers	43,599	35,964	39,175			
White-collar workers						
Average wage[a]	16,199	14,828	15,990	9.64	9.56	9.63
SD	5,735	4,739	5,435	0.33	0.29	0.31
90th percentile	23,935	21,302	23,475	10.08	9.97	10.06
10th percentile	10,145	9,903	10,400	9.22	9.20	9.25
No. of workers	267,293	277,491	296,778			
Average of firm average wage[b] (weight observations different from previous row)	15,445	14,374	15,660	9.59	9.53	9.61
SD	1,787	1,581	1,908	0.11	0.11	0.12
90th percentile	17,654	16,288	17,970	9.73	9.66	9.75
10th percentile	13,187	12,407	13,329	9.44	9.39	9.46
No. of firms	1,701	2,069	2,493			
Average of SD of wage[b]	5,066	4,161	4,895	0.31	0.27	0.29
SD	1,141	1,035	1,164	0.050	0.048	0.049
90th percentile	6,516	5,469	6,335	0.37	0.30	0.35
10th percentile	3,584	2,809	3,393	0.25	0.20	0.23
No. of firms	1,701	2,069	2,493			
Average CV of wages[b]	0.327	0.287	0.311	0.032	0.028	0.030
SD	0.058	0.056	0.058	0.005	0.005	0.005
90th percentile	0.400	0.357	0.382	0.039	0.034	0.036
10th percentile	0.253	0.211	0.235	0.026	0.021	0.024
No. of firms	1,701	2,069	2,493			
Correlation (average wage, SD of wage)[b]	0.641	0.689	0.657	0.136	0.360	0.308
Average of firm average wage[c]	15,701	14,500	15,714	9.60	9.54	9.61
SD	2,017	1,675	2,020	0.12	0.11	0.12
90th percentile	18,358	16,810	18,611	9.76	9.68	9.77
10th percentile	13,132	12,305	13,187	9.43	9.38	9.44
No. of plants	2,358	2,752	2,956			
Average of SD of wage[c]	5,142	4,184	4,926	0.31	0.27	0.29
SD	1,167	1,079	1,205	0.052	0.051	0.051
90th percentile	7,314	6,026	7,061	0.40	0.34	0.37
10th percentile	3,699	2,828	3,365	0.25	0.20	0.23
No. of plants	2,358	2,751	2,956			

Table 12.2   (continued)

	Wages in 1990 kroners			Log monthly wages in 1990 kroners		
	1974	1982	1990	1974	1982	1990
Average CV of wage[c]	0.33	0.29	0.31	0.032	0.028	0.030
SD	0.06	0.06	0.061	0.005	0.005	0.005
90th percentile	0.43	0.38	0.42	0.041	0.036	0.038
10th percentile	0.26	0.21	0.24	0.026	0.021	0.024
No. of plants	2,358	2,751	2,956			
Correlation (average wage, SD of wage)[c]	0.610	0.646	0.623	0.059	0.277	0.243
Average wage for workers between 25 and 30[a]	13,060	11,897	13,244	9.46	9.37	9.47
SD	2,750	2,233	2,813	0.20	0.18	0.20
90th percentile	16,533	14,599	16,787	9.71	9.59	9.73
10th percentile	9,957	9,391	10,100	9.21	9.15	9.22
No. of workers	41,574	28,552	37,423			
Average wage for workers between 45 and 50[a]	18,244	16,183	17,699	9.76	9.65	9.73
SD	6,155	5,059	5,948	0.31	0.29	0.32
90th percentile	27,053	23,393	26,395	10.21	10.06	10.18
10th percentile	11,986	11,014	11,500	9.39	9.31	9.35
No. of workers	29,679	31,861	46,722			

Notes: All values are kroners per month, set to 1990 values using the Swedish CPI. Data include full time and part time, men and women, no age restrictions. Only firms with twenty-five or more employees in the relevant year are included. SD = standard deviation; CV = coefficient of variation.
[a]Observation = a person.
[b]Observation = a firm.
[c]Observation = a plant.

getting smaller (and falling below the twenty-five-person floor), people moving to part-time work, and movement to the public sector (and, therefore, out of the SAF data.)

The first line of both panels shows that real wages dropped between 1974 and 1982 in this sample and then rose during the next decade. From 1974 to 1982, as bargaining remained highly centralized, wages continued to become more compressed. As a result, the accompanying reduction in real wages was felt largely by higher-income workers. This compressing of wages can be seen looking both between the two sectors and within each sector. Average white-collar wages dropped 8.5 percent, while blue-collar wages dropped only 3.4 percent, making blue- and white-collar wages less differentiated from one another. The wage drops were larger at the 90th percentile of each group (6.2 percent for blue-collar and 10.0 percent for white-collar) and smaller at the 10th percentile (an *increase* of 0.6 percent for blue-collar and a decrease of 2.4 percent for white-collar.) The compression in this period can also be seen in the reduction in standard deviation of log wages in both samples.

It appears that the relatively slow growth in the 1970s demonstrated in figures 12.2 and 12.3 actually led to lower real wages. Per capita wages conditional on working went down, while countrywide per capita income went up slightly. The difference is due to the increase in women's labor participation rates during this period, from about 60 percent to nearly 80 percent.

The period between 1982 and 1990 is somewhat different, however, as the centralized bargaining system broke down. Economic growth was fairly consistent in this period, and average wages increased considerably (by 11 percent for blue-collar workers and nearly 8 percent for white-collar workers). As would be expected given the more localized bargaining, wage variation increased slightly, as evidenced by the mild increase in the variance of log wages and by the fact that the wage growth at the 90th percentile of the distribution was stronger than at the 10th percentile. The bottom two rows of table 12.2 show that these conclusions largely hold for younger workers (between ages twenty-five and thirty) and older workers (forty-five to fifty-five). One age-specific result worth noting is that the drop in wages during the 1970s was particularly large for younger workers.

The second set of entries shows that most of the same trends that hold at the individual level hold when using a firm and its average wages as an observation. Average wages decreased from 1974 to 1982 and increased after that through 1990. Wages became more compressed within firms during the first period and less compressed during the 1980s. Average firm wages also became more compressed initially and then less compressed. This suggests that the decrease in wage variation during the 1970s and the increase in the 1980s were due to increased variation of wages *within* firms and increased variation *across* firms. Both the standard deviation of wages within firms and firms' coefficients of variation decreased during the 1970s and then increased during the 1980s. This was true for the average firm, as well as firms at the high and low ends of the distributions of these measures.

Figures 12.4 and 12.5, each of which has a blue-collar and a white-collar portion, graphically capture these changes in wage policies across firms. Figure 12.5 shows kernel density estimates of firm average wages in each of the three years captured in table 12.2. That is, it maps an estimate of the probability density function of average wage for a firm. The distribution moves to the left (as wages decrease) and gets more compressed between 1974 and 1982. However, the pattern is exactly reversed by 1990. In fact, the 1974 and 1990 densities look remarkably similar, though the 1990 density is shifted considerably to the right due to the wage growth of the 1980s.

Figure 12.6 shows a similar pattern for firm standard deviation of wages. The distribution moves to the left and compresses from 1974 to 1982 as wages get more compressed within most firms. Then the distribution reverts to roughly its 1974 shape by 1990.

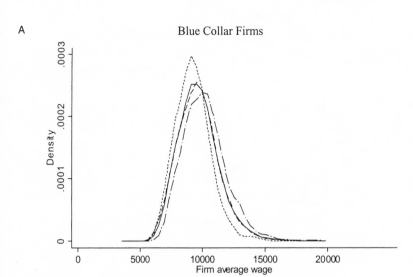

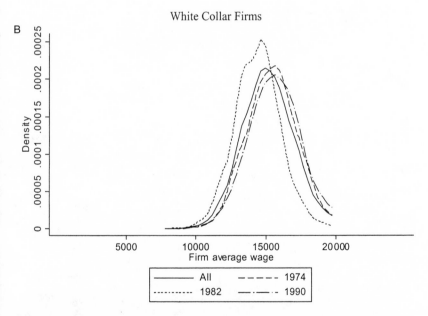

Fig. 12.5   Kernel density of firm average wage: *A*, Blue-collar firms; *B*, White-collar firms

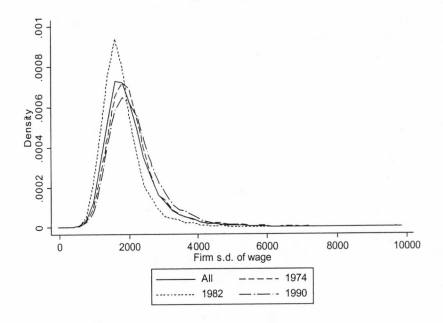

A   Blue Collar Firms

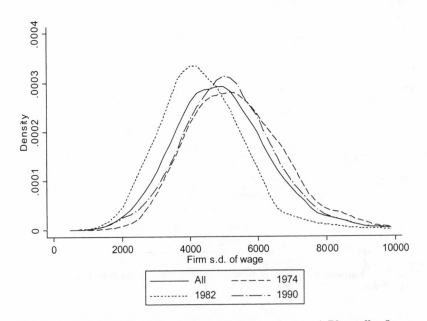

B   White Collar Firms

Fig. 12.6   Kernel density of firm standard deviation of wage: *A,* **Blue-collar firms;** *B,* **White-collar firms**

The top panel of table 12.2 shows that high-wage blue-collar firms have high variance. In levels, this relationship is strong in 1974, but gets weaker as wages compress by 1982. By 1990, wages and variance are once again highly correlated. This is to be expected as similar proportional differences in pay would lead to larger pay variance at higher pay levels. The fact that there is some positive correlation between log wages and variation of log wages by 1990 suggests that high-wage firms really are high-variance firms and that this relationship got stronger throughout the period. These correlations average a similar magnitude in the white-collar data, but there is no clear trend or connection to wage compression.

Finally, table 12.2 includes a summary of plant-level wages and wage variation. Similar to firms, a "plant" is actually the blue-collar workers in an establishment or the white-collar workers in an establishment. I only include plants with at least twenty-five employees. The results suggest that basically all firm-level conclusions hold for plants as well, so it appears that much of the change in variation over the sample period took place within individual plants. In fact, the results are so similar for the plant-level and firm-level analyses that it seems each plant (or at least the blue- or white-collar group in the plant) is a microcosm of the firm as a whole. There is as much variation within a typical plant as there is in a whole firm.

Figure 12.7 provides some basic information on what determines the variation between workers in wages. The figure displays the results of analysis of variance (ANOVA) for each type of worker (that is, blue-collar or white-collar) in each of the three years. The analysis runs a regression of log wage on indicator variables for individual firms, industry, occupation, age, and city. The graph displays the portion of the variance that the ANOVA attributes to each set of indicator variables.

For blue-collar workers, the firm effects are quite important, explaining 9 to 14 percent of the cross-sectional variation in wages. Occupation effects are somewhat more important than firm effects, explaining as much as 19 percent of the variation in wages. Age effects explain a small amount of the variation, while industry and location do not have any economically meaningful effect on blue-collar wages. The total R-squared statistics of the blue-collar regressions are generally about 40 percent.[4] However, the R-squared increases to about 60 percent when using hourly wages because a considerable amount of the monthly wage variation is due to differences in hours worked. It appears that, despite the centralized bargaining system, there is considerable variation in blue-collar pay rates across firms.

The lower graph in figure 12.7 suggests that centralized bargaining is more important in determining white-collar wages, however. While firm

4. Note that the R-squared is not simply 1 minus the variance not assigned to any specific variable because the ANOVA model does not necessarily assign all the variance that can be explained by a combination of the variables to individual variables.

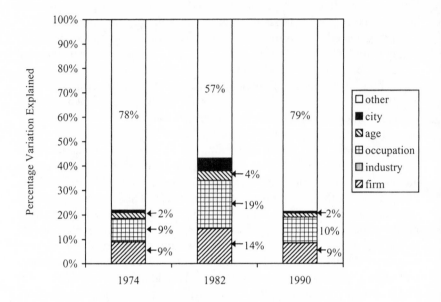

A   Blue Collar Workers

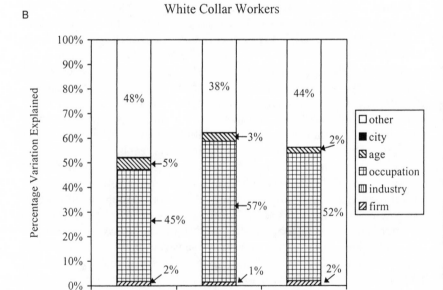

B   White Collar Workers

Fig. 12.7   Analysis of variance of log wages: *A*, Blue-collar workers; *B*, White-collar workers

effects are also important for white-collar workers, the magnitude of the occupation effects is quite dramatic. Roughly half the cross-sectional variation in white-collar wages can be explained by the 285 occupation classifications. Even though the collective bargaining system became more decentralized in the late 1980s, these occupation effects were still very strong in 1990.

Table 12.3 looks at wage changes in 1974, 1982, and 1990, with the top panel again covering blue-collar workers and the bottom panel covering white-collar workers. This table is based on calculating each individual worker's wage in the appropriate year minus his or her wage in the preceding year. The first row of the bottom panel shows that a substantial portion of the reduction in white-collar wages from 1974 to 1982 was due to a drop in the last year of this period. There were some significant real wage reductions in 1982. As wages got more variable after 1982, there continued to be greater variance in wage changes, and there were many real wage cuts again in 1990. This reflects the fact that the Swedish economy began a recession during 1990. The similarity between individual and firm-average wage changes suggests that there is a significant firm-specific component in short-term wage changes. This is consistent with the findings in Lazear and Oyer (2004), who used the white-collar SAF data to show that firm fixed effects can explain a substantial portion of year-to-year wage changes, but do not have a large effect on overall wage levels.

In both the blue-collar and white-collar panels, wage changes are different for the sample of people who change firms (and who I am able to follow between firms.) They have higher wage change, on average, suggesting that these changes are typically voluntary movement to increase wages. They are more extreme than the wage changes of stayers on the high end of the distribution and somewhat higher throughout the rest of the distribution. This suggests, as one might expect under this compressed system where it is difficult to fire unproductive workers, that some very productive workers get hired away at considerably higher wages.

The difference in wage changes by age operate in the direction one might expect, but the age differences are surprisingly small. Young workers (age twenty-five to thirty) get larger wage increases than other workers, but not by much. For blue-collar workers, the differences in wage changes for young workers, older workers (age forty-five to fifty), and all others are trivial. Though somewhat larger than the blue-collar age differences, the differences among white-collar workers are also small. For example, in 1990, the average real wage change for the sample as a whole and for older workers is negative (though very small). The average change for young workers is about 2 percent.

Differences in wage changes are also surprisingly small when looking at short-tenured and long-tenured workers. Higher-tenured workers generally get slightly smaller wage increases than low-tenured workers. As expected, relatively new workers seem to have larger productivity gains and,

Table 12.3   Wage dynamics

	Change in wages			Change in log monthly wages		
	1974	1982	1990	1974	1982	1990
	Blue-collar workers					
Average change in wage[a]	7	−42	−151	0.004	−0.002	−0.011
SD	2,198	1,881	2,446	0.22	0.19	0.22
90th percentile	2,492	2,148	2,721	0.25	0.23	0.26
10th percentile	−1,104	−2,234	−2,883	−0.25	−0.23	−0.27
No. of workers	294,978	306,686	237,178			
Average of firm average change in wage[b]	26	−97	−147	0.010	−0.007	−0.011
SD	1,118	977	1,371	0.11	0.098	0.12
90th percentile	1,206	992	1,301	0.126	0.108	0.124
10th percentile	−1,250	−1,148	−1,552	−0.115	−0.115	−0.139
No. of firms	3,222	3,350	3,509			
Average of SD of change in wage[b]	1,814	1,538	1,983	0.19	0.17	0.19
SD	975	644	865	0.069	0.053	0.061
90th percentile	2,729	2,217	2,990	0.26	0.23	0.27
10th percentile	1,049	922	1,161	0.12	0.11	0.12
No. of firms	3,219	3,343	3,503			
Average of firm average change in wage[c]	17	−110	−164	0.007	−0.008	−0.012
SD	1,134	981	1,409	0.107	0.097	0.125
90th percentile	1,307	1,036	1,395	0.130	0.109	0.126
10th percentile	−1,220	−1,152	−1,551	−0.117	−0.116	−0.140
No. of plants	4,099	4,232	4,204			
Average of SD of change in wage[c]	1,806	1,554	1,999	0.187	0.169	0.191
SD	986	668	900	0.068	0.053	0.061
90th percentile	2,801	2,308	3,118	0.262	0.232	0.274
10th percentile	1,034	926	1,160	0.123	0.114	0.124
No. of plants	4,096	4,226	4,195			
Average change in wage for people who change firms[a]	320	148	−77	0.04	0.02	−0.003
SD	3,060	2,626	2,960	0.311	0.26	0.267
90th percentile	3,869	3,119	3,254	0.43	0.34	0.32
10th percentile	−3,121	−2,731	−3,273	−0.33	−0.29	−0.32
No. of workers	18,737	10,713	33,302			
Average change in wage for workers between 25 and 30[a]	−53	−31	−154	−0.0038	−0.0013	−0.013
SD	2,319	1,952	2,616	0.216	0.201	0.233
90th percentile	2,526	2,261	2,920	0.247	0.241	0.273
10th percentile	−2,669	−2,354	−3,149	−0.263	−0.246	−0.292
No. of workers	41,542	42,963	33,349			
Average change in wage for workers between 45 and 50[a]	−73	−55	−199	−0.006	−0.003	−0.016

Table 12.3 (continued)

	Change in wages			Change in log monthly wages		
	1974	1982	1990	1974	1982	1990
SD	2,162	1,822	2,367	0.202	0.183	0.204
90th percentile	2,238	2,033	2,548	0.221	0.213	0.230
10th percentile	−2,463	−2,166	−2,773	−0.243	−0.218	−0.249
No. of workers	30,154	30,205	28,742			
Average change in wage for people with tenure <3 years[a]	243	35	48	0.035	0.008	0.010
SD	2,314	1,933	2,490	0.257	0.222	0.250
90th percentile	3,098	2,309	3,070	0.370	0.280	0.320
10th percentile	−2,455	−2,269	−2,809	−0.263	−0.260	−0.283
No. of workers	14,712	17,615	34,431			
Average change in wage for people with tenure ≥3 years[a]	−9	−36	−179	−0.002	−0.002	−0.015
SD	2,187	1,869	2,432	0.213	0.192	0.214
90th percentile	2,451	2,141	2,670	0.246	0.227	0.246
10th percentile	−2,486	−2,214	−2,898	−0.247	−0.229	−0.265
No. of workers	273,070	272,085	178,334			
	White-collar workers					
Average change in wage[a]	590	−255	−45	0.041	−0.016	−0.004
SD	862	890	1,257	0.53	0.053	0.700
90th percentile	1,307	436	1,162	0.090	0.030	0.070
10th percentile	−27	−805	−943	−0.002	−0.050	−0.060
No. of workers	224,499	242,410	226,755			
Average of firm average change in wage[b]	551	−260	54	0.041	−0.018	0.001
SD	344	320	529	0.021	0.020	0.031
90th percentile	930	66	684	0.064	0.003	0.040
10th percentile	219	−545	−470	0.019	−0.036	−0.031
No. of firms	1,615	1,955	2,282			
Average of SD of change in wage[b]	851	791	1,138	0.056	0.049	0.066
SD	552	514	606	0.027	0.027	0.029
90th percentile	1,509	1,334	1,843	0.090	0.079	0.100
10th percentile	405	335	561	0.030	0.021	0.036
No. of firms	1,615	1,954	2,280			
Average of firm average change in wage[c]	566	−269	31	0.041	−0.018	−0.0002
SD	316	274	542	0.020	0.017	0.032
90th percentile	934	25	684	0.064	0.001	0.037
10th percentile	252	−544	−480	0.020	−0.036	−0.032
No. of plants	2,204	2,550	2,627			
Average of SD of change in wage[c]	752	723	1,075	0.050	0.045	0.062
SD	514	451	602	0.026	0.024	0.029

(*continued*)

Table 12.3   (continued)

	Change in wages			Change in log monthly wages		
	1974	1982	1990	1974	1982	1990
90th percentile	1,358	1,239	1,860	0.083	0.076	0.098
10th percentile	361	301	525	0.027	0.019	0.033
No. of plants	2,203	2,546	2,627			
Average change in wage for people who change firms[a]	744	117	342	0.050	0.008	0.02
SD	1,782	1,684	1,737	0.106	0.098	0.097
90th percentile	2,486	1,950	2,330	0.172	0.126	0.140
10th percentile	−552	−1,044	−867	−0.032	−0.061	−0.055
No. of workers	9,279	9,192	29,629			
Average change in wage for workers between 25 and 30[a]	834	123	305	0.065	0.008	0.019
SD	761	756	1,225	0.052	0.058	0.082
90th percentile	1,565	832	1,520	0.119	0.067	0.109
10th percentile	250	−378	−597	0.020	−0.033	−0.049
No. of workers	31,183	22,744	24,639			
Average change in wage for workers between 45 and 50[a]	455	−368	−135	0.027	−0.023	−0.010
SD	851	780	1,265	0.042	0.042	0.063
90th percentile	1,060	126	1,036	0.063	0.008	0.054
10th percentile	−104	−866	1,006	−0.006	−0.049	−0.058
No. of workers	26,743	29,086	38,044			
Average change in wage for people with tenure <3 years[a]	680	30	246	0.064	0.003	0.017
SD	999	943	1,232	0.085	0.065	0.080
90th percentile	1,617	807	1,438	0.160	0.070	0.110
10th percentile	−140	−588	−691	−0.008	−0.044	−0.051
No. of workers	8,639	10,624	33,449			
Average change in wage for people with tenure ≥3 years[a]	590	−267	−94	0.040	−0.017	−0.008
SD	843	884	1,270	0.050	0.052	0.068
90th percentile	1,294	408	1,118	0.090	0.029	0.064
10th percentile	−15	−813	−986	−0.001	−0.048	−0.060
No. of workers	205,773	218,746	165,669			

Notes: All values are kroners set to 1990 values. SD = standard deviation. Change in wages is defined as wage in year t – wage in year $t − 1$. Change in log monthly wages is defined as log wage in year t – log wage in year $t − 1$.

[a]Observation = a person.

[b]Observation = a firm.

[c]Observation = a plant.

therefore, get larger pay increases. But these differences are not particularly large. The average raise for people with at least three years of tenure is generally within 2 percentage points of the average raise for people with less than three years of tenure.

12.5 Worker Mobility

Table 12.4 details employee entry and exit patterns. Again, the top panel provides data for blue-collar workers, and the bottom panel details white-collar mobility. Both panels include columns for 1974, 1982, and 1990 that summarize firms with at least twenty-five employees and then three columns limiting the sample to firms with at least 100 employees. The first row of the table shows the declining sample firm size. The standard deviation of firm size is substantial, reflecting the fact that there are a number of very large firms.

The blue-collar data have 1,402 possible occupations. The typical blue-collar firm only has people in ten of these occupations (about twenty for firms with 100 or more employees.) As firm size drops throughout the sample period, so does the average number of occupations within a firm. There are a total of fifty-one white-collar occupation groups and, once the various levels within each of these groups is added, 285 distinct occupation classifications in the white-collar data. The average white-collar firm in the data has employees in thirty of these occupations, again dropping as average firm size drops. The average larger firm (100 or more employees) employs people in about sixty occupations.

The third row of the bottom panel of table 12.4 shows the number of levels (out of a possible seven) of white-collar jobs represented. There is not a blue-collar equivalent to the white-collar level. There are up to seven levels within an occupation group. As mentioned earlier, high-level employees in one occupation may not be comparable (in terms of skill and wages) to high-level employees in another occupation. So the average number of levels within a firm, which can include numerous occupation groups, is at best a proxy of the number of true "levels" within any given firm. An average white-collar firm has almost four levels, and the average large firm has almost four and a half. This suggests that most firms do not have a full hierarchy that covers all possible levels. Firms tend to have workers concentrated in a few levels.

The fourth row of the blue-collar section and the fifth row of the white-collar section show the exit rate using an individual year as an observation. In order to be included in this calculation, a firm had to appear in the data in the year shown and the previous year. It also had to have at least twenty-five workers in each of those two years. I define an exit as a person who is working in a firm in year $t - 1$ but not working at that firm in year t. The sample sizes are based on year $t - 1$, while the employee cutoff that determines if the

Table 12.4 **Mobility (no. of firms)**

	All firms			Firms with 100+ employees		
	1974	1982	1990	1974	1982	1990
	Blue-collar workers					
Employees	128.1	111.9	94.8	444.0	448.3	374.9
SD	532.3	511.2	331.9	1090.3	1160.0	745.1
No. of occupations	10.4	9.2	8.3	20.0	19.5	18.8
SD	11.2	10.1	9.7	18.1	17.4	16.9
Employment growth	6.9	−1.9	2.8	8.2	−4.6	−0.1
SD	24.4	37.5	24.7	19.7	13.3	22.8
Exit rate[a]	14.8	10.7	22.6	14.3	10.3	23.5
No. of observations	265,717	351,132	320,778	204,754	269,992	235,531
Exit rate	16.1	12.1	20.2	15.2	11.8	20.5
SD	11.0	10.9	13.1	9.3	11.7	14.6
No. of firms	1,777	2,258	2,368	502	587	581
Exit rate, top quartile of firm wages	10.4	8.1	14.3	9.8	8.1	14.8
SD	12.5	12.3	15.3	10.1	12.6	16.1
Exit rate, bottom quartile of firm wages	25.3	18.9	29.7	24.2	18.3	30.1
SD	16.7	15.9	17.8	12.5	14.0	16.1
Exit rate, top decile of firm wages	9.9	8.1	14.3	9.5	8.2	14.9
SD	15.8	15.0	19.4	12.1	14.0	17.9
Exit rate, bottom decile of firm wages	29.9	22.7	34.0	29.6	22.2	34.6
SD	22.2	21.2	23.5	15.9	16.5	18.3
Entry rate	19.6	10.7	20.3	20.0	9.6	19.1
SD	12.2	11.8	13.3	11.3	11.1	13.0
Entry rate, top quartile of firm wages	10.4	7.0	12.4	11.3	6.6	11.9
SD	12.8	12.3	14.7	11.9	11.6	13.7
Entry rate, bottom quartile of firm wages	34.3	16.0	31.0	34.1	14.0	28.3
SD	19.6	16.5	19.7	15.3	13.4	16.2
Entry rate, top decile of firm wages	9.5	6.6	11.4	10.1	6.5	11.2
SD	15.8	14.6	18.0	13.1	13.0	15.2
Entry rate, bottom decile of firm wages	43.1	18.4	36.2	42.7	16.4	33.2
SD	25.6	21.5	25.4	18.6	16.0	18.1
Percentage of employees who switch jobs internally	13.1	12.9	14.0	12.9	13.4	13.6
SD	13.8	19.5	19.9	12.6	19.5	18.4
Percentage of new jobs filled internally	33.0	47.0	31.6	33.1	52.6	34.4
SD	23.2	32.5	26.1	20.2	28.4	24.6
Percentage of workers who have been at firm 3+ years	88.3	89.3	72.0	88.3	90.9	73.0
SD	9.1	9.7	13.8	7.9	6.7	12.5
Correlation (exit rate, average wage)[b]	−0.105	−0.052	−0.151	−0.068	−0.049	−0.157
Correlation (exit rate, average wage change)[b]	0.031	−0.030	−0.064	−0.059	−0.021	−0.056
Correlation (exit rate, SD of wage)[b]	0.059	0.074	−0.017	0.098	0.033	0.014

Table 12.4   (continued)

	All firms			Firms with 100+ employees		
	1974	1982	1990	1974	1982	1990
Correlation (entry rate, average wage)[b]	−0.094	0.006	−0.048	−0.079	0.062	−0.035
Correlation (entry rate, average wage change)[b]	0.076	0.066	0.058	0.120	0.042	0.127
Correlation (entry rate, SD of wage)[b]	0.048	0.170	0.080	0.039	0.243	0.151
Exit rate[c]	0.153	0.116	0.197	0.139	0.106	0.194
SD	0.108	0.108	0.135	0.084	0.103	0.139
No. of plants	2,334	3,040	2,823	596	729	602
Entry rate[c]	0.186	0.103	0.195	0.187	0.085	0.172
SD	0.120	0.113	0.133	0.104	0.099	0.122
White-collar workers						
Employees	157.1	134.1	119.0	455.2	415.0	345.3
SD	477.5	443.0	319.3	846.1	837.4	587.6
No. of occupations	30.2	28.9	25.6	60.7	59.0	49.5
SD	26.3	24.4	20.1	33.4	32.2	26.3
No. of levels	3.8	3.7	3.6	4.4	4.4	4.3
SD	0.7	0.8	0.8	0.6	0.8	0.7
Employment growth	7.5	−0.2	2.5	9.1	−1.0	−0.2
SD	26.5	16.2	48.3	38.9	13.7	17.0
Exit rate[a]	10.1	9.6	18.6	9.3	9.3	19.4
No. of observations	252,633	272,599	279,620	200,487	210,398	206,276
Exit rate	12.5	10.6	16.9	11.0	10.6	17.7
SD	10.4	11.6	14.6	8.8	12.0	17.2
No. of firms	1,540	1,814	2,105	436	492	570
Exit rate, top quartile of firm wages	9.7	10.0	15.4	8.4	10.2	16.6
SD	12.2	13.6	17.0	9.0	12.4	18.4
Exit rate, bottom quartile of firm wages	18.6	13.1	20.8	17.0	12.5	21.6
SD	15.1	15.0	17.7	11.3	13.0	17.6
Exit rate, top decile of firm wages	10.4	11.0	16.2	9.4	11.1	17.7
SD	15.9	16.9	20.9	10.3	13.8	19.9
Exit rate, bottom decile of firm wages	23.1	15.4	23.6	21.2	14.6	24.1
SD	20.7	19.5	22.2	13.3	14.9	18.7
Entry rate	15.3	9.7	17.1	14.8	9.5	15.6
SD	10.7	10.6	13.7	10.9	11.1	13.6
Entry rate, top quartile of firm wages	7.6	7.3	12.4	7.5	7.3	11.5
SD	11.4	11.4	14.9	11.0	11.4	14.0
Entry rate, bottom quartile of firm wages	29.4	14.6	24.6	29.0	14.3	22.8
SD	17.7	15.7	19.0	15.0	13.5	16.9
Entry rate, top decile of firm wages	7.5	7.4	12.7	7.6	8.0	11.7
SD	14.0	13.6	18.2	11.8	12.8	15.2
Entry rate, bottom decile of firm wages[b]	38.8	17.7	28.9	39.0	17.6	26.8
SD	24.9	21.3	24.5	19.0	16.8	19.9

(*continued*)

Table 12.4   (continued)

	All firms			Firms with 100+ employees		
	1974	1982	1990	1974	1982	1990
Percentage of employees who switch jobs internally	10.9	8.2	8.4	11.7	9.8	8.9
SD	11.5	9.5	10.7	7.9	7.2	8.5
Percentage of new jobs filled internally	32.9	42.7	27.6	39.2	52.7	34.1
SD	25.1	31.4	24.8	20.1	23.0	21.3
Percentage of workers who have been at firm 3+ years	92.4	92.3	73.7	93.4	93.1	75.7
SD	6.8	7.4	12.8	4.7	6.1	11.0
Correlation (exit rate, average wage)[b]	−0.104	0.015	0.008	−0.072	0.095	−0.026
Correlation (exit rate, average wage change)	0.026	0.141	0.139	0.067	0.155	0.187
Correlation (exit rate, SD of wage)	−0.040	0.012	0.049	−0.015	0.076	0.018
Correlation (entry rate, average wage)[b]	−0.159	−0.013	−0.009	−0.231	−0.044	−0.105
Correlation (entry rate, average wage change)[b]	0.098	0.255	0.258	−0.011	0.250	0.213
Correlation (entry rate, SD of wage)[b]	−0.028	0.013	0.010	−0.035	0.007	−0.018
Exit rate[c]	0.131	0.105	0.173	0.120	0.100	0.177
SD	0.120	0.122	0.154	0.108	0.121	0.171
No. of plants	2,079	2,331	2,393	473	477	492
Entry rate[c]	0.157	0.097	0.175	0.147	0.093	0.157
SD	0.118	0.111	0.149	0.106	0.117	0.134

Notes: All statistics are calculated at the firm level, except the first exit rate and the plant level statistics in the last two rows. SD = standard deviation.

[a]Observations = a person.

[b]Observations = a firm.

[c]Observations = a person.

firm has at least 100 employees is based on year t. The exit rate for blue- and white-collar employees in 1974 was 14.8 percent and 10.1 percent, respectively. This suggests that, though the Swedish labor market is thought to be fairly stable, about one worker in seven left his or her firm in 1974. The exit rate drops to 10.7 percent (blue-collar) and 9.6 percent (white-collar) in 1982 and then jumps to over 22 percent and 18 percent in 1990. The exit rate is quite similar for the sample with 100 or more employees.

The next row of the table shows that the average firm-level exit rate (that is, the average across all firms of the firms' exit rates) is similar to the person-level exit rate. This is to be expected because, given that there is no apparent relationship between exit rates and firm size, there is no reason to think weighting by firm would lead to a difference relative to weighting by individuals.

The standard deviation of firm exit rate, which is 10 to 11 percent in 1974 and 1982, grows to nearly 13 to 15 percent in 1990. This suggests that many firms have exit rates over 20 percent in each year, while some firms have very low exit rates. This variation in exit rates can be seen graphically in figure 12.8, which presents kernel density estimates of firm-average exit rates by year for the blue-collar and white-collar samples.

The next several rows of the table examine exit rates within wage groups at each firm. Specifically, I break each firm into quartiles and deciles by wage and then look at exit rates in the upper or lower extreme. As one might expect, exit rates are much higher in the bottom wage quartile (decile) than in the top quartile (decile). The difference is particularly stark in the blue-collar sample, where bottom-quartile exit rates are more than double top-quartile exit rates. Further, exit is particularly high in the bottom decile, which has a somewhat higher exit rate than the bottom quartile (of which, obviously, it is a subset.) On the other hand, the top decile does not have a noticeably different exit rate than the top quartile. Two other things worth noting are that all of these patterns hold both in larger firms and the sample as a whole and that turnover increased between 1982 and 1990 for every subgroup.

These results suggest that people in the low part of the wage distribution have the least to lose by changing jobs and that this relationship gets stronger all the way to the bottom of the wage distribution within firms. However, there appears to be a difference in the upper end of firms' wage distributions. While high-paid workers are less likely to leave their jobs than other workers, the very highest-paid workers are no less likely to leave (and maybe even a bit more likely to leave) than employees who are near, but not quite at, the top of their firms' wage distributions. This is consistent with there being a relatively fluid market for top performers who sometimes have to move firms to have their talents used efficiently.

The drop in exit rates between 1974 and 1982, as well as the increase from 1982 through 1990, are substantial. These two trends were likely driven by several factors. First, the Swedish economy was recovering from a significant recession in 1984, and this may have hindered the opportunity to change jobs. Second, there was a significant increase in the use of temporary workers in Sweden starting around 1990.[5] While the bulk of this increase came after 1990, temporary arrangements likely had a positive effect on turnover rates in the late 1980s. Third, as wages became more compressed in the 1970s, the gains to be had by switching firms were reduced. One of the reasons the centralized bargaining system broke down in 1983 is that firms had difficulty recruiting highly skilled workers. The resulting decentralized bargaining system led to the less compressed wage system

5. See Holmlund and Storrie (2002).

that can be seen in table 12.2, which led at least some employees to seek out the new better-paid opportunities.

Finally, the late 1980s and 1990 saw significant activity in mergers, acquisitions, and other ownership changes. The SAF data, therefore, show many people changing "firms" even when most of their coworkers are unchanged. These workers have changed jobs in that their employer, as defined as the owner of the business for which they work, has changed even if their daily job has not. However, for at least two reasons, this seems unlikely to be a primary driver of the trends in turnover. First, if a firm is taken over and all its employees go to work for another firm, that firm disappears from the data and is not included in the turnover calculations. Second, the kernel density estimates in figure 12.8 suggest that the increase in turnover in 1990 was due to a fairly consistent increase in turnover at most firms rather than a subset of firms having a dramatic increase in turnover. Thus, it appears that the 1990 increase in turnover was widespread, rather than being concentrated in firms that merged.

The next several rows of the table measure the average firm entry rate. An entry is defined as someone who works in the firm in year t but did not work in the firm in year $t - 1$. The sample for this calculation is firms that are in the sample in both year $t - 1$ and year t. The entry rates shown are firm averages. For example, the 19.6 percent entry rate in 1974 for the blue-collar sample indicates that 19.6 percent of the 1974 workers at an average firm were not employed by the firm in 1973. Not surprisingly, the entry rate is similar to the exit rate, though a bit higher as a result of the fact that surviving firms are, on average, growing.

While the exit and entry rates are quite similar, they are not as similar when looking at smaller portions of the distribution within firms. For the most part, the entry rates are noticeably higher than the exit rates at the lower end of the distribution and lower at the higher end of the distribution. This is, again, quite natural. Many of the employees who "enter" higher-paid jobs do so internally. As a result, the entry rate from outside the firm is relatively low for these jobs.

Several rows near the bottom of the table show the correlation between entry (or exit) and various firm-level wage variables. It seems reasonable to expect that firms with higher pay would have lower exit and entry rates. This tends to be true, though the results are inconsistent for white-collar workers. For white-collar workers, firm pay levels and exit rates are negatively correlated, but the level of correlation is not particularly high. In addition, for white-collar firms, those firms that provide relatively large raises actually have higher exit rates. This may reflect the fact that firms with the highest risk of losing workers give relatively large raises. This could make the exit rate lower than it otherwise would be, though still high at these firms. The final rows of the table show that entry and exit rates are very similar when measured at a plant level as at a firm level. This means that movement

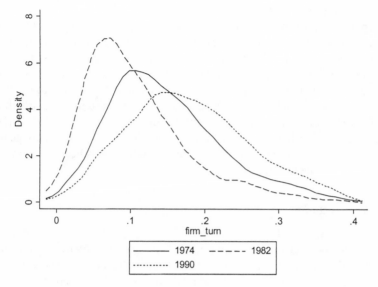

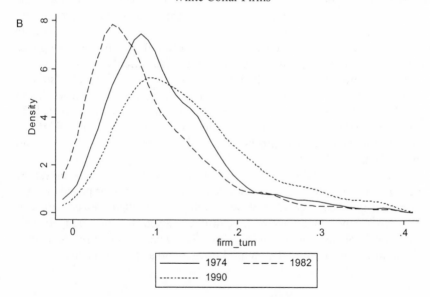

Fig. 12.8   Kernel density of firm turnover: *A*, Blue-collar firms, *B*, White-collar firms

between plants at the same firm is not an important part of total movement between jobs in the Swedish labor market.

In addition to these findings within each sample, there are some differences between the top panel blue-collar sample and the bottom panel white-collar sample. In general, there is more movement (that is, higher entry and exit rates) for white-collar workers than for blue collar workers. Blue-collar workers change jobs somewhat less frequently than white-collar workers. At least two explanations are consistent with this difference. First, there may be more competition for relatively skilled workers. Second, productivity in managerial jobs could be driven more by general human capital, so the value of long-term relationships between firms and workers may be lower.

12.6   Conclusion

Using a matched employer-employee data set, I have shown that the Swedish labor market underwent fairly dramatic changes during the 1970s and 1980s. From 1974 through 1982, wages in the already relatively egalitarian Swedish labor market became even more compressed. Wage variation decreased both within firms and across firms. However, in 1983, the highly centralized wage bargaining system that had been in place for several decades began to break down. Several unions began to negotiate wages in a more fragmented manner. As a result of this change (and possibly other changes), Swedish wages became more variable by 1990.

I also showed that, probably due to the bargaining changes, the state of the Swedish economy, and an increase in merger and acquisition activity in the late 1980s, job change became less common in Sweden between 1974 and 1982 and then became dramatically more common by 1990. Both the job turnover and wage compression trends are strong for blue-collar and white-collar workers.

The analyses in this chapter have been largely descriptive. However, they suggest numerous potential economic questions that can be posed and answered using the matched employer-employee data set employed here. Future work can help determine how different Swedish firms changed their personnel policies in reaction to changes in the bargaining process, macroeconomic conditions, and increased merger and acquisition activity.

References

Edin, Per-Anders, and Bertil Holmlund. 1995. The Swedish wage structure: The rise and fall of solidarity wage policy? In *Differences and changes in wage structure,* ed. Richard B. Freeman and Lawrence F. Katz, 307–43. Chicago: University of Chicago Press.

Edin, Per-Anders, and Robert Topel. 1997. Wage policy and restructuring: The Swedish labor market since 1960. In *The welfare state in transition,* ed. Richard B. Freeman, Robert Topel, and Birgitta Swedenborg, 155–201. Chicago: University of Chicago Press.

Ekberg, John. 2004. *Essays in empirical labor economics.* PhD diss. Stockholm University, Stockholm, Sweden.

Holmlund, Bertil, and Donald Storrie. 2002. Temporary work in turbulent times: The Swedish experience. *Economic Journal* 112:F245–F269.

Lazear, Edward P., and Paul Oyer. 2004. Internal and external labor markets: A personnel economics approach. *Labour Economics* 11:527–54.

Meyersson Milgrom, Eva M., Trond Petersen, and Vemond Snartland. 2001. Equal pay for equal work? Evidence from Sweden and a comparison with Norway and the U.S. *Scandinavian Journal of Economics* 103:559–83.

Nilsson, C. 1993. The Swedish model: Labor market institutions and contracts. In *Labor market institutions and contracts,* ed. J. Hartog and J. Theeuwes, 233–66. Amsterdam: Elsevier Science.

Contributors

John M. Abowd
School of Industrial and Labor
  Relations
Cornell University
358 East Ives Hall
Ithaca, NY 14850

Holger Alda
Sociological Research Institute
University of Goettingen
Friedländer Weg 31
37085 Göttingen, Germany

Lutz Bellmann
Institute for Employment Research
  (IAB)
Regensburger Strasse 104
D-90327 Nuremberg, Germany

Lex Borghans
Faculty of Economics and Business
  Administration
Maastricht University
P.O. Box 616
6200 MD Maastricht, The Netherlands

Bruno Contini
Department of Economics
University of Turin
Via Po, 53
10124 Turin, Italy

Per-Anders Edin
Department of Economics
Uppsala University
P.O. Box 513
S-751 20 Uppsala, Sweden

Tor Eriksson
Department of Economics and Center
  for Corporate Performance
Aarhus School of Business
Prismet, Silkeborgvej 2
DK-8000 Aarhus C, Denmark

Hermann Gartner
Institute for Employment Research
  (IAB)
Regensburger Strasse 104
D-90327 Nuremberg, Germany

John Haltiwanger
Department of Economics
University of Maryland
College Park, MD 20742

Bertil Holmlund
Department of Economics
Uppsala University
Box 513
SE-751 20 Uppsala, Sweden

Arngrim Hunnes
Department of Economics
Norwegian School of Economics and
   Business Administration
Helleveien 30
N-5045 Bergen, Norway

Francis Kramarz
CREST-INSEE
15 Boulevard Gabriel Péri
92245 Malakoff, France

Ben Kriechel
Faculty of Economics and Business
   Administration
Maastricht University
P.O. Box 616
6200 MD Maastricht, The Netherlands

Thierry Lallemand
Department of Applied Economics
   (DULBEA)
Free University of Brussels
50, Avenue F.D. Roosevelt
1050 Brussels, Belgium

Julia Lane
National Opinion Research Center
   (NORC)
University of Chicago
1155 East 60th Street
Chicago, IL 60637

Edward P. Lazear
Graduate School of Business and
   Hoover Institution
Stanford University
Stanford, CA 94305-5015

Roberto Leombruni
Laboratorio Riccardo Revelli
Via Real Collegio 30
10024 Moncalieri, Turin, Italy

Jarle Møen
Department of Finance and
   Management Science
Norwegian School of Economics and
   Business Administration
Helleveien 30
N-5045 Bergen, Norway

Paul Oyer
Graduate School of Business
Stanford University
518 Memorial Way
Stanford, CA 94305-5015

Lia Pacelli
Department of Economics and
   Finance
University of Turin
C.so Unione Sovietica 218 bis
10134 Turin, Italy

Sébastien Perez-Duarte
Statistics Development and
   Coordination
European Central Bank
Kaiserstrasse 29
60311 Frankfurt am Main, Germany

Robert Plasman
Department of Applied Economics
   (DULBEA)
Free University of Brussels
50, Avenue F.D. Roosevelt
B-1050 Brussels, Belgium

François Rycx
Department of Applied Economics
   (DULBEA)
Free University of Brussels
50, Avenue F.D. Roosevelt
1050 Brussels, Belgium

Kjell G. Salvanes
Department of Economics
Norwegian School of Economics and
   Business Administration
Helleveien 30
N-5045 Bergen, Norway

Kathryn L. Shaw
Graduate School of Business
Littlefield 339
Stanford University
Stanford, CA 94305-5015

Oskar Nordström Skans
The Institute for Labour Market Policy
   Evaluation (IFAU)
Box 513
SE-75120 Uppsala, Sweden

Roope Uusitalo
Government Institute for Economic
  Research
Pitkänsillanranta 3 A
00530 Helsinki, Finland

Juhana Vartiainen
National Institute for Economic
  Research
Box 3116
Kungsgatan 12-14
SE-103 62 Stockholm, Sweden

Lars Vilhuber
Cornell Institute for Social and
  Economic Research (CISER)
391 Pine Tree Road
Ithaca, NY 14850

Claudia Villosio
LABORatorio Riccardo Revelli
Via Real Collegio 30
10024 Moncalieri, Turin, Italy

Niels Westergaard-Nielsen
Department of Economics and Center
  for Corporate Performance
Aarhus School of Business
Aarhus University
Prismet, Silkeborgvej 2
DK-8000 Aarhus C, Denmark

Author Index

Subject Index

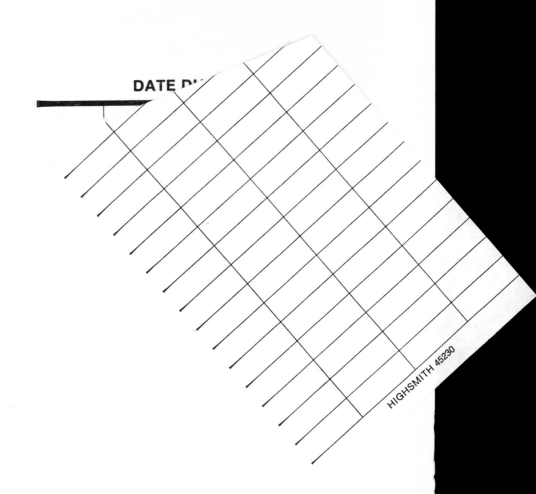

DATE DUE

HIGHSMITH 45230